# THE
# GIFT

## *the* NEW
## TESTAMENT
*with Psalms & Proverbs*

PRESENTED TO:

_____

_____

BY:

_____

_____

ON:

_____

_____

# THE GIFT

## the NEW TESTAMENT
### for NEW BELIEVERS
### with Psalms & Proverbs

HOLMAN
**CHRISTIAN STANDARD BIBLE**®

ISBN 1-5864-0023-1

Printed in Canada
2 3 4 5 6 06 05 04 03
T

# Contents

# Introduction to the HCSB®

The Bible is God's inspired word, inerrant in the original manuscripts. It is the only means of knowing God's plan of salvation and His will for our lives. It is the only hope and answer for a rebellious, searching world. Bible translation, both a science and an art, is a bridge that brings God's word from the ancient world to the world today. Depending on God to accomplish this task, Holman Bible Publishers presents the *Holman Christian Standard Bible*®, a new English translation of God's word.

## The Goals of This Translation

- to provide English-speaking people across the world with an accurate, readable Bible in contemporary English
- to equip serious Bible students with an accurate translation for personal study, private devotions, and memorization
- to give those who love God's word a text that is easy to read, visually attractive on the page, and appealing when heard
- to affirm the authority of the Scriptures as God's inerrant word and to champion its absolutes against social or cultural agendas that would compromise its accuracy

The name, *Holman Christian Standard Bible*®, embodies these goals: *Holman* Bible Publishers presents a new *Bible* translation, for the *Christian* and English-speaking communities, which will set the *standard* in Bible translations for years to come.

## Why Another English Translation of the Bible?

Many people ask: "Why another English translation of the Bible?" There are several answers to this question:

1. **Each generation needs a fresh translation of the Bible in its own language.**

   The Bible is the world's most important book, confronting each individual and each generation with issues that affect life, both now and forever. Since each new generation must be introduced to God's word in its own language, there will always be a need for new translations such as the *Holman Christian Standard Bible*® [HCSB®].

2. **English, one of the world's greatest languages, is rapidly changing, and Bible translations must keep in step with those changes.**

English is the first truly global language in history. It is the language of education, business, travel, research, and the Internet. More than 1.3 billion people around the world speak English as a primary or secondary language. The HCSB® seeks to serve a large cross-section of those people with a translation they can easily use and understand.

English is also the world's most rapidly changing language. The HCSB® seeks to reflect recent changes in English by using modern punctuation, formatting, and vocabulary, while avoiding slang, regionalisms, or changes made specifically for the sake of political or social agendas.

3. **Rapid advances in biblical research provide new data for Bible translators.**

This has been called the "information age," a term that accurately describes the field of biblical research. Never before in history has there been as much information about the Bible as there is today—from archaeological discoveries to analysis of ancient manuscripts to years of study and statistical research on individual Bible books. Translations made as recently as 10 or 20 years ago do not reflect many of these advances in biblical research. The translators of the HCSB® have sought to use as much of this new data as possible.

4. **Advances in computer technology have opened a new door for Bible translation.**

The HCSB® has used computer technology and telecommunications in its creation perhaps more than any Bible translation in history. Electronic mail was used daily and sometimes hourly for communication and transmission of manuscripts. The most advanced Bible software available has been used to create and review the translation at each step in its production. A developmental copy of the HCSB® itself was used within this software program to facilitate cross-checking during the translation process—something never done before with a Bible translation.

## Translation Philosophy

Bible translations generally follow one of three approaches to translating the original Hebrew, Aramaic, and Greek words into English:

1. <u>Formal Equivalence</u>: Often called "word for word" translation, formal equivalence seeks to represent each word of the original text with a corresponding word in the translation so that the

reader can see word for word what the original human author wrote. The merit of this approach is that the Holy Spirit did inspire the very words of Scripture in the original manuscripts. A formal equivalence translation is good to the extent that its words accurately convey the meaning of the original words. However, a literal rendering can result in awkward English or in a misunderstanding of the author's intent.

2. Dynamic Equivalence: Often called "thought for thought" translation, dynamic equivalence seeks to translate the meaning of biblical words so the text makes the same impact on modern readers that the ancient text made on its original readers. Strengths of this approach include readability and understandability, especially in places where the original is difficult to render word for word. However, some serious questions can be asked about dynamic equivalence: How can a modern translator be certain of the original author's intent? Since meaning is always conveyed by words, why not ensure accuracy by using words that are as close as possible in meaning to the original instead of words that just capture the idea? How can a modern person ever know the impact of the original text on its readers?

3. Optimal Equivalence: This approach seeks to combine the best features of both formal and dynamic equivalence. In the many places throughout Scripture where a word for word rendering is clearly understandable, a literal translation is used. In places where a literal rendering might be unclear, then a more dynamic translation is given. The HCSB® has chosen to use the balance and beauty of optimal equivalence for a fresh translation of God's word that is both faithful to the words God inspired and "user friendly" to modern readers.

## History of the *Holman Christian Standard Bible*®

After several years of preliminary development, Holman Bible Publishers, the oldest Bible publisher in America, assembled an international, interdenominational team of 90 scholars, all of whom were committed to biblical inerrancy. Smaller teams of editors, stylists, and proofreaders then corrected and polished the translation. Outside consultants contributed valuable suggestions from their areas of expertise. An executive team then reviewed the final manuscripts.

## Textual Base of the HCSB®

The textual base for the New Testament [NT] is the *Nestle-Aland Novum Testamentum Graece*, 27th edition, and the United Bible

Societies' *Greek New Testament*, 4<sup>th</sup> corrected edition. The text for the Old Testament [OT] is the *Biblia Hebraica Stuttgartensia*, 5<sup>th</sup> edition.

Significant differences among Hebrew [Hb] and Aramaic [Aram] manuscripts of the OT or among Greek [Gk] manuscripts of the NT are indicated in footnotes. In a few NT cases large square brackets indicate texts that are omitted in some ancient manuscripts. The HCSB® uses the traditional verse divisions found in most Protestant Bibles in English.

## Translation Features

In keeping with a long line of Bible publications, the *Holman Christian Standard Bible*® has retained a number of features found in traditional Bibles:

1. Traditional theological vocabulary (such as *justification, sanctification, redemption*, etc.) has been retained in the HCSB®, since such terms have no translation equivalent that adequately communicates their exact meaning.

2. Traditional spellings of names and places found in most Bibles have been used to make the HCSB® compatible with most Bible study tools.

3. To help readers easily locate the spoken words of the Lord Jesus Christ, some editions of the HCSB® will print the words of Christ in red letters.

4. Most nouns and pronouns that refer to any person of the Trinity are capitalized.

5. Descriptive headings, printed above each section of Scripture, help readers quickly identify the contents of that section.

6. Small lower corner brackets: ⌊ ⌋ indicate words supplied for clarity by the translators (but see discussion below, under <u>Agreement of Elements in Sentences</u>, about supplied words that are *not* bracketed).

## Translation Style Issues
### The Names of God

The HCSB® OT consistently translates the Hb names for God as follows:

| HCSB® English: | Hb original: |
|---|---|
| God | Elohim |
| LORD | Yahweh or YHWH |
| Lord | Adonai |
| Lord GOD | Adonai Yahweh |
| LORD of Hosts | Yahweh Sabaoth |
| God Almighty | El Shaddai |

The HCSB® uses *Yahweh,* the personal name of God in Hb, when a text emphasizes *Yahweh* as a name: *His name is Yahweh* (Ps 68:4).

## Place Names

A number of well-known places in the original text of the Bible, particularly in the OT, have a different name than the one today's Bible readers are familiar with. For example, the Euphrates River often appears in the original text simply as "the River." In cases like this, the HCSB® uses "the Euphrates River" in the text without a footnote indicating this change.

### Agreement of Elements in Sentences

The original text of the Bible does not always follow the standard rules of English grammar, especially in the agreement of subject and verb or agreement of person and number. In order to conform to standard usage, the HCSB® has often made these kinds of grammatical constructions agree in English and has not noted them using footnotes or lower corner brackets.

In addition, the Gk or Hb texts sometimes seem redundant or ambiguous by repeating nouns when we would substitute pronouns or by repeating pronouns when we would supply nouns for clarity and good style. The HCSB® sometimes changes a pronoun to its corresponding noun or a noun to its corresponding pronoun in the interests of clarity and good English style without noting this change with a footnote or lower corner brackets. For example:

The HCSB® text of Jn 1:42 reads: "And he brought Simon to Jesus . . ." [The original Gk of this sentence reads: "And he brought him to Jesus."]

## Special Formatting Features

The *Holman Christian Standard Bible*® has several distinctive formatting features:

1. OT passages quoted in the NT are set in boldface type. OT quotes less than two lines long are embedded in the Bible text. Quotes consisting of two or more lines are block indented.
2. In dialogue, a new paragraph is used for each new speaker as in most modern publications.
3. Many passages, such as 1 Co 13, have been formatted as Dynamic Prose (separate lines that are block indented like poetry) for ease in reading and comprehension.
4. A series of persons or items may be indented as a list. Examples are the genealogy of Christ (Mt 1:2-16), the 12 apostles (Mt 10:2-4), and the precious stones in the New Jerusalem (Rv 21:19-20).
5. A written inscription that was posted for people to read, such as the sign above Jesus on the cross (Mt 27:37), is placed inside a box and centered in the text.
6. Frequently used foreign, geographical, cultural, or ancient words are preceded by a superscripted bullet [˙*Abba*] and listed in alphabetical order at the back of most editions under the heading HCSB Bullet Notes™.

## Footnotes

Located at the bottom of the page, footnotes provide valuable information to help the reader understand the original biblical language or how it is translated in the HCSB®. The words of Scripture, quoted in a footnote, are always printed in italics.

### NT Textual Footnotes

NT textual notes indicate significant differences among Gk manuscripts [mss] and are normally indicated in one of three ways:

> Other mss read _____
> Other mss add _____
> Other mss omit _____

In the NT, some textual footnotes that use the word "add" or "omit" also have square brackets before and after the corresponding verses in the biblical text. See Mk 16:9-20, Jn 5:3-4, and Jn 7:53–8:11 for examples.

### OT Textual Footnotes

OT textual notes show important differences among Hb manuscripts and among ancient OT versions, such as the Septuagint (LXX) and the Vulgate (Vg). See the list of abbreviations on page xv for a complete list of other ancient versions used.

Like NT textual notes, some OT textual notes give only the alternate textual reading, but other OT textual notes list the manuscripts and versions that support a reading found in the HCSB® text and are followed by a semicolon, the alternative reading, and the manuscript evidence supporting that reading. For example, the HCSB® text of Ps 12:7 reads:

You will protect us [b] from this generation forever.

The textual footnote for this verse reads:

[b] 12:7 Some Hb mss, LXX; other Hb mss read *him*

The textual note in this example means that there are two different readings found in the Hb manuscripts: some manuscripts read us and others read *him.* The HCSB® translators decided to put the reading *us* in the text (which is also supported by the Septuagint [LXX]); the other reading *him* is placed in the footnote.

Occasionally, variations by scribal copyists in the Hb manuscript tradition will be noted as follows (in OT studies, these variations are referred to as *Kethiv/Qere* readings):

Alt Hb tradition reads _____

A few times when there is uncertainty about what the original Hb text was, the following note is used:

Hb uncertain

## Other Kinds of Footnotes

| | |
|---|---|
| Lit _____ | a very literal rendering in English of the Hebrew, Aramaic, or Greek text |
| Or _____ | an alternate English translation of the same Hebrew, Aramaic, or Greek text |
| Hb, Aram, Gk | the actual Hebrew, Aramaic, or Greek word is given using English letters |
| Hb obscure | in the OT, when the original Hebrew wording is difficult to translate |
| emend(ed) to _____ | informs the reader that the original Hb text is so difficult to translate that some scholars have conjectured what the original text was in order to translate it. |

Additional footnotes clarify the meaning of certain biblical texts or explain biblical history, persons, customs, places, activities, and weights and measures. Cross-references are given for some parallel passages or passages with similar wording, and in the NT, for passages quoted from the OT.

## HCSB® Bible Book Abbreviations

### Old Testament

| | |
|---|---|
| Gn | Genesis |
| Ex | Exodus |
| Lv | Leviticus |
| Nm | Numbers |
| Dt | Deuteronomy |
| Jos | Joshua |
| Jdg | Judges |
| Ru | Ruth |
| 1 Sm | 1 Samuel |
| 2 Sm | 2 Samuel |
| 1 Kg | 1 Kings |
| 2 Kg | 2 Kings |
| 1 Ch | 1 Chronicles |
| 2 Ch | 2 Chronicles |
| Ezr | Ezra |
| Neh | Nehemiah |
| Est | Esther |
| Jb | Job |
| Ps | Psalms |
| Pr | Proverbs |
| Ec | Ecclesiastes |
| Sg | Song of Solomon |
| Is | Isaiah |
| Jr | Jeremiah |
| Lm | Lamentations |
| Ezk | Ezekiel |
| Dn | Daniel |
| Hs | Hosea |
| Jl | Joel |
| Am | Amos |
| Ob | Obadiah |
| Jnh | Jonah |
| Mc | Micah |
| Nah | Nahum |
| Hab | Habakkuk |
| Zph | Zephaniah |
| Hg | Haggai |
| Zch | Zechariah |
| Mal | Malachi |

### New Testament

| | |
|---|---|
| Mt | Matthew |
| Mk | Mark |
| Lk | Luke |
| Jn | John |
| Ac | Acts |
| Rm | Romans |
| 1 Co | 1 Corinthians |
| 2 Co | 2 Corinthians |
| Gl | Galatians |
| Eph | Ephesians |
| Php | Philippians |
| Col | Colossians |
| 1 Th | 1 Thessalonians |
| 2 Th | 2 Thessalonians |
| 1 Tm | 1 Timothy |
| 2 Tm | 2 Timothy |
| Ti | Titus |
| Phm | Philemon |
| Heb | Hebrews |
| Jms | James |
| 1 Pt | 1 Peter |
| 2 Pt | 2 Peter |
| 1 Jn | 1 John |
| 2 Jn | 2 John |
| 3 Jn | 3 John |
| Jd | Jude |
| Rv | Revelation |

## Commonly Used Abbreviations in the HCSB®

| | |
|---|---|
| A.D. | in the year of our Lord |
| alt | alternate |
| a.m. | from midnight until noon |
| Aram | Aramaic |
| B.C. | before Christ |
| c. | circa |
| chap | chapter |
| DSS | Dead Sea Scrolls |
| Eng | English |
| Gk | Greek |
| Hb | Hebrew |
| Lat | Latin |
| Lit | Literally |
| LXX | Septuagint—an ancient translation of the Old Testament into Greek |
| MT | Masoretic Text |
| NT | New Testament |
| ms(s) | manuscript(s) |
| OT | Old Testament |
| p.m. | from noon until midnight |
| pl | plural |
| Ps(s) | psalm(s) |
| Sam | Samaritan Pentateuch |
| sg | singular |
| syn. | synonym |
| Sym | Symmachus |
| Syr | Syriac |
| Tg | Targum |
| Theod | Theodotian |
| v., vv. | verse, verses |
| Vg | Vulgate—an ancient translation of the Bible into Latin |
| vol(s). | volume(s) |

# WHAT A GIFT!

New beginnings are what give life its hope. Imagine what our years on earth would be like without ever knowing the crisp, starchy feel of a new outfit, the oniony aroma of a freshly cut lawn, a new box of cereal and the Sunday comics.

These are the kind of fresh starts we get every day, every year, every couple of weeks—times when the old and ratty is replaced by something new and unscratched, something with none of the problems and all of the possibilities.

But coming to Christ is the ultimate new beginning. Even if it's happened in the most natural way of all—a good kid growing up in a good Christian home, taking a simple step of faith in a life that's been heading God's direction all along—the prize of a saved heart puts a treasure in your hands that's smooth and gleaming, polished to a shine, a wonder you can't take your eyes off.

Or maybe you've come to Christ leaving behind a lot more damage than just little white lies and spats with your sister—with old sins that make you blush and relationships in need of repair. Still, this treasure of salvation glistens with a contrast that's almost beyond belief. You're free. You're at peace. You're starting over.

So welcome to your new beginning. This Bible is your chance to build something solid on your new foundation, to go somewhere with this new heart and a head of steam, to put God's truth underneath your next decision and never lack the living reality of His presence.

God has given you quite a gift. This book—this *Gift*—is designed to help you figure out what you have been given . . . and learn how to put it to work.

## *But First*

Before we get too much further into this, though, let's take a quick look at the simplest basics of salvation.

The Bible says that we are born with a problem: we are sinners. "All have sinned and fall short of the glory of God" (Romans 3:23). Even if we've done a lot of good things up to now, we know that our hearts have been turned toward ourselves. If they've leaned toward God at all, it has either been because we made ourselves do it or because we were told to. He is not our natural preference. We are.

Now, we could never get ourselves out of this mess, but God can. Better than that, He wants to. Jesus was sent into our world for that very purpose—"to seek and to save the lost" (Luke 19:10). He said, "I have come that they may have life and have it in abundance" (John 10:10).

Even before we had made one move toward God, "while we were still sinners Christ died for us" (Romans 5:8).

And all we have to do is receive His gift.

Besides, we could never work hard enough to get God's approval anyway. "For by grace you are saved through faith, and this is not from yourselves; it is God's gift—not from works, so that no one can boast" (Ephesians 2:8-9). We must simply say that we've had enough of our sins and the problems they've been causing us, and "this is the message of faith that we proclaim: if you confess with your mouth, 'Jesus is Lord,' and believe in your heart that God raised Him from the dead, you will be saved. . . . For everyone who calls on the name of the Lord will be saved" (Romans 10:9,13).

If you've done that, God's salvation is now yours.

If you've done that, *The Gift* is for you.

## The First 90 Days

If you'll turn just one page more, you can begin a 90-day adventure with God, where you'll soak up all kinds of information and experiences that can help you get your spiritual feet up under you.

These short devotionals (which you can read and study at your own pace) will unlock some of the mysteries of Christian faith and take you straight into the Bible where you can see the answers for yourself.

Promise yourself you won't lay this book aside until you've read every word and marked down every new discovery. This is the revealed Word of God you're holding in your hands. It contains the answers to all your questions, the reasons behind your faith, the promises you'll need every step of the way. And it'll walk with you day by day until you're ready to move on to the next level of growth.

While you're working through these devotionals, you'll also find some other helps in the back pages—a quick list of the Top 10 Truths of the Bible, along with another healthy selection of Scriptures to look up and learn from.

So what do you say we get going? We'll start slow, but we'll move fast. And in three months, you'll look back and won't believe how far God has taken you.

The worst thing you can do with a gift is shut it in a drawer and never use it.

The best thing you can do with this *Gift* is to put it in your life—and start living it.

Let's go!

## Day 1
# WHY ME? WHY NOW?
*How God Draws You to Himself*

*"No one can come to Me unless the Father who sent me draws him."*
John 6:44

Calling your conversion experience a decision for Christ doesn't begin to convey the truth of the matter. Yes, you made a decision based on your own free will. Yes, you were perfectly free to make a different choice than you did.

But look at the whole thing on balance—from God's perspective—and suddenly your decision to follow Jesus looks a lot less like a bold move on your part and a lot more like a stunning victory on His part.

He fashioned everything there is about you in His own mind. He set you in a particular time and place. He's been carefully arranging people, situations, and events in your life, waving His arms in front of your face, pleading with you to look back, to see the cross, to know the love that paid every last dime on your escalating debt of sins, to experience more freedom and joy and peace and contentment than you ever thought possible.

Looks like your hardest decision was trying to say no all this time.

*Look Up*
*John 6:35-46 (page 142)*

## Day 2
# REMEMBER YOUR ROOTS
*The Rise and Fall of Man*

*Just as sin entered the world through one man, and death through sin, in this way death spread to all men, because all sinned.*
Romans 5:12

Say hello to the deadwood in your spiritual family tree. They go by the names Adam and Eve. And they've taken you far away from your roots. Not that we'd have done any differently had we been in their bare feet, but Adam and Eve's decline into deception cost them much more than a nice, cozy home in the garden spot of the world. It cost the entire human family everything God had created it to be.

Because of their sin—or the Fall, as it's commonly called—mankind refused his rightful, original place of perfect, guilt-free fellowship with God, and landed with a thud on a dark, remote nowhere land a million miles from home—spiritually depraved, hopelessly lost.

Ever since then, the human quest has been to rediscover his lost worth, to understand why his innate desire to be better than he is—and to enjoy a relationship with a God bigger than himself—has always ended in such disappointing failure. There's only one way back. And you've found it. Say hello to Jesus Christ.

*Look Up*
*Romans 5:12-21 (page 224)*

# GOOD COP, BAD COP

*The New Man and the Old*

---

*I discover this principle: When I want to do good, evil is with me.*
Romans 7:21

---

When you welcomed Jesus into your world, He restored the blood supply to your spirit—that part of you that had been beaten and left for dead by the thugs of sin and deception. He gave you a new heart, complete with a guarantee of full protection against the punishment of hell, against the fear and finality of the grave. He placed in you His own Holy Spirit to give you a new way of thinking, a fresh awareness of God's presence, and a promise that one day your faith would pay off with a one-way ticket to paradise.

But look who's still hanging around. Your heart may be in heaven, but God's left your feet here on the ground, where the person you used to be can still have a say in your choices and remind you how much fun you used to have together.

Don't be surprised when civil war breaks out in your heart, when you're torn between the God you love and the temptations that still know how to play your song. Your sinful self is beaten, but he's not going without a fight.

*Look Up*
*Romans 7:13-25 (page 227)*

# POWER IN YOUR CORNER

*Your All-Sufficiency in Christ*

---

*I pray that the eyes of your heart may be enlightened so you may know . . . the immeasurable greatness of his power.*
Ephesians 1:18a,19a

---

Trusting God to help you overcome your sins and shortcomings sounds so spiritual, doesn't it? Turning everything over to God, letting God handle your problems, giving your burdens to the Lord . . . can't argue with the wisdom there.

But when it's just you and your bad temper, or your runaway sex drive, or your weakness for cherry cheesecake, where do you find the strength to say no?

You might not guess it to look at you, but you have available to you—right now—the same kind of power that God "demonstrated . . . in the Messiah by raising Him from the dead" (Ephesians 1:20). And as you begin facing even your toughest challenges with the weapons of prayer, Bible truth, worship, thanksgiving, accountability, and other specific strategies that you'll begin gaining through experience, you'll see sin's deception for what it is, you'll turn your back on habits that have had your number for years, and your heart for instant gratification will be changed into a heart that knows where its power lies.

*Look Up*
*Ephesians 1:15-19 (page 281)*

# ONE STEP AT A TIME

*Learning to Walk with God*

*Grow in the grace and knowledge of our Lord and Savior Jesus Christ.*
2 Peter 3:18

No one enters the Christian life as middle management. Just like there's only one way in—through belief in Jesus Christ and His death on the cross—there's only one way up. And it starts on the ground floor.

But don't worry. For at least two reasons it's anything but boring in the minimum-wage mailroom of Christian maturity:

• Your enemy, Satan, knows that your fire is burning pretty bright right now. He also knows that you're vulnerable to a relapse (modern attention spans and commitment levels being what they are). He'll have plenty of temptations to keep you busy once the new wears off.

• But on the other hand, God promises you room for steady advancement if you're willing to work hard in His training program, committing yourself to His Word, to His church, to His tried-and-true philosophy of aspiring to bigger things by being faithful in the small things. New blessings and discoveries can spring up from all over when you're just starting out. You won't find this much joy in anyone else's company.

*Look Up*
*2 Peter 3:17-18 (page 355)*

# LIKE A LITTLE CHILD

*Seeing God as Father*

*As a father has compassion on his children, so the Lord has compassion on those who fear Him.*
Psalm 103:13

When God wanted to put His love into terms we could understand, He painted Himself in the biblical imagery of a Father—not the kind who rants and raves, fussing about the way you keep your room or teaching you how to drive by pounding the dashboard every time you change lanes in traffic. Not the kind who's tied up (again) at work, or only visible from the waist down behind his morning paper, apparently unconcerned with the things that matter most to you.

Neither is He a doting grandfather, mindlessly doling out dollar bills so you can buy your fill of candy and bubble gum. This Father who asks you to walk with Him will ask more of you than anyone possibly could—your life, in fact, for the privilege of being on personal terms with the God of the universe. But in return, you'll receive a love that's so complete and unconditional, so honest and pure, so rich in mercy and long on patience, that you'll want nothing more than to please Him, to make Him proud of you, to find your reason for living in His gentle smile.

*Look Up*
*Psalm 103:11-14 (page 477)*

# WHAT WOULD JESUS DO?

*Thinking with the Mind of Christ*

*The one who says he remains in Him
should walk just as He walked.*
*1 John 2:6*

Christ's death on the cross did a lot more than tear up your rap sheet and clear your name with the Judge. By accepting His death, you have also accepted His life—the seeds of a new character that He is forming inside you as you let His words become yours, as you begin adopting His nature of purity, trust, and humility, crowding out the self-centered clutter you've been accumulating all these years.

Christ has come to clean house, to bag up the stuff that needs to go in the garbage, to throw open the windows for fresh breezes of godly insight and perspective, to shine the revealing light of His Word into every corner of your life.

As He starts to work within your everyday experiences, you'll not only begin doing things His way, but thinking the way He thinks, becoming sick to your stomach at the sight of your own unfaithfulness. You'll seek your thrills at no other place than the satisfying waters of Christian obedience and filter your daily decisions through the lens of His unselfish love.

*Look Up*
*1 John 2:3-6 (page 356)*

# INSIDE INFORMATION

*Living in the Spirit*

*We have not received the spirit of the
world, but the Spirit who is from God.*
*1 Corinthians 2:12*

That ocean of relief and refreshment you felt as you turned your back on sin and turned your life over to Jesus Christ's control was the Holy Spirit of God rushing into your heart, filling you with the raw power of everlasting life. The Bible says: "In [God] you also, when you heard the word of truth, the gospel of your salvation—in Him when you believed—were sealed with the promised Holy Spirit" (Ephesians 1:13b-14). It's sort of like earnest money on the house God's building you in heaven.

Once we get there, we'll understand all that our salvation means. We'll see why we had to go through some of the tough times we faced on earth. Maybe we'll even find out how God pulled off that Red Sea thing, or why He thought it best to put our noses smack-dab in the middle of our faces.

But until then, God has given us His Spirit so that we don't have to rely on our own vague observations and knowledge about spiritual things in order to do what He wants, to understand His plans for us, and to put ourselves into position to serve Him with power and freedom.

*Look Up*
*1 Corinthians 2:9-16 (page 243)*

# DID I DO THAT?

*Spiritual Gifts*

*According to the grace given to us, we have different gifts.*
Romans 12:6

God made you with an inborn set of natural abilities, things that have just always come easily to you. Maybe you have a nice singing voice or a flair for calligraphy. Maybe you're good with numbers or can fix anything on wheels. You've trained these abilities, honed them. But the raw materials and understanding were built into your natural makeup. They are gifts from God in every sense of the word.

Now that you've become a Christian, though, God has given you an extra set of gifts—spiritual gifts—to equip you to play the vital role He's given you in His church. Where natural gifts may dictate the kind of work you've chosen, the hobbies you enjoy, or the subjects you like most in school, spiritual gifts are designed to activate your field of ministry. They supercharge you with un-natural abilities to give, to comfort, to challenge, or to speak with boldness. They won't take the place of the things you do well, but they will open up new vistas of opportunity—and responsibility—for you to be all that God created you to be.

*Look Up*
*Romans 12:3-8 (page 234)*

# COUNTING THE COST

*The High Price of Commitment*

*"If anyone wants to be My follower, he must deny himself, take up his cross, and follow me."*
Mark 8:34

Being a Christian means everything. Everything you are, everything you have. That's why the most miserable people in the world are Christians who aren't willing to take it all the way.

To them, church is uncomfortable, because it keeps confronting them with their sins. Sin is uncomfortable, because the Spirit's taken all the guiltless fun out of it. Relationships are uncomfortable, because being a Christian in one place and a heathen in another makes life hard to keep up with. The call of God stirs their heart, but the call of the world purrs even louder. So with feet in two worlds, they know only the worst of each— the empty promises of sin and the nagging pain of an awakened conscience.

Wow. And they thought God's ways were hard.

The road to the good life is narrow and pretty steep in a lot of places, but the view is breathtaking—the experiences, unforgettable. And those who choose to walk it find everything their heart desires.

Everything.

*Look Up*
*Mark 8:34-38 (page 64)*

# Day 11
# CALLED MEETINGS
*Spending Set-Aside Time with God*

*At daybreak, Lord, You hear my voice.*
*Psalm 5:3*

You can usually tell how important something is to your Christian walk by watching how hard Satan works to prevent you from doing it. Spending quiet time with God is one of them.

Yet if there's one thing you need as a growing believer, it's the early-established, hard-fought discipline of starting each day in fellowship with God.

Jesus did. The Bible says that He "often withdrew to deserted places and prayed" (Luke 5:16). "Very early in the morning, while it was still dark, He got up, went out, and made His way to a deserted place" (Mark 1:35). Not that your time alone with God has to be in the morning, but most of us have learned that leaving quiet time off till bedtime usually results in leaving it off altogether, or at least changes it from a season of new commitments and confidence into a weepy, discouraging rehash of the messes you've made that day.

You'll make time for what matters. And this matters a lot.

# Day 12
# COMPLETELY BOOKED
*Reading Your Bible*

*The instruction of the Lord is perfect,*
*reviving the soul.*
*Psalm 19:7*

The Bible sure is a big book, isn't it? And if you try starting logically in the Old Testament—page 1—and barreling straight through to the end, you're likely to bog down somewhere in Leviticus or Numbers, not quite sure how the cleansing ritual for leprosy is going to factor into your life.

So start by reading one of the foundational books of the Bible—like the Gospel of John, or Paul's Letter to the Romans, or the Book of James. If you want to tackle more, you could set off on a journey through the New Testament, starting with Matthew. Read as much as you can, but only as much as you can understand, not being afraid to read only a verse or two a day as long as you mingle it with prayer that God will use it to shine His truth into your life.

As you read, you'll begin picking up hints of what God's nature is like, plus new understandings of the Bible's overall message. Little by little—but quicker than you think—you'll start developing a mind that thinks like God thinks, because you know what God says.

*Look Up*
*Psalm 5:1-3 (page 393)*

*Look Up*
*Psalm 19:7-11 (page 404)*

Day 13

# GET IT THROUGH YOUR HEAD

*Scripture Memory*

*I have treasured Your word in my heart
so that I may not sin against You.
Psalm 119:11*

Admit it—there are some things you've committed to memory. Either it's song lyrics, or movie lines, or your favorite player's home run totals. You pay enough attention to certain, interesting aspects of life that its minutest details have become common knowledge to you.

Know what, though? This time next year, you'll have a hard time remembering who even played in last year's Super Bowl, though at the time it seemed so important. You'll forget who ran against the governor in the previous election, though at the time you devoured every article on the race. You'll lose track of the TV story line that used to keep you awake nights trying to figure out what was going to happen next week.

"But the Counselor, the Holy Spirit, whom the Father will send in My name, will teach you all things and will remind you of everything I have told you" (John 14:26). If you'll load up on the words of life instead of filling your mind with forgettable facts, you'll place within constant reach the right word for every situation.

*Look Up*
*Psalm 119:9-16 (page 492)*

Day 14

# ANY TIME, ANY PLACE

*Prayer*

*"Keep asking,
and it will be given to you."
Matthew 7:7*

Praying comes to us pretty naturally when we accidentally start a grease fire on the stove or get caught out on the lake in a lightning storm. But those who only know the number to God's 911 hotline are missing out on the simple pleasure of picking up the phone anytime they feel like it—day or night, weekends or holidays—and sharing their hearts with someone who always has the time to listen.

Prayer is so many things and can take so many forms. It can be repeating a Bible verse that thanks God for His mercy or reassures you of His faithfulness. It can be your usual laundry list of family members and friends who need God's touch so much. It can be a request, a praise. A smile, a tear. Eyes closed, eyes open. Just you and Him.

So begin committing yourself to the practice of prayer—even when things are going smoothly, even when you feel like you've got everything under control. In prayer, He will lead you by the hand into His very presence and walk beside you every step of the way.

*Look Up*
*Matthew 7:7-11 (Page 10)*

# DIARY OF A DESTINY

*Keeping a Journal*

*I remember the days of old; I meditate on all You have done.*
*Psalm 143:5*

When life is right on top of you, when you're wrestling with every detail of your current concerns and troubles, it's hard to imagine a day when you won't be able to recall the way you feel right now or remember how difficult this certain decision was. More importantly, it seems impossible that you won't reflect on how God met you in your misery, pulling you through at the last minute, in ways you never expected.

But that day will come. And with it another new challenge, perhaps different but no less imposing, no less complex than the situation before.

Then one morning, your stomach in a knot, you'll pull out your personal journal, flip to a page dated two or three years back, and be suddenly transported to another time and place, to another crossroads conflict that seemed so huge at the time. Wow, you'd almost forgotten about it. Look how desperate you were. Feel the pain in your words. And remember the faithfulness of God—the God who's still here, to deal with the pressure that's so fresh today.

Don't you feel better now?

Look Up
Psalm 143:5-6 (page 510)

# ALL EYES ON HIM

*Praise and Worship*

*We boast in God all day long; we will praise Your name forever.*
*Psalm 44:8*

Let's face it. We're stuck on ourselves—worried about how our bonus check compares with the others, dying to get noticed for our part in the project, hoping nobody else wants the last piece of bread in the basket.

That's why worship is so important in the Christian's life, because it goes against the grain of our deep affection for ourselves. When we kick back our head in praise, when we lift our eyes away from the work of our own hands, we cross the bridge into another world. We see things the way they really are—God, in all His awesome glory, in perfect, patient control over everything that touches us. We see the source behind our strength, the provider of each penny, the fount of every blessing. We see Him fully aware of every need, ready and able to meet us at the exact moment we need an answer—this God who knows us so well, yet loves us so much.

If there was ever a cure for selfishness, it's the prescription-strength power that flows when we empty ourselves of cares and conceit and lose our grip in the face of His greatness.

Look Up
Psalm 44:4-8 (page 426)

# PEACE, BE STILL

## Meditation and Quietude

*While it was still dark, He got up, went out, and made His way to a deserted place.*
Mark 1:35

The New Agers came around, talking about focusing, finding their center, pondering their navels (and stuff like that), and made us define meditation as some heebie-jeebie, hippie holdover that feels at home on a PBS special but not on our living room sofas.

But just because someone misuses God's gift doesn't diminish its importance. Meditation is a much-needed Christian discipline. When you seek a silent place away from the pull of the newspaper or the approaching drumbeats of a work deadline, when you feast on a single verse of the Scripture, letting the Holy Spirit bring to your mind new lessons to learn, new twists on the truth, new insights to gather . . . you will learn to recognize God's voice and grow in your relationship.

You certainly don't have to look for demands and distractions. They'll find you—enough to fill every second of your life with noise and activity, yet still leave you restless and dissatisfied. Come quietly—deliberately—before God. Meditate on His Word. Enjoy His satisfying rest.

*Look Up*
*Mark 1:35-37 (page 51)*

# OUT IN THE OPEN

## Confession and Repentance

*The one who conceals his sins will not prosper.*
Proverbs 28:13

God is no pushover. His call to holy living is very clear, very firm, very hard to misunderstand. Let's not trick ourselves into thinking that His heart of compassion has made Him soft on sin.

But rest in this: "He knows what we are made of, remembering that we are dust" (Psalm 103:14). He understands the bad habits we've molded over the years, the comfortable corners we run to when we're tired or upset or discouraged. Truth is, the anger we feel pressing down on us is more ours than His, for while we could kick ourselves for caving again, He's heartbroken that we've sold ourselves out so cheaply, that we've chosen the path of pain when He has offered us the path of peace.

So as you catch yourself in compromise, confess your mistake. And promise (with God's help) that you'll turn your back on this foolishness. Confession gets your sin out in front where you can deal with it. Repentance takes it out to the curb where God can haul it off with the rest of your garbage—and leave you feeling clean again.

*Look Up*
*Proverbs 28:13-14 (page 556)*

## Day 19
# STRENGTH IN NUMBERS
*Why You Belong in Church*

*There are many parts, yet one body.*
*1 Corinthians 12:20*

Your week may be filled with sales meetings and lunch plans, with night classes and homework, with diapers and runny noses—whatever ordinary means to you. You may be having a squabble with your sister or a hassle with your landlord. You may be knee-deep in credit card bills or trying not to worry about that curious new pain in your side.

The week has a way of wearing you down, of hitting you head-on with more troubles and temptations than you were hoping to handle. You can fall into bed on Saturday night a limp rag. A sigh. A surrender. You may feel almost as far out of God's plan as you were before you gave your life to Him.

But no matter what your week's been like, you can walk into God's house on Sunday morning and know that you're right where you're supposed to be—that you're part of something bigger than yourself, a place where you belong, a member of an eternal family. You need them, and they need you. Together, you can find the strength to face another week—to go on another day.

*Look Up*
*1 Corinthians 12:12-20 (page 254)*

## Day 20
# BETWEEN FRIENDS
*Accountability*

*Encourage each other daily . . . so that none of you is hardened by sin's deception.*
*Hebrews 3:13*

"I will bless the Lord who counsels me—even at night my conscience instructs me. I keep the Lord in mind always" (Psalm 16:7-8).

He's there. Wherever you are. Whatever you're feeling. Without having to play a silly mind game or pretend something that's not real, you can just believe the fact that God is always with you, His power always within reach, His help always a word away.

But when it's late, when you've had a tough day, when a drink is sounding awfully good, or the remote control is driving your TV through a bad section of town, the features on God's face can dim a little. His invisible presence can fade into forgetfulness.

But if you've got a couple of friends you've promised to stay accountable to, if you dread the thought of facing them without a clear conscience and a good word of testimony, you can flash their faces through your mind or make a quick phone call and remember what a holy life is worth.

Look, we're all in this thing together.

*Look Up*
*Hebrews 3:12-14 (page 325)*

# SWEAT THE SMALL STUFF

*Subtle Sins*

---

*Be doers of the word
and not hearers only.
James 1:22*

---

Ever tried cleaning up a room that was totally trashed? By the time the dresser drawers won't shut and the bed disguises an unseen colony of clothes and clutter—when the last shoe has finally dropped and you've been surrounded by the law of gravity—it's time to do the big stuff first. The glaring things. The obvious things. Like making your bed. Folding up your sweaters. Returning all the plates, forks, and glasses to the kitchen.

But underneath the chief culprits lies a second layer of vandals. Dust. Corners. Baseboards. Pockets of disarray you didn't notice before, but now—with all the major problems taken care of—they cry out for correction. On and on it goes. The light exposes another. You fix, tinker, and straighten. You want to be clean.

As a growing Christian, you need to stay constantly open to the white glove of God's Word—not to keep you endlessly frustrated with your faults, but to keep unseen sins from becoming an all-day mess. What's under the rug can be more of a problem than you think.

*Look Up
James 1:19-25 (page 339)*

# FAMILIAR PLACES

*Bad Habits*

---

*All bitterness, anger and wrath, insult and slander must be removed from you.
Ephesians 4:31*

---

Every time you've gone back to your old ways of getting relief or revenge, every time you've reacted without thinking or given in when you should have toughed it out, you've widened the entrance ramp onto the easy street of compromise. You've made it that much easier to come back for a return trip next time you're worn down and upset—when things just aren't going your way.

That's really what bad habits are—wide, open highways that you know like the back of your hand. Roads you've traveled so many times that you could drive them with your eyes closed. But you know you have no business being out there. You know you'll eventually dead-end into regrets and apologies. And if you just had the strength, you'd whip that car around right now and take the straight and narrow path that could lead you to something better.

So do it, because now your "no" has the power of God behind it. And every time you lean hard into His side for the strength to resist, you close another entrance ramp. You shut down another access road. You play dead to the call of the highway. You win over habitual sin.

*Look Up
Ephesians 4:25-32 (page 285)*

# SUCKER PUNCHES

*Temptation*

*He will not allow you to be tempted
beyond what you are able.*
*1 Corinthians 10:13*

Satan didn't sleep through your salvation experience. Your sudden departure from the kingdom of darkness into the kingdom of light sent off warning flares in his security division. And He immediately set a strategic plan in motion to make sure your faith gets lost on its way to your lifestyle.

So Never underestimate the depths of his deceit. He knows a lot about you, but guess what—we know a few things about him, too.

For one, we know that God has limited the reach of Satan's temptations. The devil may hold the night stick, but God holds the leash. In fact, God can even turn the devil's schemes to your advantage, using them to toughen muscles in your character and open your eyes to places where you're trusting yourself instead of trusting God.

Remember, too, that temptation isn't sin. It just feels like it. And nowhere in the whole process are you forced to comply—even if you're not quick enough to douse the first flicker of Satan's finesse. He can make persuasive suggestions—and hope you feel guilty just by thinking about it—but he can't make you do anything.

Don't believe a word he says.

*Look Up*
*1 Corinthians 10:6-13 (page 250)*

# IT'S ALL BEHIND YOU

*Overcoming Past Guilt*

*To make you stand in the presence of
His glory, blameless and with great joy.*
*Jude 24*

If you only knew how clean your record was.

If you could only believe how much the Father loves you.

If you could finally understand that when you gave your heart to Jesus, you "put on Christ" (Galatians 3:27), so that when God looks at you now, He doesn't see that junk you used to wear, but the pure, shining garments of Christ's everlasting righteousness.

He sees you for who you really are—a full-fledged child of the living God.

Oh, you've still got some wrinkles to iron out. And as you stay open to the Spirit's conviction—through the Bible, through sermons, through the words of a true friend—you'll be drawn to new repentance. You'll want to be like Christ no matter what it costs.

But guilt gives itself away by beating you down, by presenting forgiven material into evidence, by accusing you of hypocrisy when God says you're worthy of heaven. Turn the guilt of your past into a testimony of God's power. Walk away with your head up.

*Look Up*
*Jude 24-25 (page 365)*

# Day 25
# CRITIC'S CORNER
*Other People's Perceptions*

*If they persecuted Me,
they will also persecute you.*
*John 15:20*

You may as well be on the lookout for a couple of thieves that like to prey on new Christians who are serious about being Christlike.

One is the old friend who liked you better the way you were, back when you were a lot more open to having a good time and going to church didn't interfere with every weekend.

The other one is the Christian who's seen your kind come along before and liked you better when you were still a prayer request. Now you're a ball of fire who's just crazy enough to take what you read in the Bible at face value, who thinks there's nothing God can't do through people who pray and churches who love each other. Your enthusiasm threatens them. They're supposed to be the ones helping you.

So if you haven't already, you're sure to start feeling the heat from those who want you either more like the world or more like the status quo. Just keep believing that what the Bible says is true and keep loving them the way you wish they could love you.

*Look Up*
*John 15:18-21 (page 160)*

# Day 26
# TALK, TALK, TALK, TALK
*The Tongue*

*A gentle answer turns away anger, but a harsh word stirs up wrath.*
*Proverbs 15:1*

You didn't mean to say it. It just slipped out. Everybody knows how it feels when the gossip engine is in full swing, when the camaraderie of shared complaints and put-downs makes you say things you promised yourself not to—little tidbits you'd been told in confidence, jokes and jabs you toss out for public enjoyment though you'd never speak them right to someone's face. We all understand.

But knowing that we all understand doesn't make it right. And working harder to bite your lip next time only provides temporary relief. Jesus said that "the mouth speaks from the overflow of the heart" (Matthew 12:34)—that if we want our words (or our silence) to be pure and pleasing, we must change our attitudes to match.

So . . . do you want to withstand the urge to sling the next insult? Then try loving the person who irritates you. Want to never make another idle remark at another's expense? Then pray for God to help you want the best for your grouchy neighbor. Kind words come from clean hearts.

*Look Up*
*Proverbs 15:1-2 (page 536)*

# MEASURING STICKS

*Comparing Yourself with Others*

*It is not the one commending himself
who is approved, but the one
the Lord commends.
2 Corinthians 10:18*

You may feel as though you know next to nothing about Christ. But so did everybody when they first started down this road—even the ones who can pray like they're six inches from heaven. Even the ones who can wow you with their grasp of biblical wisdom and insight. Even the ones who can send chills down people's spines in a worship service or who rarely come off a business trip without a new convert under each arm.

But you need to know this: God is always more pleased with folks who are faithful than with those who can draw a crowd.

And another thing: God's invested time and talents in you that He's just now starting to use. And as you yield them to His service—whether you get any recognition or not—you'll begin steadily growing into the ministry He wants you to perform.

God's putting a whole team together in your town or city to take His love and salvation to every person who'll listen. It's going to take all of you working together, combining your callings and pooling your abilities. So start practicing your part. Your piece is as important as anybody's.

*Look Up
2 Corinthians 10:12-18 (page 269)*

# GOOD ENOUGH

*Performance-Based Acceptance*

*After beginning with the Spirit, are you
now going to be made complete
by the flesh?
Galatians 3:3*

Maybe your dad wasn't quick with an "I love you." Maybe he said the lawn looked pretty good, but that you could have been a lot more careful around the flower bed. Maybe he was fairly pleased with your musical performance, but scolded you for being flat in a few places. He may have thought four A's and two B's wasn't too bad, but it could have been better. You could have tried harder. You could have done more.

But what you did was never enough.

So you thought getting up ten minutes early three days this week to pray and read your Bible was good. Wasn't it, Father? Of course, it could have been more like twenty minutes. And every day.

Giving an extra five dollars in your tithe check this week was pretty generous. Right, Father? Or would ten dollars have earned more of a smile?

Listen, you can always do more to return the favor God's given. There's not a person alive who can't deepen his devotion. But child of God, He loves you and accepts you right where you are. You can't work hard enough to get more. The proof is in His palm.

*Look Up
Galatians 3:1-5 (page 275)*

# WHATEVER YOU SAY

*Doing God's Will*

*"My food is to do the will of Him who
sent Me and to finish His work."*
John 4:34

God has given you the freedom of taking your best stab at life, of spreading out your own map, striking out on your own instincts, and finding your own way to the land of meaning and purpose.

But in case that responsibility leaves you feeling unsettled and ill equipped, He is more than willing to oversee your travel plans, to plot out the routes that He knows are best—no matter how out-of-the-way they may appear to you.

After all, He knows the places where you're likely to bump into lane closures and construction delays. He knows that the squiggly red line on the map that appears to cut nearly an hour off your trip disguises a sea of school zones, stop signs, and Friday night ballgame traffic. He even knows they've opened one of your favorite restaurants on a little backroad that you never would have spotted if you'd gone the way you were thinking. With a travel agent like that helping you chart your path through life, why would anybody want to trust their own sense of direction? Would you?

*Look Up*
*John 4:31-34 (page 138)*

# WHAT A BARGAIN

*Decision Making*

*Walk by the Spirit and you will not carry
out the desire of the flesh.*
Galatians 5:16

You now have a partner in life, and He is not a silent one. This new Friend who walks beside you into every decision you make has no desire to withhold the guidance you need to arrive at sound, godly decisions. Count on Him to always let you see enough of every situation to make the best choice, whether you're choosing between right and wrong or between good and better. As badly as you want to be faithful to Him, to use your life to bring Him honor, He wants you to know His will. To talk where you can hear.

But you won't always want to listen. You may be too mad to think clearly, too afraid to act boldly, or perhaps just too busy to give Him the time of day. But if you'll strip away any desire for personal gain or attention, if you'll turn to the Bible for truthful instruction, and if you'll quiet yourself before God and allow His Holy Spirit to direct and confirm your thoughts—you'll get your answer. You'll be able to step out in obedient faith, willing to make a mistake as long as you know your heart is right. Good choice.

*Look Up*
*Galatians 5:16-18 (page 279)*

# WHATEVER YOU SAY

## *Doing God's Will*

*"My food is to do with will of Him who sent Me and to finish His work."*
*John 4:34*

God has given you the freedom of taking your best stab at life, of spreading out your own map, striking out on your own instincts, and finding your own way to the land of meaning and purpose.

But in case that responsibility leaves you feeling unsettled and ill equipped, He is more than willing to oversee your travel plans, to plot out the routes that He knows are best—no matter how out-of-the-way they may appear to you.

After all, He knows the places where you're likely to bump into lane closures and construction delays. He knows that the squiggly red line on the map that appears to cut nearly an hour off your trip disguises a sea of school zones, stop signs, and Friday night ballgame traffic. He even knows they've opened one of your favorite restaurants on a little backroad that you never would have spotted if you'd gone the way you were thinking. With a travel agent like that helping you chart your path through life, why would anybody want to trust their own sense of direction? Would you?

*Look Up*
*John 4:31-34 (page 138)*

# WHAT A BARGAIN

## *Decision Making*

*Walk by the Spirit and you will not carry out the desire of the flesh.*
*Galatians 5:16*

You now have a partner in life, and He is not a silent one. This new Friend who walks beside you into every decision you make has no desire to withhold the guidance you need to arrive at sound, godly decisions. Count on Him to always let you see enough of every situation to make the best choice, whether you're choosing between right and wrong or between good and better. As badly as you want to be faithful to Him, to use your life to bring Him honor, He wants you to know His will. To talk where you can hear.

But you won't always want to listen. You may be too mad to think clearly, too afraid to act boldly, or perhaps just too busy to give Him the time of day. But if you'll strip away any desire for personal gain or attention, if you'll turn to the Bible for truthful instruction, and if you'll quiet yourself before God and allow His Holy Spirit to direct and confirm your thoughts—you'll get your answer. You'll be able to step out in obedient faith, willing to make a mistake as long as you know your heart is right. Good choice.

*Look Up*
*Galatians 5:16-18 (page 279)*

# THE BIG PICTURE

## *The Christian Worldview*

*Be careful that no one takes you captive through philosophy and empty deceit.*
*Colossians 2:8*

Beliefs have consequences, even the ones that people rarely spend time thinking about. Those, in fact, may be the scariest beliefs of all. But whether deliberately or unwittingly, people live their lives based on a set of understood principles. Their answers to the questions of where they came from, what they're doing here, and where they're going colors the decisions they make, the work they do, and the responsibility they feel for themselves and others.

They live by what is called a worldview—be it secular and self-centered, humanistic, New Age, or whatever.

So do you. As a holder of the Christian worldview, you have given up your right to mindlessly float through life on the driftwood of someone else's opinions. The Bible's revelation of who God is, what He has done to redeem fallen humanity, and the eternal nature of His heavenly kingdom should affect every position you hold on every possible issue of modern life. To know how to live, you must first know what you believe. Dig in and find out.

# FARSIGHTED

## *Long-Term Perspective*

*You need endurance, so that after you have done God's will, you may receive what was promised.*
*Hebrews 10:36*

This is the era of the quick turnaround. If we can't call tonight and have it on our desk first thing in the morning, we'll call someone else who can. That's the way the world thinks. That's the way the world runs. But that's the way you get yourself into trouble if you're expecting God to cater to your short-term demands.

It's not that He's too busy to work you into His schedule or unconcerned with the time pressure you're up against. It's just that He knows how impatient we can get, how limited our little minds are to the bigger picture of His plan, and how often we'll look back on this season of waiting as one of the most valuable experiences our faith ever endured.

If you can ever come to grips with the fact that God knows exactly what you need, when you need it, and in what measure you need to receive it, you'll be able to shrug off every thought that tempts you to begrudge His timing. After all, we've got a long time to enjoy all the things we've been waiting for.

# SIMPLE STEPS

### Steady Progress

*I pursue as my goal the prize promised by God's heavenly call in Christ Jesus.*
*Philippians 3:14*

---

Every now and then, a football team will string together a season of surprise victories on the backs of a wide-open offense and a renegade pass rush. Fans will flock to the games, reporters will descend on the campus, front pages will flash their colors and accomplishments.

But somewhere in relative obscurity, another team will be turning their usual brand of rugged discipline, quiet confidence, and basic, fundamental football into simple, unspectacular wins. 14-10. 20-17. 10-8. Nothing all that special for the 10 o'clock highlight reel. Just another win.

Like expected.

And five years later, when the glitter and sparkle of that Cinderella team has faded into a frustrating 5-and-6 finish, the boys who just block and tackle and run dives up the middle will be in the hunt for another championship. That's just the way it is.

So don't be discouraged if your victories don't win you the chance to stand in the pulpit or get applause from the crowd. Your coach likes the way you play when you give Him consistent performance.

*Look Up*
*Philippians 3:12-14 (page 292)*

# NOT ON MY OWN

### The Inadequacy of Willpower

*Humble yourselves before the Lord, and He will exalt you.*
*James 4:10*

---

You can try to dodge temptation, come up with some kind of self-talk to say, or devise some clever scheme to trick your mind into thinking about something else. But in the end, all your bluster will pop like an overblown balloon, and you'll find yourself right back in the mudhole.

Take it from people who've been there themselves.

Human willpower can accomplish a lot of things, but achieving lasting victory over your sin areas is not one of them.

That's why Christians who've gotten sick enough of continuing to sin eventually throw up their hands, lay down their unwieldy weapons, and start letting God fight their battles for them, "because the One who is in you is greater than the one who is in the world" (1 John 4:4).

So turn a deaf ear to temptation. Repeat the Scriptures that remind you to "consider yourselves dead to sin" (Romans 6:11) and not to "give the devil a foothold" (Ephesians 4:27). The battle isn't yours but God's. So stay alert, sit back, and watch Him win.

*Look Up*
*James 4:7-10 (page 342)*

# THIS IS A HOLD-UP

*God's Grace*

*He gave Himself for us ... to cleanse for Himself a special people, eager to do good works.*
*Titus 2:14*

Every one of us knows the anguish of failing the Lord. We tap our fist against our forehead, eyes closed in disbelief and disappointment. We've done it again. How are we going to explain this to God?

But we don't have to. He already knows. And after we've beaten ourselves up long enough, we finally realize that we can quit groveling in shame and turn our face toward His throne, "so that we may receive mercy and find grace to help us" (Hebrews 4:16).

Grace. There it is again. Just as sweet and refreshing as it was the first time we put it to our lips. When we first fell back into its big, strong arms and felt the peace of God's purity flowing through our veins, we thought grace had done all it was supposed to do. But like ocean waves that splash with fresh blessing from a bottomless source, God's grace keeps catching us, keeps picking us up, keeps moving us forward when we thought we'd fallen too far behind to catch up. His grace is still here, still supplying, still as amazing as ever.

# UNSUNG HEROES

*Greatness in Little Things*

*"Whoever gives just a cup of cold water to one of these little ones ... he will never lose his reward!"*
*Matthew 10:42*

Little notes written to encourage folks to keep their chin up, to remind them that God hasn't forgotten them. And neither have you.

Long, boring hours beside a hospital bed, holding the hand and whispering into the ear of a dying grandmother who may not even know you're in the room.

An hour-long, nonsensical imaginary adventure with your four-year-old (complete with your own falsetto voices) even though you were just fifty pages away from tying up the loose ends of a good mystery novel.

Great people in God's eyes are the ones who don't shun the shadows of personal ministry, but who are willing to be faithful when it doesn't show, humble when it doesn't profit, and unafraid to say no to their own self-will. "Blessed are the gentle, because they will inherit the earth" (Matthew 5:5). They will know the joy of sharing a kind word, the pleasure of buying someone a cup of coffee. They will come to know quicker than the rest of us what life is all about. Life is in the little things.

# ALWAYS ON CALL

*Becoming Others-Oriented*

*"For even the Son of Man did not come to be served, but to serve."*
*Mark 10:45*

This was supposed to be the era of the shorter work week, what with the emergence of the computer and the simpler life we'd enjoy from our modern conveniences. Our biggest challenge was supposed to be choosing how to spend all this extra time we'd have on our hands.

Very funny.

Have you ever before seen a day when people were this strung out with work demands, longer hours, tighter deadlines, breakneck schedules, and higher expectations? Whatever little energy is left at the end of earning a paycheck, running errands, and keeping our homes in working order usually ends up stretched out on the sofa with a glass of iced tea, and the hope that no one will bother us. At this pace, we just don't have time for people.

What an opportunity, then, for you to make the love of Christ stand out in a crowd—every time you forsake the sofa in order to meet a need, serve a brother, help a neighbor. The window's open for us to "shine like stars" (Philippians 2:15). And to see God's face light up.

*Look Up*
*Mark 10:42-45 (page 68)*

# A LIFE OF SERVICE

*Devotion to Ministry*

*Don't neglect to show hospitality, for by doing this some have welcomed angels as guests.*
*Hebrews 13:2*

He was 88 years old. Old enough to know what he was talking about. And you just happened to catch him on a day when he really felt like talking. You had gone with your church group to a local nursing home—sort of a ministry project. You weren't all that sure about it at first. But, as often happens when you try something new like that, God puts just the right people in your path.

And yours was a talker.

Because you are a polite person, you tried hard not to interrupt or to let on that people were waiting for you. Some of his ramblings were hard to follow, but you nodded a lot, acting genuinely interested.

Then he leaned forward in his chair, raised his crooked finger to your face, squinted his eyes through thick, heavy glasses as though he saw in you every precious moment of life he wished he could recapture, and said: "I want you to listen to this old man: Love people. Do good to people. Go out of your way to help people. People are all that matter."

Take it from a guy who knows. People are all that matter.

*Look Up*
*Hebrews 13:1-3 (page 337)*

# Day 41

## ALL IS WELL

### Peace

*He got up and rebuked the wind and the raging waves. So they ceased, and there was a great calm.*
*Luke 8:24*

Train wrecks don't appear all that often on the evening news. But if you'll look around you, in the lives of people you know (or at least people you know of), you'll see one just about every day.

That's because life can roll on fairly predictably for a long time, seducing its passengers into laying their heads back on their own self-assurance. But sooner or later, they'll encounter some kind of unexpected turbulence—a phone call at four in the morning, a chest pain that flares up out of nowhere, a teenage son who's shutting them out of his world—the frightening feeling that life is no longer in the safekeeping of cruise control.

That's when people long for peace—when in the panic of life's emergencies, help seems a million miles away—when in the lonely hours of the night, they wish they had a friend like God to talk to . . . the way you do.

You are a witness of God's peace every time you keep a cool head through one of life's hot spots. Be on your guard. Your trust is showing.

*Look Up*
*Luke 8:22-25 (page 97)*

# Day 42

## I AM SATISFIED

### Contentment

*But godliness with contentment is great gain.*
*1 Timothy 6:6*

Christian contentment goes a lot deeper than the car in your driveway or the clothes in your closet. In fact, it doesn't usually take long for us to understand—in our head, if not entirely in practice—that we can be okay with the things we've got, even if they're not the latest, the fastest, the sharpest. We learn quickly that we can't really keep pace in that game. Today's prize trophy ends up in tomorrow's yard sale.

But contentment is much more than a material matter. It's about waking up in the morning satisfied with who we are—not with what sin has done to us, but with what God has invested in us. It means being content with our basic temperament and the role God uses us to play in life. Content with the work He has given us, even if at the time it seems an improper match with the calling we feel. Content with being a person of honor and integrity, even if it seems like people are laughing at us.

You can stop searching now. In Jesus Christ, you have found life's ultimate fulfillment. Be at peace with the person He's helping you to be.

*Look Up*
*1 Timothy 6:3-10 (page 311)*

## Day 43
# DON'T THANK ME
*Humility*

*He mocks those who mock, but gives grace to the humble.*
*Proverbs 3:34*

You wouldn't know him. He lived in a small town and preached in a small church, earning a salary so small that he had to take a job at a local clothing factory to provide for his wife and family. Even in stature he was small, not the kind of man who entered a room with an immediate presence. You could have passed him in the mall or waited behind him in line at the grocery store and not have paid him much attention.

But this small man with the small life was a giant among men, backing up his Sunday morning words with a long, unassuming list of all-week-long actions. Who knows how many times his neighbors had seen him at their door with a sackful of beans and tomatoes from his garden?—or how many times an elderly widow had heard his mower starting up in her yard?—or how many strangers had literally received the shirt (and probably even the coat) right off his back?

You wouldn't know. He'd never say.

It takes big people to be truly humble.

*Look Up*
*Proverbs 3:27-35 (page 519)*

## Day 44
# WAITING YOUR TURN
*Patience*

*"Now, Master, You can dismiss Your slave in peace . . . for my eyes have seen Your salvation."*
*Luke 2:29,30*

Monday. "God, I believe this is the week I'm going to hear about that job. I'm going to be patient, though. I know you're in control."

Tuesday. "God, I was really hoping to hear something yesterday, but that's okay. I just need you to help me be patient till I hear."

Wednesday. "I've just got to hear something one way or the other. But I don't want to sound desperate or anything! I don't know, maybe I should just wait. But then they might think I'm not really interested! I don't know what to do. God, what should I do? I can't wait any longer."

Thursday. "I can't believe it. They must have chosen somebody else. God, I don't understand. I mean, here it is, 4 o'clock on Thursday afternoon, and I still don't—"

"Hello? . . . Yes, this is she. . . . I got the job? Really? . . . Sure, Monday sounds fine. . . . Okay, well, I'll talk to you then. . . . Okay! And thanks!"

"Wow! I got the job. I got the job! I can't believe it! I can't—I can't, uh—I can't believe how impatient I was with you, God. I'll learn one of these days, won't I?"

*Look Up*
*Luke 2:25-32 (page 84)*

# BETTER THAN EVER
*Joy*

*Weeping may spend the night, but there is joy in the morning.*
Psalm 30:5

You've seen people who had joy. They're the ones who know how to throw their head back and belly-laugh at a good, clean joke. They're the ones who get as much pleasure out of a bowl of vanilla ice cream and chocolate syrup as most people require of a steak and lobster dinner. They're the ones who still cry every time Travis has to shoot Ole Yeller and wonder why they can't make movies like they used to.

That's because joy is so full, so rich, so big-hearted, it can't be contained in a smile. The joy that God gives to those whose sins are forgiven, whose destiny is certain, and whose hearts beat for other people pours out through all their emotions—and showers the brightness of God's presence into scenes and situations that seem as dark as death.

As you grow deeper in His Word, more enthralled with His love, ever nearer to His side, He'll show you reasons to be glad everywhere you turn— and chances to share the exuberance with everyone you meet.

*Look Up*
*Psalm 30:1-5 (page 412)*

# KEEP IT BASIC
*Simplicity*

*Take delight in the Lord, and He will give you your heart's desires.*
Psalm 37:4

"I just wish I could simplify my life." If you've said it once, you've said it a hundred times—and watched every head in the room nod in personal agreement. This modern world with its maxed-out credit cards and multi-year car notes, with its ten-hour days and ten-point to-do lists has stripped the threads on our ability to cope and left us spinning our wheels just to stay above water.

But God has your answer. It's not a week at the beach or a thousand dollars in the mail from a rich uncle. It's a singleminded purpose to love and serve Him through every circumstance in your life.

Imagine waking up in the morning with the exact same demands and pressures but with a real confidence that God was going to use every one of them to make your life more useful to Him, to put you in the path of people who need your touch, to give you new understanding and insights that are secretly preparing you for the next big challenge you'll face. When God has your heart, He can help you handle all your headaches.

*Look Up*
*Psalm 37:1-4 (page 419)*

# TENDING THE TEMPLE
*Self-Control*

> Do you not know that your body is a
> sanctuary of the Holy Spirit?
> 1 Corinthians 6:19

There's something sacred about God's house. That's why you wouldn't feel good eating a Whopper Junior during church. Or wiping your muddy shoes on the pew cushions. Or telling a dirty joke from the pulpit. You just don't do those things in the church building. You have too much respect for it, if not for your own personal reputation. Even the Christmas and Easter crowd knows that.

But guess what? Those two eyes you're peeping out of right now are windows to the house of God. Those two ears on your head are its sound system. And everything your hands choose to do, everywhere your feet choose to go, is visible on the screen of your heart, in the sanctuary of your soul, in the living, breathing temple of the one true God. In you.

So when you're always picking candy bars over carrot sticks, when you're constantly choosing the TV over the treadmill—and when you're giving in to sexual temptation instead of walking the path of purity—you're doing it right in God's living room. Don't you ever forget it.

*Look Up*
*1 Corinthians 6:12-20 (page 246)*

# I STILL BELIEVE
*Faith*

> "Here is the endurance of the saints,
> who keep the commandments of God
> and the faith in Jesus."
> Revelation 14:12

Worst-case scenario. You've been diagnosed with a life-threatening illness. It's not a very aggressive one, but the doctors say that slowly—over time—even the most routine, ordinary activities of life will become taxing and laborious. The outlook doesn't look good.

But you go to God. And you pray with all the faith you can muster. You honestly believe that He's going to heal you. You really do.

Over the years, however, your prognosis plays out pretty much according to schedule. Yet your faith never wavers. In fact, you wish you had a dime for every time God's given you some little reason to hope—almost always at the moment that anger or depression was coming close to claiming you.

As your strength fails, your friends and family rally around to serve you. You stay upbeat, believing, being as much of a blessing to them as they are to you. You live a life free from the petty worries of the everyday person. And though you die too soon, you leave behind a legacy of faith—a faith that accomplished more than you'll ever know. Can anybody really say your faith didn't work?

*Look Up*
*Revelation 14:9-13 (page 380)*

# THANKS FOR EVERYTHING

*Gratitude*

*"Didn't any return to give glory to God
except this foreigner?"*
Luke 17:18

Yes, we live in a world where waiters can sometimes be slow getting us more coffee, where repairmen can only promise they'll be at our house sometime between eight and five, where computer terminals can mysteriously go down the moment we call needing important information.

That's life.

But, my, how this world needs a lot more thankfulness. People who can smile back into the face of a harried store worker and thank her for at least trying. People who are more willing to write a note of appreciation than to register a hotheaded complaint. People who don't forget the ones who gave them a chance when no one else gave them the time of day. People who work just as hard for five dollars an hour as they would for ten. 

If you want to make an impact for Christ on ordinary people in your world, just try being genuinely thankful for even the smallest kindnesses done to you. And it won't be long before they recognize you as a person who walks with God because you treat them like someone special.

*Look Up*
*Luke 17:11-19 (page 115)*

# THE GREATEST OF THESE

*Love*

*Let us love one another,
because love is from God.*
1 John 4:7

New Bible translations have certainly succeeded in bringing the Scriptures within everyday reach. And that's great. But sometimes in the course of communicating, they must sacrifice beauty for practicality, giving us the command (for example) to "love each other deeply," when the old King James Version puts it so eloquently: "Above all things have fervent charity among yourselves" (1 Peter 4:8).

Fervent isn't a word you'd usually place alongside love (or charity, to toss out another old-time term). You might describe a fiery political debate as fervent—or the guy who paints his face and torso in the team colors.

But how about helping a friend move on the first Saturday that you've had off this month? How about organizing two weeks of meals for the family whose newborn baby is still too sick to leave the hospital? How about replacing a water pump for free on your Sunday School teacher's car?

When your love for one another is fervent, it's thought-out, planned, and deliberate. It's a love that meets each other's needs. With a passion.

*Look Up*
*1 John 4:7-12 (page 360)*

# FAITH OVER FEELINGS

*Sound Doctrine*

*"You will know the truth, and the truth will set you free."*
John 8:32

To have nothing more than head knowledge about Jesus Christ is certainly inadequate to understand who He really is. But to have nothing more than heart knowledge is just about as dangerous . . . because if all you know is what you feel, you may later feel differently about what you think you know.

"The heart is deceitful above all things and beyond cure. Who can understand it?" (Jeremiah 17:9). Why should you trust in your own observations and experiences when God has given you written reasons for everything He is and everything you are—right out there where you can see it, read it, examine it, study it, and picture the whole thing in more detail than you've ever seen with your own eyes?

Doctrine sounds so highbrow and sophisticated, but if this faith of yours is as important as you say, don't you want to know all you can about it? Don't you want to be able to answer others' questions with confidence in the facts? Don't you want to have His Word to hold on to?

# BIGGER THAN LIFE

*God's Holiness*

*God, You are awe-inspiring in Your sanctuaries.*
Psalm 68:35

In trying to make God appetizing to a wide range of tastes, some of us have been guilty of making Him a little too warm and fuzzy. In trying to keep His high standards from coming across as too gruff or unsettling, we've been tempted to soften His message and hope people don't read the fine print until they've already committed.

We've been trying to be God's PR people.

But even though the Bible shows us a God whose love defines the true meaning of caring and compassion, it also tells us to "Worship the Lord in His holy majesty; tremble before Him, all the earth" (Psalm 96:9). His grace means nothing if it's not pictured against His perfection. His mercy loses its luster if it's not framed in His justice.

God wants you close. He's sent His Son to pave the way. But it's only as you bow before Him in humility and reverent fear, staring into the pure whiteness of His glorious face, that you can realize how much He must love you—and how much you love Him.

# PRIORITY ONE

### God's Plan of Redemption

*In Christ, God was reconciling the world to Himself.*
*2 Corinthians 5:19*

God could have wrapped this thing up years ago. He holds the keys in His hands right now that could turn out the lights on our perceived reality any second he wants, then replace it with His own eternal reality. Just that quick. Just that easy.

But that's just not His way.

"The Lord does not delay His promise, as some understand delay, but is patient with you, not wanting any to perish, but all to come to repentance" (2 Peter 3:9).

Nothing would please God more than watching the devil spend all eternity in his wicked little hell-world all by himself, with just the rats and alligators to keep him torturous company. God's passionate desire is that all people would appeal their self-imposed death sentence and embrace the full, free pardon that's offered through the blood of Jesus Christ.

He waits. He perseveres. He extends one hand to us, and points the only way home with the other, knowing that many will be humble enough to follow.

*Look Up*
*2 Corinthians 5:18-21 (page 265)*

# GOD WITH US

### The Incarnation

*"They will name Him Immanuel, which is translated 'God is with us.' "*
*Matthew 1:23*

The first-century Jews may have been anticipating the coming of their Messiah with about the same low-level assurance we feel that He's coming back this afternoon. Yes, we know it's possible. No, we don't see how things could get much worse. But few of us are expecting Him to be here before we go to bed tonight. I mean, people have been talking about this for years. What makes us so sure that ours is the chosen generation? We should be watching, but we usually aren't.

We have a pretty good idea of what it will look like when He does come. "For the Lord Himself will descend from heaven with a shout, with the archangel's voice, and with the trumpet of God" (1 Thessalonians 4:16). We know what we're looking for. They just thought they did. They were looking for a deliverer. A warrior king like their beloved David, who would rally God's people together and throw off the weight of Roman domination and years of oppression at the hands of their enemies.

Who'd have thought to look for their warrior in the baby nursery?

*Look Up*
*Matthew 1:18-23 (page 1)*

## Day 55
# CLEAN SLATE
### *Justification*

*They are justified freely by His grace through the redemption that is in Christ Jesus.*
*Romans 3:24*

The fact that you deal with your own sins every day can often cloud the fact that God dealt with them two thousand years ago—all of them—the sins you committed two years ago, the sins you'll commit two years from now, the sins you're trying really hard not to commit today. No matter how your sins stack up on the timeline of your life, every one of them was in the future tense when Christ was gasping for air on the cross, blood oozing from His hands, His head, His feet, His side. When you gave in to His love and welcomed His forgiveness into your life, He "erased the certificate of debt, with its obligations, that was against us and opposed to us, and has taken it away by nailing it to the cross" (Colossians 2:14). "Since we have now been declared righteous by His blood, we will be saved through Him from wrath" (Romans 5:9).

Justified. The books balanced. The debt paid. So that when God looks at you, he sees you "holy, faultless, and blameless before Him" (Colossians 1:22). You can't get any cleaner than that.

*Look Up*
*Romans 3:21-26 (page 222)*

## Day 56
# PICTURE PERFECT
### *Baptism*

*"Look, there's water! What would keep me from being baptized?"*
*Acts 8:36*

We could sit here and argue about whether you should be sprinkled or dunked, or about whether baptism is the moment of salvation. People who are a lot smarter than any of us have gone back and forth on these issues for centuries and are still not agreed on all the particulars. But let's not allow the incidentals to obscure the importance of this obedient act and the value it holds in the life of every Christian believer.

Could there be a more perfect, wordless way than baptism to describe what Christ has done for us or to demonstrate what has happened in our own lives by surrendering to His grace?

Christ died and was buried, but He rose again, conquering the finality of death. Our old selves, destined for hell and all its torments, have been buried but raised dripping wet in the cleansing blood of Jesus Christ to walk a clear path to glory.

If you haven't yet followed Christ's example of baptism, you really should. If you already have, use its memory to remind the devil of the day you shook the sin off your feet and turned your back on him forever.

*Look Up*
*Acts 8:36-38 (page 184)*

# A FRIEND IN HIGH PLACES

*Christ, Our High Priest*

*Because He remains forever, He holds His priesthood permanently.*
*Hebrews 7:24*

Three of the gospels report it. It must have been something to see. The moment the last breath drained out of Jesus' body, "the curtain of the sanctuary was split in two from top to bottom" (Matthew 27:51). For the first time ever, people could see behind the thick, heavily embroidered veil that hid the deep, candle-lit darkness of God's presence—the Holy of Holies. Suddenly the sacred sanctum which only the high priest could enter—and even at that, only once a year—was made available to the most common of men. No longer were people required to bring the blood of goats and bulls before God to obtain His forgiveness. The Lamb had been slain "for the removal of sin by the sacrifice of Himself" (Hebrews 9:26). The perfect High Priest had finally come.

That's why today, you can bring your prayers to the water's edge, grasp the hand of the One who bridges the impossible gap between earth and eternity, and be ushered into the throne room of God with a standing appointment. Christ, our High Priest, has cleared the way.

*Look Up*
*Hebrews 7:23-28 (page 329)*

# ONE BIG FAMILY

*The People of God*

*Once you were not a people, but now you are God's people.*
*1 Peter 2:10*

Seems like everybody is entitled to free speech these days except the poor people who dare to suggest that God's ways are right and that His Word should still pull some weight around here. Christianity has been so maligned and caricatured, so scoffed and skewered, we're tempted at times to play dumb instead of speaking out. Why not just agree to disagree instead of offering our wrists to the razor blades of rejection? Nobody'd want to hear what we have to say anyway.

Now, listen up, you guys. We may be mistreated and misunderstood. But we're the people of God. We're thousands of years old and millions of people deep. We share faith with people in nearly every nation on the globe. And our core message has stood the test of time. The world may make fun of us to our face, but our gospel is still its only cure. They may paint us as phonies, but our peace is what they long for. They may dismiss us as unimportant, but our love will never die. We're the people of God. We don't have to be afraid of this world. Or the next.

*Look Up*
*1 Peter 2:9-10 (page 346)*

# WHOLLY DEVOTED

*Consecration*

*"They are not of the world, just as I am not of the world."*
John 17:14

One world, two kingdoms: the kingdom of darkness and the kingdom of light. The spirit of the age and the God of the ages.

Those are your choices, and you've just made yours.

The problem is, though, that while your heart can be sold out to God, your feet must remain in the world—your eyes subject to its seductions, your ears within reach of its lies, your mind dangerously close to its deceptions. God has called you out from the world and its system of beliefs. He has set you apart, made you holy, consecrated you for His service. But He has plans for you while you're here. That's where the tightrope act comes in.

You'll be called on time and again to love the people of the world without being sucked into their way of thinking, to be an agent for cultural change without being changed to look like the culture, to relate to human need and speak human language without desiring human temptations. "Set apart the Messiah as Lord in your hearts" (1 Peter 3:15). And remember in Whose kingdom you're spoken for.

*Look Up*
*John 17:14-19 (page 162)*

# IN THE PROCESS

*Sanctification*

*We all . . . are being transformed.*
2 Corinthians 3:18

What do you make of this long gap between the moment of your Christian conversion and the day you finally see its heavenly results? That leaves a lot of years in between unaccounted for, a lot of opportunities to either goof it up royally or to make good, steady progress.

What'll it be?

Welcome to the sanctification lab, where God's people get to try out the natural consequences of their beliefs—where the fresh fruit of patience meets the neighbor who reports your scraggly lawn to the community board, where the lofty words of integrity and holiness find themselves on the mean streets of temptation, where the superficiality of "Bless Grandma" prayers can at times collapse into gut-wrenching cries for help.

In the midterm tests of life, God will change you from a person who says what he believes into a person who knows it from experience, from a person who can talk a good game into a person who can live it on or off the field—a person who's getting used to living with God.

*Look Up*
*2 Corinthians 3:17-18 (page 263)*

# MARCHING ORDERS

*Discipleship*

*He would explain everything to His own disciples.*
Mark 4:34

You're going to find out very soon (if you haven't already) that the Christian life is no ice-cream social in the church basement. For too many people, that's what they try to make it—a small-talk escape from the seriousness of the Sunday morning sermon, an opportunity to make an appearance as long as they're not asked to pray or anything.

If only it were that convenient to walk with Christ.

The call to discipleship goes out to every believer—no matter how old or far along on the journey—making an irrational appeal for you to come and die, to lay down everything you were and are on the altar of self-interests, and to "consider everything to be a loss in view of the surpassing value of knowing Christ Jesus my Lord" (Philippians 3:8).

But in return for this brave commitment, you receive a kind of life and depth that gives you purpose in place of potluck, passion instead of party games, and more opportunities to dish out Christian service than the lady who pours the punch. Are you hungry to be like Christ?

*Look Up*
*Mark 4:33-34 (page 56)*

# JUST THE WAY IT IS

*Absolute Truth*

*We did not follow cleverly contrived myths.*
2 Peter 1:16

Ask today's average Christian if he believes that the Bible represents the standard for personal morality, that it possesses absolute truth that applies to all people in all times and all places, and way too many of them will think you're taking this thing a little too far.

But despite the poll numbers, Christian disciples like you must realize that the Bible is your one and only authority on how to live.

The problem is: In this new age of personal expression, the subject of right and wrong has gone way out of style—even in the church. The very idea that an invisible God can arbitrarily decide what someone should do in a given situation tramples too hard on individual freedom. "Doesn't the Constitution have some kind of protection against that?"

If you choose to reject Christ's Lordship, you slam the door not only on what may be an uncomfortable demand or restriction, but also on the freedom of living in union with the One who made you, who saved you, and who only wants what's best for you. And that's the truth.

*Look Up*
*2 Peter 1:16-21 (page 352)*

# Day 63

## AWAKE AT THE WHEEL

### Spiritual Passion

*"For we are unable to stop speaking about what we have seen and heard."*
Acts 4:20

God's not looking for perfection but for passion. He's not looking for people who are afraid to make a mistake, but for people who are just bold enough to make themselves look foolish if necessary in order to express their genuine love and compassion. He's not nearly as concerned with the raunchy things you're avoiding as He is with the good and gracious things you're letting Him do through you.

Can you even begin to imagine the people you could reach with the good news of God's love if you could stop worrying about what others think and simply care about where they're headed? How many lives could you touch if you used your drive time to dream up ministry projects? How many situations could you have a hand in correcting if you replaced a mindless two-hour movie with a mighty two-hour prayer meeting? This is not some light-lunch pep talk. This is the hard-fought, rewarding reality that's yours to embrace as you start putting your passions where your faith is and living today in another world.

*Look Up*
*Acts 4:13-20 (page 176)*

# Day 64

## SURE OF ONE THING

### Avoiding Disillusionment

*Your labor in the Lord is not in vain.*
1 Corinthians 15:58

You'll know you're growing as a Christian when the dry times come. Of course, you'll think you're doing just the opposite. You'll feel like a giant failure. Ashamed of yourself. A great big hypocrite.

But whether you've been blown into the desert by the scorching winds of sin or you've just found that the journey to the next oasis of spiritual victory is taking longer than you expected, now's your chance to build some muscle.

Will you keep your old habits from calling you out, from gunning you down with one blast of temptation? Or will you realize that in Christ you can play dead to sin no matter how bold its threats are?

Will you only move your feet when the fiery sands of spiritual thrills are making you feel like dancing? Or will you walk the faithful path beaten hard by earlier travelers, even when the road takes an uneventful stretch? Keep getting back up from your fall. Keep pouring your heart out for people who need what you've found. You'll look up one day and be amazed at what God's growing in you.

*Look Up*
*1 Corinthians 15:55-58 (page 259)*

# OH, IT'S JUST YOU

### Being Yourself

*We speak, not to please men, but rather God, who examines our hearts.*
*1 Thessalonians 2:4*

The villagers stood in awed, yet awkward silence—afraid to speak, to flinch, to look anyone in the eye for fear of seeming uncultured. While everything inside them was telling them to gasp, to point, to ask the one standing next to them if he saw what they were seeing, everything on the outside was smiles, nods, and applause—a war between honesty and appearances—until a boy too young to know any better shattered the strange stillness by giving voice to the very statement no one wanted to be the first to say.

"He doesn't have anything on!" The emperor had no clothes.

Yet even though we don't live in a fairy-tale world, we are accustomed to being the villager on the street, avoiding the obvious, skirting the issue, appearing unfamiliar with others' problems that we know very well by heart but never by admission.

Let's get real. Let's be honest. Let's not be satisfied with our sin, but let's not act like it's not there. Being an open book will give others the courage to be one themselves. And to find a true friend in need.

# GUARD THE PERIMETER

### Boundaries

*Your adversary the Devil is prowling around like a roaring lion, looking for anyone he can devour.*
*1 Peter 5:8*

Test the logic in this: If you know you're going to be tempted to go for the potato chips while you watch the late news tonight, it'd be a good idea to keep them out of your pantry. If you know that sexy, seductive pictures draw your eyes like a magnet, you probably shouldn't make a habit of shopping in the magazine aisle. If you know that every time you go over to this one friend's house, you always end up doing things you shouldn't, you'd be smart to not go over there.

Boundaries. They're lines that you draw in the sand of everyday life—as much to protect yourself as to put Satan on notice. They are self-imposed security zones that alert you in advance of the areas he's most likely to strike. When you team them up with promises you've made to accountability partners who are committed to watching your back for you, they can make you doubly difficult to defeat. They won't keep out all your temptations—the devil's never above a sneak attack—but they can shield you from the worst of it and give your integrity real staying power.

*Look Up*
*1 Thessalonians 2:3-8 (page 299)*

*Look Up*
*1 Peter 5:8-9 (page 350)*

# NEEDED AT HOME

*Your Family*

*Children, obey your parents in the Lord, because this is right.*
Ephesians 6:1

Your family is your proving ground, where early morning moods and unsightly closets leave no place for Christian beliefs to hide behind, no words to sugarcoat the bald-faced lives we lead when the outside world is out of earshot . . . which can be a little scary.

But your family is also your training ground, where you can share life's most everyday challenges and experiences in the comfort of each other's company, where you can work through your shyness for bringing Sunday morning ideals into daily life by discovering how to pray as a family, how to use the Bible as a measuring stick, how to create a safe place for even the most childlike questions.

When Christ is given permission to make Himself at home at your house, you'll take pains to love your wife or husband more, to be more patient with others' mistakes, to be quicker to admit your own fault and to ask for forgiveness. You'll bite your tongue, you'll work for everyone's good, you'll give when you're tired and cranky. You'll grow. Together.

*Look Up*
*Ephesians 6:1-4 (page 286)*

# ALWAYS ON THE JOB

*Your Work*

*"If anyone isn't willing to work, he should not eat."*
2 Thessalonians 3:10

One important aspect of the Christian worldview is understanding the need for Christian men and women to be on the job in all kinds of workplaces and arenas—to be the "salt of the earth" and the "light of the world" in the courtroom and the classroom, on the assembly line and in the executive office, in the public domain as well as the pulpit.

God has given each of us a calling in life. Some of those callings spill over very naturally into the kind of jobs we do. But in case you don't feel called to the work you're doing right now (yet you realize the necessity of it at this stage of your life), you can always remain in the will of God by striving for excellence in everything you do, caring genuinely for the people you serve and work alongside, looking for opportunities to offer Christian counsel and friendship, and maintaining integrity in all your relationships.

You may have never seen anything very spiritual in turning a wrench, pecking a keyboard, doing your history homework, or running another load of towels. But your faithful performance can speak volumes if you'll let it.

*Look Up*
*2 Thessalonians 3:6-10 (page 305)*

# Day 69
# BUILDING BRIDGES
*Your Relationships*

*Walk in wisdom toward outsiders, making the most of the time.*
*Colossians 4:5*

Every time you say hello to the ringing telephone, every time you open the door to dinner company, every time you plop your milk and bread up on the checkout conveyor, you get one more chance to have a godly influence on a buddy, a neighbor, a stranger. The way you react in situations like these—be they casual, corporate, or confrontational—can paint honest, loving eyes on someone's personal picture of the Christ you serve.

It really is an awesome responsibility.

If God put us here for any other reason than to love and worship Him, it was to love and honor His children, to be a warm-eyed smile in a sea of grunts and frowns, a two-hour phone call in a world of busy signals, a lunch invitation in the middle of a long, lonely day.

Christian disciples are committed to lifting their friends a little higher, overlooking the faults of their enemies, and going out of their way to meet a need, to remember a kindness, to speak a word of encouragement. No one is insignificant to God or to the people who love Him.

*Look Up*
*Colossians 4:5-6 (page 298)*

# Day 70
# HEADS UP
*Your Thought Life*

*"A good man produces good out of the good storeroom of his heart."*
*Luke 6:45*

If you've ever wasted a whole evening trying to get to the bonus level on a video game, then you know what it's like to close your eyes at bedtime and see hostile, cartoon enemies sailing across the blank screen of your eyelids. That's because the thoughts you dwell on don't just come to visit. They come to stay. And if they're not the good kind, they can get to be very annoying company before they're done.

The same way a head cold makes your whole body feel lousy, the condition of your thought life affects your whole behavior. If you allow yourself to stew about the friend who mistreated you, you'll pass up lots of chances to mend your relationship. If you allow the movie screen to singe your ears with more rotten language than you already have to put up with at work or school, you'll start hearing it come out of your own mouth as well. But if you'll fill your mind with things that you know God would like, and if you'll plug your ears to the devil's pack of lies, your feet will walk a straight line to spiritual success. And that's worth thinking about.

*Look Up*
*Luke 6:43-45 (page 94)*

# GOING TO BAT

*Intercession*

*"Couldn't you stay awake with Me one hour? Stay awake and pray."*
*Matthew 26:40*

My, my, my.

You don't have to look far to find plenty of personal matters you can pray to God about. Between the new clutch that costs five hundred dollars you don't have, the work that's due the day after tomorrow, the sins that overtake you in the day and the worries that keep you up at night, you can talk God's ear off from now till next weekend and never get past your own little world.

But as surely as God cares about the things that concern you most (and loves it when you turn to Him for help), He wants to begin transforming your prayer life the same way He's been changing you everywhere else—from the inside out, from self to service, from me to my neighbor.

God is making you into a person who genuinely loves and cares about people other than yourself. As your heart for them begins spilling over into your prayer time, you'll find yourself continually pleading their case before a higher court, sharing the load of their sufferings, and taking their hope in Him to new heights.

*Look Up*
*Matthew 26:40-41 (page 44)*

# BREAKFAST OF CHAMPIONS

*Fasting*

*"The days will come when the groom will be taken away from them—then they will fast."*
*Luke 5:35*

You may not think fasting is for you. After all, isn't that more of an advanced skill—something more suited to those who have enough holiness in reserve to survive on 40 days of tap water and beef broth?

Actually, fasting is for anyone who's ever felt squeezed by a pressing prayer concern, anyone who battles to keep his sinful self-will from calling the shots, anyone who's woken up in the morning with his head in a blur, unable to concentrate on one thought for two seconds without being bombarded by three more.

It's for everyone.

Try it for just one meal. Or one day. You can fast with lots of things besides just food, such as a certain food group you're struggling to avoid. Or the television. Or the Internet. Or the mall. Anything that's standing between you and pure, free-flowing fellowship with the Lord.

By starving the growling appetites of the flesh and devoting the time you save into quiet times of prayer, worship, and Bible reading, you'll find yourself renewed, refreshed, restored. Back in control.

*Look Up*
*Luke 5:33-35 (page 91)*

# BRACED FOR BATTLE
## *Spiritual Warfare*

*"Look, I have given you authority . . . over all the power of the enemy."*
Luke 10:19

Even as marvelous and beyond description as God has created our minds and bodies, He has built into us certain restrictions to keep us from overloading on outside sensations and information. For example, if we could truly grasp the staggering depths of human need around the world, our hearts literally could not contain the grief. If our ears could detect every sound wave in this very room, we would run screaming into the hills.

He knows that we can only withstand so much—which makes us wonder why He'd even mention the fact that we are being opposed this minute by "the world powers of darkness" and "the spiritual forces of evil in the heavens" (Ephesians 6:12). Seems like knowledge as horrific as that would fall under the "don't-need-to-know" category.

But God must have a reason for wanting us aware. He must want the devil to understand that we're wise to his schemes. He must want us to understand that we have nothing to fear. With Christ leading the charge, we mere mortals can handle anything.

*Look Up*
*Luke 10:18-20 (page 102)*

# ONLY BELIEVE
## *Miracles*

*God testified to the message of His grace by granting that signs and wonders be performed.*
Acts 14:3

You probably don't have any problem believing that miracles still occur in our day. You may even have enough faith to believe He'll perform one for you. The biggest problem we have with miracles is understanding why He does one for this person while overlooking another. It seems so random. So arbitrary. Not at all like the deliberate God of order and justice we've discovered Him to be.

But God does perform His miracles for a purpose—the same reason Christ performed them by the thousands while He ministered here on earth: "so that you may believe Jesus is the Messiah, and by believing you may have life in His name" (John 20:31).

Healing cancer, saving lives, restoring relationships, providing cash flow, opening eyes, locating children, connecting people, salvaging ruin—these are not God's grand finales. They are merely the entry points God uses to get through to people's hearts, to capture the attention of another skeptic, to lift the faith of another doubter, to turn the eyes of the lost to their only answer in life.

*Look Up*
*Acts 14:1-3 (page 193)*

# Day 75

## SHARE THE WEALTH

### *Witnessing*

*"Don't worry beforehand what you will say. . . . Whatever is given to you in that hour—say it."*
*Mark 13:11*

"How can they call on Him in whom they have not believed? And how can they believe without hearing about Him? And how can they hear without a preacher?" (Romans 10:14).

He's got a point there.

As logical as that sounds, you'll never have to look far to find an excuse for staying silent. You're in too big of a hurry. Or you don't know your Bible well enough. Or you're not a good enough Christian to be talking. And you're pretty sure they're not interested anyway. Besides, you've got milk spoiling in the trunk.

But if you're ever able to realize that God can use you right where you are, that you're not personally responsible for how people take your word of witness, and that you can never know where the seed you plant today may sprout tomorrow, you can feel free bringing God up in conversation anywhere He says. And trusting Him to get through to the people closest to you.

*Look Up*
*Mark 13:9-11 (page 73 )*

# Day 76

## UNDER THE BRIDGE

### *Forgiveness*

*"Shouldn't you also have had mercy on your fellow slave, as I had mercy on you?"*
*Matthew 18:33*

You know how much God loves to see you in church. He smiles the whole time you're tugging yourself out of bed on Sunday morning, splashing water in your face, grabbing a bagel or biscuit, and zooming down to soak up the fellowship, enter into praise, and hear the Word explained and experienced in the flow of worship. Throw in Sunday and Wednesday nights, and you're a long way toward getting your Christian priorities in apple-pie order.

Knowing how important church attendance and involvement are in your overall spiritual health, it's worth listening carefully when Jesus says, "If you are offering your gift on the altar, and there you remember that your brother has something against you, leave your gift there in front of the altar. First go and be reconciled with your brother, and then come and offer your gift" (Matthew 5:23-24).

Your life will stay fairly empty and you'll strain to be free to worship and serve the Lord if you don't give forgiveness the chance to come first.

*Look Up*
*Matthew 18:32-35 (page 29)*

# BREAD OF LIFE

## Communion

---

*"This is my body, which is given for you.
Do this in remembrance of Me."*
Luke 22:19

---

On a crisp November noonday, a gray-haired gentleman in a navy blue vinyl windbreaker stands at solemn attention—one hand over his heart, the other brushing away a noble tear—just like every year at the Veteran's Day parade. Yet a block away, a frazzled young businessman darts his car through alleys and side roads, barking his disbelief at why they would block off a main downtown street like this in the middle of lunch hour.

The only reason customs and traditions wither into meaningless ritual is because we forget or don't understand what they represent.

When we eat the bread and drink from the cup of Communion, we're joining with millions of fellow believers across centuries and time zones, affirming our common faith and remembering the price of our salvation. We're renewing our commitment to holy living and piling up our forgiven sins at the base of the cross. And we're getting just a taste of the celebration that's in store when we gather around heaven's table at the "marriage feast of the Lamb" (Revelation 19:9).

Come and dine.

*Look Up*
*Luke 22:17-20 (page 124)*

# MORE AND MORE

## Being Spirit-Filled

---

*"If we live by the Spirit, we must also
follow the Spirit."*
Galatians 5:25

---

Yes, there is a way to operate your car without the benefit of gas. You can throw it in neutral, open the driver's side door, heave with all the isometric power you can generate from your knees and shoulders, and at least creep it to the side of the road to avoid being smashed by moving traffic. You won't go far. You won't go fast. And even if you're able to keep it rolling for a little while, you'll eventually come to a steep enough incline to bring all your hard work to a weary halt.

That's life in the slow lane—life without the Holy Spirit's power animating your actions, injecting your mind with spiritual insights, driving you to acts of unselfish love and kindness, steering you toward people in need of God's tender touch.

If you don't want to stay stranded on the shoulder of the Christian road, offer the Spirit a clean car to drive. Let Him take you for a joy ride to your chosen destination, keeping your tank filled with supreme purpose, your steps in perfect balance and alignment, your engine running on all cylinders.

*Look Up*
*John 7:37-39 (page 145)*

# I NEEDED THAT

## *God's Chastening*

*Lord, happy is the man You discipline
and teach from Your law.*
Psalm 94:12

Fathers are known for buying you ice cream and bubble gum, giving you rides on their shoulders, and teaching you how to tie a good square knot.

But fathers are also known for the belt, for the midnight questions about why you've been coming in so late, and for grounding you for a month to make sure it doesn't happen again.

Fathers who care are willing to watch you hurt, if temporary pain can save you from long-term disaster. Fathers who care are willing to watch you fall, if a sore spot on your pride can make you walk a little more carefully. Fathers who care are willing to interfere with your fun, if a word of warning can teach you that life's not a game.

And your Father cares—enough to let you face the consequences of your sin, to let you feel the pain you've caused another person, to allow things into your life that overpower your inner reserves so that like a toddler in the deep end, you'll cry out for Daddy.

And learn that you can trust Him.

# SOMETHING BORROWED

## *Stewardship*

*One person gives freely, yet gains more;
another withholds what is right,
only to become poor.*
Proverbs 11:24

In church vocabulary, *stewardship* can be code for a fund drive. But it actually cheapens the principle of Christian stewardship to limit its scope to just money. As a committed disciple of Jesus Christ, you're in charge of mountains of blessings that are yours to use, share, and invest—but never to own.

Money is certainly one of them, but so is your time and your entire package of talents and abilities. Even the words you say and the health you enjoy are gifts from the hand of God that require careful attention, wise handling, and (at times) measured restraint.

As you prove your faithfulness in managing small portions of God's resources, don't be surprised to see Him commit even more into your care, knowing that He can trust you to manage His property and be a funnel for passing the blessing along to others—the same way He's passed it along to you.

Money can't go to your head when you have God's interests at heart.

# VALUE JUDGMENTS

*Choosing Wisely*

*Wisdom is better than precious stones,
and nothing desirable
can compare with it.*
*Proverbs 8:11*

You can avoid the pain of countless regrets, disappoint yourself (and others) much less frequently, and keep your daily schedule from running your life out of control by memorizing this simple response:

"No."

There—you said it. Of course, it wasn't easy. It may have meant you had to pick the library over your Sunday School class picnic this Saturday, or stay up an extra two hours tonight to make time for your child's Little League game this afternoon, or finish up your small-group Bible study homework instead of watching the Cubs on TV. But those are the choices you have to make if you want to be the person God's grooming you to be—the person you see in your mind's eye when a sermon hits home or a book speaks right to you.

Learning to say no to the good—and okay to the better—will move you light years ahead on your Christian journey, leaving you free to enjoy the ride. And to make sure you're traveling at God's steady pace.

*Look Up*
*Proverbs 8:4-11 (page 525)*

# LIVING ON PURPOSE

*Priorities*

*Be diligent to present yourself approved
to God, a worker who doesn't need to
be ashamed.*
*2 Timothy 2:15*

Vision statements, core values, guiding principles. That's what you hear today's CEOs talking about in their board meetings and sales conferences—overarching themes that help workers evaluate their daily decisions in the light of well-thought-out criteria.

And it works—because when you can size up a situation based on something more than an immediate hunch, you can stay true to your goals and watch them take shape before your very eyes.

That's why every Christian needs to take the time to map out his personal priorities concerning faith, family, calling, careers, and daily life. Prayerful priorities can help you manage your time more productively, weigh the costs of your promises and commitments, and thwart the world's attempts at keeping you trivially minded when God wants you dealing in much more important things.

Left to itself, your life will tend to deteriorate. But led by the Spirit, you can move through life on a mission—and stay on track all the way.

*Look Up*
*2 Timothy 2:14-16 (page 314)*

# Day 83

# ABOVE
# THE FRAY

*Unity in Diversity*

*Fulfill my joy by thinking the same way,
having the same love . . . focusing on
one goal.*
Philippians 2:2

When you first come to Christ, it seems like a dream world. Everybody's so nice, so accepting, so quick to shake your hand and take an interest in your life. But the longer you hang around, and the more you discover about the people of God—even the ones who worship on the seat right next to you—you'll find that we have a lot of differences. Different backgrounds. Different callings. Different opinions and expectations. Getting all those differences to mesh into one unified body can be a stretch on our relating skills.

Enter the Holy Spirit—whose powerful capacity to love can fill your heart with patience and grace, helping you give people the freedom to live within their own temperaments, to move at their own pace, to express their own reasons for holding their particular brand of beliefs.

C. S. Lewis wrote, "When all is said about the divisions of Christendom, there remains by God's mercy an enormous common ground."

And if you can learn to be happy with that, you'll be one happy person.

*Look Up
Philippians 2:1-4 (page 290)*

# Day 84

# LOVED
# TO LIFE

*Being Patient with the Unsaved*

*Do you despise the riches of His kindness, restraint, and patience?*
Romans 2:4

The hang-ups are so much more real today. Barely a person alive hasn't felt at least a glancing blow from abuse, abandonment, divorce, disillusionment. Even some people who appear to be coasting through life can be casualties of cynicism or victims drowning in the undertow of their own low self-esteem. They find it hard to accept why God is the way He is. And if He even is at all, what would make Him want to love people like them?

That's why even those who may be hungry for the things you've found aren't likely to believe everything you say. They need to see it in your life. They need to see it with your time. They need to see it when it's not convenient or acceptable, but when it shows how much you care about their needs and concerns.

It may take months. It may take years. It may not ever click at all. But are you willing to let God lead you to the ones He's wanting nearer? Are you willing to invest yourself in the life of another person? Are you willing to go the extra mile to keep a friend from turning back?

*Look Up
Romans 2:1-4 (page 219)*

# PASSING THE TORCH

*Discipling Our Children*

*[We] must tell a future generation the praises of the Lord.*
*Psalm 78:4*

You only get them for a few years. Ask someone who's already watched their kids grow up and leave the nest, and you'll find out in a hurry how fast the time flies. They're eighteen, they're twenty-five, they've got children of their own, but in the mind's eye of a Mom or Dad, they should still need a phone book to sit up tall at the table.

So big. So fast. Kind of chokes you up just thinking about it.

So now's your chance to lay the groundwork for a child that God is depending on you to mold. No matter how busy you are with the rest of your life, no matter how unaccustomed you are to talking spiritual things in front of your family, you're being counted on to model Christ to your little boy or girl, to be the picture they get of loving authority, to be the safe place they can turn to for an honest answer, to be the living evidence that all this church talk really does carry over into everyday life.

Help them learn to submit their will to yours today so that when they're out there on their own, they'll be able to submit to God's.

*Look Up*
*Psalm 78:1-8 (page 454)*

# OPEN HANDED

*Generosity*

*The righteous give and don't hold back.*
*Proverbs 21:26*

You haven't lived until you've looked into the impoverished eyes of a homeless person and offered him the sack lunch you'd made for yourself that morning. You haven't lived until you've sensed God stirring you to give one hundred dollars to a young couple in your church and heard them tell you how hard they'd been praying for that exact amount. You haven't lived until you've learned that giving is a privilege, giving is contagious.

Giving is fun.

Just take the 10 percent (the tithe) that God asks you to invest in your church. Most people feel good about tossing a five or a few ones in the offering plate—as though they were giving God a tip. But how can you feel satisfied tossing your Master a bone after all He's faithfully done for you—after He's been keeping you up in clothes, your breakfast cereal in the pantry, your heart beating like a drum sixty times a minute. It's not a chore to pour as much as possible back into His kingdom so that others can enjoy the same things you do. It's an honor. It's a joy. Try it. You'll see.

*Look Up*
*Proverbs 21:25-26 (page 547)*

# GRAVE MISGIVINGS
### *Victory Over Death*

*"The one who endures to the end, this one will be delivered."*
Matthew 24:13

Michael was just eight. Barely tall enough to stretch to the top of the red stick that cleared him to ride the big roller coaster. We'd been pumping him all day: "You sure you want to go? It's really scary."

His words said yes. His eyes said he wasn't so sure.

He handed over his ball cap to Mom for safekeeping and took his place with Dad in the turnstiles. Inch by inch, they worked closer and closer, his laugh getting more nervous, his feet and hands a constant fidget.

Before long, the fear was all over his face. "We can go back, son. It's all right." But with a stiff shake of his head, they were locked into the car. His face was white. His knuckles clenched. For the longest 45 seconds of his young life, he clung somewhere between guts and glory—holding his breath through every dip, closing his eyes on the ratchety inclines, until it jerked to a halt back in the station, his odyssey complete . . . the fear gone. "That wasn't so bad. Thanks for taking me, Dad."

Death must be like that. It's not so bad. Thanks for taking us, Dad.

# GOING HOME
### *Heaven*

*Then he showed me the river of living water, sparkling like crystal.*
Revelation 22:1

"You've got your Christian model and your non-Christian model. Those are the only two kinds we carry."

"Well, just looking on the outside, they appear to be pretty similar. What's the difference between the two?"

"You know, you're exactly right. They are very similar. Both have healthy bodies. Both have nice-looking families. Both come equipped with the usual house, car, paying job, microwave, etc."

"Yeah, I see that. But isn't there anything different about them?"

"Well, the Christian model claims to come with more peace of mind and a lot more power. But those who've tried the non-Christian model think it's all in their head. Of course, on the other hand, people have told us that the non-Christian brand doesn't seem to hold up as well as the other one. And the warranty is a lot more vague and unreliable. So if I were you, I think I'd go with the other one."

Christians. Built to last.

*Look Up*
*Matthew 24:9-14 (page 38)*

*Look Up*
*Revelation 22:1-5 (page 389)*

# ENCORE!

*Christs Return*

---

*The Lord Himself will descend from heaven with a shout, with the archangel's voice.*
*1 Thessalonians 4:16*

---

Through no fault of our own, really, we've become so acclimated to this earth that at times the thought of Christ's return makes us wish He'd hold off for a while. We want to see our children marry. We want to take our grandkids out for pizza. We want to see our business flourish, get a home in the country, finally work our way up to a marathon, see the tulip bulbs bloom out in the spring, enjoy the only life that we know.

If we only knew.

Christ's coming to earth will be more glorious than anything we've ever experienced—more thrilling than Game Seven of a World Series, more exhilarating than the chill of a mountain spring in summertime, more beautiful than your wife's eyes behind her wedding veil. We will see Him—yes, Him!—Jesus, the Lamb of God, the Lord of glory, the Lover of our souls—face to face, eye to eye, as though He's just been breathless for the day to come when He could hold us in His arms, wrap us in His love, and take us safely home to the glorious place He's made for us. Come quickly, Lord Jesus!

# WHAT A FINISH

*Glory*

---

*"I count my life of no value to myself, so that I may finish my course."*
*Acts 20:24*

---

Life looks different through the eyes of eternity.

The game can be played without your son getting to start. The dirty laundry won't kill anyone if it's not cleaned till tomorrow. The meeting you're in charge of today won't affect the fate of the nations.

You can relax.

The bedrooms aren't in quite as big a rush to be painted. You can go to bed without having to read the newspaper. You can be thankful your old car is at least good transportation.

You can wait.

The hours you spend listening to the goofballs on radio call-in shows will seem a waste. The urgency of telling people about Jesus will burn in your spirit. The people you haven't told lately how much you love them will be the next phone call you make or the next letter you write.

You can act.

You can be holy. You can be pure. You can be real.

You can live. Oh boy, how you can live!

# MATTHEW

## The Genealogy of Jesus Christ

**1** The historical record of Jesus Christ, the Son of David, the Son of Abraham:

## From Abraham to David

2   Abraham fathered Isaac,
Isaac fathered Jacob,
Jacob fathered Judah and his
    brothers,
3   Judah fathered Perez and Zerah
    by Tamar,
Perez fathered Hezron,
Hezron fathered Aram,
4   Aram fathered Amminadab,
Amminadab fathered Nahshon,
Nahshon fathered Salmon,
5   Salmon fathered Boaz by Rahab,
Boaz fathered Obed by Ruth,
Obed fathered Jesse,
6   and Jesse fathered King David.

## From David to the Babylonian Exile

Then[a] David fathered Solomon
    by Uriah's wife,
7   Solomon fathered Rehoboam,
Rehoboam fathered Abijah,
Abijah fathered Asa,[b]
8   Asa[b] fathered Jehoshaphat,
Jehoshaphat fathered Joram,
Joram fathered Uzziah,
9   Uzziah fathered Jotham,
Jotham fathered Ahaz,
Ahaz fathered Hezekiah,
10  Hezekiah fathered Manasseh,
Manasseh fathered Amon,[c]
Amon[c] fathered Josiah,
11  and Josiah fathered Jechoniah
    and his brothers
at the time of the exile to Babylon.

## From the Exile to the Messiah

12  Then after the exile to Babylon
Jechoniah fathered Shealtiel,
Shealtiel fathered Zerubbabel,
13  Zerubbabel fathered Abiud,
Abiud fathered Eliakim,
Eliakim fathered Azor,
14  Azor fathered Zadok,
Zadok fathered Achim,
Achim fathered Eliud,
15  Eliud fathered Eleazar,
Eleazar fathered Matthan,
Matthan fathered Jacob,
16  and Jacob fathered Joseph the
    husband of Mary,
who gave birth to Jesus who is
called Messiah.

17 So all the generations from Abraham to David were 14 generations; and from David until the exile to Babylon, 14 generations; and from the exile to Babylon until the Messiah, 14 generations.

---

*"Christ, when you were in the womb of your mother, you married yourself to our mortality, that we would not remain mortal forever."*
*—Augustine*

---

## The Nativity of the Messiah

18 The birth of Jesus Christ came about this way: After His mother Mary had been engaged to Joseph, before they came together, she was found to be with child by the Holy Spirit. 19 So Joseph, her husband, being a righteous

[a]1:6 Other mss add *King*  [b]1:7-8 Other mss read *Asaph*  [c]1:10 Other mss read *Amos*

man, and not wanting to disgrace her publicly, decided to divorce her secretly.

20 But after he had considered these things, an angel of the Lord suddenly appeared to him in a dream, saying, "Joseph, son of David, don't be afraid to take Mary as your wife, because what has been conceived in her is by the Holy Spirit. 21 She will give birth to a son, and you are to name Him Jesus, because He will save His people from their sins."

---

### Matthew 1:18-23

*Our salvation came by way of a manger in Bethlehem where we witnessed the most incredible love story of all time: the God of heaven bending low to save the sons of earth. Nothing prepared the world for seeing God in such a personal way—except its need for a Savior.*

---

22 Now all this took place to fulfill what was spoken by the Lord through the prophet:

23 **See, the virgin will be with child and give birth to a son, and they will name Him Immanuel,**[a]

which is translated "God is with us." 24 When Joseph woke up from his sleep, he did as the Lord's angel had commanded him. He took his wife home, 25 but he did not know her intimately until she gave birth to a son.[b] And he named Him Jesus.

## Wise Men Seek the King

2 After Jesus was born in Bethlehem of Judea in the days of King *Herod, *wise men from the east arrived unexpectedly in Jerusalem, 2 saying, "Where is He who has been born King of the Jews? For we saw His star in the east and have come to worship Him."

3 When King Herod heard this, he was deeply disturbed, and all Jerusalem with him. 4 So he assembled all the *chief priests and *scribes of the people and asked them where the *Messiah would be born.

5 "In Bethlehem of Judea," they told him, "because this is what was written through the prophet:

6 **And you, Bethlehem,** in the land of Judah, are by no means **least among the leaders of Judah:** because out of you will come a **Leader** who will shepherd My people Israel."[c]

7 Then Herod secretly summoned the wise men and learned from them the time when the star appeared. 8 He sent them to Bethlehem and said, "Go and search carefully for the child. When you find Him, report back to me so that I too can go and worship Him." 9 After hearing the king, they went on their way. And there it was—the star they had seen in the east! It led them until it came and stopped above the place where the child was. 10 When they saw the star, they were overjoyed beyond measure. 11 Entering the house, they saw the child with Mary His mother, and falling to their knees, they worshiped Him. Then they opened their treasures and pre-

---

[a]1:23 Is 7:14   [b]1:25 Other mss read *to her firstborn son*   [c]2:6 Mc 5:2

sented Him with gifts: gold, frankincense, and myrrh. [12] And being warned in a dream not to go back to Herod, they returned to their own country by another route.

## The Flight into Egypt

[13] After they were gone, an angel of the Lord suddenly appeared to Joseph in a dream, saying, "Get up! Take the child and His mother, flee to Egypt, and stay there until I tell you. For Herod is about to search for the child to destroy Him." [14] So he got up, took the child and His mother during the night, and escaped to Egypt. [15] He stayed there until Herod's death, so that what was spoken by the Lord through the prophet might be fulfilled: **Out of Egypt I called My Son.**[a]

## The Massacre of the Innocents

[16] Then Herod, when he saw that he had been outwitted by the wise men, flew into a rage. He gave orders to massacre all the male children in and around Bethlehem who were two years old and under, in keeping with the time he had learned from the wise men. [17] Then what was spoken through Jeremiah the prophet was fulfilled:

[18] **A voice was heard in Ramah,**
**weeping,**[b] **and great mourning,**
**Rachel weeping for her children;**
**and she refused to be consoled,**
**because they were no more.**[c]

## The Holy Family in Nazareth

[19] After Herod died, an angel of the Lord suddenly appeared in a dream to Joseph in Egypt, [20] saying, "Get up! Take the child and His mother and go to the land of Israel, because those who sought the child's life are dead." [21] So he got up, took the child and His mother, and entered the land of Israel. [22] But when he heard that Archelaus was ruling over Judea in place of his father Herod, he was afraid to go there. And being warned in a dream, he withdrew to the region of Galilee. [23] Then he went and settled in a town called Nazareth to fulfill what was spoken through the prophets, that He will be called a •Nazarene.

## The Messiah's Herald

**3** In those days John the Baptist came, preaching in the wilderness of Judea [2] and saying, "Repent, because the kingdom of heaven has come near!" [3] For he is the one spoken of through the prophet Isaiah, who said:

**A voice of one crying out in the**
**wilderness:**
**"Prepare the way for the Lord;**
**make His paths straight!"**[d]

[4] John himself had a camel-hair garment with a leather belt around his waist, and his food was locusts and wild honey. [5] Then Jerusalem, all Judea, and all the vicinity of the Jordan were flocking to him, [6] and they were baptized by him in the Jordan River as they confessed their sins.

[7] When he saw many of the •Pharisees and •Sadducees coming to the place of his baptism, he said to them, "Brood of vipers! Who warned you to flee from the coming wrath? [8] Produce fruit consistent with repentance. [9] And don't presume to say to yourselves, 'We have Abraham as our father.' For I tell you that God is able to raise up children for Abraham from

[a]**2:15** Hs 11:1   [b] **2:18** Other mss read *Ramah, lamentation, and weeping,*   [c]**2:18** Jr 31:15   [d]**3:3** Is 40:3

these stones! ¹⁰ Even now the ax is ready to strike the root of the trees! Therefore, every tree that doesn't produce good fruit will be cut down and thrown into the fire.

¹¹ "I baptize you with water for repentance. But the One who is coming after me is more powerful than I; I am not worthy to take off His sandals. He Himself will baptize you with the Holy Spirit and fire. ¹² With a winnowing shovel in His hand, He will clear His threshing floor and gather His wheat into the barn, but the chaff He will burn up with fire that never goes out."

---

### Matthew 3:16-17

### God the Son

*This is one of the most interesting passages in the Bible, because here you can see the Son, the Spirit, and the Father all in one picture. Imagine the intensity of this moment! The Son is about to embark on a 3-year, earthly ministry . . . with the Spirit's power and the Father's blessing.*

---

### The Baptism of Jesus

¹³ Then Jesus came from Galilee to John at the Jordan, to be baptized by him. ¹⁴ But John tried to stop Him, saying, "I need to be baptized by You, and yet You come to me?"

¹⁵ Jesus answered him, "Allow it for now, because this is the way for us to fulfill all righteousness." Then he allowed Him |to be baptized.|

¹⁶ After Jesus was baptized, He went up immediately from the water. The heavens suddenly opened for Him,ª and He saw the Spirit of God descending like a dove and coming down on Him. ¹⁷ And there came a voice from heaven:

This is My beloved Son.
I take delight in Him!

### The Temptation of Jesus

**4** Then Jesus was led up by the Spirit into the wilderness to be tempted by the Devil. ² And after He had fasted 40 days and 40 nights, He was hungry. ³ Then the tempter approached Him and said, "If You are the Son of God, tell these stones to become bread."

⁴ But He answered, "It is written:

**Man must not live on bread alone,
but on every word that comes from the mouth of God."**ᵇ

⁵ Then the Devil took Him to the holy city, had Him stand on the pinnacle of the temple, ⁶ and said to Him, "If You are the Son of God, throw Yourself down. For it is written:

**He will give His angels orders concerning you, and,
In their hands they will lift you up,
so you will not strike your foot against a stone."**ᶜ

⁷ Jesus told him, "It is also written:

**You must not tempt the Lord your God."**ᵈ

---

ª**3:16** Other mss omit *for Him*   ᵇ**4:4** Dt 8:3   ᶜ**4:6** Ps 91:11–12   ᵈ**4:7** Dt 6:16

[8] Again, the Devil took Him to a very high mountain and showed Him all the kingdoms of the world and their splendor. [9] And he said to Him, "I will give You all these things if You will fall down and worship me."

[10] Then Jesus told him, "Go away,[a] Satan! For it is written:

> You must worship the Lord
> your God,
> and you must serve Him only."[b]

[11] Then the Devil left Him, and immediately angels came and began to serve Him.

## Ministry in Galilee

[12] But after He heard that John had been arrested, He withdrew into Galilee. [13] He left Nazareth behind and went to live in Capernaum by the sea, in the region of Zebulun and Naphtali. [14] This was to fulfill what was spoken through the prophet Isaiah:

[15] O land of Zebulun and land of
> Naphtali,
> along the sea road, beyond the
> Jordan,
> Galilee of the Gentiles!
[16] The people who live in darkness
> have seen a great light,
> and for those living in the
> shadowland of death,
> light has dawned. [c]

[17] From then on Jesus began to preach, "Repent, because the kingdom of heaven has come near!"

## The First Disciples

[18] As He was walking along the Sea of Galilee, He saw two brothers, Simon, who was called Peter, and his brother Andrew. They were casting a net into the sea, since they were fishermen. [19] "Follow Me," He told them, "and I will make you fishers of men!" [20] Immediately they left their nets and followed Him.

[21] Going on from there, He saw two other brothers, James the son of Zebedee, and his brother John. They were in a boat with Zebedee their father, mending their nets, and He called them. [22] Immediately they left the boat and their father and followed Him.

## Teaching, Preaching, and Healing

[23] Jesus was going all over Galilee, teaching in their synagogues, preaching the good news of the kingdom, and healing every disease and sickness among the people. [24] Then the news about Him spread throughout Syria. So they brought to Him all those who were afflicted, those suffering from various diseases and intense pains, the demon-possessed, the epileptics, and the paralytics. And He healed them.

---

### Matthew 4:17

### The Kingdom

*God's kingdom has always existed, yet the coming of Christ and His death and resurrection gave a new visibility to God's rule. Christ's victory over death, hell, and the grave would provide the world an up-close look at the King and make an up-close relationship with Him a reality.*

---

[a]**4:10** Other mss read *Get behind Me*   [b]**4:10** Dt 6:13   [c]**4:15–16** Is 9:1–2

25 Large crowds followed Him from Galilee, •Decapolis, Jerusalem, Judea, and beyond the Jordan.

## THE SERMON ON THE MOUNT

5 When He saw the crowds, He went up on the mountain, and after He sat down, His disciples came to Him. 2 Then He began to teach them, saying:

### The Beatitudes

3  "Blessed are the poor in spirit,
      because the kingdom of
         heaven is theirs.
4  Blessed are those who mourn,
      because they will be comforted.
5  Blessed are the gentle,
      because they will inherit the
         earth.
6  Blessed are those who hunger
         and thirst for righteousness,
      because they will be filled.
7  Blessed are the merciful,
      because they will be shown
         mercy.
8  Blessed are the pure in heart,
      because they will see God.
9  Blessed are the peacemakers,
      because they will be called sons
         of God.
10  Blessed are those who are
         persecuted for righteousness,
      because the kingdom of heaven
         is theirs.

11 "Blessed are you when they insult you and persecute you, and say every kind of evil against you falsely because of Me. 12 Be glad and rejoice, because your reward is great in heaven. For that is how they persecuted the prophets who were before you.

### Believers Are Salt and Light

13 "You are the salt of the earth. But if the salt should lose its taste, how can it be made salty? It's no longer good for anything but to be thrown out and trampled on by men.

14 "You are the light of the world. A city situated on a hill cannot be hidden. 15 No one lights a lamp and puts it under a basket, but rather on a lampstand, and it gives light for all who are in the house. 16 In the same way, let your light shine before men, so that they may see your good works and give glory to your Father in heaven.

---

### Matthew 5:17-19

### The Scriptures

*Some people wonder if the Old Testament still applies since Jesus came and made everything new. In Matthew, chapters 5-7 (known as the Sermon on the Mount), Christ teaches us that God's Word hasn't changed. It just goes deeper than some people thought it did.*

---

### Christ Fulfills the Law

17 "Don't assume that I came to destroy the Law or the Prophets. I did not come to destroy but to fulfill. 18 For •I assure you: Until heaven and earth pass away, not the smallest letter or one stroke of a letter will pass from the law until all things are accomplished. 19 Therefore, whoever breaks one of the least of these commandments and teaches people to do so will be called least in the kingdom of heaven. But whoever practices and teaches [these commandments] will be called great in the kingdom of heaven. 20 For I tell you, unless your righteousness surpasses that of the

•scribes and •Pharisees, you will never enter the kingdom of heaven.

## Murder Begins in the Heart

21 "You have heard that it was said to our ancestors, **You shall not murder,**[a] and whoever murders will be subject to judgment. 22 But I tell you, everyone who is angry with his brother[b] will be subject to judgment. And whoever says to his brother, 'Fool!' will be subject to the •Sanhedrin. But whoever says, 'You moron!' will be subject to •hellfire. 23 So if you are offering your gift on the altar, and there you remember that your brother has something against you, 24 leave your gift there in front of the altar. First go and be reconciled with your brother, and then come and offer your gift. 25 Reach a settlement quickly with your adversary while you're on the way with him, or your adversary will hand you over to the judge, the judge to[c] the officer, and you will be thrown into prison. 26 I assure you: You will never get out of there until you have paid the last penny!

## Adultery in the Heart

27 "You have heard that it was said, **You shall not commit adultery.**[d] 28 But I tell you, everyone who looks at a woman to lust for her has already committed adultery with her in his heart. 29 If your right eye causes you to sin, gouge it out and throw it away. For it is better that you lose one of your members than for your whole body to be thrown into hell. 30 And if your right hand causes you to sin, cut it off and throw it away. For it is better that you lose one of your members than for your whole body to go into hell!

## Divorce Practices Censured

31 "It was also said, **Whoever divorces his wife must give her a written notice of divorce.**[e] 32 But I tell you, everyone who divorces his wife, except in a case of sexual immorality, causes her to commit adultery. And whoever marries a divorced woman commits adultery.

## Tell the Truth

33 "Again, you have heard that it was said to our ancestors, **You must not break your oath, but you must keep your oaths to the Lord.**[f] 34 But I tell you, don't take an oath at all: either by heaven, because it is God's throne; 35 or by the earth, because it is His footstool; or by Jerusalem, because it is the city of the great King. 36 Neither should you swear by your head, because you cannot make a single hair white or black. 37 But let your word 'yes' be 'yes,' and your 'no' be 'no.' Anything more than this is from the evil one.

## Go the Second Mile

38 "You have heard that it was said, **An eye for an eye** and a **tooth for a tooth.**[g] 39 But I tell you, don't resist an evildoer. On the contrary, if anyone slaps you on your right cheek, turn the other to him also. 40 As for the one who wants to sue you and take away your shirt, let him have your coat as

[a]**5:21** Ex 20:13; Dt 5:17   [b]**5:22** Other mss add *without a cause*   [c] **5:25** Other mss read *judge will hand you over to*   [d]**5:27** Ex 20:14; Dt 5:18   [e]**5:31** Dt 24:1   [f]**5:33** Lv 19:12; Nm 30:2; Dt 23:21   [g]**5:38** Ex 21:24; Lv 24:20; Dt 19:21

well. [41] And if anyone forces you to go one mile, go with him two. [42] Give to the one who asks you, and don't turn away from the one who wants to borrow from you.

### Love Your Enemies

[43] "You have heard that it was said, **You shall love your neighbor**[a] and hate your enemy. [44] But I tell you, love your enemies,[b] and pray for those who[c] persecute you, [45] so that you may be sons of your Father in heaven. For He causes His sun to rise on the evil and the good, and sends rain on the righteous and the unrighteous. [46] For if you love those who love you, what reward will you have? Don't even the tax collectors do the same? [47] And if you greet only your brothers, what are you doing out of the ordinary? Don't even the Gentiles[d] do the same? [48] Be perfect, therefore, as your heavenly Father is perfect.

### How to Give

**6** "Be careful not to practice your righteousness[e] in front of people, to be seen by them. Otherwise, you will have no reward from your Father in heaven. [2] So whenever you give to the poor, don't sound a trumpet before you, as the hypocrites do in the synagogues and on the streets, to be applauded by people. •I assure you: They've got their reward! [3] But when you give to the poor, don't let your left hand know what your right hand is doing, [4] so that your giving may be in secret. And your Father who sees in secret will reward you.[f]

### How to Pray

[5] "Whenever you pray, you must not be like the hypocrites, because they love to pray standing in the synagogues and on the street corners to be seen by people. I assure you: They've got their reward! [6] But when you pray, go into your private room, shut your door, and pray to your Father who is in secret. And your Father who sees in secret will reward you.[g] [7] When you pray, don't babble like the idolaters, since they imagine they'll be heard for their many words. [8] Don't be like them, because your Father knows the things you need before you ask Him.

### The Model Prayer

[9] "Therefore, you should pray like this:

> Our Father in heaven,
> Your name be honored as holy.
> [10] Your kingdom come.
> Your will be done
> on earth as it is in heaven.
> [11] Give us today our daily bread.
> [12] And forgive us our debts,
> as we also have forgiven our
> debtors.
> [13] And do not bring us into
> temptation,
> but deliver us from
> the evil one.
> ⌊For Yours is the kingdom
> and the power
> and the glory forever,
> •Amen.⌋ [h]

[14] "For if you forgive people their wrongdoing, your heavenly Father will forgive you as well. [15] But if you don't forgive people,[i] your

---

[a]5:43 Lv 19:18   [b]5:44 Other mss add *bless those who curse you, do good to those who hate you,*
[c]5:44 Other mss add *mistreat you and*   [d]5:47 Other mss read *the tax collectors*   [e]6:1 Other mss read *your charitable giving*   [f]6:4 Other mss read *will Himself reward you openly*   [g]6:6 Other mss add *openly*
[h]6:13 Other mss omit bracketed text   [i]6:15 Other mss add *their wrongdoing*

Father will not forgive your wrong-doing.

## How to Fast

16 "Whenever you fast, don't be sad-faced like the hypocrites. For they make their faces unattractive so they may show their fasting to people. I assure you: They've got their reward! 17 But when you fast, brush your hair and wash your face, 18 so that you don't show your fasting to people, but to your Father who is in secret. And your Father who sees in secret will reward you.[a]

## God and Possessions

19 "Don't collect for yourselves treasures on earth, where moth and rust destroy and where thieves break in and steal. 20 But collect for yourselves treasures in heaven, where neither moth nor rust destroys, and where thieves don't break in and steal. 21 For where your treasure is, there your heart will be also.

22 "The eye is the lamp of the body. If your eye is generous, your whole body will be full of light. 23 But if your eye is stingy, your whole body will be full of darkness. So if the light within you is darkness—how deep is that darkness!

24 "No one can be a slave of two masters, since either he will hate one and love the other, or be devoted to one and despise the other. You cannot be slaves of God and of money.

## The Cure for Anxiety

25 "This is why I tell you: Don't worry about your life, what you will eat or what you will drink; or about your body, what you will wear. Isn't life more than food and the body more than clothing? 26 Look at the birds of the sky: they don't sow or reap or gather into barns, yet your heavenly Father feeds them. Aren't you worth more than they? 27 Can any of you add a single •cubit to his height by worrying? 28 And why do you worry about clothes? Learn how the wildflowers of the field grow: they don't labor or spin thread. 29 Yet I tell you that not even Solomon in all his splendor was adorned like one of these! 30 If that's how God clothes the grass of the field, which is here today and thrown into the furnace tomorrow, won't He do much more for you—you of little faith? 31 So don't worry, saying, 'What will we eat?' or 'What will we drink?' or 'What will we wear?' 32 For the Gentiles eagerly seek all these things, and your heavenly Father knows that you need them. 33 But seek first the kingdom of God[b] and His righteousness, and all these things will be provided for you. 34 Therefore don't worry about tomorrow, because tomorrow will worry about itself. Each day has enough trouble of its own.

---

### Matthew 6:31-33

### The Kingdom

*Something wonderful happens when we focus all our attention and energy on doing what God wants: He promises to make sure that everything we need will be taken care of. We're not missing out when we "seek first the kingdom." We're getting the only thing in life that's really worth having.*

---

a 6:18 Other mss add *openly*    b 6:33 Other mss omit *of God*

## Do Not Judge

**7** "Do not judge, so that you won't be judged. ² For with the judgment you use, you will be judged, and with the measure you use, it will be measured to you. ³ Why do you look at the speck in your brother's eye, but don't notice the log in your own eye? ⁴ Or how can you say to your brother, 'Let me take the speck out of your eye,' and look, there's a log in your eye? ⁵ Hypocrite! First take the log out of your eye, and then you will see clearly to take the speck out of your brother's eye. ⁶ Don't give what is holy to dogs or toss your pearls before pigs, or they will trample them with their feet, turn, and tear you to pieces.

---

### Matthew 7:7-11

*Right along with letting the Bible become a staple in your daily diet, prayer will open your life to ongoing fellowship with God and keep you going all day long. Developing an attitude of prayer will change you from an aimless wanderer to a mighty warrior.*

---

## Keep Asking, Searching, Knocking

⁷ "Keep asking, and it will be given to you. Keep searching, and you will find. Keep knocking, and the door will be opened to you. ⁸ For everyone who asks receives, and the one who searches finds, and to the one who knocks, the door will be opened.

⁹ What man among you, if his son asks him for bread, will give him a stone? ¹⁰ Or if he asks for a fish, will give him a snake? ¹¹ If you then, who are evil, know how to give good gifts to your children, how much more will your Father in heaven give good things to those who ask Him! ¹² Therefore, whatever you want others to do for you, do also the same for them—this is the Law and the Prophets.

## Entering the Kingdom

¹³ "Enter through the narrow gate; because the gate is wide and the road is broad that leads to destruction, and there are many who go through it. ¹⁴ How narrow is the gate and difficult the road that leads to life; and few find it.

¹⁵ "Beware of false prophets who come to you in sheep's clothing, but inwardly are ravaging wolves. ¹⁶ You'll recognize them by their fruit. Are grapes gathered from thornbushes or figs from thistles? ¹⁷ In the same way, every good tree produces good fruit, but a bad tree produces bad fruit. ¹⁸ A good tree can't produce bad fruit; neither can a bad tree produce good fruit. ¹⁹ Every tree that doesn't produce good fruit is cut down and thrown into the fire. ²⁰ So you'll recognize them by their fruit.

²¹ "Not everyone who says to Me, 'Lord, Lord!' will enter the kingdom of heaven, but the one who does the will of My Father in heaven. ²² On that day many will say to Me, 'Lord, Lord, didn't we prophesy in Your name, drive out demons in Your name, and do many miracles in Your name?' ²³ Then I will announce to them, 'I never knew you! **Depart from Me, you lawbreakers!**'ᵃ

ᵃ**7:23** Ps 6:8

## The Two Foundations

²⁴ "Therefore, everyone who hears these words of Mine and acts on them will be like a sensible man who built his house on the rock. ²⁵ The rain fell, the rivers rose, and the winds blew and pounded that house. Yet it didn't collapse, because its foundation was on the rock. ²⁶ But everyone who hears these words of Mine and doesn't act on them will be like a foolish man who built his house on the sand. ²⁷ The rain fell, the rivers rose, the winds blew and pounded that house, and it collapsed. And its collapse was great!"

---

*"The powers of the eternal world have been placed at prayer's disposal. It is the essence of true religion, the channel of all blessings."*
—Andrew Murray

---

²⁸ When Jesus had finished this sermon, the crowds were astonished at His teaching. ²⁹ For He was teaching them like one who had authority, and not like their •scribes.

## Cleansing a Leper

**8** When He came down from the mountain, large crowds followed Him. ² Right away a man with leprosy came up and knelt before Him, saying, "Lord, if You are willing, You can make me clean."
³ And reaching out His hand He touched him, saying, "I am willing; be made clean." Immediately his leprosy was cleansed. ⁴ Then Jesus told him, "See that you don't tell anyone; but go, show yourself to the priest, and offer the gift that Moses prescribed, as a testimony to them."

## A Centurion's Faith

⁵ When He entered Capernaum, a •centurion came to Him, pleading with Him, ⁶ "Lord, my servant is lying at home paralyzed, in terrible agony!"
⁷ "I will come and heal him," He told him.
⁸ "Lord," the centurion replied, "I am not worthy to have You come under my roof. But only say the word, and my servant will be cured. ⁹ For I too am a man under authority, having soldiers under my command. I say to this one, 'Go!' and he goes; and to another, 'Come!' and he comes; and to my slave, 'Do this!' and he does it."
¹⁰ Hearing this, Jesus was amazed and said to those following Him, "•I assure you: I have not found anyone in Israel with so great a faith! ¹¹ I tell you that many will come from east and west, and recline at the table with Abraham, Isaac, and Jacob in the kingdom of heaven. ¹² But the sons of the kingdom will be thrown into the outer darkness. In that place there will be weeping and gnashing of teeth."
¹³ Then Jesus told the centurion, "Go. As you have believed, let it be done for you." And his servant was cured that very moment.

## Healings at Capernaum

¹⁴ When Jesus went into Peter's house, He saw his mother-in-law lying in bed with a fever. ¹⁵ So He touched her hand, and the fever left her. Then she got up and began to serve Him. ¹⁶ When evening came, they brought to Him many who were demon-possessed. He drove out the spirits with a word and healed all who were sick, ¹⁷ so that what was spoken through the prophet Isaiah might be fulfilled:

**He Himself took our weaknesses and carried our diseases.**[a]

## Following Jesus

[18] When Jesus saw large crowds[b] around Him, He gave the order to go to the other side ⌊of the sea⌋. [19] A •scribe approached Him and said, "Teacher, I will follow You wherever You go!"

[20] Jesus told him, "Foxes have dens and birds of the sky have nests, but the •Son of Man has no place to lay His head."

[21] "Lord," another of His disciples said, "first let me go bury my father."

[22] But Jesus told him, "Follow Me, and let the dead bury their own dead."

## Wind and Wave Obey the Master

[23] As He got into the[c] boat, His disciples followed Him. [24] Suddenly, a violent storm arose on the sea, so that the boat was being swamped by the waves. But He was sleeping. [25] So the disciples came and woke Him up, saying, "Lord, save ⌊us⌋! We're going to die!"

[26] But He said to them, "Why are you fearful, you of little faith?" Then He got up and rebuked the winds and the sea. And there was a great calm.

[27] The men were amazed and said, "What kind of man is this?—even the winds and the sea obey Him!"

## Demons Driven Out by the Master

[28] When He had come to the other side, to the region of the Gadarenes,[d] two demon-possessed men met Him as they came out of the tombs. They were so violent that no one could pass that way. [29] Suddenly they shouted, "What do You have to do with us,[e] Son of God? Have You come here to torment us before the time?"

[30] Now a long way off from them, a large herd of pigs was feeding. [31] "If You drive us out," the demons begged Him, "send us into the herd of pigs."

[32] "Go!" He told them. So when they had come out, they entered the pigs. And suddenly the whole herd rushed down the steep bank into the sea and perished in the water. [33] Then the men who tended them fled, went into the city, and reported everything—especially what had happened to those who were demon-possessed. [34] At that, the whole town went out to meet Jesus. When they saw Him, they begged Him to leave their region.

## The Son of Man Forgives and Heals

**9** So He got into a boat, crossed over, and came to His own town. [2] Just then some men brought to Him a paralytic lying on a stretcher. Seeing their faith, Jesus told the paralytic, "Have courage, son, your sins are forgiven."

[3] At this, some of the •scribes said among themselves, "He's blaspheming!"

[4] But perceiving their thoughts, Jesus said, "Why are you thinking evil things in your hearts? [5] For which is easier: to say, 'Your sins are forgiven,' or to say, 'Get up and walk'? [6] But so you may know that the •Son of Man has authority on earth to forgive sins"—then He told the paralytic, "Get up, pick up your stretcher, and go home." [7] And he got up and went home. [8] When the crowds saw this, they were awestruck[f] and gave glory to God who had given such authority to men.

---

[a]8:17 Is 53:4   [b]8:18 Other mss read *saw a crowd*   [c] 8:23 Other mss read *into a*   [d] 8:28 Other mss read *Gergesenes*   [e] 8:29 Other mss add *Jesus*   [f] 9:8 Other mss read *they were amazed*

## The Call of Matthew

[9] As Jesus went on from there, He saw a man named Matthew sitting at the tax office, and He said to him, "Follow Me!" So he got up and followed Him.

[10] While He was reclining at the table in the house, many tax collectors and sinners came as guests with Jesus and His disciples. [11] When the •Pharisees saw this, they asked His disciples, "Why does your Teacher eat with tax collectors and sinners?"

[12] But when He heard this, He said, "Those who are well don't need a doctor, but the sick do. [13] Go and learn what this means: **I desire mercy and not sacrifice.**[a] For I didn't come to call the righteous, but sinners."[b]

## A Question about Fasting

[14] Then John's disciples came up to Him, saying, "Why do we and the Pharisees fast often, but Your disciples do not fast?"

[15] Jesus said to them, "Can the wedding guests be sad while the groom is with them? The days will come when the groom is taken away from them, and then they will fast. [16] No one patches an old garment with unshrunk cloth, because the patch pulls away from the garment and makes the tear worse. [17] And no one puts new wine into old wineskins. Otherwise, the skins burst, the wine spills out, and the skins are ruined. But they put new wine into fresh wineskins, and both are preserved."

## A Girl Restored and a Woman Healed

[18] As He was telling them these things, suddenly one of the leaders came and knelt down before Him, saying, "My daughter is near death, but come and lay Your hand on her, and she will live." [19] So Jesus and His disciples got up and followed him.

[20] Just then, a woman who had suffered from bleeding for 12 years approached from behind and touched the •tassel on His robe, [21] for she said to herself, "If I can just touch His robe, I'll be made well!"

[22] But Jesus turned and saw her. "Have courage, daughter," He said. "Your faith has made you well." And the woman was made well from that moment.

[23] When Jesus came to the leader's house, He saw the flute players and a crowd lamenting loudly. [24] "Leave," He said, "because the girl isn't dead, but sleeping." And they started laughing at Him. [25] But when the crowd had been put outside, He went in and took her by the hand, and the girl got up. [26] And this news spread throughout that whole area.

## Healing the Blind

[27] As Jesus went on from there, two blind men followed Him, shouting, "Have mercy on us, Son of David!"

[28] When He entered the house, the blind men approached Him, and Jesus said to them, "Do you believe that I can do this?"

"Yes, Lord," they answered Him.

[29] Then He touched their eyes, saying, "Let it be done for you according to your faith!" [30] And their eyes were opened. Then Jesus warned them sternly, "Be sure that no one finds out!" [31] But they went out and spread the news about Him throughout that whole area.

[a]9:13 Hs 6:6    [b]9:13 Other mss add *to repentance*

## Driving Out a Demon

[32] Just as they were going out, a demon-possessed man who was unable to speak was brought to Him. [33] When the demon had been driven out, the man spoke. And the crowds were amazed, saying, "Nothing like this has ever been seen in Israel!"

[34] The Pharisees however, said, "He drives out demons by the ruler of the demons!"

---

### Matthew 9:37-38

### Evangelism

*Each day, we go out into a harvest field. Around us are people in various stages of growth and readiness—some a few days away from fullness, others still in need of weeding, watering, and encouragement. God's job is to draw their heads toward the Son. Our job is to keep working.*

---

## The Lord of the Harvest

[35] Then Jesus went to all the towns and villages, teaching in their *synagogues, preaching the good news of the kingdom, and healing every disease and every sickness.[a] [36] When He saw the crowds, He felt compassion for them, because they were weary and worn out, like sheep without a shepherd. [37] Then He said to His disciples, "The harvest is abundant, but the workers are few. [38] Therefore, pray to the Lord of the harvest to send out workers into His harvest."

## Commissioning the Twelve

**10** Summoning His 12 disciples, He gave them authority over unclean spirits, to drive them out, and to heal every disease and every sickness. [2] These are the names of the 12 apostles:

First, Simon, who is called Peter, and Andrew his brother;
James the son of Zebedee, and John his brother;
[3] Philip and Bartholomew;
Thomas and Matthew the tax collector;
James the son of Alphaeus, and Thaddaeus;[b]
[4] Simon the Zealot, and Judas Iscariot, who also betrayed Him.

[5] Jesus sent out these 12 after giving them instructions: "Don't take the road leading to other nations, and don't enter any *Samaritan town. [6] Instead, go to the lost sheep of the house of Israel. [7] As you go, announce this: 'The kingdom of heaven has come near.' [8] Heal the sick, raise the dead, cleanse the lepers, drive out demons. You have received free of charge; give free of charge. [9] Don't take along gold, silver, or copper for your money-belts, [10] or a backpack for the road, or an extra shirt, or sandals, or a walking stick, for the worker is worthy of his food.

[11] "Whatever town or village you enter, find out who is worthy, and stay there until you leave. [12] Greet a household when you enter it, [13] and if the household is worthy, your peace should come upon it. But if it is unworthy, your peace should return to you. [14] If anyone will not welcome you or listen to your words, shake the dust off your feet when you leave that

[a] **9:35** Other mss add *among the people*   [b] **10:3** Other mss read *and Lebbaeus, whose surname was Thaddaeus*

house or town. [15] •I assure you: It will be more tolerable on the day of judgment for the land of Sodom and Gomorrah than for that town.

## Persecutions Predicted

[16] "Look, I'm sending you out like sheep among wolves. Therefore be as shrewd as serpents and harmless as doves. [17] Because people will hand you over to sanhedrins and flog you in their •synagogues, beware of them. [18] You will even be brought before governors and kings because of Me, to bear witness to them and to the nations. [19] But when they hand you over, don't worry about how or what you should speak. For you will be given what to say at that hour, [20] because you are not speaking, but the Spirit of your Father is speaking in you.

---

*"We are expected to live triumphantly without what we would naturally wish for the most. Full provision is made for that kind of life."*
—Amy Carmichael

---

[21] "Brother will betray brother to death, and a father his child. Children will even rise up against their parents and have them put to death. [22] You will be hated by everybody because of My name. And the one who endures to the end will be delivered. [23] But when they persecute you in one town, move on to another. For I assure you: You will not have covered the towns of Israel before the •Son of Man comes. [24] A disciple is not above his teacher, or a slave above his master. [25] It is enough for a disciple to become like his teacher and a slave like his master. If they called the head of the house '•Beelzebul,' how much more the members of his household!

## Fear God

[26] "Therefore, don't be afraid of them, since there is nothing covered that won't be uncovered, and nothing hidden that won't be made known. [27] What I tell you in the dark, speak in the light. What you hear in a whisper, proclaim on the housetops. [28] Don't fear those who kill the body but are not able to kill the soul; but rather, fear Him who is able to destroy both soul and body in •hell. [29] Aren't two sparrows sold for a penny? Yet not one of them falls to the ground without your Father's consent. [30] But even the hairs of your head have all been counted. [31] Don't be afraid therefore; you are worth more than many sparrows.

## Acknowledging Christ

[32] "Therefore, everyone who will acknowledge Me before men, I will also acknowledge him before My Father in heaven. [33] But whoever denies Me before men, I will also deny him before My Father in heaven. [34] Don't assume that I came to bring peace on the earth. I did not come to bring peace, but a sword. [35] For I came to turn

A man against his father,
a daughter against her
    mother,
a daughter-in-law against her
    mother-in-law;
[36] and a man's enemies will be
    the members of his
    household.[a]

[a]10:35–36 Mc 7:6

[37] The person who loves father or mother more than Me is not worthy of Me; the person who loves son or daughter more than Me is not worthy of Me. [38] And whoever doesn't take up his cross and follow Me is not worthy of Me. [39] Anyone finding his life will lose it, and anyone losing his life because of Me will find it.

---

### Matthew 10:40-42

*God sees greatness in the most out-of-the-way places, where most of us pass by without a second look, but where people are doing little things of great importance. You can never do anything too small for God. In fact, you might be surprised how big that can be.*

---

## A Cup of Cold Water

[40] "The one who welcomes you welcomes Me, and the one who welcomes Me welcomes Him who sent Me. [41] Anyone who welcomes a prophet because he is a prophet will receive a prophet's reward. And anyone who welcomes a righteous person because he's righteous will receive a righteous person's reward. [42] And whoever gives just a cup of cold water to one of these little ones because he is a disciple—I assure you: He will never lose his reward!"

## In Praise of John the Baptist

**11** When Jesus had finished giving orders to His 12 disciples, He moved on from there to teach and preach in their towns. [2] When John heard in prison what the •Messiah was doing, he sent ⌊a message⌋ by his disciples [3] and asked Him, "Are You the Coming One, or should we expect someone else?"

[4] Jesus replied to them, "Go and report to John what you hear and see: [5] the blind see, the lame walk, lepers are cleansed, the deaf hear, the dead are raised, and the poor are told the good news. [6] And if anyone is not offended because of Me, he is blessed."

[7] As these men went away, Jesus began to speak to the crowds about John: "What did you go out into the wilderness to see? A reed swaying in the wind? [8] What then did you go out to see? A man dressed in soft clothes? Look, those who wear soft clothes are in kings' palaces. [9] But what did you go out to see? A prophet? Yes, I tell you, and far more than a prophet. [10] This is the one of whom it is written:

**Look, I am sending My
   messenger ahead of You;
he will prepare Your way
   before You.**[a]

[11] "•I assure you: Among those born of women no one greater than John the Baptist has appeared, but the least in the kingdom of heaven is greater than he. [12] From the days of John the Baptist until now, the kingdom of heaven has been suffering violence, and the violent have been seizing it by force. [13] For all the prophets and the law prophesied until John; [14] if you're willing to accept it, he is the Elijah who is to come. [15] Anyone who has ears[b] should listen!

[a]11:10 Mal 3:1    [b]11:15 Other mss add *to hear*

## An Unresponsive Generation

16 "To what should I compare this generation? It's like children sitting in the marketplaces who call out to each other:

17  We played the flute for you,
    but you didn't dance;
    we sang a lament,
    but you didn't mourn!

18 For John did not come eating or drinking, and they say, 'He has a demon!' 19 The •Son of Man came eating and drinking, and they say, 'Look, a glutton and a drunkard, a friend of tax collectors and sinners!' Yet wisdom is vindicated by her deeds."[a] 20 Then He proceeded to denounce the towns where most of His miracles were done, because they did not repent: 21 "Woe to you, Chorazin! Woe to you, Bethsaida! For if the miracles that were done in you had been done in Tyre and Sidon, they would have repented in sackcloth and ashes long ago! 22 But I tell you, it will be more tolerable for Tyre and Sidon on the day of judgment than for you. 23 And you, Capernaum, will you be exalted to heaven? You will go down to •Hades. For if the miracles that were done in you had been done in Sodom, it would have remained until today. 24 But I tell you, it will be more tolerable for the land of Sodom on the day of judgment than for you."

## The Son Gives Knowledge and Rest

25 At that time Jesus said, "I praise You, Father, Lord of heaven and earth, because You have hidden these things from the wise and learned and revealed them to infants. 26 Yes, Father, because this was Your good pleasure. 27 All things have been entrusted to Me by My Father. No one knows the Son except the Father, and no one knows the Father except the Son and anyone to whom the Son desires to reveal Him.

---

### Matthew 11:25-27

### God the Father

*It's impossible to see the Son without seeing the Father, because they are one, yet distinct. That's why Jesus would often tell people that when they looked at Him, they were also looking at the Father. Only the Son really knows the Father, but in knowing the Son, we can see the Father too.*

---

28 "Come to Me, all you who are weary and burdened, and I will give you rest. 29 Take My yoke upon you and learn from Me, because I am gentle and humble in heart, and you will find rest for your souls. 30 For My yoke is easy and My burden is light."

## Lord of the Sabbath

**12** At that time Jesus passed through the grainfields on the Sabbath. His disciples were hungry and began to pick and eat some heads of grain. 2 But when the •Pharisees saw it, they said to Him, "Look, Your disciples are doing what is not lawful to do on the Sabbath!" 3 He said to them, "Haven't you read what David did when he was hungry, and those who were with him— 4 how he entered the house of God, and they ate[b] the •sacred bread, which is not

---

[a] 11:19 Other mss read *children*    [b] 12:4 Other mss read *he ate*

lawful for him or for those with him to eat, but only for the priests? [5] Or haven't you read in the law that on Sabbath days the priests in the temple violate the Sabbath and are guiltless? [6] But I tell you that something greater than the temple is here! [7] If you had known what this means: **I desire mercy and not sacrifice,**[a] you would not have condemned the guiltless. [8] For the •Son of Man is Lord of the Sabbath."

## The Man with the Paralyzed Hand

[9] Moving on from there, He entered their •synagogue. [10] There He saw a man who had a paralyzed hand. And in order to accuse Him they asked Him, "Is it lawful to heal on the Sabbath?" [11] But He said to them, "What man among you, if he had a sheep that fell into a pit on the Sabbath, wouldn't take hold of it and lift it out? [12] A man is worth far more than a sheep, so it is lawful to do good on the Sabbath." [13] Then He told the man, "Stretch out your hand." So he stretched it out, and it was restored, as good as the other. [14] But the Pharisees went out and plotted against Him, how they might destroy Him.

## The Servant of the Lord

[15] When Jesus became aware of this, He withdrew from there. Huge crowds[b] followed Him, and He healed them all. [16] He warned them not to make Him known, [17] so that what was spoken through the prophet Isaiah might be fulfilled:

[18] **Here is My Servant whom I
have chosen,
My beloved in whom My soul
delights;
I will put My Spirit upon Him,**

**and He will proclaim justice to
the nations.**
[19] **He will not argue or shout,
and no one will hear His voice
in the streets.**
[20] **He will not break a bruised reed,
and He will not put out a
smoldering wick,
until He has led justice to
victory.**
[21] **The nations will hope in His
name.**[c]

## A House Divided

[22] Then a demon-possessed man who was blind and unable to speak was brought to Him. He healed him, so that the man both spoke and saw. [23] And all the crowds were astounded and said, "Perhaps this is the Son of David!" [24] When the Pharisees heard this, they said, "The man drives out demons only by •Beelzebul, the ruler of the demons." [25] Knowing their thoughts, He told them: "Every kingdom divided against itself is headed for destruction, and no city or house divided against itself will stand. [26] If Satan drives out Satan, he is divided against himself. How then will his kingdom stand? [27] And if I drive out demons by Beelzebul, by whom do your sons drive them out? For this reason they will be your judges. [28] If I drive out demons by the Spirit of God, then the kingdom of God has come to you. [29] How can someone enter a strong man's house and steal his possessions unless he first ties up the strong man? Then he can rob his house. [30] Anyone who is not with Me is against Me, and anyone who does not gather with Me scatters. [31] Because of this, I tell you,

---

[a]**12:7** Hs 6:6   [b]**12:15** Other mss read *Many*   [c]**12:18–21** Is 42:1–4

people will be forgiven every sin and blasphemy, but the blasphemy against the Spirit will not be forgiven.ᵃ ³² Whoever speaks a word against the Son of Man, it will be forgiven him. But whoever speaks against the Holy Spirit, it will not be forgiven him, either in this age or in the one to come.

## A Tree and Its Fruit

³³ "Either make the tree good and its fruit good, or make the tree bad and its fruit bad; for a tree is known by its fruit. ³⁴ Brood of vipers! How can you speak good things when you are evil? For the mouth speaks from the overflow of the heart. ³⁵ A good man produces good things from his storeroom of good,ᵇ and an evil man produces evil things from his storeroom of evil. ³⁶ I tell you that on the day of judgment people will have to account for every careless word they speak. ³⁷ For by your words you will be acquitted, and by your words you will be condemned."

## The Sign of Jonah

³⁸ Then some of the •scribes and Pharisees said to Him, "Teacher, we want to see a sign from You."
³⁹ But He answered them, "An evil and adulterous generation demands a sign, but no sign will be given to it except the sign of the prophet Jonah. ⁴⁰ For as Jonah was in the belly of the great fish three days and three nights, so the Son of Man will be in the heart of the earth three days and three nights. ⁴¹ The men of Nineveh will stand up at the judgment with this generation and condemn it, because they repented at Jonah's proclamation; and look— something greater than Jonah is here! ⁴² The queen of the south will rise up at the judgment with this generation and condemn it, because she came from the ends of the earth to hear the wisdom of Solomon; and look—something greater than Solomon is here!

## An Unclean Spirit's Return

⁴³ "When an unclean spirit comes out of a man, it roams through waterless places looking for rest, but doesn't find any. ⁴⁴ Then it says, 'I'll go back to my house that I came from.' And when it arrives, it finds ⌊the house⌋ vacant, swept, and put in order. ⁴⁵ Then off it goes and brings with it seven other spirits more evil than itself, and they enter and settle down there. As a result, that man's last condition is worse than the first. That's how it will also be with this evil generation."

## True Relationships

⁴⁶ He was still speaking to the crowds when suddenly His mother and brothers were standing outside wanting to speak to Him. ⁴⁷ And someone told Him, "Look, Your mother and Your brothers are standing outside, wanting to speak to You."ᶜ
⁴⁸ But He replied to the one who told Him, "Who is My mother and who are My brothers?" ⁴⁹ And stretching out His hand toward His disciples, He said, "Here are My mother and My brothers! ⁵⁰ For whoever does the will of My Father in heaven, that person is My brother and sister and mother."

ᵃ 12:31 Other mss add *people*   ᵇ 12:35 Other mss read *from the storehouse of his heart*   ᶜ 12:47 Other mss omit this verse

## The Parable of the Sower

**13** On that day Jesus went out of the house and was sitting by the sea. [2] Such large crowds gathered around Him that He got into a boat and sat down, while the whole crowd stood on the shore.

[3] Then He told them many things in parables, saying: "Consider the sower who went out to sow. [4] As he was sowing, some seeds fell along the path, and the birds came and ate them up. [5] Others fell on rocky ground, where they didn't have much soil, and they sprang up quickly since they had no deep soil. [6] But when the sun came up they were scorched, and since they had no root, they withered. [7] Others fell among thorns, and the thorns came up and choked them. [8] Still others fell on good ground, and produced a crop: some 100, some 60, and some 30 times ⌊what was sown⌋. [9] Anyone who has ears[a] should listen!"

## Why Jesus Used Parables

[10] Then the disciples came up and asked Him, "Why do You speak to them in parables?"

[11] He answered them, "To know the secrets of the kingdom of heaven has been granted to you, but to them it has not been granted. [12] For whoever has, ⌊more⌋ will be given to him, and he will have more than enough. But whoever does not have, even what he has will be taken away from him. [13] For this reason I speak to them in parables, because looking they do not see, and hearing they do not listen or understand. [14] In them the prophecy of Isaiah is fulfilled that says:

You will listen and listen,
    yet never understand;
    and you will look and look,
    yet never perceive.
[15] For this people's heart has
        grown callous;
    their ears are hard of hearing,
    and they have shut their eyes;
    otherwise they might see with
        their eyes
    and hear with their ears,
    understand with their hearts
    and turn back—and I would
        cure them.[b]

[16] "But your eyes are blessed because they do see, and your ears because they do hear! [17] For •I assure you: Many prophets and righteous people longed to see the things you see, yet didn't see them; to hear the things you hear, yet didn't hear them.

## The Parable of the Sower Explained

[18] "You, then, listen to the parable of the sower: [19] When anyone hears the word about the kingdom and

---

### Matthew 13:11

### The Kingdom

*We wish sometimes that people could understand why Christ is so important to us, that they could see why serving Him is worth all the sacrifice. But there are things about the kingdom that can only be known by those who have the Spirit living inside them, teaching them, showing them.*

---

a 13:9 Other mss add *to hear*   b 13:14–15 Is 6:9–10

doesn't understand it, the evil one comes and snatches away what was sown in his heart. This is the one sown along the path. [20] And the one sown on rocky ground—this is one who hears the word and immediately receives it with joy. [21] Yet he has no root in himself, but is short-lived. When pressure or persecution comes because of the word, immediately he stumbles. [22] Now the one sown among the thorns—this is one who hears the word, but the worries of this age and the pleasure of wealth choke the word, and it becomes unfruitful. [23] But the one sown on the good ground—this is one who hears and understands the word, who does bear fruit and yields: some 100, some 60, some 30 times ⌊what was sown⌋."

## The Parable of the Wheat and the Weeds

[24] He presented another parable to them: "The kingdom of heaven may be compared to a man who sowed good seed in his field. [25] But while people were sleeping, his enemy came, sowed weeds among the wheat, and left. [26] When the plants sprouted and produced grain, then the weeds also appeared. [27] The landowner's slaves came to him and said, 'Master, didn't you sow good seed in your field? Then where did the weeds come from?'

[28] " 'An enemy did this!' he told them.

" 'So, do you want us to go and gather them up?' the slaves asked him.

[29] " 'No,' he said. 'When you gather up the weeds, you might also uproot the wheat with them. [30] Let both grow together until the harvest. At harvest time I'll tell the reapers,

"Gather the weeds first and tie them in bundles to burn them, but store the wheat in my barn." ' "

## The Parables of the Mustard Seed and of the Yeast

[31] He presented another parable to them: "The kingdom of heaven is like a mustard seed that a man took and sowed in his field. [32] It's the smallest of all the seeds, but when grown, it's taller than the vegetables and becomes a tree, so that the birds of the sky come and nest in its branches."

[33] He told them another parable: "The kingdom of heaven is like yeast that a woman took and mixed into three measures of flour until it spread through all of it."

## Using Parables Fulfills Prophecy

[34] Jesus told the crowds all these things in parables, and He would not speak anything to them without a parable, [35] so that what was spoken through the prophet might be fulfilled:

> **I will open My mouth in**
> **parables;**
> **I will declare things kept secret**
> **from the foundation**
> **of the world.**[a]

## Jesus Interprets the Wheat and the Weeds

[36] Then He dismissed the crowds and went into the house. And His disciples approached Him and said, "Explain the parable of the weeds in the field to us."

[37] He replied: "The One who sows the good seed is the •Son of Man; [38] the field is the world; and the good seed—these are the sons of the

[a]**13:35** Ps 78:2

kingdom. The weeds are the sons of the evil one, and [39] the enemy who sowed them is the Devil. The harvest is the end of the age, and the harvesters are angels. [40] Therefore just as the weeds are gathered and burned in the fire, so it will be at the end of the age. [41] The Son of Man will send out His angels, and they will gather from His kingdom everything that causes sin and those guilty of lawlessness. [42] They will throw them into the blazing furnace where there will be weeping and gnashing of teeth. [43] Then the righteous will shine like the sun in their Father's kingdom. Anyone who has ears[a] should listen!

### The Parables of the Hidden Treasure and of the Priceless Pearl

[44] "The kingdom of heaven is like treasure, buried in a field, that a man found and reburied. Then in his joy he goes and sells everything he has and buys that field.

[45] "Again, the kingdom of heaven is like a merchant in search of fine pearls. [46] When he found one priceless pearl, he went and sold everything he had, and bought it.

### The Parable of the Net

[47] "Again, the kingdom of heaven is like a large net thrown into the sea. It collected every kind ⌊of fish⌋, [48] and when it was full, they dragged it ashore, sat down, and gathered the good ⌊fish⌋ into containers, but threw out the worthless ones. [49] So it will be at the end of the age. The angels will go out, separate the evil who are among the righteous, [50] and throw them into the blazing furnace. In that place there will be weeping and gnashing of teeth.

### The Storehouse of Truth

[51] "Have you understood all these things?"[b]

"Yes," they told Him.

[52] "Therefore," He said to them, "every student of Scripture instructed in the kingdom of heaven is like a landowner who brings out of his storeroom what is new and what is old." [53] When Jesus had finished these parables, He left there.

### Rejection at Nazareth

[54] Having come to His hometown, He began to teach them in their •synagogue, so that they were astonished and said, "How did this wisdom and these miracles come to Him? [55] Isn't this the carpenter's son? Isn't His mother called Mary, and His brothers James, Joseph,[c] Simon, and Judas? [56] And His sisters, aren't they all with us? So where does He get all these things?" [57] And they were offended by Him.

But Jesus said to them, "A prophet is not without honor except in his hometown and in his household." [58] And He did not do many miracles there because of their unbelief.

### John the Baptist Beheaded

**14** At that time •Herod the tetrarch heard the report about Jesus. [2] "This is John the Baptist!" he told his servants. "He has been raised from the dead, and that's why these powers are working in him."

[3] For Herod had arrested John, chained him, and put him in prison on account of Herodias, his brother

---

[a]13:43 Other mss add *to hear*   [b]13:51 Other mss add *Jesus asked them*   [c]13:55 Other mss read *Joses*; see Mk 6:3

Philip's wife, ⁴ because John had been telling him, "It's not lawful for you to have her!" ⁵ Though he wanted to kill him, he feared the crowd, since they regarded him as a prophet.

⁶ But when Herod's birthday celebration came, Herodias' daughter danced before them and pleased Herod. ⁷ So he promised with an oath to give her whatever she might ask. ⁸ And prompted by her mother, she answered, "Give me John the Baptist's head here on a platter!" ⁹ Although the king regretted it, he commanded that it be granted because of his oaths and his guests. ¹⁰ So he sent orders and had John beheaded in the prison. ¹¹ His head was brought on a platter and given to the girl, who carried it to her mother. ¹² Then his disciples came, removed the corpse,[a] buried it, and went and reported to Jesus.

## Feeding 5,000

¹³ When Jesus heard about it, He withdrew from there by boat to a remote place to be alone. When the crowds heard this, they followed Him on foot from the towns. ¹⁴ As He stepped ashore, He saw a huge crowd, felt compassion for them, and healed their sick.

¹⁵ When evening came, the disciples approached Him and said, "This place is a wilderness, and the hour is already late. Send the crowds away so they can go into the villages and buy food for themselves."

¹⁶ "They don't need to go away," Jesus told them. "You give them something to eat."

¹⁷ "But we only have five loaves and two fish here," they said to Him.

¹⁸ "Bring them here to Me," He said. ¹⁹ Then He commanded the crowds to sit down on the grass. He took the five loaves and the two fish, and looking up to heaven, He blessed them. He broke the loaves and gave them to the disciples, and the disciples ⌊gave them⌋ to the crowds. ²⁰ Everyone ate and was filled. Then they picked up 12 baskets full of leftover pieces! ²¹ Now those who ate were about 5,000 men, besides women and children.

## Walking on the Water

²² Immediately He[b] made the disciples get into the boat and go ahead of Him to the other side, while He dismissed the crowds. ²³ After dismissing the crowds, He went up on the mountain by Himself to pray. When evening came, He was there alone. ²⁴ But the boat was already over a mile from land,[c] battered by the waves, because the wind was against them. ²⁵ Around three in the morning, He came toward them walking on the sea. ²⁶ When the disciples saw Him walking on the sea, they were terrified. "It's a ghost!" they said, and cried out in fear.

²⁷ Immediately Jesus spoke to them. "Have courage! It is I. Don't be afraid."

²⁸ "Lord, if it's You," Peter answered Him, "command me to come to You on the water."

²⁹ "Come!" He said.

And climbing out of the boat, Peter started walking on the water and came toward Jesus. ³⁰ But when he saw the strength of the wind,[d] he was afraid. And beginning to sink he cried out, "Lord, save me!"

³¹ Immediately Jesus reached out His hand, caught hold of him, and said to him, "You of little faith, why did you doubt?" ³² When they got into the

[a]14:12 Other mss read *body*   [b]14:22 Other mss read *Jesus*   [c]14:24 Other mss read *already in the middle of the sea*   [d]14:30 Other mss read *he saw the wind*

boat, the wind ceased. [33] Then those in the boat worshiped Him and said, "Truly You are the Son of God!"

## Miraculous Healings

[34] Once they crossed over, they came to land at Gennesaret. [35] When the men of that place recognized Him, they alerted the whole vicinity and brought to Him all who were sick. [36] They were begging Him that they might only touch the *tassel on His robe. And as many as touched it were made perfectly well.

## The Tradition of the Elders

**15** Then *Pharisees and *scribes came from Jerusalem to Jesus and asked, [2] "Why do Your disciples break the tradition of the elders? For they don't wash their hands when they eat!"
[3] He answered them, "And why do you break God's commandment because of your tradition? [4] For God said:[a]

**Honor your father and your mother;[b] and,
The one who speaks evil of father or mother must be put to death.[c]**

[5] But you say, 'Whoever tells his father or mother, "Whatever benefit you might have received from me is a gift ⌊committed to the temple⌋"— [6] he does not have to honor his father.'[d] In this way, you have revoked God's word[e] because of your tradition. [7] Hypocrites! Isaiah prophesied correctly about you when he said:

[8] **This people[g] honors Me with their lips,
   but their heart is far from Me.
[9] They worship Me in vain,
   teaching as doctrines the commands of men."[f]**

## Defilement Is from Within

[10] Summoning the crowd, He told them, "Listen and understand: [11] It's not what goes into the mouth that defiles a man, but what comes out of the mouth, this defiles a man."
[12] Then the disciples came up and told Him, "Do You know that the Pharisees took offense when they heard this statement?"
[13] He replied, "Every plant that My heavenly Father didn't plant will be uprooted. [14] Leave them alone! They are blind guides.[h] And if the blind guide the blind, both will fall into a pit."
[15] Then Peter replied to Him, "Explain this parable to us."
[16] "Are even you still lacking in understanding?" He[i] asked. [17] "Don't you realize[j] that whatever goes into the mouth passes into the stomach and is eliminated? [18] But what comes out of the mouth comes from the heart, and this defiles a man. [19] For from the heart come evil thoughts, murders, adulteries, sexual immoralities, thefts, false testimonies, blasphemies. [20] These are the things that defile a man, but eating with unwashed hands does not defile a man."

## A Gentile Mother's Faith

[21] When Jesus left there, He withdrew to the area of Tyre and Sidon. [22] Just then a Canaanite woman from

---

[a]15:4 Other mss read *commanded, saying*   [b]15:4 Ex 20:12; Dt 5:16   [c]15:4 Ex 21:17; Lv 20:9
[d]15:6 Other mss read *then he does not have to honor his father or mother*   [e]15:6 Other mss read *commandment*   [f]15:8 -9 Is 29:13 LXX   [g]15:8 Other mss add *draws near to Me with their mouths, and*
[h]15:14 Other mss add *for the blind*   [i] 15:16 Other mss read *Jesus*   [j]5:17 Other mss add *yet*

that region came and kept crying out,[a] "Have mercy on me, Lord, Son of David! My daughter is cruelly tormented by a demon."

23 Yet He did not say a word to her. So His disciples approached Him and urged Him, "Send her away, because she cries out after us."

24 He replied, "I was sent only to the lost sheep of the house of Israel."

25 But she came, knelt before Him, and said, "Lord, help me!"

26 He answered, "It isn't right to take the children's bread and throw it to their dogs."

27 "Yes, Lord," she said, "yet even the dogs eat the crumbs that fall from their masters' table!"

28 Then Jesus replied to her, "Woman, your faith is great. Let it be done for you as you want." And from that moment her daughter was cured.

## Healing Many People

29 Moving on from there, Jesus passed along the Sea of Galilee. He went up on a mountain and sat there, 30 and large crowds came to Him, having with them the lame, the blind, the deformed, those unable to speak, and many others. They put them at His feet, and He healed them. 31 So the crowd was amazed when they saw those unable to speak talking, the deformed restored, the lame walking, and the blind seeing. And they gave glory to the God of Israel.

## Feeding the 4,000

32 Now Jesus summoned His disciples and said, "I have compassion on the crowd, because they've already stayed with Me three days and have nothing to eat. I don't want to send them away hungry; otherwise they might collapse on the way."

33 The disciples said to Him, "Where could we get enough bread in this desolate place to fill such a crowd?"

34 "How many loaves do you have?" Jesus asked them.

"Seven," they said, "and a few small fish."

35 After commanding the crowd to sit down on the ground, 36 He took the seven loaves and the fish, and He gave thanks, broke them, and kept on giving them to the disciples, and the disciples ⌊gave them⌋ to the crowds. 37 They all ate and were filled. Then they collected the leftover pieces—seven large baskets full. 38 Now those who ate were 4,000 men, besides women and children. 39 After dismissing the crowds, He got into the boat and went to the region of Magadan.[b]

## The Yeast of the Pharisees and the Sadducees

**16** The •Pharisees and •Sadducees approached, and as a test, asked Him to show them a sign from heaven.

2 He answered them: "When evening comes you say, 'It will be good weather, because the sky is red.' 3 And in the morning, 'Today will be stormy because the sky is red and threatening.' You[c] know how to read the appearance of the sky, but you can't read the signs of the times.[d] 4 An evil and adulterous generation wants a sign, but no sign will be given to it except the sign of[e]

a 15:22 Other mss read and cried out to Him   b 15:39 Other mss read Magdala   c 16:3 Other mss read Hypocrites! You   d 16:2-3 Other mss omit When (v. 2) through end of v. 3   e 16:4 Other mss add the prophet

Jonah." Then He left them and went away.

⁵ When the disciples reached the other shore, they had forgotten to take bread.

⁶ Then Jesus told them, "Watch out and beware of the yeast of the Pharisees and Sadducees."

⁷ And they discussed among themselves, "We didn't bring any bread!"

⁸ Aware of this, Jesus said, "You of little faith! Why are you discussing among yourselves that you do not have bread? ⁹ Don't you understand yet? Don't you remember the five loaves for the 5,000 and how many baskets you collected? ¹⁰ Or the seven loaves for the 4,000 and how many large baskets you collected? ¹¹ Why is it you don't understand that when I told you, 'Beware of the yeast of the Pharisees and Sadducees,' it wasn't about bread?" ¹² Then they understood that He did not tell them to beware of the yeast in bread, but of the teaching of the Pharisees and Sadducees.

## Peter's Confession of the Messiah

¹³ When Jesus came to the region of Caesarea Philippi, He asked His disciples, "Who do people say that the •Son of Man is?"[a]

¹⁴ And they said, "Some say John the Baptist; others, Elijah; still others, Jeremiah or one of the prophets."

¹⁵ "But you," He asked them, "who do you say that I am?"

¹⁶ Simon Peter answered, "You are the •Messiah, the Son of the living God!"

¹⁷ And Jesus responded, "Blessed are you, Simon son of Jonah, because flesh and blood did not reveal this to you, but My Father in heaven. ¹⁸ And

---

### Matthew 16:13-18

### God the Son

*Up until now, Jesus' followers had been inspired by Him, awed by Him, and impressed by Him. But ask them privately, and you'd be hard pressed for a straight answer about who He was. Leave it to Peter to make this bold declaration, to sign His name on the line as a follower of "the Son of the living God."*

---

I also say to you that you are Peter, and on this rock I will build My church, and the forces of •Hades will not overpower it. ¹⁹ I will give you the keys of the kingdom of heaven, and whatever you bind on earth will have been bound in heaven, and whatever you loose on earth will have been loosed in heaven."

²⁰ And He gave the disciples orders to tell no one that He was[b] the Messiah.

## His Death and Resurrection Predicted

²¹ From then on Jesus began to point out to His disciples that He must go to Jerusalem and suffer many things from the elders, •chief priests, and •scribes, be killed, and be raised the third day. ²² Then Peter took Him aside and began to rebuke Him, "Oh no, Lord! This will never happen to You!"

²³ But He turned and told Peter, "Get behind Me, Satan! You are an offense to Me, because you're not thinking about God's concerns, but man's."

---

[a] **16:13** Other mss read *that I, the Son of Man, am*   [b] **16:20** Other mss add *Jesus*

## Take Up Your Cross

²⁴ Then Jesus said to His disciples, "If anyone wants to come with Me, he must deny himself, take up his cross, and follow Me. ²⁵ For whoever wants to save his life will lose it, but whoever loses his life because of Me will find it. ²⁶ What will it benefit a man if he gains the whole world yet loses his life? Or what will a man give in exchange for his life? ²⁷ For the Son of Man is going to come with His angels in the glory of His Father, and then He will reward each according to what he has done. ²⁸ •I assure you: There are some of those standing here who will not taste death until they see the Son of Man coming in His kingdom."

## The Transfiguration

**17** After six days Jesus took Peter, James, and his brother John, and led them up on a high mountain by themselves. ² He was transformed in front of them, and His face shone like the sun. Even His clothes became as white as the light. ³ Suddenly, Moses and Elijah appeared to them, talking with Him.

⁴ Then Peter said to Jesus, "Lord, it's good for us to be here! If You wish, I will makeᵃ three •tabernacles here: one for You, one for Moses, and one for Elijah."

⁵ While he was still speaking, suddenly a bright cloud covered them, and a voice from the cloud said:

This is My beloved Son.
I take delight in Him.
Listen to Him!

⁶ When the disciples heard it, they fell on their faces and were terrified.

⁷ Then Jesus came up, touched them, and said, "Get up; don't be afraid." ⁸ When they looked up they saw no one except Jesus Himselfᵇ alone. ⁹ As they were coming down from the mountain, Jesus commanded them, "Don't tell anyone about the vision until the •Son of Man is raisedᶜ from the dead."

¹⁰ So the disciples questioned Him, "Why then do the •scribes say that Elijah must come first?"

¹¹ "Elijah is comingᵈ and will restore everything," He replied.ᵉ ¹² "But I tell you: Elijah has already come, and they didn't recognize him. On the contrary, they did whatever they pleased to him. In the same way the Son of Man is going to suffer at their hands." ¹³ Then the disciples understood that He spoke to them about John the Baptist.

## The Power of Faith over a Demon

¹⁴ When they reached the crowd, a man approached and knelt down before Him. ¹⁵ "Lord," he said, "have mercy on my son, because he has seizures and suffers severely. He often falls into the fire and often into the water. ¹⁶ I brought him to Your disciples, but they couldn't heal him."

¹⁷ Jesus replied, "O unbelieving and rebellious generation! How long will I be with you? How long must I put up with you? Bring him here to Me." ¹⁸ Then Jesus rebuked the demon, and it came out of him, and from that moment the boy was healed.

¹⁹ Then the disciples approached Jesus privately and said, "Why couldn't we drive it out?"

---

ᵃ17:4 Other mss read *wish, let's make*  ᵇ17:8 Other mss omit *Himself*  ᶜ17:9 Other mss read *Man has risen*
ᵈ17:11 Other mss add *first*  ᵉ17:11 Other mss read *Jesus said to them*

20 "Because of your little faith," Hea told them. "For *I assure you: If you have faith the size of a mustard seed, you will tell this mountain, 'Move from here to there,' and it will move. Nothing will be impossible for you. ⌊21 However, this kind does not come out except by prayer and fasting."⌋b

## The Second Prediction of His Death

22 As they were meetingc in Galilee, Jesus told them, "The Son of Man is about to be betrayed into the hands of men. 23 They will kill Him, and on the third day He will be raised up." And they were deeply distressed.

## Paying the Temple Tax

24 When they came to Capernaum, those who collected the double-drachma tax approached Peter and said, "Doesn't your Teacher pay the double-drachma tax?"

25 "Yes," he said.

When he went into the house, Jesus spoke to him first, "What do you think, Simon? From whom do earthly kings collect tariffs or taxes? From their sons or from strangers?"

26 "From strangers," he said.d

"Then the sons are free," Jesus told him. 27 "But, so we won't offend them, go to the sea, cast in a fishhook, and catch the first fish that comes up. When you open its mouth you'll find a coin. Take it and give it to them for Me and you."

## Who Is the Greatest?

**18** At that time the disciples came to Jesus and said, "Who is greatest in the kingdom of heaven?"

2 Then He called a child to Him and had him stand among them. 3 "*I assure you," He said, "unless you are converted and become like children, you will never enter the kingdom of heaven. 4 Therefore, whoever humbles himself like this child—this one is the greatest in the kingdom of heaven. 5 And whoever welcomes one child like this in My name welcomes Me.

6 "But whoever causes the downfall of one of these little ones who believe in Me—it would be better for him if a heavy millstone were hung around his neck and he were drowned in the depths of the sea! 7 Woe to the world because of offenses. For offenses must come, but woe to that man by whom the offense comes. 8 If your hand or your foot causes your downfall, cut it off and throw it away. It is better for you to enter life maimed or lame, than to have two hands or two feet and be thrown into the eternal fire. 9 And if your eye causes your downfall, gouge it out and throw it away. It is better for you to enter life with one eye, rather than to have two eyes and be thrown into *hellfire!

## The Parable of the Lost Sheep

10 "See that you don't look down on one of these little ones, because I tell you that in heaven their angels continually view the face of My Father in heaven. ⌊11 For the *Son of Man has come to save the lost.⌋e 12 What do you think? If a man has 100 sheep, and one of them goes astray, won't he leave the 99 on the hillside, and go and search for the stray? 13 And if he finds it, I assure you: He rejoices over that sheep more than over the

---

a17:20 Other mss read your unbelief," Jesus    b17:21 Other mss omit bracketed text; see Mk 9:29    c17:22 Other mss read were staying    d17:26 Other mss read Peter said to Him    e18:11 Other mss omit bracketed text

> *"Our principal weapon in the crises we face in the world is love, and love operates only in a state of reconciliation and forgiveness."*
> —Pat Robertson

99 that did not go astray. [14] In the same way, it is not the will of your Father in heaven that one of these little ones perish.

### Restoring a Brother

[15] "If your brother sins against you,[a] go and rebuke him in private. If he listens to you, you have won your brother. [16] But if he won't listen, take one or two more with you, so that **by the testimony of two or three witnesses every fact may be established.**[b] [17] If he pays no attention to them, tell the church. But if he doesn't pay attention even to the church, let him be like an unbeliever and a tax collector to you. [18] I assure you: Whatever you bind on earth will have been bound in heaven, and whatever you loose on earth will have been loosed in heaven. [19] Again, I assure you: If two of you on earth agree about any matter that you pray for, it will be done for you by My Father in heaven. [20] For where two or three are gathered together in My name, I am there among them."

### The Parable of the Unforgiving Slave

[21] Then Peter came to Him and said, "Lord, how many times could my brother sin against me and I forgive him? As many as seven times?"

[22] "I tell you, not as many as seven," Jesus said to him, "but 70 times seven. [23] For this reason, the kingdom of heaven can be compared to a king who wanted to settle accounts with his slaves. [24] When he began to settle accounts, one who owed 10,000 talents was brought before him. [25] Since he had no way to pay it back, his master commanded that he, his wife, his children, and everything he had be sold to pay the debt.

[26] "At this, the slave fell down on his face before him and said, 'Be patient with me, and I will pay you everything!' [27] Then the master of that slave had compassion, released him, and forgave him the loan.

[28] "But that slave went out and found one of his fellow slaves who owed him 100 denarii. He grabbed him, started choking him, and said, 'Pay what you owe!'

[29] "At this, his fellow slave fell down[c] and began begging him, 'Be patient with me, and I will pay you back.' [30] But he wasn't willing. On the contrary, he went and threw him into prison until he could pay what was owed. [31] When the other slaves saw what had taken place, they were deeply distressed and went and reported to their master everything that had happened.

[32] "Then, after he had summoned him, his master said to him, 'You wicked slave! I forgave you all that debt because you begged me. [33] Shouldn't you also have had mercy on your fellow slave, as I had mercy on you?' [34] And his master got angry and handed him over to the jailers until he could pay everything that was owed. [35] So My heavenly Father will also do

[a]**18:15** Other mss omit *against you*    [b]**18:16** Dt 19:15    [c]**18:29** Other mss add *at his feet*

---

### Matthew 18:32-35

*We all know that love is the unifying force which turns our faithfulness into effectiveness. But trailing along at a close second is another key ingredient: forgiveness. You'll learn how to forgive, or you'll live a life of inadequate blessing and short-circuited ministry.*

---

to you if each of you does not forgive his brother[a] from his heart."

### The Question of Divorce

**19** When Jesus had finished this instruction, He departed from Galilee and went to the region of Judea across the Jordan. [2] Large crowds followed Him, and He healed them there. [3] Some •Pharisees approached Him to test Him. They asked, "Is it lawful for a man to divorce his wife on any grounds?"

[4] "Haven't you read," He replied, "that He who created[b] them in the beginning **made them male and female,**[c] [5] and He also said:

**For this reason a man will leave
   his father and mother
and be joined to his wife,
and the two will become one
   flesh?[d]**

[6] So they are no longer two, but one flesh. Therefore what God has joined together, man must not separate."

[7] "Why then," they asked Him, "did Moses command ⌊us⌋ to give divorce papers and to send her away?"

[8] He told them, "Moses permitted you to divorce your wives because of the hardness of your hearts. But it was not like that from the beginning. [9] And I tell you, whoever divorces his wife, except for sexual immorality, and marries another, commits adultery."[e]

[10] His disciples said to Him, "If the relationship of a man with his wife is like this, it's better not to marry!"

[11] But He told them, "Not everyone can accept this saying, but only those to whom it has been given. [12] For there are eunuchs who were born that way from their mother's womb, there are eunuchs who were made by men, and there are eunuchs who have made themselves that way because of the kingdom of heaven. Let anyone accept this who can."

### Blessing the Children

[13] Then children were brought to Him so He might put His hands on them and pray. But the disciples rebuked them. [14] Then Jesus said, "Leave the children alone, and don't try to keep them from coming to Me, because the kingdom of heaven is made up of people like this." [15] After putting His hands on them, He went on from there.

### The Rich Young Ruler

[16] Just then someone came up and asked Him, "Teacher, what good must I do to have eternal life?"

[17] "Why do you ask Me about what is good?"[f] He said to him. "There is

---

[a]**18:35** Other mss add *his trespasses*   [b]**19:4** Other mss read *made*   [c]**19:4** Gn 1:27; 5:2   [d]**19:5** Gn 2:24
[e]**19:9** Other mss add *Also whoever marries a divorced woman commits adultery;* see Mt 5:32   [f]**19:17** Other mss read *Why do you call Me good?*

only One who is good.ª If you want to enter into life, keep the commandments."

¹⁸ "Which ones?" he asked Him. Jesus answered,

> You shall not murder;
> you shall not commit adultery;
> you shall not steal;
> you shall not bear false witness;
> ¹⁹ honor your father and your
>     mother;
> and you shall love your
>     neighbor as yourself.ᵇ

²⁰ "I have kept all these,"ᶜ the young man told Him. "What do I still lack?"

²¹"If you want to be perfect," Jesus said to him, "go, sell your belongings and give to the poor, and you will have treasure in heaven. Then come, follow Me."

²² When the young man heard that command, he went away grieving, because he had many possessions.

## Possessions and the Kingdom

²³ Then Jesus said to His disciples, "•I assure you: It is hard for a rich person to enter the kingdom of heaven! ²⁴ Again I tell you, it is easier for a camel to go through the eye of a needle than for a rich person to enter the kingdom of God."

²⁵ When the disciples heard this, they were utterly astonished and asked, "Then who can be saved?"

²⁶ But Jesus looked at them and said, "With men this is impossible, but with God all things are possible."

²⁷ Then Peter responded to Him, "Look, we have left everything and followed You. So what will there be for us?"

²⁸ Jesus said to them, "I assure you: In the Messianic Age, when the •Son of Man sits on His glorious throne, you who have followed Me will also sit on 12 thrones, judging the 12 tribes of Israel. ²⁹ And everyone who has left houses, brothers or sisters, father or mother,ᵈ children, or fields because of My name will receive 100 times more and will inherit eternal life. ³⁰ But many who are first will be last, and the last first.

## The Parable of the Vineyard Workers

**20** "For the kingdom of heaven is like a landowner who went out early in the morning to hire workers for his vineyard. ² After agreeing with the workers on one •denarius for the day, he sent them into his vineyard. ³ When he went out about nine in the morning, he saw others standing in the marketplace doing nothing. ⁴ To those men he said, 'You also go to my vineyard, and I'll give you whatever is right.' So off they went. ⁵ About noon and at three, he went out again and did the same thing. ⁶ Then about five he went and found others standing around,ᵉ and said to them, 'Why have you been standing here all day doing nothing?'

⁷ " 'Because no one hired us,' they said to him.

" 'You also go to my vineyard,' he told them.ᶠ ⁸ When evening came, the owner of the vineyard told his foreman, 'Call the workers and give them their pay, starting with the last and ending with the first.'

⁹ "When those who were hired about five came, they each received one denarius. ¹⁰ So when the first ones came, they assumed they would get more, but they also received a denarius each. ¹¹ When they received it, they began to complain to the landowner: ¹² 'These last men put in one

---

ª**19:17** Other mss read *No one is good but One—God*   ᵇ**19:18–19** Ex 20:12–16; Dt 5:16–20; Lv 19:18
ᶜ**19:20** Other mss add *from my youth*   ᵈ**19:29** Other mss add *or wife*   ᵉ**20:6** Other mss add *doing nothing*
ᶠ**20:7** Other mss add *'and you'll get whatever is right.'*

hour, and you made them equal to us who bore the burden of the day and the burning heat!'

¹³ "He replied to one of them, 'Friend, I'm doing you no wrong. Didn't you agree with me on a denarius? ¹⁴ Take what's yours and go. I want to give this last man the same as I gave you. ¹⁵ Don't I have the right to do what I want with my business? Are you jealous because I'm generous?'

¹⁶ "So the last will be first, and the first last."ᵃ

## The Third Prediction of His Death

¹⁷ While going up to Jerusalem, Jesus took the 12 disciples aside privately and said to them on the way: ¹⁸ "Listen! We are going up to Jerusalem. The •Son of Man will be handed over to the •chief priests and •scribes, and they will condemn Him to death. ¹⁹ Then they will hand Him over to the Gentiles to be mocked, flogged, and crucified, and He will be resurrectedᵇ on the third day."

## Suffering and Service

²⁰ Then the mother of Zebedee's sons approached Him with her sons. She knelt down to ask Him for something. ²¹ "What do you want?" He asked her.

"Promise," she said to Him, "that these two sons of mine may sit, one on Your right and the other on Your left, in Your kingdom."

²² But Jesus answered, "You don't know what you're asking. Are you able to drink the cup that I am about to drink?"ᶜ

"We are able," they said to Him.

²³ He told them, "You will indeed drink My cup.ᵈ But to sit at My right and left is not Mine to give; instead, it belongs to those for whom it has been prepared by My Father." ²⁴ When the 10 ⌊disciples⌋ heard this, they became indignant with the two brothers. ²⁵ But Jesus called them over and said, "You know that the rulers of the Gentiles dominate them, and the men of high position exercise power over them. ²⁶ It must not be like that among you. On the contrary, whoever wants to become great among you must be your servant, ²⁷ and whoever wants to be first among you must be your slave; ²⁸ just as the Son of Man did not come to be served, but to serve, and to give His life—a ransom for many."

## Two Blind Men Healed

²⁹ As they were leaving Jericho, a large crowd followed Him. ³⁰ There were two blind men sitting by the road. When they heard that Jesus was passing by, they cried out, "Lord, have mercy on us, Son of David!" ³¹ The crowd told them to keep quiet, but they cried out all the more, "Lord, have mercy on us, Son of David!"

³² Jesus stopped, called them, and said, "What do you want Me to do for you?"

³³ "Lord," they said to Him, "open our eyes!" ³⁴ Moved with compassion, Jesus touched their eyes. Immediately they could see, and they followed Him.

## The Triumphal Entry

**21** When they approached Jerusalem and came to Bethphage at the

---

ᵃ**20:16** Other mss add *For many are called, but few are chosen.*    ᵇ**20:19** Other mss read *will rise again*
ᶜ**20:22** Other mss add *and (or) to be baptized with the baptism that I am baptized with*    ᵈ**20:23** Other mss add *and be baptized with the baptism that I am baptized with*

•Mount of Olives, Jesus then sent two disciples, <sup>2</sup> telling them, "Go into the village ahead of you. At once you will find a donkey tied there, and a colt with her. Untie them and bring them to Me. <sup>3</sup> If anyone says anything to you, you should say that the Lord needs them, and immediately he will send them."

<sup>4</sup> This took place so that what was spoken through the prophet might be fulfilled:

<sup>5</sup> **Tell the Daughter of Zion,
"See, your King is coming to you,
gentle, and mounted on a
donkey,
even on a colt, the foal of a beast
of burden."**<sup>a</sup>

<sup>6</sup> The disciples went and did just as Jesus directed them. <sup>7</sup> They brought the donkey and the colt, laid their robes on them, and He sat on them. <sup>8</sup> A very large crowd spread their robes on the road; others were cutting branches from the trees and spreading them on the road. <sup>9</sup> Then the crowds who went before Him and those who followed kept shouting:

•*Hosanna* **to the Son of David!
Blessed is He who comes in the
name of the Lord!**<sup>b</sup>
*Hosanna* **in the highest
heaven!**

<sup>10</sup> When He entered Jerusalem, the whole city was shaken, saying, "Who is this?" <sup>11</sup> And the crowds kept saying, "This is the prophet Jesus from Nazareth in Galilee!"

## Cleansing the Temple Complex

<sup>12</sup> Jesus went into the •temple complex<sup>c</sup> and drove out all those buying and selling in the temple. He overturned the money changers' tables and the chairs of those selling doves. <sup>13</sup> And He said to them, "It is written, **My house will be called a house of prayer.**<sup>d</sup> But you are making it **'a den of thieves!'**<sup>e</sup>

## Children Cheer Jesus

<sup>14</sup> The blind and the lame came to Him in the temple complex, and He healed them. <sup>15</sup> When the •chief priests and the •scribes saw the wonders that He did, and the children in the temple complex cheering, "*Hosanna* to the Son of David!" they were indignant <sup>16</sup> and said to Him, "Do You hear what these ⌊children⌋ are saying?"

"Yes," Jesus told them. "Have you never read:

**From the mouths of children
and nursing infants
You have prepared praise?"**<sup>f</sup>

<sup>17</sup> Then He left them, went out of the city to Bethany, and spent the night there.

## The Barren Fig Tree

<sup>18</sup> Early in the morning, as He was returning to the city, He was hungry. <sup>19</sup> Seeing a lone fig tree by the road, He went up to it and found nothing on it except leaves. And He said to it, "May no fruit ever come from you again!" At once the fig tree withered.

<sup>20</sup> When the disciples saw it, they were amazed and said, "How did the fig tree wither so quickly?"

<sup>21</sup> Jesus answered them, "•I assure you: If you have faith and do not doubt, you will not only do what was done to the fig tree, but even if you tell

<sup>a</sup>**21:5** Is 62:11; Zch 9:9    <sup>b</sup>**21:9** Ps 118:25–26    <sup>c</sup>**21:12** Other mss add *of God*    <sup>d</sup>**21:13** Is 56:7
<sup>e</sup>**21:13** Jr 7:11    <sup>f</sup>**21:16** Ps 8:3 LXX

this mountain, 'Be lifted up and thrown into the sea,' it will be done. [22] And everything—whatever you ask in prayer, believing—you will receive."

## Messiah's Authority Challenged

[23] When He entered the temple complex, the chief priests and the elders of the people came up to Him as He was teaching and said, "By what authority are You doing these things? Who gave You this authority?" [24] Jesus answered them, "I will also ask you one question, and if you answer it for Me, then I will tell you by what authority I do these things. [25] Where did John's baptism come from? From heaven or from men?"

They began to argue among themselves, "If we say, 'From heaven,' He will say to us, 'Then why didn't you believe him?' [26] But if we say, 'From men,' we're afraid of the crowd, because everyone holds John to be a prophet." [27] So they answered Jesus, "We don't know."

And He said to them, "Neither will I tell you by what authority I do these things.

## The Parable of the Two Sons

[28] "But what do you think? A man had two sons. He went to the first and said, 'My son, go, work in the vineyard today.'

[29] "He answered, 'I don't want to!' Yet later he changed his mind and went. [30] Then the man went to the other and said the same thing.

" 'I will, sir,' he answered. But he didn't go.

[31] "Which of the two did his father's will?"

"The first," they said.

Jesus said to them, "I assure you: Tax collectors and prostitutes are

entering the kingdom of God before you! [32] For John came to you in the way of righteousness, and you didn't believe him. Tax collectors and prostitutes did believe him, but you, when you saw it, didn't even change your minds then and believe him.

## The Parable of the Vineyard Owner

[33] "Listen to another parable: There was a man, a landowner, who planted a vineyard, put a fence around it, dug a winepress in it, and built a watchtower. He leased it to tenant farmers and went away. [34] When the grape harvest drew near, he sent his slaves to the farmers to collect his fruit. [35] But the farmers took his slaves, beat one, killed another, and stoned a third. [36] Again, he sent other slaves, more than the first group, and they did the same to them. [37] Finally, he sent his son to them. 'They will respect my son,' he said.

[38] "But when the tenant farmers saw the son, they said among themselves, 'This is the heir. Come, let's kill him and seize his inheritance!' [39] So they seized him and threw him out of the vineyard, and killed him. [40] Therefore, when the owner of the vineyard comes, what will he do to those farmers?"

[41] "He will destroy those terrible men in a terrible way," they told Him, "and lease his vineyard to other farmers who will give him his produce at the harvest."

[42] Jesus said to them, "Have you never read in the Scriptures:

**The stone that the builders rejected,
this has become the cornerstone.
This cornerstone came from the Lord
and is wonderful in our eyes?**[a]

[a] **21:42** Ps 118:22–23

[43] Therefore I tell you, the kingdom of God will be taken away from you and given to a nation producing its fruit. [44] Whoever falls on this stone will be broken to pieces; but on whomever it falls, it will grind him to powder!"[a]

[45] When the chief priests and the •Pharisees heard His parables, they knew He was speaking about them. [46] Although they were looking for a way to arrest Him, they feared the crowds, because they regarded Him as a prophet.

## The Parable of the Wedding Banquet

**22** Once more Jesus spoke to them in parables: [2] "The kingdom of heaven may be compared to a king who gave a wedding banquet for his son. [3] He sent out his slaves to summon those invited to the banquet, but they didn't want to come. [4] Again, he sent out other slaves, and said, 'Tell those who are invited, "Look, I've prepared my dinner; my oxen and fattened cattle have been slaughtered, and everything is ready. Come to the wedding banquet."'

[5] "But they paid no attention and went away, one to his own farm, another to his business. [6] And the others seized his slaves, treated them outrageously and killed them. [7] The king[b] was enraged, so he sent out his troops, destroyed those murderers, and burned down their city.

[8] "Then he told his slaves, 'The banquet is ready, but those who were invited were not worthy. [9] Therefore, go to where the roads exit the city and invite everyone you find to the banquet.' [10] So those slaves went out on the roads and gathered everyone they found, both evil and good. The wedding banquet was filled with guests.

[11] But when the king came in to view the guests, he saw a man there who was not dressed for a wedding. [12] So he said to him, 'Friend, how did you get in here without wedding clothes?' The man was speechless.

[13] "Then the king told the attendants, 'Tie him up hand and foot,[c] and throw him into the outer darkness, where there will be weeping and gnashing of teeth.'

[14] "For many are invited, but few are chosen."

## God and Caesar

[15] Then the •Pharisees went and plotted how to trap Him by what He said. [16] They sent their disciples to Him, with the •Herodians. "Teacher," they said, "we know that You are truthful and teach the way of God in truth. You defer to no one, for You don't show partiality. [17] Tell us, therefore, what You think. Is it lawful to pay taxes to Caesar or not?"

[18] But perceiving their malice, Jesus said, "Why are you testing Me, hypocrites? [19] Show Me the coin used for the tax." So they brought Him a •denarius. [20] "Whose image and inscription is this?" He asked them.

[21] "Caesar's," they said to Him.

Then He said to them, "Therefore, give back to Caesar the things that are Caesar's, and to God the things that are God's." [22] When they heard this, they were amazed. So they left Him and went away.

## The Sadducees and the Resurrection

[23] The same day some •Sadducees, who say there is no resurrection, came up to Him and questioned Him:

[a]**21:44** Other mss omit this verse.    [b]**22:7** Other mss read *But when the (that) king heard about it he*
[c]**22:13** Other mss add *take him away*

24 "Teacher, Moses said, **if a man dies, having no children, his brother is to marry his wife and raise up offspring for his brother.**[a] 25 Now there were seven brothers among us. The first got married and died. Having no offspring, he left his wife to his brother. 26 The same happened to the second also, and the third, and so to all seven. 27 Then last of all the woman died. 28 Therefore, in the resurrection, whose wife will she be of the seven? For they all had married her."

29 Jesus answered them, "You are deceived, because you don't know the Scriptures or the power of God. 30 For in the resurrection they neither marry nor are given in marriage, but are like[b] angels in heaven. 31 Now concerning the resurrection of the dead, haven't you read what was spoken to you by God: 32 **I am the God of Abraham and the God of Isaac and the God of Jacob?**[c] He[d] is not the God of the dead, but of the living."

33 And when the crowds heard this, they were astonished at His teaching.

---

### Matthew 22:29

### The Scriptures

*It's human nature to look for loopholes in the Scriptures, to want no authority over us other than our own wishes. The guys in this passage resorted to riddles to try spotting a flaw in Jesus' teaching. They could have avoided being embarrassed if they'd just believed what they'd read.*

---

### The Primary Commandments

34 When the Pharisees heard that He had silenced the Sadducees, they came together in the same place. 35 And one of them, an expert in the law, asked a question to test Him: 36 "Teacher, which commandment in the law is the greatest?"

37 He said to him, " **You shall love the Lord your God with all your heart, with all your soul, and with all your mind.**[e] 38 This is the greatest and most important commandment. 39 The second is like it: **You shall love your neighbor as yourself.**[f] 40 All the Law and the Prophets depend on these two commandments."

### The Question about the Messiah

41 While the Pharisees were together, Jesus questioned them, 42 "What do you think about the •Messiah? Whose Son is He?"

"David's," they told Him.

43 He asked them, "How is it then that David, inspired by the Spirit, calls Him 'Lord':

44 **The Lord said to my Lord, 'Sit at My right hand until I put Your enemies under Your feet'?**[g][h]

45 "If, then, David calls Him 'Lord,' how is He his Son?" 46 No one was able to answer Him at all, and from that day no one dared to question Him any more.

### Religious Hypocrites Denounced

**23** Then Jesus spoke to the crowds and to His disciples: 2 "The •scribes and the •Pharisees are seated

---

[a]**22:24** Dt 25:5    [b]**22:30** Other mss add *God's*    [c]**22:32** Ex 3:6, 15–16    [d]**22:32** Other mss read *God*
[e]**22:37** Dt 6:5    [f]**22:39** Lv 19:18    [g]**22:44** Other mss read *until I make Your enemies Your footstool*
[h]**22:44** Ps 110:1

in the chair of Moses. ³ Therefore do and observe whatever they tell you. But don't do what they do, because they don't do what they say. ⁴ They tie up heavy loads that are hard to carryᵃ and put them on people's shoulders, but they themselves aren't willing to lift a finger to move them. ⁵ They do everything to be observed by others: They enlarge their phylacteries and lengthen their •tassels.ᵇ ⁶ They love the place of honor at banquets, the front seats in the •synagogues, ⁷ greetings in the marketplaces, and to be called "•Rabbi' by people.

⁸"But as for you, do not be called 'Rabbi,' because you have one Teacher,ᶜ and you are all brothers. ⁹ Do not call anyone on earth your father, because you have one Father, who is in heaven. ¹⁰ And do not be called masters either, because you have one Master, the •Messiah. ¹¹ The greatest among you will be your servant. ¹² Whoever exalts himself will be humbled, and whoever humbles himself will be exalted.

¹³"But woe to you, scribes and Pharisees, hypocrites! You lock up the kingdom of heaven from people. For you don't go in, and you don't allow those entering to go in.

⌊¹⁴"Woe to you, scribes and Pharisees, hypocrites! You devour widows' houses, and make long prayers just for show. This is why you will receive a harsher punishment.⌋ᵈ

¹⁵"Woe to you, scribes and Pharisees, hypocrites! You travel over land and sea to make one •convert, and when he becomes one, you make him twice as fit for •hell as you are!

¹⁶"Woe to you, blind guides, who say, 'Whoever takes an oath by the sanctuary, it is nothing. But whoever takes an oath by the gold of the sanc-

tuary is bound by his oath.' ¹⁷ Blind fools! For which is greater, the gold or the sanctuary that sanctified the gold? ¹⁸ Also, 'Whoever takes an oath by the altar, it is nothing. But whoever takes an oath by the gift that is on it is bound by his oath.' ¹⁹ Blind people!ᵉ For which is greater, the gift or the altar that sanctifies the gift? ²⁰ Therefore the one who takes an oath by the altar takes an oath by it and by everything on it. ²¹ The one who takes an oath by the sanctuary takes an oath by it and by Him who dwells in it. ²² And the one who takes an oath by heaven takes an oath by God's throne and by Him who sits on it.

²³"Woe to you, scribes and Pharisees, hypocrites! You pay a tenth of mint, dill, and cumin, yet you have neglected the more important matters of the law—justice, mercy, and faith. These things should have been done without neglecting the others. ²⁴ Blind guides! You strain out a gnat, yet gulp down a camel!

²⁵"Woe to you, scribes and Pharisees, hypocrites! You clean the outside of the cup and dish, but inside they are full of greed and self-indulgence! ²⁶ Blind Pharisee! First clean the inside of the cup,ᶠ so the outside of itᵍ may also become clean.

²⁷"Woe to you, scribes and Pharisees, hypocrites! You are like whitewashed tombs, which appear beautiful on the outside, but inside are full of dead men's bones and every impurity. ²⁸ In the same way, on the outside you seem righteous to people, but inside you are full of hypocrisy and lawlessness.

²⁹"Woe to you, scribes and Pharisees, hypocrites! You build the tombs of the prophets and decorate the monuments of the righteous, ³⁰ and you say, 'If we had lived in the

ᵃ23:4 Other mss omit *that are hard to carry*   ᵇ23:5 Other mss add *on their robes*   ᶜ23:8 Other mss add *the Messiah*   ᵈ23:14 Other mss omit bracketed text   ᵉ23:19 Other mss read *Fools and blind*   ᶠ23:26 Other mss add *and dish*   ᵍ23:26 Other mss read *of them*

days of our fathers, we wouldn't have taken part with them in shedding the prophets' blood.' ³¹ You therefore testify against yourselves that you are sons of those who murdered the prophets. ³² Fill up, then, the measure of your fathers' sins!

³³ "Snakes! Brood of vipers! How can you escape being condemned to hell? ³⁴ This is why I am sending you prophets, sages, and scribes. Some of them you will kill and crucify, and some of them you will flog in your synagogues and hound from town to town. ³⁵ So all the righteous blood shed on the earth will be charged to you, from the blood of righteous Abel to the blood of Zechariah, son of Berechiah, whom you murdered between the sanctuary and the altar. ³⁶ •I assure you: All these things will come on this generation!

### Jesus' Lamentation over Jerusalem

³⁷ "O Jerusalem! Jerusalem that kills the prophets and stones those who are sent to her! How often I wanted to gather your children together, as a hen gathers her chicks under her wings, yet you were not willing! ³⁸ See! Your house is left to you desolate. ³⁹ For I tell you, you will never see Me again until you say, **Blessed is He who comes in the name of the Lord!**"ᵃ

### Destruction of the Temple Predicted

**24** As Jesus left and was going out of the •temple complex, His disciples came up and called His attention to the temple buildings. ² Then He replied to them, "Do you not see all these things? •I assure you: Not one

stone will be left here on another that will not be thrown down!"

Of all the things you can be thankful to God for, what about the freedom of knowing that death is but a door, that your reward is waiting— just on the other side? The devil can scream and holler and stamp his feet all he wants to. He can't have this little soul.

### Signs of the End of the Age

³ While He was sitting on the •Mount of Olives, the disciples approached Him privately and said, "Tell us, when will these things happen? And what is the sign of Your coming and of the end of the age?" ⁴ Then Jesus replied to them: "Watch out that no one deceives you. ⁵ For many will come in My name, saying, 'I am the •Messiah,' and they will deceive many. ⁶ You are going to hear of wars and rumors of wars. See that you are not alarmed, because these things must take place, but the end is not yet. ⁷ For nation will rise up against nation, and kingdom against kingdom. There will be faminesᵇ and earthquakes in various places. ⁸ All these events are the beginning of birth pains.

### Persecutions Predicted

⁹ "Then they will hand you over to persecution, and they will kill you.

---

ᵃ**23:39** Ps 118:26   ᵇ **24:7** Other mss add *epidemics*

You will be hated by all nations because of My name. [10] Then many will take offense, betray one another and hate one another. [11] Many false prophets will rise up and deceive many. [12] And because lawlessness will multiply, the love of many will grow cold. [13] But the one who endures to the end, this one will be delivered. [14] This good news of the kingdom will be proclaimed in all the world as a testimony to all nations. And then the end will come.

## The Great Tribulation

[15]"So when you see **the abomination that causes desolation,**[a] spoken of by the prophet Daniel, standing in the holy place" (let the reader understand), [16]"then those in Judea must flee to the mountains! [17] A man on the housetop must not come down to get things out of his house. [18] And a man in the field must not go back to get his clothes. [19] Woe to pregnant women and nursing mothers in those days! [20] Pray that your escape may not be in winter or on a Sabbath. [21] For at that time there will be great tribulation, the kind that hasn't taken place since the beginning of the world until now, and never will again! [22] Unless those days were cut short, no one would survive. But because of the elect those days will be cut short.

[23]"If anyone tells you then, 'Look, here is the Messiah!' or, 'Over here!' do not believe it! [24] False messiahs and false prophets will arise and perform great signs and wonders to lead astray, if possible, even the elect. [25] Take note: I have told you in advance. [26] So if they tell you, 'Look, he's in the wilderness!' don't go out; 'Look, he's in the inner rooms!' do not believe it. [27] For as the lightning comes from the east and

flashes as far as the west, so will be the coming of the •Son of Man. [28] Wherever the carcass is, there the vultures will gather.

---

*"Long did we seek you, freedom—*
*in discipline, action, and suffering.*
*Now that we die, in the face of*
*God Himself we behold you."*
—*Dietrich Bonhoeffer*

---

## The Coming of the Son of Man

[29]"Immediately after the tribulation of those days,

> The sun will be darkened,
> and the moon will not shed her
> light;
> the stars will fall from the sky,
> and the celestial powers will be
> shaken.

[30]"Then the sign of the Son of Man will appear in the sky, and then all the tribes of the land will mourn; and they will see the Son of Man coming on the clouds of heaven with power and great glory. [31] He will send out His angels with a loud trumpet, and they will gather His elect from the four winds, from one end of the sky to the other.

## The Parable of the Fig Tree

[32]"Now from the fig tree learn this parable: As soon as its branch becomes tender and sprouts leaves, you know that summer is near. [33] In the same way, when you see all these things, know that He is near—at the door! [34] I assure you: This generation will certainly not pass away until all these

[a]**24:15** Dn 9:27

things take place. [35] Heaven and earth will pass away, but My words will never pass away.

## No One Knows the Day or Hour

[36]"Now concerning that day and hour no one knows—neither the angels in heaven, nor the Son[a]—except the Father only. [37] As the days of Noah were, so the coming of the Son of Man will be. [38] For in those days before the flood they were eating and drinking, marrying and giving in marriage, until the day Noah boarded the ark. [39] They didn't know until the flood came and swept them all away. So this is the way the coming of the Son of Man will be: [40] Then two men will be in the field: one will be taken and one left. [41] Two women will be grinding at the mill: one will be taken and one left. [42] Therefore be alert, since you don't know what day[b] your Lord is coming. [43] But know this: If the homeowner had known what time the thief was coming, he would have stayed alert and not let his house be broken into. [44] This is why you also should get ready, because the Son of Man is coming at an hour you do not expect.

## Faithful Service to the Messiah

[45]"Who then is a faithful and sensible slave, whom his master has put in charge of his household, to give them food at the proper time? [46] Blessed is that slave whom his master, when he comes, will find working. [47] I assure you: He will put him in charge of all his possessions. [48] But if that wicked slave says in his heart, 'My master is delayed,' [49] and starts to beat his fellow slaves, and eats and drinks with drunkards, [50] that slave's master will come on a day he does not expect and at a time he does not know. [51] He will cut him to pieces and assign him a place with the hypocrites. In that place there will be weeping and gnashing of teeth.

## The Parable of the 10 Virgins

**25** "Then the kingdom of heaven will be like 10 virgins who took their lamps and went out to meet the groom. [2] Five of them were foolish and five were sensible. [3] When the foolish took their lamps, they didn't take oil with them. [4] But the sensible ones took oil in their flasks with their lamps. [5] Since the groom was delayed, they all became drowsy and fell asleep.

---

### Matthew 25:34

### God's Grace

*Even before He created the world, God's grace had already looked down the corridors of history and seen your face, your heart, your faith in His Son. He had made a place for you to live with Him forever and ever. That is total, all-consuming, never-say-die, everlasting grace.*

---

[6]"In the middle of the night there was a shout: 'Here's the groom! Come out to meet him.'
[7]"Then all those virgins got up and trimmed their lamps. [8] But the foolish ones said to the sensible ones, 'Give us some of your oil, because our lamps are going out.'

[a]**24:36** Other mss omit *nor the Son*   [b]**24:42** Other mss read *hour;* that is, time

9"The sensible ones answered, 'No, there won't be enough for us and for you. Go instead to those who sell, and buy oil for yourselves.'

10"When they had gone to buy some, the groom arrived. Then those who were ready went in with him to the wedding banquet, and the door was shut.

11"Later the rest of the virgins also came and said, 'Master, master, open up for us!'

12"But he replied, '•I assure you: I do not know you!'

13"Therefore be alert, because you don't know either the day or the hour.ᵃ

## The Parable of the Talents

14"For it is just like a man going on a journey. He called his own slaves and turned over his possessions to them. 15 To one he gave five talents; to another, two; and to another, one—to each according to his own ability. Then he went on a journey. Immediately 16 the man who had received five talents went, put them to work, and earned five more. 17 In the same way the man with two earned two more. 18 But the man who had received one talent went off, dug a hole in the ground, and hid his master's money.

19"After a long time the master of those slaves came and settled accounts with them. 20 The man who had received five talents approached, presented five more talents, and said, 'Master, you gave me five talents. Look, I've earned five more talents.'

21"His master said to him, 'Well done, good and faithful slave! You were faithful over a few things; I will put you in charge of many things. Enter your master's joy!'

22"Then the man with two talents also approached. He said, 'Master, you gave me two talents. Look, I've earned two more talents.'

23"His master said to him, 'Well done, good and faithful slave! You were faithful over a few things; I will put you in charge of many things. Enter your master's joy!'

24"Then the man who had received one talent also approached and said, 'Master, I know you. You're a difficult man, reaping where you haven't sown and gathering where you haven't scattered seed. 25 So I was afraid and went off and hid your talent in the ground. Look, you have what is yours.'

26"But his master replied to him, 'You evil, lazy slave! If you knew that I reap where I haven't sown and gather where I haven't scattered, 27 then you should have deposited my money with the bankers. And when I returned I would have received my money back with interest.

28"'So take the talent from him and give it to the one who has 10 talents. 29 For to everyone who has, more will be given, and he will have more than enough. But from the one who does not have, even what he has will be taken away from him. 30 And throw this good-for-nothing slave into the outer darkness. In that place there will be weeping and gnashing of teeth.'

## The Sheep and the Goats

31"When the •Son of Man comes in His glory, and all the angelsᵇ with Him, then He will sit on the throne of His glory. 32 All the nations will be gathered before Him, and He will separate them one from another, just as a shepherd separates the sheep from the goats. 33 He will put the sheep on

ᵃ25:13 Other mss add *in which the Son of Man is coming.*    ᵇ25:31 Other mss read *holy angels*

His right, and the goats on the left. [34] Then the King will say to those on His right, 'Come, you who are blessed by My Father, inherit the kingdom prepared for you from the foundation of the world.

[35] For I was hungry and you gave
    Me something to eat;
  I was thirsty and you gave Me
    something to drink;
  I was a stranger and you took
    Me in;
[36] I was naked and you clothed
    Me;
  I was sick and you took care of
    Me;
  I was in prison and you visited
    Me.'

[37] "Then the righteous will answer Him, 'Lord, when did we see You hungry and feed You, or thirsty and give You something to drink? [38] When did we see You a stranger and take You in, or without clothes and clothe You? [39] When did we see You sick, or in prison, and visit You?' [40] "And the King will answer them, 'I assure you: Whatever you did for one of the least of these brothers of Mine, you did for Me.' [41] Then He will also say to those on the left, 'Depart from Me, you who are cursed, into the eternal fire prepared for the Devil and his angels!

[42] For I was hungry and you gave
    Me nothing to eat;
  I was thirsty and you gave Me
    nothing to drink;
[43] I was a stranger and you didn't
    take Me in;
  I was naked and you didn't
    clothe Me,
  sick and in prison and you didn't
    take care of Me.'

[44] "Then they too will answer, 'Lord, when did we see You hungry, or thirsty, or a stranger, or without clothes, or sick, or in prison, and not help You?' [45] "Then He will answer them, 'I assure you: Whatever you did not do for one of the least of these, you did not do for Me either.' [46] "And they will go away into eternal punishment, but the righteous into eternal life."

### The Plot to Kill Jesus

**26** When Jesus had finished saying all this, He told His disciples, [2] "You know that the •Passover takes place after two days, and the •Son of Man will be handed over to be crucified." [3] Then the chief priests[a] and the elders of the people assembled in the •palace of the high priest, who was called Caiaphas, [4] and they conspired to arrest Jesus by deceit and kill Him. [5] "Not during the festival," they said, "so there won't be rioting among the people."

### The Anointing at Bethany

[6] While Jesus was in Bethany at the house of Simon the leper, [7] a woman approached Him with an alabaster jar of very expensive fragrant oil. She poured it on His head as He was reclining at the table. [8] When the disciples saw it, they were indignant. "Why this waste?" they asked. [9] "This might have been sold for a great deal and given to the poor." [10] But Jesus, aware of this, said to them, "Why are you bothering this woman? She has done a noble thing for Me. [11] You always have the poor with you, but you do not always have

---

[a]**26:3** Other mss add *and the scribes*

Me. [12] By pouring this fragrant oil on My body, she has prepared Me for burial. [13] •I assure you: Wherever this gospel is proclaimed in the whole world, what this woman has done will also be told in memory of her."

[14] Then one of the Twelve—the man called Judas Iscariot—went to the •chief priests [15] and said, "What are you willing to give me if I hand Him over to you?" So they weighed out 30 pieces of silver for him. [16] And from that time he started looking for a good opportunity to betray Him.

## Betrayal at the Passover

[17] On the first day of •Unleavened Bread the disciples came to Jesus and asked, "Where do You want us to prepare the Passover so You may eat it?" [18] "Go into the city to a certain man," He said, "and tell him, 'The Teacher says, "My time is near; I am celebrating the Passover at your place with My disciples."'" [19] So the disciples did as Jesus had directed them and prepared the Passover. [20] When evening came, He was reclining at the table with the Twelve. [21] While they were eating, He said, "I assure you: One of you will betray Me."

[22] Deeply distressed, each one began to say to Him, "Surely not I, Lord?"

[23] He replied, "The one who dipped his hand with Me in the bowl—he will betray Me. [24] The Son of Man will go just as it is written about Him, but woe to that man by whom the Son of Man is betrayed! It would have been better for that man if he had not been born."

[25] Then Judas, His betrayer, replied, "Surely not I, •Rabbi?"

"You have said it," He told him.

## The First Lord's Supper

[26] As they were eating, Jesus took bread, blessed and broke it, gave it to the disciples, and said, "Take, eat; this is My body." [27] Then He took a cup, and after giving thanks, He gave it to them and said, "Drink from it, all of you. [28] For this is My blood of the covenant,[a] which is shed for many for the forgiveness of sins. [29] But I tell you, from this moment I will not drink of this fruit of the vine until that day when I drink it new in My Father's kingdom with you." [30] After singing psalms, they went out to the •Mount of Olives.

## Peter's Denial Predicted

[31] Then Jesus said to them, "Tonight all of you will fall because of Me, for it is written:

**I will strike the shepherd,
and the sheep of the flock will
be scattered.**[b]

[32] But after I have been resurrected, I will go ahead of you to Galilee."

[33] Peter told Him, "Even if everyone falls because of You, I will never fall!"

[34] "I assure you," Jesus said to him, "tonight—before the rooster crows, you will deny Me three times!"

[35] "Even if I have to die with You," Peter told Him, "I will never deny You!" And all the disciples said the same thing.

## The Prayer in the Garden

[36] Then Jesus came with them to a place called Gethsemane, and He told the disciples, "Sit here while I go over there and pray." [37] Taking along Peter and the two sons of Zebedee, He began

---

[a]**26:28** Other mss read *new covenant*    [b]**26:31** Zch 13:7

# CLEAN SLATE
## *Justification*

They are justified freely by His grace
through the redemption that is
in Christ Jesus.
Romans 3:24

The fact that you deal with your own sins every day can often cloud the fact that God dealt with them two thousand years ago—all of them—the sins you committed two years ago, the sins you'll commit two years from now, the sins you're trying really hard not to commit today. No matter how your sins stack up on the timeline of your life, every one of them was in the future tense when Christ was gasping for air on the cross, blood oozing from His hands, His head, His feet, His side. When you gave in to His love and welcomed His forgiveness into your life, He "erased the certificate of debt, with its obligations, that was against us and opposed to us, and has taken it away by nailing it to the cross" (Colossians 2:14). "Since we have now been declared righteous by His blood, we will be saved through Him from wrath" (Romans 5:9).

Justified. The books balanced. The debt paid. So that when God looks at you, he sees you "holy, faultless, and blameless before Him" (Colossians 1:22). You can't get any cleaner than that.

*Look Up*
*Romans 3:21-26 (page 222)*

# PICTURE PERFECT
## *Baptism*

"Look, there's water! What would keep
me from being baptized?"
Acts 8:36

People sit around and argue about whether you should be sprinkled or dunked, or whether baptism itself brings the moment of salvation. These are important issues, and we could knock you over with our arguments. But let's not allow these questions to obscure the importance of this obedient act and the value it holds in the life of every Christian believer.

Could there be a more perfect, wordless way than baptism to describe what Christ has done for us or to demonstrate what has happened in our own lives by surrendering to His grace?

Christ died and was buried, but He rose again, conquering the finality of death. Our old selves, destined for hell and all its torments, have been buried but raised dripping wet in the cleansing blood of Jesus Christ to walk a clear path to glory.

If you haven't yet followed Christ's example of baptism, you really should. If you already have, use its memory to remind the devil of the day you shook the sin off your feet and turned your back on him forever.

*Look Up*
*Acts 8:36-38 (page 184)*

the high priest's courtyard. He went in and was sitting with the temple police to see the outcome.

[59] The chief priests and the whole •Sanhedrin were looking for false testimony against Jesus so they could put Him to death. [60] But they could not find any, even though many false witnesses came forward.[a] Finally, two[b] who came forward [61] stated, "This man said, 'I can demolish God's sanctuary and rebuild it in three days.' "

---

*"Talking to men for God is a great thing, but talking to God for men is still greater."*

*—E. M. Bounds*

---

[62] The high priest then stood up and said to Him, "Don't You have an answer to what these men are testifying against You?" [63] But Jesus kept silent. Then the high priest said to Him, "By the living God I place You under oath: tell us if You are the •Messiah, the Son of God!"

[64]"You have said it," Jesus told him. "But I tell you, in the future you will see **the Son of Man seated at the right hand** of the Power, and **coming on the clouds of heaven.**"[c]

[65] Then the high priest tore his robes and said, "He has blasphemed! Why do we still need witnesses? Look, now you've heard the blasphemy! [66] What is your decision?"

They answered, "He deserves death!" [67] Then they spit in His face and beat Him; and others slapped Him [68] and said, "Prophesy to us, You Messiah! Who hit You?"

## Peter Denies His Lord

[69] Now Peter was sitting outside in the courtyard. A servant approached him and she said, "You were with Jesus the Galilean too."

[70] But he denied it in front of everyone: "I don't know what you're talking about!"

[71] When he had gone out to the gateway, another woman saw him and told those who were there, "This man was with Jesus the •Nazarene!"

[72] And again he denied it with an oath, "I don't know the man!"

[73] After a little while those standing there approached and said to Peter, "You certainly are one of them, since even your accent gives you away."

[74] Then he started to curse and to swear with an oath, "I do not know the man!" Immediately a rooster crowed. [75] And Peter remembered the words Jesus had spoken, "Before the rooster crows, you will deny Me three times." And he went outside and wept bitterly.

## Jesus Handed Over to Pilate

**27** When daybreak came, all the •chief priests and the elders of the people plotted against Jesus to put Him to death. [2] After tying Him up, they led Him away and handed Him over to •Pilate,[d] the governor.

## Judas Hangs Himself

[3] Then Judas, His betrayer, seeing that He had been condemned, was full of remorse and returned the 30 pieces of silver to the chief priests and to the elders. [4]"I have sinned by betraying innocent blood," he said.

---

[a]**26:60** Other mss add *they found none*    [b]**26:60** Other mss add *false witnesses*    [c]**26:64** Ps 110:1; Dn 7:13
[d]**27:2** Other mss read *Pontius Pilate*

"What's that to us?" they said. "See to it yourself!"

⁵ So he threw the silver into the sanctuary and departed. Then he went and hanged himself.

⁶ The chief priests took the silver and said, "It's not lawful to put it into the temple treasury, since it is blood money." ⁷ So they conferred together and bought the potter's field with it as a burial place for foreigners. ⁸ Therefore that field has been called "Blood Field" to this day. ⁹ Then what was spoken through the prophet Jeremiah was fulfilled:

**They took the 30 pieces of silver, the price of Him whose price was set by the sons of Israel, ¹⁰ and they gave them for the potter's field, as the Lord directed me.**[a]

## Jesus Faces the Governor

¹¹ Now Jesus stood before the governor. "Are You the King of the Jews?" the governor asked Him.

Jesus answered, "You have said it." ¹² And while He was being accused by the chief priests and elders, He didn't answer.

¹³ Then Pilate said to Him, "Don't You hear how much they are testifying against You?" ¹⁴ But He didn't answer him on even one charge, so that the governor was greatly amazed.

## Jesus or Barabbas

¹⁵ At the festival the governor's custom was to release to the crowd one prisoner whom they wanted. ¹⁶ At that time they had a notorious prisoner called Barabbas.[b] ¹⁷ So when they had gathered together, Pilate said to them, "Whom do you want me to release for you—Barabbas,[b] or Jesus who is called *Messiah?" ¹⁸ For he knew they had handed Him over because of envy.

¹⁹ While he was sitting on the judge's bench, his wife sent word to him, "Have nothing to do with that righteous man, for today I've suffered terribly in a dream because of Him!"

²⁰ The chief priests and the elders, however, persuaded the crowds to ask for Barabbas and to execute Jesus. ²¹ The governor asked them, "Which of the two do you want me to release for you?"

"Barabbas!" they answered.

²² Pilate asked them, "What should I do then with Jesus, who is called Messiah?"

They all answered, "Crucify Him!"

²³ Then he said, "Why? What has He done wrong?"

But they kept shouting, "Crucify Him!" all the more.

²⁴ When Pilate saw that he was getting nowhere, but that a riot was starting instead, he took some water, washed his hands in front of the crowd, and said, "I am innocent of this man's blood.[c] See to it yourselves!"

²⁵ All the people answered, "His blood be on us and on our children!" ²⁶ Then he released Barabbas to them. But after having Jesus flogged, he handed Him over to be crucified.

## Mocked by the Military

²⁷ Then the governor's soldiers took Jesus into *headquarters and gathered the whole *company around Him. ²⁸ They stripped Him and dressed Him in a scarlet robe. ²⁹ They twisted a crown out of thorns, put it on His

[a]**27:9-10** Jr 32:6-9; Zch 11:12-13   [b]**27:16-17** Other mss read *Jesus Barabbas*   [c]**27:24** Other mss read *this righteous man's blood*

head, and placed a reed in His right hand. And they knelt down before Him and mocked Him: "Hail, King of the Jews!" [30] Then they spit at Him, took the reed, and kept hitting Him on the head. [31] When they had mocked Him, they stripped Him of the robe, put His clothes on Him, and led Him away to crucify Him.

### Crucified Between Two Criminals

[32] As they were going out, they found a Cyrenian man named Simon. They forced this man to carry His cross. [33] When they came to a place called *Golgotha* (which means Skull Place), [34] they gave Him wine[a] mixed with gall to drink. But when He tasted it, He would not drink it. [35] After crucifying Him they divided His clothes by casting lots.[b] [36] Then they sat down and were guarding Him there. [37] Above His head they put up the charge against Him in writing:

> **THIS IS JESUS
> THE KING OF THE JEWS**

[38] Then two criminals were crucified with Him, one on the right and one on the left. [39] Those who passed by were yelling insults at Him, shaking their heads [40] and saying, "The One who would demolish the sanctuary and rebuild it in three days, save Yourself! If You are the Son of God, come down from the cross!" [41] In the same way the chief priests, with the •scribes and elders,[c] mocked Him and said, [42]"He saved others, but He cannot save Himself! He is the King of Israel! Let Him[d] come down now from the cross, and we will believe in Him. [43] He has put His trust in God; let God

rescue Him now—if He wants Him! For He said, 'I am God's Son.' "[44] In the same way even the criminals who were crucified with Him kept taunting Him.

### The Death of Jesus

[45] From noon until three in the afternoon darkness came over the whole land. [46] At about three in the afternoon Jesus cried out with a loud voice, *Elí, Elí, lemá sabachtháni?* that is, **My God, My God, why have You forsaken Me?**"[e] [47] When some of those standing there heard this, they said, "He's calling for Elijah!" [48] Immediately one of them ran and got a sponge, filled it with sour wine, fixed it on a reed, and offered Him a drink. [49] But the rest said, "Let us see if Elijah comes to save Him!" [50] Jesus shouted again with a loud voice and gave up His spirit. [51] Suddenly, the curtain of the sanctuary was split in two from top to bottom; the earth quaked and the rocks were split. [52] The tombs also were opened and many bodies of the saints who had gone to their rest were raised. [53] And they came out of the tombs after His resurrection, entered the holy city, and appeared to many. [54] When the •centurion and those with him, who were guarding Jesus, saw the earthquake and the things that had happened, they were terrified and said, "This man really was God's Son!" [55] Many women who had followed Jesus from Galilee and ministered to Him were there, looking on from a distance. [56] Among them were •Mary

---

[a]**27:34** Other mss read *sour wine*   [b]**27:35** Other mss add *that what was spoken by the prophet might be fulfilled: "They divided My clothes among them, and for My clothing they cast lots."*   [c]**27:41** Other mss add *and Pharisees*   [d]**27:42** Other mss read *If He . . . Israel, let Him*   [e]**27:46** Ps 22:1

*Matthew 27:54*

*God the Son*

*Jesus had been tried, convicted, and executed for claiming to be the Son of God—something the people were sure He was not. But barely had the life left His body before some people were starting to realize they had made a big mistake. Jesus was who He claimed to be.*

Magdalene, Mary the mother of James and Joseph, and the mother of Zebedee's sons.

## The Burial of Jesus

[57] When it was evening, a rich man from Arimathea named Joseph came, who himself had also become a disciple of Jesus. [58] He approached Pilate and asked for Jesus' body. Then Pilate ordered that it[a] be released. [59] So Joseph took the body, wrapped it in clean, fine linen, [60] and placed it in his new tomb, which he had cut into the rock. He left after rolling a great stone against the entrance of the tomb. [61] Mary Magdalene and the other Mary were seated there, facing the tomb.

## The Closely Guarded Tomb

[62] The next day, which followed the preparation day, the chief priests and the •Pharisees gathered before Pilate [63] and said, "Sir, we remember that while this deceiver was still alive, He said, 'After three days I will rise again.' [64] Therefore give orders that the tomb be made secure until the third day. Otherwise, His disciples may come, steal Him, and tell the people, 'He has been raised from the dead.' Then the last deception will be worse than the first."

[65] "You have a guard ⌊of soldiers⌋," Pilate told them. "Go and make it as secure as you know how." [66] Then they went and made the tomb secure by sealing the stone and setting the guard.

## Resurrection Morning

**28** After the Sabbath, as the first day of the week was dawning, •Mary Magdalene and the other Mary went to view the tomb. [2] Suddenly there was a violent earthquake, because an angel of the Lord descended from heaven and approached ⌊the tomb⌋. He rolled back the stone and was sitting on it. [3] His appearance was like lightning, and his robe was as white as snow. [4] The guards were so shaken from fear of him that they became like dead men.

[5] But the angel told the women, "Don't be afraid, because I know you are looking for Jesus who was crucified. [6] He is not here! For He has been resurrected, just as He said. Come and see the place where He lay. [7] Then go quickly and tell His disciples, 'He has been raised from the dead. In fact, He is going ahead of you to Galilee; you will see Him there.' Listen, I have told you." [8] So, departing quickly from the tomb with fear and great joy, they ran to tell His disciples the news. [9] Just then[b] Jesus met them and said, "Rejoice!" They came up, took hold of His feet, and worshiped Him. [10] Then

---

[a]**27:58** Other mss read *that the body*   [b]**28:9** Other mss add *as they were on their way to tell the news to His disciples*

Jesus told them, "Do not be afraid. Go and tell My brothers to leave for Galilee, and they will see Me there."

## The Soldiers Are Bribed to Lie

[11] As they were on their way, some of the guard came into the city and reported to the •chief priests everything that had happened. [12] After the priests had assembled with the elders and agreed on a plan, they gave the soldiers a large sum of money [13] and told them, "Say this, 'His disciples came during the night and stole Him while we were sleeping.' [14] If this reaches the governor's ears, we will deal with him and keep you out of trouble." [15] So they took the money and did as they were instructed. And this story has been spread among Jewish people to this day.

## The Great Commission

[16] The 11 disciples traveled to Galilee, to the mountain where Jesus had directed them. [17] When they saw Him, they worshiped,[a] but some doubted. [18] Then Jesus came near and said to them, "All authority has been given to Me in heaven and on earth. [19] Go, therefore, and make disciples of all nations, baptizing them in the name of the Father and of the Son and of the Holy Spirit, [20] teaching them to observe everything I have commanded you. And remember, I am with you always, to the end of the age."

---

*Matthew 28:19-20*

*Evangelism*

*These parting words of Christ (known as The Great Commission) are meant for all of us. It doesn't mean, however, that all of us should go to Thailand or Tanzania. But it does mean that the whole church should have a heart for people everywhere who need to know Jesus.*

---

[a]**28:17** Other mss add *Him*

# MARK

## The Messiah's Herald

**1** The beginning of the gospel of Jesus Christ, the Son of God. ² As it is written in Isaiah the prophet:[a]

> **Look, I am sending My**
> **messenger ahead of You,**
> **who will prepare Your way.[b]**
> ³ **A voice of one crying out in the**
> **wilderness:**
> **"Prepare the way for the Lord;**
> **make His paths straight!"[c]**

⁴ John came baptizing in the wilderness and preaching a baptism of repentance for the forgiveness of sins. ⁵ The whole Judean countryside and all the people of Jerusalem were flocking to him, and they were baptized by him in the Jordan River as they confessed their sins. ⁶ John wore a camel-hair garment with a leather belt around his waist, and ate locusts and wild honey. ⁷ He was preaching: "Someone more powerful than I will come after me. I am not worthy to stoop down and untie the strap of His sandals. ⁸ I have baptized you with water, but He will baptize you with the Holy Spirit."

## The Baptism of Jesus

⁹ In those days Jesus came from Nazareth in Galilee and was baptized in the Jordan by John. ¹⁰ As soon as He came up out of the water, He saw the heavens being torn open and the Spirit descending to Him like a dove. ¹¹ And a voice came from heaven:

> You are My beloved Son;
> In You I take delight!

## The Temptation of Jesus

¹² Immediately the Spirit drove Him into the wilderness. ¹³ He was in the wilderness 40 days, being tempted by Satan. He was with the wild animals, and the angels began to serve Him.

---

*"We must carefully plan solitude. We do not take the spiritual life seriously if we do not set aside some time to be with, and listen to, God."*
—*Henri Nouwen*

---

## Ministry in Galilee

¹⁴ But after John was arrested, Jesus went to Galilee, preaching the good news[d] of God: ¹⁵ "The time is fulfilled, and the kingdom of God has come near. Repent and believe in the good news!"

## The First Disciples

¹⁶ As He was passing along by the Sea of Galilee, He saw Simon and Andrew, Simon's brother. They were casting a net into the sea, since they were fishermen. ¹⁷ "Follow Me," Jesus told them, "and I will make you into fishers of men!" ¹⁸ Immediately they left their nets and followed Him. ¹⁹ Going on a little farther, He saw James the son of

[a]**1:2** Other mss read *in the prophets*  [b]**1:2** Other mss add *before You*  [c]**1:2–3** Mal 3:1; Is 40:3  [d]**1:14** Other mss add *of the kingdom*

Zebedee and his brother John. They were in their boat mending their nets. <sup>20</sup> Immediately He called them, and they left their father Zebedee in the boat with the hired men and followed Him.

## Driving Out an Unclean Spirit

<sup>21</sup> Then they went into Capernaum, and right away He entered the •synagogue on the Sabbath and began to teach. <sup>22</sup> They were astonished at His teaching because, unlike the •scribes, He was teaching them as one having authority.

<sup>23</sup> Just then a man with an unclean spirit was in their synagogue. He cried out,<sup>a</sup> <sup>24</sup> "What do You have to do with us, Jesus—•Nazarene? Have You come to destroy us? I know who You are—the Holy One of God!"

<sup>25</sup> But Jesus rebuked him and said, "Be quiet, and come out of him!" <sup>26</sup> And the unclean spirit convulsed him, shouted with a loud voice, and came out of him.

<sup>27</sup> Then they were all amazed, so they began to argue with one another, saying, "What is this? A new teaching with authority!<sup>b</sup> He commands even the unclean spirits, and they obey Him." <sup>28</sup> His fame then spread throughout the entire vicinity of Galilee.

## Healings at Capernaum

<sup>29</sup> As soon as they left the synagogue, they went into Simon and Andrew's house with James and John. <sup>30</sup> Simon's mother-in-law was lying in bed with a fever, and they told Him about her at once. <sup>31</sup> So He went to her, took her by the hand, and raised her up. The fever left her,<sup>c</sup> and she began to serve them.

<sup>32</sup> When evening came, after the sun had set, they began bringing to Him all those who were sick and those who were demon-possessed. <sup>33</sup> The whole town was assembled at the door, <sup>34</sup> and He healed many who were sick with various diseases, and drove out many demons. But He would not permit the demons to speak, because they knew Him.

## Preaching in Galilee

<sup>35</sup> Very early in the morning, while it was still dark, He got up, went out, and made His way to a deserted place. And He was praying there. <sup>36</sup> Simon and his companions went searching for Him. <sup>37</sup> They found Him and said, "Everyone's looking for You!"

<sup>38</sup> And He said to them, "Let's go on to the neighboring villages, so that I may preach there too. This is why I have come." <sup>39</sup> So He went into all of Galilee, preaching in their synagogues and driving out demons.

---

### Mark 1:35-37

*Jesus invites you to enjoy something that's been sadly lost in the mad dash of modern life—the sweet simplicity of a quiet moment to think, to read, to pray, to go deeper with God. There's a quiet place beyond the buzz of the TV and the telephone. And God's saving you a seat.*

---

<sup>a</sup>1:23 Other mss add to the beginning of v. 24: *"Leave us alone.*  <sup>b</sup>1:27 Other mss read *What is this? What is this new teaching? For with authority*  <sup>c</sup>1:31 Other mss add *at once*

## Cleansing a Leper

40 Then a leper came to Him, and begged on his knees before[a] Him, saying, "If You are willing, You can make me clean."
41 Moved with compassion, Jesus reached out His hand and touched him. "I am willing," He told him. "Be made clean." 42 Immediately the leprosy left him, and he was made clean. 43 Then He sternly warned him and sent him away at once, 44 telling him, "See that you say nothing to anyone; but go and show yourself to the priest, and offer what Moses prescribed for your cleansing, as a testimony to them." 45 Yet he went out and began to proclaim it widely and to spread the news, with the result that Jesus could no longer enter a town openly. But He was out in deserted places, and they would come to Him from everywhere.

## The Son of Man Forgives and Heals

2 When He entered Capernaum again after some days, it was reported that He was at home. 2 So many people gathered together that there was no more room, even near the door, and He was speaking the message to them. 3 Then they came to Him bringing a paralytic, carried by four men. 4 Since they were not able to bring him to[b] Jesus because of the crowd, they removed the roof above where He was. And when they had broken through, they lowered the stretcher on which the paralytic was lying. 5 Seeing their faith, Jesus told the paralytic, "Son, your sins are forgiven."
6 But some of the •scribes were sitting there, reasoning in their hearts:

7 "Why does He speak like this? He's blaspheming! Who can forgive sins but God alone?"
8 Right away Jesus understood in His spirit that they were reasoning like this within themselves, and said to them, "Why are you reasoning these things in your hearts? 9 Which is easier: to say to the paralytic, 'Your sins are forgiven,' or to say, 'Get up, pick up your stretcher, and walk'? 10 But so you may know that the •Son of Man has authority on earth to forgive sins," He told the paralytic, 11 "I tell you: get up, pick up your stretcher, and go home."
12 Immediately he got up, picked up the stretcher, and went out in front of everyone. As a result, they were all astounded and gave glory to God, saying, "We have never seen anything like this!"

## The Call of Matthew

13 Then Jesus went out again beside the sea. The whole crowd was coming to Him, and He taught them. 14 Then, moving on, He saw Levi the son of Alphaeus sitting at the tax office, and He said to him, "Follow Me!" So he got up and followed Him.

## Dining with Sinners

15 While He was reclining at the table in Levi's house, many tax collectors and sinners were also guests with Jesus and His disciples, because there were many who were following Him. 16 When the scribes of the Pharisees[c] saw that He was eating with sinners and tax collectors, they asked His disciples, "Why does He eat[d] with tax collectors and sinners?"

---

[a]1:40 Other mss omit on his knees before   [b]2:4 Other mss read able to get near   [c]2:16 Other mss read scribes and Pharisees   [d]2:16 Other mss add and drink

[17] When Jesus heard this, He told them, "Those who are well don't need a doctor, but the sick ⌊do need⌋ one. I didn't come to call the righteous, but sinners."

## A Question about Fasting

[18] Now John's disciples and the Pharisees[a] were fasting. People came and asked Him, "Why do John's disciples and the •Pharisees' disciples fast, but Your disciples do not fast?"
[19] Jesus said to them, "The wedding guests cannot fast while the groom is with them, can they? As long as they have the groom with them, they cannot fast. [20] But the time will come when the groom is taken away from them, and then they will fast in that day. [21] No one sews a patch of unshrunk cloth on an old garment. Otherwise, the new patch pulls away from the old cloth, and a worse tear is made. [22] And no one puts new wine into old wineskins. Otherwise, the wine will burst the skins, and the wine is lost as well as the skins.[b] But new wine is for fresh wineskins."

## Lord of the Sabbath

[23] On the Sabbath He was going through the grainfields, and His disciples began to make their way picking some heads of grain. [24] The •Pharisees said to Him, "Look, why are they doing what is not lawful on the Sabbath?"
[25] And He said to them, "Have you never read what David did when he was in need and hungry, he and his companions: [26] how he entered the house of God in the time of Abiathar the high priest and ate the •sacred bread—which is not lawful for anyone to eat except the priests—and

also gave some to his companions?" [27] Then He told them, "The Sabbath was made for man, and not man for the Sabbath. [28] Therefore the Son of Man is Lord even of the Sabbath."

## The Man with the Paralyzed Hand

**3** Now He entered the •synagogue again, and a man was there who had a paralyzed hand. [2] In order to accuse Him, they were watching Him closely to see whether He would heal him on the Sabbath. [3] He told the man with the paralyzed hand, "Stand before us." [4] Then He said to them, "Is it lawful on the Sabbath to do good or to do evil, to save life or to kill?" But they were silent. [5] After looking around at them with anger and sorrow at the hardness of their hearts, He told the man, "Stretch out your hand." So he stretched it out, and his hand was restored. [6] Immediately the •Pharisees went out and started plotting with the •Herodians against Him, how they might destroy Him.

## Ministering to the Multitude

[7] Jesus departed with His disciples to the sea, and a great multitude followed from Galilee, Judea, [8] Jerusalem, Idumea, beyond the Jordan, and around Tyre and Sidon. The great multitude came to Him because they heard everything He was doing. [9] Then He told His disciples to have a small boat ready for Him, so the crowd would not crush Him. [10] Since He had healed many, all who had diseases were pressing toward Him to touch Him. [11] Whenever the unclean spirits saw Him, they would fall down before Him and cry out, "You are the Son of

---

[a]**2:18** Other mss read *the disciples of John and of the Pharisees*   [b]**2:22** Other mss read *the wine spills out and the skins will be ruined*

God!" ¹² And He would strongly warn them not to make Him known.

## The 12 Apostles

¹³ Then He went up the mountain and summoned those He wanted, and they came to Him. ¹⁴ He appointed 12, whom He also named apostles,ᵃ that they might be with Him and that He might send them out to preach ¹⁵ and to have authority toᵇ drive out demons. ¹⁶He appointed the Twelve:ᶜ

> To Simon, He gave the name Peter;
> ¹⁷ and to James the son of Zebedee, and to his brother John,
> He gave the name "Boanerges" (that is, "Sons of Thunder");
> ¹⁸ Andrew;
> Philip and Bartholomew;
> Matthew and Thomas;
> James the son of Alphaeus, and Thaddaeus;
> Simon the Zealot, ¹⁹ and Judas Iscariot, who also betrayed Him.

## A House Divided

²⁰ Then He went into a house, and the crowd gathered again so that they were not even able to eat. ²¹ When His family heard this, they set out to restrain Him, because they said, "He's out of His mind."
²² And the •scribes who had come down from Jerusalem said, "He has •Beelzebul in Him!" and, "He drives out demons by the ruler of the demons!"
²³ So He summoned them and spoke to them in parables: "How can Satan drive out Satan? ²⁴ If a kingdom is divided against itself, that kingdom cannot stand. ²⁵ If a house is divided against itself, that house cannot stand. ²⁶ And if Satan rebels against himself and is divided, he cannot stand but is finished!

²⁷ "On the other hand, no one can enter a strong man's house and rob his possessions unless he first ties up the strong man. Then he will rob his house. ²⁸ •I assure you: People will be forgiven for all sins and whatever blasphemies they may blaspheme. ²⁹ But whoever blasphemes against the Holy Spirit never has forgiveness, but is guilty of an eternal sin"ᵈ— ³⁰ because they were saying, "He has an unclean spirit."

## True Relationships

³¹ Then His mother and His brothers came, and standing outside, they sent word to Him and called Him. ³² A crowd was sitting around Him and told Him, "Look, Your mother, Your brothers, and Your sistersᵉ are outside asking for You."
³³ He replied to them, "Who are My mother and My brothers?" ³⁴ And looking about at those who were sitting in a circle around Him, He said, "Here are My mother and My brothers! ³⁵ Whoever does the will of God is My brother and sister and mother."

## The Parable of the Sower

4 Again He began to teach by the sea, and a very large crowd gathered around Him. So He got into a boat on the sea and sat down, while the whole crowd was on the shore fac-

ᵃ3:14 Other mss omit *whom He also named apostles*   ᵇ3:15 Other mss add *heal diseases, and to*   ᶜ3:16 Other mss omit *He appointed the Twelve*   ᵈ3:29 Other mss read *is subject to eternal judgment*   ᵉ3:32 Other mss omit *and Your sisters*

ing the sea. [2] He taught them many things in parables, and in His teaching He said to them: [3] "Listen! Consider the sower who went out to sow. [4] As he sowed, this occurred: Some seed fell along the path, and the birds came and ate it up. [5] Other seed fell on rocky ground where it didn't have much soil, and it sprang up right away, since it didn't have deep soil. [6] When the sun came up, it was scorched, and since it didn't have a root, it withered. [7] Other seed fell among thorns, and the thorns came up and choked it, and it didn't produce a crop. [8] Still others fell on good ground and produced a crop that increased 30, 60, and 100 times ⌊what was sown⌋." [9] Then He said, "Anyone who has ears to hear should listen!"

---

*"Christianity without discipleship is Christianity without Christ. In such a religion there is trust in God, but no following of Christ."*
*—Dietrich Bonhoeffer*

---

## Why Jesus Used Parables

[10] When He was in private, those who were around Him, along with the Twelve, asked Him about the parables. [11] He answered them, "The secret of the kingdom of God has been granted to you, but to those outside, everything comes in parables [12] so that

**they may look and look, yet not perceive;**
**they may listen and listen, yet**

**not understand;**
**otherwise, they might turn back—**
**and be forgiven."**[a][b]

## The Parable of the Sower Explained

[13] Then He said to them: "Do you not understand this parable? How then will you understand all the parables? [14] The sower sows the word. [15] These are the ones along the path where the word is sown: when they hear, immediately Satan comes and takes away the word sown in them.[c] [16] And these are[d] the ones sown on rocky ground: when they hear the word, immediately they receive it with joy. [17] But they have no root in themselves; they are short-lived. And when affliction or persecution comes because of the word, they stumble immediately. [18] Others are sown among thorns; these are the ones who hear the word, [19] but the worries of this age, the pleasure of wealth, and the desires for other things enter in and choke the word, and it becomes unfruitful. [20] But the ones sown on good ground are those who hear the word, welcome it, and produce a crop: 30, 60, and 100 times ⌊what was sown⌋."

## Using Your Light

[21] He also said to them, "Is a lamp brought in to be put under a basket or under a bed? Isn't it to be put on a lampstand? [22] For nothing is concealed except to be revealed, and nothing hidden except to come to light. [23] If anyone has ears to hear, he should listen!" [24] Then He said to them, "Pay attention to what you hear. By the measure you use, it will

[a]**4:12** Other mss read *and their sins be forgiven them*   [b]**4:12** Is 6:9–10   [c]**4:15** Other mss read *in their hearts*
[d]**4:16** Other mss read *are like*

be measured and added to you. <sup>25</sup> For to the one who has, it will be given, and from the one who does not have, even what he has will be taken away."

## The Parable of the Growing Seed

<sup>26</sup> "The kingdom of God is like this," He said. "A man scatters seed on the ground; <sup>27</sup> night and day he sleeps and gets up, and the seed sprouts and grows—he doesn't know how. <sup>28</sup> The soil produces a crop by itself—first the blade, then the head, and then the ripe grain on the head. <sup>29</sup> But as soon as the crop is ready, he sends for the sickle, because harvest has come."

## The Parable of the Mustard Seed

<sup>30</sup> And He said: "How can we illustrate the kingdom of God, or with what parable should we describe it? <sup>31</sup> It's like a mustard seed that, when sown in the soil, is smaller than all the seeds on the ground. <sup>32</sup> But when sown, it comes up and grows taller than all the vegetables, and produces large branches, so that the birds of the sky can nest in its shade."

## Using Parables

<sup>33</sup> He would speak the word to them with many parables like these, as they were able to hear. <sup>34</sup> And He did not speak to them without a parable. Privately, however, He would explain everything to His own disciples.

## Wind and Wave Obey the Master

<sup>35</sup> On that day, when evening had come, He told them, "Let's cross over

---

*Mark 4:33-34*

*Growing deeper in Christ is not an automatic process, but a deliberate decision to learn what following God is all about. It's called discipleship. Disciples want nothing more than to be like their masters. Yours just happens to be the best there is.*

---

to the other side ⌊of the lake⌋." <sup>36</sup> So they left the crowd and took Him along since He was in the boat. And other boats were with Him. <sup>37</sup> A fierce windstorm arose, and the waves were breaking over the boat, so that the boat was already being swamped. <sup>38</sup> But He was in the stern, sleeping on the cushion. So they woke Him up and said to Him, "Teacher! Don't you care we're going to die?"

<sup>39</sup> He got up, rebuked the wind, and said to the sea, "Silence! Be still!" The wind ceased, and there was a great calm. <sup>40</sup> Then He said to them, "Why are you fearful? Do you still have no faith?"

<sup>41</sup> And they were terrified and said to one another, "Who then is this? Even the wind and the sea obey Him!"

## Demons Driven Out by the Master

**5** Then they came to the other side of the sea, to the region of the Gerasenes.<sup>a</sup> <sup>2</sup> As soon as He got out of the boat, a man with an unclean spirit came out of the tombs and met Him. <sup>3</sup> He lived in the tombs; and no one was able to restrain him any more— even with chains— <sup>4</sup> because he often

---

<sup>a</sup>**5:1** Other mss read *Gadarenes*; other mss read *Gergesenes*

had been bound with shackles and chains, but had snapped off the chains and smashed the shackles. No one was strong enough to subdue him. [5] And always, night and day, among the tombs and in the mountains, he was crying out and cutting himself with stones.

[6] When he saw Jesus from a distance, he ran and knelt down before Him. [7] And he cried out with a loud voice, "What do You have to do with me, Jesus, Son of the Most High God? I beg You before God, don't torment me!" [8] For He had told him, "Come out of the man, you unclean spirit!"

[9] "What is your name?" He asked him.

"My name is Legion," he answered Him, "because we are many." [10] And he kept begging Him not to send them out of the region.

[11] Now a large herd of pigs was there, feeding on the hillside. [12] The demons[a] begged Him, "Send us to the pigs, so we may enter them." [13] And He gave them permission. Then the unclean spirits came out and entered the pigs, and the herd of about two thousand rushed down the steep bank into the sea and drowned there. [14] The men who tended them[b] ran off and reported it in the town and the countryside, and people went to see what had happened. [15] They came to Jesus and saw the man who had been demon-possessed by the legion sitting there, dressed and in his right mind; and they were afraid. [16] The eyewitnesses described to them what had happened to the demon-possessed man and ⌊told⌋ about the pigs. [17] Then they began to beg Him to leave their region.

[18] As He was getting into the boat, the man who had been demon-possessed kept begging Him to be with Him. [19] But He would not let him; instead, He told him, "Go back home to your own people, and report to them how much the Lord has done for you and how He has had mercy on you." [20] So he went out and began to proclaim in the *Decapolis how much Jesus had done for him; and they were all amazed.

## A Girl Restored and a Woman Healed

[21] When Jesus had crossed over again by boat to the other side, a large crowd gathered around Him while He was by the sea. [22] One of the *synagogue leaders, named Jairus, came, and when he saw Jesus, he fell at His feet [23] and kept begging Him, "My little daughter is at death's door. Come and lay Your hands on her, so that she may get well and live."

[24] So Jesus went with him, and a large crowd was following and pressing against Him. [25] A woman suffering from bleeding for 12 years [26] had endured much under many doctors. She had spent everything she had, and was not helped at all. On the contrary, she became worse. [27] Having heard about Jesus, she came behind Him in the crowd and touched His robe. [28] For she said, "If I can just touch His robes, I'll be made well!" [29] Instantly her flow of blood ceased, and she sensed in her body that she was cured of her affliction.

[30] At once Jesus realized in Himself that power had gone out from Him. He turned around in the crowd and said, "Who touched My robes?"

[31] His disciples said to Him, "You see the crowd pressing against You, and You say, 'Who touched Me?' "

[32] So He was looking around to see who had done this. [33] Then the woman, knowing what had happened

[a]5:12 Other mss read *All the demons*   [b]5:14 Other mss read *tended the pigs*

to her, came with fear and trembling, fell down before Him, and told Him the whole truth. [34] "Daughter," He said to her, "your faith has made you well. Go in peace and be free from your affliction."

[35] While He was still speaking, people came from the synagogue leader's house and said, "Your daughter is dead. Why bother the Teacher any more?"

[36] But when Jesus overheard what was said, He told the synagogue leader, "Don't be afraid. Only believe." [37] He did not let anyone accompany Him except Peter, James, and John, James' brother. [38] They came to the synagogue leader's house, and He saw a commotion—people weeping and wailing loudly. [39] He went in and said to them, "Why are you making a commotion and weeping? The child is not dead but •asleep."

[40] They started laughing at Him, but He put them all outside. He took the child's father, mother, and those who were with Him, and entered the place where the child was. [41] Then He took the child by the hand and said to her, *"Talitha koum!"* (which is translated, "Little girl, I say to you, get up!"). [42] Immediately the girl got up and began to walk. (She was 12 years old.) At this they were utterly astounded. [43] Then He gave them strict orders that no one should know about this, and said that she should be given something to eat.

## Rejection at Nazareth

**6** He went away from there and came to His hometown, and His disciples followed Him. [2] When the Sabbath came, He began to teach in the •synagogue, and many who heard

---

### Mark 6:7

### Evangelism

*From near the beginning of His earthly ministry, Jesus began sending His followers out in groups to tell others that Christ Himself had come from them. The effort was difficult then, as it can be difficult now, but those who obeyed got to see the power of God working through them.*

---

Him were astonished. "Where did this man get these things?" they said. "What is this wisdom given to Him, and these miracles performed by His hands? [3] Isn't this the carpenter, the son of Mary, and the brother of James, Joses, Judas, and Simon? And aren't His sisters here with us?" So they were offended by Him.

[4] Then Jesus said to them, "A prophet is not without honor except in his hometown, among his relatives, and in his household." [5] So He was not able to do any miracles there, except that He laid His hands on a few sick people and healed them. [6] And He was amazed at their unbelief.

### Commissioning the Twelve

Now He was going around the villages in a circuit, teaching. [7] He summoned the Twelve and began to send them out in pairs, and gave them authority over unclean spirits. [8] He instructed them to take nothing for the road except a walking stick: no bread, no backpack, no money in their belts, [9] but to wear sandals, and not to put on an extra shirt. [10] Then He said to them, "Whenever you enter a house, stay there until you leave that place. [11] Whatever place will not welcome you, and people refuse to listen to you, when you leave there, shake the dust off your feet as a testimony against them."[a]

[12] So they went out and preached that people should repent. [13] And they were driving out many demons, anointing many sick people with oil, and healing.

## John the Baptist Beheaded

[14] King •Herod heard of this, because Jesus' name had become well known. Some[b] said, "John the Baptist has been raised from the dead, and that's why these powers are working in him." [15] But others said, "He's Elijah." Still others said, "He's a prophet—like one of the prophets."

[16] When Herod heard of it, he said, "John, the one I beheaded, has been raised!" [17] For Herod himself had given orders to arrest John and to chain him in prison on account of Herodias, his brother Philip's wife, whom he had married. [18] John had been telling Herod, "It is not lawful for you to have your brother's wife!" [19] So Herodias held a grudge against him and wanted to kill him. But she could not, [20] because Herod was in awe of John and was protecting him, knowing he was a righteous and holy man. When Herod heard him he would be very disturbed,[c] yet would hear him gladly.

[21] Now an opportune day came on his birthday, when Herod gave a banquet for his nobles, military commanders, and the leading men of Galilee. [22] When Herodias' own daughter[d] came in and danced, she pleased Herod and his guests. The king said to the girl, "Ask me whatever you want, and I'll give it to you." [23] So he swore oaths to her: "Whatever you ask me I will give you, up to half my kingdom."

[24] Then she went out and said to her mother, "What should I ask for?"

"John the Baptist's head!" she said.

[25] Immediately she hurried to the king and said, "I want you to give me John the Baptist's head on a platter—right now!"

[26] Though the king was deeply distressed, because of his oaths and the guests he did not want to refuse her. [27] The king immediately sent for an executioner and commanded him to bring John's head. So he went and beheaded him in prison, [28] brought his head on a platter, and gave it to the girl. Then the girl gave it to her mother. [29] When his disciples heard about it, they came and removed his corpse and placed it in a tomb.

## Feeding 5,000

[30] The apostles gathered around Jesus and reported to Him all that they had done and taught. [31] He said to them, "Come away by yourselves to a remote place and rest a little." For many people were coming and going, and they did not even have time to eat. [32] So they went away in the boat by themselves to a remote place, [33] but many saw them leaving and recognized them. Then they ran there on foot from all the towns and arrived ahead of them.[e] [34] So as He stepped ashore, He saw a huge crowd and had compassion on them, because they were like sheep without a shepherd. Then He began to teach them many things.

---

[a]6:11 Other mss add *I assure you, it will be more tolerable for Sodom or Gomorrah on judgment day than for that town.*   [b]6:14 Other mss read *He*   [c]6:20 Other mss read *When he heard him, he did many things*
[d]6:22 Other mss read *When his daughter Herodias*   [e]6:33 Other mss add *and gathered around Him*

35 When it was already late, His disciples approached Him and said, "This place is a wilderness, and the hour is already late! 36 Send them away, so they can go into the surrounding countryside and villages to buy themselves something to eat."

37 "You give them something to eat," He responded.

They said to Him, "Should we go and buy 200 denarii worth of bread and give them something to eat?"

38 And He asked them, "How many loaves do you have? Go look."

When they found out they said, "Five, and two fish."

39 Then He instructed them to have all the people sit down in groups on the green grass. 40 So they sat down in ranks of hundreds and fifties. 41 Then He took the five loaves and the two fish, and looking up to heaven, He blessed and broke the loaves. And He kept giving them to His disciples to set before the people. He also divided the two fish among them all. 42 Everyone ate and was filled. 43 Then they picked up 12 baskets full of pieces of bread and fish. 44 Now those who ate the loaves were 5,000 men.

## Walking on the Water

45 Immediately He made His disciples get into the boat and go ahead of Him to the other side, to Bethsaida, while He dismissed the crowd. 46 Having said good-bye to them, He went away to the mountain to pray. 47 When evening came, the boat was in the middle of the sea, and He was alone on the land. 48 He saw them being battered as they rowed, because the wind was against them. Around three in the morning He came toward them walking on the sea, and wanted to pass by them. 49 When they saw Him walking on the sea, they thought it was a ghost and cried out; 50 for they all saw Him and were terrified. Immediately He spoke with them and said, "Have courage! It is I. Don't be afraid." 51 Then He got into the boat with them, and the wind ceased. They were completely astounded, 52 because they did not understand about the loaves. Instead, their hearts were hardened.

## Miraculous Healings

53 When they had crossed over, they came to land at Gennesaret and beached the boat. 54 As they got out of the boat, immediately people recognized Him. 55 They hurried throughout that vicinity and began to carry the sick on stretchers to wherever they heard He was. 56 Wherever He would go, into villages, towns, or the country, they laid the sick in the marketplaces and begged Him that they might touch just the •tassel of His robe. And everyone who touched it was made well.

## The Traditions of the Elders

7 The •Pharisees and some of the •scribes who had come from Jerusalem gathered around Him. 2 They observed that some of His disciples were eating their bread with unclean—that is, unwashed—hands. 3 (For the Pharisees, in fact all the Jews, will not eat unless they wash their hands ritually, keeping the tradition of the elders. 4 When they come from the marketplace, they do not eat unless they have washed. And there are many other customs they have received and keep, like the washing of

cups, jugs, copper utensils, and dining couches.ª) [5] Then the Pharisees and the scribes asked Him, "Why don't Your disciples live according to the tradition of the elders, instead of eating bread with ritually unclean[b] hands?"

[6] But He said to them, "Isaiah prophesied correctly about you hypocrites, as it is written:

> This people honors Me with
>     their lips,
> but their heart is far from
>     Me.
> [7] They worship Me in vain,
> teaching as doctrines the
>     commands of men.[c]

[8] Disregarding the commandment of God, you keep the tradition of men."[d] [9] He also said to them, "You splendidly disregard God's commandment, so that you may maintain[e] your tradition! [10] For Moses said:

> Honor your father and your
>     mother;[f] and,
> Whoever speaks evil of father
>     or mother must be put to
>     death.[g]

[11] But you say, 'If a man tells his father or mother, "Whatever benefit you might have received from me is *Corban*" ' " (that is, a gift [committed to the temple]), [12] "you no longer let him do anything for his father or mother. [13] You revoke God's word by your tradition that you have handed down. And you do many other similar things." [14] Summoning the crowd again, He told them, "Listen to Me, all of you, and understand: [15] Nothing that goes into a man from outside can defile him, but the things that come out of a man are what defile a man. [16] If anyone has ears to hear, he should listen!"[h]

[17] When He went into the house away from the crowd, the disciples asked Him about the parable. [18] And He said to them, "Are you also as lacking in understanding? Don't you realize that nothing going into a man from the outside can defile him? [19] For it doesn't go into his heart but into the stomach, and is eliminated." (As a result, He made all foods clean.[i]) [20] Then He said, "What comes out of a man—that defiles a man. [21] For from within, out of people's hearts, come evil thoughts, sexual immoralities, thefts, murders, [22] adulteries, greed, evil actions, deceit, lewdness, stinginess, blasphemy, pride, and foolishness. [23] All these evil things come from within and defile a man."

## A Gentile Mother's Faith

[24] From there He got up and departed to the region of Tyre and Sidon.[j] He entered a house and did not want anyone to know it, but He could not escape notice. [25] Instead, immediately after hearing about Him, a woman whose little daughter had an unclean spirit came and fell at His feet. [26] Now the woman was Greek, a Syrophoenician by birth, and she kept asking Him to drive the demon out of her daughter. [27] And He said to her, "Allow the children to be satisfied first, because it isn't right to take the children's bread and throw it to the dogs."

---

[a]**7:4** Other mss omit *and dining couches*   [b]**7:5** Other mss read *with unwashed*   [c]**7:6–7** Is 29:13   [d]**7:8** Other mss add *The washing of jugs, and cups, and many other similar things you practice.*   [e]**7:9** Other mss read *may establish*   [f]**7:10** Ex 20:12; Dt 5:16   [g]**7:10** Ex 21:17; Lv 20:9   [h]**7:16** Other mss omit this verse   [i]**7:19** Other mss read *is eliminated, making all foods clean*   [j]**7:24** Other mss omit *and Sidon*

28 But she replied to Him, "Lord, even the dogs under the table eat the children's crumbs."

29 Then He told her, "Because of this reply, you may go. The demon has gone out of your daughter." 30 When she went back to her home, she found her child lying on the bed, and the demon was gone.

## Jesus Does Everything Well

31 Again, leaving the region of Tyre, He went by way of Sidon to the Sea of Galilee, through the region of the •Decapolis. 32 And they brought to Him a deaf man who also had a speech difficulty, and begged Him to lay His hand on him. 33 So He took him away from the crowd privately. After putting His fingers in the man's ears and spitting, He touched his tongue. 34 Then, looking up to heaven, He sighed deeply and said to him, *"Ephphatha!"* (that is, "Be opened!"). 35 Immediately his ears were opened, his speech difficulty was removed, and he began to speak clearly. 36 Then He ordered them to tell no one, but the more He would order them, the more they would proclaim it.

37 They were extremely astonished and said, "He has done everything well! He even makes deaf people hear, and people unable to speak, talk!"

## Feeding 4,000

**8** In those days there was again a large crowd, and they had nothing to eat. He summoned the disciples and said to them, 2 "I have compassion on the crowd, because they've already stayed with Me three days and have nothing to eat. 3 If I send them home famished, they will collapse on the way, and some of them have come a long distance."

4 His disciples answered Him, "Where can anyone get enough bread here in this desolate place to fill these people?"

5 "How many loaves do you have?" He asked them.

"Seven," they said. 6 Then He commanded the crowd to sit down on the ground. Taking the seven loaves, He gave thanks, broke the ⌊loaves⌋, and kept on giving them to His disciples to set before them. So they served the ⌊loaves⌋ to the crowd. 7 They also had a few small fish, and when He had blessed them, He said these were to be served as well. 8 They ate and were filled. Then they collected seven large baskets of leftover pieces. 9 About 4,000 were there. He dismissed them 10 and immediately got into the boat with His disciples and went to the district of Dalmanutha.

---

*"God nowhere tells us to give up things for the sake of giving them up. He tells us to give them up for the sake of the only thing worth having."*
—Oswald Chambers

---

## The Yeast of the Pharisees and Herod

11 The •Pharisees came out and began to argue with Him, demanding of Him a sign from heaven to test Him. 12 But sighing deeply in His spirit, He said, "Why does this generation demand a sign? •I assure you: No sign will be given to this generation!" 13 Then He left them, got on board ⌊the boat⌋ again, and went to the other side.

14 They had forgotten to take bread and had only one loaf with them in the boat. 15 Then He began to give them strict orders: "Watch out! Beware of the yeast of the Pharisees and the yeast of •Herod."

16 They were discussing among themselves that they did not have any bread. 17 Aware of this, He said to them, "Why are you discussing that you do not have any bread? Do you not yet understand or comprehend? Is your heart hardened? 18 **Do you have eyes, and not see, and do you have ears, and not hear?**a And do you not remember? 19 When I broke the five loaves for the 5,000, how many baskets full of pieces of bread did you collect?"

"Twelve," they told Him.

20 "When I broke the seven loaves for the 4,000, how many large baskets full of pieces of bread did you collect?"

"Seven," they said.

21 And He said to them, "Don't you understand yet?"

## Healing a Blind Man

22 Then they came to Bethsaida. They brought a blind man to Him and begged Him to touch him. 23 He took the blind man by the hand and brought him out of the village. Spitting on his eyes and laying His hands on him, He asked him, "Do you see anything?"

24 He looked up and said, "I see people—they look to me like trees walking."

25 Again He placed His hands on his eyes, and he saw distinctly. He was cured and could see everything clearly. 26 Then He sent him home, saying, "Don't even go into the village."b

## Peter's Confession of the Messiah

27 Jesus went out with His disciples to the villages of Caesarea Philippi. And on the road He asked His disciples, "Who do people say that I am?"

28 And they answered Him, "John the Baptist; others, Elijah; still others, one of the prophets."

29 "But you," He asked them again, "who do you say that I am?"

Peter answered Him, "You are the •Messiah!"

30 And He strictly warned them to tell no one about Him.

## His Death and Resurrection Predicted

31 Then He began to teach them that the •Son of Man must suffer many things, and be rejected by the elders, the •chief priests, and the •scribes, be killed, and rise after three days. 32 And He was openly talking about this. So Peter took Him aside and began to rebuke Him.

33 But turning around and looking at His disciples, He rebuked Peter and said, "Get behind Me, Satan, because

a8:18 Jr 5:21; Ezk 12:2   b8:26 Other mss add *or tell anyone in the village*

you're not thinking about God's concerns, but man's!"

## Take Up Your Cross

34 Summoning the crowd along with His disciples, He said to them, "If anyone wants to be My follower, he must deny himself, take up his cross, and follow Me. 35 For whoever wants to save his life will lose it, but whoever loses his life because of Me and the gospel will save it. 36 For what does it benefit a man to gain the whole world yet lose his life? 37 What can a man give in exchange for his life? 38 For whoever is ashamed of Me and of My words in this adulterous and sinful generation, the Son of Man will also be ashamed of him when He comes in the glory of His Father with the holy angels."

9 Then He said to them, "•I assure you: There are some of those standing here who will not taste death until they see the kingdom of God come in power."

## The Transfiguration

2 After six days Jesus took Peter, James, and John, and led them up on a high mountain by themselves to be alone. He was transformed in front of them, 3 and His clothes became dazzling, extremely white, as no launderer on earth could whiten them. 4 Elijah appeared to them with Moses, and they were talking with Jesus.

5 Then Peter said to Jesus, "•Rabbi, it is good for us to be here! Let us make three •tabernacles: one for You, one for Moses, and one for Elijah"— 6 because he did not know what he should say, since they were terrified.

7 A cloud appeared, overshadowing them, and a voice came from the cloud:

This is My beloved Son;
listen to Him!

8 Then suddenly, looking around, they no longer saw anyone with them except Jesus alone.

9 As they were coming down from the mountain, He ordered them to tell no one what they had seen until the •Son of Man had risen from the dead. 10 They kept this word to themselves, discussing what "rising from the dead" meant.

11 Then they began to question Him, "Why do the •scribes say that Elijah must come first?"

12 "Elijah does come first and restores everything," He replied. "How then is it written about the Son of Man that He must suffer many things and be treated with contempt? 13 But I tell you that Elijah really has come, and they did to him whatever they wanted, just as it is written about him."

## The Power of Faith over a Demon

14 When they came to the disciples, they saw a large crowd around them and scribes disputing with them. 15 All of a sudden, when the whole crowd saw Him, they were amazed and ran to greet Him. 16 Then He asked them, "What are you arguing with them about?"

17 Out of the crowd, one man answered Him, "Teacher, I brought my son to You. He has a spirit that makes him unable to speak. 18 Wherever it seizes him, it throws him down, and he foams at the mouth, grinds his teeth, and becomes rigid. So I asked Your disciples to drive it out, but they couldn't."

[19] He replied to them, "O, unbelieving generation! How long will I be with you? How long must I put up with you? Bring him to Me." [20] So they brought him to Him. When the spirit saw Him, it immediately convulsed the boy. He fell to the ground and rolled around, foaming at the mouth. [21] "How long has this been happening to him?" Jesus asked his father.

"From childhood," he said. [22] "And many times it has thrown him into fire or water to destroy him. But if You can do anything, have compassion on us and help us."

[23] Then Jesus said to him, " 'If You can?'[a] Everything is possible to the one who believes."

[24] Immediately the father of the boy cried out, "I do believe! Help my unbelief."

[25] When Jesus saw that a crowd was rapidly coming together, He rebuked the unclean spirit, saying to it, "You mute and deaf spirit, I command you: come out of him and never enter him again!"

[26] Then it came out, shrieking and convulsing him violently. The boy became like a corpse, so that many said, "He's dead." [27] But Jesus, taking him by the hand, raised him, and he stood up. [28] After He went into a house, His disciples asked Him privately, "Why couldn't we drive it out?"

[29] And He told them, "This kind can come out by nothing but prayer ⌊and fasting."⌋[b]

## The Second Prediction of His Death

[30] Then they left that place and made their way through Galilee, but He did not want anyone to know it. [31] For He was teaching His disciples and telling them, "The Son of Man is being betrayed into the hands of men. They will kill Him, and after He is killed, He will rise three days later." [32] But they did not understand this statement, and they were afraid to ask Him.

## Who Is the Greatest?

[33] Then they came to Capernaum. When He was in the house, He asked them, "What were you arguing about on the way?" [34] But they were silent, because on the way they had been arguing with one another about who was the greatest. [35] Sitting down, He called the Twelve and said to them, "If anyone wants to be first, he must be last of all and servant of all." [36] Then He took a child, had him stand among them, and taking him in His arms, He said to them, [37] "Whoever welcomes one little child such as this in My name welcomes Me. And whoever welcomes Me does not welcome Me, but Him who sent Me."

## In His Name

[38] John said to Him, "Teacher, we saw someone[c] driving out demons in Your name, and we tried to stop him because he wasn't following us."

[39] "Don't stop him," said Jesus, "because there is no one who will perform a miracle in My name who can soon afterward speak evil of Me. [40] For whoever is not against us is for us. [41] And whoever gives you a cup of water to drink because of My name, since you belong to the •Messiah—•I assure you: He will never lose his reward.

[a]9:23 Other mss add *believe*   [b]9:29 Other mss omit bracketed text   [c]9:38 Other mss add *who didn't go along with us*

## Warnings from Jesus

42 "But whoever causes the downfall of one of these little ones who believe in Me—it would be better for him if a heavy millstone were hung around his neck and he were thrown into the sea. 43 And if your hand causes your downfall, cut it off. It is better for you to enter life maimed than to have two hands and go to *hell—the unquenchable fire, ⌊44 where

> **Their worm does not die,**
> **and the fire is not quenched.**⌋ab

45 And if your foot causes your downfall, cut it off. It is better for you to enter life lame than to have two feet and be thrown into hell— ⌊the unquenchable fire, 46 where

> **Their worm does not die,**
> **and the fire is not quenched.**⌋ac

47 And if your eye causes your downfall, gouge it out. It is better for you to enter the kingdom of God with one eye than to have two eyes and be thrown into hell, 48 where

> **Their worm does not die,**
> **and the fire is not quenched.**

49 For everyone will be salted with fire.de 50 Salt is good, but if the salt should lose its flavor, how can you make it salty? Have salt among yourselves and be at peace with one another."

## The Question of Divorce

**10** He set out from there and went to the region of Judea and across the Jordan. Then crowds converged on Him again and, as He usually did, He began teaching them once more. 2 Some *Pharisees approached Him to test Him. They asked, "Is it lawful for a man to divorce ⌊his⌋ wife?"
3 He replied to them, "What did Moses command you?"
4 They said, "Moses permitted us to write divorce papers and send her away."
5 But Jesus told them, "He wrote this commandment for you because of the hardness of your hearts. 6 But from the beginning of creation Godf made them male and female.g

> 7 **For this reason a man will**
> **leave his father and**
> **mother**
> ⌊**and be joined to his wife,**⌋g
> 8 **and the two will become**
> **one flesh.**h

So they are no longer two, but one flesh. 9 Therefore what God has joined together, man must not separate."
10 Now in the house the disciples questioned Him again about this matter. 11 And He said to them, "Whoever divorces his wife and marries another commits adultery against her. 12 Also, if she divorces her husband and marries another, she commits adultery."

## Blessing the Children

13 Some people were bringing little children to Him so He might touch them. But His disciples rebuked them. 14 When Jesus saw it, He was indignant and said to them, "Let the little children come to Me; don't stop them, for the kingdom of God belongs to such as these. 15 *I assure

a9:44,46 Other mss omit bracketed text   b9:44 Is 66:24   c9:46 Is 66:24   d9:49 Other mss add and every sacrifice will be salted with salt   e9:49 Lv 2:16; Ezk 43:24   f10:6 Other mss omit God   g10:6 Gn 1:27; 5:2 10:7 Other mss omit bracketed text   h10:7–8 Gn 2:24

you: Whoever does not welcome the kingdom of God like a little child will never enter it." [16] After taking them in His arms, He laid His hands on them and blessed them.

## The Rich Young Ruler

[17] As He was going out on the road, a man ran up, knelt down before Him, and asked Him, "Good Teacher, what must I do to inherit eternal life?" [18] But Jesus asked him, "Why do you call Me good? No one is good but One—God. [19] You know the commandments:

> **Do not murder;**
> **do not commit adultery;**
> **do not steal;**
> **do not bear false witness;**
> **do not defraud;**
> **honor your father and**
>     **mother."[a]**

[20] He said to Him, "Teacher, I have kept all these from my youth." [21] Then, looking at him, Jesus loved him and said to him, "You lack one thing: Go, sell all you have and give to the poor, and you will have treasure in heaven. Then come,[b] follow Me." [22] But he was stunned at this demand, and he went away grieving, because he had many possessions.

---

*"As we give ourselves to God, He gives back to us a wonderful present—the power to demonstrate Christ's love to those He sends our way."*

*—Doris Greig*

---

## Possessions and the Kingdom

[23] Jesus looked around and said to His disciples, "How hard it is for those who have wealth to enter the kingdom of God!" [24] But the disciples were astonished at His words. Again Jesus said to them, "Children, how hard it is[c] to enter the kingdom of God! [25] It is easier for a camel to go through the eye of a needle than for a rich person to enter the kingdom of God." [26] But they were even more astonished, saying to one another, "Then who can be saved?" [27] Looking at them, Jesus said, "With men it is impossible, but not with God, because all things are possible with God." [28] Peter began to tell Him, "Look, we have left everything and followed You." [29] "I assure you," Jesus said, "there is no one who has left house, brothers or sisters, mother or father,[d] children, or fields because of Me and the gospel, [30] who will not receive 100 times more, now at this time—houses, brothers and sisters, mothers and children, and fields, with persecutions—and eternal life in the age to come. [31] But many who are first will be last, and the last first."

## The Third Prediction of His Death

[32] They were on the road, going up to Jerusalem, and Jesus was walking ahead of them. They were astonished, but those who followed Him were afraid. And taking the Twelve aside again, He began to tell them the things that would happen to Him. [33] "Listen! We are going up to Jerusalem. The •Son of Man will be

---

[a]10:19 Ex 20:12–16; Dt 5:16–20   [b]10:21 Other mss add *taking up the cross, and*   [c]10:24 Other mss add *for those trusting in wealth*   [d]10:29 Other mss add *or wife*

handed over to the •chief priests and the •scribes, and they will condemn Him to death. Then they will hand Him over to the Gentiles, 34 and they will mock Him, spit on Him, flog Him, and kill Him, and He will rise after three days."

## Suffering and Service

35 Then James and John, the sons of Zebedee, approached Him and said, "Teacher, we want You to do something for us if we ask You."

36 "What do you want Me to do for you?" He asked them.

37 "Grant us," they answered Him, "that we may sit at Your right and at Your left in Your glory."

38 But Jesus said to them, "You don't know what you're asking. Are you able to drink the cup I drink, or to be baptized with the baptism I am baptized with?"

39 "We are able," they told Him.

But Jesus said to them, "You will drink the cup I drink, and you will be baptized with the baptism I am baptized with. 40 But to sit at My right or left is not Mine to give, but it is for those for whom it has been prepared." 41 When the ⌊other⌋ 10 ⌊disciples⌋ heard this, they began to be indignant with James and John.

42 And Jesus called them over and said to them, "You know that those who are regarded as rulers of the Gentiles dominate them, and their men of high positions exercise power over them. 43 But it must not be like that among you. On the contrary, whoever wants to become great among you must be your servant, 44 and whoever wants to be first among you must be a slave to all. 45 For even the Son of Man did not come to be served, but to serve, and to give His life—a ransom for many."

---

### Mark 10:42-45

*Becoming drawn to the unnoticed aspects of ministry will slowly turn the focus of your life off yourself— and into the faces and futures of those within your reach. Your will has been a tyrant all your life. It's time to start thinking about someone else for a change.*

---

## A Blind Man Healed

46 They came to Jericho. And as He was leaving Jericho with His disciples and a large crowd, Bartimaeus (the son of Timaeus), a blind beggar, was sitting by the road. 47 When he heard that it was Jesus the •Nazarene, he began to cry out, "Son of David, Jesus, have mercy on me!" 48 Many people told him to keep quiet, but he was crying out all the more, "Have mercy on me, Son of David!"

49 Jesus stopped and said, "Call him."

So they called the blind man and said to him, "Have courage! Get up; He's calling for you." 50 He threw off his coat, jumped up, and came to Jesus.

51 Then Jesus answered him, "What do you want Me to do for you?"

*"Rabbouni,"* the blind man told Him, "I want to see!"

52 "Go your way," Jesus told him. "Your faith has healed you." Immediately he could see and began to follow Him on the road.

## The Triumphal Entry

**11** When they approached Jerusalem, at Bethphage and Bethany, near the •Mount of Olives, He sent two of His disciples ² and told them, "Go into the village ahead of you. As soon as you enter it, you will find a young donkey tied there, on which nobody has ever sat. Untie it and bring it here. ³ If anyone says to you, 'Why are you doing this?' say, 'The Lord needs it and will send it back here right away.' "

⁴ So they went and found a young donkey outside in the street, tied by a door. They untied it, ⁵ and some of those standing there said to them, "What are you doing, untying the donkey?" ⁶ Then they answered them just as Jesus had said, so they let them go. ⁷ And they brought the donkey to Jesus and threw their robes on it, and He sat on it.

⁸ Many people spread their robes on the road, and others spread leafy branches cut from the fields.ᵃ

⁹ Then those who went before and those who followed kept shouting:

•*Hosanna!*
**Blessed is He who comes in
the name of the Lord!**ᵇ

¹⁰ Blessed is the coming
kingdom of our father David!
*Hosanna* in the highest
heaven!

¹¹ And He went into Jerusalem and into the •temple complex. After looking around at everything, since the hour was already late, He went out to Bethany with the Twelve.

## The Barren Fig Tree Is Cursed

¹² The next day, when they came out from Bethany, He was hungry. ¹³ After seeing in the distance a fig tree with leaves, He went to find out if there was anything on it. When He came to it, He found nothing but leaves, because it was not the season for figs. ¹⁴ And He said to it, "May no one ever eat fruit from you again!" And His disciples heard it.

## Cleansing the Temple Complex

¹⁵ They came to Jerusalem, and He went into the temple complex and began to throw out those buying and selling in the temple. He overturned the money changers' tables and the chairs of those selling doves, ¹⁶ and would not permit anyone to carry goods through the temple complex. ¹⁷ Then He began to teach them: "Is it not written, **My house will be called a house of prayer for all nations**?ᶜ But you have made it **a den of thieves!**"ᵈ ¹⁸ Then the •chief priests and the •scribes heard it and started looking for a way to destroy Him. For they were afraid of Him, because the whole crowd was astonished by His teaching.

¹⁹ And whenever evening came, they would go out of the city.

## The Barren Fig Tree Is Withered

²⁰ Early in the morning, as they were passing by, they saw the fig tree withered from the roots up. ²¹ Then Peter remembered and said to Him, "•Rabbi, look! The fig tree that You cursed is withered."

ᵃ11:8 Other mss read *others were cutting leafy branches from the trees and spreading them on the road*
ᵇ11:9 Ps 118:26   ᶜ11:17 Is 56:7   ᵈ11:17 Jr 7:11

22 Jesus replied to them, "Have faith in God. 23 •I assure you: If anyone says to this mountain, 'Be lifted up and thrown into the sea,' and does not doubt in his heart, but believes that what he says will happen, it will be done for him. 24 Therefore, I tell you, all the things you pray and ask for—believe that you have received[a] them, and you will have them. 25 And whenever you stand praying, if you have anything against anyone, forgive him, so that your Father in heaven may also forgive you your wrongdoing. ⌊26 But if you don't forgive, neither will your Father in heaven forgive your wrongdoing."⌋[b]

## Messiah's Authority Challenged

27 They came again to Jerusalem. As He was walking in the temple complex, the chief priests, the scribes, and the elders came and asked Him, 28 "By what authority are You doing these things? Who gave You this authority to do these things?"
29 Jesus said to them, "I will ask you one question; then answer Me, and I will tell you by what authority I am doing these things. 30 Was John's baptism from heaven or from men? Answer Me."
31 They began to argue among themselves: "If we say, 'From heaven,' He will say, 'Then why didn't you believe him?' 32 But if we say, 'From men' "— they were afraid of the crowd, because everyone thought that John was a genuine prophet. 33 So they answered Jesus, "We don't know."
And Jesus said to them, "Neither will I tell you by what authority I do these things."

## The Parable of the Vineyard Owner

12 Then He began to speak to them in parables: "A man planted a vineyard, put a fence around it, dug out a pit for a winepress, and built a watchtower. Then he leased it to tenant farmers and went away. 2 At harvest time he sent a slave to the farmers so that he might collect some of the fruit of the vineyard from the farmers. 3 But they took him, beat him, and sent him away empty-handed. 4 And again he sent another slave to them, and they[c] hit him on the head and treated him shamefully.[d] 5 Then he sent another, and that one they killed. ⌊He⌋ also ⌊sent⌋ many others; they beat some and they killed some.
6 "He still had one to send, a beloved son. Finally he sent him to them, saying, 'They will respect my son.'
7 "But those tenant farmers said among themselves, 'This is the heir. Come, let's kill him, and the inheritance will be ours!' 8 So they seized him and killed him, and threw him out of the vineyard.
9 "Therefore, what will the owner of the vineyard do? He will come and destroy the farmers and give the vineyard to others. 10 Haven't you read this Scripture:

The stone that the builders rejected,
this has become the cornerstone.
11 This cornerstone came from the Lord
and is wonderful in our eyes?"[e]

12 Because they knew He had said this parable against them, they were

---

[a]11:24 Other mss read *you receive*; other mss read *you will receive*   [b]11:26 Other mss omit bracketed text
[c]12:4 Other mss add *threw stones and*   [d]12:4 Other mss add *and sent him off*   [e]12:10–11 Ps 118:22–23

looking for a way to arrest Him, but they were afraid of the crowd. So they left Him and went away.

## God and Caesar

[13] Then they sent some of the •Pharisees and the •Herodians to Him in order to trap Him by what He said. [14] When they came, they said to Him, "Teacher, we know You are truthful and defer to no one, for You don't show partiality, but teach the way of God in truth. Is it lawful to pay taxes to Caesar or not? [15] Should we pay, or should we not pay?"

But knowing their hypocrisy, He said to them, "Why are you testing Me? Bring Me a •denarius to look at." [16] So they brought one. "Whose image and inscription is this?" He asked them.

"Caesar's," they said.

[17] Then Jesus told them, "Give back to Caesar the things that are Caesar's, and to God the things that are God's." And they were amazed at Him.

## The Sadducees and the Resurrection

[18] Some •Sadducees, who say there is no resurrection, came to Him and questioned Him: [19] "Teacher, Moses wrote for us that **if a man's brother dies,** leaves his wife behind, and **leaves no child, his brother should take the wife and produce offspring for his brother.**[a] [20] There were seven brothers. The first took a wife, and dying, left no offspring. [21] The second also took her, and he died, leaving no offspring. And the third likewise. [22] The seven also[b] left no offspring. Last of all, the woman died too. [23] In the resurrection, when they rise,[c]

whose wife will she be, since the seven had married her?"

[24] Jesus told them, "Are you not deceived because you don't know the Scriptures or the power of God? [25] For when they rise from the dead, they neither marry nor are given in marriage, but are like angels in heaven. [26] Now concerning the dead being raised—haven't you read in the book of Moses, in the passage about the burning bush, how God spoke to him: **I am the God of Abraham and the God of Isaac and the God of Jacob**?[d] [27] He is not God of the dead, but of the living. You are badly deceived."

## The Primary Commandments

[28] One of the •scribes approached. When he heard them debating and saw that Jesus answered them well, he asked Him, "Which commandment is the most important of all?"

[29] "This is the most important,"[e] Jesus answered:

> **Hear, O Israel! The Lord our God is one Lord.** [30] **And you shall love the Lord your God with all your heart, with all your soul, with all your mind, and with all your strength.**[f][g]

[31] "The second is: **You shall love your neighbor as yourself.**[h] There is no other commandment greater than these."

[32] Then the scribe said to Him, "Well said, Teacher! You have spoken in truth that He is one, and there is no one else except Him. [33] And to love Him with all the heart, with all the understanding,[i] and with all the strength, and to love one's neighbor as

---

[a]**12:19** Gn 38:8; Dt 25:5   [b]**12:22** Other mss add *had taken her and*   [c]**12:23** Other mss omit *when they rise*
[d]**12:26** Ex 3:6,15–16   [e]**12:29** Other mss add *of all the commandments*   [f]**12:30** Other mss add *This is the first commandment.*   [g]**12:30** Dt 6:4–5; Jos 22:5   [h]**12:31** Lv 19:18   [i]**12:33** Other mss add *with all the soul*

oneself, is far more ⌊important⌋ than all the burnt offerings and sacrifices."

³⁴ When Jesus saw that he answered intelligently, He said to him, "You are not far from the kingdom of God." And no one dared to question Him any longer.

## The Question about the Messiah

³⁵ So Jesus asked this question as He taught in the •temple complex, "How can the scribes say that the •Messiah is the Son of David? ³⁶ David himself says by the Holy Spirit:

**The Lord said to my Lord,
'Sit at My right hand
until I put Your enemies
under Your feet.'**ᵃ

³⁷ David himself calls Him 'Lord'; so how is He his Son?" And the large crowd was listening to Him with delight.

## Warning against the Scribes

³⁸ He also said in His teaching, "Beware of the scribes, who want to go around in long robes, and who want greetings in the marketplaces, ³⁹ the front seats in the •synagogues, and the places of honor at banquets. ⁴⁰ They devour widows' houses and say long prayers just for show. These will receive harsher punishment."

## The Widow's Gift

⁴¹ Sitting across from the temple treasury, He watched how the crowd dropped money into the treasury. Many rich people were putting in large sums. ⁴² And a poor widow came and dropped in two tiny coins worth very little. ⁴³ Summoning His

disciples, He said to them, "•I assure you: This poor widow has put in more than all those giving to the temple treasury. ⁴⁴ For they all gave out of their surplus, but she out of her poverty has put in everything she possessed—all she had to live on."

## Destruction of the Temple Predicted

**13** As He was going out of the •temple complex, one of His disciples said to Him, "Teacher, look! What massive stones! What impressive buildings!"

² Jesus said to him, "You see these great buildings? Not one stone will be left here on another that will not be thrown down!"

---

*"Be willing to enter their world to tell them about Christ, rather than bringing them into your world before you can talk."*
*—John Kramp*

---

## Signs of the End of the Age

³ While He was sitting on the •Mount of Olives across from the temple complex, Peter, James, John, and Andrew asked Him privately, ⁴ "Tell us, when will these things happen? And what will be the sign when all these things are about to take place?"

⁵ Then Jesus began by telling them: "Watch out that no one deceives you. ⁶ Many will come in My name, saying, 'I am He,' and they will deceive many. ⁷ When you hear of wars and rumors of wars, don't be alarmed; these things must

ᵃ**12:36** Ps. 110:1

take place, but the end is not yet. [8] For nation will rise up against nation, and kingdom against kingdom. There will be earthquakes in various places, and famines.[a] These are the beginning of birth pains.

## Persecutions Predicted

[9] "But you, be on your guard! They will hand you over to sanhedrins, and you will be flogged in the *synagogues. You will stand before governors and kings because of Me, as a witness to them. [10] And the good news must first be proclaimed to all nations. [11] So when they arrest you and hand you over, don't worry beforehand what you will say. On the contrary, whatever is given to you in that hour—say it. For it isn't you who are speaking, but the Holy Spirit. [12] Then brother will betray brother to death, and a father his child. Children will rise up against parents and put them to death. [13] And you will be hated by all because of My name. But the one who endures to the end, this one will be delivered.

---

### Mark 13:9-11

*If you're willing to open your mouth, God will give you the words to say—and an audience that He's already primed to hear what Jesus Christ has done for you. You have a story that'll speak volumes to someone, and a God who can put the two of you together.*

---

## The Great Tribulation

[14] "When you see the **abomination that causes desolation**[b] standing where it should not" (let the reader understand), "then those in Judea must flee to the mountains! [15] A man on the housetop must not come down, or go in to get anything out of his house. [16] And a man in the field must not go back to get his clothes. [17] Woe to pregnant women and nursing mothers in those days! [18] Pray that it[c] may not be in winter. [19] For those days will be a tribulation, the kind that hasn't been since the beginning of the world, which God created, until now, and never will be again! [20] Unless the Lord cut short those days, no one would survive.    But because of the elect, whom He chose, He cut short those days.

[21] "Then if anyone tells you, 'Look, here is the *Messiah! Look—there!' do not believe it! [22] For false messiahs and false prophets will rise up and will perform signs and wonders to lead astray, if possible, the elect. [23] And you must watch! I have told you everything in advance.

## The Coming of the Son of Man

[24] "But in those days, after that tribulation,

> The sun will be darkened,
> and the moon will not shed her
>     light;
> [25] the stars will be falling from the
>     sky,
> and the celestial powers will be
>     shaken.

[26] Then they will see the *Son of Man coming in clouds with great power

---

[a]13:8 Other mss add *and disturbances*    [b]13:14 Dn 9:27    [c]13:18 Other mss read *your escape*

and glory. [27] He will send out the angels and gather His elect from the four winds, from the end of the earth to the end of the sky.

## The Parable of the Fig Tree

[28] "Learn this parable from the fig tree: As soon as its branch becomes tender and sprouts leaves, you know that summer is near. [29] In the same way, when you see these things happening, know that He is near—at the door! [30] •I assure you: This generation will certainly not pass away until all these things take place. [31] Heaven and earth will pass away, but My words will never pass away.

## No One Knows the Day or Hour

[32] "Now concerning that day or hour no one knows—neither the angels in heaven, nor the Son—except the Father. [33] Watch! Be alert![a] For you don't know when the time is ⌊coming⌋. [34] It is like a man on a journey, who left his house, gave authority to his slaves, gave each one his work, and commanded the doorkeeper to be alert. [35] Therefore be alert, since you don't know when the master of the house is coming—whether in the evening, or at midnight, or at the crowing of the rooster, or early in the morning. [36] Otherwise, he might come suddenly and find you sleeping. [37] And what I say to you, I say to everyone: Be alert!"

## The Plot to Kill Jesus

**14** After two days it was the •Passover and the Festival of •Unleavened Bread. The •chief priests and the •scribes were looking for a way to arrest Him by deceit and kill Him. [2] "Not during the festival," they said, "or there may be rioting among the people."

## The Anointing at Bethany

[3] While He was in Bethany at the house of Simon the leper, as He was reclining at the table, a woman came with an alabaster jar of pure and expensive fragrant oil of nard. She broke the jar and poured it on His head. [4] But some were expressing indignation to one another: "Why has this fragrant oil been wasted? [5] For this oil might have been sold for more than 300 denarii and given to the poor." And they began to scold her. [6] Then Jesus said, "Leave her alone. Why are you bothering her? She has done a noble thing for Me. [7] You always have the poor with you, and you can do good for them whenever you want, but you do not always have Me. [8] She has done what she could; she has anointed My body in advance for burial. [9] •I assure you: Wherever the gospel is proclaimed in the whole world, what this woman has done will also be told in memory of her."

[10] Then Judas Iscariot, one of the Twelve, went to the chief priests to hand Him over to them. [11] And when they heard this, they were glad and promised to give him silver. So he started looking for a good opportunity to betray Him.

## Preparation for Passover

[12] On the first day of Unleavened Bread, when they sacrifice the Passover lamb, His disciples asked Him, "Where do You want us to go and prepare the Passover so You may eat it?"

[a]**13:33** Other mss add *and pray*

13 So He sent two of His disciples and told them, "Go into the city, and a man carrying a water jug will meet you. Follow him. 14 Wherever he enters, tell the owner of the house, 'The Teacher says, "Where is the guest room for Me to eat the Passover with My disciples?" ' 15 He will show you a large room upstairs, furnished and ready. Make the preparations for us there." 16 So the disciples went out, entered the city, and found it just as He had told them, and they prepared the Passover.

## Betrayal at the Passover

17 When evening came, He arrived with the Twelve. 18 While they were reclining and eating, Jesus said, "I assure you: One of you will betray Me—one who is eating with Me!" 19 They began to be distressed and to say to Him one by one, "Surely not I?" 20 He said to them, "⌊It is⌋ one of the Twelve—the one who is dipping ⌊bread⌋ with Me in the bowl. 21 For the •Son of Man will go just as it is written about Him, but woe to that man by whom the Son of Man is betrayed! It would have been better for that man if he had not been born."

## The First Lord's Supper

22 As they were eating, He took bread, blessed and broke it, gave it to them, and said, "Take ⌊it⌋;a this is My body." 23 Then He took a cup, and after giving thanks, He gave it to them, and so they all drank from it. 24 He said to them, "This is My blood of the covenant,b which is shed for many. 25 I assure you: I will no longer drink of the fruit of the vine until that day when I drink it new in the kingdom of God." 26 After singing psalms, they went out to the •Mount of Olives.

## Peter's Denial Predicted

27 Then Jesus said to them, "All of you will fall,c because it is written:

**I will strike the shepherd,
and the sheep will be
scattered.d**

28 But after I have been resurrected, I will go ahead of you to Galilee." 29 Peter told Him, "Even if everyone falls, yet I will not!" 30 "I assure you," Jesus said to him, "today, this very night, before the rooster crows twice, you will deny Me three times!" 31 But he kept insisting, "If I have to die with You, I will never deny You!" And they all said the same thing.

## The Prayer in the Garden

32 Then they came to a place named Gethsemane, and He told His disciples, "Sit here while I pray." 33 He took Peter, James, and John with Him, and He began to be horrified and deeply distressed. 34 Then He said to them, "My soul is swallowed up in sorrow—to the point of death. Remain here and stay awake." 35 Then He went a little farther, fell to the ground, and began to pray that if it were possible, the hour might pass from Him. 36 And He said, "•Abba, Father! All things are possible for You. Take this cup away from Me. Nevertheless, not what I will, but what You will." 37 Then He came and found them sleeping. "Simon, are you sleeping?"

---

a14:22 Other mss add eat;   b14:24 Other mss read the new covenant   c14:27 Other mss add because of Me this night   d14:27 Zch 13:7

He asked Peter. "Couldn't you stay awake one hour? [38] Stay awake and pray, so that you won't enter into temptation. The spirit is willing, but the flesh is weak."

[39] Once again He went away and prayed, saying the same thing. [40] And He came again and found them sleeping, because they could not keep their eyes open. They did not know what to say to Him. [41] Then He came a third time and said to them, "Are you still sleeping and resting? Enough! The time has come. Look, the Son of Man is being betrayed into the hands of sinners. [42] Get up; let's go! See—My betrayer is near."

## The Judas Kiss

[43] While He was still speaking, Judas, one of the Twelve, suddenly arrived. With him was a mob, with swords and clubs, from the chief priests, the scribes, and the elders. [44] His betrayer had given them a signal. "The one I kiss," he said, "He's the one; arrest Him and get Him securely away." [45] So when he came, he went right up to Him and said, "•Rabbi!"—and kissed Him. [46] Then they laid hands on Him and arrested Him. [47] And one of those who stood by drew his sword, struck the high priest's slave, and cut off his ear. [48] But Jesus said to them, "Have you come out with swords and clubs, as though I were a criminal, to capture Me? [49] Every day I was among you, teaching in the •temple complex, and you didn't arrest Me. But the Scriptures must be fulfilled." [50] Then they all deserted Him and ran away.

[51] Now a certain young man, having a linen cloth wrapped around his naked body, was following Him. And they caught hold of him. [52] But he left the linen cloth behind and ran away naked.

## Jesus Faces the Sanhedrin

[53] They led Jesus away to the high priest, and all the chief priests, the elders, and the scribes convened. [54] Peter followed Him at a distance, right into the high priest's courtyard. And he was sitting with the temple police, warming himself by the fire.

[55] The chief priests and the whole •Sanhedrin were looking for testimony against Jesus to put Him to death. But they could find none. [56] For many were giving false testimony against Him, but the testimonies did not agree. [57] Some stood up and were giving false testimony against Him, stating, [58] "We heard Him say, 'I will demolish this sanctuary made by hands, and in three days I will build another not made by hands.' " [59] But not even on this did their testimony agree.

[60] Then the high priest stood up before them all and questioned Jesus, "Don't You have an answer to what these men are testifying against You?" [61] But He kept silent and did not answer anything. Again the high priest questioned Him, "Are You the •Messiah, the Son of the Blessed One?"

[62] "I am," said Jesus, "and all of you will see **the Son of Man seated at the right hand** of the Power and **coming with the clouds of heaven.**"[a]

[63] Then the high priest tore his robes and said, "Why do we still need witnesses? [64] You have heard the blasphemy! What is your decision?"

And they all condemned Him to be deserving of death. [65] Then some

[a]**14:62** Ps 110:1; Dn 7:13

began to spit on Him, to blindfold Him, and to beat Him, saying, "Prophesy!" Even the temple police took Him and slapped Him.

## Peter Denies His Lord

⁶⁶ Now as Peter was in the courtyard below, one of the high priest's servants came. ⁶⁷ When she saw Peter warming himself, she looked at him and said, "You also were with that •Nazarene, Jesus."

⁶⁸ But he denied it: "I don't know or understand what you're talking about!" Then he went out to the entryway, and a rooster crowed.ᵃ

⁶⁹ When the servant saw him again she began to tell those standing nearby, "This man is one of them!"

⁷⁰ But again he denied it. After a little while those standing there said to Peter again, "You certainly are one of them, since you're a Galilean also!"ᵇ

⁷¹ Then he started to curse and to swear with an oath, "I don't know this man you're talking about!"

⁷² Immediately a rooster crowed a second time. So Peter remembered when Jesus had spoken the word to him, "Before the rooster crows twice, you will deny Me three times." When he thought about it, he began to weep.

## Jesus Faces Pilate

**15** As soon as it was morning, the •chief priests had a meeting with the elders, •scribes, and the whole •Sanhedrin. After tying Jesus up, they led Him away and handed Him over to •Pilate.

² So Pilate asked Him, "Are You the King of the Jews?"

He answered him, "You have said it."

³ And the chief priests began to accuse Him of many things. ⁴ Then Pilate questioned Him again, "Are You not answering anything? Look how many things they are accusing You of!" ⁵ But Jesus still did not answer anything, so Pilate was amazed.

## Jesus or Barabbas

⁶ At the festival it was Pilate's custom to release for them one prisoner whom they requested. ⁷ There was one named Barabbas, who was in prison with rebels who had committed murder in the rebellion. ⁸ The crowd came up and began to ask [Pilate] to do for them as was his custom. ⁹ So Pilate answered them, "Do you want me to release the King of the Jews for you?" ¹⁰ For he knew it was because of envy that the chief priests had handed Him over. ¹¹ But the chief priests stirred up the crowd so that he would release Barabbas to them instead.

¹² Pilate asked them again, "Then what do you want me to do with the One you call the King of the Jews?"

¹³ And again they shouted, "Crucify Him!"

¹⁴ Then Pilate said to them, "Why? What has He done wrong?"

But they shouted, "Crucify Him!" all the more.

¹⁵ Then, willing to gratify the crowd, Pilate released Barabbas to them. And after having Jesus flogged, he handed Him over to be crucified.

## Mocked by the Military

¹⁶ Then the soldiers led Him away into the courtyard (that is, •headquarters) and called the whole •company together. ¹⁷ They dressed Him

---

ᵃ14:68 Other mss omit *and a rooster crowed*    ᵇ14:70 Other mss add *and your speech shows it*

in a purple robe, twisted a crown out of thorns, and put it on Him. [18] And they began to salute Him, "Hail, King of the Jews!" [19] They kept hitting Him on the head with a reed and spitting on Him. And getting down on their knees, they were paying Him homage. [20] When they had mocked Him, they stripped Him of the purple robe, put His clothes on Him, and led Him out to crucify Him.

### Crucified between Two Criminals

[21] They forced a passer-by coming in from the country to carry His cross—Simon, a Cyrenian, the father of Alexander and Rufus. [22] And they brought Him to the place called *Golgotha* (which means Skull Place). [23] They tried to give Him wine mixed with myrrh, but He did not take it. [24] Then they crucified Him and divided His clothes, casting lots for them to decide what each would get. [25] Now it was nine in the morning when they crucified Him. [26] The inscription of the charge written against Him was:

---

### THE KING OF THE JEWS

---

[27] They crucified two criminals with Him, one on His right and one on His left. ⌊[28] So the Scripture was fulfilled that says: **And He was counted among outlaws.**⌋[ab] [29] Those who passed by were yelling insults at Him, shaking their heads, and saying, "Ha! The One who would demolish the sanctuary and build it in three days, [30] save Yourself by coming down from the cross!" [31] In the same way, the •chief priests with the scribes were mocking Him to one another and saying, "He saved others; He cannot save Himself! [32] Let the •Messiah, the King

of Israel, come down now from the cross, so that we may see and believe." Even those who were crucified with Him were taunting Him.

### The Death of Jesus

[33] When it was noon, darkness came over the whole land until three in the afternoon. [34] And at three Jesus cried out with a loud voice, *"Eloi, Eloi, lemá[c] sabachtháni?"* which is translated, **"My God, My God, why have You forsaken Me?"**[d] [35] When some of those standing there heard this, they said, "Look, He's calling for Elijah!" [36] Someone ran and filled a sponge with sour wine, fixed it on a reed, offered Him a drink, and said, "Let us see if Elijah comes to take Him down!"

[37] But Jesus let out a loud cry and breathed His last. [38] Then the curtain of the sanctuary was split in two from top to bottom. [39] When the •centurion, who was standing opposite Him, saw the way He[e] breathed His last, he said, "This man really was God's Son!"

[40] There were also women looking on from a distance. Among them were •Mary Magdalene, Mary the mother of James the younger and of Joses, and Salome. [41] When He was in Galilee, they would follow Him and minister to Him. Many other women had come up with Him to Jerusalem.

### The Burial of Jesus

[42] When it was already evening, because it was preparation day (that is, the day before the Sabbath), [43] Joseph of Arimathea, a prominent member of the Sanhedrin who was himself looking forward to the kingdom of God, came and boldly went in to Pilate and asked for Jesus' body. [44] Pilate was surprised that He was already dead. Summoning the •centu-

---

[a]15:28 Other mss omit bracketed text   [b]15:28 Is 53:12   [c]15:34 Other mss read *lama*; other mss read *lima*
[d]15:34 Ps 22:1   [e]15:39 Other mss read *saw that He cried out like this and*

rion, he asked him whether He had already died. [45] When he found out from the centurion, he granted the corpse to Joseph. [46] After he bought some fine linen, he took Him down and wrapped Him in the linen. Then he placed Him in a tomb cut out of the rock, and rolled a stone against the entrance to the tomb. [47] Now Mary Magdalene and Mary the mother of Joses were watching where He was placed.

## Resurrection Morning

**16** When the Sabbath was over, •Mary Magdalene, Mary the mother of James, and Salome bought spices, so that they might go and anoint Him. [2] Very early in the morning, on the first day of the week, they went to the tomb at sunrise. [3] And they were saying to one another, "Who will roll away the stone from the entrance to the tomb for us?" [4] Looking up, they observed that the stone—which was very large—had been rolled away. [5] When they entered the tomb, they saw a young man dressed in a long white robe sitting on the right side; they were amazed and alarmed.

[6] "Don't be alarmed," he told them. "You are looking for Jesus the •Nazarene, who was crucified. He has been resurrected! He is not here! See the place where they put Him. [7] But go, tell His disciples and Peter, 'He is going ahead of you to Galilee; you will see Him there just as He told you.' "

[8] So they went out and started running from the tomb, because trembling and astonishment had gripped them. And they said nothing to anyone, since they were afraid.

## Appearances of the Risen Lord

⌊[9] Early on the first day of the week, after He had risen, He appeared first to Mary Magdalene, out of whom He had driven seven demons. [10] She went and reported to those who had been with Him, as they were mourning and weeping. [11] Yet, when they heard that He was alive and had been seen by her, they did not believe it. [12] Then after this, He appeared in a different form to two of them walking on their way into the country. [13] And they went and reported it to the rest, who did not believe them either.

## The Great Commission

[14] Later, He appeared to the Eleven themselves as they were reclining at the table. And He rebuked their unbelief and hardness of heart, because they did not believe those who saw Him after He had been resurrected. [15] Then He said to them, "Go into all the world and preach the gospel to the whole creation. [16] Whoever believes and is baptized will be saved, but whoever does not believe will be condemned. [17] And these signs will accompany those who believe: In My name they will drive out demons; they will speak in new languages; [18] they will pick up snakes;[a] if they should drink anything deadly, it will never harm them; they will lay hands on the sick, and they will get well."

## The Ascension

[19] Then after speaking to them, the Lord Jesus was taken up into heaven and sat down at the right hand of God. [20] And they went out and preached everywhere, the Lord working with them and confirming the word by the accompanying signs.⌋ [b]

---

[a]**16:18** Other mss add *with their hands*   [b]**16:9-20** Other mss omit bracketed text.

# LUKE

## The Dedication to Theophilus

**1** Since many have undertaken to compile a narrative about the events that have been fulfilled among us, [2] just as the original eyewitnesses and servants of the word handed them down to us, [3] it also seemed good to me, having carefully investigated everything from the very first, to write to you in orderly sequence, most honorable Theophilus, [4] so that you may know the certainty of the things about which you have been instructed.

## Gabriel Predicts John's Birth

[5] In the days of King •Herod of Judea, there was a priest of Abijah's division named Zechariah. His wife was from the daughters of Aaron, and her name was Elizabeth. [6] Both were righteous in God's sight, living without blame according to all the commandments and requirements of the Lord. [7] But they had no children because Elizabeth could not conceive, and both of them were well along in years.

[8] When his division was on duty, and he was serving as priest before God, [9] it happened that he was chosen by lot, according to the custom of the priesthood, to enter the sanctuary of the Lord and burn incense. [10] At the hour of incense the whole assembly of the people was praying outside. [11] An angel of the Lord appeared to him, standing to the right of the altar of incense. [12] When Zechariah saw him, he was startled and overcome with fear. [13] But the angel said to him:

Do not be afraid, Zechariah,
because your prayer has been heard.
Your wife Elizabeth will bear you a son,
and you will name him John.
[14] There will be joy and delight for you,
and many will rejoice at his birth.
[15] For he will be great in the sight of the Lord,
and will never drink wine or beer.
And he will be filled with the Holy Spirit
while still in his mother's womb.
[16] He will turn many of the sons of Israel
to the Lord their God.
[17] And he will go before Him
in the spirit and power of Elijah,
to turn the hearts of fathers to their children,
and the disobedient to the understanding of the righteous,
to make ready for the Lord a prepared people.

[18] "How can I know this?" Zechariah asked the angel. "For I am an old man, and my wife is well along in years."

[19] The angel answered him, "I am Gabriel, who stands in the presence of God, and I was sent to speak to you and tell you this good news. [20] Now listen! You will become silent and unable to speak until the day these things take place, because you did not believe my words, which will be fulfilled in their proper time."

²¹ Meanwhile, the people were waiting for Zechariah, amazed that he stayed so long in the sanctuary. ²² When he did come out, he could not speak to them. Then they realized that he had seen a vision in the sanctuary. He kept making signs to them and remained speechless. ²³ And when the days of his ministry were completed, he went back home.

²⁴ After these days his wife Elizabeth conceived, and kept herself in seclusion for five months. She said, ²⁵ "The Lord has done this for me. He has looked with favor in these days to take away my disgrace among the people."

## Gabriel Predicts Jesus' Birth

²⁶ In the sixth month, the angel Gabriel was sent by God to a town in Galilee called Nazareth, ²⁷ to a virgin •engaged to a man named Joseph, of the house of David. The virgin's name was Mary. ²⁸ And he[a] came to her and said, "Rejoice, favored woman! The Lord is with you."[b] ²⁹ But she was deeply troubled by this statement and was wondering what kind of greeting this could be. ³⁰ Then the angel told her:

> Do not be afraid, Mary, for you
>     have found favor with God.
> ³¹ Now listen: You will conceive
>     and give birth to a son,
> and you will call His name
>     JESUS.
> ³² He will be great
> and will be called the Son of
>     the Most High,
> and the Lord God will give Him
>     the throne of His father
>     David.

³³ He will reign over the house of
    Jacob forever,
    and His kingdom will have
    no end.

---

### Luke 1:31-35

### God the Son

*Jesus was born of a virgin, a woman who had never been intimate with a man. Mark this as not only extremely unusual but extremely important. If Jesus were born to a man and woman, He wouldn't be God, He'd have no right to forgive us, and we'd be up a creek without a paddle.*

---

³⁴ Mary asked the angel, "How can this be, since I have not been intimate with a man?"
³⁵ The angel replied to her:

> The Holy Spirit will come
>     upon you,
> and the power of the Most High
>     will overshadow you.
> Therefore the holy child to be
>     born
> will be called the Son of God.

³⁶ And consider Elizabeth your relative—even she has conceived a son in her old age, and this is the sixth month for her who was called barren. ³⁷ For nothing will be impossible with God."
³⁸ "Consider me the Lord's slave," said Mary. "May it be done to me according to your word." Then the angel left her.

---

[a]1:28 Other mss read *And the angel*    [b]1:28 Other mss add *blessed are you among women*

## Mary's Visit to Elizabeth

39 In those days Mary set out and hurried to a town in the hill country of Judah, 40 where she entered Zechariah's house and greeted Elizabeth. 41 When Elizabeth heard Mary's greeting, the baby leaped inside her, and Elizabeth was filled with the Holy Spirit. 42 Then she exclaimed with a loud cry:

Blessed are you among women, and blessed is your offspring!

43 How could this happen to me, that the mother of my Lord should come to me? 44 For you see, when the sound of your greeting reached my ears, the baby leaped for joy inside me! 45 Blessed is she who has believed that what was spoken to her by the Lord will be fulfilled!"

## Mary's Praise

46 And Mary said:

My soul proclaims the
    greatness of the Lord,
47 and my spirit has rejoiced in
    God my Savior,
48 because He has looked with favor
    on the humble condition of His
    slave.
    Surely, from now on all
    generations will call
    me blessed,
49 because the Mighty One has
    done great things for me,
    and holy is His name.
50 His mercy is from generation
    to generation
    on those who fear Him.
51 He has done a mighty deed
    with His arm;
    He has scattered the proud
    because of the thoughts of
    their hearts;
52 He has toppled the mighty
    from their thrones

and exalted the lowly.
53 He has satisfied the hungry
    with good things
    and sent the rich away empty.
54 He has helped His servant
    Israel,
    mindful of His mercy,
55 just as He spoke to our
    forefathers,
    to Abraham and his
    descendants forever.

56 And Mary stayed with her about three months; then she returned to her home.

## The Birth and Naming of John

57 Now the time for Elizabeth to give birth was completed, and she bore a son. 58 Then her neighbors and relatives heard that the Lord had shown her His great mercy, and they rejoiced with her.

59 When they came to circumcise the child on the eighth day, they were going to name him Zechariah, after his father. 60 But his mother responded, "No! He will be called John."

61 Then they said to her, "None of your relatives has that name." 62 So they motioned to his father to find out what he wanted him to be called. 63 He asked for a writing tablet and wrote:

| His name is John |
| --- |

And they were all amazed. 64 Immediately his mouth was opened and his tongue freed, and he began to speak, praising God. 65 Fear came upon all those who lived around them, and all these things were being talked about throughout the hill country of Judea. 66 All who heard took them to heart, saying, "What then will this child become?" For, indeed, the Lord's hand was with him.

## Zechariah's Prophecy

<sup>67</sup> Then his father Zechariah was filled with the Holy Spirit and prophesied:

<sup>68</sup> Blessed is the Lord, the God
of Israel,
because He has visited and
provided redemption
for His people.
<sup>69</sup> He has raised up a horn of
salvation for us
in the house of His servant
David,
<sup>70</sup> just as He spoke by the
mouth of His holy
prophets of old:
<sup>71</sup> salvation from our enemies
and from the clutches
of those who hate us.
<sup>72</sup> He has dealt mercifully with
our fathers
and remembered His holy
covenant—
<sup>73</sup> the oath that He swore to our
father Abraham.
He has granted us that,
<sup>74</sup> having been rescued from
our enemies' clutches,
we might serve Him without
fear
<sup>75</sup> in holiness and righteousness
in His presence all our days.
<sup>76</sup> And you, child, will be called
a prophet of the Most High,
for you will go before the
Lord to prepare His ways,
<sup>77</sup> to give His people knowledge
of salvation
through the forgiveness of
their sins,
<sup>78</sup> because of our God's
merciful compassion
by which the Dawn from on
high will visit us,
<sup>79</sup> to shine on those who live in

darkness and the shadow
of death,
to guide our feet into the way
of peace.

<sup>80</sup> The child grew up and became strong in spirit, and he was in the wilderness until the day of his public appearance to Israel.

## The Birth of Jesus

**2** In those days a decree went out from Caesar Augustus that the whole empire should be registered. <sup>2</sup> This first registration took place while Quirinius was governing Syria. <sup>3</sup> So everyone went to be registered, each to his own town.

<sup>4</sup> And Joseph also went up from the town of Nazareth in Galilee, to Judea, to the city of David, which is called Bethlehem, because he was of the house and family line of David, <sup>5</sup> to be registered along with Mary, who was •engaged to him[a] and was pregnant. <sup>6</sup> While they were there, it happened that the days were completed for her to give birth. <sup>7</sup> Then she gave birth to her firstborn Son, and she wrapped Him snugly in cloth and laid Him in a manger—because there was no room for them at the inn.

## The Shepherds and the Angels

<sup>8</sup> In the same region, shepherds were living out in the fields and keeping watch at night over their flock. <sup>9</sup> Then an angel of the Lord stood before them, and the glory of the Lord shone around them, and they were terrified. <sup>10</sup> But the angel said to them, "Do not be afraid, for you see, I announce to you good news of great joy that will be for all the people:

<sup>a</sup>**2:5** Other mss read *was his engaged wife*

> *"God uses the time while we are waiting for His promises to be fulfilled to make us ready for the answer."*
>
> —Neva Coyle

[11] because today in the city of David was born for you a Savior, who is Christ the Lord. [12] This will be the sign for you: you will find a baby wrapped snugly in cloth and lying in a manger."

[13] Suddenly there was a multitude of the heavenly host with the angel, praising God and saying:

[14]  Glory to God in the highest
       heaven,
       and peace on earth to people
       He favors![a]

[15] When the angels had left them and returned to heaven, the shepherds said to one another, "Let's go straight to Bethlehem and see this thing that has taken place, which the Lord has made known to us."

[16] And they hurried off and found both Mary and Joseph, and the baby who was lying in the manger. [17] After seeing ⌊them⌋, they reported the message they were told about this child, [18] and all who heard it were amazed at what the shepherds said to them. [19] But Mary was treasuring up all these things in her heart and meditating on them. [20] The shepherds returned, glorifying and praising God for all they had seen and heard, just as they had been told.

## The Circumcision and Presentation of Jesus

[21] When the eight days were completed for His circumcision, He was named JESUS—the name given by the angel before He was conceived. [22] And when the days of their purification according to the law of Moses were completed, they brought Him up to Jerusalem to present Him to the Lord [23] (just as it is written in the law of the Lord: **Every firstborn male will be called holy to the Lord**)[b] [24] and to offer a sacrifice (according to what is stated in the law of the Lord: **a pair of turtledoves or two young pigeons**).[c]

## Simeon's Prophetic Praise

[25] There was a man in Jerusalem whose name was Simeon. This man was righteous and devout, looking forward to Israel's consolation, and the Holy Spirit was upon him. [26] It had been revealed to him by the Holy Spirit that he would not see death before he saw the Lord's •Messiah. [27] Guided by the Spirit, he entered the •temple complex. When the parents brought in the child Jesus to perform for Him what was customary under the law, [28] Simeon took Him up in his arms, praised God, and said:

[29]  Now, Master, You can
       dismiss Your slave in peace,
       according to Your word.
[30]  For my eyes have seen Your
       salvation,
[31]  which You have prepared in
       the presence of all peoples—
[32]  a light for revelation to the
       Gentiles
       and glory to Your people
       Israel.

---

[a]**2:14** Other mss read *earth good will to people*    [b]**2:23** Ex 13:2,12    [c]**2:24** Lv 5:11; 12:8

[33] His father and mother[a] were amazed at what was being said about Him. [34] Then Simeon blessed them and told His mother Mary: "Indeed, this child is destined to cause the fall and rise of many in Israel, and to be a sign that will be opposed— [35] and a sword will pierce your own soul— that the thoughts of many hearts may be revealed."

## Anna's Testimony

[36] There was also a prophetess, Anna, a daughter of Phanuel, of the tribe of Asher. She was well along in years, having lived with her husband seven years after her marriage, [37] and was a widow for 84 years. She did not leave the temple complex, serving God night and day with fastings and prayers. [38] At that very moment, she came up and began to thank God and to speak about Him to all who were looking forward to the redemption of Jerusalem.[b]

## The Family's Return to Nazareth

[39] When they had completed everything according to the law of the Lord, they returned to Galilee, to their own town of Nazareth. [40] The boy grew up and became strong, filled with wisdom, and God's grace was on Him.

## In His Father's House

[41] Every year His parents traveled to Jerusalem for the •Passover Festival. [42] When He was 12 years old, they went up according to the custom of the festival. [43] After those days were over, as they were returning, the boy Jesus stayed behind in Jerusalem, but His parents[c] did not know it.

[44] Assuming He was in the traveling party, they went a day's journey. Then they began looking for Him among their relatives and friends. [45] When they did not find Him, they returned to Jerusalem to search for Him. [46] After three days, they found Him in the temple complex sitting among the teachers, listening to them and asking them questions. [47] And all those who heard Him were astounded at His understanding and His answers. [48] When His parents saw Him, they were astonished, and His mother said to Him, "Son, why have You treated us like this? Your father and I have been anxiously searching for You."

---

### Luke 2:25-32

*If peace is God's answer to panic, if contentment is His answer to greed, if humility is His answer to personal recognition, what's His answer to worry? Be patient. The light will eventually turn green for you, and you'll understand why you needed to wait so long.*

---

[49] "Why were you searching for Me?" He asked them. "Didn't you know that I must be involved in My Father's interests?" [50] But they did not understand what He said to them.

## In Favor with God and with People

[51] Then He went down with them and came to Nazareth, and was obedient to them. His mother kept all these things in her heart. [52] And Jesus increased in wisdom and

[a]2:33 Other mss read *But Joseph and His mother*   [b]2:38 Other mss read *in Jerusalem*   [c]2:43 Other mss read *but Joseph and His mother*

stature, and in favor with God and with people.

## The Messiah's Herald

**3** In the fifteenth year of the reign of Tiberius Caesar, while Pontius •Pilate was governor of Judea, •Herod was tetrarch of Galilee, his brother Philip tetrarch of the region of Iturea and Trachonitis, and Lysanias tetrarch of Abilene, [2] during the high priesthood of Annas and Caiaphas, God's word came to John the son of Zechariah in the wilderness. [3] He went into all the vicinity of the Jordan, preaching a baptism of repentance for the forgiveness of sins, [4] as it is written in the book of the words of the prophet Isaiah:

A voice of one crying out in
the wilderness:
"Prepare the way for the Lord;
make His paths straight!
[5] Every valley will be filled,
and every mountain and hill
will be made low;
the crooked will become
straight,
the rough ways smooth,
[6] and everyone will see the
salvation of God."[a]

[7] He then said to the crowds who came out to be baptized by him, "Brood of vipers! Who warned you to flee from the coming wrath? [8] Therefore produce fruit consistent with repentance. And don't start saying to yourselves, 'We have Abraham as our father,' for I tell you that God is able to raise up children for Abraham from these stones! [9] Even now the ax is ready to strike the root of the trees! Therefore every tree that doesn't produce good fruit will be cut down and thrown into the fire."

[10] "What then should we do?" the crowds were asking him.

[11] He replied to them, "The one who has two shirts must share with someone who has none, and the one who has food must do the same."

[12] Tax collectors also came to be baptized, and they asked him, "Teacher, what should we do?"

[13] He told them, "Don't collect any more than what you have been authorized."

[14] Some soldiers also questioned him: "What should we do?"

He said to them, "Don't take money from anyone by force or false accusation; be satisfied with your wages."

[15] Now the people were waiting expectantly, and all of them were debating in their minds whether John might be the •Messiah. [16] John answered them all, "I baptize you with water. But One is coming who is more powerful than I. I am not worthy to untie the strap of His sandals. He will baptize you with the Holy Spirit and fire. [17] His winnowing shovel is in His hand to clear His threshing floor and gather the wheat into His barn, but the chaff He will burn up with a fire that never goes out." [18] Then, along with many other exhortations, he announced good news to the people. [19] But Herod the tetrarch, being rebuked by him about Herodias, his brother's wife, and about all the evil things Herod had done, [20] added this to everything else—he locked John up in prison.

## The Baptism of Jesus

[21] When all the people were baptized, Jesus also was baptized. As He was praying, heaven opened, [22] and the Holy Spirit descended on Him in a

[a]**3:4–6** Is 40:3–5

physical appearance like a dove. And a voice came from heaven:

You are My beloved Son.
I take delight in You!

## The Genealogy of Jesus Christ

23 As He began His ministry, Jesus was about 30 years old and was thought to be the son of Joseph, son of Heli,

24son of Matthat, son of Levi, son of Melchi, son of Jannai,
son of Joseph,
25son of Mattathias, son of Amos, son of Nahum, son of Esli,
son of Naggai, 26son of Maath, son of Mattathias, son of Semein, son of Josech, son of Joda,
27son of Joanan, son of Rhesa, son of Zerubbabel,
son of Shealtiel, son of Neri,
28son of Melchi, son of Addi, son of Cosam, son of Elmadam, son of Er, 29son of Joshua, son of Eliezer, son of Jorim, son of Matthat, son of Levi,
30son of Simeon, son of Judah, son of Joseph, son of Jonan, son of Eliakim, 31son of Melea, son of Menna, son of Mattatha, son of Nathan, son of David,
32son of Jesse, son of Obed, son of Boaz, son of Salmon,a son of Nahshon,
33son of Amminadab,
son of Ram,b son of Hezron, son of Perez, son of Judah,
34son of Jacob, son of Isaac, son of Abraham, son of Terah, son of Nahor, 35son of Serug, son of Reu, son of Peleg,

son of Eber, son of Shelah,
36son of Cainan,
son of Arphaxad, son of Shem, son of Noah, son of Lamech,
37son of Methuselah,
son of Enoch, son of Jared, son of Mahalaleel,
son of Cainan, 38son of Enos, son of Seth, son of Adam, son of God.

## The Temptation of Jesus

4 Then Jesus returned from the Jordan, full of the Holy Spirit, and was led by the Spirit in the wilderness 2 for 40 days to be tempted by the Devil. He ate nothing during those days, and when they were over, He was hungry. 3 The Devil said to Him, "If You are the Son of God, tell this stone to become bread."
4 But Jesus answered him, "It is written: **Man must not live on bread alone.**"c d
5 So he took Him upe and showed Him all the kingdoms of the world in a moment of time. 6 The Devil said to Him, "I will give You their splendor and all this authority, because it has been given over to me, and I can give it to anyone I want. 7 If You, then, will worship me, all will be Yours."
8 And Jesus answered him,f "It is written:

**You shall worship the Lord your God,
and Him alone you shall serve.**"g

9 So he took Him to Jerusalem, had Him stand on the pinnacle of the

---

a3:32 Other mss read *Sala*   b3:33 Other mss read *Amminadab, son of Aram, son of Joram;* other mss read *Amminadab son of Admin, son of Arni*   c4:4 Other mss add *but on every word of God*   d4:4 Dt 8:3
e4:5 Other mss read *So the Devil took Him up on a high mountain*   f4:8 Other mss add *"Get behind Me, Satan!*
g4:8 Dt 6:13

temple, and said to Him, "If You are the Son of God, throw Yourself down from here. [10] For it is written:

He will give His angels orders concerning you,
to protect you,[a]

[11] and,

In their hands they will lift you up,
so you will not strike your foot against a stone."[b]

[12] And Jesus answered him, "It is said: You must not tempt the Lord your God."[c]

[13] After the Devil had finished every temptation, he departed from Him for a time.

---

### Luke 4:18-21

#### God the Holy Spirit

*Jesus began His public ministry after the Spirit came on Him at His baptism. Though He was God the Son from all eternity, as man He depended on the Spirit in temptation, in His authoritative teaching, and in His ministry of healing. If Jesus Himself relied on the Spirit in order to serve the Father, how much more should we rely on His empowerment!*

---

### Ministry in Galilee

[14] Then Jesus returned to Galilee in the power of the Spirit, and news about Him spread throughout the entire vicinity. [15] He was teaching in their *synagogues, being acclaimed by everyone.

### Rejection at Nazareth

[16] He came to Nazareth, where He had been brought up. As usual, He entered the synagogue on the Sabbath day and stood up to read. [17] The scroll of the prophet Isaiah was given to Him, and unrolling the scroll, He found the place where it was written:

[18] The Spirit of the Lord is upon Me,
because He has anointed Me
to preach good news to the poor.
He has sent Me[d] to proclaim freedom to the captives
and recovery of sight to the blind,
to set free the oppressed,
[19] to proclaim the year of the Lord's favor.[e]

[20] He then rolled up the scroll, gave it back to the attendant, and sat down. And the eyes of everyone in the synagogue were fixed on Him. [21] He began by saying to them, "Today this Scripture has been fulfilled in your hearing."

[22] They were all speaking well of Him and were amazed by the gracious words that came from His mouth, yet they said, "Isn't this Joseph's son?"

[23] Then He said to them, "No doubt you will quote this proverb to Me: 'Doctor, heal yourself.' 'All we've heard that took place in Capernaum, do here in Your hometown also.' "

[24] He also said, "•I assure you: No prophet is accepted in his hometown.

---

[a]4:10 Ps 91:11   [b]4:11 Ps 91:12   [c]4:12 Dt 6:16   [d]4:18 Other mss add *to heal the brokenhearted,*
[e]4:18-19 Is 61:1-2

25 But I say to you, there were certainly many widows in Israel in Elijah's days, when the sky was shut up for three years and six months while a great famine came over all the land. 26 Yet Elijah was not sent to any of them—but to a widow at Zarephath in Sidon. 27 And there were many lepers in Israel in the prophet Elisha's time, yet not one of them was cleansed— but only Naaman the Syrian."

28 When they heard this, all who were in the synagogue were enraged. 29 They got up, drove Him out of town, and brought Him to the edge of the hill on which their town was built, intending to hurl Him over the cliff. 30 But He passed right through the crowd and went on His way.

## Driving Out an Unclean Spirit

31 Then He went down to Capernaum, a town in Galilee, and was teaching them on the Sabbath. 32 And they were astonished at His teaching because His message had authority. 33 In the synagogue there was a man with an unclean demonic spirit who cried out with a loud voice, 34 "Leave us alone! What do You have to do with us, Jesus—•Nazarene? Have You come to destroy us? I know who You are—the Holy One of God!"

35 But Jesus rebuked him and said, "Be quiet and come out of him!"

And throwing him down before them, the demon came out of him without hurting him at all. 36 They were all struck with amazement and kept saying to one another, "What is this message? For with authority and power He commands the unclean spirits, and they come out!" 37 And news about Him began to go out to every place in the vicinity.

## Healings at Capernaum

38 After He left the synagogue, He entered Simon's house. Simon's mother-in-law was suffering from a high fever, and they asked Him about her. 39 So He stood over her and rebuked the fever, and it left her. She got up immediately and began to serve them.

40 When the sun was setting, all those who had anyone sick with various diseases brought them to Him. As He laid His hands on each one of them, He would heal them. 41 Also, demons were coming out of many, shouting and saying, "You are the Son of God!" But He rebuked them and would not allow them to speak, because they knew He was the •Messiah.

## Preaching in Galilee

42 When it was day, He went out and made His way to a deserted place. But the crowds were searching for Him. They came to Him and tried to keep Him from leaving them. 43 But He said to them, "I must proclaim the good news about the kingdom of God to the other towns also, because I was sent for this purpose." 44 And He was preaching in the synagogues of Galilee.[a]

## The First Disciples

5 As the crowd was pressing in on Jesus to hear God's word, He was standing by Lake Gennesaret. 2 He saw two boats at the edge of the lake; the fishermen had left them and were washing their nets. 3 He got into one of the boats, which belonged to Simon, and asked him to put out a little from the land. Then He sat down and was teaching the crowds from the boat.

a4:44 Other mss read Judea

⁴ When He had finished speaking, He said to Simon, "Put out into deep water and let down your nets for a catch."

⁵ "Master," Simon replied, "we've worked hard all night long and caught nothing! But at Your word, I'll let down the nets."ᵃ

⁶ When they did this, they caught a great number of fish, and their netsᵃ began to tear. ⁷ So they signaled to their partners in the other boat to come and help them; they came and filled both boats so full that they began to sink.

⁸ When Simon Peter saw this, he fell at Jesus' knees and said, "Depart from me, because I'm a sinful man, Lord!" ⁹ For he and all those with him were amazed at the catch of fish they took, ¹⁰ and so also James and John, Zebedee's sons, who were Simon's partners.

"Don't be afraid," Jesus told Simon. "From now on you will be catching people!" ¹¹ Then they brought the boats to land, left everything, and followed Him.

### Cleansing a Leper

¹² While He was in one of the towns, a man covered with leprosy was there. He saw Jesus, fell on his face, and begged Him: "Lord, if You are willing, You can make me clean."

¹³ Reaching out His hand, He touched him, saying, "I am willing; be made clean," and immediately the leprosy left him. ¹⁴ Then He ordered him to tell no one: "But go and show yourself to the priest, and offer what Moses prescribed for your cleansing as a testimony to them."

¹⁵ But the news about Him spread even more, and large crowds would come together to hear Him and to be healed of their sicknesses. ¹⁶ Yet He often withdrew to deserted places and prayed.

> *"Fasting allows us to subordinate our body's needs to our spiritual need for God. It helps us to control our appetites before they control us."*
>
> —James Houston

### The Son of Man Forgives and Heals

¹⁷ On one of those days while He was teaching, •Pharisees and teachers of the law were sitting there who had come from every village of Galilee and Judea, and also from Jerusalem. And the Lord's power to heal was in Him. ¹⁸ Just then some men came, carrying on a stretcher a man who was paralyzed. They tried to bring him in and set him down before Him. ¹⁹ Since they could not find a way to bring him in because of the crowd, they went up on the roof and lowered him on the stretcher through the roof tiles into the middle of the crowd before Jesus.

²⁰ Seeing their faith He said, "Friend, your sins are forgiven you."

²¹ Then the •scribes and the Pharisees began to reason: "Who is this man who speaks blasphemies? Who can forgive sins but God alone?"

²² But perceiving their thoughts, Jesus replied to them, "Why are you

ᵃ5:5-6 Other mss read *net* (Gk sg)

reasoning this in your hearts? [23] Which is easier: to say, 'Your sins are forgiven you,' or to say, 'Get up and walk'? [24] But so you may know that the *Son of Man has authority on earth to forgive sins"—He told the paralyzed man, "I tell you: get up, pick up your stretcher, and go home."

[25] Immediately he got up before them, picked up what he had been lying on, and went home glorifying God. [26] Then everyone was astounded, and they were giving glory to God. And they were filled with awe and said, "We have seen incredible things today!"

## The Call of Levi

[27] After this, Jesus went out and saw a tax collector named Levi sitting at the tax office, and He said to him, "Follow Me!" [28] So, leaving everything behind, he got up and began to follow Him.

## Dining with Sinners

[29] Then Levi hosted a grand banquet for Him at his house. Now there was a large crowd of tax collectors and others who were guests with them. [30] But the Pharisees and their scribes were complaining to His disciples, "Why do you eat and drink with tax collectors and sinners?" [31] Jesus replied to them, "The healthy don't need a doctor, but the sick do. [32] I have not come to call the righteous, but sinners to repentance."

## A Question about Fasting

[33] Then they said to Him, "John's disciples fast often and say prayers,

---

### Luke 5:33-35

*Some people aren't all that high on the discipline of fasting, but the one protesting the loudest is that old flesh inside you that wants its way about everything. Once you've gotten yourself filled up at God's table, you won't be hungry for anything else.*

---

and those of the Pharisees do the same, but Yours eat and drink."[a]

[34] Jesus said to them, "You can't make the wedding guests fast while the groom is with them, can you? [35] But the days will come when the groom will be taken away from them—then they will fast in those days."

[36] He also told them a parable: "No one tears a patch from a new garment and puts it on an old garment. Otherwise, not only will he tear the new, but also the piece from the new garment will not match the old. [37] And no one puts new wine into old wineskins. Otherwise, the new wine will burst the skins, it will spill, and the skins will be ruined. [38] But new wine should be put into fresh wineskins.[b] [39] And no one, after drinking old wine, wants new, because he says, 'The old is better.' "[c]

## Lord of the Sabbath

**6** On a Sabbath,[d] He passed through the grainfields. His disciples were picking heads of grain, rubbing them in their hands, and eating them. [2] But some of the *Pharisees said, "Why are

---

[a]**5:33** Other mss read *"Why do John's . . . drink?"* (as a question)   [b]**5:38** Other mss add *And so both are preserved.*   [c]**5:39** Other mss read *is good*   [d]**6:1** Other mss read *a second-first Sabbath*; perhaps a special sabbath

you doing what is not lawful on the Sabbath?"

³ And Jesus answered them, "Haven't you read what David did when he was hungry, he and those who were with him— ⁴ how he entered the house of God, and took and ate the •sacred bread, which is not lawful for any but the priests to eat? He even gave some to those who were with him." ⁵ Then He told them, "The •Son of Man is Lord of the Sabbath."

## The Man with the Paralyzed Hand

⁶ On another Sabbath He entered the •synagogue and was teaching. A man was there whose right hand was paralyzed. ⁷ The •scribes and Pharisees were watching Him closely, to see if He would heal on the Sabbath, so that they might find a charge against Him. ⁸ But He knew their thoughts and told the man with the paralyzed hand, "Get up and stand here." So he got up and stood there. ⁹ Then Jesus said to them, "I ask you: is it lawful on the Sabbath to do good or to do evil, to save life or to destroy it?" ¹⁰ After looking around at them all, He told him, "Stretch out your hand." He did so, and his hand was restored.ᵃ ¹¹ They, however, were filled with rage, and started discussing with one another what they might do to Jesus.

## The 12 Apostles

¹² During those days He went out to the mountain to pray, and spent all night in prayer to God. ¹³ When daylight came, He summoned His disciples, and from them He chose 12, whom He also named apostles:

¹⁴ Simon, whom He also named

Peter, and Andrew his brother; James and John; Philip and Bartholomew;
¹⁵ Matthew and Thomas; James the son of Alphaeus, and Simon called the Zealot;
¹⁶ Judas the son of James, and Judas Iscariot, who became a traitor.

## Teaching and Healing

¹⁷ After coming down with them, He stood on a level place with a large crowd of His disciples and a great multitude of people from all Judea and Jerusalem and from the seacoast of Tyre and Sidon. ¹⁸ They came to hear Him and to be healed of their diseases; and those tormented by unclean spirits were made well. ¹⁹ The whole crowd was trying to touch Him, because power was coming out from Him and healing them all.

## The Beatitudes

²⁰ Then looking up at His disciples, He said:

Blessed are you who are poor,
because the kingdom of God is yours.
²¹ Blessed are you who are hungry now,
because you will be filled.
Blessed are you who weep now,
because you will laugh.
²² Blessed are you when people hate you,
when they exclude you, insult you,
and slander your name as evil,
because of the Son of Man.

ᵃ6:10 Other mss add *as sound as the other*

> *"We must face the fact that a war is on. And unless we fight, how can we retake the fortresses of the enemy which are in the mind?"*
> —*Watchman Nee*

23 "Rejoice in that day and leap for joy! Take note—your reward is great in heaven, because this is the way their forefathers used to treat the prophets.

## Woe to the Self-satisfied

24  But woe to you who are rich,
       because you have received
          your comfort.
25  Woe to you who are full now,
       because you will be hungry.
     Woe to you[a] who are
          laughing now,
       because you will mourn
          and weep.
26  Woe to you[a] when all
          people speak well of you,
       because this is the way their
          forefathers
     used to treat the false
          prophets.

## Love Your Enemies

27 "But I say to you who listen: Love your enemies, do good to those who hate you, 28 bless those who curse you, pray for those who mistreat you. 29 If anyone hits you on the cheek, offer the other also. And if anyone takes away your coat, don't hold back your shirt either. 30 Give to everyone who asks from you, and from one who takes away your things, don't ask for

them back. 31 Just as you want others to do for you, do the same for them. 32 If you love those who love you, what credit is that to you? Even sinners love those who love them. 33 If you do good to those who do good to you, what credit is that to you? Even sinners do that. 34 And if you lend to those from whom you expect to receive, what credit is that to you? Even sinners lend to sinners to be repaid in full. 35 But love your enemies, do good, and lend, expecting nothing in return. Then your reward will be great, and you will be sons of the Most High. For He is gracious to the ungrateful and evil. 36 Be merciful, just as your Father also is merciful.

## Do Not Judge

37 "Do not judge, and you will not be judged. Do not condemn, and you will not be condemned. Forgive, and you will be forgiven. 38 Give, and it will be given to you; a good measure, pressed down, shaken together, and running over will be poured into your lap. For with the measure that you use, it will be measured back to you."

39 He also told them a parable: "Can the blind guide the blind? Won't they both fall into a pit? 40 A disciple is not above his teacher, but everyone who is fully trained will be like his teacher.

41 "Why do you look at the speck in your brother's eye, but don't notice the log in your own eye? 42 Or how can you say to your brother, 'Brother, let me take out the speck that is in your eye,' when you yourself don't see the log in your eye? Hypocrite! First take the log out of your eye, and then you will see clearly to take out the speck in your brother's eye.

[a]6:25-26 Other mss omit *to you*

## A Tree and Its Fruit

43 "A good tree doesn't produce bad fruit, nor again does a bad tree produce good fruit. 44 For each tree is known by its own fruit. Figs aren't gathered from thornbushes, or grapes picked from a bramble bush. 45 A good man produces good out of the good storeroom of his heart, and an evil man produces evil out of the evil storeroom. For his mouth speaks from the overflow of the heart.

---

### Luke 6:43-45

*You have ears, you have eyes, you have time, you have television— you have all kinds of ways to get all kinds of stuff into your head, but only one way to control it. The biggest battle you'll face as a Christian will take place every day—right between your ears.*

---

## The Two Foundations

46 "Why do you call Me 'Lord, Lord,' and don't do the things I say? 47 I will show you what someone is like who comes to Me, hears My words, and acts on them: 48 He is like a man building a house, who dug deep and laid the foundation on the rock. When the flood rose, the river crashed against that house and couldn't shake it, because it was well built. 49 But the one who hears and does not act is like a man who built a house on the ground without a foundation. The river crashed against it, and immediately it collapsed. And the destruction of that house was great!"

## A Centurion's Faith

7 When He had concluded all His sayings in the hearing of the people, He entered Capernaum. 2 A *centurion's slave, who was highly valued by him, was sick and about to die. 3 Having heard about Jesus, he sent some Jewish elders to Him, requesting Him to come and save his slave's life. 4 When they reached Jesus, they pleaded with Him earnestly, saying, "He is worthy for You to grant this, 5 because he loves our nation and has built us a *synagogue." 6 Jesus went with them, and when He was not far from the house, the centurion sent friends to tell Him, "Lord, don't trouble Yourself, since I am not worthy to have You come under my roof. 7 That is why I didn't even consider myself worthy to come to You. But say the word, and my servant will be cured.[a] 8 For I too am a man placed under authority, having soldiers under my command. I say to this one, 'Go!' and he goes; and to another, 'Come!' and he comes; and to my slave, 'Do this!' and he does it."

9 Hearing this, Jesus was amazed at him, and turning to the crowd following Him, said, "I tell you, I have not found so great a faith even in Israel!" 10 When those who had been sent returned to the house, they found the slave in good health.

## A Widow's Son Raised to Life

11 Soon afterward He was on His way to a town called Nain. His disci-

a7:7 Other mss read *and let my servant be cured*

ples and a large crowd were traveling with Him. [12] Just as He neared the gate of the town, a dead man was being carried out. He was his mother's only son, and she was a widow. A large crowd from the city was also with her. [13] When the Lord saw her, He had compassion on her and said, "Don't cry." [14] Then He came up and touched the open coffin, and the pallbearers stopped. And He said, "Young man, I tell you, get up!" [15] The dead man sat up and began to speak, and Jesus gave him to his mother. [16] Then fear came over everyone, and they glorified God, saying, "A great prophet has risen among us," and "God has visited His people." [17] This report about Him went throughout Judea and all the vicinity.

## In Praise of John the Baptist

[18] Then John's disciples told him about all these things. So John summoned two of his disciples [19] and sent them to the Lord, asking, "Are You the Coming One, or should we look for someone else?"

[20] When the men reached Him, they said, "John the Baptist sent us to ask You, 'Are You the Coming One, or should we look for someone else?' "

[21] At that time Jesus healed many people of diseases, plagues, and evil spirits, and He granted sight to many blind people. [22] He replied to them, "Go and report to John the things you have seen and heard: The blind receive their sight, the lame walk, lepers are cleansed, the deaf hear, the dead are raised, and the poor have the good news preached to them. [23] And blessed is anyone who is not offended because of Me." [24] After John's messengers left, He

began to speak to the crowds about John: "What did you go out into the wilderness to see? A reed swaying in the wind? [25] But what did you go out to see? A man dressed in soft robes? Look, those who are splendidly dressed and live in luxury are in royal palaces. [26] But what did you go out to see? A prophet? Yes, I tell you, and far more than a prophet. [27] This is the one of whom it is written:

> **Look, I am sending My**
> **    messenger ahead of You;**
> **he will prepare Your way**
> **    before You.**[a]

[28] I tell you, among those born of women no one is greater than John;[b] but the least in the kingdom of God is greater than he."

[29] (And when all the people, including the tax collectors, heard this, they acknowledged God's way of righteousness, because they had been baptized with John's baptism. [30] But since the •Pharisees and experts in the law had not been baptized by him, they rejected the plan of God for themselves.)

## An Unresponsive Generation

[31] "To what then should I compare the people of this generation, and what are they like? [32] They are like children sitting in the marketplace and calling to each other:

> We played the flute for you,
> but you didn't dance;
> we sang a lament,
> but you didn't weep!

[33] For John the Baptist did not come eating bread or drinking wine, and you say, 'He has a demon!' [34] The

[a]**7:27** Mal 3:1    [b]**7:28** Other mss read *women is not a greater prophet than John the Baptist*

•Son of Man has come eating and drinking, and you say, 'Look, a glutton and a drunkard, a friend of tax collectors and sinners!' ³⁵ Yet wisdom is vindicated by all her children."

## Much Forgiveness, Much Love

³⁶ Then one of the Pharisees invited Him to eat with him. He entered the Pharisee's house and reclined at the table. ³⁷ And a woman in the town who was a sinner found out that Jesus was reclining at the table in the Pharisee's house. She brought an alabaster flask of fragrant oil ³⁸ and stood behind Him at His feet, weeping, and began to wash His feet with her tears. She wiped His feet with the hair of her head, kissing them and anointing them with the fragrant oil.

³⁹ When the Pharisee who had invited Him saw this, he said to himself, "This man, if He were a prophet, would know who and what kind of woman this is who is touching Him— that she's a sinner!"

⁴⁰ Jesus replied to him, "Simon, I have something to say to you."

"Teacher," he said, "say it."

⁴¹ "A creditor had two debtors. One owed 500 denarii, and the other 50. ⁴² Since they could not pay it back, he graciously forgave them both. So, which of them will love him more?"

⁴³ Simon answered, "I suppose the one he forgave more."

"You have judged correctly," He told him. ⁴⁴ Turning to the woman, He said to Simon, "Do you see this woman? I entered your house; you gave Me no water for My feet, but she, with her tears, has washed My feet and wiped them with her hair. ⁴⁵ You gave Me no kiss, but she hasn't stopped kissing My feet since I came in. ⁴⁶ You didn't anoint My head with oil, but she has anointed My feet with fragrant oil. ⁴⁷ Therefore I tell you, her many sins have been forgiven; that's why she loved much. But the one who is forgiven little, loves little." ⁴⁸ Then He said to her, "Your sins are forgiven."

⁴⁹ Those who were at the table with Him began to say among themselves, "Who is this man who even forgives sins?"

⁵⁰ And He said to the woman, "Your faith has saved you. Go in peace."

## Many Women Support Christ's Work

**8** Soon afterward He was traveling from one town and village to another, preaching and telling the good news of the kingdom of God. The Twelve were with Him, ² and also some women who had been healed of evil spirits and sicknesses: Mary, called Magdalene, from whom seven demons had come out; ³ Joanna the wife of Chuza, •Herod's steward; Susanna; and many others who were supporting them from their possessions.

## The Parable of the Sower

⁴ As a large crowd was gathering, and people were flocking to Him from every town, He said in a parable: ⁵ "A sower went out to sow his seed. As he was sowing, some fell along the path; it was trampled on, and the birds of the sky ate it up. ⁶ Other seed fell on the rock; when it sprang up, it withered, since it lacked moisture. ⁷ Other seed fell among thorns; the thorns sprang up with it and choked it. ⁸ Still other seed fell on good ground; when it sprang up, it produced a

crop: 100 times what was sown."
As He said this, He called out,
"Anyone who has ears to hear
should listen!"

## Why Jesus Used Parables

[9] Then His disciples asked Him what
this parable might mean. [10] So He said,
"To know the secrets of the kingdom of
God has been granted to you, but to the
rest it is in parables, so that

**Looking they may not see,
and hearing they may not
understand.[a]**

## The Parable of the Sower Explained

[11] "This is the meaning of the parable: The seed is the word of God.
[12] The seeds along the path are those
who have heard. Then the Devil
comes and takes away the word from
their hearts, so that they may not
believe and be saved. [13] And the
seeds on the rock are those who,
when they hear, welcome the word
with joy. Having no root, these
believe for a while and depart in a
time of testing. [14] As for the seed that
fell among thorns, these are the ones
who, when they have heard, go on
their way and are choked with worries, riches, and pleasures of life, and
produce no mature fruit. [15] But the
seed in the good ground—these are
the ones who, having heard the word
with an honest and good heart, hold
on to it and bear fruit with endurance.

## Using Your Light

[16] "No one, after lighting a lamp, covers it with a basket or puts it under a
bed, but puts it on a lampstand, so that
those who come in may see the light.
[17] For nothing is concealed that won't
be revealed, and nothing hidden that
won't be made known and come to
light. [18] Therefore, take care how you
listen. For whoever has, more will be
given to him; and whoever does not
have, even what he thinks he has will
be taken away from him."

## True Relationships

[19] Then His mother and brothers
came to Him, but they could not meet
with Him because of the crowd. [20] He
was told, "Your mother and Your
brothers are standing outside, wanting to see You."
[21] But He replied to them, "My
mother and My brothers are those
who hear and do the word of God."

## Wind and Wave Obey the Master

[22] One day He and His disciples got
into a boat, and He told them, "Let's
cross over to the other side of the
lake." So they set out, [23] and as they
were sailing He fell asleep. Then a
fierce windstorm came down on the
lake; they were being swamped and
were in danger. [24] They came and
woke Him up, saying, "Master, Master, we're going to die!" Then He got
up and rebuked the wind and the raging waves. So they ceased, and there
was a calm. [25] He said to them, "Where
is your faith?"
They were fearful and amazed, saying to one another, "Who can this be?
He commands even the winds and the
waves, and they obey Him!"

## Demons Driven Out by the Master

[26] Then they sailed to the region of
the Gerasenes,[b] which is opposite

[a]8:10 Is 6:9   [b]8:26 Other mss read the Gadarenes

*Luke 8:22-25*

*You don't have to know how every-
thing is going to turn out. You just
have to trust that the One who is
in the boat with you has everything
under control. Knowing that Jesus
Christ is in charge can put you at
ease in life's most unsettling
situations.*

Galilee. [27] When He got out on land, a man from the town who had demons met Him. For a long time he had worn no clothes and did not stay in a house but in the tombs. [28] When he saw Jesus, he cried out, fell down before Him, and said in a loud voice, "What do You have to do with me, Jesus, You Son of the Most High God? I beg You, don't torment me!" [29] For He had commanded the unclean spirit to come out of the man. Many times it had seized him, and although he was guarded, bound by chains and shackles, he would snap the restraints and be driven by the demon into deserted places.

[30] "What is your name?" Jesus asked him.

"Legion," he said—because many demons had entered him. [31] And they begged Him not to banish them to the •abyss.

[32] A large herd of pigs was there, feeding on the hillside. The demons begged Him to permit them to enter the pigs, and He gave them permission. [33] The demons came out of the man and entered the pigs, and the herd rushed down the steep bank into the lake and drowned. [34] When the men who tended them saw what had happened, they ran off and reported it in the town and in the countryside. [35] Then people went out to see what had happened. They came to Jesus and found the man from whom the demons had departed, sitting at Jesus' feet, dressed and in his right mind. And they were afraid. [36] Meanwhile the eyewitnesses reported to them how the demon-possessed man was delivered. [37] Then all the people of the Gerasene region[a] asked Him to leave them, because they were gripped by great fear. So getting into the boat, He returned.

[38] The man from whom the demons had departed kept begging Him to be with Him. But He sent him away and said, [39] "Go back to your home, and tell all that God has done for you." And off he went, proclaiming throughout the town all that Jesus had done for him.

## A Girl Restored and a Woman Healed

[40] When Jesus returned, the crowd welcomed Him, for they were all expecting Him. [41] Just then, a man named Jairus came. He was a leader of the •synagogue. He fell down at Jesus' feet and pleaded with Him to come to his house, [42] because he had an only daughter about 12 years old, and she was at death's door.

While He was going, the crowds were nearly crushing Him. [43] A woman suffering from bleeding for 12 years, who had spent all she had on doctors[b] yet could not be healed by any, [44] approached from behind and touched the •tassel of His robe. Instantly her bleeding stopped.

[45] "Who touched Me?" Jesus asked.

When they all denied it, Peter[c] said, "Master, the crowds are hemming You in and pressing against You."[d]

[a]8:37 Other mss read *the Gadarenes*   [b]8:43 Other mss omit *who had spent all she had on doctors*
[c]8:45 Other mss add *and those with him*   [d]8:45 Other mss add *and You say, 'Who touched Me?'*

⁴⁶ "Somebody did touch Me," said Jesus. "I know that power has gone out from Me." ⁴⁷ When the woman saw that she was discovered, she came trembling and fell down before Him. In the presence of all the people, she declared the reason she had touched Him and how she was instantly cured. ⁴⁸ "Daughter," He said to her, "your faith has made you well. Go in peace."

---

*"A mark of spiritual maturity is the quiet confidence that God is in control—without the need to understand why He does what He does."*
—Charles Swindoll

---

⁴⁹ While He was still speaking, someone came from the synagogue leader's house, saying, "Your daughter is dead. Don't bother the Teacher anymore."

⁵⁰ But when Jesus heard it, He answered him, "Don't be afraid. Only believe, and she will be made well." ⁵¹ When He came to the house, He let no one enter with Him except Peter, John, James, and the child's father and mother. ⁵² And all were weeping and mourning for her. But He said, "Stop weeping; for she is not dead but asleep."

⁵³ They started laughing at Him, because they knew she was dead. ⁵⁴ But He[a] took her by the hand and called out, "Child, get up!" ⁵⁵ Her spirit returned, and she got up at once. Then He gave orders that she be given something to eat. ⁵⁶ Her parents were astounded, but He instructed them to tell no one what had happened.

## Commissioning the Twelve

**9** Summoning the Twelve, He gave them power and authority over all the demons, and to heal diseases. ² Then He sent them to proclaim the kingdom of God and to heal the sick. ³ "Take nothing for the road," He told them, "no walking stick, no backpack, no bread, no money; and don't have an extra shirt. ⁴ Whatever house you enter, stay there and leave from there. ⁵ Wherever they do not welcome you, when you leave that town, shake off the dust from your feet as a testimony against them." ⁶ So they went out and traveled from village to village, proclaiming the good news and healing everywhere.

## Herod's Desire to See Jesus

⁷ •Herod the tetrarch heard about everything that was going on. He was perplexed, because some said that John had been raised from the dead, ⁸ some that Elijah had appeared, and others that one of the ancient prophets had risen. ⁹ "I beheaded John," Herod said. "But who is this I hear such things about?" And he wanted to see Him.

## Feeding 5,000

¹⁰ When the apostles returned, they reported to Jesus all that they had done. He took them along and withdrew privately to a[b] town called Bethsaida. ¹¹ When the crowds found out, they followed Him. He welcomed them, spoke to them about the kingdom of God, and cured those who needed healing.

¹² Late in the day, the Twelve approached and said to Him, "Send the crowd away, so they can go into the surrounding villages and country-

---

[a]8:54 Other mss add *having put them all outside*    [b]9:10 Other mss add *deserted place near a*

side to find food and lodging, because we are in a deserted place here."

¹³ "You give them something to eat," He told them.

"We have no more than five loaves and two fish," they said, "unless we go and buy food for all these people." ¹⁴ (For about 5,000 men were there.)

Then He told His disciples, "Have them sit down in groups of about 50 each." ¹⁵ They did so, and had them all sit down. ¹⁶ Then He took the five loaves and the two fish, and looking up to heaven, He blessed and broke them. He kept giving them to the disciples to set before the crowd. ¹⁷ Everyone ate and was filled. Then they picked up 12 baskets of leftover pieces.

## Peter's Confession of the Messiah

¹⁸ Once when He was praying in private, and His disciples were with Him, He asked them, "Who do the crowds say that I am?"

¹⁹ And they answered, "John the Baptist; others, Elijah; still others, that one of the ancient prophets has come back."

²⁰ "But you," He asked them, "who do you say that I am?"

Peter answered, "God's •Messiah!"

## His Death and Resurrection Predicted

²¹ But He strictly warned and instructed them to tell this to no one, ²² saying, "The •Son of Man must suffer many things and be rejected by the elders, •chief priests, and •scribes, be killed, and be raised the third day."

## Take Up Your Cross

²³ Then He said to them all, "If anyone wants to come with Me, he must deny himself, take up his cross daily,ᵃ and follow Me. ²⁴ For whoever wants to save his •life will lose it, but whoever loses his life because of Me will save it. ²⁵ What is a man benefited if he gains the whole world, yet loses or forfeits himself? ²⁶ For whoever is ashamed of Me and My words, the Son of Man will be ashamed of him when He comes with His glory, and with the glory of the Father, and of the holy angels. ²⁷ I tell you the truth: there are some standing here who will not taste death until they see the kingdom of God."

## The Transfiguration

²⁸ About eight days after these words, He took along Peter, John, and James, and went up on the mountain to pray. ²⁹ As He was praying, the appearance of His face changed, and His clothes became dazzling white. ³⁰ Suddenly, two men were talking with Him—none other than Moses and Elijah. ³¹ They appeared in glory and were speaking of His death, which He was about to accomplish in Jerusalem.

³² Peter and those with him were in a deep sleep, and when they became fully awake, they saw His glory and the two men who were standing with Him. ³³ As the two men were departing from Him, Peter said to Jesus, "Master, it's good for us to be here! Let us make three •tabernacles: one for You, one for Moses, and one for Elijah"—not knowing what he said. ³⁴ While he was saying this, a cloud appeared and overshadowed them. They became afraid as they entered the cloud. ³⁵ Then a voice came from the cloud, saying:

This is My Son, the Chosen One;ᵇ listen to Him!

ᵃ9:23 Other mss omit *daily*   ᵇ9:35 Other mss read *the Beloved*

[36] After the voice had spoken, only Jesus was found. They kept silent, and in those days told no one what they had seen.

## The Power of Faith over a Demon

[37] The next day, when they came down from the mountain, a large crowd met Him. [38] Just then a man from the crowd cried out, "Teacher, I beg You to look at my son, because he's my only child. [39] Often a spirit seizes him; suddenly he shrieks, and it throws him into convulsions until he foams at the mouth; wounding him, it hardly ever leaves him. [40] I begged Your disciples to drive it out, but they couldn't."

[41] Jesus replied, "O unbelieving and rebellious generation! How long will I be with you and put up with you? Bring your son here."

[42] As the boy was still approaching, the demon knocked him down and threw him into severe convulsions. But Jesus rebuked the unclean spirit, cured the boy, and gave him back to his father. [43] And they were all astonished at the greatness of God.

## The Second Prediction of His Death

While everyone was amazed at all the things He was doing, He told His disciples, [44] "Let these words sink in: the Son of Man is about to be betrayed into the hands of men."

[45] But they did not understand this statement; it was concealed from them so that they could not grasp it, and they were afraid to ask Him about it.

## Who Is the Greatest?

[46] Then an argument started among them about who would be the greatest of them. [47] But Jesus, knowing the thoughts of their hearts, took a little child and had him stand next to Him.

[48] He told them, "Whoever welcomes this little child in My name welcomes Me. And whoever welcomes Me welcomes Him who sent Me. For whoever is least among you all—this one is great."

## In His Name

[49] John responded, "Master, we saw someone driving out demons in Your name, and we tried to stop him because he does not follow with us."

[50] "Don't stop him," Jesus told him, "because whoever is not against you is for you."[a]

## The Journey to Jerusalem

[51] When the days were coming to a close for Him to be taken up, He was determined to journey to Jerusalem. [52] He sent messengers ahead of Him, and on the way they entered a village of the •Samaritans to make preparations for Him. [53] But they did not welcome Him, because He was determined to journey to Jerusalem. [54] When the disciples James and John saw this, they said, "Lord, do You want us to call down fire from heaven to consume them?"[b]

[55] But He turned and rebuked them,[c] [56] and they went to another village.

## Following Jesus

[57] As they were traveling on the road someone said to Him, "I will follow You wherever You go!"

[58] Jesus told him, "Foxes have dens, and birds of the sky have nests, but the Son of Man has no place to lay His head." [59] Then He said to another, "Follow Me."

"Lord," he said, "first let me go to bury my father."

---

[a]9:50 Other mss read *against us is for us*  [b]9:54 Other mss add *as Elijah also did*  [c]9:55 Other mss add *and said, "You don't know what kind of spirit you belong to.* [56] *For the Son of Man did not come to destroy people's lives but to save them."*

⁶⁰ But He told him, "Let the dead bury their own dead, but you go and spread the news of the kingdom of God."

⁶¹ Another also said, "I will follow You, Lord, but first let me go and say good-bye to those at my house."

⁶² But Jesus said to him, "No one who puts his hand to the plow and looks back is fit for the kingdom of God."

## Sending Out the Seventy

**10** After this the Lord appointed 70ᵃ others, and He sent them ahead of Him in pairs to every town and place where He Himself was about to go. ² He told them: "The harvest is abundant, but the workers are few. Therefore, pray to the Lord of the harvest to send out workers into His harvest. ³ Now go; I'm sending you out like lambs among wolves. ⁴ Don't carry a money-bag, backpack, or sandals; don't greet anyone along the road. ⁵ Whatever house you enter, first say, 'Peace to this household.' ⁶ If a son of peace is there, your peace will rest on him; but if not, it will return to you. ⁷ Remain in the same house, eating and drinking what they offer, for the worker is worthy of his wages. Don't be moving from house to house. ⁸ Whatever town you enter, and they welcome you, eat the things set before you. ⁹ Heal the sick who are there, and tell them, 'The kingdom of God has come near you.' ¹⁰ But whatever town you enter, and they don't welcome you, go out into its streets and say, ¹¹ 'Even the dust of your town that clings to our feet we wipe off against you. But know this: the kingdom of God has come near.' ¹² I tell you, on that day it will be more tolerable for Sodom than for that town.

## Unrepentant Towns

¹³ "Woe to you, Chorazin! Woe to you, Bethsaida! For if the miracles that were done in you had been done in Tyre and Sidon, they would have repented long ago, sitting in sackcloth and ashes! ¹⁴ But it will be more tolerable for Tyre and Sidon at the judgment than for you. ¹⁵ And you, Capernaum, will you be exalted to heaven? No, you will go down to •Hades! ¹⁶ Whoever listens to you listens to Me. Whoever rejects you rejects Me. And whoever rejects Me rejects the One who sent Me."

### Luke 10:18-20

*You may not like to think about harmful spiritual forces having you in their crosshairs, but you'd be delighted to know that you've got them outmanned. Go ahead and talk up where the devil can hear you, and remind him Who's fighting on your side.*

## The Return of the Seventy

¹⁷ The Seventyᵇ returned with joy, saying, "Lord, even the demons submit to us in Your name."

¹⁸ He said to them, "I watched Satan fall from heaven like a lightning flash. ¹⁹ Look, I have given you the authority to trample on snakes and scorpions and over all the power of the enemy; nothing will ever harm you. ²⁰ However, don't rejoice that the spirits submit to you, but rejoice that your names are written in heaven."

ᵃ10:1 Other mss read *72*    ᵇ10:17 Other mss read *Seventy-two*

## The Son Reveals the Father

21 In that same hour He[a] rejoiced in the Holy[b] Spirit and said, "I praise You, Father, Lord of heaven and earth, because You have hidden these things from the wise and the learned and have revealed them to infants. Yes, Father, because this was Your good pleasure. 22 All things have[c] been entrusted to Me by My Father. No one knows who the Son is except the Father, and who the Father is except the Son, and anyone to whom the Son desires to reveal Him."

23 Then turning to His disciples He said privately, "Blessed are the eyes that see the things you see! 24 For I tell you that many prophets and kings wanted to see the things you see, yet didn't see them; to hear the things you hear, yet didn't hear them."

## The Parable of the Good Samaritan

25 Just then an expert in the law stood up to test Him, saying, "Teacher, what must I do to inherit eternal life?"

26 "What is written in the law?" He asked him. "How do you read it?"

27 He answered:

> You shall love the Lord your
>     God
> with all your heart, with all
>     your soul,
> with all your strength, and
>     with all your mind;
> and your neighbor as
>     yourself.[d]

28 "You've answered correctly," He told him. "Do this and you will live."

29 But wanting to justify himself, he asked Jesus, "And who is my neighbor?"

---

*"The devil is not frightened by our human efforts. But he knows his kingdom will be damaged when we lift up our hearts to God."*

—Jim Cymbala

---

30 Jesus took up the question and said: "A man was going down from Jerusalem to Jericho and fell into the hands of robbers. They stripped him, beat him up, and fled, leaving him half dead. 31 A priest happened to be going down that road. When he saw him, he passed by on the other side. 32 In the same way, a Levite, when he arrived at the place and saw him, passed by on the other side. 33 But a •Samaritan, while traveling, came up to him; and when he saw the man, he had compassion. 34 He went over to him and bandaged his wounds, pouring on oil and wine. Then he put him on his own animal, brought him to an inn, and took care of him. 35 The next day[e] he took out two denarii, gave them to the innkeeper, and said, 'Take care of him; and when I come back I'll reimburse you for whatever extra you spend.'

36 "Which of these three do you think proved to be a neighbor to the man who fell into the hands of the robbers?"

37 "The one who showed mercy to him," he said.

Then Jesus told him, "Go and do the same."

---

[a]10:21 Other mss read *Jesus*  [b]10:21 Other mss omit *Holy*  [c]10:22 Other mss read *And turning to the disciples, He said, "Everything has*  [d]10:27 Dt 6:5; Lv 19:18  [e]10:35 Other mss add *as he was leaving*

## Martha and Mary

[38] While they were traveling, He entered a village, and a woman named Martha welcomed Him into her home.[a] [39] She had a sister named Mary, who also sat at the Lord's[b] feet and was listening to what He said. [40] But Martha was distracted by her many tasks, and she came up and asked, "Lord, don't You care that my sister has left me to serve alone? So tell her to give me a hand."

[41] The Lord[c] answered her, "Martha, Martha, you are worried and upset about many things, [42] but one thing is necessary. Mary has made the right choice, and it will not be taken away from her."

## The Model Prayer

**11** He was praying in a certain place, and when He finished, one of His disciples said to Him, "Lord, teach us to pray, just as John also taught his disciples."

[2] He said to them, "Whenever you pray, say:

> Father,[d] Your name be
> honored as holy.
> Your kingdom come.[e]
> [3] Give us each day our daily
> bread.
> [4] And forgive us our sins,
> for we ourselves also forgive
> everyone in debt to us.
> And do not bring us into
> temptation."[f]

## Keep Asking, Searching, Knocking

[5] He also said to them: "Suppose one of you has a friend and goes to him at midnight and says to him, 'Friend, lend me three loaves of bread, [6] because a friend of mine on a journey has come to me, and I don't have anything to offer him.' [7] Then he will answer from inside and say, 'Don't bother me! The door is already locked, and my children and I have gone to bed. I can't get up to give you anything.' [8] I tell you, even though he won't get up and give him anything because he is his friend, yet because of his persistence, he will get up and give him as much as he needs.

---

### Luke 11:11-13

### God the Holy Spirit

*How hard is it for someone to receive the Holy Spirit into their lives? About as hard as asking their father to please pass them the fish, or the eggs, knowing that he won't hand them a plate of snakes or scorpions. It is the heavenly Father's desire that we ask—and He willingly gives.*

---

[9] "So I say to you, keep asking, and it will be given to you. Keep searching, and you will find. Keep knocking, and the door will be opened to you. [10] For everyone who asks receives, and the one who searches finds, and to the one who knocks, the door will be opened. [11] What father among you, if his son[g] asks for a fish, will, instead of a fish, give him a snake? [12] Or if he asks for an egg, will give him a scorpion? [13] If you then, who are evil,

[a]10:38 Other mss omit *into her home*  [b]10:39 Other mss read *at Jesus'*  [c]10:41 Other mss read *Jesus*
[d]11:2 Other mss read *Our Father in heaven*  [e]11:2 Other mss add *Your will be done on earth as it is in heaven*  [f]11:4 Other mss add *But deliver us from the evil one*  [g]11:11 Other mss read *son asks for bread, would give him a stone? Or if he*

know how to give good gifts to your children, how much more will the heavenly Father give the Holy Spirit to those who ask Him?"

## A House Divided

14 Now He was driving out a demon that was mute. When the demon came out, the man spoke who had been unable to speak, and the crowds were amazed. 15 But some of them said, "He drives out demons by •Beelzebul, the ruler of the demons!" 16 And others, as a test, were demanding of Him a sign from heaven.

17 Knowing their thoughts, He told them: "Every kingdom divided against itself is headed for destruction, and a house divided against itself falls. 18 If Satan also is divided against himself, how will his kingdom stand? For you say I drive out demons by Beelzebul. 19 And if I drive out demons by Beelzebul, by whom do your sons drive them out? For this reason they will be your judges. 20 If I drive out demons by the finger of God, then the kingdom of God has come to you. 21 When a strong man, fully armed, guards his estate, his possessions are secure. 22 But when one stronger than he attacks and overpowers him, he takes from him all his weapons in which he trusted, and divides up his plunder. 23 Anyone who is not with Me is against Me, and anyone who does not gather with Me scatters.

## An Unclean Spirit's Return

24 "When an unclean spirit comes out of a man, it roams through waterless places looking for rest, and not finding rest, it then[a] says, 'I'll go back to my house where I came from.' 25 And returning, it finds the house swept and put in order. 26 Then it goes and brings seven other spirits more evil than itself, and they enter and settle down there. As a result, that man's last condition is worse than the first."

## True Blessedness

27 As He was saying these things, a woman from the crowd raised her voice and said to Him, "Blessed is the womb that bore You, and the breasts that nursed You!" 28 He said, "More blessed still are those who hear the word of God and keep it!"

## The Sign of Jonah

29 As the crowds were increasing, He began saying: "This generation is an evil generation. It demands a sign, but no sign will be given to it except the sign of Jonah.[b] 30 For just as Jonah became a sign to the people of Nineveh, so also the •Son of Man will be to this generation. 31 The queen of the south will rise up at the judgment with the men of this generation and condemn them, because she came from the ends of the earth to hear the wisdom of Solomon; and look—something greater than Solomon is here! 32 The men of Nineveh will rise up at the judgment with this generation and condemn it, because they repented at Jonah's proclamation; and look—something greater than Jonah is here!

## The Lamp of the Body

33 "No one lights a lamp and puts it in the cellar or under a basket,[c] but on a lampstand, so that those who come in may see its light. 34 Your eye

[a]11:24 Other mss omit *then*   [b]11:29 Other mss add *the prophet*   [c]11:33 Other mss omit *or under a basket*

is the lamp of the body. When your eye is good, your whole body is also full of light. But when it is bad, your body is also full of darkness. <sup>35</sup> Take care then, that the light in you is not darkness. <sup>36</sup> If therefore your whole body is full of light, with no part of it in darkness, the whole body will be full of light, as when a lamp shines its light on you."

## Religious Hypocrisy Denounced

<sup>37</sup> As He was speaking, a •Pharisee asked Him to dine with him. So He went in and reclined at the table. <sup>38</sup> When the Pharisee saw this, he was amazed that He did not first perform the ritual washing before dinner. <sup>39</sup> But the Lord said to him: "Now you Pharisees clean the outside of the cup and dish, but inside you are full of greed and evil. <sup>40</sup> Fools! Didn't He who made the outside make the inside too? <sup>41</sup> But give to charity what is within, and then everything is clean for you.

<sup>42</sup> "But woe to you Pharisees! You give a tenth of mint, rue, and every kind of herb, and you bypass justice and love for God. These things you should have done without neglecting the others.

<sup>43</sup> "Woe to you Pharisees! You love the front seat in the •synagogues and greetings in the marketplaces.

<sup>44</sup> "Woe to you!<sup>a</sup> You are like unmarked graves; the people who walk over them don't know it."

<sup>45</sup> One of the experts in the law answered Him, "Teacher, when You say these things You insult us too."

<sup>46</sup> And He said: "Woe to you experts in the law as well! You load people with burdens that are hard to carry, yet you yourselves don't touch these burdens with one of your fingers.

<sup>47</sup> "Woe to you! You build monuments to the prophets, and your fathers killed them. <sup>48</sup> Therefore you are witnesses that you approve the deeds of your fathers, for they killed them, and you build their monuments.<sup>b</sup> <sup>49</sup> And because of this, the wisdom of God said, 'I will send them prophets and apostles, and some of them they will kill and persecute,' <sup>50</sup> so that this generation may be held responsible for the blood of all the prophets shed since the foundation of the world, <sup>51</sup> from the blood of Abel to the blood of Zechariah, who perished between the altar and the sanctuary.

"Yes, I tell you, this generation will be held responsible.

<sup>52</sup> "Woe to you experts in the law! You have taken away the key of knowledge! You didn't go in yourselves, and you hindered those who were going in."

<sup>53</sup> When He left there,<sup>c</sup> the •scribes and the Pharisees began to oppose Him fiercely and to cross-examine Him about many things; <sup>54</sup> they were lying in wait for Him to trap Him in something He said.<sup>d</sup>

## Beware of Religious Hypocrisy

**12** In these circumstances, a crowd of many thousands came together, so that they were trampling on one another. He began to say to His disciples first: "Be on your guard against the yeast of the •Pharisees, which is hypocrisy. <sup>2</sup> There is nothing covered that won't be uncovered; nothing hidden that won't be made known.

---

<sup>a</sup>11:44 Other mss read *you scribes and Pharisees, hypocrites!*   <sup>b</sup>11:48 Other mss omit *their monuments*
<sup>c</sup>11:53 Other mss read *And as He was saying these things to them*   <sup>d</sup>11:54 Other mss add *so that they might bring charges against Him*

³ Therefore whatever you have said in the dark will be heard in the light, and what you have whispered in an ear in private rooms will be proclaimed on the housetops.

## Fear God

⁴ "And I say to you, My friends, don't fear those who kill the body, and after that can do nothing more. ⁵ But I will show you the One to fear: Fear Him who, after He has killed, has authority to throw into *hell. Yes, I say to you, this is the One to fear! ⁶ Aren't five sparrows sold for two pennies? Yet not one of them is forgotten in God's sight. ⁷ But even the hairs of your head are all counted. Don't be afraid; you are worth more than many sparrows!

---

*Luke 12:11-12*

### God the Holy Spirit

*Talk about a fantastic promise! It doesn't mean we should slack off our Bible study or never think through our reasons for believing. When others need to know what Jesus Christ is like, how comforting it is to know that the Holy Spirit will give us the right words at the right time.*

---

## Acknowledging Christ

⁸ "And I say to you, anyone who acknowledges Me before men, the *Son of Man will also acknowledge him before the angels of God; ⁹ but whoever denies Me before men will be denied before the angels of God. ¹⁰ Anyone who speaks a word against the Son of Man will be forgiven; but the one who blasphemes against the Holy Spirit will not be forgiven. ¹¹ Whenever they bring you before *synagogues and rulers and authorities, don't worry about how you should defend yourselves or what you should say. ¹² For the Holy Spirit will teach you at that very hour what must be said."

## The Parable of the Rich Fool

¹³ Someone from the crowd said to Him, "Teacher, tell my brother to divide the inheritance with me."

¹⁴ "Friend," He said to him, "who appointed Me a judge or arbitrator over you?" ¹⁵ And He told them, "Watch out and be on guard against all greed, because one's life is not in the abundance of his possessions."

¹⁶ Then He told them a parable: "A rich man's land was very productive. ¹⁷ He thought to himself, 'What should I do, since I don't have anywhere to store my crops? ¹⁸ I will do this,' he said. 'I'll tear down my barns and build bigger ones, and store all my grain and my goods there. ¹⁹ Then I'll say to myself, "You have many goods stored up for many years. Take it easy; eat, drink, and enjoy yourself." '

²⁰ "But God said to him, 'You fool! This very night your *life is demanded of you. And the things you have prepared—whose will they be?'

²¹ "That's how it is with the one who stores up treasure for himself and is not rich toward God."

## The Cure for Anxiety

²² Then He said to His disciples: "Therefore I tell you, don't worry about your life, what you will eat; or about the body, what you will wear. ²³ For life is more than food and the body more than clothing. ²⁴ Consider

the ravens: they don't sow or reap; they don't have a storeroom or a barn; yet God feeds them. Aren't you worth much more than the birds? 25 Can any of you add a *cubit to his height by worrying? 26 If then you're not able to do even a little thing, why worry about the rest?

27 "Consider how the wildflowers grow: they don't labor or spin thread. Yet I tell you, not even Solomon in all his splendor was adorned like one of these! 28 If that's how God clothes the grass, which is in the field today and is thrown into the furnace tomorrow, how much more will He do for you—you of little faith? 29 Don't keep striving for what you should eat and what you should drink, and do not be anxious. 30 For the Gentile world eagerly seeks all these things, and your Father knows that you need them.

31 "But seek His kingdom, and these things will be provided for you. 32 Don't be afraid, little flock, because your Father delights to give you the kingdom. 33 Sell your possessions and give to the poor. Make money-bags for yourselves that won't grow old, an inexhaustible treasure in heaven, where no thief comes near and no moth destroys. 34 For where your treasure is, there your heart will be also.

## Ready for the Master's Return

35 "Be ready for service and have your lamps lit. 36 You must be like people waiting for their master to return from the wedding banquet so that when he comes and knocks, they can open the door for him at once. 37 Blessed are those slaves whom the master will find alert when he comes. *I assure you: He will get ready, have them recline at the table, then come and serve them. 38 If he comes in the middle of the night, or even near dawn, and finds them alert, blessed are those slaves. 39 But know this: if the homeowner had known at what hour the thief was coming, he would not have let his house be broken into. 40 You also be ready, because the Son of Man is coming at an hour that you do not expect."

## Rewards and Punishment

41 "Lord," Peter asked, "are You telling this parable to us or to everyone?" 42 The Lord said: "Who then is the faithful and sensible manager whom his master will put in charge of his household servants to give them their allotted food at the proper time? 43 Blessed is that slave whom his master, when he comes, will find at work. 44 I tell you the truth: he will put him in charge of all his possessions. 45 But if that slave says in his heart, 'My master is delaying his coming,' and starts to beat the male and female slaves, and to eat and drink and get drunk, 46 that slave's master will come on a day he does not expect him and at an hour he does not know. He will cut him to pieces and assign him a place with the unbelievers. 47 And that slave who knew his master's will, and didn't prepare himself or do it, will be severely beaten. 48 But the one who did not know, and did things deserving of blows, will be beaten lightly. Much will be required of everyone who has been given much. And even more will be expected of the one who has been entrusted with more.

## Not Peace but Division

49 "I came to bring fire on the earth, and how I wish it were already set ablaze! 50 But I have a baptism to be baptized with, and how it consumes

Me until it is finished! [51] Do you think that I came here to give peace to the earth? No, I tell you, but rather division! [52] From now on, five in one household will be divided: three against two, and two against three.

[53] **They will be divided, father against son,
son against father,
mother against daughter,
daughter against mother,
mother-in-law against her daughter-in-law,
and daughter-in-law against mother-in-law."**[a]

## Interpreting the Time

[54] He also said to the crowds: "When you see a cloud rising in the west, right away you say, 'A storm is coming,' and so it does. [55] And when the south wind is blowing, you say, 'It's going to be a scorcher!' and it is. [56] Hypocrites! You know how to interpret the appearance of the earth and the sky, but why don't you know how to interpret this time?

## Settling Accounts

[57] "Why don't you judge for yourselves what is right? [58] As you are going with your adversary to the ruler, make an effort to settle with him on the way. Then he won't drag you before the judge, the judge hand you over to the bailiff, and the bailiff throw you into prison. [59] I tell you, you will never get out of there until you have paid the last cent."

## Repent or Perish

**13** At that time, some people came and reported to Him about the Galileans whose blood *Pilate had mixed with their sacrifices. [2] And He[b] responded to them, "Do you think that these Galileans were more sinful than all Galileans because they suffered these things? [3] No, I tell you; but unless you repent, you will all perish as well! [4] Or those 18 that the tower in Siloam fell on and killed— do you think they were more sinful than all the people who live in Jerusalem? [5] No, I tell you; but unless you repent, you will all perish as well!"

## The Parable of the Barren Fig Tree

[6] And He told this parable: "A man had a fig tree that was planted in his vineyard. He came looking for fruit on it and found none. [7] He told the vineyard worker, 'Listen, for three years I have come looking for fruit on this fig tree and haven't found any. Cut it down! Why should it even waste the soil?' [8] "But he replied to him, 'Sir, leave it this year also, until I dig around it and fertilize it. [9] Perhaps it will bear fruit next year, but if not, you can cut it down.' "

## Healing a Daughter of Abraham

[10] As He was teaching in one of the *synagogues on the Sabbath, [11] a woman was there who had been disabled by a spirit for over 18 years. She was bent over and could not straighten up at all. [12] When Jesus saw her, He called out to her, "Woman, you are free of your disability." [13] Then He laid His hands on her, and instantly she was restored and began to glorify God. [14] But the leader of the synagogue, indignant because Jesus had healed on the Sabbath, responded by telling the

[a]**12:53** Mc 7:6    [b]**13:2** Other mss read *Jesus*

crowd, "There are six days when work should be done; therefore come on those days and be healed, and not on the Sabbath day."

¹⁵ But the Lord answered him and said, "Hypocrites! Doesn't each one of you untie his ox or donkey from the manger on the Sabbath, and lead it to water? ¹⁶ And this woman, a daughter of Abraham, whom Satan has bound for 18 years—shouldn't she be untied from this bondage on the Sabbath day?"

¹⁷ When He had said these things, all His adversaries were humiliated, but the whole crowd was rejoicing over all the glorious things He was doing.

## The Parables of the Mustard Seed and of the Yeast

¹⁸ He said therefore, "What is the kingdom of God like, and to what should I compare it? ¹⁹ It's like a mustard seed that a man took and sowed in his garden. It grew and became a tree, and the birds of the sky nested in its branches."

²⁰ Again He said, "To what should I compare the kingdom of God? ²¹ It's like yeast that a woman took and mixed into 50 pounds of flour until it spread through the entire mixture."

## The Narrow Way

²² He went through one town and village after another, teaching and making His way to Jerusalem. ²³ "Lord," someone asked Him, "are there few being saved?"

He said to them, ²⁴ "Make every effort to enter through the narrow door, because I tell you, many will try to enter and won't be able ²⁵ once the homeowner gets up and shuts the door. Then you will stand outside and knock on the door, saying, 'Lord,

open up for us!' He will answer you, 'I don't know you or where you're from.' ²⁶ Then you will say, 'We ate and drank in Your presence, and You taught in our streets!' ²⁷ But He will say, 'I tell you, I don't know you or where you're from. Get away from Me, all you workers of unrighteousness!' ²⁸ There will be weeping and gnashing of teeth in that place, when you see Abraham, Isaac, Jacob, and all the prophets in the kingdom of God but yourselves thrown out. ²⁹ They will come from east and west, from north and south, and recline at the table in the kingdom of God. ³⁰ Note this: some are last who will be first, and some are first who will be last."

## Jesus and Herod Antipas

³¹ At that time some •Pharisees came and told Him, "Go, get out of here! •Herod wants to kill You!"

³² And He said to them, "Go tell that fox, 'Look! I'm driving out demons and performing healings today and tomorrow, and on the third day I will complete My work.' ³³ Yet I must travel today, tomorrow, and the next day, because it is not possible for a prophet to perish outside of Jerusalem!

## Jesus' Lamentation over Jerusalem

³⁴ "O Jerusalem! Jerusalem! The city who kills the prophets and stones those who are sent to her! How often I wanted to gather your children together, as a hen gathers her chicks under her wings, but you were not willing! ³⁵ See! Your house is abandoned to you. And I tell you, you will not see Me until the time comes when you say, '**Blessed is He who comes in the name of the Lord!**' "a

ᵃ**13:35** Ps 118:26

## A Sabbath Controversy

**14** One Sabbath, when He went to eat at the house of one of the leading •Pharisees, they were watching Him closely. [2] There in front of Him was a man whose body was swollen with fluid. [3] In response, Jesus asked the law experts and the Pharisees, "Is it lawful to heal on the Sabbath or not?" [4] But they kept silent. He took the man, healed him, and sent him away. [5] And to them, He said, "Which of you whose son or ox falls into a well, will not immediately pull him out on the Sabbath day?" [6] To this they could find no answer.

## Teachings on Humility

[7] He told a parable to those who were invited, when He noticed how they would choose the best places for themselves: [8] "When you are invited by someone to a wedding banquet, don't recline at the best place, because a more distinguished person than you may have been invited by your host. [9] The one who invited both of you may come and say to you, 'Give your place to this man,' and then in humiliation, you will proceed to take the lowest place. [10] "But when you are invited, go and recline in the lowest place, so that when the one who invited you comes, he will say to you, 'Friend, move up higher.' You will then be honored in the presence of all the other guests. [11] For everyone who exalts himself will be humbled, and the one who humbles himself will be exalted."

[12] He also said to the one who had invited Him, "When you give a lunch or a dinner, don't invite your friends, your brothers, your relatives, or your rich neighbors, because they might invite you back, and you would be repaid. [13] On the contrary, when you host a banquet, invite those who are poor, maimed, lame, or blind. [14] And you will be blessed, because they cannot repay you; for you will be repaid at the resurrection of the righteous."

## The Parable of the Large Banquet

[15] When one of those who reclined at the table with Him heard these things, he said to Him, "Blessed is the one who will eat bread in the kingdom of God!"

[16] Then He told him: "A man was giving a large banquet and invited many. [17] At the time of the banquet, he sent his slave to tell those who were invited, 'Come, because everything is now ready.'

[18] "But without exception they all began to make excuses. The first one said to him, 'I have bought a field, and I must go out and see it. I ask you to excuse me.'

[19] "Another said, 'I have bought five yoke of oxen, and I'm going to try them out. I ask you to excuse me.'

[20] "And another said, 'I just got married, and therefore I'm unable to come.'

[21] "So the slave came back and reported these things to his master. Then in anger, the master of the house told his slave, 'Go out quickly into the streets and alleys of the city, and bring in here the poor, maimed, blind, and lame!'

[22] " 'Master,' the slave said, 'what you ordered has been done, and there's still room.'

[23] "Then the master told the slave, 'Go out into the highways and lanes and make them come in, so that my house may be filled. [24] For I tell you,

not one of those men who were invited will enjoy my banquet!' "

## The Cost of Following Jesus

25 Now great crowds were traveling with Him. So He turned and said to them: 26 "If anyone comes to Me and does not hate his own father and mother, wife and children, brothers and sisters—yes, and even his own life—he cannot be My disciple. 27 Whoever does not bear his own cross and come after Me cannot be My disciple.

28 "For which of you, wanting to build a tower, doesn't first sit down and calculate the cost, to see if he has enough to complete it? 29 Otherwise, after he has laid the foundation and cannot finish it, all the onlookers will begin to make fun of him, 30 saying, 'This man started to build and wasn't able to finish.'

31 "Or what king, going to war against another king, will not first sit down and decide if he is able with 10,000 to oppose the one who comes against him with 20,000? 32 If not, while the other is still far off, he sends a delegation and asks for terms of peace. 33 In the same way, therefore, every one of you who does not say good-bye to all his possessions cannot be My disciple.

34 "Now, salt is good, but if salt should lose its taste, how will it be made salty? 35 It isn't fit for the soil or for the manure pile; they throw it out. Anyone who has ears to hear should listen!"

## The Parable of the Lost Sheep

**15** All the tax collectors and sinners were drawing near to listen to Him. 2 And the •Pharisees and •scribes were complaining, "This man welcomes sinners and eats with them!"

3 So He told them this parable: 4 "What man among you, who has 100 sheep and loses one of them, does not leave the 99 in the open field and go after the lost one until he finds it? 5 When he has found it, he joyfully puts it on his shoulders, 6 and coming home, he calls his friends and neighbors together, saying to them, 'Rejoice with me, because I have found my lost sheep!' 7 I tell you, in the same way, there will be more joy in heaven over one sinner who repents than over 99 righteous people who don't need repentance.

## The Parable of the Lost Coin

8 "Or what woman who has 10 silver coins, if she loses one coin, does not light a lamp, sweep the house, and search carefully until she finds it? 9 When she finds it, she calls her women friends and neighbors together, saying, 'Rejoice with me, because I have found the silver coin I lost!' 10 I tell you, in the same way, there is joy in the presence of God's angels over one sinner who repents."

## The Parable of the Lost Son

11 He also said: "A man had two sons. 12 The younger of them said to his father, 'Father, give me the share of the estate I have coming to me.' So he distributed the assets to them. 13 Not many days later, the younger son gathered together all he had and traveled to a distant country, where he squandered his estate in foolish living. 14 After he had spent everything, a severe famine struck that country, and he had nothing. 15 Then he went to work for one of the citi-

zens of that country, who sent him into his fields to feed pigs. [16] He longed to eat his fill from[a] the carob pods the pigs were eating, and no one would give him any. [17] But when he came to his senses, he said, 'How many of my father's hired hands have more than enough food, and here I am dying of hunger! [18] I'll get up, go to my father, and say to him, "Father, I have sinned against heaven and in your sight. [19] I'm no longer worthy to be called your son. Make me like one of your hired hands." ' [20] So he got up and went to his father. But while the son was still a long way off, his father saw him and was filled with compassion. He ran, threw his arms around his neck, and kissed him. [21] The son said to him, 'Father, I have sinned against heaven and in your sight. I'm no longer worthy to be called your son.'

[22] "But the father told his slaves, 'Quick! Bring out the best robe and put it on him; put a ring on his finger and sandals on his feet. [23] Then bring the fattened calf and slaughter it, and let's celebrate with a feast, [24] because this son of mine was dead and is alive again; he was lost and is found!' So they began to celebrate.

[25] "Now his older son was in the field; as he came near the house, he heard music and dancing. [26] So he summoned one of the servants and asked what these things meant. [27] 'Your brother is here,' he told him, 'and your father has slaughtered the fattened calf because he has him back safe and sound.'

[28] "Then he became angry and didn't want to go in. So his father came out and pleaded with him. [29] But he replied to his father, 'Look, I have been slaving many years for you, and I have never disobeyed your orders; yet you never gave me a young goat so I could celebrate with my friends. [30] But when this son of yours came, who has devoured your assets with prostitutes, you slaughtered the fattened calf for him.'

[31] " 'Son,' he said to him, 'you are always with me, and everything I have is yours. [32] But we had to celebrate and rejoice, because this brother of yours was dead and is alive again; he was lost and is found.' "

## The Parable of the Dishonest Manager

**16** He also said to the disciples: "There was a rich man who received an accusation that his manager was squandering his possessions. [2] So he called the manager in and asked, 'What is this I hear about you? Give an account of your management, because you can no longer be my manager.'

[3] "Then the manager said to himself, 'What should I do, since my master is taking the management away from me? I'm not strong enough to dig; I'm ashamed to beg. [4] I know what I'll do so that when I'm removed from management, people will welcome me into their homes.'

[5] "So he summoned each one of his master's debtors. 'How much do you owe my master?' he asked the first one.

[6] " 'A hundred measures of oil,' he said.

" 'Take your invoice,' he told him, 'sit down quickly, and write 50.'

[7] "Next he asked another, 'How much do you owe?'

" 'A hundred measures of wheat,' he said.

" 'Take your invoice,' he told him, 'and write 80.'

[8] "The master praised the unrighteous manager because he had acted

---

[a]15:16 Other mss read *to fill his stomach with*

astutely. For the sons of this age are more astute than the sons of light in dealing with their own people. [9] And I tell you, make friends for yourselves by means of the money of unrighteousness, so that when it fails,[a] they may welcome you into eternal dwellings. [10] Whoever is faithful in very little is also faithful in much; and whoever is unrighteous in very little is also unrighteous in much. [11] So if you have not been faithful with the unrighteous money, who will trust you with what is genuine? [12] And if you have not been faithful with what belongs to someone else, who will give you what is your own? [13] No servant can be the slave of two masters, since either he will hate one and love the other, or he will be devoted to one and despise the other. You can't be slaves to both God and money."

## Kingdom Values

[14] The *Pharisees, who were lovers of money, were listening to all these things and scoffing at Him. [15] And He told them: "You are the ones who justify yourselves in the sight of others, but God knows your hearts. For what is highly admired by people is revolting in God's sight.

[16] "The Law and the Prophets were until John; since then, the good news of the kingdom of God has been proclaimed, and everyone is strongly urged to enter it. [17] But it is easier for heaven and earth to pass away than for one stroke of a letter in the law to drop out.

[18] "Everyone who divorces his wife and marries another woman commits adultery, and everyone who marries a woman divorced from her husband commits adultery.

## The Rich Man and Lazarus

[19] "There was a rich man who would dress in purple and fine linen, feasting lavishly every day. [20] But at his gate was left a poor man named Lazarus, covered with sores. [21] He longed to be filled with what fell from the rich man's table, but instead the dogs would come and lick his sores. [22] One day the poor man died and was carried away by the angels to Abraham's side. The rich man also died and was buried. [23] And being in torment in *Hades, he looked up and saw Abraham a long way off, with Lazarus at his side. [24] 'Father Abraham!' he called out, 'Have mercy on me and send Lazarus to dip the tip of his finger in water and cool my tongue, because I am in agony in this flame!'

[25] " 'Son,' Abraham said, 'remember that during your life you received your good things, just as Lazarus received bad things; but now he is comforted here, while you are in agony. [26] Besides all this, a great chasm has been fixed between us and you, so that those who want to pass over from here to you cannot; neither can those from there cross over to us.'

[27] " 'Father,' he said, 'then I beg you to send him to my father's house— [28] because I have five brothers—to warn them, so they won't also come to this place of torment.'

[29] "But Abraham said, 'They have Moses and the prophets; they should listen to them.'

[30] " 'No, father Abraham,' he said. 'But if someone from the dead goes to them, they will repent.'

[31] "But he told him, 'If they don't listen to Moses and the prophets,

---

[a] 16:9 Other mss read *when you fail* or *pass away*

they will not be persuaded if someone rises from the dead.' "

## Warnings from Jesus

**17** He said to His disciples, "Offenses will certainly come, but woe to him through whom they come! [2] It would be better for him if a millstone were hung around his neck and he were thrown into the sea than for him to cause one of these little ones to stumble. [3] Be on your guard. If your brother sins,[a] rebuke him; and if he repents, forgive him. [4] And if he sins against you seven times in a day, and comes back to you seven times, saying, 'I repent,' you must forgive him."

## Faith and Duty

[5] The apostles said to the Lord, "Increase our faith."

[6] "If you have faith the size of a mustard seed," the Lord said, "you could say to this mulberry tree, 'Be uprooted and planted in the sea,' and it would obey you.

[7] "Which one of you having a slave plowing or tending sheep, would say to him when he comes in from the field, 'Come at once and sit down to eat'? [8] Instead, would he not tell him, 'Prepare something for me to eat, get ready, and serve me while I eat and drink; later you may eat and drink'? [9] Does he thank that slave because he did what was commanded?[b] [10] In the same way, when you have done all that you were commanded, you should say, 'We are good-for-nothing slaves; we've only done our duty.' "

## The 10 Lepers

[11] While traveling to Jerusalem, He passed between Samaria and Galilee.

---

*Luke 17:11-19*

*One of the trademark traits of the Christian life is the ability to be truly thankful—thankful to God, thankful to others, thankful for everything that comes your way. Going out of your way to thank someone will go a long way toward growing your character.*

---

[12] As He entered a village, 10 men with leprosy met Him. They stood at a distance [13] and raised their voices, saying, "Jesus, Master, have mercy on us!"

[14] When He saw them, He told them, "Go and show yourselves to the priests." And while they were going, they were cleansed.

[15] But one of them, seeing that he was healed, returned and, with a loud voice, gave glory to God. [16] He fell on his face at His feet, thanking Him. And he was a *Samaritan.

[17] Then Jesus said, "Were not 10 cleansed? Where are the nine? [18] Didn't any return to give glory to God except this foreigner?" [19] And He told him, "Get up and go on your way. Your faith has made you well."

## The Coming of the Kingdom

[20] Being asked by the *Pharisees when the kingdom of God will come, He answered them, "The kingdom of God is not coming with something observable; [21] no one will say, 'Look here!' or 'There!' For you see, the kingdom of God is among you."

[a]17:3 Other mss add *against you*   [b]17:9 Other mss add *I don't think so*

22 Then He told the disciples: "The days are coming when you will long to see one of the days of the •Son of Man, but you won't see it. 23 They will say to you, 'Look there!' or 'Look here!' Don't follow or run after them. 24 For as the lightning flashes from horizon to horizon and lights up the sky, so the Son of Man will be in His day. 25 But first He must suffer many things and be rejected by this generation.

---

*"Our receiving of things isn't dependent on our giving thanks, but oh—how it pleases God when we simply look up and say, 'Thank you.' "*

*—Gigi Graham Tchividijan*

---

26 "Just as it was in the days of Noah, so it will be in the days of the Son of Man: 27 people went on eating, drinking, marrying and giving in marriage until the day Noah boarded the ark, and the flood came and destroyed them all. 28 It will be the same as it was in the days of Lot: people went on eating, drinking, buying, selling, planting, building; 29 but on the day Lot left Sodom, fire and sulfur rained from heaven and destroyed them all. 30 It will be like that on the day the Son of Man is revealed. 31 On that day, a man on the housetop, whose belongings are in the house, must not come down to get them. And likewise the man who is in the field must not turn back. 32 Remember Lot's wife! 33 Whoever tries to make his •life secure[a] will lose it, and whoever loses his life will preserve it. 34 I tell you, on that night two will be in one bed: one will be taken and the other will be left. 35 Two women will be grinding grain together: one will be taken and the other left. ⌊36 Two will be in a field: one will be taken, and the other will be left."⌋ [b]

37 "Where, Lord?" they asked Him.

He said to them, "Where the corpse is, there also the vultures will be gathered."

## The Parable of the Persistent Widow

18 He then told them a parable on the need for them to pray always and not become discouraged: 2 "There was a judge in one town who didn't fear God or respect man. 3 And a widow in that town kept coming to him, saying, 'Give me justice against my adversary.'

4 "For a while he was unwilling; but later he said to himself, 'Even though I don't fear God or respect man, 5 yet because this widow keeps pestering me, I will give her justice, so she doesn't wear me out by her persistent coming.' "

6 Then the Lord said, "Listen to what the unjust judge says. 7 Will not God grant justice to His elect who cry out to Him day and night? Will He delay to help them? 8 I tell you that He will swiftly grant them justice. Nevertheless, when the •Son of Man comes, will He find that faith on earth?"

## The Parable of the Pharisee and the Tax Collector

9 He also told this parable to some who trusted in themselves that they were righteous and looked down on everyone else: 10 "Two men went up to the •temple complex to pray, one a •Pharisee and the other a tax collec-

[a]17:33 Other mss read *to save his life*   [b]17:36 Other mss omit bracketed text

tor. [11] The Pharisee took his stand and was praying like this: 'God, I thank You that I'm not like other people—greedy, unrighteous, adulterers, or even like this tax collector. [12] I fast twice a week; I give a tenth of everything I get.'

[13] "But the tax collector, standing far off, would not even raise his eyes to heaven, but kept striking his chest and saying, 'O God, turn Your wrath from me—a sinner!' [14] I tell you, this one went down to his house justified rather than the other; because everyone who exalts himself will be humbled, but the one who humbles himself will be exalted."

## Blessing the Children

[15] Some people even were bringing infants to Him so He might touch them, but when the disciples saw it, they rebuked them. [16] Jesus, however, invited them: "Let the little children come to Me, and don't stop them, because the kingdom of God belongs to such as these. [17] •I assure you: Whoever does not welcome the kingdom of God like a little child will never enter it."

## The Rich Young Ruler

[18] A ruler asked Him, "Good Teacher, what must I do to inherit eternal life?" [19] "Why do you call Me good?" Jesus asked him. "No one is good but One—God. [20] You know the commandments:

> Do not commit adultery;
>   do not murder;
> do not steal;
>   do not bear false witness;
> honor your father and
>   mother."[a]

[21] "I have kept all these from my youth," he said.

[22] When Jesus heard this, He told him, "You still lack one thing: sell all that you have and distribute it to the poor, and you will have treasure in heaven. Then come, follow Me."

[23] After he heard this, he became extremely sad, because he was very rich.

## Possessions and the Kingdom

[24] Seeing that he became sad,[b] Jesus said, "How hard it is for those who have wealth to enter the kingdom of God! [25] For it is easier for a camel to go through the eye of a needle than for a rich person to enter the kingdom of God."

[26] Those who heard this asked, "Then who can be saved?"

[27] He replied, "What is impossible with men is possible with God."

[28] Then Peter said, "Look, we have left what we had and followed You."

[29] So He said to them, "I assure you: There is no one who has left a house, wife or brothers, parents or children because of the kingdom of God, [30] who will not receive many times more at this time, and eternal life in the age to come."

## The Third Prediction of His Death

[31] Then He took the Twelve aside and told them, "Listen! We are going up to Jerusalem. Everything that is written through the prophets about the Son of Man will be accomplished. [32] For He will be handed over to the Gentiles, and He will be mocked, insulted, spit on; [33] and after they flog Him, they will kill Him, and He will rise on the third day."

[a]18:20 Ex 20:12–16; Dt 5:16–20    [b]18:24 Other mss omit *he became sad*

**34** They understood none of these things. This saying was hidden from them, and they did not grasp what was said.

### A Blind Man Receives His Sight

**35** As He drew near Jericho, a blind man was sitting by the road begging. **36** Hearing a crowd passing by, he inquired what this meant. **37** "Jesus the •Nazarene is passing by," they told him.

**38** So he called out, "Jesus, Son of David, have mercy on me!" **39** Then those in front told him to keep quiet, but he was crying out all the more, "Son of David, have mercy on me!"

**40** Jesus stopped and commanded that he be brought to Him. When he drew near, He asked him, **41** "What do you want Me to do for you?"

"Lord," he said, "I want to see!"

**42** "Receive your sight!" Jesus told him. "Your faith has healed you." **43** Instantly he could see, and he began to follow Him, glorifying God. All the people, when they saw it, gave praise to God.

### Jesus Visits Zacchaeus

**19** He entered Jericho and was passing through. **2** There was a man named Zacchaeus who was a chief tax collector, and he was rich. **3** He was trying to see who Jesus was, but he was not able because of the crowd, since he was a short man. **4** So running ahead, he climbed up a sycamore tree to see Jesus, since He was about to pass that way. **5** When Jesus came to the place, He looked up and said to him, "Zacchaeus, hurry and come down, because today I must stay at your house."

**6** So he quickly came down and welcomed Him joyfully. **7** All who saw it began to complain, "He's gone to lodge with a sinful man!"

**8** But Zacchaeus stood there and said to the Lord, "Look, I'll give half of my possessions to the poor, Lord! And if I have extorted anything from anyone, I'll pay back four times as much!"

**9** "Today salvation has come to this house," Jesus told him, "because he too is a son of Abraham. **10** For the •Son of Man has come to seek and to save the lost."

### The Parable of the 10 Minas

**11** As they were listening to this, He went on to tell a parable, because He was near Jerusalem, and they thought the kingdom of God was going to appear right away.

---

*Luke 19:9-10*

*God's Grace*

*The point of Christ's coming to earth was to bring God's grace within reach, to make available the blessing of salvation to all people, wherever they may be found. And still today, Christ does the seeking—and the saving—and people everywhere are swept into His kingdom.*

---

**12** Therefore He said: "A nobleman traveled to a far country to receive for himself authority to be king, and then return; **13** and having called 10 of his slaves, he gave them 10 •minas and told them, 'Do business until I come back.'

<sup>14</sup> "But his subjects hated him and sent a delegation after him, saying, 'We don't want this man to rule over us!'

<sup>15</sup> "At his return, having received the authority to be king, he summoned those slaves to whom he had given the money so that he could find out how much they had made in business. <sup>16</sup> The first came forward and said, 'Master, your mina has earned 10 more minas.'

<sup>17</sup> " 'Well done, good slave!' he told him. 'Because you have been faithful in a very small matter, have authority over 10 towns.'

<sup>18</sup> "The second came and said, 'Master, your mina has made five minas.'

<sup>19</sup> "So he said to him, 'You will be over five towns.'

<sup>20</sup> "And another came and said, 'Master, here is your mina. I have kept it hidden away in a cloth <sup>21</sup> because I was afraid of you, for you're a tough man: you collect what you didn't deposit and reap what you didn't sow.'

<sup>22</sup> "He told him, 'I will judge you by what you have said, you evil slave! If you knew I was a tough man, collecting what I didn't deposit and reaping what I didn't sow, <sup>23</sup> why didn't you put my money in the bank? And when I returned, I would have collected it with interest!' <sup>24</sup> So he said to those standing there, 'Take the mina away from him and give it to the one who has 10 minas.'

<sup>25</sup> "But they said to him, 'Master, he has 10 minas.'

<sup>26</sup> " 'I tell you, that to everyone who has, more will be given; and from the one who does not have, even what he does have will be taken away. <sup>27</sup> But bring here these enemies of mine, who did not want me to rule over them, and slaughter them in my presence.' "

## The Triumphal Entry

<sup>28</sup> When He had said these things, He went on ahead, going up to Jerusalem. <sup>29</sup> As He approached Bethphage and Bethany, at the place called the •Mount of Olives, He sent two of the disciples <sup>30</sup> and said, "Go into the village ahead of you. As you enter it, you will find a young donkey tied there, on which no one has ever sat. Untie it and bring it here. <sup>31</sup> And if anyone asks you, 'Why are you untying it?' say this: 'The Lord needs it.' "

<sup>32</sup> So those who were sent left and found it just as He had told them. <sup>33</sup> As they were untying the young donkey, its owners said to them, "Why are you untying the donkey?"

<sup>34</sup> "The Lord needs it," they said. <sup>35</sup> Then they brought it to Jesus, and after throwing their robes on the donkey, they helped Jesus get on it. <sup>36</sup> As He was going along, they were spreading their robes on the road. <sup>37</sup> Now He came near the path down the •Mount of Olives, and the whole crowd of the disciples began to praise God joyfully with a loud voice for all the miracles they had seen:

<sup>38</sup> **Blessed is the King who comes**
   **in the name of the Lord.**[a]
   Peace in heaven and glory in the
   highest heaven!

<sup>39</sup> And some of the •Pharisees from the crowd told Him, "Teacher, rebuke Your disciples."

<sup>40</sup> He answered, "I tell you, if they were to keep silent, the stones would cry out!"

[a]19:38 Ps 118:26

## Jesus' Love for Jerusalem

[41] As He approached and saw the city, He wept over it, [42] saying, "If you knew this day what leads to peace—but now it is hidden from your eyes. [43] For the days will come upon you when your enemies will build an embankment against you, surround you, and hem you in on every side. [44] They will crush you and your children within you to the ground, and they will not leave one stone on another in you, because you did not recognize the time of your visitation."

## Cleansing the Temple Complex

[45] He went into the •temple complex and began to throw out those who were selling,[a] [46] and He said, "It is written, **My house will be a house of prayer**, but you have made it **a den of thieves!** "[b]

[47] Every day He was teaching in the temple complex. The •chief priests, the •scribes, and the leaders of the people were looking for a way to destroy Him, [48] but they could not find a way to do it, because all the people were captivated by what they heard.

## The Authority of Jesus Challenged

**20** One day as He was teaching the people in the •temple complex and proclaiming the good news, the •chief priests and the •scribes, with the elders, came up [2] and said to Him: "Tell us, by what authority are You doing these things? Who is it who gave You this authority?"

[3] He answered them, "I will also ask you a question. Tell Me, [4] was the baptism of John from heaven or from men?"

[5] They discussed it among themselves: "If we say, 'From heaven,' He will say, 'Why didn't you believe him?' [6] But if we say, 'From men,' all the people will stone us, because they are convinced that John was a prophet."

[7] So they answered that they did not know its origin.

[8] And Jesus said to them, "Neither will I tell you by what authority I do these things."

## The Parable of the Vineyard Owner

[9] Then He began to tell the people this parable: "A man planted a vineyard, leased it to tenant farmers, and went away for a long time. [10] At harvest time he sent a slave to the farmers so that they might give him some fruit from the vineyard. But the farmers beat him and sent him away empty-handed. [11] He sent yet another slave, but they beat that one too, treated him shamefully, and sent him away empty-handed. [12] And he sent yet a third; but they wounded this one too, and threw him out.

[13] "Then the owner of the vineyard said, 'What should I do? I will send my beloved son. Perhaps[c] they will respect him.'

[14] "But when the tenant farmers saw him, they discussed it among themselves and said, 'This is the heir. Let's kill him, so that the inheritance may be ours!' [15] So they threw him out of the vineyard and killed him.

"Therefore, what will the owner of the vineyard do to them? [16] He will come and destroy those farmers and give the vineyard to others."

---

[a]**19:45** Other mss add *and buying in it*   [b]**19:46** Is 56:7; Jr 7:11   [c]**20:13** Other mss add *when they see him*

But when they heard this they said, "No—never!"

17 But He looked at them and said, "Then what is the meaning of this Scripture:

> The stone that the builders
> rejected,
> this has become the
> cornerstone?[a]

18 Everyone who falls on that stone will be broken to pieces, and if it falls on anyone, it will grind him to powder!"

19 Then the scribes and the chief priests looked for a way to get their hands on Him that very hour, because they knew He had told this parable against them, but they feared the people.

## God and Caesar

20 They watched closely and sent spies who pretended to be righteous, so they could catch Him in what He said, to hand Him over to the governor's rule and authority. 21 They questioned Him, "Teacher, we know that You speak and teach correctly, and You don't show partiality, but teach the way of God in truth. 22 Is it lawful for us to pay taxes to Caesar or not?"

23 But detecting their craftiness, He said to them,[b] 24 "Show Me a •denarius. Whose image and inscription does it have?"

"Caesar's," they said.

25 "Well then," He told them, "give back to Caesar the things that are Caesar's, and to God the things that are God's."

26 They were not able to catch Him in what He said in public, and being amazed at His answer, they became silent.

## The Sadducees and the Resurrection

27 Some of the •Sadducees, who say there is no resurrection, came up and questioned Him: 28 "Teacher, Moses wrote for us that **if a man's brother dies** having a wife, and he **is without children, his brother should take the wife and produce offspring for his brother.**[c] 29 Now there were seven brothers. The first took a wife, and died without children. 30 Also the second[d] 31 and the third took her. In the same way, all seven died and left no children. 32 Finally, the woman died too. 33 Therefore, in the resurrection, whose wife will the woman be? For all seven had married her."

34 Jesus told them, "The children of this age marry and are given in marriage. 35 But those who are counted worthy to take part in that age and the resurrection from the dead neither marry nor are given in marriage. 36 For they cannot die anymore, because they are like angels and are children of God, since they are children of the resurrection. 37 But even Moses indicated in the passage about the burning bush that the dead are raised, where he calls the Lord **the God of Abraham and the God of Isaac and the God of Jacob.**[e] 38 He is not God of the dead but of the living, because all are living to Him."

39 Some of the scribes answered, "Teacher, You have spoken well." 40 And they no longer dared to ask Him anything.

---

[a]20:17 Ps 118:22   [b]20:23 Other mss add *"Why are you testing Me?*   [c]20:28 Dt 25:5   [d]20:30 Other mss add *took her as wife, and he died without children*   [e]20:37 Ex 3:6,15

## The Question about the Messiah

41 Then He said to them, "How can they say that the •Messiah is the Son of David? 42 For David himself says in the Book of Psalms:

**The Lord said to my Lord,
'Sit at My right hand,**
43 **until I make Your enemies
Your footstool.'ᵃ**

44 David, then, calls Him 'Lord'; so how is He his Son?"

## Warning against the Scribes

45 While all the people were listening, He said to His disciples, 46 "Beware of the scribes, who want to go around in long robes, and who love greetings in the marketplaces, the front seats in the •synagogues, and the places of honor at banquets. 47 They devour widows' houses and say long prayers just for show. These will receive greater punishment."

## The Widow's Gift

**21** He looked up and saw the rich dropping their offerings into the temple treasury. 2 He also saw a poor widow dropping in two tiny coins. 3 "I tell you the truth," He said. "This poor widow has put in more than all of them. 4 For all these people have put in gifts out of their surplus, but she out of her poverty has put in all she had to live on."

## Destruction of the Temple Predicted

5 As some were talking about the •temple complex, how it was adorned with beautiful stones and gifts dedicated to God, He said, 6 "These things that you see—the days will come when not one stone will be left on another that will not be thrown down!"

## Signs of the End of the Age

7 "Teacher," they asked Him, "so when will these things be? And what will be the sign when these things are about to take place?"

8 Then He said, "Watch out that you are not deceived. For many will come in My name, saying, 'I am He,' and, 'The time is near.' Don't follow them. 9 When you hear of wars and rebellions, don't be alarmed; because these things must take place first, but the end won't come right away."

10 Then He told them: "Nation will be raised up against nation, and kingdom against kingdom. 11 There will be violent earthquakes, and famines and plagues in various places, and there will be terrifying sights and great signs from heaven. 12 But before all these things, they will lay their hands on you and persecute you. They will hand you over to the •synagogues and prisons, and you will be brought before kings and governors because of My name. 13 It will lead to an opportunity for you to witness. 14 Therefore make up your minds not to prepare your defense ahead of time, 15 for I will give you such words and a wisdom that none of your adversaries will be able to resist or contradict. 16 You will even be betrayed by parents, brothers, relatives, and friends; and they will kill some of you. 17 And you will be hated by all because of My name. 18 But not a hair of your head will be lost. 19 By your endurance gainᵇ your lives.

ᵃ20:42–43 Ps 110:1     ᵇ21:19 Other mss read *endurance you will gain*

## The Destruction of Jerusalem

20 "But when you see Jerusalem surrounded by armies, then know that its desolation has come near. 21 Then those in Judea must flee to the mountains! Those inside the city must leave it, and those who are in the country must not enter it, 22 because these are days of vengeance to fulfill all the things that are written. 23 Woe to pregnant women and nursing mothers in those days, for there will be great distress in the land and wrath against this people. 24 They will fall by the edge of the sword and be led captive into all the nations; and Jerusalem will be trampled by the Gentiles until the times of the Gentiles are fulfilled.

---

### Luke 21:33

### The Scriptures

*Ask anyone who has read the Bible for years and they'll tell you it never stops speaking. New things pop out of it all the time. You can read every word every year, yet the next day you might notice something you've never seen before. The Bible is a living book. Its truth is here to stay.*

---

## The Coming of the Son of Man

25 "Then there will be signs in the sun, moon, and stars; and there will be anguish on the earth among nations, bewildered by the roaring sea and waves. 26 People will faint from fear and expectation of the things that are coming on the world, because the celestial powers will be shaken. 27 Then they will see the •Son of Man coming in a cloud with power and great glory. 28 But when these things begin to take place, stand up and lift up your heads, because your redemption is near!"

## The Parable of the Fig Tree

29 Then He told them a parable: "Look at the fig tree, and all the trees. 30 As soon as they put out leaves you can see and know for yourselves that summer is already near. 31 In the same way, when you see these things happening, know that the kingdom of God is near. 32 •I assure you: This generation will certainly not pass away until all things take place. 33 Heaven and earth will pass away, but My words will never pass away.

## The Need for Watchfulness

34 "Be on your guard, so that your minds are not dulled from carousing, drunkenness, and worries of life, or that day will come on you unexpectedly 35 like a trap. For it will come on all who live on the face of the whole earth. 36 But be alert at all times, praying that you may have strength[a] to escape all these things that are going to take place, and to stand before the Son of Man."

37 During the day, He was teaching in the temple complex, but in the evening He would go out and spend the night on what is called the •Mount of Olives. 38 Then all the people would come early in the morning to hear Him in the temple complex.

[a]21:36 Other mss read *you may be counted worthy*

## The Plot to Kill Jesus

**22** The Festival of *Unleavened Bread, which is called *Passover, was drawing near. [2] The *chief priests and the *scribes were looking for a way to put Him to death, because they were afraid of the people.

[3] Then Satan entered Judas, called Iscariot, who was numbered among the Twelve. [4] He went away and discussed with the chief priests and temple police how he could hand Him over to them. [5] They were glad, and agreed to give him silver. [6] So he accepted the offer and started looking for a good opportunity to betray Him to them when the crowd was not present.

## Preparation for Passover

[7] Then the Day of Unleavened Bread came, on which the Passover lamb had to be sacrificed. [8] Jesus sent Peter and John, saying, "Go and prepare the Passover meal for us, so we may eat it."

[9] "Where do You want us to prepare it?" they asked Him.

[10] "Listen," He said to them, "when you've entered the city, a man carrying a water jug will meet you. Follow him into the house that he enters. [11] Tell the owner of the house, 'The Teacher asks you, "Where is the guest room where I may eat the Passover with My disciples?" ' [12] Then he will show you a large, furnished room upstairs. Make the preparations there."

[13] So they went and found it just as He had told them, and they prepared the Passover.

---

### Luke 22:17-20

*One of the most holy moments in the entire Christian experience is the observance of Communion or the Lord's Supper. Don't miss its deeper messages. Every time you receive the bread and the wine, you're a witness to life's most incredible mystery.*

---

## The First Lord's Supper

[14] When the hour came, He reclined at the table, and the apostles with Him. [15] Then He said to them, "I have fervently desired to eat this Passover with you before I suffer. [16] For I tell you, I will not eat it again[a] until it is fulfilled in the kingdom of God." [17] Then He took a cup, and after giving thanks, He said, "Take this and share it among yourselves. [18] For I tell you, from now on I will not drink of the fruit of the vine until the kingdom of God comes."

[19] And He took bread, gave thanks, broke it, gave it to them, and said, "This is My body, which is given for you. Do this in remembrance of Me."

[20] In the same way He also took the cup after supper and said, "This cup is the new covenant in My blood, which is shed for you.[b] [21] But look, the hand of the one betraying Me is at the table with Me! [22] For the *Son of Man will go away as it has been determined, but woe to that man by whom He is betrayed!"

---

[a] 22:16 Other mss omit *again*    [b] 22:19-20 Other mss omit *which is given for you* (v. 19) through the end of v. 20

23 So they began to argue among themselves which of them it could be who was going to do this thing.

## The Dispute over Greatness

24 Then a dispute also arose among them about who should be considered the greatest. 25 But He said to them, "The kings of the Gentiles dominate them, and those who have authority over them are called 'Benefactors.' 26 But it must not be like that among you. On the contrary, whoever is greatest among you must become like the youngest, and whoever leads, like the one serving. 27 For who is greater, the one at the table or the one serving? Isn't it the one at the table? But I am among you as the One who serves. 28 You are the ones who stood by Me in My trials. 29 I grant you a kingdom, just as My Father granted one to Me, 30 so that you may eat and drink at My table in My kingdom. And you will sit on thrones judging the 12 tribes of Israel.

## Peter's Denial Predicted

31 "Simon,a Simon, look out! Satan has asked to sift you like wheat. 32 But I have prayed for you, that your faith may not fail. And you, when you have turned back, strengthen your brothers."
33 "Lord," he told Him, "I'm ready to go with You both to prison and to death!"
34 "I tell you, Peter," He said, "the rooster will not crow today untilb you deny three times that you know Me!"

## Money-bag, Backpack, and Sword

35 He also said to them, "When I sent you out without money-bag, backpack, or sandals, did you lack anything?"
"Not a thing," they said.
36 Then He said to them, "But now, whoever has a money-bag should take it, and also a backpack. And whoever doesn't have a sword should sell his robe and buy one. 37 For I tell you, what is written must be fulfilled in Me: **And He was counted among the outlaws**.c Yes, what is written about Me is coming to its fulfillment."
38 "Lord," they said, "look, here are two swords."
"Enough of that!" He told them.

*"The Lord's supper is memorative, and so it has the nature and use of a pledge or token of love, left by a dying man to a dear surviving friend."*
*—John Flavel*

## The Prayer in the Garden

39 He went out and made His way as usual to the •Mount of Olives, and the disciples also followed Him. 40 When He reached the place, He told them, "Pray that you may not enter into temptation." 41 Then He withdrew from them about a stone's throw, knelt down, and began to pray, 42 "Father, if You are willing, take this cup away from Me—nevertheless, not My will, but Yours, be done."
[43 Then an angel from heaven appeared to Him, strengthening Him. 44 Being in anguish, He prayed more fervently, and His sweat became like drops of blood falling to the ground.]d

a22:31 Other mss read *Then the Lord said, "Simon, Simon*   b22:34 Other mss read *before*   c22:37 Is 53:12
d22:43-44 Other mss omit bracketed text

45 When He got up from prayer and came to the disciples, He found them sleeping, exhausted from their grief. 46 "Why are you sleeping?" He asked them. "Get up and pray, so that you may not enter into temptation."

## The Judas Kiss

47 While He was still speaking, suddenly a mob was there, and one of the Twelve named Judas was leading them. He came near Jesus to kiss Him, 48 but Jesus said to him, "Judas, are you betraying the Son of Man with a kiss?" 49 When those around Him saw what was going to happen, they asked, "Lord, should we strike with the sword?" 50 Then one of them struck the high priest's slave and cut off his right ear.

51 But Jesus responded, "No more of this!" And touching his ear, He healed him. 52 Then Jesus said to the chief priests, temple police, and the elders who had come for Him, "Have you come out with swords and clubs as if I were a criminal? 53 Every day while I was with you in the *temple complex, you never laid a hand on Me. But this is your hour—and the dominion of darkness."

## Peter Denies His Lord

54 They seized Him, led Him away, and brought Him into the high priest's house. Meanwhile Peter was following at a distance. 55 When they had lit a fire in the middle of the courtyard and sat down together, Peter sat among them. 56 When a servant saw him sitting in the firelight, and looked closely at him, she said, "This man was with Him too."

57 But he denied it: "Woman, I don't know Him!"

58 After a little while, someone else saw him and said, "You're one of them too!"

"Man, I am not!" Peter said.

59 About an hour later, another kept insisting, "This man was certainly with Him, since he's also a Galilean."

60 But Peter said, "Man, I don't know what you're talking about!" Immediately, while he was still speaking, a rooster crowed. 61 Then the Lord turned and looked at Peter. So Peter remembered the word of the Lord, how He had said to him, "Before the rooster crows today, you will deny Me three times." 62 And he went outside and wept bitterly.

## Jesus Mocked and Beaten

63 The men who were holding Jesus started mocking and beating Him. 64 After blindfolding Him, they kept[a] asking, "Prophesy! Who hit You?" 65 And they were saying many other blasphemous things against Him.

## Jesus Faces the Sanhedrin

66 When daylight came, the elders of the people, both the chief priests and the scribes, convened and brought Him before their *Sanhedrin. 67 They said, "If You are the *Messiah, tell us."

But He said to them, "If I do tell you, you will not believe. 68 And if I ask you, you will not answer. 69 But from now on, the Son of Man will be seated at the right hand of the Power of God."

70 They all asked, "Are You, then, the Son of God?"

And He said to them, "You say that I am."

71 "Why do we need any more testimony," they said, "since we've heard it ourselves from His mouth?"

a 22:64 Other mss add *striking Him on the face and*

## Jesus Faces Pilate

**23** Then their whole assembly rose up and brought Him before •Pilate. ² They began to accuse Him, saying, "We found this man subverting our nation, opposing payment of taxes to Caesar, and saying that He Himself is the •Messiah, a King."

³ So Pilate asked Him, "Are You the King of the Jews?"

He answered him, "You have said it."

⁴ Pilate then told the •chief priests and the crowds, "I find no grounds for charging this man."

⁵ But they kept insisting, "He stirs up the people, teaching throughout all Judea, from Galilee where He started even to here."

## Jesus Faces Herod Antipas

⁶ When Pilate heard this,ᵃ he asked if the man was a Galilean. ⁷ Finding that He was under •Herod's jurisdiction, he sent Him to Herod, who was also in Jerusalem during those days. ⁸ Herod was very glad to see Jesus; for a long time he had wanted to see Him, because he had heard about Him and was hoping to see some miracle performed by Him. ⁹ So he kept asking Him questions, but Jesus did not answer him. ¹⁰ The chief priests and the •scribes stood by, vehemently accusing Him. ¹¹ Then Herod, with his soldiers, treated Him with contempt, mocked Him, dressed Him in a brilliant robe, and sent Him back to Pilate. ¹² That very day Herod and Pilate became friends. Previously, they had been hostile toward each other.

## Jesus or Barabbas

¹³ Pilate called together the chief priests, the leaders, and the people, ¹⁴ and said to them, "You have brought me this man as one who subverts the people. But in fact, after examining Him in your presence, I have found no grounds to charge this man with those things you accuse Him of. ¹⁵ Neither has Herod, because he sent Him back to us. Clearly, He has done nothing to deserve death. ¹⁶ Therefore I will have Him whipped and release Him." ⌊¹⁷ For according to the festival he had to release someone to them.⌋ᵇ

¹⁸ Then they all cried out together, "Take this man away! Release Barabbas to us!" ¹⁹ (He had been thrown into prison for a rebellion that had taken place in the city, and for murder.) ²⁰ Pilate, wanting to release Jesus, addressed them again, ²¹ but they kept shouting, "Crucify! Crucify Him!"

²² A third time he said to them, "Why? What has this man done wrong? I have found in Him no grounds for the death penalty. Therefore I will have Him whipped and release Him."

²³ But they kept up the pressure, demanding with loud voices that He be crucified. And their voicesᶜ won out. ²⁴ So Pilate decided to grant their demand ²⁵ and released the one they were asking for, who had been thrown into prison for rebellion and murder. But he handed Jesus over to their will.

## The Way to the Cross

²⁶ As they led Him away, they seized Simon, a Cyrenian, who was coming in from the country, and laid the cross

---

ᵃ**23:6** Other mss read *heard "Galilee"*   ᵇ**23:17** Other mss omit bracketed text   ᶜ**23:23** Other mss add *and those of the chief priests*

on him to carry behind Jesus. 27 A great multitude of the people followed Him, including women who were mourning and lamenting Him. 28 But turning to them, Jesus said, "Daughters of Jerusalem, do not weep for Me, but weep for yourselves and your children. 29 Look, the days are coming when they will say, 'Blessed are the barren, the wombs that never bore, and the breasts that never nursed!' 30 Then they will begin **to say to the mountains, 'Fall on us!' and to the hills, 'Cover us!'**a 31 For if they do these things when the wood is green, what will happen when it is dry?"

### Crucified between Two Criminals

32 Two others—criminals—were also led away to be executed with Him. 33 When they arrived at the place called The Skull, they crucified Him there, along with the criminals, one on the right and one on the left. [34 Then Jesus said, "Father, forgive them, because they do not know what they are doing."] b And they divided His clothes and cast lots.

35 The people stood watching, and even the leaders kept scoffing: "He saved others; let Him save Himself if this is God's Messiah, the Chosen One!" 36 The soldiers also mocked Him. They came offering Him sour wine 37 and said, "If You are the King of the Jews, save Yourself!"

38 An inscription was above Him:c

> **THIS IS
> THE KING OF THE JEWS**

39 Then one of the criminals hanging there began to yell insults at Him:

"Aren't You the Messiah? Save Yourself and us!"

40 But the other answered, rebuking him: "Don't you even fear God, since you are undergoing the same punishment? 41 We are punished justly, because we're getting back what we deserve for the things we did, but this man has done nothing wrong." 42 Then he said, "Jesus, remember med when You come into Your kingdom!"

43 And He said to him, "•I assure you: Today you will be with Me in paradise."

---

### Luke 23:42-43

### The Kingdom

*The kingdom of God is a present reality. We are living in it right now, employed as its ambassadors, looking to Jesus as our final authority. But Christ's kingdom is also yet to come—a future reality where all who have received Him as Lord will live with Him forever in paradise.*

---

### The Death of Jesus

44 It was now about noon, and darkness came over the whole land until three, 45 because the sun's light failed.e The curtain of the sanctuary was split down the middle. 46 And Jesus called out with a loud voice, "Father, **into Your hands I entrust My spirit.**"f Saying this, He breathed His last.

a**23:30** Hs 10:8  b**23:34** Other mss omit bracketed text  c**23:38** Other mss add *written in Greek, Latin, and Hebrew letters*  d**23:42** Other mss add *Lord*  e**23:45** Other mss read *three, and the sun was darkened*  f**23:46** Ps 31:5

[47] When the •centurion saw what happened, he began to glorify God, saying, "This man really was righteous!" [48] All the crowds that had gathered for this spectacle, when they saw what had taken place, went home, striking their chests. [49] But all who knew Him, including the women who had followed Him from Galilee, stood at a distance, watching these things.

## The Burial of Jesus

[50] There was a good and righteous man named Joseph, a member of the •Sanhedrin, [51] who had not agreed with their plan and action. He was from Arimathea, a Judean town, and was looking forward to the kingdom of God. [52] He approached Pilate and asked for Jesus' body. [53] Taking it down, he wrapped it in fine linen and placed it in a tomb cut into the rock, where no one had ever been placed. [54] It was preparation day, and the Sabbath was about to begin. [55] The women who had come with Him from Galilee followed along and observed the tomb and how His body was placed. [56] Then they returned and prepared spices and perfumes. And they rested on the Sabbath according to the commandment.

## Resurrection Morning

**24** On the first day of the week, very early in the morning, they[a] came to the tomb, bringing the spices they had prepared. [2] They found the stone rolled away from the tomb. [3] They went in but did not find the body of the Lord Jesus. [4] While they were perplexed about this, suddenly two men stood by them in dazzling clothes. [5] So the women were terrified and bowed down to the ground.

"Why are you looking for the living among the dead?" asked the men. [6] "He is not here, but He has been resurrected! Remember how He spoke to you when He was still in Galilee, [7] saying, 'The •Son of Man must be betrayed into the hands of sinful men, be crucified, and rise on the third day'?" [8] And they remembered His words.

[9] Returning from the tomb, they reported all these things to the Eleven and to all the rest. [10] •Mary Magdalene, Joanna, Mary the mother of James, and the other women with them were telling the apostles these things. [11] But these words seemed like nonsense to them, and they did not believe the women. [12] Peter, however, got up and ran to the tomb. When he stooped to look in, he saw only the linen cloths.[b] So he went home, amazed at what had happened.

## The Emmaus Disciples

[13] Now that same day two of them were on their way to a village called Emmaus, which was about seven miles from Jerusalem. [14] Together they were discussing everything that had taken place. [15] And while they were discussing and arguing, Jesus Himself came near and began to walk along with them. [16] But they were prevented from recognizing Him. [17] Then He asked them, "What is this dispute that you're having with each other as you are walking?" And they stopped walking and looked discouraged.

[18] The one named Cleopas answered Him, "Are You the only visitor in Jerusalem who doesn't know the things that happened there in these days?"

[19] "What things?" He asked them.

---

[a]**24:1** Other mss add *and other women with them*   [b]**24:12** Other mss add *lying there*

So they said to Him, "The things concerning Jesus the •Nazarene, who was a Prophet powerful in action and speech before God and all the people, [20] and how our •chief priests and leaders handed Him over to be sentenced to death, and they crucified Him. [21] But we were hoping that He was the One who was about to redeem Israel. Besides all this, it's the third day since these things happened. [22] Moreover, some women from our group astounded us. They arrived early at the tomb, [23] and when they didn't find His body, they came and reported that they had seen a vision of angels who said He was alive. [24] Some of those who were with us went to the tomb and found it just as the women had said, but they didn't see Him."

[25] He said to them, "O how unwise and slow you are to believe in your hearts all that the prophets have spoken! [26] Didn't the •Messiah have to suffer these things and enter into His glory?" [27] Then beginning with Moses and all the Prophets, He interpreted for them in all the Scriptures the things concerning Himself.

[28] They came near the village where they were going, and He gave the impression that He was going farther. [29] But they urged Him: "Stay with us, because it's almost evening, and now the day is almost over." So He went in to stay with them.

[30] It was as He reclined at the table with them that He took the bread, blessed and broke it, and gave it to them. [31] Then their eyes were opened, and they recognized Him; but He disappeared from their sight. [32] So they said to each other, "Weren't our hearts ablaze within us while He was talking with us on the road and explaining the Scriptures to us?" [33] That very hour they got up and returned to Jerusalem.

They found the Eleven and those with them gathered together, [34] who said, "The Lord has certainly been raised, and has appeared to Simon!" [35] Then they began to describe what had happened on the road, and how He was made known to them in the breaking of the bread.

---

## Luke 24:44-48

### The Scriptures

*Hindsight is 20/20, right? In one of the final scenes from Jesus' life on earth, He tells His followers to look back, to remember what He had said before. There was the cross, then three days in the tomb. Think back even further, to everything that was written before. It was all about Him. And what He would do for us.*

---

## The Reality of the Risen Jesus

[36] And as they were saying these things, He Himself stood among them. He said to them, "Peace to you!" [37] But they were startled and terrified and thought they were seeing a ghost. [38] "Why are you troubled?" He asked them. "And why do doubts arise in your hearts? [39] Look at My hands and My feet, that it is I Myself! Touch Me and see, because a ghost does not have flesh and bones as you can see I have." [40] Having said this, He showed them His hands and feet. [41] But while they still could not believe for joy, and were amazed, He asked them, "Do you have anything here to eat?" [42] So they gave Him a piece of a

broiled fish,[a] [43] and He took it and ate in their presence.

[44] Then He told them, "These are My words that I spoke to you while I was still with you, that everything written about Me in the Law of Moses, the Prophets, and the Psalms must be fulfilled." [45] Then He opened their minds to understand the Scriptures. [46] He also said to them, "This is what is written:[b] the Messiah would suffer and rise from the dead the third day, [47] and repentance for[c] forgiveness of sins would be proclaimed in His name to all the nations, beginning at Jerusalem. [48] You are witnesses of these things. [49] And look, I am sending you what My Father promised. As for you, stay in the city[d] until you are empowered from on high."

## The Ascension of Jesus

[50] Then He led them out as far as Bethany, and lifting up His hands He blessed them. [51] And while He was blessing them, He left them and was carried up into heaven. [52] After worshiping Him, they returned to Jerusalem with great joy. [53] And they were continually in the •temple complex blessing God.[e]

---

[a]**24:42** Other mss add *and some honeycomb*   [b]**24:46** Other mss add *and thus it was necessary that*
[c]**24:47** Other mss read *repentance and*   [d]**24:49** Other mss add *of Jerusalem*   [e]**24:53** Other mss read *praising and blessing God. Amen.*

# JOHN

*Prologue*

**1** In the beginning was the
    Word;
  and the Word was with
    God,
  and the Word was God.
2 He was with God in the
    beginning.
3 All things were created through
    Him,
  and apart from Him not one
    thing was created
    that has been created.
4 In Him was life,[a]
  and that life was the light of
    men.
5 That light shines in the
    darkness,
  yet the darkness did not
    overcome it.

6 There was a man named John
  who was sent from God.
7 He came as a witness
  to testify about the light,
  so that all might believe through
    him.
8 He was not the light,
  but he came to testify about the
    light.
9 The true light, who gives light to
    everyone,
  was coming into the world.

10 He was in the world,
  and the world was created
    through Him,
  yet the world did not know
    Him.
11 He came to His own,
  and His own people did not
    receive Him.

12 But to all who did receive
    Him,
  He gave them the right to be
    children of God,
  to those who believe in His
    name,
13 who were born,
  not of blood,
  or of the will of the flesh,
  or of the will of man,
  but of God.
14 The Word became flesh
  and took up residence among
    us.
  We observed His glory,
  the glory as the •One and Only
    Son from the Father,
  full of grace and truth.

---

*John 1:12-13*

*Salvation*

*Our salvation was in the mind of
God before the foundation of the
world. Understand that for the miracle it is! The process He put in
place to bring about our passage
from death to eternal life came
about, not because we deserved it,
but because that's the way He
wanted it.*

---

15 (John testified concerning Him
    and exclaimed,
  "This was the One of whom I
    said,
  'The One coming after me

[a] **1:3-4** Other punctuation is possible: . . . *not one thing was created. What was created in Him was life*

has surpassed me,
because He existed before
me.' ")

16 For we have all received
grace after grace
from His fullness.

17 For the law was given through
Moses;
grace and truth came through
Jesus Christ.

18 No one has ever seen God.
The •One and Only Son[a]—
the One who is at the Father's
side—
He has revealed Him.

## John the Baptist's Testimony

19 This is John's testimony when the
Jews from Jerusalem sent priests and
Levites to ask him, "Who are you?"
20 He confessed and did not deny,
declaring, "I am not the •Messiah."
21 "What then?" they asked him.
"Are you Elijah?"
"I am not," he said.
"Are you the Prophet?"
"No," he answered.
22 "Who are you, then?" they asked.
"We need to give an answer to those
who sent us. What can you tell us
about yourself?"
23 He said, "I am a **voice of one crying out in the wilderness: Make
straight the way of the Lord**[b]—just
as Isaiah the prophet said."
24 Now they had been sent from the
•Pharisees. 25 So they asked him,
"Why then do you baptize if you
aren't the Messiah, or Elijah, or the
Prophet?"
26 "I baptize with water," John
answered them. "But among you
stands Someone you don't know. 27 He
is the One coming after me,[c] whose
sandal strap I'm not worthy to untie."

28 All this happened in Bethany[d]
across the Jordan, where John was
baptizing.

## The Lamb of God

29 The next day John saw Jesus coming toward him and said, "Here is the
Lamb of God, who takes away the sin
of the world! 30 This is the One I told
you about: 'After me comes a man
who has surpassed me, because He
existed before me.' 31 I didn't know
Him, but I came baptizing with water
so He might be revealed to Israel."
32 And John testified, "I watched the
Spirit descending from heaven like a
dove, and He rested upon Him. 33 I
didn't know Him, but He who sent me
to baptize with water told me, 'The
One on whom you see the Spirit
descending and resting—He is the
One baptizing with the Holy Spirit.'
34 I have seen and testified that He is
the Son of God!"[e]
35 Again the next day, John was
standing with two of his disciples.
36 When he saw Jesus passing by, he
said, "Look! The Lamb of God!"
37 The two disciples heard him say
this and followed Jesus. 38 When Jesus
turned and noticed them following
Him, He asked them, "What are you
looking for?"
They said to Him, "•Rabbi" (which
means "Teacher"), "where are You
staying?"
39 "Come and you'll see," He
replied. So they went and saw where
He was staying, and they stayed with
Him that day. It was about 10 in the
morning.
40 Andrew, Simon Peter's brother,
was one of the two who heard John
and followed Him. 41 He first found
his own brother Simon and told him,

---

[a]1:18 Other mss read *God*   [b]1:23 Is 40:3   [c]1:27 Other mss add *who came before me*   [d]1:28 Other mss read
*in Bethabara*   [e]1:34 Other mss read *is the Chosen One of God*

"We have found the Messiah!" (which means "Anointed One"), [42] and he brought ⌊Simon⌋ to Jesus.

When Jesus saw him, He said, "You are Simon, son of John.[a] You will be called •Cephas" (which means "Rock").

## Philip and Nathanael

[43] The next day He decided to leave for Galilee. Jesus found Philip and told him, "Follow Me!"

[44] Now Philip was from Bethsaida, the hometown of Andrew and Peter. [45] Philip found Nathanael and told him, "We have found the One of whom Moses wrote in the law (and so did the prophets): Jesus the son of Joseph, from Nazareth!"

[46] "Can anything good come out of Nazareth?" Nathanael asked him.

"Come and see," Philip answered.

[47] Then Jesus saw Nathanael coming toward Him and said about him, "Here is a true Israelite in whom is no deceit."

[48] "How do you know me?" Nathanael asked.

"Before Philip called you, when you were under the fig tree, I saw you," Jesus answered.

[49] "Rabbi," Nathanael replied, "You are the Son of God! You are the King of Israel!"

[50] Jesus responded to him, "Do you believe ⌊only⌋ because I told you I saw you under the fig tree? You will see greater things than this." [51] Then He said, "•I assure you: You will see heaven opened and the angels of God ascending and descending upon the •Son of Man."

## The First Sign: Turning Water into Wine

**2** On the third day a wedding took place in Cana of Galilee. Jesus' mother was there, and [2] Jesus and His disciples were invited to the wedding as well. [3] When the wine ran out, Jesus' mother told Him, "They don't have any wine."

[4] "What has this concern of yours to do with Me, woman?" Jesus asked. "My hour has not yet come."

[5] "Do whatever He tells you," His mother told the servants.

[6] Now six stone water jars had been set there for Jewish purification. Each contained 20 or 30 gallons.

[7] "Fill the jars with water," Jesus told them. So they filled them to the brim. [8] Then He said to them, "Now draw some out and take it to the chief servant." And they did.

[9] When the chief servant tasted the water (after it had become wine), he did not know where it came from— though the servants who had drawn the water knew. He called the groom [10] and told him, "Everybody sets out the fine wine first, then, after people have drunk freely, the inferior. But you have kept the fine wine until now."

[11] Jesus performed this first sign in Cana of Galilee. He displayed His glory, and His disciples believed in Him.

[12] After this He went down to Capernaum, together with His mother, His brothers, and His disciples, and they stayed there only a few days.

## Cleansing the Temple Complex

[13] The Jewish •Passover was near, so Jesus went up to Jerusalem. [14] In the

---

[a]1:42 Other mss read *Simon, son of Jonah*

•temple complex He found people selling oxen, sheep, and doves, and ⌊He also found⌋ the money changers sitting there. [15] After making a whip out of cords, He drove everyone out of the temple complex with their sheep and oxen. He also poured out the money changers' coins and overturned the tables. [16] He told those who were selling doves, "Get these things out of here! Stop turning my Father's house into a marketplace!"

[17] And His disciples remembered that it is written: **Zeal for Your house will consume Me.**[a]

[18] So the Jews replied to Him, "What sign ⌊of authority⌋ will You show us for doing these things?"

[19] Jesus answered, "Destroy this sanctuary, and I will raise it up in three days."

[20] Therefore the Jews said, "This sanctuary took 46 years to build, and will You raise it up in three days?"

[21] But He was speaking about the sanctuary of His body. [22] So when He was raised from the dead, His disciples remembered that He had said this. And they believed the Scripture and the statement Jesus had made.

[23] While He was in Jerusalem at the Passover Festival, many trusted in His name when they saw the signs He was doing. [24] Jesus, however, would not entrust Himself to them, since He knew them all [25] and because He did not need anyone to testify about man; for He Himself knew what was in man.

### Jesus and Nicodemus

3 There was a man from the •Pharisees named Nicodemus, a ruler of the Jews. [2] This man came to Him at night and said, "•Rabbi, we know that You have come from God as a teacher, for no one could perform these signs You do unless God were with him."

[3] Jesus replied, "•I assure you: Unless someone is born again, he cannot see the kingdom of God."

---

*John 3:4-6*

*Salvation*

*This explanation baffled the religious leader who approached Jesus under cover of darkness to find out what He was all about. What a great description of what happens to us at salvation. We begin again as new people in Christ, no longer living as a slave of sin but as a child of God.*

---

[4] "But how can anyone be born when he is old?" Nicodemus asked Him. "Can he enter his mother's womb a second time and be born?"

[5] Jesus answered, "I assure you: Unless someone is born of water and the Spirit, he cannot enter the kingdom of God. [6] Whatever is born of the flesh is flesh, and whatever is born of the Spirit is spirit. [7] Do not be amazed that I told you that you must be born again. [8] The wind blows where it pleases, and you hear its sound, but you don't know where it comes from or where it is going. So it is with everyone born of the Spirit."

[9] "How can these things be?" asked Nicodemus.

[10] "Are you a teacher of Israel and don't know these things?" Jesus replied. [11] "I assure you: We speak what We know and We testify to

---
[a]2:17 Ps 69:9

what We have seen, but you do not accept Our testimony. [12] If I have told you about things that happen on earth and you don't believe, how will you believe if I tell you about things of heaven? [13] No one has ascended into heaven except the One who descended from heaven—the *Son of Man.[a] [14] Just as Moses lifted up the serpent in the wilderness, so the *Son of Man must be lifted up, [15] so that everyone who believes in Him will[b] have eternal life.

---

### John 3:16-18

### Salvation

*You might recognize these as some of the Bible's most well-known verses, and for good reason. In the matter of a few phrases, it gives us a vivid description of God's great love for us—a love that motivated Him to give of Himself in order that we might not get what was coming to us.*

---

[16] "For God loved the world in this way: He gave His *One and Only Son, so that everyone who believes in Him will not perish but have eternal life. [17] For God did not send His Son into the world that He might judge the world, but that the world might be saved through Him. [18] Anyone who believes in Him is not judged, but anyone who does not believe is already judged, because he has not believed in the name of the *One and Only Son of God.

[19] "This, then, is the judgment: the light has come into the world, and people loved darkness rather than the light because their deeds were evil. [20] For everyone who practices wicked things hates the light and avoids it, so that his deeds may not be exposed. [21] But anyone who lives by the truth comes to the light, so that his works may be shown to be accomplished by God."

### Jesus and John the Baptist

[22] After this Jesus and His disciples went to the Judean countryside, where He spent time with them and baptized. [23] John also was baptizing in Aenon near Salim, because there was plenty of water there. And people were coming and being baptized, [24] since John had not yet been thrown into prison.

[25] Then a dispute arose between John's disciples and a Jew[c] about purification. [26] So they came to John and told him, "Rabbi, the One you testified about, and who was with you across the Jordan, is baptizing—and everyone is flocking to Him."

[27] John responded, "No one can receive a single thing unless it's given to him from heaven. [28] You yourselves can testify that I said, 'I am not the *Messiah, but I've been sent ahead of Him.' [29] He who has the bride is the groom. But the groom's friend, who stands by and listens for him, rejoices greatly at the groom's voice. So this joy of mine is complete. [30] He must increase, but I must decrease."

### The One from Heaven

[31] The One who comes from above is above all. The one who is from the earth is earthly and speaks in earthly terms. The One who comes from heaven is above all. [32] He testifies to

---

[a]3:13 Other mss add *who is in heaven*   [b]3:15 Other mss add *not perish, but*   [c]3:25 Other mss read *and the Jews*

what He has seen and heard, yet no one accepts His testimony. [33] The one who has accepted His testimony has affirmed that God is true. [34] For He whom God sent speaks God's words, since He[a] gives the Spirit without measure. [35] The Father loves the Son and has given all things into His hands. [36] The one who believes in the Son has eternal life, but the one who refuses to believe in the Son will not see life; instead, the wrath of God remains on him.

## Jesus and the Samaritan Woman

**4** When Jesus[b] knew that the •Pharisees heard He was making and baptizing more disciples than John [2] (though Jesus Himself was not baptizing, but His disciples were), [3] He left Judea and went again to Galilee. [4] He had to travel through Samaria, [5] so He came to a town of Samaria called Sychar near the property that Jacob had given his son Joseph. [6] Jacob's well was there, and Jesus, worn out from His journey, sat down at the well. It was about six in the evening.

[7] A woman of Samaria came to draw water.

"Give Me a drink," Jesus said to her, [8] for His disciples had gone into town to buy food.

[9] "How is it that You, a Jew, ask for a drink from me, a •Samaritan woman?" she asked. For Jews do not associate with Samaritans.[c]

[10] Jesus answered, "If you knew the gift of God, and who is saying to you, 'Give Me a drink,' you would ask Him, and He would give you living water."

[11] "Sir," said the woman, "You don't even have a bucket, and the well is deep. So where do you get this 'living water'? [12] You aren't greater than our father Jacob, are you? He gave us the well and drank from it himself, as did his sons and livestock."

[13] Jesus said, "Everyone who drinks from this water will get thirsty again. [14] But whoever drinks from the water that I will give him will never get thirsty again—ever! In fact, the water I will give him will become a well of water springing up within him for eternal life."

[15] "Sir," the woman said to Him, "give me this water so I won't get thirsty and come here to draw water."

[16] "Go call your husband," He told her, "and come back here."

[17] "I don't have a husband," she answered.

> "Until you are ready to make any adjustment necessary to follow and obey what God has said, you will be of little use to God."
> —Henry Blackaby

"You have correctly said, 'I don't have a husband,' " Jesus said. [18] "For you've had five husbands, and the man you now have is not your husband. What you have said is true."

[19] "Sir," the woman replied, "I see that You are a prophet. [20] Our fathers worshiped on this mountain, yet you [Jews] say that the place to worship is in Jerusalem."

[21] Jesus told her, "Believe Me, woman, an hour is coming when you will worship the Father neither on this mountain nor in Jerusalem. [22] You Samaritans worship what you do not know. We worship what we do know, because salvation is from

---

[a]**3:34** Other mss read *since God*   [b]**4:1** Other mss read *the Lord*   [c]**4:9** Other mss omit *For Jews do not associate with Samaritans.*

the Jews. [23] But an hour is coming, and is now here, when the true worshipers will worship the Father in spirit and truth. Yes, the Father wants such people to worship Him. [24] God is Spirit, and those who worship Him must worship in spirit and truth."

[25] The woman said to Him, "I know that •Messiah is coming" (who is called Christ). "When He comes, He will explain everything to us."

[26] "I am He," Jesus told her, "the One speaking to you."

## The Ripened Harvest

[27] Just then His disciples arrived, and they were amazed that He was talking with a woman. Yet no one said, "What do You want?" or "Why are You talking with her?"

[28] Then the woman left her water jar, went into town, and told the men, [29] "Come, see a man who told me everything I ever did! Could this be the Messiah?" [30] They left the town and made their way to Him.

[31] In the meantime the disciples kept urging Him, "•Rabbi, eat something."

[32] But He said, "I have food to eat that you don't know about."

[33] The disciples said to one another, "Could someone have brought Him something to eat?"

[34] "My food is to do the will of Him who sent Me and to finish His work," Jesus told them. [35] "Don't you say, 'There are still four more months, then comes the harvest'? Listen to what I'm telling you: Open your eyes and look at the fields, for they are ready for harvest. [36] The reaper is already receiving pay and gathering fruit for eternal life, so the sower and reaper can rejoice together. [37] For in this case the saying is true: 'One sows and another reaps.' [38] I sent you to reap what you didn't labor for; others have labored, and you have benefited from their labor."

## The Savior of the World

[39] Now many Samaritans from that town believed in Him because of what the woman said when she testified, "He told me everything I ever did." [40] Therefore, when the Samaritans came to Him, they asked Him to stay with them, and He stayed there two days. [41] Many more believed because of what He said. [42] And they told the woman, "We no longer believe because of what you said, for we have heard for ourselves and know that this really is the Savior of the world."[a]

---

### John 4:31-34

*God looks at things differently than we do. In His kingdom, leaders serve. Givers receive. Those who pour their lives out in service to others find their own cup filled to overflowing. Wanting your own way starts early in life, but the sooner you start giving it up, the better off you'll be.*

---

## A Galilean Welcome

[43] After two days He left there for Galilee. [44] Jesus Himself testified that a prophet has no honor in his own country. [45] When they entered Galilee, the Galileans welcomed Him because they had seen everything He

[a]**4:42** Other mss add *the Messiah*

did in Jerusalem during the festival. For they also had gone to the festival.

## The Second Sign: Healing an Official's Son

46 Then He went again to Cana of Galilee, where He had turned the water into wine. There was a certain royal official whose son was ill at Capernaum. 47 When this man heard that Jesus had come from Judea into Galilee, he went to Him and pleaded with Him to come down and heal his son, for he was about to die. 48 Jesus told him, "Unless you |people| see signs and wonders, you will not believe." 49 "Sir," the official said to Him, "come down before my boy dies!" 50 "Go," Jesus told him, "your son will live." The man believed what Jesus said to him and departed. 51 While he was still going down, his slaves met him saying that his boy was alive. 52 He asked them at what time he got better. "Yesterday at seven in the morning the fever left him," they answered. 53 The father realized this was the very hour at which Jesus had told him, "Your son will live." Then he himself believed, along with his whole household. 54 This therefore was the second sign Jesus performed after He came from Judea to Galilee.

## The Third Sign: Healing the Sick

5 After this a Jewish festival took place, and Jesus went up to Jerusalem. 2 By the Sheep Gate in Jerusalem there is a pool, called Bethesda[a] in Hebrew, which has five colonnades. 3 Within these lay a multitude of the sick—blind, lame, and paralyzed |—waiting for the moving of the water, 4 because an angel would go down into the pool from time to time and stir up the water. Then the first one who got in after the water was stirred up recovered from whatever ailment he had|.[b] 5 One man was there who had been sick for 38 years. 6 When Jesus saw him lying there and knew he had already been there a long time, He said to him, "Do you want to get well?" 7 "Sir," the sick man answered, "I don't have a man to put me into the pool when the water is stirred up, but while I'm coming, someone goes down ahead of me." 8 "Get up," Jesus told him, "pick up your bedroll and walk!" 9 Instantly the man got well, picked up his bedroll, and started to walk.

Now that day was the Sabbath, 10 so the Jews said to the man who had been healed, "This is the Sabbath! It's illegal for you to pick up your bedroll." 11 He replied, "The man who made me well told me, 'Pick up your bedroll and walk.'" 12 "Who is this man who told you, 'Pick up |your bedroll| and walk?'" they asked. 13 But the man who was cured did not know who it was, because Jesus had slipped away into the crowd that was there. 14 After this Jesus found him in the •temple complex and said to him, "See, you are well. Do not sin any more, so that something worse doesn't happen to you." 15 The man went and reported to the Jews that it was Jesus who had made him well.

## Honoring the Father and the Son

16 Therefore, the Jews began persecuting Jesus[c] because He was doing these things on the Sabbath. 17 But

---

a 5:2 Other mss read *Bethzatha*; others read *Bethsaida*   b 5:3-4 Other mss omit bracketed text   c 5:16 Other mss add *and trying to kill Him*

Jesus responded to them, "My Father is still working, and I also am working." [18] This is why the Jews began trying all the more to kill Him: not only was He breaking the Sabbath, but He was even calling God His own Father, making Himself equal with God.

[19] Then Jesus replied, "•I assure you: The Son is not able to do anything on His own, but only what He sees the Father doing. For whatever the Father does, these things the Son also does in the same way. [20] For the Father loves the Son and shows Him everything He is doing, and He will show Him greater works than these so that you will be amazed. [21] And just as the Father raises the dead and gives them life, so also the Son gives life to whomever He wishes. [22] The Father, in fact, judges no one but has given all judgment to the Son, [23] so that all people will honor the Son just as they honor the Father. Anyone who does not honor the Son does not honor the Father who sent Him.

## Life and Judgment

[24] "I assure you: Anyone who hears My word and believes Him who sent Me has eternal life and will not come under judgment, but has passed from death to life.

[25] "I assure you: An hour is coming, and is now here, when the dead will hear the voice of the Son of God, and those who hear will live. [26] For just as the Father has life in Himself, so also He has granted to the Son to have life in Himself. [27] And He has granted Him the right to pass judgment, because He is the •Son of Man. [28] Do not be amazed at this, because a time is coming when all who are in the graves will hear His voice [29] and come out—those who have done good things, to the resurrection of

life, but those who have done wicked things, to the resurrection of judgment.

[30] "I can do nothing on My own. Only as I hear do I judge, and My judgment is righteous, because I do not seek My own will, but the will of Him who sent Me.

════════════════════

### John 5:24

### Salvation

*This "passing" from death to life is one of the great pictures of salvation. Receiving God's grace is like passing through an open door, leaving behind a world where death and emptiness hide in every corner, walking into a breezy, sunlit world of joy, unfailing love, and lasting purpose.*

════════════════════

## Four Witnesses to Jesus

[31] "If I testify about Myself, My testimony is not valid. [32] There is Another who testifies about Me, and I know that the testimony He gives about Me is valid. [33] You ⌊people⌋ have sent ⌊messengers⌋ to John, and he has testified to the truth. [34] I don't receive man's testimony, but I say these things so that you may be saved. [35] John was a burning and shining lamp, and for an hour you were willing to enjoy his light.

[36] "But I have a greater testimony than John's because of the works that the Father has given Me to accomplish. These very works I am doing testify about Me that the Father has sent Me. [37] The Father who sent Me has Himself testified about Me. You have not heard

His voice at any time, and you haven't seen His form. [38] You don't have His word living in you, because you don't believe the One He sent. [39] You pore over the Scriptures because you think you have eternal life in them, yet they testify about Me. [40] And you are not willing to come to Me that you may have life.

[41] "I do not accept glory from men, [42] but I know you—that you have no love for God within you. [43] I have come in My Father's name, yet you don't accept Me. If someone else comes in his own name, you will accept him. [44] How can you believe? While accepting glory from one another, you don't seek the glory that comes from the only God. [45] Do not think that I will accuse you to the Father. Your accuser is Moses, on whom you have set your hope. [46] For if you believed Moses, you would believe Me, because he wrote about Me. [47] But if you don't believe his writings, how will you believe My words?"

## The Fourth Sign: Feeding 5,000

**6** After this Jesus crossed the Sea of Galilee (or Tiberias). [2] And a huge crowd was following Him because they saw the signs that He was performing on the sick. [3] So Jesus went up a mountain and sat down there with His disciples.

[4] Now the •Passover, a Jewish festival, was near. [5] Therefore, when Jesus raised His eyes and noticed a huge crowd coming toward Him, He asked Philip, "Where will we buy bread so these people can eat?" [6] He asked this to test him, for He Himself knew what He was going to do.

[7] Philip answered, "Two hundred denarii worth of bread wouldn't be enough for each of them to have a little."

[8] One of His disciples, Andrew, Simon Peter's brother, said to Him, [9] "There's a boy here who has five barley loaves and two fish—but what are they for so many?"

[10] Then Jesus said, "Have the people sit down."

There was plenty of grass in that place, so the men sat down, numbering about 5,000. [11] Then Jesus took the loaves, and after giving thanks He distributed them to those who were seated; so also with the fish, as much as they wanted.

[12] When they were full, He told His disciples, "Collect the leftovers so that nothing is wasted." [13] So they collected them and filled 12 baskets with the pieces from the five barley loaves that were left over by those who had eaten.

[14] When the people saw the sign[a] He had done, they said, "This really is the Prophet who was to come into the world!" [15] Therefore, when Jesus knew that they were about to come and take Him by force to make Him king, He withdrew again to the mountain by Himself.

## The Fifth Sign: Walking on Water

[16] When evening came, His disciples went down to the sea, [17] got into a boat, and started across the sea to Capernaum. Darkness had already set in, but Jesus had not yet come to them. [18] Then a high wind arose, and the sea began to churn. [19] After they had rowed about three or four miles, they saw Jesus walking on the sea. He was coming near the boat, and they were afraid.

[a]6:14 Other mss read *signs*

20 But He said to them, "It is I. Don't be afraid!" 21 Then they were willing to take Him on board, and at once the boat was at the shore where they were heading.

## The Bread of Life

22 The next day, the crowd that had stayed on the other side of the sea knew there had been only one boat.ᵃ [They also knew] that Jesus had not boarded the boat with His disciples, but His disciples had gone off alone. 23 Some boats from Tiberias came near the place where they ate the bread after the Lord gave thanks. 24 When the crowd saw that neither Jesus nor His disciples were there, they got into the boats and went to Capernaum, looking for Jesus. 25 When they found Him on the other side of the sea, they said to Him, "•Rabbi, when did You get here?" 26 Jesus answered, "•I assure you: You are looking for Me, not because you saw the signs, but because you ate the loaves and were filled. 27 Don't work for the food that perishes but for the food that lasts for eternal life, which the •Son of Man will give you, because on Him God the Father has set His seal of approval."

28 "What can we do to perform the works of God?" they asked.

29 Jesus replied, "This is the work of God: that you believe in the One He has sent."

30 "Then what sign are You going to do so we may see and believe You?" they asked. "What are You going to perform? 31 Our fathers ate the manna in the desert, just as it is written: **He gave them bread from heaven to eat.**"ᵇ

32 Jesus said to them, "I assure you: Moses didn't give you the bread from heaven, but My Father gives you the true bread from heaven. 33 For the bread of God is the One who comes down from heaven and gives life to the world."

34 Then they said, "Sir, give us this bread always!"

35 "I am the bread of life," Jesus told them. "No one who comes to Me will ever be hungry, and no one who believes in Me will ever be thirsty again. 36 But as I told you, you've seen Me,ᶜ and yet you do not believe. 37 Everyone the Father gives Me will come to Me, and the one who comes to Me I will never cast out. 38 For I have come down from heaven, not to do My will, but the will of Him who sent Me. 39 This is the will of Him who sent Me: that I should lose none of those He has given Me but should raise them up on the last day. 40 For this is the will of My Father: that everyone who sees the Son and believes in Him may have eternal life, and I will raise him up on the last day."

---

### John 6:35-46

*You may have felt like you were the one doing all the chasing, that you were the one weighing your options and giving God a chance to show what He can do. But God's been after you a long time, hounding you with a love that wouldn't let up until you were safely home.*

---

41 Therefore the Jews started complaining about Him, because He said, "I

---

am the bread that came down from heaven." [42] They were saying, "Isn't this Jesus the son of Joseph, whose father and mother we know? How can He now say, 'I have come down from heaven'?"

[43] Jesus answered them, "Stop complaining among yourselves. [44] No one can come to Me unless the Father who sent Me draws him, and I will raise him up on the last day. [45] It is written in the Prophets: **And they will all be taught by God.**[a] Everyone who has listened to and learned from the Father comes to Me— [46] not that anyone has seen the Father except the One who is from God. He has seen the Father.

[47] "I assure you: Anyone who believes[b] has eternal life. [48] I am the bread of life. [49] Your fathers ate the manna in the desert, and they died. [50] This is the bread that comes down from heaven so that anyone may eat of it and not die. [51] I am the living bread that came down from heaven. If anyone eats of this bread he will live forever. The bread that I will give for the life of the world is My flesh."

[52] At that, the Jews argued among themselves, "How can this man give us His flesh to eat?"

[53] So Jesus said to them, "I assure you: Unless you eat the flesh of the Son of Man and drink His blood, you do not have life in yourselves. [54] Anyone who eats My flesh and drinks My blood has eternal life, and I will raise him up on the last day, [55] because My flesh is true food and My blood is true drink. [56] The one who eats My flesh and drinks My blood lives in Me, and I in him. [57] Just as the living Father sent Me and I live because of the Father, so the one who feeds on Me will live because of Me. [58] This is the bread that came down from heaven; it is not like the manna[c] your fathers ate—and they died. The one who eats this bread will live forever."

[59] He said these things while teaching in the *synagogue in Capernaum.

---

*"How could the initiative lie on my side? If Shakespeare and Hamlet could ever meet, it must be Shakespeare's doing."*
—C. S. Lewis

---

## Many Disciples Desert Jesus

[60] Therefore, when many of His disciples heard this, they said, "This teaching is hard! Who can accept it?"

[61] Jesus, knowing in Himself that His disciples were complaining about this, asked them, "Does this offend you? [62] Then what if you were to observe the Son of Man ascending to where He was before? [63] The Spirit is the One who gives life. The flesh doesn't help at all. The words that I have spoken to you are spirit and are life. [64] But there are some among you who don't believe." (For Jesus knew from the beginning those who would not[d] believe and the one who would betray Him.) [65] He said, "This is why I told you that no one can come to Me unless it is granted to him by the Father."

[66] From that moment many of His disciples turned back and no longer walked with Him. [67] Therefore Jesus said to the Twelve, "You don't want to go away too, do you?"

[68] Simon Peter answered, "Lord, to whom should we go? You have the words of eternal life. [69] And we have

[a]6:45 Is 54:13  [b]6:47 Other mss add *in Me*  [c]6:58 Other mss omit *the manna*  [d]6:64 Other mss omit *not*

come to believe and know that You are the Holy One of God!"[a]

[70] Jesus replied to them, "Didn't I choose you, the Twelve? Yet one of you is the Devil!" [71] He was referring to Judas, Simon Iscariot's son,[b] one of the Twelve, because he was going to betray Him.

## The Unbelief of Jesus' Brothers

**7** After this Jesus traveled in Galilee, since He did not want to travel in Judea because the Jews were trying to kill Him. [2] The Jewish Festival of *Tabernacles was near, [3] so His brothers said to Him, "Leave here and go to Judea so Your disciples can see Your works that You are doing. [4] For no one does anything in secret while he's seeking public recognition. If You do these things, show Yourself to the world." [5] (For not even His brothers believed in Him.)

[6] Jesus told them, "My time has not yet arrived, but your time is always at hand. [7] The world cannot hate you, but it does hate Me because I testify about it—that its deeds are evil. [8] Go up to the festival yourselves. I'm not going up to the festival yet,[c] because My time has not yet fully come." [9] After He had said these things, He stayed in Galilee.

---

*"The way to cultivate true graces of character is by submitting ourselves utterly to the Spirit to do His work and to bear His fruit."*

—R. A. Torrey

---

## Jesus at the Festival of Tabernacles

[10] When His brothers had gone up to the festival, then He also went up, not openly but secretly. [11] The Jews were looking for Him at the festival and saying, "Where is He?" [12] And there was a lot of discussion about Him among the crowds. Some were saying, "He's a good man." Others were saying, "No, on the contrary, He's deceiving the people." [13] Still, nobody was talking publicly about Him because they feared the Jews.

[14] When the festival was already half over, Jesus went up into the *temple complex and began to teach. [15] Then the Jews were amazed and said, "How does He know the Scriptures, since He hasn't been trained?"

[16] Jesus answered them, "My teaching isn't Mine, but is from the One who sent Me. [17] If anyone wants to do His will, he will understand whether the teaching is from God or if I am speaking on My own. [18] The one who speaks for himself seeks his own glory. But He who seeks the glory of the One who sent Him is true, and unrighteousness is not in Him. [19] Didn't Moses give you the law? Yet none of you keeps the law! Why do you want to kill Me?"

[20] "You have a demon!" the crowd responded. "Who wants to kill You?"

[21] "I did one work, and you are all amazed," Jesus answered. [22] "Consider this: Moses has given you circumcision—not that it comes from Moses but from the fathers—and you circumcise a man on the Sabbath. [23] If a man receives circumcision on the Sabbath so that the law of Moses won't be broken, are you angry at Me because I made a man entirely well on the Sabbath? [24] Stop

---

[a]**6:69** Other mss read *You are the Messiah, the Son of the Living God*    [b]**6:71** Other mss read *Judas Iscariot, Simon's son*    [c]**7:8** Other mss omit *yet*

judging according to outward appearances; rather judge according to righteous judgment."

## The Identity of the Messiah

[25] Some of the people of Jerusalem were saying, "Isn't this the man they want to kill? [26] Yet, look! He's speaking publicly and they're saying nothing to Him. Can it be true that the authorities know He is the •Messiah? [27] But we know where this man is from. When the Messiah comes, nobody will know where He is from."

[28] As He was teaching in the temple complex, Jesus cried out, "You know Me and you know where I am from. Yet I have not come on My own, but the One who sent Me is true. You don't know Him; [29] I know Him because I am from Him, and He sent Me."

[30] Therefore they tried to seize Him. Yet no one laid a hand on Him because His hour had not yet come. [31] However, many from the crowd believed in Him and said, "When the Messiah comes, He won't perform more signs than this man has done, will He?"

[32] The •Pharisees heard the crowd muttering these things about Him, so the •chief priests and the Pharisees sent temple police to arrest Him.

[33] Therefore Jesus said, "I am only with you for a short time. Then I'm going to the One who sent Me. [34] You will look for Me, and you will not find Me; and where I am, you cannot come."

[35] Then the Jews said to one another, "Where does He intend to go so we won't find Him? He doesn't intend to go to the Dispersion among the Greeks and teach the Greeks, does He? [36] What is this remark He made: 'You will look for Me, and you will not find Me; and where I am, you cannot come'?"

## The Promise of the Spirit

[37] On the last and most important day of the festival, Jesus stood up and cried out, "If anyone is thirsty, he should come to Me[a] and drink! [38] The one who believes in Me, as the Scripture has said, will have streams of living water flow from deep within him." [39] He said this about the Spirit, whom those who believed in Him were going to receive, for the Spirit[b] had not yet been received,[c] because Jesus had not yet been glorified.

---

### John 7:37-39

*In order for you to be all that God wants you to become, you'll need much more than a sturdy resolve. You'll need the Holy Spirit of God. He has a way of empowering you that's better than anything you can come up with on your own.*

---

## The People Are Divided over Jesus

[40] When some from the crowd heard these words, they said, "This really is the Prophet!" [41] Others said, "This is the Messiah!" But some said, "Surely the Messiah doesn't come from Galilee, does He? [42] Doesn't the Scripture say that the Messiah comes from David's offspring and from the town of Bethlehem, where David once lived?" [43] So a division occurred among the crowd because of Him.

[a]7:37 Other mss omit *to Me*   [b]7:39 Other mss read *Holy Spirit*   [c]7:39 Other mss read *had not yet been given*

44 Some of them wanted to seize Him, but no one laid hands on Him.

## Debate over Jesus' Claims

45 Then the temple police came to the chief priests and Pharisees, who asked them, "Why haven't you brought Him?"

46 The police answered, "No man ever spoke like this!"[a]

47 Then the Pharisees responded to them: "Are you fooled too? 48 Have any of the rulers believed in Him? Or any of the Pharisees? 49 But this crowd, which doesn't know the law, is accursed!"

50 Nicodemus—the one who came to Him previously, being one of them—said to them, 51 "Our law doesn't judge a man before it hears from him and knows what he's doing, does it?"

52 "You aren't from Galilee too, are you?" they replied. "Search and see: no prophet arises from Galilee."

⌊53 So each one went to his house.

**8** 1 But Jesus went to the •Mount of Olives.

## An Adulteress Forgiven

2 At dawn He went to the •temple complex again, and all the people were coming to Him. He sat down and began to teach them.

3 Then the •scribes and the •Pharisees brought a woman caught in adultery, making her stand in the center. 4 "Teacher," they said to Him, "this woman was caught in the act of committing adultery. 5 In the law Moses commanded us to stone such women. So what do You say?" 6 They asked this to trap Him, in order that they might have evidence to accuse Him.

Jesus stooped down and started writing on the ground with His finger. 7 When they persisted in questioning Him, He stood up and said to them, "The one without sin among you should be the first to throw a stone at her."

8 Then He stooped down again and continued writing on the ground. 9 When they heard this, they left one by one, starting with the older men. Only He was left, with the woman in the center. 10 When Jesus stood up, He said to her, "Woman, where are they? Has no one condemned you?"

11 "No one, Lord," she answered.

"Neither do I condemn you," said Jesus. "Go, and from now on do not sin any more."⌋[b]

12 Then Jesus spoke to them again: "I am the light of the world. Anyone who follows Me will never walk in the darkness, but will have the light of life."

## Jesus' Self-witness

13 So the Pharisees said to Him, "You are testifying about Yourself. Your testimony is not valid."

14 "Even if I testify about Myself," Jesus replied, "My testimony is valid, because I know where I came from and where I'm going. But you don't know where I come from or where I'm going. 15 You judge by human standards. I judge no one. 16 And if I do judge, My judgment is true, because I am not alone, but I and the Father who sent Me ⌊judge together⌋. 17 Even in your law it is written that the witness of two men is valid. 18 I am the One who testifies about Myself, and the Father who sent Me testifies about Me."

a7:46 Other mss read *like this man*   b8:11 Other mss omit bracketed text

¹⁹ Then they asked Him, "Where is Your Father?"

"You know neither Me nor My Father," Jesus answered. "If you knew Me, you would also know My Father." ²⁰ He spoke these words by the treasury, while teaching in the temple complex. But no one seized Him, because His hour had not come.

### Jesus Predicts His Departure

²¹ Then He said to them again, "I'm going away; you will look for Me, and you will die in your sin. Where I'm going, you cannot come."

²² So the Jews said again, "He won't kill Himself, will He, since He says, 'Where I'm going, you cannot come'?"

²³ "You are from below," He told them, "I am from above. You are of this world; I am not of this world. ²⁴ Therefore I told you that you will die in your sins. For if you do not believe that I am He, you will die in your sins."

²⁵ "Who are You?" they questioned.

"Precisely what I've been telling you from the very beginning," Jesus told them. ²⁶ "I have many things to say and to judge about you, but the One who sent Me is true, and what I have heard from Him—these things I tell the world."

²⁷ They did not know He was speaking to them about the Father. ²⁸ So Jesus said to them, "When you lift up the •Son of Man, then you will know that I am He, and that I do nothing on My own. But just as the Father taught Me, I say these things. ²⁹ The One who sent Me is with Me. He has not left Me alone, because I always do what pleases Him."

---

*John 8:25-32*

*If all you have to go on is your own experience, you don't have much more to say about your faith than anyone who claims to believe anything. But when your words are based on the timeless Word of God, you have a real leg to stand on.*

---

### Truth and Freedom

³⁰ As He was saying these things, many believed in Him. ³¹ So Jesus said to the Jews who had believed Him, "If you continue in My word, you really are My disciples. ³² You will know the truth, and the truth will set you free."

³³ "We are descendants of Abraham," they answered Him, "and we have never been enslaved to anyone. How can You say, 'You will become free'?"

³⁴ Jesus responded, "•I assure you: Everyone who commits sin is a slave of sin. ³⁵ A slave does not remain in the household forever, but a son does remain forever. ³⁶ Therefore if the Son sets you free, you really will be free. ³⁷ I know you are descendants of Abraham, but you are trying to kill Me because My word is not welcome among you. ³⁸ I speak what I have seen in the presence of the Father,ᵃ and therefore you do what you have heard from your father."

³⁹ "Our father is Abraham!" they replied.

"If you were Abraham's children," Jesus told them, "you would do what Abraham did. ⁴⁰ But now you are

ᵃ8:38 Other mss read *of My Father*

trying to kill Me, a man who has told you the truth that I heard from God. Abraham did not do this! [41] You're doing what your father does."

"We weren't born of sexual immorality," they said. "We have one Father—God."

[42] Jesus said to them, "If God were your Father, you would love Me, because I came from God and I am here. For I didn't come on My own, but He sent Me. [43] Why don't you understand what I say? Because you cannot listen to My word. [44] You are of your father the Devil, and you want to carry out your father's desires. He was a murderer from the beginning and has not stood in the truth, because there is no truth in him. When he tells a lie, he speaks from his own nature, because he is a liar and the father of liars. [45] Yet because I tell the truth, you do not believe Me. [46] Who among you can convict Me of sin? If I tell the truth, why don't you believe Me? [47] The one who is from God listens to God's words. This is why you don't listen, because you are not from God."

> "We need theology, not to replace experience, but to give it definition and to ensure its spiritual health."
> —Dan Scott

## Jesus and Abraham

[48] The Jews responded to Him, "Aren't we right in saying that You're a •Samaritan and have a demon?"

[49] "I do not have a demon," Jesus answered. "On the contrary, I honor My Father and you dishonor Me. [50] I do not seek My glory; the One who seeks it also judges. [51] I assure you: If anyone keeps My word, he will never see death—ever!"

[52] Then the Jews said, "Now we know You have a demon. Abraham died and so did the prophets. You say, 'If anyone keeps My word, he will never taste death—ever!' [53] Are You greater than our father Abraham who died? Even the prophets died. Who do You pretend to be?"

[54] "If I glorify Myself," Jesus answered, "My glory is nothing. My Father is the One who glorifies Me, of whom you say, 'He is our God.' [55] You've never known Him, but I know Him. If I were to say I don't know Him, I would be a liar like you. But I do know Him, and I keep His word. [56] Your father Abraham was overjoyed that he would see My day; he saw it and rejoiced."

[57] The Jews replied, "You aren't 50 years old yet, and You've seen Abraham?"[a]

[58] Jesus said to them, "I assure you: Before Abraham was, I am."

[59] At that, they picked up stones to throw at Him. But Jesus was hidden and went out of the temple complex.[b]

## The Sixth Sign: Healing a Man Born Blind

9 As He was passing by, He saw a man blind from birth. [2] His disciples questioned Him: "•Rabbi, who sinned, this man or his parents, that he was born blind?"

[3] "Neither this man sinned nor his parents," Jesus answered. "[This came about] so that God's works might be displayed in him. [4] We[c] must do the works of Him who sent Me[d] while it is

day. Night is coming when no one can work. [5] As long as I am in the world, I am the light of the world."

[6] After He said these things He spit on the ground, made some mud from the saliva, and spread the mud on his eyes. [7] "Go," He told him, "wash in the pool of Siloam" (which means "Sent"). So he left, washed, and came back seeing.

[8] His neighbors and those who formerly had seen him as a beggar said, "Isn't this the man who sat begging?" [9] Some said, "He's the one." "No," others were saying, "but he looks like him." He kept saying, "I'm the one!"

[10] Therefore they asked him, "Then how were your eyes opened?"

[11] He answered, "The man called Jesus made mud, spread it on my eyes, and told me, 'Go to Siloam and wash.' So when I went and washed I received my sight."

[12] "Where is He?" they asked.

"I don't know," he said.

## The Healed Man's Testimony

[13] They brought to the •Pharisees the man who used to be blind. [14] The day that Jesus made the mud and opened his eyes was a Sabbath. [15] So again the Pharisees asked him how he received his sight.

"He put mud on my eyes," he told them. "I washed and I can see."

[16] Therefore some of the Pharisees said, "This man is not from God, for He doesn't keep the Sabbath!" But others were saying, "How can a sinful man perform such signs?" And there was a division among them.

[17] Again they asked the blind man, "What do you say about Him, since He opened your eyes?"

"He's a prophet," he said.

[18] The Jews did not believe this about him—that he was blind and received sight—until they summoned the parents of the one who had received his sight.

[19] They asked them, "Is this your son, whom you say was born blind? How then does he now see?"

[20] "We know this is our son and that he was born blind," his parents answered. [21] "But we don't know how he now sees, and we don't know who opened his eyes. Ask him; he's of age. He will speak for himself." [22] His parents said these things because they were afraid of the Jews, since the Jews had already agreed that if anyone confessed Him as •Messiah, he would be banned from the •synagogue. [23] This is why his parents said, "He's of age; ask him."

[24] So a second time they summoned the man who had been blind and told him, "Give glory to God. We know that this man is a sinner!"

[25] He answered, "Whether or not He's a sinner, I don't know. One thing I do know: I was blind, and now I can see!"

[26] Then they asked him, "What did He do to you? How did He open your eyes?"

[27] "I already told you," he said, "and you didn't listen. Why do you want to hear it again? You don't want to become His disciples too, do you?"

[28] They ridiculed him: "You're that man's disciple, but we're Moses' disciples. [29] We know that God has spoken to Moses. But this man—we don't know where He's from!"

[30] "This is an amazing thing," the man told them. "You don't know where He is from; yet He opened my eyes! [31] We know that God doesn't listen to sinners; but if anyone is God-fearing and does His will, He listens to

him. [32] Throughout history no one has ever heard of someone opening the eyes of a person born blind. [33] If this man were not from God, He wouldn't be able to do anything."

[34] "You were born entirely in sin," they replied, "and are you trying to teach us?" Then they threw him out.

## The Blind Man's Sight and the Pharisees' Blindness

[35] When Jesus heard that they had thrown the man out, He found him and asked, "Do you believe in the •Son of Man?"[a]

[36] "Who is He, Sir, that I may believe in Him?" he asked in return.

[37] Jesus answered, "You have both seen Him and He is the One speaking with you."

[38] "I believe, Lord!" he said, and he worshiped Him.

[39] Jesus said, "I came into this world for judgment, in order that those who do not see may see and those who do see may become blind."

[40] Some of the Pharisees who were with Him heard these things and asked Him, "We aren't blind too, are we?"

[41] "If you were blind," Jesus told them, "you wouldn't have sin. But now that you say, 'We see'—your sin remains.

## The Ideal Shepherd

**10** "•I assure you: Anyone who doesn't enter the sheep pen by the door, but climbs in some other way, is a thief and a robber. [2] The one who enters by the door is the shepherd of the sheep. [3] The doorkeeper opens it for him, and the sheep hear his voice. He calls his own sheep by name and leads them out. [4] When he

has brought all his own outside, he goes ahead of them. The sheep follow him because they recognize his voice. [5] They will never follow a stranger; instead they will run away from him, because they don't recognize the voice of strangers."

[6] Jesus gave them this illustration, but they did not understand what He was telling them.

## The Good Shepherd

[7] So Jesus said again, "I assure you: I am the door of the sheep. [8] All who came before Me[b] are thieves and robbers, but the sheep didn't listen to them. [9] I am the door. If anyone enters by Me, he will be saved, and will come in and go out and find pasture. [10] A thief comes only to steal and to kill and to destroy. I have come that they may have life and have it in abundance.

[11] "I am the good shepherd. The good shepherd lays down his life for the sheep. [12] The hired man, since he's not the shepherd and doesn't own the sheep, leaves them and runs away when he sees a wolf coming. The wolf then snatches and scatters them. [13] ⌊This happens⌋ because he is a hired man and doesn't care about the sheep.

[14] "I am the good shepherd. I know My own sheep, and they know Me, [15] as the Father knows Me, and I know the Father. I lay down My life for the sheep. [16] But I have other sheep that are not of this fold; I must bring them also, and they will listen to My voice. Then there will be one flock, one shepherd. [17] This is why the Father loves Me, because I am laying down My life that I may take it up again. [18] No one takes it from Me, but I lay it down on My own. I have the right to lay it down, and I have the right to take it up again.

[a]9:35 Other mss read *the Son of God*   [b]10:8 Other mss omit *before Me*

I have received this command from My Father."

¹⁹ Again a division took place among the Jews because of these words. ²⁰ Many of them were saying, "He has a demon and He's crazy! Why do you listen to Him?" ²¹ Others were saying, "These aren't the words of someone demon-possessed. Can a demon open the eyes of the blind?"

### Jesus at the Festival of Dedication

²² Then the Festival of Dedication took place in Jerusalem; and it was winter. ²³ Jesus was walking in the •temple complex in Solomon's Colonnade. ²⁴ Then the Jews surrounded Him and asked, "How long are You going to keep us in suspense? If You are the •Messiah, tell us plainly."
²⁵ "I did tell you and you don't believe," Jesus answered them. "The works that I do in My Father's name testify about Me. ²⁶ But you don't believe because you are not My sheep.ᵃ ²⁷ My sheep hear My voice, I know them, and they follow Me. ²⁸ I give them eternal life, and they will never perish—ever! No one will snatch them out of My hand. ²⁹ My Father, who has given them to Me, is greater than all. No one is able to snatch them out of the Father's hand. ³⁰ The Father and I are one."

### Renewed Efforts to Stone Jesus

³¹ Again the Jews picked up rocks to stone Him.
³² Jesus replied, "I have shown you many good works from the Father. For which of these works are you stoning Me?"
³³ "We aren't stoning You for a good work," the Jews answered, "but for

blasphemy, and because You—being a man—make Yourself God."
³⁴ Jesus answered them, "Isn't it written in your law,ᵇ **I said, you are gods?**ᶜ ³⁵ If He called those to whom the word of God came 'gods'—and the Scripture cannot be broken— ³⁶ do you say, 'You are blaspheming' to the One the Father set apart and sent into the world, because I said 'I am the Son of God'? ³⁷ If I am not doing My Father's works, don't believe Me. ³⁸ But if I am doing them and you don't believe Me, believe the works. This way you will know and understandᵈ that the Father is in Me and I in the Father." ³⁹ Then they were trying again to seize Him, yet He eluded their grasp.

---

*John 10:27-30*

*God's Assurance*

*There is no safer place in the world than in the center of God's grace. Jesus Christ, the Shepherd of our souls, guards the way in and out, letting nothing and no one call our salvation into question or threaten to remove us from His care. We are in, and we're staying in.*

---

### Many beyond the Jordan Believe in Jesus

⁴⁰ So He departed again across the Jordan to the place where John had been baptizing earlier, and He remained there. ⁴¹ Many came to Him and said, "John never did a sign, but everything John said about this

---

ᵃ10:26 Other mss add *just as I told you*   ᵇ10:34 Other mss read *in the law*   ᶜ10:34 Ps 82:6   ᵈ10:38 Other mss read *know and believe*

man was true." [42] And many believed in Him there.

## Lazarus Dies at Bethany

**11** Now a man was sick, Lazarus, from Bethany, the village of Mary and her sister Martha. [2] Mary was the one who anointed the Lord with fragrant oil and wiped His feet with her hair, and it was her brother Lazarus who was sick. [3] So the sisters sent a message to Him: "Lord, the one You love is sick."

[4] When Jesus heard it, He said, "This sickness will not end in death, but is for the glory of God, so that the Son of God may be glorified through it." [5] (Jesus loved Martha, her sister, and Lazarus.) [6] So when He heard that he was sick, He stayed two more days in the place where He was. [7] Then after that, He said to the disciples, "Let's go to Judea again."

[8] "•Rabbi," the disciples told Him, "just now the Jews tried to stone You, and You're going there again?"

[9] "Aren't there 12 hours in a day?" Jesus answered. "If anyone walks during the day, he doesn't stumble, because he sees the light of this world. [10] If anyone walks during the night, he does stumble, because the light is not in him." [11] He said this, and then He told them, "Our friend Lazarus has fallen asleep, but I'm on My way to wake him up."

[12] Then the disciples said to Him, "Lord, if he has fallen •asleep, he will get well."

[13] Jesus, however, was speaking about his death, but they thought He was speaking about natural sleep. [14] So Jesus then told them plainly, "Lazarus has died. [15] I'm glad for you that I wasn't there, so that you may believe. But let's go to him."

[16] Then Thomas (called "Twin") said to his fellow disciples, "Let's go so that we may die with Him."

## The Resurrection and the Life

[17] When Jesus arrived, He found that Lazarus had already been in the tomb four days. [18] Bethany was near Jerusalem (about two miles away). [19] Many of the Jews had come to Martha and Mary to comfort them about their brother. [20] As soon as Martha heard that Jesus was coming, she went to meet Him. But Mary remained seated in the house.

[21] Then Martha said to Jesus, "Lord, if You had been here, my brother wouldn't have died. [22] Yet even now I know that whatever You ask from God, God will give You."

[23] "Your brother will rise again," Jesus told her.

[24] Martha said, "I know that he will rise again in the resurrection at the last day."

[25] Jesus said to her, "I am the resurrection and the life. The one who believes in Me, even if he dies, will live. [26] Everyone who lives and believes in Me will never die—ever. Do you believe this?"

[27] "Yes, Lord," she told Him, "I believe You are the •Messiah, the Son of God, who was to come into the world."

## Jesus Shares the Sorrow of Death

[28] Having said this, she went back and called her sister Mary, saying in private, "The Teacher is here and is calling for you."

[29] As soon as she heard this, she got up quickly and went to Him. [30] Jesus had not yet come into the village, but was still in the place where Martha had met Him. [31] The Jews who were with her in the house consoling her saw that Mary got up quickly and

went out. So they followed her, supposing that she was going to the tomb to cry there.

<sup></sup>32 When Mary came to where Jesus was and saw Him, she fell at His feet and told Him, "Lord, if You had been here, my brother would not have died!"

33 When Jesus saw her crying, and the Jews who had come with her crying, He was angry in His spirit and deeply moved. 34 "Where have you put him?" He asked.

"Lord," they told Him, "come and see."

35 Jesus wept.

36 So the Jews said, "See how He loved him!" 37 But some of them said, "Couldn't He who opened the blind man's eyes also have kept this man from dying?"

## The Seventh Sign: Raising Lazarus from the Dead

38 Then Jesus, angry in Himself again, came to the tomb. It was a cave, and a stone was lying against it. 39 "Remove the stone," Jesus said.

Martha, the dead man's sister, told Him, "Lord, he already stinks. It's been four days."

40 Jesus said to her, "Did I not tell you that if you believed you would see the glory of God?"

41 So they removed the stone. Then Jesus raised His eyes and said, "Father, I thank You that You heard Me. 42 I know that You always hear Me, but because of the crowd standing here I said this, so they may believe You sent Me." 43 After He said this, He shouted with a loud voice, "Lazarus, come out!" 44 The dead man came out bound hand and foot with linen strips and with his face wrapped in a cloth. Jesus said to them, "Loose him and let him go."

a11:50 Other mss read to our

## The Plot to Kill Jesus

45 Therefore many of the Jews who came to Mary and saw what He did believed in Him. 46 But some of them went to the •Pharisees and told them what Jesus had done.

47 So the •chief priests and the Pharisees convened the •Sanhedrin and said, "What are we going to do since this man does many signs? 48 If we let Him continue in this way, everybody will believe in Him! Then the Romans will come and remove both our place and our nation."

49 One of them, Caiaphas, who was high priest that year, said to them, "You know nothing at all! 50 You're not considering that it is to your<sup>a</sup> advantage that one man should die for the people rather than the whole nation perish." 51 He did not say this on his own; but being high priest that year he prophesied that Jesus was going to die for the nation, 52 and not for the nation only, but also to unite the scattered children of God. 53 So from that day on they plotted to kill Him. 54 Therefore Jesus no longer walked openly among the Jews, but departed from there to the countryside near the wilderness, to a town called Ephraim. And He stayed there with the disciples.

55 Now the Jewish •Passover was near, and before the Passover many went up to Jerusalem from the country to purify themselves. 56 They were looking for Jesus, and asking one another as they stood in the •temple complex: "What do you think? He won't come to the festival, will He?"

57 The chief priests and the Pharisees had given orders that if anyone knew where He was, he should report it so they could arrest Him.

## The Anointing at Bethany

**12** Six days before the •Passover, Jesus came to Bethany where Lazarus[a] was, whom Jesus had raised from the dead. [2] So they gave a dinner for Him there; Martha was serving them, and Lazarus was one of those reclining at the table with Him. [3] Then Mary took a pound of fragrant oil—pure and expensive nard—anointed Jesus' feet, and wiped His feet with her hair. So the house was filled with the fragrance of the oil.

[4] Then one of His disciples, Judas Iscariot (who was about to betray Him), said, [5] "Why wasn't this fragrant oil sold for 300 denarii and given to the poor?" [6] He didn't say this because he cared about the poor, but because he was a thief. He was in charge of the money-bag and would steal part of what was put in it.

[7] Jesus answered, "Leave her alone; she has kept it for the day of My burial. [8] For you always have the poor with you, but you do not always have Me."

## The Decision to Kill Lazarus

[9] Then a large crowd of the Jews learned that He was there. They came not only because of Jesus, but also to see Lazarus whom He had raised from the dead. [10] Therefore the •chief priests decided to kill Lazarus too, [11] because he was the reason many of the Jews were deserting them and believing in Jesus.

## The Triumphal Entry

[12] The next day, when the large crowd that had come to the festival heard that Jesus was coming to Jerusalem, [13] they took palm branches and went out to meet Him. They kept shouting: "•*Hosanna*! Blessed is He who comes in the name of the Lord[b]—the King of Israel!"

[14] Jesus found a young donkey and sat on it, just as it is written: [15] **Fear no more, daughter of Zion; look! your King is coming, sitting on a donkey's colt.**[c]

[16] His disciples did not understand these things at first. However, when Jesus was glorified, then they remembered that these things had been written about Him and that they had done these things to Him. [17] Meanwhile the crowd, which had been with Him when He called Lazarus out of the tomb and raised him from the dead, continued to testify.[d] [18] This is also why the crowd met Him, because they heard He had done this sign.

[19] Then the •Pharisees said to one another, "You see? You've accomplished nothing. Look—the world has gone after Him!"

## Jesus Predicts His Crucifixion

[20] Now among those who went up to worship at the festival were some Greeks. [21] So they came to Philip, who was from Bethsaida in Galilee, and requested of him, "Sir, we want to see Jesus."

[22] Philip went and told Andrew; then Andrew and Philip went and told Jesus. [23] Jesus replied to them, "The hour has come for the •Son of Man to be glorified. [24] "•I assure you: Unless a grain of wheat falls into the ground and dies, it remains by itself. But if it dies, it produces a large crop. [25] The one who loves his life will lose it, and the one who hates his life in this world will keep it for eternal life. [26] If anyone serves Me, he must follow Me.

Where I am, there My servant also will be. If anyone serves Me, the Father will honor him.

27 "Now My soul is troubled. What should I say—'Father, save Me from this hour'? But that is why I came to this hour. 28 Father, glorify Your name!"a

Then a voice came from heaven: "I have glorified it, and I will glorify it again!"

29 The crowd standing there heard it and said it was thunder. Others said, "An angel has spoken to Him!"

30 Jesus responded, "This voice came, not for Me, but for you. 31 Now is the judgment of this world. Now the ruler of this world will be cast out. 32 As for Me, if I am lifted up from the earth I will draw all ⌊people⌋ to Myself." 33 He said this to signify what kind of death He was about to die.

34 Then the crowd replied to Him, "We have heard from the law that the •Messiah would remain forever. So how can You say, 'The Son of Man must be lifted up'? Who is this Son of Man?"

35 Jesus answered, "The light will be with you only a little longer. Walk while you have the light, so that darkness doesn't overtake you. The one who walks in darkness doesn't know where he's going. 36 While you have the light, believe in the light, so that you may become sons of light." Jesus said this, then went away and hid from them.

## Isaiah's Prophecies Fulfilled

37 Even though He had performed so many signs in their presence, they did not believe in Him. 38 But this was to fulfill the word of Isaiah the prophet, who said:

Lord, who has believed our
    message?
And to whom has the arm of
    the Lord been revealed?b

39 This is why they were unable to believe, because Isaiah also said:

40 He has blinded their eyes
    and hardened their hearts,
    so that they would not see
        with their eyes
    or understand with their
        hearts,
    and be converted,
    and I would heal them.c

41 Isaiah said these things becaused he saw His glory and spoke about Him.

42 Nevertheless, many did believe in Him even among the rulers, but because of the Pharisees they did not confess Him, so they would not be banned from the •synagogue. 43 For they loved praise from men more than praise from God.

## A Summary of Jesus' Mission

44 Then Jesus cried out, "The one who believes in Me believes not in Me, but in Him who sent Me. 45 And the one who sees Me sees Him who sent Me. 46 I have come as a light into the world, so that everyone who believes in Me would not remain in darkness. 47 If anyone hears My words and doesn't keep them, I do not judge him; for I did not come to judge the world, but to save the world. 48 The one who rejects Me and doesn't accept My sayings has this as his judge: the word I have spoken will judge him on the last day. 49 For I have not spoken on My own, but the Father Himself who sent Me

a12:28 Other mss read *Your Son*   b12:38 Is 53:1   c12:40 Is 6:10   d12:41 Other mss read *when* has given Me a command as to what I should say and what I should speak. ⁵⁰ I know that His command is eternal life. So the things that I speak, I speak just as the Father has told Me."

## Jesus Washes His Disciples' Feet

**13** Before the •Passover Festival, Jesus knew that His hour had come to depart from this world to the Father. Having loved His own who were in the world, He loved them to the end. ² Now by the time of supper, the Devil had already put it into the heart of Judas, Simon Iscariot's son, to betray Him. ³ Jesus knew that the Father had given everything into His hands, that He had come from God, and that He was going back to God. ⁴ So He got up from supper, laid aside His robe, took a towel, and tied it around Himself. ⁵ Next, He poured water into a basin and began to wash His disciples' feet and to dry them with the towel tied around Him.

⁶ He came to Simon Peter, who asked Him, "Lord, are You going to wash my feet?"

⁷ Jesus answered him, "What I'm doing you don't understand now, but afterward you will know."

⁸ "You will never wash my feet—ever!" Peter said.

Jesus replied, "If I don't wash you, you have no part with Me."

⁹ Simon Peter said to Him, "Lord, not only my feet, but also my hands and my head."

¹⁰ "One who has bathed," Jesus told him, "doesn't need to wash anything except his feet, but he is completely clean. You are clean, but not all of you." ¹¹ For He knew who would betray Him. This is why He said, "You are not all clean."

## The Meaning of Footwashing

¹² When Jesus had washed their feet and put on His robe, He reclined again and said to them, "Do you know what I have done for you? ¹³ You call Me Teacher and Lord. This is well said, for I am. ¹⁴ So if I, your Lord and Teacher, have washed your feet, you also ought to wash one another's feet. ¹⁵ For I have given you an example that you also should do just as I have done for you.

¹⁶ "•I assure you: A slave is not greater than his master, and a messenger is not greater than the one who sent him. ¹⁷ If you know these things, you are blessed if you do them. ¹⁸ I'm not speaking about all of you; I know those I have chosen. But the Scripture must be fulfilled: **The one who eats My bread**ᵃ **has raised his heel against Me.**ᵇ

¹⁹ "I am telling you now before it happens, so that when it does happen you will believe that I am He. ²⁰ I assure you: The one who receives whomever I send receives Me, and the one who receives Me receives Him who sent Me."

## Judas' Betrayal Predicted

²¹ When Jesus had said this, He was troubled in His spirit and testified, "I assure you: One of you will betray Me!" ²² The disciples started looking at one another—at a loss as to which one He was speaking about. ²³ One of His disciples, whom Jesus loved, was reclining close beside Jesus. ²⁴ Simon Peter motioned to him to find out who it was He was talking about.

---

ᵃ13:18 Other mss read *eats bread with Me*    ᵇ13:18 Ps 41:9

25 So he leaned back against Jesus and asked Him, "Lord, who is it?"

26 Jesus replied, "He's the one I give the piece of bread to after I have dipped it." When He had dipped the bread, He gave it to Judas, Simon Iscariot's son.ᵃ 27 After ⌊Judas ate⌋ the piece of bread, Satan entered him. Therefore Jesus told him, "What you're doing, do quickly."

28 None of those reclining at the table knew why He told him this. 29 Since Judas kept the money-bag, some thought that Jesus was telling him, "Buy what we need for the festival," or that he should give something to the poor. 30 After receiving the piece of bread, he went out immediately. And it was night.

## The New Commandment

31 When he had gone out, Jesus said, "Now the •Son of Man is glorified, and God is glorified in Him. 32 If God is glorified in Him,ᵇ God will also glorify Him in Himself, and will glorify Him at once.

33 "Children, I am with you a little while longer. You will look for Me, and just as I told the Jews, 'Where I am going you cannot come,' so now I tell you.

34 "I give you a new commandment: that you love one another. Just as I have loved you, you should also love one another. 35 By this all people will know that you are My disciples, if you have love for one another."

## Peter's Denials Predicted

36 "Lord," Simon Peter said to Him, "where are You going?"

Jesus answered, "Where I am going you cannot follow Me now; but you will follow later."

37 "Lord," Peter asked, "why can't I follow You now? I will lay down my life for You!"

38 Jesus replied, "Will you lay down your life for Me? I assure you: A rooster will not crow until you have denied Me three times.

---

### John 14:6

### God the Son

*Many people don't believe that faith in Christ is the only way to be saved. Some people in the church today question it. But from Jesus' own mouth comes the statement that He alone is able to provide us access to God's approval. Who are you going to believe?*

---

## The Way to the Father

14 "Your heart must not be troubled. Believe in God; believe also in Me. 2 In My Father's house are many dwelling places; if not, I would have told you. I am going away to prepare a place for you. 3 If I go away and prepare a place for you, I will come back and receive you to Myself, so that where I am you may be also. 4 You know the way where I am going."ᶜ

5 "Lord," Thomas said, "we don't know where You're going. How can we know the way?"

6 Jesus told him, "I am the way, the truth, and the life. No one comes to the Father except through Me.

---

ᵃ13:26 Other mss read *Judas Iscariot, Simon's son*    ᵇ13:32 Other mss omit *If God is glorified in Him*
ᶜ14:4 Other mss read this verse: *And you know where I am going, and you know the way*

## Jesus Reveals the Father

7 "If you know Me, you will also know[a] My Father. From now on you do know Him and have seen Him."

8 "Lord," said Philip, "show us the Father, and that's enough for us."

9 Jesus said to him, "Have I been among you all this time without your knowing Me, Philip? The one who has seen Me has seen the Father. How can you say, 'Show us the Father'? 10 Don't you believe that I am in the Father and the Father is in Me? The words I speak to you I do not speak on My own. The Father who lives in Me does His works. 11 Believe Me that I am in the Father and the Father is in Me. Otherwise, believe[b] because of the works themselves.

## Praying in Jesus' Name

12 "•I assure you: The one who believes in Me will also do the works that I do. And he will do even greater works than these, because I am going to the Father. 13 Whatever you ask in My name, I will do it, so that the Father may be glorified in the Son. 14 If you ask Me[c] anything in My name, I will do it.[d]

## Another Counselor Promised

15 "If you love Me, you will keep[e] My commandments. 16 And I will ask the Father, and He will give you another •Counselor to be with you forever. 17 He is the Spirit of truth, whom the world is unable to receive because it doesn't see Him or know Him. But you do know Him, because He remains with you and will be[f] in you. 18 I will not leave you as orphans; I am coming to you.

## The Father, the Son, and the Holy Spirit

19 "In a little while the world will see Me no longer, but you will see Me. Because I live, you will live too. 20 In that day you will know that I am in My Father, you are in Me, and I am in you. 21 The one who has My commandments and keeps them is the one who loves Me. And the one who loves Me will be loved by My Father. I also will love him and will reveal Myself to him."

22 Judas (not Iscariot) said to Him, "Lord, how is it You're going to reveal Yourself to us and not to the world?"

23 Jesus answered, "If anyone loves Me, he will keep My word. My Father will love him, and We will come to him and make Our home with him. 24 The one who doesn't love Me will not keep My words. The word that you hear is not Mine, but is from the Father who sent Me.

25 "I have spoken these things to you while I remain with you. 26 But the Counselor, the Holy Spirit, whom the Father will send in My name, will teach you all things and remind you of everything I have told you.

## Jesus' Gift of Peace

27 "Peace I leave with you. My peace I give to you. I do not give to you as the world gives. Your heart must not be troubled or fearful. 28 You have heard Me tell you, 'I am going away and I am coming to you.' If you loved Me, you would have rejoiced that I am going to the Father, because the Father is greater than I. 29 I have told you now before it happens, so that when it does happen you may believe. 30 I will not talk

[a]14:7 Other mss read *If you had known Me, you would have known*      [b]14:11 Other mss read *believe Me*
[c]14:14 Other mss omit *Me*      [d]14:14 Other mss omit all of v. 14      [e]14:15 Other mss read *If you love Me, keep*
(as a command)      [f]14:17 Other mss read *and is*

with you much longer, because the ruler of the world is coming. He has no power over Me. [31] On the contrary, ⌊I am going away⌋ so that the world may know that I love the Father. Just as the Father commanded Me, so I do.

"Get up; let's leave this place.

## The Vine and the Branches

**15** "I am the true vine, and My Father is the vineyard keeper. [2] Every branch in Me that does not produce fruit He removes, and He prunes every branch that produces fruit so that it will produce more fruit. [3] You are already clean because of the word I have spoken to you. [4] Remain in Me, and I in you. Just as a branch is unable to produce fruit by itself unless it remains on the vine, so neither can you unless you remain in Me.

---

*John 15:18-21*

*When your faith is young and exuberance spills over easily into life, some people won't be crazy about who you're becoming. But you'd be crazy to listen to them. Lots of people may have lots of opinions about you. But you're only playing for an audience of One.*

---

[5] "I am the vine; you are the branches. The one who remains in Me and I in him produces much fruit, because you can do nothing without Me. [6] If anyone does not remain in Me, he is thrown aside like a branch and he withers. They gather them, throw them into the fire, and they are burned. [7] If you remain in Me and My words remain in you, ask whatever you want and it will be done for you. [8] My Father is glorified by this: that you produce much fruit and prove to be My disciples.

---

*"Conformity is a joy thief, but fixing our eyes on Jesus is a joyful, life-giving exercise."*
*—Ed Young*

---

## Christlike Love

[9] "Just as the Father has loved Me, I also have loved you. Remain in My love. [10] If you keep My commandments you will remain in My love, just as I have kept My Father's commandments and remain in His love.

[11] "I have spoken these things to you so that My joy may be in you and your joy may be complete. [12] This is My commandment: that you love one another just as I have loved you. [13] No one has greater love than this, that someone would lay down his life for his friends. [14] You are My friends if you do what I command you. [15] I do not call you slaves anymore, because a slave doesn't know what his master is doing. I have called you friends, because I have made known to you everything I have heard from My Father. [16] You did not choose Me, but I chose you. I appointed you that you should go out and produce fruit, and that your fruit should remain, so that whatever you ask the Father in My name, He will give you. [17] This is what I command you: that you love one another.

## Persecutions Predicted

18 "If the world hates you, understand that it hated Me before it hated you. 19 If you were of the world, the world would love ⌊you as⌋ its own. However, because you are not of the world, but I have chosen you out of the world, this is why the world hates you. 20 Remember the word I spoke to you: 'A slave is not greater than his master.' If they persecuted Me, they will also persecute you. If they kept My word, they will also keep yours. 21 But they will do all these things to you on account of My name, because they don't know the One who sent Me. 22 If I had not come and spoken to them, they would not have sin. Now they have no excuse for their sin. 23 The one who hates Me also hates My Father. 24 If I had not done the works among them that no one else has done, they would not have sin. Now they have seen and hated both Me and My Father. 25 But ⌊this happened⌋ so that the statement written in their law might be fulfilled: **They hated Me for no reason.**ᵃ

## Coming Testimony and Rejection

26 "When the •Counselor comes, whom I will send to you from the Father—the Spirit of truth who proceeds from the Father—He will testify about Me. 27 You also will testify, because you have been with Me from the beginning.

16 "I have told you these things to keep you from stumbling. 2 They will ban you from the •synagogues. In fact, a time is coming when anyone who kills you will think he is offering service to God. 3 They will do these things because they haven't known the Father or Me.

4 But I have told you these things so that when their timeᵇ comes you may remember I told them to you. I didn't tell you these things from the beginning, because I was with you.

*John 16:12-15*

### God the Holy Spirit

*Granted, the Bible is hard to understand sometimes. And for those who don't have the Spirit living in them, it never gets any easier. But for us, the Holy Spirit is our guide to going deeper in the Word. He may want us to dig a little, but He'll bring the truth closer to the surface.*

## The Counselor's Ministry

5 "But now I am going away to Him who sent Me, and not one of you asks Me, 'Where are You going?' 6 Yet, because I have spoken these things to you, sorrow has filled your heart. 7 Nevertheless, I am telling you the truth. It is for your benefit that I go away, because if I don't go away the •Counselor will not come to you. If I go, I will send Him to you. 8 When He comes, He will convict the world about sin, righteousness, and judgment: 9 about sin, because they do not believe in Me; 10 about righteousness, because I am going to the Father and you will no longer see Me; 11 and about judgment, because the ruler of this world has been judged. 12 "I still have many things to tell you, but you can't bear them now.

ᵃ15:25 Ps 69:4   ᵇ16:4 Other mss read *when the time*

[13] When the Spirit of truth comes, He will guide you into all the truth. For He will not speak on His own, but He will speak whatever He hears. He will also declare to you what is to come. [14] He will glorify Me, because He will take from what is Mine and declare it to you. [15] Everything the Father has is Mine. This is why I told you that He takes from what is Mine and will declare it to you.

## Sorrow Turned to Joy

[16] "A little while and you will no longer see Me; again a little while and you will see Me."[a]

[17] Therefore some of His disciples said to one another, "What is this He tells us: 'A little while and you will not see Me; again a little while and you will see Me'; and, 'because I am going to the Father'?" [18] They said, "What is this He is saying,[b] 'A little while'? We don't know what He's talking about!"

[19] Jesus knew they wanted to question Him, so He said to them, "Are you asking one another about what I said, 'A little while and you will not see Me; again a little while and you will see Me'?

[20] "•I assure you: You will weep and wail, but the world will rejoice. You will become sorrowful, but your sorrow will turn to joy. [21] When a woman is in labor she has pain because her time has come. But when she has given birth to a child, she no longer remembers the suffering because of the joy that a person has been born into the world. [22] So you also have sorrow[c] now. But I will see you again. Your hearts will rejoice, and no one will rob you of your joy. [23] In that day you will not ask Me anything.

"I assure you: Anything you ask the Father in My name, He will give you. [24] Until now you have asked for nothing in My name. Ask and you will receive, that your joy may be complete.

## Jesus the Victor

[25] "I have spoken these things to you in figures of speech. A time is coming when I will no longer speak to you in figures, but I will tell you plainly about the Father. [26] In that day you will ask in My name. I am not telling you that I will make requests to the Father on your behalf. [27] For the Father Himself loves you, because you have loved Me and have believed that I came from God.[d] [28] I came from the Father and have come into the world. Again, I am leaving the world and going to the Father."

[29] "Ah!" His disciples said. "Now You're speaking plainly and not using any figurative language. [30] Now we know that You know everything and don't need anyone to question You. By this we believe that You came from God."

[31] Jesus responded to them, "Do you now believe? [32] Look: An hour is coming, and has come, when you will be scattered each to his own home, and you will leave Me alone. Yet I am not alone, because the Father is with Me. [33] I have told you these things so that in Me you may have peace. In the world you have suffering. Be courageous! I have conquered the world."

## Jesus Prays for Himself

**17** Jesus spoke these things, then raised His eyes to heaven, and said:

---

[a]16:16 Other mss add *because I am going to the Father*   [b]16:18 Other mss omit *He is saying*   [c]16:22 Other mss read *will have sorrow*   [d]16:27 Other mss read *from the Father*

Father,
the hour has come.
Glorify Your Son
so that the Son may glorify You,
2 just as You gave Him
    authority over all flesh;
so that He may give eternal
    life
to all You have given Him.
3 This is eternal life:
that they may know You, the
    only true God,
and the One You have sent—
    Jesus Christ.
4 I have glorified You on the
    earth
by completing the work You
    gave Me to do.
5 Now, Father, glorify Me in
    Your presence
with that glory I had with You
before the world existed.

---

*John 17:3-5*

*God the Father*

*The Father and the Son have
always existed, sharing their glory
with one another and with the
Spirit, living in perfect love and fellowship, needing nothing, fully satisfied. But God the Father loved
the world, and He sent His Son to
save it. That is eternal love. His gift
is eternal life.*

---

## Jesus Prays for His Disciples

6 I have revealed Your name
to the men You gave Me
    from the world.
They were Yours,
You gave them to Me,

and they have kept Your
    word.
7 Now they know that all things
You have given to Me are from
    You,
8 because the words that You
    gave to Me,
I have given to them.
They have received them and
    have known for certain
that I came from You.
They have believed that You
    sent Me.
9 I pray for them.
I am not praying for the world
but for those You have given
    Me,
because they are Yours.
10 All My things are Yours,
    and Yours are Mine,
and I have been glorified in
    them.
11 I am no longer in the world,
but they are in the world,
and I am coming to You.
Holy Father, protect them by
    Your name
that You have given Me,
so that they may be one just as
    We are.
12 While I was with them I was
    protecting them
by Your name that You have
    given Me.
I guarded them and not one
    of them is lost,
except the son of destruction,
that the Scripture may be
    fulfilled.
13 Now I am coming to You,
and I speak these things in
    the world
so that they may have
My joy completed in them.
14 I have given them Your
    word.
The world hated them

---

*John 17:14-19*

*This world is not our home. We're strangers in a foreign land, aliens from a distant planet, ambassadors of a heavenly country. We are set apart to serve God's kingdom in enemy-occupied territory. We have given up our rights to citizenship. But not to responsibility.*

---

because they are not of
the world,
just as I am not of the world.
<sup>15</sup> I am not praying
that You take them out of the
world,
but that You protect them
from the evil one.
<sup>16</sup> They are not of the world,
just as I am not of the world.
<sup>17</sup> Sanctify them by the truth;
Your word is truth.
<sup>18</sup> Just as You sent Me into the
world,
I also have sent them into the
world.
<sup>19</sup> I sanctify Myself for them,
so they also may be sanctified
by the truth.

### Jesus Prays for All Believers

<sup>20</sup> I pray not only for these, but
also for those
who believe in Me through
their message.
<sup>21</sup> May they all be one, just as
You, Father,
are in Me and I am in You.
May they also be one[a] in Us,

so that the world may believe
You sent Me.
<sup>22</sup> I have given them the glory
that You have given to
Me.
May they be one just as We
are one.
<sup>23</sup> I am in them and You are in
Me.
May they be made completely
one,
so that the world may know
You sent Me
and that You have loved
them
just as You have loved Me.
<sup>24</sup> Father, I desire those You
have given Me
to be with Me where I am.
Then they may see My glory,
which You have given Me
because You loved Me
before the world's foundation.
<sup>25</sup> Righteous Father!
The world has not known You.
However, I have known You,
and these have known that
You sent Me.
<sup>26</sup> I made Your name known to
them
and will make it known,
so that the love with which You
have loved Me
may be in them,
and that I may be in them.

---

*"We are to keep the world from ruling our hearts by letting Christ rule there instead. The separation happens inside of us, not outside."*
*—John Fischer*

---

[a]**17:21** Other mss omit *one*

## Jesus Betrayed

**18** After Jesus had said these things, He went out with His disciples across the Kidron ravine, where there was a garden into which He and His disciples entered. ² Judas, who betrayed Him, also knew the place, because Jesus often met there with His disciples. ³ So Judas took a •company of soldiers and some temple police from the •chief priests and the •Pharisees and came there with lanterns, torches, and weapons.

⁴ Then Jesus, knowing everything that was about to happen to Him, went out and said to them, "Who is it you're looking for?"

⁵ "Jesus the •Nazarene," they answered.

"I am He," Jesus told them.

Judas, who betrayed Him, was also standing with them. ⁶ When He told them, "I am He," they stepped back and fell to the ground.

⁷ Then He asked them again, "Who is it you're looking for?"

"Jesus the Nazarene," they said.

⁸ "I told you I am He," Jesus replied. "So if you're looking for Me, let these men go." ⁹ This was to fulfill the words He had said: "I have not lost one of those You have given Me."

¹⁰ Then Simon Peter, who had a sword, drew it, struck the high priest's slave, and cut off his right ear. (The slave's name was Malchus.) ¹¹ At that, Jesus said to Peter, "Sheathe your sword! Should I not drink the cup that the Father has given Me?"

## Jesus Arrested and Taken to Annas

¹² Then the detachment of soldiers, the captain, and the Jewish temple police arrested Jesus and tied Him up. ¹³ First they led Him to Annas, for he was the father-in-law of Caiaphas, who was high priest that year. ¹⁴ Caiaphas was the one who had advised the Jews that it was advantageous that one man should die for the people.

## Peter Denies Jesus

¹⁵ Meanwhile Simon Peter was following Jesus, as was another disciple. That disciple was an acquaintance of the high priest; so he went with Jesus into the high priest's courtyard. ¹⁶ But Peter remained standing outside by the door. So the other disciple, the one known to the high priest, went out and spoke to the girl who kept the door, and brought Peter in.

¹⁷ Then the slave-girl who kept the door said to Peter, "You aren't one of this man's disciples too, are you?"

"I am not!" he said. ¹⁸ Now the slaves and the temple police had made a charcoal fire, because it was cold. They were standing there warming themselves, and Peter was standing with them and warming himself.

## Jesus before Annas

¹⁹ The high priest questioned Jesus about His disciples and about His teaching.

²⁰ "I have spoken openly to the world," Jesus answered him. "I have always taught in the •synagogue and in the •temple complex, where all the Jews congregate, and I haven't spoken anything in secret. ²¹ Why do you question Me? Question those who heard what I told them. Look, they know what I said."

²² When He had said these things, one of the temple police standing by slapped Jesus, saying, "Is this the way you answer the high priest?"

23 "If I have spoken wrongly," Jesus answered him, "give evidence about the wrong; but if rightly, why do you hit Me?"

24 Then Annas sent Him bound to Caiaphas the high priest.

## Peter Denies Jesus Twice More

25 Now Simon Peter was standing and warming himself. They said to him, "You aren't one of His disciples too, are you?"

He denied it and said, "I am not!"

26 One of the high priest's slaves, a relative of the man whose ear Peter had cut off, said, "Didn't I see you with Him in the garden?"

27 Peter then denied it again. Immediately a rooster crowed.

---

### John 18:36

### The Kingdom

*There is a restraint we can enjoy when we are pushed to defend our faith or to take our case for truth and righteousness to the county courthouse. For even if we do not earn temporary victory in our efforts today, we know that our ultimate victory is coming and assured . . . in another world.*

---

## Jesus before Pilate

28 Then they took Jesus from Caiaphas to the governor's •headquarters. It was early morning. They did not enter the headquarters themselves; otherwise they would be defiled and unable to eat the •Passover.

29 Then •Pilate came out to them and said, "What charge do you bring against this man?"

30 They answered him, "If this man weren't a criminal, we wouldn't have handed Him over to you."

31 So Pilate told them, "Take Him yourselves and judge Him according to your law."

"It's not legal for us to put anyone to death," the Jews declared. 32 They said this so that Jesus' words might be fulfilled signifying what sort of death He was going to die.

33 Then Pilate went back into the headquarters, summoned Jesus, and said to Him, "Are You the King of the Jews?"

34 Jesus answered, "Are you asking this on your own, or have others told you about Me?"

35 "I'm not a Jew, am I?" Pilate replied. "Your own nation and the chief priests handed You over to me. What have You done?"

36 "My kingdom is not of this world," said Jesus. "If My kingdom were of this world, My servants would fight, so that I wouldn't be handed over to the Jews. As it is, My kingdom does not have its origin here."

37 "You are a king then?" Pilate asked.

"You say that I'm a king," Jesus replied. "I was born for this, and I have come into the world for this: to testify to the truth. Everyone who is of the truth listens to My voice."

38 "What is truth?" said Pilate.

## Jesus or Barabbas

After he had said this, he went out to the Jews again and told them, "I find no grounds for charging Him. 39 You have a custom that I release one [prisoner] to you at the Passover.

So, do you want me to release to you the King of the Jews?"

40 They shouted back, "Not this man, but Barabbas!" Now Barabbas was a revolutionary.

## Jesus Flogged and Mocked

**19** Then •Pilate took Jesus and had Him flogged. 2 The soldiers also twisted a crown out of thorns, put it on His head, and threw a purple robe around Him. 3 And they repeatedly came up to Him and said, "Hail, King of the Jews!" and were slapping His face.

4 Pilate went outside again and said to them, "Look, I'm bringing Him outside to you to let you know I find no grounds for charging Him."

## Pilate Sentences Jesus to Death

5 Then Jesus came out wearing the crown of thorns and the purple robe. Pilate said to them, "Here is the man!"

6 When the •chief priests and the temple police saw Him, they shouted, "Crucify! Crucify!"

Pilate responded, "Take Him and crucify Him yourselves, for I find no grounds for charging Him."

7 "We have a law," the Jews replied to him, "and according to that law He must die, because He made Himself the Son of God."

8 When Pilate heard this statement, he was more afraid than ever. 9 He went back into the •headquarters and asked Jesus, "Where are You from?" But Jesus did not give him an answer. 10 So Pilate said to Him, "You're not talking to me? Don't You know that I have the authority to release You and the authority to crucify You?"

11 "You would have no authority over Me at all," Jesus answered him, "if it hadn't been given you from above. This is why the one who handed Me over to you has the greater sin."

12 From that moment Pilate made every effort to release Him. But the Jews shouted, "If you release this man, you are not Caesar's friend. Anyone who makes himself a king opposes Caesar!"

13 When Pilate heard these words, he brought Jesus outside. He sat down on the judge's bench in a place called the Stone Pavement (but in Hebrew *Gabbatha*). 14 It was the preparation day for the •Passover, and it was about six in the morning. Then he told the Jews, "Here is your king!"

15 But they shouted, "Take Him away! Take Him away! Crucify Him!"

Pilate said to them, "Should I crucify your king?"

"We have no king but Caesar!" the chief priests answered.

16 So then, because of them, he handed Him over to be crucified.

## The Crucifixion

Therefore they took Jesus away.[a] 17 Carrying His own cross, He went out to what is called Skull Place, which in Hebrew is called *Golgotha*. 18 There they crucified Him and two others with Him, one on either side, with Jesus in the middle. 19 Pilate also had a sign lettered and put on the cross. The inscription was:

> **JESUS THE NAZARENE THE KING OF THE JEWS**

20 Many of the Jews read this sign, because the place where Jesus was

[a]19:16 Other mss add *and led Him out*

crucified was near the city; and it was written in Hebrew, Latin, and Greek. [21] So the chief priests of the Jews said to Pilate, "Don't write, 'The King of the Jews,' but that he said, 'I am the King of the Jews.' "

[22] Pilate replied, "What I have written, I have written."

[23] When the soldiers crucified Jesus, they took His clothes and divided them into four parts, a part for each soldier. They also took the tunic, which was seamless, woven in one piece from the top. [24] So they said to one another, "Let's not tear it, but toss for it, to see who gets it." ⌊They did this⌋ to fulfill the Scripture that says: **They divided My clothes among themselves, and they cast lots for My clothing.**[a] And this is what the soldiers did.

## Jesus' Provision for His Mother

[25] Standing by the cross of Jesus were His mother, His mother's sister, Mary the wife of Clopas, and •Mary Magdalene. [26] When Jesus saw His mother and the disciple He loved standing there, He said to His mother, "Woman, here is your son." [27] Then He said to the disciple, "Here is your mother." And from that hour the disciple took her into his home.

## The Finished Work of Jesus

[28] After this, when Jesus knew that everything was now accomplished, that the Scripture might be fulfilled, He said, "I'm thirsty!" [29] A vessel full of sour wine was sitting there; so they fixed a sponge full of sour wine on hyssop and held it up to His mouth. [30] When Jesus had received the sour wine, He said, "It is finished!" Then bowing His head, He yielded up His spirit.

## Jesus' Side Pierced

[31] Since it was the preparation day, the Jews did not want the bodies to remain on the cross on the Sabbath (for that Sabbath was a special day). They requested that Pilate have the men's legs broken and that ⌊their bodies⌋ be taken away. [32] So the soldiers came and broke the legs of the first man and of the other one who had been crucified with Him. [33] When they came to Jesus, they did not break His legs since they saw that He was already dead. [34] But one of the soldiers pierced His side with a spear, and at once blood and water came out. [35] He who saw this has testified so that you also may believe. His testimony is true, and he knows he is telling the truth. [36] For these things happened so that the Scripture may be fulfilled: **Not one of His bones will be broken.**[b] [37] Also, another Scripture says: **They will look at the One they pierced.**[c]

## Jesus' Burial

[38] After this, Joseph of Arimathea, who was a disciple of Jesus—but secretly because of his fear of the Jews—asked Pilate that he might remove Jesus' body. Pilate gave him permission, so he came and took His body away. [39] Nicodemus (who had previously come to Him at night) also came, bringing a mixture of about 75 pounds of myrrh and aloes. [40] Then they took Jesus' body and wrapped it in linen cloths with the aromatic spices, according to the burial custom of the Jews. [41] There was a garden in

[a]**19:24** Ps 22:18   [b]**19:36** Ex 12:46; Nm 9:12; Ps 34:20   [c]**19:37** Zch 12:10

the place where He was crucified. And in the garden was a new tomb in which no one had yet been placed. [42] So because of the Jewish preparation day, since the tomb was nearby, they placed Jesus there.

---

*"Our loving Heavenly Father desires our presence even if it means pouring out our hearts in anger, frustration, and fear."*
—Sandra Glahn

---

## The Empty Tomb

**20** On the first day of the week Mary Magdalene came to the tomb early, while it was still dark. She saw that the stone had been removed from the tomb. [2] So she ran to Simon Peter and to the other disciple, whom Jesus loved, and said to them, "They have taken the Lord out of the tomb, and we don't know where they have put Him!" [3] At that, Peter and the other disciple went out, heading for the tomb. [4] The two were running together, but the other disciple outran Peter and got to the tomb first. [5] Stooping down, he saw the linen cloths lying there, yet he did not go in. [6] Then, following him, Simon Peter came also. He entered the tomb and saw the linen cloths lying there. [7] The wrapping that had been on His head was not lying with the linen cloths but folded up in a separate place by itself. [8] The other disciple, who had reached the tomb first, then entered the tomb, saw, and believed. [9] For they still did not understand the Scripture that He must rise from the dead. [10] Then the disciples went home again.

## Mary Magdalene Sees the Risen Lord

[11] But Mary stood outside facing the tomb, crying. As she was crying, she stooped to look into the tomb. [12] She saw two angels in white sitting there, one at the head and one at the feet, where Jesus' body had been lying. [13] They said to her, "Woman, why are you crying?"

"Because they've taken away my Lord," she told them, "and I don't know where they've put Him." [14] Having said this, she turned around and saw Jesus standing there, though she did not know it was Jesus.

[15] "Woman," Jesus said to her, "why are you crying? Who is it you are looking for?"

Supposing He was the gardener, she replied, "Sir, if you've removed Him, tell me where you've put Him, and I will take Him away."

[16] "Mary!" Jesus said.

Turning around, she said to Him in Hebrew, *"Rabbouni!"*—which means "Teacher."

[17] "Don't cling to Me," Jesus told her, "for I have not yet ascended to the Father. But go to My brothers and tell them that I am ascending to My Father and your Father—to My God and your God."

[18] Mary Magdalene went and announced to the disciples, "I have seen the Lord!" And she told them what He had said to her.

## The Disciples Commissioned

[19] In the evening of that first day of the week, the disciples were ⌊gathered together⌋ with the doors locked because of their fear of the Jews. Then Jesus came, stood among them, and said to them, "Peace to you!"

[20] Having said this, He showed them His hands and His side. So the disciples rejoiced when they saw the Lord.

<sup>21</sup> Jesus said to them again, "Peace to you! Just as the Father has sent Me, I also send you." <sup>22</sup> After saying this, He breathed on them and said, "Receive the Holy Spirit. <sup>23</sup> If you forgive the sins of any, they are forgiven them; if you retain [the sins of] any, they are retained."

## Thomas Sees and Believes

<sup>24</sup> But one of the Twelve, Thomas (called "Twin"), was not with them when Jesus came. <sup>25</sup> So the other disciples kept telling him, "We have seen the Lord!"

But he said to them, "If I don't see the mark of the nails in His hands, put my finger into the mark of the nails, and put my hand into His side, I will never believe!"

<sup>26</sup> After eight days His disciples were indoors again, and Thomas was with them. Even though the doors were locked, Jesus came and stood among them. He said, "Peace to you!" <sup>27</sup> Then He said to Thomas, "Put your finger here and observe My hands. Reach out your hand and put it into My side. Don't be an unbeliever, but a believer."

<sup>28</sup> Thomas responded to Him, "My Lord and my God!"

<sup>29</sup> Jesus said, "Because you have seen Me, you have believed. Blessed are those who believe without seeing."

## The Purpose of This Gospel

<sup>30</sup> Jesus performed many other signs in the presence of His disciples that are not written in this book. <sup>31</sup> But these are written so that you may believe Jesus is the •Messiah, the Son of God, and by believing you may have life in His name.

---

### John 20:24-29

*You're sold on Christ and certain you've done the right thing, but sometimes you wonder how you can really be sure. Is that allowed after you've already committed? Well, you can ask God any question, as long as you understand that He knows when you need the answer.*

---

## Jesus' Third Appearance to the Disciples

**21** After this, Jesus revealed Himself again to His disciples by the Sea of Tiberias. He revealed Himself in this way: <sup>2</sup> Simon Peter, Thomas (called "Twin"), Nathanael from Cana of Galilee, Zebedee's sons, and two others of His disciples were together. <sup>3</sup> "I'm going fishing," Simon Peter said to them.

"We're coming with you," they told him. They went out and got into the boat; but that night they caught nothing.

<sup>4</sup> When daybreak came, Jesus stood on the shore. However, the disciples did not know that it was Jesus. <sup>5</sup> "Men," Jesus called to them, "you don't have any fish, do you?"

"No," they answered.

<sup>6</sup> "Cast the net on the right side of the boat," He told them, "and you'll find some." So they did, and they were unable to haul it in because of the large number of fish. <sup>7</sup> Therefore the disciple whom Jesus loved said to Peter, "It's the Lord!"

When Simon Peter heard that it was the Lord, he tied his outer garment around him (for he was stripped) and plunged into the sea. <sup>8</sup> But since they were not far from land (about 100 yards away), the other disciples came in the boat, dragging the net full of fish. <sup>9</sup> When they got out on land, they saw a charcoal fire there, with fish lying on it, and bread.

<sup>10</sup> "Bring some of the fish you've just caught," Jesus told them. <sup>11</sup> So Simon Peter got up and hauled the net ashore, full of large fish—153 of them. Even though there were so many, the net was not torn.

<sup>12</sup> "Come and have breakfast," Jesus told them. None of the disciples dared ask Him, "Who are You?" because they knew it was the Lord. <sup>13</sup> Jesus came, took the bread, and gave it to them. He did the same with the fish.

<sup>14</sup> This was now the third time Jesus appeared to the disciples after He was raised from the dead.

### Jesus' Threefold Restoration of Peter

<sup>15</sup> When they had eaten breakfast, Jesus asked Simon Peter, "Simon, son of John,<sup>a</sup> do you love Me more than these?"

"Yes, Lord," he said to Him, "You know that I love You."

"Feed My lambs," He told him.

<sup>16</sup> A second time He asked him, "Simon, son of John, do you love Me?"

"Yes, Lord," he said to Him, "You know that I love You."

"Shepherd My sheep," He told him.

<sup>17</sup> He asked him the third time, "Simon, son of John, do you love Me?" Peter was grieved that He asked him the third time, "Do you love Me?" He said, "Lord, You know everything! You know that I love You."

"Feed My sheep," Jesus said. <sup>18</sup> "•I assure you: When you were young, you would tie your belt and walk wherever you wanted. But when you grow old, you will stretch out your hands and someone else will tie you and carry you where you don't want to go." <sup>19</sup> He said this to signify by what kind of death he would glorify God. After saying this, He told him, "Follow Me!"

### Correcting a False Report

<sup>20</sup> So Peter turned around and saw the disciple Jesus loved following them. ⌊That disciple⌋ was the one who had leaned back against Jesus at the supper and asked, "Lord, who is the one that's going to betray You?" <sup>21</sup> When Peter saw him, he said to Jesus, "Lord—what about him?"

<sup>22</sup> "If I want him to remain until I come," Jesus answered, "what is that to you? As for you, follow Me."

<sup>23</sup> So this report spread to the brothers that this disciple would not die. Yet Jesus did not tell him that he would not die, but, "If I want him to remain until I come, what is that to you?"

### Epilogue

<sup>24</sup> This is the disciple who testifies to these things and who wrote them down. We know that his testimony is true.

<sup>25</sup> And there are also many other things that Jesus did, which, if they were written one by one, I suppose not even the world itself could contain the books that would be written.

<sup>a</sup>**21:15-17** Other mss read *Simon, son of Jonah*; see Jn 1:42; Mt 16:17

# ACTS

## Prologue

**1** I wrote the first narrative, Theophilus, about all that Jesus began to do and teach [2] until the day He was taken up, after He had given orders through the Holy Spirit to the apostles whom He had chosen. [3] After He had suffered, He also presented Himself alive to them by many convincing proofs, appearing to them during 40 days and speaking about the kingdom of God.

## The Holy Spirit Promised

[4] While He was together with them, He commanded them not to leave Jerusalem, but to wait for the Father's promise. "This," ⌊He said, "is what⌋ you heard from Me; [5] for John baptized with water, but you will be baptized with the Holy Spirit not many days from now."

[6] So when they had come together, they asked Him, "Lord, at this time are You restoring the kingdom to Israel?"

[7] He said to them, "It is not for you to know times or periods that the Father has set by His own authority. [8] But you will receive power when the Holy Spirit has come upon you, and you will be My witnesses in Jerusalem, in all Judea and Samaria, and to the ends of the earth."

## The Ascension

[9] After He had said this, He was taken up as they were watching, and a cloud received Him out of their sight. [10] While He was going, they were gazing into heaven, and suddenly two men in white clothes stood by them.

[11] They said, "Men of Galilee, why do you stand looking up into heaven? This Jesus, who has been taken from you into heaven, will come in the same way that you have seen Him going into heaven."

## United in Prayer

[12] Then they returned to Jerusalem from the mount called Olive Grove, which is near Jerusalem—a Sabbath day's journey away. [13] When they arrived, they went to the room upstairs where they were staying: Peter, John, James, Andrew, Philip, Thomas, Bartholomew, Matthew, James the son of Alphaeus, Simon the Zealot, and Judas the son of James. [14] All these were continually united in prayer,[a] along with the women, including Mary the mother of Jesus, and His brothers.

## Matthias Chosen

[15] During these days Peter stood up among the brothers[b]—the number of people who were together was about 120—and said: [16] "Brothers, the Scripture had to be fulfilled that the Holy Spirit through the mouth of David spoke in advance about Judas, who became a guide to those who arrested Jesus. [17] For he was one of our number and was allotted a share in this ministry." [18] Now this man acquired a field with his unrighteous wages; and falling headfirst, he burst open in the middle, and all his insides spilled out. [19] This became known to all the residents of Jerusalem, so that in their own language that field is

called *Hakeldama,* that is, Field of Blood. [20] "For it is written in the Book of Psalms:

> **Let his dwelling become**
> **desolate;**
> **let no one live in it;**[a] and
> **Let someone else take his**
> **position.**[b]

[21] "Therefore, from among the men who have accompanied us during the whole time the Lord Jesus went in and out among us— [22] beginning from the baptism of John until the day He was taken up from us—from among these, it is necessary that one become a witness with us of His resurrection."

[23] So they proposed two: Joseph, called Barsabbas, who was also known as Justus, and Matthias. [24] Then they prayed, "You, Lord, know the hearts of all; show which of these two You have chosen [25] to take the place[c] in this apostolic service that Judas left to go to his own place." [26] Then they cast lots for them, and the lot fell to Matthias. So he was numbered with the 11 apostles.

## Pentecost

**2** When the day of Pentecost had arrived, they were all together in one place. [2] Suddenly a sound like that of a violent rushing wind came from heaven, and it filled the whole house where they were staying. [3] And tongues, like flames of fire that were divided, appeared to them and rested on each one of them. [4] Then they were all filled with the Holy Spirit and began to speak in different languages, as the Spirit gave them ability for speech.

[5] There were Jews living in Jerusalem, devout men from every nation under heaven. [6] When this sound occurred, the multitude came together and was confused because each one heard them speaking in his own language. [7] And they were astounded and amazed, saying,[d] "Look, aren't all these who are speaking Galileans? [8] How is it that we hear, each of us, in our own native language? [9] Parthians, Medes, Elamites; those who live in Mesopotamia, in Judea and Cappadocia, Pontus and Asia, [10] Phrygia and Pamphylia, Egypt and the parts of Libya near Cyrene; visitors from Rome, both Jews and proselytes, [11] Cretans and Arabs—we hear them speaking in our own languages the magnificent acts of God." [12] And they were all astounded and perplexed, saying to one another, "What could this be?" [13] But some sneered and said, "They're full of new wine!"

## Peter's Sermon

[14] But Peter stood up with the Eleven, raised his voice, and proclaimed to them: "Jewish men and all you residents of Jerusalem, let this be known to you and pay attention to my words. [15] For these people are not drunk, as you suppose, since it's only nine in the morning. [16] On the contrary, this is what was spoken through the prophet Joel:

> [17] **And it will be** in the last days,
>      says God,
>    that **I will pour out My Spirit**
>      **on all humanity;**
>    **then your sons and your**
>      **daughters will prophesy,**
>    **your young men will see**
>      **visions,**
>    **and your old men will dream**
>      **dreams.**
> [18] **I will even pour out My Spirit**
>    **on My male and female**

---

[a] 1:20 Ps 69:25.  [b] 1:20 Ps 109:8  [c] 1:25 Other mss read *to share*  [d] 2:7 Other mss add *to one another*

slaves in those days,
and they will prophesy.
<sup>19</sup> I will display wonders in the
      heaven above
and signs on the earth below:
blood and fire and a cloud of
      smoke.
<sup>20</sup> The sun will be turned to
      darkness,
and the moon to blood,
before the great and
      remarkable day of the
      Lord comes;
<sup>21</sup> then whoever calls on the
      name of the Lord will
      be saved.<sup>a</sup>

<sup>22</sup> "Men of Israel, listen to these
words: This Jesus the •Nazarene
was a man pointed out to you by
God with miracles, wonders, and
signs that God did among you
through Him, just as you yourselves know. <sup>23</sup> Though He was
delivered up according to God's
determined plan and foreknowl-
edge, you used<sup>b</sup> lawless people to
nail Him to a cross and kill Him.
<sup>24</sup> God raised Him up, ending the
pains of death, because it was not
possible for Him to be held by it.
<sup>25</sup> For David says of Him:

I saw the Lord ever before
      me;
because He is at my right
      hand,
I will not be shaken.
<sup>26</sup> Therefore my heart was
      glad,
and my tongue rejoiced.
Moreover my flesh will rest
      in hope,
<sup>27</sup> because You will not leave
      my soul in •Hades,
or allow Your Holy One to

see decay.
<sup>28</sup> You have revealed
      the paths of life to me;
You will fill me with gladness
      in Your presence.<sup>c</sup>

<sup>29</sup> "Brothers, I can confidently speak
to you about the patriarch David: he is
both dead and buried, and his tomb is
with us to this day. <sup>30</sup> Since he was a
prophet, he knew that God had sworn
an oath to him to seat one of his
descendants<sup>d</sup> on his throne. <sup>31</sup> Seeing
this in advance, he spoke concerning
the resurrection of the •Messiah:

He<sup>e</sup> was not left in Hades,
and His flesh did not
      experience decay.<sup>f</sup>

<sup>32</sup> "God has resurrected this Jesus.
We are all witnesses of this.
<sup>33</sup> Therefore, since He has been
exalted to the right hand of God and
has received from the Father the
promised Holy Spirit, He has poured
out what you both see and hear.
<sup>34</sup> For it was not David who ascended
into the heavens, but he himself says:

The Lord said to my Lord,
'Sit at My right hand
<sup>35</sup> until I make Your enemies
      Your footstool.'<sup>g</sup>

<sup>36</sup> "Therefore let all the house of
Israel know with certainty that God
has made this Jesus, whom you crucified, both Lord and Messiah!"

## Forgiveness through the Messiah

<sup>37</sup> When they heard this, they were
pierced to the heart and said to Peter
and the rest of the apostles: "Brothers,
what must we do?"

<sup>a</sup>2:17–21 Jl 2:28–32   <sup>b</sup>2:23 Other mss read *you have taken*   <sup>c</sup>2:25–28 Ps 16:8–11   <sup>d</sup>2:30 Other mss
add *according to the flesh to raise up the Messiah*   <sup>e</sup>2:31 Other mss read *His soul*   <sup>f</sup>2:31 Ps 16:10
<sup>g</sup>2:34–35 Ps 110:1

## Acts 2:38-39

### God the Holy Spirit

*The Holy Spirit comes to live in us the moment we invite Jesus into our lives. Through the regular practice of repentance—turning deliberately away from sin and turning head-on into the path of obedience toward God—we make His new home a roomier place to live and work.*

[38] "Repent," Peter said to them, "and be baptized, each of you, in the name of Jesus the Messiah for the forgiveness of your sins, and you will receive the gift of the Holy Spirit. [39] For the promise is for you and for your children, and for all who are far off, as many as the Lord our God will call." [40] And with many other words he testified and strongly urged them, saying, "Be saved from this corrupt generation!"

### A Generous and Growing Church

[41] So those who accepted his message were baptized, and that day about 3,000 people were added to them. [42] And they devoted themselves to the apostles' teaching, to fellowship, to the breaking of bread, and to prayers. [43] Then fear came over everyone, and many wonders and signs were being performed through the apostles. [44] Now all the believers were together and had everything in common. [45] So they sold their possessions and property and distributed the proceeds to all, as anyone had a need. [46] And every day they devoted themselves [to meeting] together in the *temple complex, and broke bread from house to house. They ate their food with gladness and simplicity of heart, [47] praising God and having favor with all the people. And every day the Lord added those being saved to them.[a]

### Healing of a Lame Man

**3** Now Peter and John were going up together to the *temple complex at the hour of prayer at three in the afternoon. [2] And a man who was lame from his mother's womb was carried there and placed every day at the temple gate called Beautiful, so he could beg from those entering the temple complex. [3] When he saw Peter and John about to enter the temple complex, he asked for help. [4] Peter, along with John, looked at him intently and said, "Look at us." [5] So he turned to them, expecting to get something from them. [6] But Peter said, "I have neither silver nor gold, but what I have, I give to you: In the name of Jesus Christ the *Nazarene, get up and walk!" [7] Then, taking him by the right hand he raised him up, and at once his feet and ankles became strong. [8] So he jumped up, stood, and started to walk, and he entered the temple complex with them—walking, leaping, and praising God. [9] All the people saw him walking and praising God, [10] and they recognized that he was the one who used to sit and beg at the Beautiful Gate of the temple complex. So they were filled with awe and astonishment at what had happened to him.

[a]**2:47** Other mss read *to the church*

### Preaching in Solomon's Colonnade

[11] While he[a] was holding on to Peter and John, all the people, greatly amazed, ran toward them in what is called Solomon's Colonnade. [12] When Peter saw this, he addressed the people: "Men of Israel, why are you amazed at this? Or why do you stare at us, as though by our own power or godliness we had made him walk? [13] The God of Abraham, Isaac, and Jacob, the God of our fathers, has glorified His Servant Jesus, whom you handed over and denied in the presence of •Pilate, when he had decided to release Him. [14] But you denied the Holy and Righteous One, and asked to have a murderer given to you. [15] And you killed the source of life, whom God raised from the dead; we are witnesses of this. [16] By faith in His name, His name has made this man strong, whom you see and know. So the faith that comes through Him has given him this perfect health in front of all of you.

[17] "And now, brothers, I know that you did it in ignorance, just as your leaders also did. [18] But what God predicted through the mouth of all the prophets—that His •Messiah would suffer—He has fulfilled in this way. [19] Therefore repent and turn back, that your sins may be wiped out so that seasons of refreshing may come from the presence of the Lord, [20] and He may send Jesus, who has been appointed Messiah for you. [21] Heaven must welcome Him until the times of the restoration of all things, which God spoke about by the mouth of His holy prophets from the beginning. [22] Moses said:[b]

**The Lord your God will raise up for you a Prophet like me** from among your brothers. You must listen to Him in everything He will say to you. [23] And it will be that everyone who will not listen to that Prophet will be completely cut off from the people.[c]

[24] "In addition, all the prophets who have spoken, from Samuel and those after him, have also announced these days. [25] You are the sons of the prophets and of the covenant that God made with your forefathers, saying to Abraham, **And in your seed all the families of the earth will be blessed.**[d] [26] God raised up His Servant[e] and sent Him first to you to bless you by turning each of you from your evil ways."

### Peter and John Arrested

**4** Now as they were speaking to the people, the priests, the commander of the temple guard, and the •Sadducees confronted them, [2] because they were provoked that they were teaching the people and proclaiming in the person of Jesus the resurrection from the dead. [3] So they seized them and put them in custody until the next day, since it was already evening. [4] But many of those who heard the message believed, and the number of the men came to about 5,000.

### Peter and John Face the Jewish Leadership

[5] The next day, their rulers, elders, and •scribes assembled in Jerusalem [6] with Annas the high priest, Caiaphas, John and Alexander, and all the members of the high-priestly family. [7] After they had Peter and John

[a]**3:11** Other mss read *the lame man who was healed*     [b]**3:22** Other mss add *to the fathers*
[c]**3:22–23** Dt 18:15–19     [d]**3:25** Gn 12:3; 18:18; 22:18; 26:4     [e]**3:26** Other mss add *Jesus*

stand before them, they asked the question: "By what power or in what name have you done this?"

[8] Then Peter was filled with the Holy Spirit and said to them, "Rulers of the people and elders:[a] [9] If we are being examined today about a good deed done to a disabled man—by what means he was healed— [10] let it be known to all of you and to all the people of Israel, that by the name of Jesus Christ the •Nazarene—whom you crucified and whom God raised from the dead—by Him this man is standing here before you healthy. [11] This ⌊Jesus⌋ is

**The stone despised by you
    builders,
who has become the
    cornerstone.**[b]

[12] There is salvation in no one else, for there is no other name under heaven given to people by which we must be saved."

---

### Acts 4:13-20

*You're getting that look in your eye, that fire in your belly, that skip in your step that tells the world you've never been this serious about anything in your life. There's only one way to live the Christian life right, and that's to do it with all you've got.*

---

### The Name Forbidden

[13] Observing the boldness of Peter and John and realizing them to be uneducated and untrained men, they were amazed and knew that they had been with Jesus. [14] And since they saw the man who had been healed standing with them, they had nothing to say in response. [15] After they had ordered them to leave the •Sanhedrin, they conferred among themselves, [16] saying, "What should we do with these men? For an obvious sign, evident to all who live in Jerusalem, has been done through them, and we cannot deny it! [17] But so this does not spread any further among the people, let's threaten them against speaking to anyone in this name again." [18] So they called for them and ordered them not to preach or teach at all in the name of Jesus.

[19] But Peter and John answered them, "Whether it's right in the sight of God ⌊for us⌋ to listen to you rather than to God, you decide; [20] for we are unable to stop speaking about what we have seen and heard."

[21] After threatening them further, they released them. They found no way to punish them, because the people were all giving glory to God over what had been done; [22] for the man was over 40 years old on whom this sign of healing had been performed.

### Prayer for Boldness

[23] After they were released, they went to their own fellowship and reported all that the •chief priests and the elders had said to them. [24] When they heard this, they raised their voices to God unanimously and said, "Master, You are the One who made the heaven, the earth, and the sea, and everything in them. [25] You said through the Holy Spirit, by the mouth of our father David Your servant:[c]

[a]4:8 Other mss add *of Israel*   [b]4:11 Ps 118:22   [c]4:25 Other mss read *through the mouth of David Your servant*

Why did the Gentiles rage,
and the peoples plot futile
things?
26 The kings of the earth took
their stand,
and the rulers assembled
together
against the Lord and against
His •Messiah.[a]

27 "For, in fact, in this city both •Herod and Pontius •Pilate, with the Gentiles and the peoples of Israel, assembled together against Your holy Servant Jesus, whom You anointed, 28 to do whatever Your hand and Your plan had predestined to take place. 29 And now, Lord, consider their threats, and grant that Your slaves may speak Your message with complete boldness, 30 while You stretch out Your hand for healing, signs, and wonders to be performed through the name of Your holy Servant Jesus." 31 When they had prayed, the place where they were assembled was shaken, and they were all filled with the Holy Spirit and began to speak God's message with boldness.

---

*"The Christian story is that of restoration of intimacy with God and the passion which comes from renewing our choice to respond to His wishes."*
—*Gordon MacDonald*

---

## Believers Sharing

32 Now the multitude of those who believed were of one heart and soul, and no one said that any of his possessions was his own, but instead they held everything in common. 33 And with great power the apostles were giving testimony to the resurrection of the Lord Jesus, and great grace was on all of them. 34 For there was not a needy person among them, because all those who owned lands or houses sold them, brought the proceeds of the things that were sold, 35 and laid them at the apostles' feet. This was then distributed to each person as anyone had a need.

36 Joseph, who was named by the apostles Barnabas, which is translated Son of Encouragement, a Levite and a Cypriot by birth, 37 sold a field he owned, brought the money, and laid it at the apostles' feet.

## Lying to the Holy Spirit

5 But a man named Ananias, with Sapphira his wife, sold a piece of property. 2 However, he kept back part of the proceeds with his wife's knowledge, and brought a portion of it and laid it at the apostles' feet.

3 Then Peter said, "Ananias, why has Satan filled your heart to lie to the Holy Spirit and keep back part of the proceeds from the field? 4 Wasn't it yours while you possessed it? And after it was sold, wasn't it at your disposal? Why is it that you planned this thing in your heart? You have not lied to men but to God!" 5 When he heard these words, Ananias dropped dead, and a great fear came on all who heard. 6 The young men got up, wrapped ⌊his body⌋, carried him out, and buried him.

7 There was an interval of about three hours; then his wife came in, not knowing what had happened. 8 "Tell me," Peter asked her, "did you sell the field for this price?"

"Yes," she said, "for that price."

[a]4:25–26 Ps 2:1–2

9 Then Peter said to her, "Why did you agree to test the Spirit of the Lord? Look! The feet of those who have buried your husband are at the door, and they will carry you out!"

10 Instantly she dropped dead at his feet. When the young men came in, they found her dead, carried her out, and buried her beside her husband. 11 Then great fear came on the whole church and on all who heard these things.

---

## Acts 5:12-14

### The Church

*The church is its people, not its building. It is not confined to a street address or a Sunday morning. But it is confined to those who believe in Jesus Christ, who are out in the world every day living for their Lord and Savior. And it grows as God brings more people into its fellowship.*

---

## Apostolic Signs and Wonders

12 Many signs and wonders were being done among the people through the hands of the apostles. By common consent they would all meet in Solomon's Colonnade. 13 None of the rest dared to join them, but the people praised them highly. 14 Believers were added to the Lord in increasing numbers—crowds of both men and women. 15 As a result, they would carry the sick out into the streets and lay them on beds and pallets so that when Peter came by, at least his shadow might fall on some of them. 16 In addition, a multitude came together from the towns surrounding Jerusalem, bringing sick people and those who were tormented by unclean spirits, and they were all healed.

## In and Out of Prison

17 Then the high priest took action. He and all his colleagues, those who belonged to the party of the •Sadducees, were filled with jealousy. 18 So they arrested the apostles and put them in the city jail. 19 But an angel of the Lord opened the doors of the jail during the night, brought them out, and said, 20 "Go and stand in the •temple complex, and tell the people all about this life." 21 In obedience to this, they entered the temple complex at daybreak and began to teach.

## The Apostles on Trial Again

When the high priest and those who were with him arrived, they convened the •Sanhedrin—the full Senate of the sons of Israel—and sent to the jail to have them brought. 22 But when the temple police got there, they did not find them in the jail, so they returned and reported, 23 "We found the jail securely locked, with the guards standing in front of the doors; but when we opened them, we found no one inside!" 24 As[a] the captain of the temple police and the •chief priests heard these things, they were baffled about them, as to what could come of this.

25 Someone came and reported to them, "Look! The men you put in jail are standing in the temple complex and teaching the people." 26 Then the captain went with the temple police

[a]5:24 Other mss add *the high priest and*

and brought them in without force, because they were afraid the people might stone them. [27] When they had brought them in, they had them stand before the Sanhedrin, and the high priest asked, [28] "Didn't we strictly order you not to teach in this name? And look, you have filled Jerusalem with your teaching and are determined to bring this man's blood on us!"

[29] But Peter and the apostles replied, "We must obey God rather than men. [30] The God of our fathers raised up Jesus, whom you had murdered by hanging Him on a tree. [31] God exalted this man to His right hand as ruler and Savior, to grant repentance to Israel, and forgiveness of sins. [32] We are witnesses of these things, and so is the Holy Spirit whom God has given to those who obey Him."

## Gamaliel's Advice

[33] When they heard this, they were enraged and wanted to kill them. [34] A *Pharisee named Gamaliel, a teacher of the law who was respected by all the people, stood up in the Sanhedrin and ordered the men[a] to be taken outside for a little while. [35] He said to them, "Men of Israel, be careful about what you're going to do to these men. [36] Not long ago Theudas rose up, claiming to be somebody, and a group of about 400 men rallied to him. He was killed, and all his partisans were dispersed and came to nothing. [37] After this man, Judas the Galilean rose up in the days of the census and attracted a following. That man also perished, and all his partisans were scattered. [38] And now, I tell you, stay away from these men and leave them alone. For if this plan or this work is of men, it will be overthrown; [39] but if it is of God, you will not be able to overthrow them. You may even be found fighting against God." So they were persuaded by him. [40] After they called in the apostles and had them flogged, they ordered them not to speak in the name of Jesus and released them. [41] Then they went out from the presence of the Sanhedrin, rejoicing that they were counted worthy to be dishonored on behalf of the name.[b] [42] Every day in the temple complex, and in various homes, they continued teaching and proclaiming the good news that the *Messiah is Jesus.

---

### Acts 6:3-4

### The Church

*Not everybody does the same thing in the church. Some preach. Some keep records. Some teach. Some change diapers. Some serve. Some lead. Some pray. Some pay visits. And when the church is working the way it's supposed to, everybody does the job God has placed them there to do.*

---

## Seven Chosen to Serve

6 In those days, as the number of the disciples was multiplying, there arose a complaint by the Hellenistic Jews against the Hebraic Jews that their widows were being overlooked in the daily distribution. [2] Then the Twelve summoned the whole *company of the disciples and said, "It would not be right for us to give up preaching about God to wait

[a]5:34 Other mss read *apostles*   [b]5:41 Other mss add *of Jesus,* or *of Christ*

on tables. ³ Therefore, brothers, select from among you seven men of good reputation, full of the Spirit and wisdom, whom we can appoint to this duty. ⁴ But we will devote ourselves to prayer and to the preaching ministry." ⁵ The proposal pleased the whole company. So they chose Stephen, a man full of faith and the Holy Spirit, and Philip, Prochorus, Nicanor, Timon, Parmenas, and Nicolaus, a proselyte from Antioch. ⁶ They had them stand before the apostles, who prayed and laid their hands on them.

⁷ So the preaching about God flourished, the number of the disciples in Jerusalem multiplied greatly, and a large group of priests became obedient to the faith.

## Stephen Accused of Blasphemy

⁸ Stephen, full of grace and power, was performing great wonders and signs among the people. ⁹ Then some from what is called the Freedmen's •Synagogue, composed of both Cyrenians and Alexandrians, and some from Cilicia and Asia, came forward and disputed with Stephen. ¹⁰ But they were unable to stand up against the wisdom and the Spirit by whom he spoke. ¹¹ Then they induced men to say, "We heard him speaking blasphemous words against Moses and God!" ¹² They stirred up the people, the elders, and the •scribes; so they came up, dragged him off, and took him to the •Sanhedrin. ¹³ They also presented false witnesses who said, "This man does not stop speaking blasphemous words against this holy place and the law. ¹⁴ For we heard him say that Jesus, this •Nazarene, will destroy this place and change the customs that Moses handed down to us." ¹⁵ And all

who were sitting in the Sanhedrin looked intently at him and saw that his face was like the face of an angel.

## Stephen's Address

**7** "Is this true?" the high priest asked.
² "Brothers and fathers," he said, "listen: The God of glory appeared to our father Abraham when he was in Mesopotamia, before he settled in Haran, ³ and said to him:

> **Get out of your country and
> away from your relatives,
> and come to the land that I
> will show you.**ᵃ

⁴ "Then he came out of the land of the Chaldeans and settled in Haran. And from there, after his father died, God had him move to this land in which you now live. ⁵ He didn't give him an inheritance in it, not even a foot of ground, but He promised to give it to him as a possession, and to his descendants after him, even though he was childless. ⁶ God spoke in this way:

> **His descendants would be
> aliens in a foreign country,
> and they would enslave and
> oppress them for 400
> years.**
> ⁷ **I will judge the nation that
> they will serve as slaves,**
> God said.
> **After this they will come out
> and worship Me in this
> place.**ᵇ

⁸ Then He gave him the covenant of circumcision. This being so, he fathered Isaac and circumcised him on the eighth day; Isaac did the same

ᵃ**7:3** Gn 12:1    ᵇ**7:6–7** Gn 15:13–14

with Jacob, and Jacob with the 12 patriarchs.

## The Patriarchs in Egypt

9 "The patriarchs became jealous of Joseph and sold him into Egypt, but God was with him 10 and rescued him out of all his troubles. He gave him favor and wisdom in the sight of Pharaoh, king of Egypt, who appointed him governor over Egypt and over his whole household. 11 Then a famine came over all of Egypt and Canaan, with great suffering, and our forefathers could find no food. 12 When Jacob heard there was grain in Egypt, he sent our forefathers the first time. 13 The second time, Joseph was revealed to his brothers, and Joseph's family became known to Pharaoh. 14 Joseph then invited his father Jacob and all his relatives, 75 people in all, 15 and Jacob went down to Egypt. He and our forefathers died there, 16 were carried back to Shechem, and were placed in the tomb that Abraham had bought for a sum of silver from the sons of Hamor in Shechem.

## Moses, a Rejected Savior

17 "As the time was drawing near to fulfill the promise that God had made to Abraham, the people flourished and multiplied in Egypt 18 until a different king ruled over Egypt[a] who did not know Joseph. 19 He dealt deceitfully with our race and oppressed our forefathers by making them leave their infants outside so they wouldn't survive. 20 At this time Moses was born, and he was beautiful before God. He was nursed in his father's home three months, 21 and when he was left outside, Pharaoh's daughter adopted and raised him as her own son. 22 So

Moses was educated in all the wisdom of the Egyptians, and was powerful in his speech and actions.

23 "As he was approaching the age of 40, he decided to visit his brothers, the sons of Israel. 24 When he saw one of them being mistreated, he came to his rescue and avenged the oppressed man by striking down the Egyptian. 25 He assumed his brothers would understand that God would give them deliverance through him, but they did not understand. 26 The next day he showed up while they were fighting and tried to reconcile them peacefully, saying, 'Men, you are brothers. Why are you mistreating each other?'

27 "But the one who was mistreating his neighbor pushed him away, saying:

**Who appointed you a ruler and a judge over us? 28 Do you want to kill me, the same way you killed the Egyptian yesterday?**[b]

29 "At this disclosure, Moses fled and became an exile in the land of Midian, where he had two sons. 30 After 40 years had passed, an angel[c] appeared to him in the desert of Mount Sinai, in the flame of a burning bush. 31 When Moses saw it, he was amazed at the sight. As he was approaching to look at it, the voice of the Lord came: 32 **I am the God of your forefathers—the God of Abraham, of Isaac, and of Jacob.**[d] So Moses began to tremble and did not dare to look.

33 "Then the Lord said to him:

**Take the sandals off your feet, because the place where you are standing is holy ground. 34 I have certainly seen the oppression of My people in Egypt; I**

[a]7:18 Other mss omit *over Egypt*   [b]7:27–28 Ex 2:14   [c]7:30 Other mss add *of the Lord*   [d]7:32 Ex 3:6,15

have heard their groaning and have come down to rescue them. And now, come, I will send you to Egypt.[a]

[35] "This Moses, whom they rejected when they said, **Who appointed you a ruler and a judge?**[b]—this one God sent as a ruler and a redeemer by means of the angel who appeared to him in the bush. [36] This man led them out and performed wonders and signs in the land of Egypt, at the Red Sea, and in the desert for 40 years.

## Israel's Rebellion against God

[37] "This is the Moses who said to the sons of Israel, **God**[c] **will raise up for you a Prophet like me from among your brothers.**[d] [38] He is the one who was in the congregation in the desert together with the angel who spoke to him on Mount Sinai, and with our forefathers. He received living oracles to give to us. [39] Our forefathers were unwilling to obey him, but pushed him away, and in their hearts turned back to Egypt. [40] They told Aaron:

**Make us gods who will go before us. As for this Moses who brought us out of the land of Egypt, we don't know what's become of him.**[e]

[41] They even made a calf in those days, offered sacrifice to the idol, and were celebrating what their hands had made. [42] Then God turned away and gave them up to worship the host of heaven, as it is written in the book of the prophets:

**Did you bring Me offerings and sacrifices**

for 40 years in the desert,
O house of Israel?
[43] No, you took up the tent of Moloch
and the star of your god Rephan,
the images that you made to worship.
So I will deport you beyond Babylon![f]

## God's Real Tabernacle

[44] "Our forefathers had the •tabernacle of the testimony in the desert, just as He who spoke to Moses commanded him to make it according to the pattern he had seen. [45] Our forefathers in turn received it and with Joshua brought it in when they dispossessed the nations that God drove out before our fathers, until the days of David. [46] He found favor in God's sight and asked that he might provide a dwelling place for the God[g] of Jacob. [47] But it was Solomon who built Him a house. [48] However, the Most High does not dwell in sanctuaries made with hands, as the prophet says:

[49] Heaven is My throne,
and earth My footstool.
What sort of house will you
build for Me? says the Lord,
or what is My resting place?
[50] Did not My hand make all
these things?[h]

## Resisting the Holy Spirit

[51] "You stiff-necked people with uncircumcised hearts and ears! You are always resisting the Holy Spirit; as your forefathers did, so do you. [52] Which of the prophets did your fathers not persecute? They even killed those who

[a]**7:33–34** Ex 3:5,7–8,10   [b]**7:35** Ex 2:14   [c]**7:37** Other mss read *'The Lord your God*   [d]**7:37** Dt 18:15
[e]**7:40** Ex 32:1,23   [f]**7:42–43** Am 5:25–27   [g]**7:46** Other mss read *house*   [h]**7:49–50** Is 66:1–2

announced beforehand the coming of the Righteous One, whose betrayers and murderers you have now become. [53] You received the law under the direction of angels and yet have not kept it."

## The First Christian Martyr

[54] Hearing these things, they were enraged in their hearts and gnashed their teeth because of him. [55] But being full of the Holy Spirit, he gazed into heaven and saw God's glory, and Jesus standing at the right hand of God, and he said, [56] "Look! I see the heavens opened and the •Son of Man standing at the right hand of God!"
[57] Then they screamed at the top of their voices, stopped their ears, and rushed together against him. [58] They threw him out of the city and began to stone him. And the witnesses laid their robes at the feet of a young man named Saul. [59] They were stoning Stephen as he called out: "Lord Jesus, receive my spirit!" [60] Then he knelt down and cried out with a loud voice, "Lord, do not charge them with this sin!" And saying this, he fell •asleep.

## Saul the Persecutor

**8** Saul agreed with putting him to death.
On that day a severe persecution broke out against the church in Jerusalem, and all except the apostles were scattered throughout the land of Judea and Samaria. [2] But devout men buried Stephen and mourned deeply over him. [3] Saul, however, was ravaging the church, and he would enter house after house, drag off men and women, and put them in prison.

## Philip in Samaria

[4] So those who were scattered went on their way proclaiming the message of good news. [5] Philip went down to a[a] city in Samaria and preached the •Messiah to them. [6] The crowds paid attention with one mind to what Philip said, as they heard and saw the signs he was performing. [7] For unclean spirits, crying out with a loud voice, came out of many who were possessed, and many who were paralyzed and lame were healed. [8] So there was great joy in that city.

---

*"We are united to Jesus and to one another. We died His death and have been raised in His resurrection. Now we can follow Him."*
*—Larry Richards*

---

## The Response of Simon

[9] A man named Simon had previously practiced sorcery in that city and astounded the •Samaritan people, while claiming to be somebody great. [10] They all paid attention to him, from the least of them to the greatest, and they said, "This man is called the Great Power of God!" [11] They were attentive to him because he had astounded them with his sorceries for a long time. [12] But when they believed Philip, as he proclaimed the good news about the kingdom of God and the name of Jesus Christ, both men and women were baptized. [13] Then even Simon himself believed. And after he was baptized, he went around constantly with Philip and was astounded as he observed the

[a]8:5 Other mss read *the*

signs and great miracles that were being performed.

## Simon's Sin

14 When the apostles who were at Jerusalem heard that Samaria had welcomed God's message, they sent Peter and John to them. 15 After they went down there, they prayed for them, that they might receive the Holy Spirit. 16 For He had not yet come down on any of them; they had only been baptized in the name of the Lord Jesus. 17 Then Peter and John laid their hands on them, and they received the Holy Spirit.

18 When Simon saw that the Holy[a] Spirit was given through the laying on of the apostles' hands, he offered them money, 19 saying, "Give me this power too, so that anyone I lay hands on may receive the Holy Spirit."

20 But Peter told him, "May your silver be destroyed with you, because you thought the gift of God could be obtained with money! 21 You have no part or share in this matter, because your heart is not right before God. 22 Therefore repent of this wickedness of yours, and pray to the Lord that the intent of your heart may be forgiven you. 23 For I see you are poisoned by bitterness and bound by iniquity."

24 "Please pray to the Lord for me," Simon replied, "so that nothing you have said may happen to me."

25 Then, after they had testified and spoken the message of the Lord, they traveled back to Jerusalem, evangelizing many villages of the Samaritans.

## The Conversion of the Ethiopian Official

26 An angel of the Lord spoke to Philip: "Get up and go south to the road that goes down from Jerusalem to desert Gaza." 27 So he got up and went. There was an Ethiopian man, a eunuch and high official of Candace, queen of the Ethiopians, who was in charge of her entire treasury. He had come to worship in Jerusalem 28 and was sitting in his chariot on his way home, reading the prophet Isaiah aloud.

29 The Spirit told Philip, "Go and join that chariot."

30 When Philip ran up to it, he heard him reading the prophet Isaiah, and said, "Do you understand what you're reading?"

31 "How can I," he said, "unless someone guides me?" So he invited Philip to come up and sit with him. 32 Now the Scripture passage he was reading was this:

He was led like a sheep to
  the slaughter,
and as a lamb is silent before
  its shearer,
so He does not open His
  mouth.
33 In His humiliation justice
  was denied Him.
Who will describe His
  generation?
For His life is taken from the
  earth.[b]

34 The eunuch replied to Philip, "I ask you, who is the prophet saying this about—himself or another person?" 35 So Philip proceeded to tell him the good news about Jesus, beginning from that Scripture.

36 As they were traveling down the road, they came to some water. The eunuch said, "Look, there's water! What would keep me from being baptized?" [37 And Philip said, "If you believe with all your heart you may."

a8:18 Other mss omit Holy    b8:32–33 Is 53:7–8

---

### Acts 8:36-38

*You painted a beautiful, living picture of salvation the moment you slipped under the waters of baptism and washed your sins into oblivion. Even though different churches handle it different ways, baptism unites us all with the family of God.*

---

And he replied, "I believe that Jesus Christ is the Son of God."]ᵃ ³⁸ Then he ordered the chariot to stop, and both Philip and the eunuch went down into the water, and he baptized him. ³⁹ When they came up out of the water, the Spirit of the Lord carried Philip away, and the eunuch did not see him any longer. But he went on his way rejoicing. ⁴⁰ Philip appeared in Azotus, and passing through, he was evangelizing all the towns until he came to Caesarea.

### The Damascus Road

**9** Meanwhile Saul, still breathing threats and murder against the disciples of the Lord, went to the high priest ² and requested letters from him to the •synagogues in Damascus, so that if he found any who belonged to the Way, either men or women, he might bring them as prisoners to Jerusalem. ³ As he traveled and was nearing Damascus, a light from heaven suddenly flashed around him. ⁴ Falling to the ground, he heard a voice saying to him, "Saul, Saul, why are you persecuting Me?"

⁵ "Who are You, Lord?" he said.

"I am Jesus, whom you are persecuting," He replied. ⁶ "But get up and go into the city, and you will be told what you must do."

⁷ The men who were traveling with him stood speechless, hearing the sound but seeing no one. ⁸ Then Saul got up from the ground, and though his eyes were open, he could see nothing. So they took him by the hand and led him into Damascus. ⁹ He was unable to see for three days, and did not eat or drink.

### Saul's Baptism

¹⁰ Now in Damascus there was a disciple named Ananias. And the Lord said to him in a vision, "Ananias!"

"Here I am, Lord!" he said.

¹¹ "Get up and go to the street called Straight," the Lord said to him, "to the house of Judas, and ask for a man from Tarsus named Saul, since he is praying there. ¹² In a visionᵇ he has seen a man named Ananias coming in and placing his hands on him so he may regain his sight."

¹³ "Lord," Ananias answered, "I have heard from many people about this man, how much harm he has done to Your saints in Jerusalem. ¹⁴ And he has authority here from the •chief priests to arrest all who call on Your name."

¹⁵ But the Lord said to him, "Go! For this man is My chosen instrument to carry My name before Gentiles, kings, and the sons of Israel. ¹⁶ I will certainly show him how much he must suffer for My name!"

¹⁷ So Ananias left and entered the house. Then he placed his hands on him and said, "Brother Saul, the Lord Jesus, who appeared to you on the road you were traveling, has sent me so you may regain your sight and be filled with the Holy Spirit."

---

ᵃ**8:37** Other mss omit bracketed text    ᵇ**9:12** Other mss omit *In a vision*

¹⁸ At once something like scales fell from his eyes, and he regained his sight. Then he got up and was baptized. ¹⁹ And after taking some food, he regained his strength.

## Saul Proclaiming the Messiah

Saul was with the disciples in Damascus for some days. ²⁰ Immediately he began proclaiming Jesus in the synagogues: "He is the Son of God."

²¹ But all who heard him were astounded and said, "Isn't this the man who, in Jerusalem, was destroying those who called on this name, and then came here for the purpose of taking them as prisoners to the chief priests?"

²² But Saul grew more capable, and kept confounding the Jews who lived in Damascus by proving that this One is the •Messiah.

²³ After many days had passed, the Jews conspired to kill him, ²⁴ but their plot became known to Saul. So they were watching the gates day and night intending to kill him, ²⁵ but his disciples took him by night and lowered him in a large basket through ⌊an opening in⌋ the wall.

## Saul in Jerusalem

²⁶ When he arrived in Jerusalem, he tried to associate with the disciples, but they were all afraid of him, since they did not believe he was a disciple. ²⁷ Barnabas, however, took him and brought him to the apostles and explained to them how, on the road, Saul had seen the Lord, and that He had talked to him, and how in Damascus he had spoken boldly in the name of Jesus. ²⁸ Saul was coming and going with them in Jerusalem, speaking boldly in the name of the Lord. ²⁹ He conversed and debated with the Hellenistic Jews, but they attempted to kill him. ³⁰ When the brothers found out, they took him down to Caesarea and sent him off to Tarsus.

³¹ So the church throughout all Judea, Galilee, and Samaria had peace, being built up and walking in the fear of the Lord and in the encouragement of the Holy Spirit, and it increased in numbers.

## The Healing of Aeneas

³² As Peter was traveling from place to place, he also came down to the saints who lived in Lydda. ³³ There he found a man named Aeneas, who was paralyzed and had been bedridden for eight years. ³⁴ Peter said to him, "Aeneas, Jesus Christ heals you. Get up and make your own bed," and immediately he got up. ³⁵ So all who lived in Lydda and Sharon saw him and turned to the Lord.

## Dorcas Restored to Life

³⁶ In Joppa there was a disciple named Tabitha, which is translated Dorcas. She was always doing good works and acts of charity. ³⁷ In those days she became sick and died. After washing her, they placed her in a room upstairs. ³⁸ Since Lydda was near Joppa, the disciples heard that Peter was there and sent two men to him who begged him, "Don't delay in coming with us." ³⁹ So Peter got up and went with them. When he arrived, they led him to the room upstairs. And all the widows approached him, weeping and showing him the robes and clothes that Dorcas had made while she was with them. ⁴⁰ Then Peter sent them all out of the room. He knelt down, prayed, and turning toward the body said, "Tabitha, get up!" She opened her eyes, saw Peter, and sat up. ⁴¹ He gave her his hand and helped her stand up. Then he called the saints and widows and presented her alive. ⁴² This became known throughout all Joppa, and many

believed in the Lord. [43] And Peter stayed on many days in Joppa with Simon, a leather tanner.

## Cornelius' Vision

**10** There was a man in Caesarea named Cornelius, a •centurion of what was called the Italian •Regiment. [2] He was a devout man and feared God along with his whole household. He did many charitable deeds for the ⌊Jewish⌋ people and always prayed to God. [3] At about three in the afternoon he distinctly saw in a vision an angel of God who came in and said to him, "Cornelius!"

[4] Looking intently at him, he became afraid and said, "What is it, Lord?"

And he told him, "Your prayers and your acts of charity have come up as a memorial offering before God. [5] Now send men to Joppa and call for Simon, who is also named Peter. [6] He is lodging with Simon, a tanner, whose house is by the sea."

[7] When the angel who spoke to him had gone, he called two of his household servants and a devout soldier, who was one of those who attended him. [8] After explaining everything to them, he sent them to Joppa.

## Peter's Vision

[9] The next day, as they were traveling and nearing the city, Peter went up to pray on the housetop at about noon. [10] Then he became hungry and wanted to eat, but while they were preparing something he went into a visionary state. [11] He saw heaven opened and an object coming down that resembled a large sheet being lowered to the earth by its four corners. [12] In it were all the four-footed animals and reptiles of the earth, and the birds of the sky. [13] Then

a voice said to him, "Get up, Peter; kill and eat!"

[14] "No, Lord!" Peter said. "For I have never eaten anything common and unclean!"

[15] Again, a second time, a voice said to him, "What God has made clean, you must not call common." [16] This happened three times, and then the object was taken up into heaven.

## Peter Visits Cornelius

[17] While Peter was deeply perplexed about what the vision he had seen might mean, the men who had been sent by Cornelius, having asked directions to Simon's house, stood at the gate. [18] They called out, asking if Simon, who was also named Peter, was lodging there.

[19] While Peter was thinking about the vision, the Spirit told him, "Three men are here looking for you. [20] Get up, go downstairs, and accompany them with no doubts at all, because I have sent them."

[21] Then Peter went down to the men and said, "Here I am, the one you're looking for. What is the reason you're here?"

[22] They said, "Cornelius, a centurion, an upright and God-fearing man, who has a good reputation with the whole Jewish nation, was divinely directed by a holy angel to call you to his house and to hear a message from you." [23] Peter then invited them in and gave them lodging.

The next day he got up and set out with them, and some of the brothers from Joppa went with him. [24] The following day he entered Caesarea. Now Cornelius was expecting them and had called together his relatives and close friends. [25] When Peter entered, Cornelius met him, fell at his feet, and worshiped him.

26 But Peter helped him up and said, "Stand up! I myself am also a man." 27 While talking with him, he went on in and found that many had come together there. 28 Peter said to them, "You know it's forbidden for a Jewish man to associate with or visit a foreigner. But God has shown me that I must not call any person common or unclean. 29 That's why I came without any objection when I was sent for. So I ask, 'Why did you send for me?' "

30 Cornelius replied, "Four days ago at this hour, at three in the afternoon, I wasª praying in my house. Just then a man in a dazzling robe stood before me 31 and said, 'Cornelius, your prayer has been heard, and your acts of charity have been remembered in God's sight. 32 Therefore send someone to Joppa and invite Simon here, who is also named Peter. He is lodging in Simon the tanner's house by the sea.'ᵇ 33 Therefore I immediately sent for you, and you did the right thing in coming. So we are all present before God, to hear everything you have been commanded by the Lord."

## Good News for Gentiles

34 Then Peter began to speak: "In truth, I understand that God doesn't show favoritism, 35 but in every nation the person who fears Him and does righteousness is acceptable to Him. 36 He sent the message to the sons of Israel, proclaiming the good news of peace through Jesus Christ—He is Lord of all. 37 You know the events that took place throughout all Judea, beginning from Galilee after the baptism that John preached: 38 how God anointed Jesus of Nazareth with the Holy Spirit and with power, and how He went about doing good and curing all who were under the tyranny of the Devil, because God was with Him. 39 We ourselves are witnesses of everything He did in both the Judean country and in Jerusalem; yet they killed Him by hanging Him on a tree. 40 God raised up this man on the third day and permitted Him to be seen, 41 not by all the people, but by us, witnesses appointed beforehand by God, who ate and drank with Him after He rose from the dead. 42 He commanded us to preach to the people, and to solemnly testify that He is the One appointed by God to be the Judge of the living and the dead. 43 All the prophets testify about Him that through His name everyone who believes in Him will receive forgiveness of sins."

## Gentile Conversion and Baptism

44 While Peter was still speaking these words, the Holy Spirit came down on all those who heard the message. 45 The circumcised believers who had come with Peter were astounded, because the gift of the Holy Spirit had been poured out on the Gentiles also. 46 For they heard them speaking ⌊other⌋ languages and declaring the greatness of God.

Then Peter responded, 47 "Can anyone withhold water and prevent these from being baptized, who have received the Holy Spirit just as we have?" 48 And he commanded them to be baptized in the name of Jesus Christ. Then they asked him to stay for a few days.

## Gentile Salvation Defended

11 The apostles and the brothers who were throughout Judea

ª10:30 Other mss add *fasting and*    ᵇ10:32 Other mss add *When he arrives, he will speak to you.*

heard that the Gentiles had welcomed God's message also. [2] When Peter went up to Jerusalem, those who stressed circumcision argued with him, [3] saying, "You visited uncircumcised men and ate with them!"

[4] Peter began to explain to them in an orderly sequence, saying: [5] "I was in the town of Joppa praying, and I saw, in a visionary state, an object coming down that resembled a large sheet being lowered from heaven by its four corners, and it came to me. [6] When I looked closely and considered it, I saw the four-footed animals of the earth, the wild beasts, the reptiles, and the birds of the sky. [7] Then I also heard a voice telling me, 'Get up, Peter; kill and eat!'

[8] " 'No, Lord!' I said. 'For nothing common or unclean has ever entered my mouth!' [9] But a voice answered from heaven a second time, 'What God has made clean, you must not call common.'

[10] "Now this happened three times, and then everything was drawn up again into heaven. [11] At that very moment, three men who had been sent to me from Caesarea arrived at the house where we were. [12] Then the Spirit told me to go with them with no doubts at all. These six brothers accompanied me, and we went into the man's house. [13] He reported to us how he had seen the angel standing in his house and saying, 'Send[a] to Joppa, and call for Simon, who is also named Peter. [14] He will speak words to you by which you and all your household will be saved.'

[15] "As I began to speak, the Holy Spirit came down on them, just as on us at the beginning. [16] Then I remembered the word of the Lord, how He said, 'John baptized with water, but you will be baptized with the Holy Spirit.' [17] Therefore, if God gave them the same gift that He also gave to us when we believed on the Lord Jesus Christ, how could I possibly hinder God?"

[18] When they heard this they became silent. Then they glorified God, saying, "So God has granted repentance resulting in life to even the Gentiles!"

## The Church in Antioch

[19] Those who had been scattered as a result of the persecution that started because of Stephen made their way as far as Phoenicia, Cyprus, and Antioch, speaking the message to no one except Jews. [20] But there were some of them, Cypriot and Cyrenian men, who came to Antioch and began speaking to the Hellenists,[b] proclaiming the good news about the Lord Jesus. [21] The Lord's hand was with them, and a large number who believed turned to the Lord. [22] Then the report about them reached the ears of the church in Jerusalem, and they sent out Barnabas to travel[c] as far as Antioch. [23] When he arrived and saw the grace of God, he was glad, and he encouraged all of them to remain true to the Lord with a firm resolve of the heart— [24] for he was a good man, full of the Holy Spirit and of faith—and large numbers of people were added to the Lord. [25] Then he[d] went to Tarsus to search for Saul, [26] and when he found him he brought him to Antioch. For a whole year they met with the church and taught large numbers, and the disciples were first called Christians in Antioch.

## Acts 11:25

## The Church

*Some people look at the church
and see nothing but hypocrisy.
They see neighbors who can't get
along, couples who won't stay
married, teenagers who aren't a lot
different than anybody else. But
when people look at the church,
they should see people who've
been changed by Jesus Christ.*

### Famine Relief

27 In those days some prophets came
down from Jerusalem to Antioch.
28 Then one of them, named Agabus,
stood up and predicted by the Spirit
that there would be a severe famine
throughout the Roman world. This
took place during the time of Claudius. 29 So each of the disciples,
according to his ability, determined to
send relief to the brothers who lived
in Judea. 30 This they did, sending it to
the elders by means of Barnabas and
Saul.

### James Martyred and Peter Jailed

**12** About that time King •Herod
cruelly attacked some who belonged to the church, 2 and he killed
James, John's brother, with the
sword. 3 When he saw that it
pleased the Jews, he proceeded to
arrest Peter too, during the days of
•Unleavened Bread. 4 After the arrest, he put him in prison and assigned four squads of four soldiers
each to guard him, intending to
bring him out to the people after the
•Passover. 5 So Peter was kept in
prison, but prayer was being made
earnestly to God for him by the
church.

### Peter Rescued

6 On the night before Herod was to
bring him out [for execution], Peter
was sleeping between two soldiers,
bound with two chains, while the sen-
tries in front of the door guarded the
prison. 7 Suddenly an angel of the Lord
appeared, and a light shone in the cell.
Striking Peter on the side, he woke
him up and said, "Quick, get up!"
Then the chains fell off his wrists.
8 "Get dressed," the angel told him,
"and put on your sandals." And he did
so. "Wrap your cloak around you," he
told him, "and follow me." 9 So he
went out and followed, and he did not
know that what took place through
the angel was real, but thought he was
seeing a vision. 10 After they passed
the first and second guard posts, they
came to the iron gate that leads into
the city, which opened to them by
itself. They went outside and passed
one street, and immediately the angel
left him.

11 Then Peter came to himself and
said, "Now I know for certain that the
Lord has sent His angel and rescued
me from Herod's grasp and from all
that the Jewish people expected."
12 When he realized this, he went to
the house of Mary, the mother of John
Mark, where many had assembled
and were praying. 13 He knocked at
the door in the gateway, and a servant
named Rhoda came to answer. 14 She
recognized Peter's voice, and because
of her joy she did not open the gate,
but ran in and announced that Peter
was standing at the gateway.

[15] "You're crazy!" they told her. But she kept insisting that it was true. Then they said, "It's his angel!" [16] Peter, however, kept on knocking, and when they opened the door and saw him, they were astounded. [17] Motioning to them with his hand to be silent, he explained to them how the Lord had brought him out of the prison. "Report these things to James and the brothers," he said. Then he departed and went to a different place. [18] At daylight, there was a great commotion among the soldiers as to what could have become of Peter. [19] After Herod had searched and did not find him, he interrogated the guards and ordered their execution. Then he went down from Judea to Caesarea and stayed there.

## Herod's Death

[20] He had been very angry with the Tyrians and Sidonians. Together they presented themselves before him, and having won over Blastus, who was in charge of the king's bedroom, they asked for peace, because their country was supplied with food from the king's country. [21] So on an appointed day, dressed in royal robes and seated on the throne, Herod delivered a public address to them. [22] The populace began to shout, "It's the voice of a god and not of a man!" [23] At once an angel of the Lord struck him because he did not give the glory to God, and he became infected with worms and died. [24] Then God's message flourished and multiplied. [25] And Barnabas and Saul returned to[a] Jerusalem after they had completed their relief mission, on which they took John Mark.

## Preparing for the Mission Field

**13** In the local church at Antioch there were prophets and teachers: Barnabas, Simeon who was called Niger, Lucius the Cyrenian, Manaen, a close friend of *Herod the tetrarch, and Saul. [2] As they were ministering to the Lord and fasting, the Holy Spirit said, "Set apart for Me Barnabas and Saul for the work that I have called them to." [3] Then, after they had fasted, prayed, and laid hands on them, they sent them off.

## The Mission to Cyprus

[4] Being sent out by the Holy Spirit, they came down to Seleucia, and from there they sailed to Cyprus. [5] Arriving in Salamis, they proclaimed God's message in the Jewish *synagogues. They also had John as their assistant. [6] When they had gone through the whole island as far as Paphos, they came across a sorcerer, a Jewish false prophet named Bar-Jesus. [7] He was with the *proconsul, Sergius Paulus, an intelligent man. This man summoned Barnabas and Saul and desired to hear God's message. [8] But Elymas, the sorcerer, which is how his name is translated, opposed them and tried to turn the proconsul away from the faith. [9] Then Saul—also called Paul—filled with the Holy Spirit, stared straight at the sorcerer [10] and said, "You son of the Devil, full of all deceit and all fraud, enemy of all righteousness! Won't you ever stop perverting the straight paths of the Lord? [11] Now, look! The Lord's hand is against you: you are going to be blind, and will not see the sun for a time." Suddenly a mist and darkness

a[12:25] Other mss read *from*

fell on him, and he went around seeking someone to lead him by the hand. ¹² Then the proconsul, seeing what happened, believed and was astonished at the teaching about the Lord.

## Paul's Sermon in Antioch of Pisidia

¹³ Paul and his companions set sail from Paphos and came to Perga in Pamphylia. John, however, left them and went back to Jerusalem. ¹⁴ They continued their journey from Perga and reached Antioch in Pisidia. On the Sabbath day they went into the synagogue and sat down. ¹⁵ After the reading of the Law and the Prophets, the leaders of the synagogue sent ⌊word⌋ to them, saying, "Brothers, if you have any message of encouragement for the people, you can speak."

¹⁶ Then standing up, Paul motioned with his hand and spoke: "Men of Israel, and you who fear God, listen! ¹⁷ The God of this people Israel chose our forefathers, exalted the people during their stay in the land of Egypt, and led them out of it with a mighty arm. ¹⁸ And for about 40 years He put up with them[a] in the desert; ¹⁹ then after destroying seven nations in the land of Canaan, He gave their land to them as an inheritance. ²⁰ This all took about 450 years. After this He gave them judges until Samuel the prophet. ²¹ Then they asked for a king, so God gave them Saul the son of Kish, a man of the tribe of Benjamin, for 40 years. ²² After removing him, He raised up David as their king, of whom He testified: 'I have found David the son of Jesse, a man after My heart,[b] who will carry out all My will.'

²³ "From this man's descendants, according to the promise, God brought the Savior, Jesus,[c] to Israel. ²⁴ Before He came to public attention, John had previously proclaimed a baptism of repentance to all the people of Israel. ²⁵ Then as John was completing his life work, he said, 'Who do you think I am? I am not the One. But look! Someone is coming after me, and I am not worthy to untie the sandals on His feet.'

²⁶ "Brothers, sons of Abraham's race, and those among you who fear God, the message of this salvation has been sent to us. ²⁷ For the residents of Jerusalem and their rulers, since they did not recognize Him or the voices of the prophets that are read every Sabbath, have fulfilled their words by condemning Him. ²⁸ Though they found no grounds for the death penalty, they asked •Pilate to have Him killed. ²⁹ When they had fulfilled all that had been written about Him, they took Him down from the tree and put Him in a tomb. ³⁰ But God raised Him from the dead, ³¹ and He appeared for many days to those who came up with Him from Galilee to Jerusalem, who are now His witnesses to the people. ³² And we ourselves proclaim to you the good news of the promise that was made to our forefathers. ³³ God has fulfilled this to us their children by raising up Jesus, as it is written in the second Psalm:

> You are My Son;
> today I have become Your
> Father.[d]

³⁴ Since He raised Him from the dead, never to return to decay, He has spoken in this way, **I will grant you the faithful covenant blessings made to David.**[e] ³⁵ Therefore He also says in another passage, **You will not allow Your Holy One to see decay.**[f] ³⁶ For

---

[a]**13:18** Other mss read *He cared for them*     [b]**13:22** 1 Sm 13:14; Ps 89:20     [c]**13:23** Other mss read *brought salvation*     [d]**13:33** Ps 2:7     [e]**13:34** Is 55:3     [f]**13:35** Ps 16:10

David, after serving his own generation in God's plan, fell •asleep, was buried with his fathers, and decayed. [37] But the One whom God raised up did not decay. [38] Therefore, let it be known to you, brothers, that through this man forgiveness of sins is being proclaimed to you, [39] and everyone who believes in Him is justified from everything, which you could not be justified from through the law of Moses. [40] So beware that what is said in the prophets does not happen to you:

[41] **Look, you scoffers,**
**marvel and vanish away,**
**because I am doing a work in**
**your days,**
**a work that you will never**
**believe,**
**even if someone were to**
**explain it to you."[a]**

## Paul and Barnabas in Antioch

[42] As they were leaving, they[b] begged that these matters be presented to them the following Sabbath. [43] After the synagogue had been dismissed, many of the Jews and devout proselytes followed Paul and Barnabas, who were speaking with them and persuading them to continue in the grace of God.

[44] The following Sabbath almost the whole town assembled to hear the message of the Lord.[c] [45] But when the Jews saw the crowds, they were filled with jealousy and began to oppose what Paul was saying by insulting him.

[46] Then Paul and Barnabas boldly said: "It was necessary that God's message be spoken to you first. But since you reject it, and consider yourselves unworthy of eternal life, we now turn to the Gentiles! [47] For this is what the Lord has commanded us:

**I have appointed you as a**
**light for the Gentiles,**
**to bring salvation to the ends**
**of the earth."[d]**

[48] When the Gentiles heard this, they rejoiced and glorified the message of the Lord, and all who had been appointed to eternal life believed. [49] So the message of the Lord spread through the whole region. [50] But the Jews incited the religious women of high standing and the leading men of the city. They stirred up persecution against Paul and Barnabas and expelled them from their district. [51] But shaking the dust off their feet against them, they proceeded to Iconium. [52] And the disciples were filled with joy and the Holy Spirit.

## Growth and Persecution in Iconium

**14** The same thing happened in Iconium; they entered the Jewish •synagogue and spoke in such a way that a great number of both Jews and Greeks believed. [2] But the Jews who refused to believe stirred up and poisoned the minds of the Gentiles against the brothers. [3] So they stayed there for some time and spoke boldly, in reliance on the Lord, who testified to the message of His grace by granting that signs and wonders be performed through them. [4] But the people of the city were divided, some siding with the Jews and some with the apostles. [5] When an attempt was made by both the Gentiles and Jews, with

[a]**13:41** Hab 1:5   [b]**13:42** Other mss read *they were leaving the synagogue of the Jews, the Gentiles*
[c]**13:44** Other mss read *of God*   [d]**13:47** Is 49:6

---

*Acts 14:1-3*

*Unless God was just buttering us up with wishful thinking, we have a right to trust Him for anything. But He has more in mind for His miracles than answering our wish lists. He uses His wonder-working power to make bold statements about who He really is.*

---

their rulers, to assault and stone them, [6] they found out about it and fled to the Lycaonian towns called Lystra and Derbe, and to the surrounding countryside. [7] And there they kept evangelizing.

## Mistaken for Gods in Lystra

[8] In Lystra a man without strength in his feet, lame from birth, and who had never walked, sat [9] and heard Paul speaking. After observing him closely and seeing that he had faith to be healed, [10] ⌊Paul⌋ said in a loud voice, "Stand up straight on your feet!" And he jumped up and started to walk around.
[11] When the crowds saw what Paul had done, they raised their voices, saying in the Lycaonian language, "The gods have come down to us in the form of men!" [12] And they started to call Barnabas, Zeus, and Paul, Hermes, because he was the main speaker. [13] Then the priest of Zeus, whose temple was just outside the town, brought oxen and garlands to the gates. He, with the crowds, intended to offer sacrifice.

[14] The apostles Barnabas and Paul tore their robes when they heard this and rushed into the crowd, shouting: [15] "Men! Why are you doing these things? We are men also, with the same nature as you, and we are proclaiming good news to you, that you should turn from these worthless things to the living God, **who made the heaven, the earth, the sea, and everything in them.**[a] [16] In past generations He allowed all the nations to go their own way, [17] although He did not leave Himself without a witness, since He did good: giving you rain from heaven and fruitful seasons, and satisfying your[b] hearts with food and happiness." [18] Even though they said these things, they barely stopped the crowds from sacrificing to them.
[19] Then some Jews came from Antioch and Iconium, and when they had won over the crowds and stoned Paul, they dragged him out of the city, thinking he was dead. [20] After the disciples surrounded him, he got up and went into the town. The next day he left with Barnabas for Derbe.

## Church Planting

[21] After they had evangelized that town and made many disciples, they returned to Lystra, to Iconium, and to Antioch, [22] strengthening the hearts of the disciples by encouraging them to continue in the faith, and by telling them, "It is necessary to pass through many troubles on our way into the kingdom of God." [23] When they had appointed elders in every church and prayed with fasting, they committed them to the Lord in whom they had believed. [24] Then they passed through Pisidia and came to Pamphylia. [25] After they spoke the message in Perga, they went down to

[a]**14:15** Ex 20:11; Ps 146:6    [b]**14:17** Other mss read *our*

Attalia. [26] From there they sailed back to Antioch where they had been entrusted to the grace of God for the work they had completed. [27] After they arrived and gathered the church together, they reported everything God had done with them, and that He had opened the door of faith to the Gentiles. [28] And they spent a considerable time with the disciples.

## Dispute in Antioch

**15** Some men came down from Judea and began to teach the brothers: "Unless you are circumcised according to the custom prescribed by Moses, you cannot be saved!" [2] But after Paul and Barnabas had engaged them in serious argument and debate, they arranged for Paul and Barnabas and some others of them to go up to the apostles and elders in Jerusalem concerning this controversy. [3] When they had been sent on their way by the church, they passed through both Phoenicia and Samaria, explaining in detail the conversion of the Gentiles, and they created great joy among all the brothers.

[4] When they arrived at Jerusalem, they were welcomed by the church, the apostles, and the elders, and they reported all that God had done with

---

*"Signs do not take us away from reality. They are focal points at which more reality becomes visible to us than we ordinarily see all at once."*

—*C. S. Lewis*

---

them. [5] But some of the believers from the party of the •Pharisees stood up and said, "It is necessary to circumcise them and to command them to keep the law of Moses!"

## The Jerusalem Council

[6] Then the apostles and the elders assembled to consider this matter. [7] After there had been much debate, Peter stood up and said to them: "Brothers, you are aware that in the early days God made a choice among you,[a] that by my mouth the Gentiles would hear the gospel message and believe. [8] And God, who knows the heart, testified to them by giving[b] the Holy Spirit, just as He also did to us. [9] He made no distinction between us and them, cleansing their hearts by faith. [10] Why, then, are you now testing God by putting on the disciples' necks a yoke that neither our forefathers nor we have been able to bear? [11] On the contrary, we believe we are saved through the grace of the Lord Jesus, in the same way they are."

[12] Then the whole assembly fell silent and listened to Barnabas and Paul describing all the signs and wonders God had done through them among the Gentiles. [13] After they stopped speaking, James responded: "Brothers, listen to me! [14] Simeon has reported how God first intervened to take from the Gentiles a people for His name. [15] And the words of the prophets agree with this, as it is written:

[16] **After these things I will return
and will rebuild David's tent,
which has fallen down.
I will rebuild its ruins and
will set it up again,**
[17] **so that those who are left of
mankind may seek the Lord—
even all the Gentiles who are
called by My name,**

---

[a]15:7 Other mss read *us*   [b]15:8 Other mss add *them*

says the Lord who does
    these things,
[18] **which have been known
    from long ago.**[a][b]

[19] Therefore, in my judgment, we should not cause difficulties for those who turn to God from among the Gentiles, [20] but instead we should write to them to abstain from things polluted by idols, from sexual immorality, from eating anything that has been strangled, and from blood. [21] For since ancient times, Moses has had in every city those who proclaim him, and he is read aloud in the *synagogues every Sabbath day."

## The Letter to the Gentile Believers

[22] Then the apostles and the elders, with the whole church, decided to select men from among them and to send them to Antioch with Paul and Barnabas: Judas, called Barsabbas, and Silas, both leading men among the brothers. [23] They wrote this letter to be delivered by them:

From the apostles and the elders,
    your brothers,

To the brothers from among the Gentiles in Antioch, Syria, and Cilicia:

Greetings.

[24] Because we have heard that some to whom we gave no authorization went out from us and troubled you with their words and unsettled your hearts,[c] [25] we have unanimously decided to select men and

send them to you along with our beloved Barnabas and Paul, [26] who have risked their lives for the name of our Lord Jesus Christ. [27] Therefore we have sent Judas and Silas, who will personally report the same things by word of mouth. [28] For it was the Holy Spirit's decision—and ours—to put no greater burden on you than these necessary things: [29] that you abstain from food offered to idols, from blood, from eating anything that has been strangled, and from sexual immorality. If you keep yourselves from these things, you will do well.

Farewell.

## The Outcome of the Jerusalem Letter

[30] Then, being sent off, they went down to Antioch, and after gathering the assembly, they delivered the letter. [31] When they read it, they rejoiced because of its encouragement. [32] Both Judas and Silas, who were also prophets themselves, encouraged the brothers and strengthened them with a long message. [33] After spending some time there, they were sent back in peace by the brothers to those who had sent them.[d] [e] [35] But Paul and Barnabas, along with many others, remained in Antioch teaching and proclaiming the message of the Lord.

## Paul and Barnabas Part Company

[36] After some time had passed, Paul said to Barnabas, "Let's go back and visit the brothers in every town where we have preached the message of the

---

[a]15:17-18 Other mss read *says the Lord who does all these things. Known to God from long ago are all His works.*
[b]15:16–18 Am 9:11–12; Is 45:21    [c]15:24 Other mss add *by saying, "Be circumcised and keep the law,"*
[d]15:33 Other mss read *the brothers to the apostles*    [e]15:33 Other mss add v. 34: *But Silas decided to stay there.*

Lord, and see how they're doing." [37] Barnabas wanted to take along John Mark. [38] But Paul did not think it appropriate to take along this man who had deserted them in Pamphylia and had not gone on with them to the work. [39] There was such a sharp disagreement that they parted company, and Barnabas took Mark with him and sailed off to Cyprus. [40] Then Paul chose Silas and departed, after being commended to the grace of the Lord by the brothers. [41] He traveled through Syria and Cilicia, strengthening the churches.

## Paul Selects Timothy

**16** Then he went on to Derbe and Lystra, where there was a disciple named Timothy, the son of a believing Jewish woman, but his father was a Greek. [2] The brothers at Lystra and Iconium spoke highly of him. [3] Paul wanted Timothy to go with him, so he took him and circumcised him because of the Jews who were in those places, since they all knew that his father was a Greek. [4] As they traveled through the towns, they delivered to them the decisions reached by the apostles and elders at Jerusalem. [5] So the churches were strengthened in the faith and were increased in number daily.

## Evangelization of Europe

[6] They went through the region of Phrygia and Galatia and were prevented by the Holy Spirit from speaking the message in the province of Asia. [7] When they came to Mysia, they tried to go into Bithynia, but the Spirit of Jesus did not allow them. [8] So, bypassing Mysia, they came down to Troas. [9] During the night a vision appeared to Paul: a Macedonian man was standing and pleading with him, "Cross over to Macedonia and help us!" [10] After he had seen the vision, we immediately made efforts to set out for Macedonia, concluding that God had called us to evangelize them.

## Lydia's Conversion

[11] Then, setting sail from Troas, we ran a straight course to Samothrace, the next day to Neapolis, [12] and from there to Philippi, a Roman colony, which is a leading city of that district of Macedonia. We stayed in that city for a number of days. [13] On the Sabbath day we went outside the city gate by the river, where we thought there was a place of prayer. We sat down and spoke to the women gathered there. [14] A woman named Lydia, a dealer in purple cloth from the city of Thyatira, who worshiped God, was listening. The Lord opened her heart to pay attention to what was spoken by Paul. [15] After she and her household were baptized, she urged us, "If you consider me a believer in the Lord, come and stay at my house." And she persuaded us.

## Paul and Silas in Prison

[16] Once, as we were on our way to prayer, a slave girl met us who had a spirit of prediction and made a large profit for her owners by fortune-telling. [17] As she followed Paul and us she cried out, "These men are the slaves of the Most High God, who are proclaiming to you[a] the way of salvation." [18] And she did this for many days.

But Paul was greatly aggravated, and turning to the spirit, said, "I

[a]16:17 Other mss read *us*

command you in the name of Jesus Christ to come out of her!" And it came out right away.

[19] When her owners saw that their hope of profit was gone, they seized Paul and Silas and dragged them into the marketplace to the authorities. [20] And bringing them before the chief magistrates, they said, "These men are seriously disturbing our city. They are Jews, [21] and are promoting customs that are not legal for us as Romans to adopt or practice."

[22] Then the mob joined in the attack against them, and the chief magistrates stripped off their clothes and ordered them to be beaten with rods. [23] After they had inflicted many blows on them, they threw them in jail, ordering the jailer to keep them securely guarded. [24] Receiving such an order, he put them into the inner prison and secured their feet in the stocks.

## A Midnight Deliverance

[25] About midnight Paul and Silas were praying and singing hymns to God, and the prisoners were listening to them. [26] Suddenly there was such a violent earthquake that the foundations of the jail were shaken, and immediately all the doors were opened, and everyone's chains came loose. [27] When the jailer woke up and saw the doors of the prison open, he drew his sword and was going to kill himself, since he thought the prisoners had escaped.

[28] But Paul called out in a loud voice, "Don't harm yourself, because all of us are here!"

[29] Then the jailer called for lights, rushed in, and fell down trembling before Paul and Silas. [30] Then he escorted them out and said, "Sirs, what must I do to be saved?"

[31] So they said, "Believe on the Lord Jesus, and you will be saved—you and your household." [32] Then they spoke the message of the Lord to him along with everyone in his house. [33] He took them the same hour of the night and washed their wounds. Right away he and all his family were baptized. [34] He brought them up into his house, set a meal before them, and rejoiced because he had believed God with his entire household.

## An Official Apology

[35] When daylight came, the chief magistrates sent the police to say, "Release those men!"

[36] The jailer reported these words to Paul: "The magistrates have sent orders for you to be released. So come out now and go in peace."

[37] But Paul said to them, "They beat us in public without a trial, although we are Roman citizens, and threw us in jail. And now are they going to smuggle us out secretly? Certainly not! On the contrary, let them come themselves and escort us out!"

[38] Then the police reported these words to the magistrates. And they were afraid when they heard that Paul and Silas were Roman citizens. [39] So they came and apologized to them, and escorting them out, they urged them to leave town. [40] After leaving the jail, they came to Lydia's house where they saw and encouraged the brothers, and departed.

## A Short Ministry in Thessalonica

**17** Then they traveled through Amphipolis and Apollonia and came to Thessalonica, where there was a Jewish •synagogue. [2] As usual, Paul went to them, and on three Sabbath days reasoned with them from the Scriptures, [3] explaining and showing that the •Messiah had to suffer and rise from the dead, and saying: "This is the Messiah, Jesus, whom I am proclaiming to you." [4] Then some of them were persuaded and joined Paul and Silas, including a great number of God-fearing Greeks, as well as a number of the leading women.

## The Assault on Jason's House

[5] But the Jews became jealous, and when they had brought together some scoundrels from the marketplace and formed a mob, they set the city in an uproar. Attacking Jason's house, they searched for them to bring them out to the public assembly. [6] When they did not find them, they dragged Jason and some of the brothers before the city officials, shouting, "These men who have turned the world upside down have come here too, [7] and Jason has received them as guests! They are all acting contrary to Caesar's decrees, saying that there is another king— Jesus!" [8] The Jews stirred up the crowd and the city officials who heard these things. [9] So taking a security bond from Jason and the others, they released them.

## The Beroeans Search the Scriptures

[10] As soon as it was night, the brothers sent Paul and Silas off to Beroea. On arrival, they went into the synagogue of the Jews. [11] The people here were more open-minded than those in Thessalonica, since they welcomed the message with eagerness and examined the Scriptures daily to see if these things were so. [12] Consequently, many of them be-

### Acts 17:11

### The Scriptures

*Some people's ideas can sound so right, their reasons for feeling that way so persuasive, we don't see how in the world they could possibly be wrong. But the only way to really tell if something is true or not is to run it by the Bible. After God has weighed in, the case is closed.*

lieved, including a number of the prominent Greek women as well as men. [13] But when the Jews from Thessalonica found out that God's message had been proclaimed by Paul at Beroea, they came there too, agitating and disturbing[a] the crowds. [14] Then the brothers immediately sent Paul away to go to the sea, but Silas and Timothy stayed on there. [15] Those who escorted Paul brought him as far as Athens, and after receiving instructions for Silas and Timothy to come to him as quickly as possible, they departed.

## Paul in Athens

[16] While Paul was waiting for them in Athens, his spirit was troubled within him when he saw that the city was full of idols. [17] So he reasoned in the synagogue with the Jews and with those who worshiped God, and in the marketplace every day with those who happened to be there. [18] Then also, some of the Epicurean and Stoic philosophers argued with him. Some

[a]17:13 Other mss omit *and disturbing*

said, "What is this pseudo-intellectual trying to say?"

Others replied, "He seems to be a preacher of foreign deities"—because he was telling the good news about Jesus and the resurrection. [19] They took him and brought him to the Areopagus, and said, "May we learn about this new teaching you're speaking of? [20] For what you say sounds strange to us, and we want to know what these ideas mean." [21] Now all the Athenians and the foreigners residing there spent their time on nothing else but telling or hearing something new.

### The Areopagus Address

[22] Then Paul stood in the middle of the Areopagus and said: "Men of Athens! I see that you are extremely religious in every respect. [23] For as I was passing through and observing the objects of your worship, I even found an altar on which was inscribed:

> TO AN UNKNOWN GOD

Therefore, what you worship in ignorance, this I proclaim to you. [24] The God who made the world and everything in it—He is Lord of heaven and earth and does not live in shrines made by hands. [25] Neither is He served by human hands, as though He needed anything, since He Himself gives everyone life and breath and all things. [26] From one man[a] He has made every nation of men to live all over the earth and has determined their appointed times and the boundaries of where they live, [27] so that they might seek God, and perhaps they might reach out and find Him, though He is not far from each one of us. [28] For in Him we live and move and exist, as

even some of your own poets have said, 'For we are also His offspring.' [29] Being God's offspring, then, we shouldn't think that the divine nature is like gold or silver or stone, an image fashioned by human art and imagination. [30] "Therefore, having overlooked the times of ignorance, God now commands all people everywhere to repent, [31] because He has set a day on which He is going to judge the world in righteousness by the Man He has appointed. He has provided proof of this to everyone by raising Him from the dead."

[32] When they heard about resurrection of the dead, some began to ridicule him. But others said, "We will hear you about this again." [33] So Paul went out from their presence. [34] However, some men joined him and believed, among whom were Dionysius the Areopagite, a woman named Damaris, and others with them.

### Founding the Corinthian Church

**18** After this he[b] left from Athens and went to Corinth, [2] where he found a Jewish man named Aquila, a native of Pontus, who had recently come from Italy with his wife Priscilla because Claudius had ordered all the Jews to leave Rome. Paul came to them, [3] and being of the same occupation, stayed with them and worked, for they were tentmakers by trade. [4] He reasoned in the *synagogue every Sabbath and tried to persuade both Jews and Greeks.

[5] When Silas and Timothy came down from Macedonia, Paul was occupied with preaching the message[c] and solemnly testified to the Jews that the *Messiah is Jesus. [6] But when they re-

sisted and blasphemed, he shook out his clothes and told them, "Your blood is on your own heads! I am clean. From now on I will go to the Gentiles." [7] So he left there and went to the house of a man named Titius Justus, a worshiper of God, whose house was next door to the synagogue. [8] Crispus, the leader of the synagogue, believed the Lord, along with his whole household; and many of the Corinthians, when they heard, believed and were baptized.

[9] Then the Lord said to Paul in a night vision, "Don't be afraid, but keep on speaking and don't be silent. [10] For I am with you, and no one will lay a hand on you to hurt you, because I have many people in this city." [11] And he stayed there a year and six months, teaching the word of God among them.

[12] While Gallio was •proconsul of Achaia, the Jews made a united attack against Paul and brought him to the judge's bench. [13] "This man," they said, "persuades people to worship God contrary to the law!"

[14] And as Paul was about to open his mouth, Gallio said to the Jews, "If it were a matter of a crime or of moral evil, it would be reasonable for me to put up with you Jews. [15] But if these are questions about words, names, and your own law, see to it yourselves. I don't want to be a judge of such things." [16] So he drove them from the judge's bench. [17] Then they all[a] seized Sosthenes, the leader of the synagogue, and beat him in front of the judge's bench. But none of these things concerned Gallio.

## The Return Trip to Antioch

[18] So Paul, having stayed on for many days, said good-bye to the broth-ers and sailed away to Syria. Priscilla and Aquila were with him. He shaved his head at Cenchreae, because he had taken a vow. [19] When they reached Ephesus he left them there, but he himself entered the synagogue and engaged in discussion with the Jews. [20] And though they asked him to stay for a longer time, he declined, [21] but said good-bye and stated,[b] "I'll come back to you again, if God wills." Then he set sail from Ephesus.

[22] On landing at Caesarea, he went up and greeted the church, and went down to Antioch. [23] He set out, traveling through one place after another in the Galatian territory and Phrygia, strengthening all the disciples.

## The Eloquent Apollos

[24] A Jew named Apollos, a native Alexandrian, an eloquent man who was powerful in the Scriptures, arrived in Ephesus. [25] This man had been instructed in the way of the Lord; and being fervent in spirit, he spoke and taught the things about Jesus accurately, although he knew only John's baptism. [26] He began to speak boldly in the synagogue. After Priscilla and Aquila heard him, they took him home and explained the way of God to him more accurately. [27] When he wanted to cross over to Achaia, the brothers wrote to the disciples urging them to welcome him. After he arrived, he greatly helped those who had believed through grace. [28] For he vigorously refuted the Jews in public, demonstrating through the Scriptures that Jesus is the Messiah.

## Twelve Disciples of John the Baptist

**19** While Apollos was in Corinth, Paul traveled through the interior

---

[a]18:17 Other mss read *Then all the Greeks*  [b]18:21 Other mss add *"By all means it is necessary to keep the coming festival in Jerusalem. But*

regions and came to Ephesus. He found some disciples [2] and asked them, "Did you receive the Holy Spirit when you believed?"

"No," they told him, "we haven't even heard that there is a Holy Spirit."

[3] "Then with what ⌊baptism⌋ were you baptized?" he asked them.

"With John's baptism," they replied.

[4] Paul said, "John baptized with a baptism of repentance, telling the people that they should believe in the One who would come after him, that is, in Jesus."

[5] On hearing this, they were baptized in the name of the Lord Jesus. [6] And when Paul had laid his hands on them, the Holy Spirit came on them, and they began to speak with ⌊other⌋ languages and to prophesy. [7] Now there were about 12 men in all.

## In the Lecture Hall of Tyrannus

[8] Then he entered the *synagogue and spoke boldly over a period of three months, engaging in discussion and trying to persuade them about the things related to the kingdom of God. [9] But when some became hardened and would not believe, slandering the Way in front of the crowd, he withdrew from them and met separately with the disciples, conducting discussions every day in the lecture hall of Tyrannus. [10] And this went on for two years, so that all the inhabitants of the province of Asia, both Jews and Greeks, heard the word of the Lord.

## Demonism Defeated at Ephesus

[11] God was performing extraordinary miracles by Paul's hands, [12] so that even facecloths or work aprons that had touched his skin were brought to the sick, and the diseases left them, and the evil spirits came out of them.

[13] Then some of the itinerant Jewish exorcists attempted to pronounce the name of the Lord Jesus over those who had evil spirits, saying, "I command you by the Jesus whom Paul preaches!" [14] Seven sons of Sceva, a Jewish *chief priest, were doing this. [15] The evil spirit answered them, "Jesus I know, and Paul I recognize—but who are you?" [16] Then the man who had the evil spirit leaped on them, overpowered them all, and prevailed against them, so that they ran out of that house naked and wounded. [17] This became known to everyone who lived in Ephesus, both Jews and Greeks. Then fear fell on all of them, and the name of the Lord Jesus was magnified. [18] And many who had become believers came confessing and disclosing their practices, [19] while many of those who had practiced magic collected their books and burned them in front of everyone. So they calculated their value, and found it to be 50,000 pieces of silver. [20] In this way the Lord's message flourished and prevailed.

## The Riot in Ephesus

[21] When these events were over, Paul resolved in the Spirit to pass through Macedonia and Achaia and go to Jerusalem. "After I've been there," he said, "I must see Rome as well!" [22] So after sending two of those who assisted him, Timothy and Erastus, to Macedonia, he himself stayed in the province of Asia for a while.

[23] During that time there was a major disturbance about the Way. [24] For a person named Demetrius, a silversmith who made silver shrines of Artemis, provided a great deal of business for the craftsmen. [25] When he had assembled them, as well as the workers engaged in this type of business, he said: "Men, you know that

our prosperity is derived from this business. ²⁶ You both see and hear that not only in Ephesus, but in almost the whole province of Asia, this man Paul has persuaded and misled a considerable number of people by saying that gods made by hand are not gods! ²⁷ So not only do we run a risk that our business may be discredited, but also that the temple of the great goddess Artemis may be despised and her magnificence come to the verge of ruin— the very one whom the whole province of Asia and the world adore."

²⁸ When they had heard this, they were filled with rage and began to cry out, "Great is Artemis of the Ephesians!" ²⁹ So the city was filled with confusion; and they rushed all together into the amphitheater, dragging along Gaius and Aristarchus, Macedonians who were Paul's traveling companions. ³⁰ Though Paul wanted to go in before the people, the disciples did not let him. ³¹ Even some of the provincial officials of Asia, who were his friends, sent word to him, pleading with him not to take a chance by going into the amphitheater. ³² Meanwhile, some were shouting one thing and some another, because the assembly was in confusion, and most of them did not know why they had come together. ³³ Then some of the crowd gave Alexander advice when the Jews pushed him to the front. So motioning with his hand, Alexander wanted to make his defense to the people. ³⁴ But when they recognized that he was a Jew, a united cry went up from all of them for about two hours: "Great is Artemis of the Ephesians!"

³⁵ However, when the city clerk had calmed the crowd down, he said, "Men of Ephesus! What man is there who doesn't know that the city of the Ephesians is the temple guardian of the great[a] Artemis, and of the image that fell from heaven? ³⁶ Therefore, since these things are undeniable, you must keep calm and not do anything rash. ³⁷ For you have brought these men here who are not temple robbers or blasphemers of our[b] goddess. ³⁸ So if Demetrius and the craftsmen who are with him have a case against anyone, the courts are in session, and there are proconsuls. Let them bring charges against one another. ³⁹ But if you want something else, it must be decided in a legal assembly. ⁴⁰ In fact, we run a risk of being charged with rioting for what happened today, since there is no justification that we can give as a reason for this disorderly gathering." ⁴¹ After saying this, he dismissed the assembly.

## Paul in Macedonia

**20** After the uproar was over, Paul sent for the disciples, encouraged them, and after saying good-bye, departed to go to Macedonia. ² And when he had passed through those areas and exhorted them at length, he came to Greece ³ and stayed three months. When he was about to set sail for Syria, a plot was devised against him by the Jews, so a decision was made to go back through Macedonia. ⁴ He was accompanied[c] by Sopater, son of Pyrrhus,[d] from Beroea, Aristarchus and Secundus from Thessalonica, Gaius from Derbe, Timothy, and Tychicus and Trophimus from Asia. ⁵ These men went on ahead and waited for us in Troas, ⁶ but we sailed away from Philippi after the days of •Unleavened Bread. In five days we reached them at Troas, where we spent seven days.

> *"Our inheritance is as sure as morning. Why are we so reluctant to leave this dingy world? Things really are better further on."*
> —Calvin Miller

## Eutychus Revived at Troas

[7] On the first day of the week, we[a] assembled to break bread. Paul spoke to them, and since he was about to depart the next day, he extended his message until midnight. [8] There were many lamps in the room upstairs where we were assembled, [9] and a young man named Eutychus was sitting on a window sill and sank into a deep sleep as Paul kept on speaking. When he was overcome by sleep he fell down from the third story, and was picked up dead. [10] But Paul went down, threw himself on him, embraced him, and said, "Don't be alarmed, for his 'life is in him!" [11] After going upstairs, breaking the bread, and eating, he conversed a considerable time until dawn. Then he left. [12] They brought the boy home alive and were greatly comforted.

## From Troas to Miletus

[13] Then we went on ahead to the ship and sailed for Assos, from there intending to take Paul on board. For these were his instructions, since he himself was going by land. [14] When he met us at Assos, we took him on board and came to Mitylene. [15] Sailing from there, the next day we arrived off Chios. The following day we crossed over to Samos, and[b] the day after, we came to Miletus. [16] For Paul had decided to sail past Ephesus so he would not have to spend time in the province of Asia, because he was hurrying to be in Jerusalem, if possible, for the day of Pentecost.

## Farewell Address to the Ephesian Elders

[17] Now from Miletus, he sent to Ephesus and called for the elders of the church. [18] And when they came to him, he said to them: "You know, from the first day I set foot in Asia, how I was with you the whole time— [19] serving the Lord with all humility, with tears, and with the trials that came to me through the plots of the Jews— [20] and that I did not shrink back from proclaiming to you anything that was profitable, or from teaching it to you in public and from house to house. [21] I testified to both Jews and Greeks about repentance toward God and faith in our Lord Jesus.

### Acts 20:22-24

> *They can make you breathe the air down here. They can make you drink the water. But they can't make your heart feel at home anymore. You belong somewhere else. If people say you've got your head in the clouds, tell them not to knock it till they've been there.*

[22] "And now I am on my way to Jerusalem, bound in my spirit, not knowing what I will encounter there,

---

[a]20:7 Other mss read *the disciples*　　[b]20:15 Other mss add *after staying at Trogyllium*

23 except that in town after town the Holy Spirit testifies to me that chains and afflictions are waiting for me. 24 But I count my life of no value to myself, so that I may finish my course[a] and the ministry I received from the Lord Jesus, to testify to the gospel of God's grace.

25 "And now I know that none of you, among whom I went about preaching the kingdom, will ever see my face again. 26 Therefore I testify to you this day that I am innocent of everyone's blood, 27 for I did not shrink back from declaring to you the whole plan of God. 28 Be on guard for yourselves and for all the flock, among whom the Holy Spirit has appointed you as *overseers, to shepherd the church of God,[b] which He purchased with His own blood. 29 I know that after my departure savage wolves will come in among you, not sparing the flock. 30 And men from among yourselves will rise up with deviant doctrines to lure the disciples into following them. 31 Therefore be on the alert, remembering that night and day for three years I did not stop warning each one of you with tears.

32 "And now[c] I commit you to God and to the message of His grace, which is able to build you up and to give you an inheritance among all who are sanctified. 33 I have not coveted anyone's silver or gold or clothing. 34 You yourselves know that these hands have provided for my needs, and for those who were with me. 35 In every way I've shown you that by laboring like this, it is necessary to help the weak and to keep in mind the words of the Lord Jesus, for He said, 'It is more blessed to give than to receive.'"

36 After he said this, he knelt down and prayed with all of them. 37 There was a great deal of weeping by everyone. And embracing Paul, they kissed him, 38 grieving most of all over his statement that they would never see his face again. Then they escorted him to the ship.

## Warnings on the Journey to Jerusalem

21 After we tore ourselves away from them and set sail, we came by a direct route to Cos, the next day to Rhodes, and from there to Patara. 2 Finding a ship crossing over to Phoenicia, we boarded and set sail. 3 After we sighted Cyprus, leaving it on the left, we sailed on to Syria and arrived at Tyre, because the ship was to unload its cargo there. 4 So we found some disciples and stayed there seven days. They said to Paul through the Spirit not to go to Jerusalem. 5 When our days there were over, we left to continue our journey, while all of them, with their wives and children, escorted us out of the city. After kneeling down on the beach to pray, 6 we said good-bye to one another. Then we boarded the ship, and they returned home.

7 When we completed our voyage from Tyre, we reached Ptolemais, where we greeted the brothers and stayed with them one day. 8 The next day we left and came to Caesarea, where we entered the house of Philip the evangelist, who was one of the Seven, and stayed with him. 9 This man had four virgin daughters who prophesied.

10 While we were staying there many days, a prophet named Agabus came down from Judea. 11 He came to us, took Paul's belt, tied his own feet and hands, and said, "This is what the

a20:24 Other mss add with joy  b20:28 Other mss read church of the Lord; other mss read church of the Lord and God  c20:32 Other mss add brothers,

Holy Spirit says: 'In this way the Jews in Jerusalem will bind the man who owns this belt, and deliver him into Gentile hands.' " [12] When we heard this, both we and the local people begged him not to go up to Jerusalem. [13] Then Paul replied, "What are you doing, weeping and breaking my heart? For I am ready not only to be bound, but also to die in Jerusalem for the name of the Lord Jesus."

[14] Since he would not be persuaded, we stopped talking and simply said, "The Lord's will be done!"

## Conflict over the Gentile Mission

[15] After these days we got ready and went up to Jerusalem. [16] Some of the disciples from Caesarea also went with us and brought us to Mnason, a Cypriot, an early disciple, with whom we were to stay.

[17] When we reached Jerusalem, the brothers welcomed us gladly. [18] The following day Paul went in with us to James, and all the elders were present. [19] After greeting them, he related one by one what God did among the Gentiles through his ministry.

[20] When they heard it, they glorified God and said, "You see, brother, how many thousands of Jews there are who have believed, and they are all zealous for the law. [21] But they have been told about you that you teach all the Jews who are among the Gentiles to abandon Moses, by telling them not to circumcise their children or to walk in our customs. [22] So what is to be done?[a] They will certainly hear that you've come. [23] Therefore do what we tell you: We have four men who have obligated themselves with a vow. [24] Take these men, purify yourself along with them, and pay for

them to get their heads shaved. Then everyone will know that what they were told about you amounts to nothing, but that you yourself are also careful about observing the law. [25] With regard to the Gentiles who have believed, we have written a letter containing our decision that[b] they should keep themselves from food sacrificed to idols, from blood, from what is strangled, and from sexual immorality."

## The Riot in the Temple Complex

[26] Then the next day, Paul took the men, having purified himself along with them, and entered the temple, announcing the completion of the purification days when the offering for each of them would be made. [27] As the seven days were about to end, the Jews from the province of Asia saw him in the •temple complex, stirred up the whole crowd, and seized him, [28] shouting, "Men of Israel, help! This is the man who teaches everyone everywhere against our people, our law, and this place. What's more, he also brought Greeks into the temple and has profaned this holy place." [29] For they had previously seen Trophimus the Ephesian in the city with him, and they supposed that Paul had brought him into the temple complex. [30] The whole city was stirred up, and the people rushed together. They seized Paul, dragged him out of the temple complex, and at once the gates were shut. [31] As they were trying to kill him, word went up to the commander of the •regiment that all Jerusalem was in chaos. [32] Taking along soldiers and centurions, he immediately ran down to them. Seeing the commander and

[a]21:22 Other mss add *A multitude has to come together, since*    [b]21:25 Other mss add *they should observe no such thing, except that*

the soldiers, they stopped beating Paul. <sup>33</sup> Then the commander came up, took him into custody, and ordered him to be bound with two chains. He asked who he was and what he had done. <sup>34</sup> Some in the mob were shouting one thing and some another. Since he was not able to get reliable information because of the uproar, he ordered him to be taken into the barracks. <sup>35</sup> When Paul got to the steps, he had to be carried by the soldiers because of the mob's violence, <sup>36</sup> for the mass of people were following and yelling, "Kill him!"

## Paul's Defense before the Jerusalem Mob

<sup>37</sup> As he was about to be brought into the barracks, Paul said to the commander, "Am I allowed to say something to you?"

He replied, "Do you know Greek? <sup>38</sup> Aren't you the Egyptian who raised a rebellion some time ago and led 4,000 Assassins into the desert?"

<sup>39</sup> Paul said, "I am a Jewish man from Tarsus of Cilicia, a citizen of an important city. Now I ask you, let me speak to the people."

<sup>40</sup> After he had given permission, Paul stood on the steps and motioned with his hand to the people. When there was a great hush, he addressed them in the Hebrew language:

**22** <sup>1</sup> "Brothers and fathers, listen now to my defense before you." <sup>2</sup> When they heard that he was addressing them in the Hebrew language, they became even quieter. <sup>3</sup> He continued, "I am a Jewish man, born in Tarsus of Cilicia, but brought up in this city at the feet of Gamaliel, and educated according to the strict view of our patriarchal law. Being zealous

for God, just as all of you are today, <sup>4</sup> I persecuted this Way to the death, binding and putting both men and women in jail, <sup>5</sup> as both the high priest and the whole council of elders can testify about me. Having received letters from them to the brothers, I was traveling to Damascus to bring those who were prisoners there to be punished in Jerusalem.

## Paul's Testimony

<sup>6</sup> "As I was traveling and near Damascus, about noon an intense light from heaven suddenly flashed around me. <sup>7</sup> I fell to the ground and heard a voice saying to me, 'Saul, Saul, why are you persecuting Me?'

<sup>8</sup> "I answered, 'Who are You, Lord?'

"He said to me, 'I am Jesus the *Nazarene, whom you are persecuting!' <sup>9</sup> Now those who were with me saw the light,<sup>a</sup> but they did not hear the voice of the One who was speaking to me.

<sup>10</sup> "Then I said, 'What should I do, Lord?'

"And the Lord told me, 'Get up and go into Damascus, and there you will be told about everything that is assigned for you to do.'

<sup>11</sup> "Since I couldn't see because of the brightness of that light, I was led by the hand by those who were with me, and came into Damascus. <sup>12</sup> Someone named Ananias, a devout man according to the law, having a good reputation with all the Jews residing there, <sup>13</sup> came to me, stood by me, and said, 'Brother Saul, regain your sight.' And in that very hour I looked up and saw him. <sup>14</sup> Then he said, 'The God of our fathers has appointed you to know His will, to see the Righteous One, and to hear the sound of His voice. <sup>15</sup> For you will be a witness for Him to all people of what

<sup>a</sup>**22:9** Other mss add *and were afraid*

you have seen and heard. [16] And now, why delay? Get up and be baptized, and wash away your sins by calling on His name.'

[17] "After I came back to Jerusalem and was praying in the *temple complex, I went into a visionary state [18] and saw Him telling me, 'Hurry and get out of Jerusalem quickly, because they will not accept your testimony about Me!'

[19] "But I said, 'Lord, they know that in *synagogue after synagogue I had those who believed in You imprisoned and beaten. [20] And when the blood of Your witness Stephen was being shed, I myself was standing by and approving,[a] and I guarded the clothes of those who killed him.'

[21] "Then He said to me, 'Go, because I will send you far away to the Gentiles.' "

## Paul's Roman Protection

[22] They listened to him up to this word. Then they raised their voices, shouting, "Wipe this person off the earth—it's a disgrace for him to live!" [23] As they were yelling and flinging aside their robes and throwing dust into the air, [24] the commander ordered him to be brought into the barracks, directing that he be examined with the scourge, so he could discover the reason they were shouting against him like this. [25] As they stretched him out for the lash, Paul said to the *centurion standing by, "Is it legal for you to scourge a man who is a Roman citizen and is uncondemned?"

[26] When the centurion heard this, he went and reported to the commander, saying, "What are you going to do? For this man is a Roman citizen."

[27] The commander came and said to him, "Tell me—are you a Roman citizen?"

"Yes," he said.

[28] The commander replied, "I bought this citizenship for a large amount of money."

"But I myself was born a citizen," Paul said.

[29] Therefore, those who were about to examine him withdrew from him at once. The commander too was alarmed when he realized Paul was a Roman citizen and he had bound him.

## Paul before the Sanhedrin

[30] The next day, since he wanted to find out exactly why Paul was being accused by the Jews, he released him[b] and instructed the *chief priests and all the *Sanhedrin to convene. Then he brought Paul down and placed him

**23** before them. [1] Paul looked intently at the *Sanhedrin and said, "Brothers, I have lived my life before God in all good conscience until this day." [2] But the high priest Ananias ordered those who were standing next to him to strike him on the mouth. [3] Then Paul said to him, "God is going to strike you, you whitewashed wall! You are sitting there judging me according to the law, and in violation of the law are you ordering me to be struck?"

[4] And those standing nearby said, "Do you dare revile God's high priest?"

[5] "I did not know, brothers," Paul said, "that it was the high priest. For it is written, **You must not speak evil of a ruler of your people.**"[c] [6] When Paul realized that one part of them were *Sadducees and the other part were *Pharisees, he cried out in the Sanhedrin, "Brothers, I am a Pharisee,

a son of Pharisees! I am being judged because of the hope of the resurrection of the dead!" [7] When he said this, a dispute broke out between the Pharisees and the Sadducees, and the assembly was divided. [8] For the Sadducees say there is no resurrection, and no angel or spirit, but the Pharisees affirm them all.

[9] The shouting grew loud, and some of the *scribes of the Pharisees' party got up and argued vehemently: "We find nothing evil in this man. What if a spirit or an angel has spoken to him?"[a] [10] When the dispute became violent, the commander feared that Paul might be torn apart by them and ordered the troops to go down, rescue him from them, and bring him into the barracks.

## The Plot against Paul

[11] The following night, the Lord stood by him and said, "Have courage! For as you have testified about Me in Jerusalem, so you must also testify in Rome."

[12] When it was day, the Jews formed a conspiracy and bound themselves under a curse neither to eat nor to drink until they had killed Paul. [13] There were more than 40 who had formed this plot. [14] These men went to the *chief priests and elders and said, "We have bound ourselves under a solemn curse that we won't eat anything until we have killed Paul. [15] So now you, along with the Sanhedrin, make a request to the commander that he bring him down to you[b] as if you were going to investigate his case more thoroughly. However, before he gets near, we are ready to kill him."

[16] But the son of Paul's sister, hearing about their ambush, came and entered the barracks and reported it to Paul. [17] Then Paul called one of the centurions and said, "Take this young man to the commander, because he has something to report to him."

[18] So he took him, brought him to the commander, and said, "The prisoner Paul called me and asked me to bring this young man to you, because he has something to tell you."

[19] Then the commander took him by the hand, led him aside, and inquired privately, "What is it you have to report to me?"

[20] "The Jews," he said, "have agreed to ask you to bring Paul down to the Sanhedrin tomorrow, as though they are going to hold a somewhat more careful inquiry about him. [21] Don't let them persuade you, because there are more than 40 of them arranging to ambush him, men who have bound themselves under a curse not to eat or drink until they kill him. Now they are ready, waiting for a commitment from you."

[22] So the commander dismissed the young man and instructed him, "Don't tell anyone that you have informed me about this."

## To Caesarea by Night

[23] He summoned two of his centurions and said, "Get 200 soldiers ready with 70 cavalry and 200 spearmen to go to Caesarea at nine tonight. [24] Also provide mounts so they can put Paul on them and bring him safely to Felix the governor."

[25] He wrote a letter of this kind:

[26] Claudius Lysias,

To the most excellent governor Felix:

Greetings.

---

[a]**23:9** Other mss add *Let us not fight God.*    [b]**23:15** Other mss add *tomorrow*

[27] When this man had been seized by the Jews and was about to be killed by them, I arrived with my troops and rescued him because I learned that he is a Roman citizen. [28] Wanting to know the charge for which they were accusing him, I brought him down before their Sanhedrin. [29] I found out that the accusations were about disputed matters in their law, and that there was no charge that merited death or chains. [30] When I was informed that there was a plot against the man,[a] I sent him to you right away. I also ordered his accusers to state their case against him in your presence.[b]

[31] Therefore, during the night, the soldiers took Paul and brought him to Antipatris as they were ordered. [32] The next day, they returned to the barracks, allowing the cavalry to go on with him. [33] When these men entered Caesarea and delivered the letter to the governor, they also presented Paul to him. [34] After he[c] read it, he asked what province he was from. So when he learned he was from Cilicia, [35] he said, "I will give you a hearing whenever your accusers get here too." And he ordered that he be kept under guard in •Herod's •palace.

## The Accusation against Paul

**24** After five days Ananias the high priest came down with some elders and a lawyer named Tertullus. These men presented their case against Paul to the governor. [2] When he was called in, Tertullus began to accuse him and said: "Since we enjoy great peace because of you, and reforms are taking place for the benefit of this nation by your foresight, [3] we gratefully receive them always and in all places, most excellent Felix, with all thankfulness. [4] However, so that I will not burden you any further, I beg you in your graciousness to give us a brief hearing. [5] For we have found this man to be a plague, an agitator among all the Jews throughout the Roman world, and a ringleader of the sect of the Nazarenes! [6] He even tried to desecrate the temple, so we apprehended him ⌊and wanted to judge him according to our law. [7] But Lysias the commander came and took him from our hands, commanding his accusers to come to you.⌋[d] [8] By examining him yourself you will be able to discern all these things of which we accuse him." [9] The Jews also joined in the attack, alleging that these things were so.

## Paul's Defense before Felix

[10] When the governor motioned to him to speak, Paul replied: "Because I know you have been a judge of this nation for many years, I am glad to offer my defense in what concerns me. [11] You are able to determine that it is no more than 12 days since I went up to worship in Jerusalem. [12] And they didn't find me disputing with anyone or causing a disturbance among the crowd, either in the •temple complex or in the •synagogues, or anywhere in the city. [13] Neither can they provide evidence to you of what they now bring against me. [14] But I confess this to you: that according to the Way, which they call a sect, so I worship my fathers' God, believing all the things that are written in the Law and in the Prophets. [15] And I have a hope in God, which these men themselves also accept, that there is going to be a resurrection,[e]

---

[a]23:30 Other mss add *by the Jews*   [b]23:30 Other mss add *Farewell*   [c]23:34 Other mss read *the governor*
[d]24:6-7 Other mss omit bracketed text   [e]24:15 Other mss add *of the dead*

both of the righteous and the unrighteous. [16] I always do my best to have a clear conscience toward God and men. [17] After many years, I came to bring charitable gifts and offerings to my nation, [18] and while I was doing this, some Jews from the province of Asia found me ritually purified in the temple, without a crowd and without any uproar. [19] It is they who ought to be here before you to bring charges, if they have anything against me. [20] Either let these men here state what wrongdoing they found in me when I stood before the •Sanhedrin, [21] or about this one statement I cried out while standing among them, 'Today I am being judged before you concerning the resurrection of the dead.' "

## The Verdict Postponed

[22] Since Felix was accurately informed about the Way, he adjourned the hearing, saying, "When Lysias the commander comes down, I will decide your case." [23] He ordered that the •centurion keep Paul under guard, though he could have some freedom, and that he should not prevent any of his friends from serving[a] him.

[24] After some days, when Felix came with his wife Drusilla, who was Jewish, he sent for Paul and listened to him on the subject of faith in Christ Jesus. [25] Now as he spoke about righteousness, self-control, and the judgment to come, Felix became afraid and replied, "Leave for now, but when I find time I'll call for you." [26] At the same time he was also hoping that money would be given to him by Paul.[b] For this reason he sent for him quite often and conversed with him.

[27] After two years had passed, Felix received a successor, Porcius Festus,

and because he wished to do a favor for the Jews, Felix left Paul in prison.

## Appeal to Caesar

**25** Three days after Festus arrived in the province, he went up to Jerusalem from Caesarea. [2] Then the •chief priests and the leaders of the Jews presented their case against Paul to him; and they appealed, [3] asking him to do them a favor against Paul, that he might summon him to Jerusalem. They were preparing an ambush along the road to kill him. [4] However, Festus answered that Paul should be kept at Caesarea, and that he himself was about to go there shortly. [5] "Therefore," he said, "let the men of authority among you go down with me and accuse him, if there is any wrong in this man."

[6] When he had spent not more than eight or 10 days among them, he went down to Caesarea. The next day, seated at the judge's bench, he commanded Paul to be brought in. [7] When he arrived, the Jews who had come down from Jerusalem stood around him and brought many serious charges that they were not able to prove, [8] while Paul made the defense that, "Neither against the Jewish law, nor against the temple, nor against Caesar have I sinned at all."

[9] Then Festus, wanting to do a favor for the Jews, replied to Paul, "Are you willing to go up to Jerusalem, there to be tried before me on these charges?"

[10] But Paul said: "I am standing at Caesar's tribunal, where I ought to be tried. I have done no wrong to the Jews, as even you can see very well. [11] If then I am doing wrong, or have done anything deserving of death, I do not refuse to die, but if there is nothing

[a]24:23 Other mss add *or visiting*    [b]24:26 Other mss add *so that he might release him*

to what these men accuse me of, no one can give me up to them. I appeal to Caesar!"

[12] After Festus conferred with his council, he replied, "You have appealed to Caesar; to Caesar you will go!"

## King Agrippa and Bernice Visit Festus

[13] After some days had passed, King Agrippa and Bernice arrived in Caesarea and paid a courtesy call on Festus. [14] Since they stayed there many days, Festus presented Paul's case to the king, saying, "There's a man who was left as a prisoner by Felix. [15] When I was in Jerusalem, the chief priests and the elders of the Jews presented their case and asked for a judgment against him. [16] I answered them that it's not the Romans' custom to give any man up[a] before the accused confronts the accusers face to face and has an opportunity to give a defense concerning the charge. [17] Therefore, when they had assembled here, I did not delay. The next day I sat at the judge's bench and ordered the man to be brought in. [18] Concerning him, the accusers stood up and brought no charge of the sort I was expecting. [19] Instead they had some disagreements with him about their own religion and about a certain Jesus, a dead man whom Paul claimed to be alive. [20] Since I was at a loss in a dispute over such things, I asked him if he wished to go to Jerusalem and be tried there concerning these matters. [21] But when Paul appealed to be held for trial by the Emperor, I ordered him to be kept in custody until I could send him to Caesar."

[22] Then Agrippa said to Festus, "I would like to hear the man myself."

"Tomorrow," he said, "you will hear him."

## Paul before Agrippa

[23] So the next day, Agrippa and Bernice came with great pomp and entered the auditorium with the commanders and prominent men of the city. When Festus gave the command, Paul was brought in. [24] Then Festus said: "King Agrippa and all men present with us, you see this man about whom the whole Jewish community has appealed to me, both in Jerusalem and here, shouting that he should not live any longer. [25] Now I realized that he had not done anything deserving of death, but when he himself appealed to the Emperor, I decided to send him. [26] I have nothing definite to write to the Emperor about him. Therefore, I have brought him before all of you, and especially before you, King Agrippa, so that after this examination is over, I may have something to write. [27] For it seems unreasonable to me to send a prisoner and not to indicate the charges against him."

## Paul's Defense before Agrippa

**26** Agrippa said to Paul, "It is permitted for you to speak for yourself."

Then Paul stretched out his hand and began his defense: [2] "I consider myself fortunate, King Agrippa, that today I am going to make a defense before you about everything I am accused of by the Jews, [3] especially since you are an expert in all the Jewish customs and controversies. Therefore I beg you to listen to me patiently. [4] "All the Jews know my way of life from my youth, which was spent from

a25:16 Other mss add to destruction

the beginning among my own nation and in Jerusalem. [5] They had previously known me for quite some time, if they were willing to testify, that according to the strictest party of our religion I lived as a •Pharisee. [6] And now I stand on trial for the hope of the promise made by God to our fathers, [7] ⌊the promise⌋ our 12 tribes hope to attain as they earnestly serve Him night and day. Because of this hope I am being accused by the Jews, O king! [8] Why is it considered incredible by any of you that God raises the dead? [9] In fact, I myself supposed it was necessary to do many things in opposition to the name of Jesus the •Nazarene. [10] This I actually did in Jerusalem, and I locked up many of the saints in prison, since I had received authority for that from the •chief priests. When they were put to death, I cast my vote against them. [11] In all the •synagogues I often tried to make them blaspheme by punishing them. Being greatly enraged at them, I even pursued them to foreign cities.

## Paul's Account of His Conversion and Commission

[12] "Under these circumstances I was traveling to Damascus with authority and a commission from the chief priests. [13] At midday, while on the road, O king, I saw a light from heaven brighter than the sun, shining around me and those traveling with me. [14] When we had all fallen to the ground, I heard a voice speaking to me in the Hebrew language, 'Saul, Saul, why are you persecuting Me? It is hard for you to kick against the goads.'

[15] "But I said, 'Who are You, Lord?'

"And the Lord replied: 'I am Jesus, whom you are persecuting. [16] But get up and stand on your feet. For I have appeared to you for this purpose, to appoint you as a servant and a witness of things you have seen,[a] and of things in which I will appear to you. [17] I will rescue you from the people and from the Gentiles, to whom I now send you, [18] to open their eyes that they may turn from darkness to light and from the power of Satan to God, that they may receive forgiveness of sins and a share among those who are sanctified by faith in Me.'

[19] "Therefore, King Agrippa, I was not disobedient to the heavenly vision. [20] Instead, I preached to those in Damascus first, and to those in Jerusalem and in all the region of Judea, and to the Gentiles, that they should repent and turn to God, and do works worthy of repentance. [21] For this reason the Jews seized me in the •temple complex and were trying to kill me. [22] Since I have obtained help that comes from God, to this day I stand and testify to both small and great, saying nothing else than what the prophets and Moses said would take place— [23] that the •Messiah must suffer, and that as the first to rise from the dead, He would proclaim light to our people and to the Gentiles."

## Not Quite Persuaded

[24] As he was making his defense this way, Festus exclaimed in a loud voice, "You're out of your mind, Paul! Too much study is driving you mad!"

[25] But Paul replied, "I'm not out of my mind, most excellent Festus. On the contrary, I'm speaking words of truth and good judgment. [26] For the king knows about these matters. It is to him I am actually speaking boldly. For I'm not convinced that any of these things escapes his notice, since

[a]**26:16** Other mss read *things in which you have seen Me*

this was not done in a corner! [27] King Agrippa, do you believe the prophets? I know you believe."

[28] Then Agrippa said to Paul, "Are you going to persuade me to become a Christian so easily?"

[29] "I wish before God," replied Paul, "that whether easily or with difficulty, not only you but all who listen to me today might become as I am—except for these chains."

[30] So the king, the governor, Bernice, and those sitting with them got up, [31] and when they had left they talked with each other and said, "This man is doing nothing that deserves death or chains."

[32] Then Agrippa said to Festus, "This man could have been released if he had not appealed to Caesar."

## Sailing for Rome

**27** When it was decided that we were to sail to Italy, they handed over Paul and some other prisoners to a •centurion named Julius, of the Imperial •Regiment. [2] So when we had boarded a ship of Adramyttium, we put to sea, intending to sail to ports along the coast of the Province of Asia. Aristarchus, a Macedonian of Thessalonica, was with us. [3] The next day we put in at Sidon, and Julius treated Paul kindly and allowed him to go to his friends to receive their care. [4] When we had put out to sea from there, we sailed along the northern coast of Cyprus because the winds were against us. [5] After sailing through the open sea off Cilicia and Pamphylia, we reached Myra in Lycia. [6] There the centurion found an Alexandrian ship sailing for Italy and put us on board. [7] Sailing slowly for many days, we came with difficulty as far as Cnidus. But since the wind did not allow us to approach

it, we sailed along the south side of Crete off Salmone. [8] With yet more difficulty we sailed along the coast, and came to a place called Fair Havens near the city of Lasea.

## Paul's Advice Ignored

[9] By now much time had passed, and the voyage was already dangerous. Since the Fast was already over, Paul gave his advice [10] and told them, "Men, I can see that this voyage is headed toward damage and heavy loss, not only of the cargo and the ship, but also of our lives." [11] But the centurion paid attention to the captain and the owner of the ship rather than to what Paul said. [12] Since the harbor was unsuitable to winter in, the majority decided to set sail from there, hoping somehow to reach Phoenix, a harbor on Crete open to the southwest and northwest, and to winter there.

## Storm-tossed Vessel

[13] When a gentle south wind sprang up, they thought they had achieved their purpose; they weighed anchor and sailed along the shore of Crete. [14] But not long afterwards, a fierce wind called the "northeaster" rushed down from the island. [15] Since the ship was caught and was unable to head into the wind, we gave way to it and were driven along. [16] After running under the shelter of a little island called Cauda, we were barely able to get control of the skiff. [17] After hoisting it up, they used ropes and tackle and girded the ship. Then, fearing they would run aground on the Syrtis, they lowered the drift-anchor, and in this way they were driven along. [18] Because we were being severely battered by the storm, they began to jettison the cargo the next day. [19] On

the third day, they threw the ship's gear overboard with their own hands.

[20] For many days neither sun nor stars appeared, and the severe storm kept raging; finally all hope that we would be saved was disappearing. [21] Since many were going without food, Paul stood up among them and said, "You men should have followed my advice not to sail from Crete and sustain this damage and loss. [22] Now I urge you to take courage, because there will be no loss of any of your lives, but only of the ship. [23] For this night an angel of the God I belong to and serve stood by me, [24] saying, 'Don't be afraid, Paul. You must stand before Caesar. And, look! God has graciously given you all those who are sailing with you.' [25] Therefore, take courage, men, because I believe God that it will be just the way it was told to me. [26] However, we must run aground on a certain island."

[27] When the fourteenth night came, we were drifting in the Adriatic Sea, and in the middle of the night the sailors thought they were approaching land. [28] They took a sounding and found it to be 120 feet deep; when they had sailed a little farther and sounded again, they found it to be 90 feet deep. [29] Then, fearing we might run aground in some rocky place, they dropped four anchors from the stern and prayed for daylight to come.

[30] Some sailors tried to escape from the ship; they had let down the skiff into the sea, pretending that they were going to put out anchors from the bow. [31] Paul said to the centurion and the soldiers, "Unless these men stay in the ship, you cannot be saved." [32] Then the soldiers cut the ropes holding the skiff and let it drop away.

[33] When it was just about daylight, Paul urged them all to take food, saying, "Today is the fourteenth day that you have been waiting and going without food, having eaten nothing. [34] Therefore I urge you to take some food. For this has to do with your survival, since not a hair will be lost from the head of any of you." [35] After he said these things and had taken some bread, he gave thanks to God in the presence of them all, and when he had broken it, he began to eat. [36] They all became encouraged and took food themselves. [37] In all there were 276 of us on the ship. [38] And having eaten enough food, they began to lighten the ship by throwing the grain overboard into the sea.

## Shipwreck

[39] When daylight came, they did not recognize the land, but sighted a bay with a beach. They planned to run the ship ashore if they could. [40] After casting off the anchors, they left them in the sea, at the same time loosening the ropes that held the rudders. Then they hoisted the foresail to the wind and headed for the beach. [41] But they struck a sandbar and ran the ship aground. The bow jammed fast and remained immovable, but the stern began to break up with the pounding of the waves.

[42] The soldiers' plan was to kill the prisoners so that no one could swim off and escape. [43] But the centurion kept them from carrying out their plan because he wanted to save Paul, so he ordered those who could swim to jump overboard first and get to land. [44] The rest were to follow, some on planks and some on debris from the ship. In this way, all got safely to land.

## Malta's Hospitality

**28** Safely ashore, we then learned that the island was called Malta.

2 The local people showed us extraordinary kindness, for they lit a fire and took us all in, since rain was falling and it was cold. 3 As Paul gathered a bundle of brushwood and put it on the fire, a viper came out because of the heat and fastened itself to his hand. 4 When the local people saw the creature hanging from his hand, they said to one another, "This man is probably a murderer, and though he has escaped the sea, Justice does not allow him to live!" 5 However, he shook the creature off into the fire and suffered no harm. 6 They expected that he would swell up or suddenly drop dead. But after they waited a long time and saw nothing unusual happen to him, they changed their minds and said he was a god.

## Ministry in Malta

7 Now in the area around that place was an estate belonging to the leading man of the island, named Publius, who welcomed us and entertained us hospitably for three days. 8 It happened that Publius' father was in bed suffering from fever and dysentery. Paul went to him, and praying and laying his hands on him, he healed him. 9 After this, the rest of those on the island who had diseases also came and were cured. 10 So they heaped many honors on us, and when we sailed, they gave us what we needed.

## Rome at Last

11 After three months we set sail in an Alexandrian ship that had wintered at the island, with the Twin Brothers as its figurehead. 12 Putting in at Syracuse, we stayed three days. 13 From there, after making a circuit along the coast,[a] we reached Rhegium. After one day a south wind sprang up, and the second day we came to Puteoli. 14 There we found believers and were invited to stay with them for seven days.

And so we came to Rome. 15 Now the believers from there had heard the news about us and had come to meet us as far as Forum of Appius and Three Taverns. When Paul saw them, he thanked God and took courage. 16 And when we entered Rome,[b] Paul was permitted to stay by himself with the soldier who guarded him.

## Paul's First Interview with Roman Jews

17 After three days he called together the leaders of the Jews. And when they had gathered he said to them: "Brothers, although I have done nothing against our people or the customs of our forefathers, I was delivered as a prisoner from Jerusalem into the hands of the Romans 18 who, after examining me, wanted to release me, since I had not committed a capital offense. 19 Because the Jews objected, I was compelled to appeal to Caesar; it was not as though I had any accusation against my nation. 20 So, for this reason I've asked to see you and speak to you. In fact, it is for the hope of Israel that I'm wearing this chain."

21 And they said to him, "We haven't received any letters about you from Judea; none of the brothers has come and reported or spoken anything evil about you. 22 But we consider it suitable to hear from you what you think. For concerning this sect, we are aware that it is spoken against everywhere."

a28:13 Other mss read *From there, casting off*   b28:16 Other mss add *the centurion turned the prisoners over to the military commander; but*

## The Response to Paul's Message

<sup>23</sup> After arranging a day with him, many came to him at his lodging. From dawn to dusk he expounded and witnessed about the kingdom of God. He persuaded them concerning Jesus from both the Law of Moses and the Prophets. <sup>24</sup> Some were persuaded by what he said, but others did not believe.

<sup>25</sup> Disagreeing among themselves, they began to leave after Paul made one statement: "The Holy Spirit correctly spoke through the prophet Isaiah to your[a] forefathers <sup>26</sup> when He said,

Go to this people and say:
'You will listen and listen,
yet never understand;
and you will look and look,
yet never perceive.
<sup>27</sup> For this people's heart has
grown callous,
their ears are hard of
hearing,
and they have shut their
eyes;
otherwise they might see
with their eyes
and hear with their ears,
understand with their heart,
and be converted—
and I would heal them.'[b]

<sup>28</sup> Therefore, let it be known to you that this saving work of God has been sent to the Gentiles; they will listen!" [<sup>29</sup> After he said these things, the Jews departed, while engaging in a prolonged debate among themselves.][c]

## Paul's Ministry Unhindered

<sup>30</sup> Then he stayed two whole years in his own rented house. And he welcomed all who visited him, <sup>31</sup> proclaiming the kingdom of God and teaching the things concerning the Lord Jesus Christ with full boldness and without hindrance.

[a]28:25 Other mss read *our*    [b]28:26–27 Is 6:9–10    [c]28:29 Other mss omit bracketed text

# ROMANS

## God's Good News for Rome

**1** Paul, a slave of Christ Jesus, called as an apostle and singled out for God's good news—[2] which He promised long ago through His prophets in the Holy Scriptures—[3] concerning His Son, Jesus Christ our Lord, who was a descendant of David according to the flesh [4] and was established as the powerful Son of God by the resurrection from the dead according to the Spirit of holiness. [5] We have received grace and apostleship through Him to bring about the obedience of faith among all the nations, on behalf of His name, [6] including yourselves who are also Jesus Christ's by calling:

[7] To all who are in Rome, loved by God, called as saints.

Grace to you and peace from God our Father and the Lord Jesus Christ.

## The Apostle's Desire to Visit Rome

[8] First, I thank my God through Jesus Christ for all of you because the news of your faith is being reported in all the world. [9] For God, whom I serve with my spirit in |telling| the good news about His Son, is my witness that I constantly mention you, [10] always asking in my prayers that if it is somehow in God's will, I may now at last succeed in coming to you. [11] For I want very much to see you, that I may impart to you some spiritual gift to strengthen you, [12] that is, to be mutually encouraged by each other's faith, both yours and mine.

[13] Now I want you to know, brothers, that I often planned to come to you (but was prevented until now) in order that I might have a fruitful ministry among you, just as among the rest of the Gentiles. [14] I am obligated both to Greeks and barbarians, both to the wise and the foolish. [15] So I am eager to preach the good news to you also who are in Rome.

## The Righteous Will Live by Faith

[16] For I am not ashamed of the gospel,[a] because it is God's power for salvation to everyone who believes, first to the Jew, and also to the Greek. [17] For in it God's righteousness is revealed from faith to faith, just as it is written: **The righteous will live by faith.**[b]

---

*Romans 1:18-21*

### Man

*What about those who've never read a Bible? Never heard a preacher? Never heard the name of Jesus? We know God will deal justly with them, according to His character, but we know that in their inner being, they are aware of the One who made them. We are all without excuse.*

---

[a]1:16 Other mss add *of Christ*　[b]1:17 Hab 2:4

## The Guilt of the Gentile World

[18] For God's wrath is revealed from heaven against all godlessness and unrighteousness of people who by their unrighteousness suppress the truth, [19] since what can be known about God is evident among them, because God has shown it to them. [20] From the creation of the world His invisible attributes, that is, His eternal power and divine nature, have been clearly seen, being understood through what He has made. As a result, people are without excuse. [21] For though they knew God, they did not glorify Him as God or show gratitude. Instead, their thinking became nonsense, and their senseless minds were darkened. [22] Claiming to be wise, they became fools [23] and exchanged the glory of the immortal God for images resembling mortal man, birds, four-footed animals, and reptiles.

[24] Therefore God delivered them over in the cravings of their hearts to sexual impurity, so that their bodies were degraded among themselves. [25] They exchanged the truth of God for a lie, and worshiped and served something created instead of the Creator, who is blessed forever. •Amen.

## From Idolatry to Depravity

[26] This is why God delivered them over to degrading passions. For even their females exchanged natural sexual intercourse for what is unnatural. [27] The males in the same way also left natural sexual intercourse with females and were inflamed in their lust for one another. Males committed shameless acts with males and re-ceived in their own persons the appropriate penalty for their perversion.

[28] And because they did not think it worthwhile to have God in their knowledge, God delivered them over to a worthless mind to do what is morally wrong. [29] They are filled with all unrighteousness,[a] evil, greed, and wickedness. They are full of envy, murder, disputes, deceit, and malice. They are gossips, [30] slanderers, God-haters, arrogant, proud, boastful, inventors of evil, disobedient to parents, [31] undiscerning, untrustworthy, unloving,[b] and unmerciful. [32] Although they know full well God's just sentence—that those who practice such things deserve to die—they not only do them, but even applaud others who practice them.

---

### Romans 2:1-4

*No telling how many unsaved friends you have—people who are curious about your newfound faith, but not sure they're ready for it. Hang in there. Love them through it. The Lord may have waited on you for a pretty long time. How long are you willing to wait on your friends?*

---

## God's Righteous Judgment

**2** Therefore, anyone of you who judges is without excuse. For when you judge another, you condemn yourself, since you, the judge, do the same things. [2] We know that God's judgment on those who do

[a]1:29 Other mss add *sexual immorality*    [b]1:31 Other mss add *unforgiving*

such things is based on the truth. [3] Do you really think—anyone of you who judges those who do such things yet do the same—that you will escape God's judgment? [4] Or do you despise the riches of His kindness, restraint, and patience, not recognizing that God's kindness is intended to lead you to repentance? [5] But because of your hardness and unrepentant heart you are storing up wrath for yourself in the day of wrath, when God's righteous judgment is revealed. [6] He **will repay each one according to his works:**[a] [7] eternal life to those who by patiently doing good seek for glory, honor, and immortality; [8] but wrath and indignation to those who are self-seeking and disobey the truth, but are obeying unrighteousness; [9] affliction and distress for every human being who does evil, first to the Jew, and also to the Greek; [10] but glory, honor, and peace for everyone who does good, first to the Jew, and also to the Greek. [11] There is no favoritism with God.

[12] All those who sinned without the law will also perish without the law, and all those who sinned under the law will be judged by the law. [13] For the hearers of the law are not righteous before God, but the doers of the law will be declared righteous. [14] So, when Gentiles, who do not have the law, instinctively do what the law demands, they are a law to themselves even though they do not have the law. [15] They show that the work of the law is written on their hearts. Their consciences testify in support of this, and their competing thoughts either accuse or excuse them [16] on the day when God judges what people have kept secret, according to my gospel through Christ Jesus.

> "Our aim is not to force people to live like Christians, but to persuade them to consider Christ."
> —John Fischer

## Jewish Violation of the Law

[17] Now if[b] you call yourself a Jew, and rest in the law, and boast in God, [18] and know His will, and approve the things that are superior, being instructed from the law, [19] and are convinced that you are a guide for the blind, a light to those in darkness, [20] an instructor of the ignorant, a teacher of the immature, having in the law the full expression of knowledge and truth— [21] you then, who teach another, do you not teach yourself? You who preach, "You must not steal"—do you steal? [22] You who say, "You must not commit adultery"—do you commit adultery? You who detest idols, do you rob their temples? [23] You who boast in the law, do you dishonor God by breaking the law? [24] For, as it is written: **The name of God is blasphemed among the Gentiles because of you.**[c]

## Circumcision of the Heart

[25] For circumcision benefits you if you observe the law, but if you are a lawbreaker, your circumcision has become uncircumcision. [26] Therefore if an uncircumcised man keeps the law's requirements, will his uncircumcision not be counted as circumcision? [27] A man who is physically uncircumcised, but who fulfills the law, will judge you who are a lawbreaker in

[a]**2:6** Ps 62:12; Pr 24:12    [b]**2:17** Other mss read *Look—*    [c]**2:24** Is 52:5

spite of having the letter ⌊of the law⌋ and circumcision. ²⁸ For a person is not a Jew who is one outwardly, and ⌊true⌋ circumcision is not something visible in the flesh. ²⁹ On the contrary, a person is a Jew who is one inwardly, and circumcision is of the heart—by the Spirit, not the letter. His praise is not from men but from God.

*"Let it be accounted folly, frenzy, fury, or whatever. We care for no knowledge in the world but this: that man hath sinned and God hath suffered."*
*—Richard Hooker*

## Paul Answers an Objection

**3** So what advantage does the Jew have? Or what is the benefit of circumcision? ² Considerable in every way. First, they were entrusted with the spoken words of God. ³ What then? If some did not believe, will their unbelief cancel God's faithfulness? ⁴ Absolutely not! God must be true, but every man a liar, as it is written:

> That You may be justified in
>    Your words
> and triumph when You
>    judge.ª

⁵ But if our unrighteousness highlights God's righteousness, what are we to say? I use a human argument: Is God unrighteous to inflict wrath? ⁶ Absolutely not! Otherwise, how will God judge the world? ⁷ But if by my lie God's truth is amplified to His glory, why am I also still judged as a sinner? ⁸ And why not say, just as some people slanderously claim we say, "Let us do evil so that good may come"? Their condemnation is deserved!

## The Whole World Guilty before God

⁹ What then? Are we any better? Not at all! For we have previously charged that both Jews and Gentiles are all under sin, ¹⁰ as it is written:

> There is no one righteous,
>    not even one;
> ¹¹ there is no one who
>    understands,
> there is no one who seeks
>    God.
> ¹² All have turned away,
>    together they have become
>    useless;
> there is no one who does
>    good,
> there is not even one.ᵇ
> ¹³ Their throat is an open
>    grave;
> they deceive with their
>    tongues.
> Vipers' venom is under their
>    lips.ᶜ ᵈ
> ¹⁴ Their mouth is full of cursing
>    and bitterness.ᵉ
> ¹⁵ Their feet are swift to shed
>    blood;
> ¹⁶ ruin and wretchedness are in
>    their paths,
> ¹⁷ and the path of peace they
>    have not known.ᶠ
> ¹⁸ There is no fear of God
>    before their eyes.ᵍ

¹⁹ Now we know that whatever the law says speaks to those who are subject to the law, so that every mouth may be shut and the whole world may become subject to God's

---

ª**3:4** Ps 51:4   ᵇ**3:10–12** Ps 14:1–3; 53:1–3; see Ec 7:20   ᶜ**3:13** Ps 5:9   ᵈ**3:13** Ps 140:3   ᵉ**3:14** Ps 10:7
ᶠ**3:15–17** Is 59:7–8   ᵍ**3:18** Ps 36:1

judgment. [20] For no flesh will be justified in His sight by the works of the law, for through the law ⌊comes⌋ the knowledge of sin.

=====================

### Romans 3:21-26

*Do you realize what Christ's coming did for you? Do you understand how clean you are from the stain of sin? Do you know what God sees when He looks at you? There's a book in God's library that lists all the sins He's holding against you. Your page is blank.*

=====================

### God's Righteousness through Faith

[21] But now, apart from the law, God's righteousness has been revealed—attested by the Law and the Prophets [22] —that is, God's righteousness through faith in Jesus Christ, to all who believe, since there is no distinction. [23] For all have sinned and fall short of the glory of God. [24] They are justified freely by His grace through the redemption that is in Christ Jesus. [25] God presented Him as a propitiation through faith in His blood, to demonstrate His righteousness, because in His restraint God passed over the sins previously committed. [26] He presented Him to demonstrate His righteousness at the present time, so that He would be righteous and declare righteous the one who has faith in Jesus.

### Boasting Excluded

[27] Where then is boasting? It is excluded. By what kind of law? By one of works? No, on the contrary, by a law of faith. [28] For we conclude that a man is justified by faith apart from works of law. [29] Or is God for Jews only? Is He not also for Gentiles? Yes, for Gentiles too, [30] since there is one God who will justify the circumcised by faith and the uncircumcised through faith. [31] Do we then cancel the law through faith? Absolutely not! On the contrary, we uphold the law.

### Abraham Justified by Faith

4 What then can we say that Abraham, our forefather according to the flesh, has found? [2] If Abraham was justified by works, then he has something to brag about—but not before God. [3] For what does the Scripture say?

> **Abraham believed God,**
> **and it was credited to him for**
> **righteousness.**[a]

[4] Now to the one who works, pay is not considered as a gift, but as something owed. [5] But to the one who does not work, but believes on Him who declares righteous the ungodly, his faith is credited for righteousness.

### David Celebrating the Same Truth

[6] Likewise, David also speaks of the blessing of the man to whom God credits righteousness apart from works:

> [7] **How happy are those whose**
> **lawless acts are forgiven**
> **and whose sins are covered!**
> [8] **How happy is the man whom**
> **the Lord will never charge**
> **with sin!**[b]

[a]4:3 Gn 15:6   [b]4:7–8 Ps 32:1–2

## Abraham Justified before Circumcision

[9] Is this blessing only for the circumcised, then? Or is it also for the uncircumcised? For we say, **Faith was credited to Abraham for righteousness.**[a] [10] How then was it credited—while he was circumcised, or uncircumcised? Not while he was circumcised, but uncircumcised. [11] And he received the sign of circumcision as a seal of the righteousness that he had by faith while still uncircumcised. This was to make him the father of all who believe but are not circumcised, so that righteousness may be credited to them also. [12] And he became the father of the circumcised, not only to those who are circumcised, but also to those who follow in the footsteps of the faith our father Abraham had while still uncircumcised.

---

### Romans 4:1-5

### Salvation

*You may wonder how God will deal with those who lived before Jesus came. Are they just out of luck for being born at the wrong time? Will they be held accountable for not trusting a Savior they didn't even know existed? Faith in God has always been rewarded with His blessing.*

---

## The Promise Granted through Faith

[13] For the promise to Abraham or to his descendants that he would inherit the world was not through the law, but through the righteousness that comes by faith. [14] If those who are of the law are heirs, faith is made empty and the promise is canceled. [15] For the law produces wrath; but where there is no law, there is no transgression. [16] This is why the promise is by faith, so that it may be according to grace, to guarantee it to all the descendants—not only to those who are of the law, but also to those who are of Abraham's faith. He is the father of us all [17] in God's sight. As it is written: **I have made you the father of many nations.**[b] He believed in God, who gives life to the dead and calls things into existence that do not exist. [18] Against hope, with hope he believed, so that he became **the father of many nations,**[c] according to what had been spoken: **So will your descendants be.**[d] [19] He considered[e] his own body to be already dead (since he was about 100 years old), and the deadness of Sarah's womb, without weakening in the faith. [20] He did not waver in unbelief at God's promise, but was strengthened in his faith and gave glory to God, [21] because he was fully convinced that what He had promised He was also able to perform. [22] Therefore, **it was credited to him for righteousness.**[f] [23] Now **it was credited to him,** was not written for Abraham alone, [24] but also for us. It will be credited to us who believe in Him who raised Jesus our Lord from the dead. [25] He was delivered up for our trespasses and raised for our justification.

---

[a]4:9 Gn 15:6    [b]4:17 Gn 17:5    [c]4:18 Gn 17:5    [d]4:18 Gn 15:5    [e]4:19 Other mss read *He did not consider*
[f]4:22 Gn 15:6

## Faith Triumphs

**5** Therefore, since we have been declared righteous by faith, we have peace[a] with God through our Lord Jesus Christ. [2] Also through Him, we have obtained access by faith[b] into this grace in which we stand, and we rejoice in the hope of the glory of God. [3] And not only that, but we also rejoice in our afflictions, because we know that affliction produces endurance, [4] endurance produces proven character, and proven character produces hope. [5] This hope does not disappoint, because God's love has been poured out in our hearts through the Holy Spirit who was given to us.

---

### Romans 5:12-21

*Before you can get too far down the road of Christian living, you must first take a good, hard look at yourself and see why you needed His help to begin with. You see, God created man in His own image. But it didn't take us long to think we could cut a better deal.*

---

## Those Declared Righteous Are Reconciled

[6] For while we were still helpless, at the appointed moment, Christ died for the ungodly. [7] For rarely will someone die for a just person— though for a good person perhaps someone might even dare to die. [8] But God proves His own love for us in that while we were still sinners Christ died for us! [9] Much more then, since we have now been declared righteous by His blood, we will be saved through Him from wrath. [10] For if, while we were enemies, we were reconciled to God through the death of His Son, ⌊then how⌋ much more, having been reconciled, will we be saved by His life! [11] And not only that, but we also rejoice in God through our Lord Jesus Christ, through whom we have now received reconciliation.

## Death through Adam and Life through Christ

[12] Therefore, just as sin entered the world through one man, and death through sin, in this way death spread to all men, because all sinned. [13] In fact, sin was in the world before the law, but sin is not charged to one's account when there is no law. [14] Nevertheless, death reigned from Adam to Moses, even over those who did not sin in the likeness of Adam's transgression. He is a prototype of the Coming One.

[15] But the gift is not like the trespass. For if by the one man's trespass the many died, how much more have the grace of God and the gift overflowed to the many by the grace of the one man, Jesus Christ. [16] And the gift is not like the one man's sin, because from one sin came the judgment, resulting in condemnation, but from many trespasses came the gift, resulting in justification. [17] Since by the one man's trespass, death reigned through that one man, how much more will those who receive the overflow of grace and the gift of righteousness reign in life through the one man, Jesus Christ.

[a]**5:1** Other mss read *faith, let us have peace,* which can also be translated *faith, let us grasp the fact that we have peace*
[b]**5:2** Other mss omit *by faith*

> *"The Bible enables people to solve the dilemma facing them. They can understand both their greatness and their cruelty."*
> —*Francis Schaeffer*

[18] So then, as through one trespass there is condemnation for everyone, so also through one righteous act there is life-giving justification for everyone. [19] For just as through one man's disobedience the many were made sinners, so also through the one man's obedience the many will be made righteous. [20] The law came along to multiply the trespass. But where sin multiplied, grace multiplied even more, [21] so that, just as sin reigned in death, so also grace will reign through righteousness, resulting in eternal life through Jesus Christ our Lord.

## The New Life in Christ

**6** What should we say then? Should we continue in sin in order that grace may multiply? [2] Absolutely not! How can we who died to sin still live in it? [3] Or are you unaware that all of us who were baptized into Christ Jesus were baptized into His death? [4] Therefore we were buried with Him by baptism into death, in order that, just as Christ was raised from the dead by the glory of the Father, so we too may •walk in a new way of life. [5] For if we have been joined with Him in the likeness of His death, we will certainly also be in the likeness of His resurrection. [6] For we know that our old self was crucified with Him in order that

sin's dominion over the body may be abolished, so that we may no longer be enslaved to sin, [7] since a person who has died is freed from sin's claims. [8] Now if we died with Christ, we believe that we will also live with Him, [9] because we know that Christ, having been raised from the dead, no longer dies. Death no longer rules over Him. [10] For in that He died, He died to sin once for all; but in that He lives, He lives to God. [11] So, you too consider yourselves dead to sin, but alive to God in Christ Jesus.[a]

[12] Therefore do not let sin reign in your mortal body, so that you obey[b] its desires. [13] And do not offer any parts of it to sin as weapons for unrighteousness. But as those who are alive from the dead, offer yourselves to God, and all the parts of yourselves to God as weapons for righteousness. [14] For sin will not rule over you, because you are not under law but under grace.

## From Slaves of Sin to Slaves of God

[15] What then? Should we sin because we are not under law but under grace? Absolutely not! [16] Do you not know that if you offer yourselves to someone as obedient slaves, you are slaves of that one you obey—either of sin leading to death or of obedience leading to righteousness? [17] But thank God that, although you used to be slaves of sin, you obeyed from the heart that pattern of teaching you were entrusted to, [18] and having been liberated from sin, you became enslaved to righteousness. [19] I am using a human analogy because of the weakness of your flesh. For just as you offered the parts of yourselves as slaves to moral impurity, and to greater and greater lawlessness, so now

[a]6:11 Other mss add *our Lord*   [b]6:12 Other mss add *sin* (lit *it*) *in*

offer them as slaves to righteousness, which results in sanctification. [20] For when you were slaves of sin, you were free from allegiance to righteousness. [21] And what fruit was produced then from the things you are now ashamed of? For the end of those things is death. [22] But now, since you have been liberated from sin and become enslaved to God, you have your fruit, which results in sanctification—and the end is eternal life! [23] For the wages of sin is death, but the gift of God is eternal life in Christ Jesus our Lord.

---

*"God will no longer be a cause of dread to me. I very soon find, however, that I am going to be a great cause of trouble to myself."*

*—Watchman Nee*

---

## An Illustration from Marriage

**7** Since I am speaking to those who understand law, brothers, are you unaware that the law has authority over someone as long as he lives? [2] For example, a married woman is legally bound to her husband while he lives. But if her husband dies, she is released from the law regarding the husband. [3] So then, if she gives herself to another man while her husband is living, she will be called an adulteress. But if her husband dies, she is free from that law. Then, if she gives herself to another man, she is not an adulteress. [4] Therefore, my brothers, you also were put to death in relation to the law through the ⌊crucified⌋ body of the •Messiah, so that you may belong to another—to Him who was raised from the dead—that we may bear fruit for God. [5] For when we were in the flesh, the sinful passions operated through the law in every part of us and bore fruit for death. [6] But now we have been released from the law, since we have died to what held us, so that we may serve in the new way of the Spirit and not in the old letter of the law.

## Sin's Use of the Law

[7] What should we say then? Is the law sin? Absolutely not! On the contrary, I would not have known sin if it were not for the law. For example, I would not have known what it is to covet if the law had not said, **You shall not covet.**[a] [8] And sin, seizing an opportunity through the commandment, produced in me coveting of every kind. For apart from the law sin is dead. [9] Once I was alive apart from the law, but when the commandment came, sin sprang to life [10] and I died. The commandment that was meant for life resulted in death for me. [11] For sin, seizing an opportunity through the commandment, deceived me, and through it killed me. [12] So then, the law is holy, and the commandment is holy and just and good.

---

### Romans 7:13-25

*Through the sacrifice of the cross, that fallen person that used to be you has now been reinstated with your heavenly Father. But it doesn't always feel like it, because now this is war. You're right in the middle of it, and choosing sides is going to be an everyday battle.*

---

[a]7:7 Ex 20:17

## The Problem of Sin in Us

[13] Therefore, did what is good cause my death? Absolutely not! On the contrary, sin, in order to be recognized as sin, was producing death in me through what is good, so that through the commandment sin might become sinful beyond measure. [14] For we know that the law is spiritual; but I am made out of flesh,[a] sold into sin's power. [15] For I do not understand what I am doing, because I do not practice what I want to do, but I do what I hate. [16] And if I do what I do not want to do, I agree with the law that it is good. [17] So now I am no longer the one doing it, but it is sin living in me. [18] For I know that nothing good lives in me, that is, in my flesh. For the desire to do what is good is with me, but there is no ability to do it. [19] For I do not do the good that I want to do, but I practice the evil that I do not want to do. [20] Now if I do what I do not want, I am no longer the one doing it, but it is the sin that lives in me. [21] So I discover this principle: when I want to do good, evil is with me. [22] For in my inner self I joyfully agree with God's law. [23] But I see a different law in the parts of my body, waging war against the law of my mind and taking me prisoner to the law of sin in the parts of my body. [24] What a wretched man I am! Who will rescue me from this body of death? [25] I thank God through Jesus Christ our Lord! So then, with my mind I myself am a slave to the law of God, but with my flesh, to the law of sin.

## The Life-giving Spirit

**8** Therefore, no condemnation now exists for those in Christ Jesus,[b]

### Romans 8:8-11

### God the Holy Spirit

*The Son did the hard work of dying for our sins, but the Spirit does the glorious work of making that transformation complete in us. The old nature is no longer the dominate force in our lives, and we who used to be as good as dead become alive in Christ.*

[2] because the Spirit's law of life in Christ Jesus has set you[c] free from the law of sin and of death. [3] What the law could not do since it was limited by the flesh, God did. He condemned sin in the flesh by sending His own Son in flesh like ours under sin's domain, and as a sin offering, [4] in order that the law's requirement would be accomplished in us who do not •walk according to the flesh but according to the Spirit. [5] For those whose lives are according to the flesh think about the things of the flesh, but those whose lives are according to the Spirit, about the things of the Spirit. [6] For the mind-set of the flesh is death, but the mind-set of the Spirit is life and peace. [7] For the mind-set of the flesh is hostile to God because it does not submit itself to God's law, for it is unable to do so. [8] Those whose lives are in the flesh are unable to please God. [9] You, however, are not in the flesh, but in the Spirit, since the Spirit of God lives in you. But if anyone does not have the Spirit of Christ, he does not belong to Him.

[a]7:14 Other mss read *I am carnal*  [b]8:1 Other mss add *who do not walk according to the flesh but according to the Spirit*  [c]8:2 Other mss read *me*

[10] Now if Christ is in you, the body is dead because of sin, but the Spirit is life because of righteousness. [11] And if the Spirit of Him who raised Jesus from the dead lives in you, then He who raised Christ from the dead will also bring your mortal bodies to life through[a] His Spirit who lives in you.

## The Holy Spirit's Ministries

[12] So then, brothers, we are not obligated to the flesh to live according to the flesh, [13] for if you live according to the flesh, you are going to die. But if by the Spirit you put to death the deeds of the body, you will live. [14] All those led by God's Spirit are God's sons. [15] For you did not receive a spirit of slavery to fall back into fear, but you received the Spirit of adoption, by whom we cry out, "•Abba, Father!" [16] The Spirit Himself testifies together with our spirit that we are God's children, [17] and if children, also heirs— heirs of God and co-heirs with Christ— seeing that we suffer with Him so that we may also be glorified with Him.

## From Groans to Glory

[18] For I consider that the sufferings of this present time are not worth comparing with the glory that is going to be revealed to us. [19] For the creation eagerly waits with anticipation for God's sons to be revealed. [20] For the creation was subjected to futility—not willingly, but because of Him who subjected it—in the hope [21] that the creation itself will also be set free from the bondage of corruption into the glorious freedom of God's children. [22] For we know that the whole creation has been groaning together with labor pains until now. [23] And not only that, but we ourselves who have the Spirit as the •firstfruits—we also groan within ourselves, eagerly waiting for adoption, the redemption of our bodies. [24] Now in this hope we were saved, yet hope that is seen is not hope, because who hopes for what he sees? [25] But if we hope for what we do not see, we eagerly wait for it with patience.

---

### Romans 8:26-27

### God the Holy Spirit

*Another of the great benefits of having the Spirit in our hearts is the freedom He brings to our prayer life. Obviously, we sometimes just don't know what to pray for. But we're assured that the Spirit turns our prayer in the direction of God's will and begins praying for us to the Father.*

---

[26] In the same way the Spirit also joins to help in our weakness, because we do not know what to pray for as we should, but the Spirit Himself intercedes for us[b] with unspoken groanings. [27] And He who searches the hearts knows the Spirit's mind-set, because He intercedes for the saints according to the will of God.
[28] We know that all things work together[c] for the good of those who love God: those who are called according to His purpose. [29] For those He foreknew He also predestined to be conformed to the image of His Son, so that He would be the

---

[a]8:11 Other mss read *because of*   [b]8:26 Some mss omit *for us*   [c]8:28 Other mss read *that God works together in all things*

firstborn among many brothers. <sup>30</sup> And those He predestined, He also called; and those He called, He also justified; and those He justified, He also glorified.

### The Believer's Triumph

<sup>31</sup> What then are we to say about these things?
If God is for us, who is against us?
<sup>32</sup> He did not even spare His own Son,
but offered Him up for us all;
how will He not also with Him grant us everything?
<sup>33</sup> Who can bring an accusation against God's elect?
God is the One who justifies.
<sup>34</sup> Who is the one who condemns?
Christ Jesus is the One who died, but even more, has been raised;
He also is at the right hand of God and intercedes for us.
<sup>35</sup> Who can separate us from the love of Christ?
Can affliction or anguish or persecution
or famine or nakedness or danger or sword?
<sup>36</sup> As it is written:
**Because of You we are being put to death all day long;
we are counted as sheep to be slaughtered.**<sup>a</sup>
<sup>37</sup> No, in all these things we are more than victorious through Him who loved us.
<sup>38</sup> For I am persuaded that neither death nor life,
nor angels nor rulers,
nor things present, nor things to come, nor

powers,
<sup>39</sup> nor height, nor depth, nor any other created thing
will have the power to separate us
from the love of God that is in Christ Jesus our Lord!

### Israel's Rejection of Christ

**9** I speak the truth in Christ—I am not lying; my conscience is testifying to me with the Holy Spirit— <sup>2</sup> that I have intense sorrow and continual anguish in my heart. <sup>3</sup> For I could wish that I myself were cursed and cut off from the •Messiah for the benefit of my brothers, my countrymen by physical descent. <sup>4</sup> They are Israelites, and to them belong the adoption, the glory, the covenants, the giving of the law, the temple service, and the promises. <sup>5</sup> The forefathers are theirs, and from them, by physical descent, came the Messiah, who is God over all, blessed forever. •Amen.

### God's Gracious Election of Israel

<sup>6</sup> But it is not as though the word of God has failed. For not all who are descended from Israel are Israel. <sup>7</sup> Neither are they all children because they are Abraham's descendants. On the contrary, **in Isaac your seed will be called.**<sup>b</sup> <sup>8</sup> That is, it is not the children by physical descent who are God's children, but the children of the promise are considered seed. <sup>9</sup> For this is the statement of the promise: **At this time I will come, and Sarah will have a son.**<sup>c</sup> <sup>10</sup> And not only that, but also when Rebekah became pregnant by Isaac our forefather <sup>11</sup> (for though they had not been born yet or done anything good or bad, so that

<sup>a</sup>**8:36** Ps 44:22; see Is 53:7; Zch 11:4,7   <sup>b</sup>**9:7** Gn 21:12   <sup>c</sup>**9:9** Gn 18:10,14

God's purpose according to election might stand, <sup>12</sup> not from works but from the One who calls) she was told: **The older will serve the younger.**<sup>a</sup> <sup>13</sup> As it is written: **Jacob I have loved, but Esau I have hated.**<sup>b</sup>

## God's Selection Is Just

<sup>14</sup> What should we say then? Is there injustice with God? Absolutely not! <sup>15</sup> For He tells Moses:

> I will show mercy to whom I
>   show mercy,
> and I will have compassion
>   on whom I have
>   compassion.<sup>c</sup>

<sup>16</sup> So then it does not depend on human will or effort, but on God who shows mercy. <sup>17</sup> For the Scripture tells Pharaoh:

> For this reason I raised you
>   up:
> so that I may display My
>   power in you,
> and that My name may be
>   proclaimed in all
>   the earth.<sup>d</sup>

<sup>18</sup> So then, He shows mercy to whom He wills, and He hardens whom He wills. <sup>19</sup> You will say to me, therefore, "Why then does He still find fault? For who can resist His will?" <sup>20</sup> But who are you—anyone who talks back to God? Will what is formed say to the one who formed it, "Why did you make me like this?" <sup>21</sup> Or has the potter no right over His clay, to make from the same lump one piece of pottery for honor and another for dishonor? <sup>22</sup> And what if God, desiring to display His wrath and to make His power known, endured with much patience objects of wrath ready for destruction? <sup>23</sup> And ⌊what if⌋ He did this to make known the riches of His glory on objects of mercy that He prepared beforehand for glory— <sup>24</sup> on us whom He also called, not only from the Jews but also from the Gentiles? <sup>25</sup> As He also says in Hosea:

> I will call "Not-My-People,"
>   "My-People,"
> and she who is "Unloved,"
>   "Beloved."<sup>e</sup>
> <sup>26</sup> And it will be in the place
>   where they were told,
> you are not My people,
>   there they will be called sons
>   of the living God.<sup>f</sup>

<sup>27</sup> But Isaiah cries out concerning Israel:

> Though the number of
>   Israel's sons is like the
>   sand of the sea,
> only the remnant will be saved;
> <sup>28</sup> for the Lord will execute His
>   sentence
> completely and decisively on
>   the earth.<sup>g</sup>

<sup>29</sup> And just as Isaiah predicted:

> If the Lord of Hosts had
>   not left us a seed,
> we would have become like
>   Sodom,
> and we would have been
>   made like Gomorrah.<sup>h</sup>

## Israel's Present State

<sup>30</sup> What should we say then? Gentiles, who did not pursue righteous-

---

<sup>a</sup>**9:12** Gn 25:23    <sup>b</sup>**9:13** Mal 1:2–3    <sup>c</sup>**9:15** Ex 33:19    <sup>d</sup>**9:17** Ex 9:16    <sup>e</sup>**9:25** Hs 2:23    <sup>f</sup>**9:26** Hs 1:10
<sup>g</sup>**9:27–28** Is 10:22–23; 28:22; Hs 1:10    <sup>h</sup>**9:29** Is 1:9

ness, have obtained righteousness—namely the righteousness that comes from faith. [31] But Israel, pursuing the law for righteousness, has not achieved the law.[a] [32] Why is that? Because they did not pursue it by faith, but as if it were by works.[b] They stumbled over the stumbling stone. [33] As it is written:

> Look! I am putting a stone
>    in Zion to stumble
>    over,
> and a rock to trip over,
> yet the one who believes on
>    Him will not be put to
>    shame.[c]

## Righteousness by Faith Alone

**10** Brothers, my heart's desire and prayer to God concerning them[d] is for their salvation! [2] I can testify about them that they have zeal for God, but not according to knowledge. [3] Because they disregarded the righteousness from God and attempted to establish their own righteousness, they have not submitted to God's righteousness. [4] For Christ is the end of the law for righteousness to everyone who believes. [5] For Moses writes about the righteousness that is from the law: **The one who does these things will live by them.**[e] [6] But the righteousness that comes from faith speaks like this: **Do not say in your heart, "Who will go up to heaven?"**[f] that is, to bring Christ down [7] or, **"Who will go down into the ·abyss?"**[g] that is, to bring Christ up from the dead. [8] On the contrary, what does it say? **The message is near you, in your mouth and in your heart"**[h] This is the message of faith that we proclaim: [9] if you confess with your mouth, **"Jesus is Lord,"** and believe in your heart that God raised Him from the dead, you will be saved. [10] With the heart one believes, resulting in righteousness, and with the mouth one confesses, resulting in salvation. [11] Now the Scripture says, **No one who believes on Him will be put to shame,**[i] [12] for there is no distinction between Jew and Greek, since the same Lord of all is rich to all who call on Him. [13] For **everyone who calls on the name of the Lord will be saved.**[j]

---

*Romans 10:8-10*

*Salvation*

*In one way, being a Christian is hard. It means changing old habits, giving up some of our old ways of thinking and doing things. But isn't it incredible that receiving something as momentous as our eternal salvation is about as hard as falling off a log? See what you think.*

---

## Israel's Rejection of the Message

[14] But how can they call on Him in whom they have not believed? And how can they believe without hearing about Him? And how can they hear without a preacher? [15] And how can they preach unless they are sent? As it is written: **How welcome are the feet of those**[k] **who announce the gospel of good things!**[l] [16] But all did not obey the gospel. For Isaiah

---

[a]9:31 Other mss read *the law for righteousness*   [b]9:32 Other mss add *of the law*   [c]9:33 Is 8:14; 28:16
[d]10:1 Other mss read *God for Israel*   [e]10:5 Lv 18:5   [f]10:6 Dt 9:4; 30:12   [g]10:7 Dt 30:13   [h]10:8 Dt 30:14
[i]10:11 Is 28:16   [j]10:13 Jl 2:32   [k]10:15 Other mss read *feet of those who announce the gospel of peace, of those*   [l]10:15 Is 52:7; Nah 1:15

says, **Lord, who has believed our message?**[a] [17] So faith comes from what is heard, and what is heard comes through the message about Christ.[b] [18] But I ask, "Did they not hear?" Yes, they did:

> **Their voice has gone out to all the earth,**
> **and their words to the ends of the inhabited world.**[c]

[19] But I ask, "Did Israel not understand?" First, Moses said:

> **I will make you jealous of those who are not a nation;**
> **I will make you angry by a nation that lacks understanding.**[d]

[20] And Isaiah says boldly:

> **I was found by those who were not looking for Me;**
> **I revealed Myself to those who were not asking for Me.**[e]

[21] But to Israel he says: **All day long I have spread out My hands to a disobedient and defiant people.**[f]

### Israel's Rejection Not Total

**11** I ask, then, has God rejected His people? Absolutely not! For I too am an Israelite, a descendant of Abraham, from the tribe of Benjamin. [2] God has not rejected His people whom He foreknew. Or do you not know what the Scripture says in the Elijah section—how he pleads with God against Israel?

> [3] **Lord, they have killed Your prophets, torn down Your altars;**
> **and I am the only one left, and they are trying to take my life!**[g]

[4] But what was God's reply to him? **I have left 7,000 men for Myself who have not bowed down to Baal.**[h] [5] In the same way, then, there is also at the present time a remnant chosen by grace. [6] Now if by grace, then it is not by works; otherwise grace ceases to be grace.[i]

[7] What then? Israel did not find what it was looking for, but the elect did find it. The rest were hardened, [8] as it is written:

> **God gave them a spirit of stupor,**
> **eyes that cannot see and ears that cannot hear,**
> **to this day.**[j]

[9] And David says:

> **Let their feasting become a snare and a trap,**
> **a pitfall and a retribution to them.**
> [10] **Let their eyes be darkened so they cannot see,**
> **and their backs be bent continually.**[k]

### Israel's Rejection Not Final

[11] I ask, then, have they stumbled so as to fall? Absolutely not! On the contrary, by their stumbling, salvation has come to the Gentiles to make Israel jealous. [12] Now if their stumbling brings riches for the world, and their failure riches for the Gentiles, how

[a]10:16 Is 53:1  [b]10:17 Other mss read *God*  [c]10:18 Ps 19:4  [d]10:19 Dt 32:21  [e]10:20 Is 65:1  [f]10:21 Is 65:2  [g]11:3 1 Kg 19:10,14  [h]11:4 1 Kg 19:18  [i]11:6 Other mss add *But if of works it is no longer grace; otherwise work is no longer work.*  [j]11:8 Dt 29:4; Is 29:10  [k]11:9–10 Ps 69:22–23

much more will their full number bring!

13 Now I am speaking to you Gentiles. In view of the fact that I am an apostle to the Gentiles, I magnify my ministry, 14 if I can somehow make my own people jealous and save some of them. 15 For if their being rejected is world reconciliation, what will their acceptance mean but life from the dead? 16 Now if the •firstfruits offered up are holy, so is the whole batch. And if the root is holy, so are the branches.

17 Now if some of the branches were broken off, and you, though a wild olive branch, were grafted in among them, and have come to share in the rich root[a] of the cultivated olive tree, 18 do not brag that you are better than those branches. But if you do brag—you do not sustain the root, but the root sustains you. 19 Then you will say, "Branches were broken off so that I might be grafted in." 20 True enough; they were broken off by unbelief, but you stand by faith. Do not be arrogant, but be afraid. 21 For if God did not spare the natural branches, He will not spare you either. 22 Therefore, consider God's kindness and severity: severity toward those who have fallen, but God's kindness toward you—if you remain in His kindness. Otherwise you too will be cut off. 23 And even they, if they do not remain in unbelief, will be grafted in, because God has the power to graft them in again. 24 For if you were cut off from your native wild olive, and against nature were grafted into a cultivated olive tree, how much more will these—the natural branches—be grafted into their own olive tree?

25 So that you will not be conceited, brothers, I do not want you to be unaware of this secret: a partial hardening has come to Israel until the full number of the Gentiles has come in. 26 And in this way all Israel will be saved, as it is written:

The Liberator will come
  from Zion;
He will turn away
  godlessness from Jacob.
27 And this will be My covenant
  with them,
when I take away their sins.[b][c]

28 Regarding the gospel, they are enemies for your advantage, but regarding election, they are loved because of their forefathers, 29 since God's gracious gifts and calling are irrevocable. 30 As you once disobeyed God, but now have received mercy through their disobedience, 31 so they too have now disobeyed, [resulting] in mercy to you, so that they also now[d] may receive mercy. 32 For God has imprisoned all in disobedience, so that He may have mercy on all.

---

*Romans 11:33-36*

*God's Grace*

*God has revealed in His Word all the information we need to know about His grace and our salvation. Yet exactly how He does it, exactly how it works, exactly why He chooses to love us after all we've been and done is a marvelous mystery. Some things are left for only God to know.*

---

[a]11:17 Other mss read *the root and the richness*   [b]11:26–27 Is 59:20–21   [c]11:27 Jr 31:31–34
[d]11:31 Other mss omit *now*

## A Hymn of Praise

33 Oh, the depth of the riches
both of the wisdom and the
knowledge of God!
How unsearchable His
judgments
and untraceable His ways!
34 **For who has known the mind
of the Lord?
Or who has been His
counselor?**
35 **Or who has ever first given
to Him,
and has to be repaid?**[a]
36 For from Him and through
Him and to Him are all
things.
To Him be the glory forever,
•amen.

## A Living Sacrifice

**12** Therefore, brothers, by the mercies of God, I urge you to present your bodies as a living sacrifice, holy and pleasing to God; this is your spiritual worship.[b] 2 Do not be conformed to this age, but be transformed by the renewing of your mind, so that you may discern what is the good, pleasing, and perfect will of God.

## Many Gifts but One Body

3 For by the grace given to me, I tell everyone among you not to think of himself more highly than he should think. Instead, think sensibly, as God has distributed a measure of faith to each one. 4 Now as we have many parts in one body, and all the parts do not have the same function, 5 in the same way we who are many are one body in Christ and individually members of one another. 6 According to the grace given to us, we have different gifts:

If prophecy, use it according
to the standard of faith;
7 if service, in service;
if teaching, in teaching;
8 if exhorting, in exhortation;
giving, with generosity;
leading, with diligence;
showing mercy, with
cheerfulness.

## Christian Ethics

9 Love must be without hypocrisy. Detest evil; cling to what is good. 10 Show family affection to one another with brotherly love. Outdo one another in showing honor. 11 Do not lack diligence; be fervent in spirit; serve the Lord. 12 Rejoice in hope; be patient in affliction; be persistent in prayer. 13 Share with the saints in their needs; pursue hospitality. 14 Bless those who persecute you; bless and do not curse. 15 Rejoice with those who rejoice; weep with those who weep. 16 Be in agreement with one another. Do not be proud; instead, associate with the humble. Do not be wise in your own estima-

---

### Romans 12:3-8

*Along with the gift of the Holy Spirit in your life comes your own custom-made package of spiritual gifts, which can take you far beyond your natural abilities. You already had a nice little handful of talents before you came to God. But look at you now!*

---

[a]11:34–35 Is 40:13; Jb 41:11; Jr 23:18　　[b]12:1 Or *your reasonable service*

> *"Every member of the Body has the*
> *potential to be—and should be led*
> *and fed toward functioning as—a*
> *fully equipped agent of*
> *Jesus Christ."*
> —*Jack Hayford*

tion. ¹⁷ Do not repay anyone evil for evil. Try to do what is honorable in everyone's eyes. ¹⁸ If possible, on your part, live at peace with everyone. ¹⁹ Friends, do not avenge yourselves; instead, leave room for His wrath. For it is written: **Vengeance belongs to Me; I will repay,**ᵃ says the Lord. ²⁰ But

> **If your enemy is hungry, feed**
> **him.**
> **If he is thirsty, give him**
> **something to drink.**
> **For in so doing you will be**
> **heaping fiery coals**
> **on his head.**ᵇ

²¹ Do not be conquered by evil, but conquer evil with good.

## A Christian's Duties to the State

**13** Everyone must submit to the governing authorities, for there is no authority except from God, and those that exist are instituted by God. ² So then, the one who resists the authority is opposing God's command, and those who oppose it will bring judgment on themselves. ³ For rulers are not a terror to good conduct, but to bad. Do you want to be unafraid of the authority? Do good and you will have its approval. ⁴ For government is God's servant to you for good. But if you do wrong, be afraid, because it does not carry the sword for no reason. For government is God's servant, an avenger that brings wrath on the one who does wrong. ⁵ Therefore, you must submit, not only because of wrath, but also because of your conscience. ⁶ And for this reason you pay taxes, since the ⌊authorities⌋ are God's public servants, continually attending to these tasks. ⁷ Pay your obligations to everyone: taxes to those you owe taxes, tolls to those you owe tolls, respect to those you owe respect, and honor to those you owe honor.

## Love Our Primary Duty

⁸ Do not owe anyone anything, except to love one another, for the one who loves another has fulfilled the law. ⁹ The commandments:

> **You shall not commit**
> **adultery,**
> **you shall not murder,**
> **you shall not steal,**ᶜ
> **you shall not covet,**ᵈ

and if there is any other commandment—all are summed up by this: **You shall love your neighbor as yourself.**ᵉ ¹⁰ Love does no wrong to a neighbor. Love, therefore, is the fulfillment of the law.

## Put On Christ

¹¹ Besides this, knowing the time, it is already the hour for youᶠ to wake up from sleep, for now our salvation is nearer than when we first believed. ¹² The night is nearly over, and the daylight is near, so let us discard the deeds of darkness and put on the armor of light. ¹³ Let us •walk with decency, as in the daylight: not in carousing and

ᵃ**12:19** Dt 32:35   ᵇ**12:20** Pr 25:21–22   ᶜ**13:9** Other mss add *you shall not bear false witness*   ᵈ**13:9** Ex 20:13–17; Dt 5:17–21   ᵉ**13:9** Lv 19:18   ᶠ**13:11** Other mss read *for us*

drunkenness; not in sexual impurity and promiscuity; not in quarreling and jealousy. [14] But put on the Lord Jesus Christ, and make no plans to satisfy the fleshly desires.

### The Law of Liberty

**14** Accept anyone who is weak in faith, but don't argue about doubtful issues. [2] One person believes he may eat anything, but one who is weak eats only vegetables. [3] One who eats must not look down on one who does not eat; and one who does not eat must not criticize one who does, because God has accepted him. [4] Who are you to criticize another's servant? Before his own Lord he stands or falls. And stand he will! For the Lord is able[a] to make him stand.

[5] One person considers one day to be above another day. Someone else considers every day to be the same. Each one must be fully convinced in his own mind. [6] Whoever observes the day, observes it to the Lord.[b] Who-

---

### Romans 13:11

### Salvation

*The Bible talks in various places about our "having been saved," about the fact the we "are saved," and—here, as well as in other places—the idea that we "will be saved." So which is it? Well, it's all of them. Today we live by God's promise, but one day our salvation will be a visible reality.*

---

ever eats, eats to the Lord, since he gives thanks to God; and whoever does not eat, it is to the Lord that he does not eat, yet he thanks God. [7] For none of us lives to himself, and no one dies to himself. [8] If we live, we live to the Lord; and if we die, we die to the Lord. Therefore, whether we live or die, we belong to the Lord. [9] Christ died and came to life for this: that He might rule over both the dead and the living. [10] But you, why do you criticize your brother? Or you, why do you look down on your brother? For we will all stand before the judgment seat of God.[c] [11] For it is written:

> **As I live, says the Lord,**
> **every knee will bow to Me,**
> **and every tongue will give**
> **praise to God.**[d]

[12] So then, each of us will give an account of himself to God.

### The Law of Love

[13] Therefore, let us no longer criticize one another, but instead decide not to put a stumbling block or pitfall in your brother's way. [14] (I know and am persuaded by the Lord Jesus that nothing is unclean in itself. Still, to someone who considers a thing to be unclean, to that one it is unclean.) [15] For if your brother is hurt by what you eat, you are no longer walking according to love. By what you eat, do not destroy that one for whom Christ died. [16] Therefore, do not let your good be slandered, [17] for the kingdom of God is not eating and drinking, but righteousness, peace, and joy in the Holy Spirit. [18] Whoever serves the •Messiah in this way is acceptable to God and approved by men.

---

[a]**14:4** Other mss read *For God has the power*   [b]**14:6** Other mss add *but whoever does not observe the day, it is to the Lord that he does not observe it*   [c]**14:10** Other mss read *of Christ*   [d]**14:11** Is 45:23; 49:18

[19] So then, we must pursue what promotes peace and what builds up one another. [20] Do not tear down God's work because of food. Everything is clean, but it is wrong for a man to cause stumbling by what he eats. [21] It is a noble thing not to eat meat, or drink wine, or do anything that makes your brother stumble.[a] [22] Do you have faith? Keep it to yourself before God. Blessed is the man who does not condemn himself by what he approves. [23] But whoever doubts stands condemned if he eats, because his eating is not from faith, and everything that is not from faith is sin.

## Pleasing Others, Not Ourselves

**15** Now we who are strong have an obligation to bear the weaknesses of those without strength, and not to please ourselves. [2] Each one of us must please his neighbor for his good, in order to build him up. [3] For even the *Messiah did not please Himself. On the contrary, as it is written, **The insults of those who insult You have fallen on Me.**[b] [4] For whatever was written before was written for our instruction, so that through our endurance and through the encouragement of the Scriptures we may have hope. [5] Now may the God of endurance and encouragement grant you agreement with one another, according to Christ Jesus, [6] so that you may glorify the God and Father of our Lord Jesus Christ with a united mind and voice.

## Glorifying God Together

[7] Therefore accept one another, just as the Messiah also accepted you, to the glory of God. [8] Now I say that Christ has become a servant of the circumcised on behalf of the truth of God, to confirm the promises to the fathers, [9] and so that Gentiles may glorify God for His mercy. As it is written:

> **Therefore I will praise You among the Gentiles,**
> **and I will sing psalms to Your name.**[c]

[10] Again it says: **Rejoice, you Gentiles, with His people!**[d] [11] And again:

> **Praise the Lord, all you Gentiles;**
> **all the peoples should praise Him!**[e]

[12] And again, Isaiah says:

> **The root of Jesse will appear, the One who rises to rule the Gentiles;**
> **in Him the Gentiles will hope.**[f]

---

### Romans 15:1-2

### Christian Influence

*As Christians, we don't need to think less of ourselves, but we need to spend less time thinking about ourselves—our wants, our hungers, our itches that aren't being scratched. We need to free up the time we waste on ourselves and invest it in those around us who need what we have.*

---

[a]**14:21** Other mss add *or offended or weakened*   [b]**15:3** Ps 69:9   [c]**15:9** 2 Sm 22:50; Ps 18:49
[d]**15:10** Dt 32:43   [e]**15:11** Ps 117:1   [f]**15:12** Is 11:10

[13] Now may the God of hope fill you with all joy and peace in believing, so that you may overflow with hope by the power of the Holy Spirit.

## From Jerusalem to Illyricum

[14] Now, my brothers, I myself am convinced about you that you also are full of goodness, filled with all knowledge, and able to instruct one another. [15] Nevertheless, to remind you, I have written to you more boldly on some points[a] because of the grace given me by God [16] to be a minister of Christ Jesus to the Gentiles, serving as a priest of God's good news. My purpose is that the offering of the Gentiles may be acceptable, sanctified by the Holy Spirit. [17] Therefore I have reason to boast in Christ Jesus regarding what pertains to God. [18] For I would not dare say anything except what Christ has accomplished through me to make the Gentiles obedient by word and deed, [19] by the power of miraculous signs and wonders, and by the power of God's Spirit. As a result, I have fully proclaimed the good news about the Messiah from Jerusalem all the way around to Illyricum. [20] So my aim is to evangelize where Christ has not been named, in order that I will not be building on someone else's foundation, [21] but, as it is written:

> Those who had no report of
>    Him will see,
> and those who have not
>    heard will understand.[b]

## Paul's Travel Plans

[22] That is why I have been prevented many times from coming to you. [23] But now I no longer have any work to do in these provinces, and I have strongly desired for many years to come to you [24] whenever I travel to Spain.[c] For I do hope to see you when I pass through, and to be sent on my way there by you, once I have first enjoyed your company for a while. [25] Now, however, I am traveling to Jerusalem to serve the saints; [26] for Macedonia and Achaia were pleased to make a contribution to the poor among the saints in Jerusalem. [27] Yes, they were pleased, and they are indebted to them. For if the Gentiles have shared in their spiritual benefits, then they are obligated to minister to Jews in material needs. [28] So when I have finished this and safely delivered the funds to them, I will go by way of you to Spain. [29] But I know that when I come to you, I will come in the fullness of the blessing[d] of Christ.

[30] Now I implore you, brothers, through the Lord Jesus Christ and through the love of the Spirit, to agonize together with me in your prayers to God on my behalf: [31] that I may be rescued from the unbelievers in Judea, that my service for Jerusalem may be acceptable to the saints, [32] and that, by God's will, I may come to you with joy and be refreshed together with you.

[33] The God of peace be with all of you. •Amen.

## Paul's Commendation of Phoebe

**16** I commend to you our sister Phoebe, who is a servant of the church in Cenchreae. [2] So you should welcome her in the Lord in a manner worthy of the saints, and assist her in whatever matter she may require your help. For indeed

[a]**15:15** Other mss add *brothers*   [b]**15:21** Is 52:15   [c]**15:24** Other mss add *I will come to you.*   [d]**15:29** Other mss add *of the gospel*

she has been a benefactor of many—
and of me also.

## Greeting to Roman Christians

3 Give my greetings to Prisca and
Aquila, my co-workers in
Christ Jesus, 4 who risked
their own necks for my life.
Not only do I thank them,
but so do all the Gentile
churches.
5 Greet also the church that meets
in their home.
Greet my dear friend Epaenetus,
who is the first convert to
Christ from Asia.[a]
6 Greet Mary,[b] who has worked
very hard for you.[c]
7 Greet Andronicus and Junia, my
fellow countrymen and fellow prisoners. They are out-
standing among the
apostles, and they were also
in Christ before me.
8 Greet Ampliatus, my dear friend
in the Lord.
9 Greet Urbanus, our co-worker
in Christ, and my dear
friend Stachys.
10 Greet Apelles, who is approved
in Christ.
Greet those who belong to the
household of Aristobulus.
11 Greet Herodion, my fellow
countryman.
Greet those who belong to the
household of Narcissus who
are in the Lord.
12 Greet Tryphaena and Tryphosa,
who have worked hard in
the Lord.
Greet my dear friend Persis,
who has worked very hard
in the Lord.

13 Greet Rufus, chosen in the Lord;
also his mother—and mine.
14 Greet Asyncritus, Phlegon, Hermes, Patrobas, Hermas, and
the brothers who are with
them.
15 Greet Philologus and Julia,
Nereus and his sister, and
Olympas, and all the saints
who are with them.
16 Greet one another with a holy
kiss.
All the churches of Christ send
you greetings.

## Warning against Divisive People

17 Now I implore you, brothers,
watch out for those who cause dissensions and pitfalls contrary to the doctrine you have learned. Avoid them;
18 for such people do not serve our
Lord Christ but their own appetites,
and by smooth talk and flattering
words they deceive the hearts of the
unsuspecting.

## Paul's Gracious Conclusion

19 The report of your obedience has
reached everyone. Therefore I rejoice
over you. But I want you to be wise
about what is good, yet innocent
about what is evil. 20 The God of peace
will soon crush Satan under your feet.
The grace of our Lord Jesus be with
you.
21 Timothy, my co-worker, and Lucius, Jason, and Sosipater, my fellow
countrymen, greet you.
22 I Tertius, who penned this epistle
in the Lord, greet you.
23 Gaius, who is host to me and to
the whole church, greets you. Erastus,
the city treasurer, and our brother
Quartus greet you.

[a]16:5 Other mss read *Achaia*   [b]16:6 Or *Maria*   [c]16:6 Other mss read *us*

⌊²⁴ The grace of our Lord Jesus Christ be with you all.⌋ ᵃ

*Glory to God*

²⁵ Now to Him who has power to strengthen you according to my gospel and the proclamation of Jesus Christ, according to the revelation of the sacred secret kept silent for long ages, ²⁶ but now revealed and made known through the prophetic Scriptures, according to the command of the eternal God, to advance the obedience of faith among all nations— ²⁷ to the only wise God, through Jesus Christ—to Him be the glory forever!ᵇ •Amen.

---

ᵃ16:24 Other mss omit bracketed text; see v. 20    ᵇ16:25-27 Other mss have these vv. at the end of chap 14 or 15.

# 1 CORINTHIANS

## Greeting

**1** Paul, called as an apostle of Christ Jesus by God's will, and our brother Sosthenes:

[2] To God's church at Corinth, to those who are sanctified in Christ Jesus and called as saints, with all those in every place who call on the name of Jesus Christ our Lord—theirs and ours.

[3] Grace to you and peace from God our Father and the Lord Jesus Christ.

## Thanksgiving

[4] I always thank my God for you because of God's grace given to you in Christ Jesus, [5] that by Him you were made rich in everything—in all speaking and all knowledge— [6] as the testimony about Christ was confirmed among you, [7] so that you do not lack any spiritual gift as you eagerly wait for the revelation of our Lord Jesus Christ. [8] He will also confirm you to the end, blameless in the day of our Lord Jesus Christ. [9] God is faithful; by Him you were called into fellowship with His Son, Jesus Christ our Lord.

## Divisions at Corinth

[10] Now I urge you, brothers, in the name of our Lord Jesus Christ, that you all say the same thing, that there be no divisions among you, and that you be united with the same understanding and the same conviction. [11] For it has been reported to me about you, my brothers, by members of Chloe's household, that there are quarrels among you. [12] What I am saying is this: each of you says, "I'm with Paul," or "I'm with Apollos," or "I'm with *Cephas," or "I'm with Christ." [13] Is Christ divided? Was it Paul who was crucified for you? Or were you baptized in Paul's name? [14] I thank God[a] that I baptized none of you except Crispus and Gaius, [15] so that no one can say you had been baptized in my name. [16] I did, in fact, baptize the household of Stephanas; beyond that, I don't know if I baptized anyone else. [17] For Christ did not send me to baptize, but to preach the gospel—not with clever words, so that the cross of Christ will not be emptied ⌊of its effect⌋.

## Christ the Power and Wisdom of God

[18] For to those who are perishing the message of the cross is foolishness, but to us who are being saved it is God's power. [19] For it is written:

> I will destroy the wisdom of
> the wise,
> and I will set aside the
> understanding of the
> experts.[b]

[20] Where is the philosopher? Where is the scholar? Where is the debater of this age? Hasn't God made the world's wisdom foolish? [21] For since, in God's wisdom, the world did not know God through wisdom, God was pleased to save those who believe through the foolishness of the message preached. [22] For the Jews

[a]1:14 Other mss omit *God*   [b]1:19 Is 29:14

---

### 1 Corinthians 1:20-25

### Man

*For those who are waiting to figure everything out, quit trying. For those who are hung up on little nit-picky points of doctrine, take a rest. A God who could be fully understood by a human mind would be no God at all. And a person who can't believe with knowing is the biggest fool of all.*

---

ask for signs and the Greeks seek wisdom, [23] but we preach Christ crucified, a stumbling block to the Jews and foolishness to the Gentiles.[a] [24] Yet to those who are called, both Jews and Greeks, Christ is God's power and God's wisdom, [25] because God's foolishness is wiser than human wisdom, and God's weakness is stronger than human strength.

### Boasting Only in the Lord

[26] Brothers, consider your calling: not many are wise from a human perspective, not many powerful, not many of noble birth. [27] Instead, God has chosen the world's foolish things to shame the wise, and God has chosen the world's weak things to shame the strong. [28] God has chosen the world's insignificant and despised things—the things viewed as nothing—so He might bring to nothing the things that are viewed as something, [29] so that no one can boast in His presence. [30] But from Him you are in Christ Jesus, who for us became

wisdom from God, as well as righteousness, sanctification, and redemption, [31] in order that, as it is written: **The one who boasts must boast in the Lord.**[b]

### Paul's Proclamation

**2** When I came to you, brothers, announcing the testimony[c] of God to you, I did not come with brilliance of speech or wisdom. [2] For I determined to know nothing among you except Jesus Christ and Him crucified. [3] And I was with you in weakness, in fear, and in much trembling. [4] My speech and my proclamation were not with persuasive words of wisdom,[d] but with a demonstration of the Spirit and power, [5] so that your faith might not be based on men's wisdom but on God's power.

### Spiritual Wisdom

[6] However, among the mature we do speak a wisdom, but not a wisdom of this age, or of the rulers of this age, who are coming to nothing. [7] On the contrary, we speak

---

### 1 Corinthians 2:9-16

*Once you've known the Father's love and felt the Son's transforming embrace, you can open your life to the sweet presence and safeguarding of the Holy Spirit. When the Spirit of the living God dwells inside you, you're a whole lot smarter than you think.*

---

[a]**1:23** Other mss read *Greeks*  [b]**1:31** Jr 9:24  [c]**2:1** Other mss read *mystery*  [d]**2:4** Other mss read *human wisdom*

God's hidden wisdom in a •mystery, which God predestined before the ages for our glory. [8] None of the rulers of this age knew it, for if they had known it, they would not have crucified the Lord of glory. [9] But as it is written:

> What no eye has seen and no
> ear has heard,
> and what has never come
> into a man's heart,
> is what God has prepared for
> those who love Him.[a]

[10] Now God has revealed them to us by the Spirit, for the Spirit searches everything, even the deep things of God. [11] For who among men knows the concerns of a man except the spirit of the man that is in him? In the same way, no one knows the concerns of God except the Spirit of God. [12] Now we have not received the spirit of the world, but the Spirit who is from God, in order to know what has been freely given to us by God. [13] We also speak these things, not in words taught by human wisdom, but in those taught by the Spirit, explaining spiritual things to spiritual people. [14] But the natural man does not welcome what comes from God's Spirit, because it is foolishness to him; he is not able to know it since it is evaluated spiritually. [15] The spiritual person, however, can evaluate everything, yet he himself cannot be evaluated by anyone. [16] For:

> who has known the Lord's
> mind,
> that he may instruct Him?[b]

But we have the mind of Christ.

> *"There is no one who magnifies Christ as the Holy Spirit does. His most intense desire is to reveal Jesus Christ to men."*
> —*R. A. Torrey*

## The Problem of Immaturity

**3** Brothers, I was not able to speak to you as spiritual people but as people of the flesh, as babies in Christ. [2] I fed you milk, not solid food, because you were not yet able to receive it. In fact, you are still not able, [3] because you are still fleshly. For since there is envy and strife[c] among you, are you not fleshly and living like ordinary people? [4] For whenever someone says, "I'm with Paul," and another, "I'm with Apollos," are you not ⌊typical⌋ men?[d]

## The Role of God's Servants

[5] So, what is Apollos? And what is Paul? They are servants through whom you believed, and each has the role the Lord has given. [6] I planted, Apollos watered, but God gave the growth. [7] So then neither the one who plants nor the one who waters is anything, but only God who gives the growth. [8] Now the one who plants and the one who waters are equal, and each will receive his own reward according to his own labor. [9] For we are God's co-workers. You are God's field, God's building. [10] According to God's grace that was given to me, as a skilled master builder I have laid a foundation, and another builds on it.

[a]**2:9** Is 52:15; 64:4    [b]**2:16** Is 40:13    [c]**3:3** Other mss add *and divisions*    [d]**3:4** Other mss read *are you not carnal*

But each one must be careful how he builds on it, [11] because no one can lay any other foundation than what has been laid—that is, Jesus Christ. [12] If anyone builds on the foundation with gold, silver, costly stones, wood, hay, or straw, [13] each one's work will become obvious, for the day will disclose it, because it will be revealed by fire; the fire will test the quality of each one's work. [14] If anyone's work that he has built survives, he will receive a reward. [15] If anyone's work is burned up, it will be lost, but he will be saved; yet it will be like an escape through fire.

[16] Don't you know that you are God's sanctuary and that the Spirit of God lives in you? [17] If anyone ruins God's sanctuary, God will ruin him; for God's sanctuary is holy, and that is what you are.

## The Folly of Human Wisdom

[18] No one should deceive himself. If anyone among you thinks he is wise in this age, he must become foolish so that he can become wise. [19] For the wisdom of this world is foolishness with God, since it is written: **He catches the wise in their craftiness**—[a] [20] and again, **The Lord knows the reasonings of the wise, that they are futile.**[b] [21] So no one should boast in men, for all things are yours: [22] whether Paul or Apollos or •Cephas or the world or life or death or things present or things to come— all are yours, [23] and you belong to Christ, and Christ to God.

## The Faithful Manager

**4** A person should consider us in this way: as servants of Christ and managers of God's mysteries. [2] In this regard, it is expected of managers that each one be found faithful. [3] It is of little importance that I should be evaluated by you or by a human court. In fact, I don't even evaluate myself. [4] For I am not conscious of anything against myself, but I am not justified by this. The One who evaluates me is the Lord. [5] Therefore don't judge anything prematurely, before the Lord comes, who will both bring to light what is hidden in darkness and reveal the intentions of the hearts. And then praise will come to each one from God.

---

### 1 Corinthians 4:3-5

### Last Things

*If others misunderstand you and misread your motives, that's okay. One day it will all be revealed. If people around are getting away with pretending to be someone they're not, give it time. It'll show. We will all one day stand before God's throne with no place to hide but His mercy.*

---

## The Apostles' Example of Humility

[6] Now, brothers, I have applied these things to myself and Apollos for your benefit, so that you may learn from us the saying: "Nothing beyond what is written." The purpose is that none of you will be inflated with pride in favor of one person over another. [7] For who makes you so superior? What do you have that you

---

[a]3:19 Jb 5:13    [b]3:20 Ps 94:11

didn't receive? If, in fact, you did receive it, why do you boast as if you hadn't received it? [8] Already you are full! Already you are rich! You have begun to reign as kings without us— and I wish you did reign, so that we also could reign with you! [9] For I think God has displayed us, the apostles, in last place, like men condemned to die: we have become a spectacle to the world and to angels and to men. [10] We are fools for Christ, but you are wise in Christ! We are weak, but you are strong! You are distinguished, but we are dishonored! [11] Up to the present hour we are both hungry and thirsty; we are poorly clothed, roughly treated, homeless; [12] we labor, working with our own hands. When we are reviled, we bless; when we are persecuted, we endure it; [13] when we are slandered, we entreat. We are, even now, like the world's garbage, like the filth of all things.

## Paul's Fatherly Care

[14] I'm not writing this to shame you, but to warn you as my dear children. [15] For you can have 10,000 instructors in Christ, but you can't have many fathers. Now I have fathered you in Christ Jesus through the gospel. [16] Therefore I urge you, be imitators of me. [17] This is why I have sent to you Timothy, who is my beloved and faithful child in the Lord. He will remind you about my ways in Christ Jesus, just as I teach everywhere in every church. [18] Now some are inflated with pride, as though I were not coming to you. [19] But I will come to you soon, if the Lord wills, and I will know not the talk but the power of those who are

inflated with pride. [20] For the kingdom of God is not in talk but in power. [21] What do you want? Should I come to you with a rod, or in love and a spirit of gentleness?

## Immoral Church Members

**5** It is widely reported that there is sexual immorality among you, and the kind of sexual immorality that is not even condoned[a] among the Gentiles—a man is living with his father's wife. [2] And you are inflated with pride, instead of filled with grief so that he who has committed this act might be removed from among you. [3] For though absent in body but present in spirit, I have already decided about him who has done this thing as though I were present. [4] In the name of our Lord Jesus, when you are assembled, along with my spirit and with the power of our Lord Jesus, [5] turn that one over to Satan for the destruction of the flesh, so that his spirit may be saved in the Day of the Lord.

[6] Your boasting is not good. Don't you know that a little yeast permeates the whole batch of dough? [7] Clean out the old yeast so that you may be a new batch, since you are unleavened. For Christ our •Passover has been sacrificed.[b] [8] Therefore, let us observe the feast, not with old yeast, or with the yeast of malice and evil, but with the unleavened bread of sincerity and truth.

## Church Discipline

[9] I wrote to you in a letter not to associate with sexually immoral people— [10] by no means referring to this world's immoral people, or to the greedy and swindlers, or to idolaters;

> *"We were purchased out of the slavemarket of sin by Jesus Christ Himself. We have no right to injure property that doesn't belong to us."*
>
> —O. S. Hawkins

otherwise you would have to leave the world. [11] But now I am writing you not to associate with anyone who bears the name of brother who is sexually immoral or greedy, an idolater or a reviler, a drunkard or a swindler. Do not even eat with such a person. [12] For what is it to me to judge outsiders? Do you not judge those who are inside? [13] But God judges outsiders. **Put away the evil person from among yourselves.**[a]

## Lawsuits among Believers

6 Does any of you who has a complaint against someone dare go to law before the unrighteous, and not before the saints? [2] Or do you not know that the saints will judge the world? And if the world is judged by you, are you unworthy to judge the smallest cases? [3] Do you not know that we will judge angels—not to speak of things pertaining to this life? [4] So if you have cases pertaining to this life, do you select those who have no standing in the church to judge? [5] I say this to your shame! Can it be that there is not one person among you who will be able to arbitrate between his brothers? [6] Instead, brother goes to law against brother, and that before unbelievers!

[7] Therefore, it is already a total defeat for you that you have lawsuits against one another. Why not rather put up with injustice? Why not rather be cheated? [8] Instead, you act unjustly and cheat—and this to brothers! [9] Do you not know that the unjust will not inherit God's kingdom? Do not be deceived: no sexually immoral people, idolaters, adulterers, male prostitutes, homosexuals, [10] thieves, greedy people, drunkards, revilers, or swindlers will inherit God's kingdom. [11] Some of you were like this; but you were washed, you were sanctified, you were justified in the name of the Lord Jesus Christ and by the Spirit of our God.

## Glorifying God in Body and Spirit

[12] "Everything is permissible for me," but not everything is helpful. "Everything is permissible for me," but I will not be brought under the control of anything. [13] "Foods for the stomach and the stomach for foods," but God will do away with both of them. The body is not for sexual immorality but for the Lord, and the Lord for the body. [14] God raised up the Lord and will also raise us up by His power. [15] Do you not know that your bodies are the members of Christ? So should I take the members of Christ and make them members of a prostitute? Absolutely not! [16] Do you not know that anyone joined to a prostitute is one body with her? For it says, **The two will become one flesh.**[b] [17] But anyone joined to the Lord is one spirit with Him.

[18] Flee from sexual immorality! "Every sin a person can commit is out-

---

[a]5:13 Dt 17:7    [b]6:16 Gn 2:24

---

## 1 Corinthians 6:12-20

*Even your physical body has received a new touch from God through your salvation experience with Christ. And you have a responsibility to keep it clean. You may not be all that crazy about the body God gave you, but it's His house now. Don't junk it up.*

---

side the body," but the person who is sexually immoral sins against his own body. [19] Do you not know that your body is a sanctuary of the Holy Spirit who is in you, whom you have from God? You are not your own, [20] for you were bought at a price; therefore glorify God in your body.[a]

## Principles of Marriage

**7** About the things you wrote:[b] "It is good for a man not to have relations with a woman." [2] But because of sexual immorality, each man should have his own wife, and each woman should have her own husband. [3] A husband should fulfill his marital duty to his wife, and likewise a wife to her husband. [4] A wife does not have authority over her own body, but her husband does. Equally, a husband does not have authority over his own body, but his wife does. [5] Do not deprive one another—except when you agree, for a time, to devote yourselves to[c] prayer. Then come together again; otherwise, Satan may tempt you because of your lack of self-control. [6] I say this as a concession, not as a command. [7] I wish that all people

were just like me. But each has his own gift from God, one this and another that.

## A Word to the Unmarried

[8] I say to the unmarried and to widows: It is good for them if they remain as I am. [9] But if they do not have self-control, they should marry, for it is better to marry than to burn with desire.

## Advice to Married People

[10] I command the married—not I, but the Lord—a wife is not to leave her husband. [11] But if she does leave, she must remain unmarried or be reconciled to her husband—and a husband is not to leave his wife. [12] But to the rest I, not the Lord, say: If any brother has an unbelieving wife, and she is willing to live with him, he must not leave her. [13] Also, if any woman has an unbelieving husband, and he is willing to live with her, she must not leave her husband. [14] For the unbelieving husband is sanctified by the wife, and the unbelieving wife is sanctified by the Christian husband. Otherwise your children would be unclean, but now they are holy. [15] But if the unbeliever leaves, let him leave. A brother or a sister is not bound in such cases. God has called you[d] to peace. [16] For you, wife, how do you know whether you will save your husband? Or you, husband, how do you know whether you will save your wife?

## Various Situations of Life

[17] However, each one must live his life in the situation the Lord assigned

---

[a]**6:20** Other mss add *and in your spirit, which belong to God.*    [b]**7:1** Other mss add *to me*    [c]**7:5** Other mss add *fasting and to*    [d]**7:15** Other mss read *us*

when God called him. This is what I command in all the churches. [18] Was anyone already circumcised when he was called? He should not undo his circumcision. Was anyone called while uncircumcised? He should not get circumcised. [19] Circumcision does not matter and uncircumcision does not matter, but keeping God's commandments does. [20] Each person should remain in the life situation in which he was called. [21] Were you called while a slave? It should not be a concern to you. But if you can become free, by all means take the opportunity. [22] For he who is called by the Lord as a slave is the Lord's freedman. Likewise he who is called as a free man is Christ's slave. [23] You were bought at a price; do not become slaves of men. [24] Brothers, each person should remain with God in whatever situation he was called.

## About the Unmarried and Widows

[25] About virgins: I have no command from the Lord, but I do give an opinion as one who by the Lord's mercy is trustworthy. [26] Therefore I consider this to be good because of the present distress: it is fine for a man to stay as he is. [27] Are you bound to a wife? Do not seek to be loosed. Are you loosed from a wife? Do not seek a wife. [28] However, if you do get married, you have not sinned, and if a virgin marries, she has not sinned. But such people will have trouble in this life, and I am trying to spare you. [29] And I say this, brothers: the time is limited, so from now on those who have wives should be as though they had none, [30] those who weep as though they did not weep, those who rejoice as though they did not rejoice, those who buy as though they did not

possess, [31] and those who use the world as though they did not make full use of it. For this world in its current form is passing away.

[32] I want you to be without concerns. An unmarried man is concerned about the things of the Lord— how he may please the Lord. [33] But a married man is concerned about the things of the world—how he may please his wife— [34] and he is divided. An unmarried woman or a virgin is concerned about the things of the Lord, so that she may be holy both in body and in spirit. But a married woman is concerned about the things of the world—how she may please her husband. [35] Now I am saying this for your own benefit, not to put a restraint on you, but because of what is proper, and so that you may be devoted to the Lord without distraction.

[36] But if any man thinks he is acting improperly toward his virgin, if she is past marriageable age, and so it must be, he can do what he wants. He is not sinning; they can get married. [37] But he who stands firm in his heart (who is under no compulsion, but has control over his own will) and has decided in his heart to keep his own virgin, will do well. [38] So then he who marries his virgin does well, but he who does not marry will do better.

[39] A wife is bound[a] as long as her husband is living. But if her husband dies, she is free to be married to anyone she wants—only in the Lord. [40] But she is happier if she remains as she is, in my opinion. And I think that I also have the Spirit of God.

## Food Offered to Idols

**8** About food offered to idols: We know that "we all have knowl-

---

[a]**7:39** Other mss add *by law*

---

*1 Corinthians 8:6*

*God the Father*

*You'll find this mentioned more often than just the first few chapters of Genesis. The Bible is full of declarations that God was in the beginning, that He made all there is, that the Son and the Spirit were involved in the process of creation. Everything comes from God. Everything.*

---

edge." Knowledge inflates with pride, but love builds up. ² If anyone thinks he knows anything, he does not yet know it as he ought to know it. ³ But if anyone loves God, he is known by Him.

⁴ About eating food offered to idols, then, we know that "an idol is nothing in the world," and that "there is no God but one." ⁵ For even if there are so-called gods, whether in heaven or on earth—as there are many "gods" and many "lords"—

⁶ yet for us there is one God,
 the Father,
 from whom are all things, and
  we for Him;
 and one Lord, Jesus Christ,
 through whom are all things,
  and we through Him.

⁷ However, not everyone has this knowledge. In fact, some have been so used to idolatry up until now, that when they eat food offered to an idol, their conscience, being weak, is de-

filed. ⁸ Food will not make us acceptable to God. We are not inferior if we don't eat, and we are not better if we do eat. ⁹ But be careful that this right of yours in no way becomes a stumbling block to the weak. ¹⁰ For if somebody sees you, the one who has this knowledge, dining in an idol's temple, won't his weak conscience be encouraged to eat food offered to idols? ¹¹ Then the weak person, the brother for whom Christ died, is ruined by your knowledge. ¹² Now when you sin like this against the brothers and wound their weak conscience, you are sinning against Christ. ¹³ Therefore, if food causes my brother to fall, I will never again eat meat, so that I won't cause my brother to fall.

## Paul's Example as an Apostle

**9** Am I not free? Am I not an apostle? Have I not seen Jesus our Lord? Are you not my work in the Lord? ² If I am not an apostle to others, at least I am to you, for you are the seal of my apostleship in the Lord. ³ My defense to those who examine me is this: ⁴ Don't we have the right to eat and drink? ⁵ Don't we have the right to be accompanied by a Christian wife, like the other apostles, the Lord's brothers, and •Cephas? ⁶ Or is it only Barnabas and I who have no right to refrain from working? ⁷ Who ever goes to war at his own expense? Who plants a vineyard and does not eat its fruit? Or who shepherds a flock and does not drink the milk from the flock? ⁸ Am I saying this from a human perspective? Doesn't the law also say the same thing? ⁹ For it is written in the law of Moses, **Do not muzzle an ox while it treads out the grain.**[a] Is God really concerned with oxen?

[a] 9:9 Dt 25:4

[10] Or isn't He really saying it for us? Yes, this is written for us, because he who plows ought to plow in hope, and he who threshes should do so in hope of sharing the crop. [11] If we have sown spiritual things for you, is it too much if we reap material things from you? [12] If others share this authority over you, don't we even more?

However, we have not used this authority; instead we endure everything so that we will not hinder the gospel of Christ. [13] Do you not know that those who perform the temple services eat the food from the temple, and those who serve at the altar share in the offerings of the altar? [14] In the same way, the Lord has commanded that those who preach the gospel should earn their living by the gospel.

[15] But I have used none of these rights, and I have not written this to make it happen that way for me. For it would be better for me to die than for anyone to deprive me of my boast! [16] For if I preach the gospel, I have no reason to boast, because an obligation is placed on me. And woe to me if I do not preach the gospel! [17] For if I do this willingly, I have a reward; but if unwillingly, I am entrusted with a stewardship. [18] What then is my reward? To preach the gospel and offer it free of charge, and not make full use of my authority in the gospel.

[19] For although I am free from all people, I have made myself a slave to all, in order to win more people. [20] To the Jews I became like a Jew, to win Jews; to those under the law, like one under the law—though I myself am not under the law[a]—to win those under the law. [21] To those who are outside the law, like one outside the law—not being outside God's law, but under the law of Christ—to win those outside the law. [22] To the weak I became weak, in order to win the weak. I have become all things to all people, so that I may by all means save some. [23] Now I do all this because of the gospel, that I may become a partner in its benefits.

[24] Do you not know that the runners in a stadium all race, but only one receives the prize? Run in such a way that you may win. [25] Now everyone who competes exercises self-control in everything. However, they do it to receive a perishable crown, but we an imperishable one. [26] Therefore I do not run like one who runs aimlessly, or box like one who beats the air. [27] Instead, I discipline my body and bring it under strict control, so that after preaching to others, I myself will not be disqualified.

## Warnings from Israel's Past

**10** Now I want you to know, brothers, that our fathers were all under the cloud, all passed through the sea, [2] and all were baptized into Moses in the cloud and in the sea. [3] They all ate the same spiritual food, [4] and all drank the same spiritual drink. For they drank from a spiritual rock that followed them, and that rock was Christ. [5] But God was not pleased with most of them, for they were struck down in the desert.

> "The devil knows that if he can get our minds to dwell on certain sins, then it will be just a matter of time before those sins are acted out."
>
> —Greg Laurie

[6] Now these things became examples for us, so that we will not desire evil as they did. [7] Don't become idol-

---

[a]9:20 Other mss omit *though I myself am not under law*

aters as some of them were; as it is written, **The people sat down to eat and drink, and got up to play.**[a] [8] Let us not commit sexual immorality as some of them did, and in a single day 23,000 people fell dead. [9] Let us not tempt Christ as some of them did, and were destroyed by snakes. [10] Nor should we complain as some of them did, and were killed by the destroyer. [11] Now these things happened to them as examples, and they were written as a warning to us, on whom the ends of the ages have come. [12] Therefore, whoever thinks he stands must be careful not to fall! [13] No temptation has overtaken you except what is common to humanity. God is faithful and He will not allow you to be tempted beyond what you are able, but with the temptation He will also provide a way of escape, so that you are able to bear it.

## Warning against Idolatry

[14] Therefore, my dear friends, flee from idolatry. [15] I am speaking as to wise people. Judge for yourselves what I say. [16] The cup of blessing that we bless, is it not a sharing in the blood of Christ? The bread that we break, is it not a sharing in the body of Christ? [17] Because there is one bread, we who are many are one body, for all of us share that one bread. [18] Look at the people of Israel. Are not those who eat the sacrifices partners in the altar? [19] What am I saying then? That food offered to idols is anything, or that an idol is anything? [20] No, but I do say that what they[b] sacrifice, they sacrifice to demons and not to God. I do not want you to be partners with demons! [21] You cannot drink the cup of the

*1 Corinthians 10:6-13*

*Temptation can be a tough customer, but with the power of prayer and the truth of God's Word, you're prepared to tackle any of them—even when they slip in unnoticed. Temptation can strike when you least expect it, but it's only as strong as the time you waste on it.*

Lord and the cup of demons. You cannot share in the Lord's table and the table of demons. [22] Or are we provoking the Lord to jealousy? Are we stronger than He?

## Christian Liberty

[23] "Everything is permissible,"[c] but not everything is helpful. "Everything is permissible,"[c] but not everything builds up. [24] No one should seek his own ⌊good⌋, but ⌊the good⌋ of the other person.
[25] Eat everything that is sold in the meat market, asking no questions for conscience' sake, for [26] **the earth is the Lord's, and all that is in it.**[d] [27] If one of the unbelievers invites you over and you want to go, eat everything that is set before you, without raising questions of conscience. [28] But if someone says to you, "This is food offered to an idol," do not eat it, out of consideration for the one who told you, and for conscience' sake.[e] [29] I do not mean your own conscience, but the other person's. For why is my freedom judged by another person's conscience? [30] If

---
[a]10:7 Ex 32:6  [b]10:20 Other mss read *Gentiles*  [c]10:23 Other mss add *for me*  [d]10:26 Ps 24:1  [e]10:28 Other mss add *"For the earth is the Lord's and all that is in it."*

I partake with thanks, why am I slandered because of something for which I give thanks?

<sup>31</sup> Therefore, whether you eat or drink, or whatever you do, do everything for God's glory. <sup>32</sup> Give no offense to the Jews or the Greeks or the church of God, <sup>33</sup> just as I also try to please all people in all things, not seeking my own profit, but the profit of many, that they may be saved. **11** Be imitators of me, as I also am of Christ.

## Instructions about Head Coverings

<sup>2</sup> Now I praise you[a] because you remember me in all things and keep the traditions just as I delivered them to you. <sup>3</sup> But I want you to know that Christ is the head of every man, and the man is the head of the woman, and God is the head of Christ. <sup>4</sup> Every man who prays or prophesies with something on his head dishonors his head. <sup>5</sup> But every woman who prays or prophesies with her head uncovered dishonors her head, since that is one and the same as having her head shaved. <sup>6</sup> So if a woman's head is not covered, her hair should be cut off. But if it is disgraceful for a woman to have her hair cut off or her head shaved, she should be covered.

<sup>7</sup> A man, in fact, should not cover his head, because he is God's image and glory, but woman is man's glory. <sup>8</sup> For man did not come from woman, but woman came from man; <sup>9</sup> and man was not created for woman, but woman for man. <sup>10</sup> This is why a woman should have ⌊a symbol of⌋ authority on her head: because of the angels. <sup>11</sup> However, in the Lord, woman is not independent of man, and man is not independent of woman. <sup>12</sup> For just as

woman came from man, so man comes through woman, and all things come from God.

<sup>13</sup> Judge for yourselves: Is it proper for a woman to pray to God with her head uncovered? <sup>14</sup> Does not even nature itself teach you that if a man has long hair it is a disgrace to him, <sup>15</sup> but that if a woman has long hair, it is her glory? For her hair is given to her[b] as a covering. <sup>16</sup> But if anyone wants to argue about this, we have no other custom, nor do the churches of God.

## The Lord's Supper

<sup>17</sup> Now in giving the following instruction I do not praise you, since you come together not for the better but for the worse. <sup>18</sup> For, to begin with, I hear that when you come together as a church there are divisions among you, and in part I believe it. <sup>19</sup> There must, indeed, be factions among you, so that the approved among you may be recognized. <sup>20</sup> Therefore when you come together in one place, it is not really to eat the Lord's Supper. <sup>21</sup> For in eating, each one takes his own supper ahead of others, and one person is hungry while another is drunk! <sup>22</sup> Don't you have houses to eat and drink in? Or do you look down on the church of God and embarrass those who have nothing? What should I say to you? Should I praise you? I do not praise you for this!

<sup>23</sup> For I received from the Lord what I also passed on to you: on the night when He was betrayed, the Lord Jesus took bread, <sup>24</sup> gave thanks, broke it, and said,[c] "This is My body, which is[d] for you. Do this in remembrance of Me."

<sup>25</sup> In the same way ⌊He⌋ also ⌊took⌋ the cup, after supper, and said, "This

[a]11:2 Other mss add *brothers,* [b]11:15 Other mss omit *to her* [c]11:24 Other mss add *"Take, eat.*
[d]11:24 Other mss add *broken*

cup is the new covenant in My blood. Do this, as often as you drink it, in remembrance of Me." [26] For as often as you eat this bread and drink the cup, you proclaim the Lord's death until He comes.

## Self-examination

[27] Therefore, whoever eats the bread or drinks the cup of the Lord in an unworthy way will be guilty of sin against the body and blood of the Lord. [28] So a man should examine himself; in this way he should eat of the bread and drink of the cup. [29] For whoever eats and drinks without recognizing the body,[a] eats and drinks judgment on himself. [30] This is why many are sick and ill among you, and many have fallen •asleep. [31] If we were properly evaluating ourselves, we would not be judged, [32] but when we are judged, we are disciplined by the Lord, so that we may not be condemned with the world. [33] Therefore, my brothers, when you come together to eat, wait for one another. [34] If anyone is hungry, he should eat at home, so that you can come together and not cause judgment. And I will give instructions about the other matters whenever I come.

## Diversity of Spiritual Gifts

**12** About matters of the spirit: brothers, I do not want you to be unaware. [2] You know how, when you were pagans, you were led to dumb idols—being led astray. [3] Therefore I am informing you that no one speaking by the Spirit of God says, "Jesus is cursed," and no one can say, "Jesus is Lord," except by the Holy Spirit.

[4] Now there are different gifts, but the same Spirit. [5] There are different ministries, but the same Lord. [6] And there are different activities, but the same God is active in everyone and everything. [7] A manifestation of the Spirit is given to each person to produce what is beneficial:

[8] to one is given a message of
wisdom through the Spirit,
to another, a message of
knowledge by the same
Spirit,
[9] to another, faith by the same
Spirit,
to another, gifts of healing by
the one Spirit,
[10] to another, the performing of
miracles,
to another, prophecy,
to another, distinguishing
between spirits,
to another, different kinds of
languages,
to another, interpretation of
languages.

[11] But one and the same Spirit is active in all these, distributing to each one as He wills.

---

### 1 Corinthians 12:12-20

*God hasn't saved you just so you could enjoy life in a better mood. He has placed you in a community of faith, where your little part can be multiplied in ministry. Lone Rangers look pretty tough on the big screen. But underneath, they're nothing but palefaces.*

---

[a]**11:29** Other mss read *drinks unworthily, not discerning the Lord's body*

> *"It's only as we, as a body of Christians, grow together in Jesus Christ that we will truly reflect faith, hope, and love."*
> —*Gene Getz*

## Unity Yet Diversity in the Body

¹² For as the body is one and has many parts, and all the parts of that body, though many, are one body—so also is Christ. ¹³ For we were all baptized by one Spirit into one body—whether Jews or Greeks, whether slaves or free—and we were all made to drink of one Spirit. ¹⁴ So the body is not one part but many. ¹⁵ If the foot should say, "Because I'm not a hand, I don't belong to the body," in spite of this it still belongs to the body. ¹⁶ And if the ear should say, "Because I'm not an eye, I don't belong to the body," in spite of this it still belongs to the body. ¹⁷ If the whole body were an eye, where would the hearing be? If the whole were an ear, where would be the sense of smell? ¹⁸ But now God has placed the parts, each one of them, in the body just as He wanted. ¹⁹ And if they were all the same part, where would the body be? ²⁰ Now there are many parts, yet one body.

²¹ So the eye cannot say to the hand, "I don't need you!" nor again the head to the feet, "I don't need you!" ²² On the contrary, all the more, those parts of the body that seem to be weaker are necessary. ²³ And those parts of the body that we think to be less honorable, we clothe these with greater honor, and our unpresentable parts have a better presentation. ²⁴ But our presentable parts have no need ⌊of clothing⌋. Instead, God has put the body together, giving greater honor to the less honorable, ²⁵ so that there would be no division in the body, but that the members would have the same concern for each other. ²⁶ So if one member suffers, all the members suffer with it; if one member is honored, all the members rejoice with it.

²⁷ Now you are the body of Christ, and individual members of it. ²⁸ And God has placed these in the church:

first apostles, second prophets,
third teachers, next, miracles,
then gifts of healing, helping,
managing, various kinds of
   languages.
²⁹ Are all apostles?
Are all prophets?
Are all teachers?
Do all do miracles?
³⁰ Do all have gifts of healing?
Do all speak in languages?
Do all interpret?

³¹ But desire the greater gifts. And I will show you an even better way.

## Love: The Superior Way

**13** If I speak the languages of
   men and of angels,
   but do not have love,
   I am a sounding gong or a
   clanging cymbal.
² If I have ⌊the gift of⌋ prophecy,
   and understand all mysteries
   and all knowledge,
   and if I have all faith,
   so that I can move mountains,
   but do not have love,
   I am nothing.
³ And if I donate all my goods to

feed the poor,
and if I give my body to be
    burned,[a]
but do not have love,
I gain nothing.

4 Love is patient; love is kind.
Love does not envy;
is not boastful; is not
    conceited;

5 does not act improperly;
is not selfish; is not
    provoked;
does not keep a record of
    wrongs;

6 finds no joy in
    unrighteousness,
but rejoices in the truth;

7 bears all things, believes all
    things,
hopes all things, endures all
    things.

8 Love never ends.
But as for prophecies, they
    will come to an end;
as for languages, they will
    cease;
as for knowledge, it will
    come to an end.

9 For we know in part,
and we prophesy in part.

10 But when the perfect comes,
the partial will come to an
    end.

11 When I was a child, I spoke
    like a child,
I thought like a child, I
    reasoned like a child.
When I became a man, I put
    aside childish things.

12 For now we see indistinctly,
    as in a mirror,
but then face to face.
Now I know in part,
but then I will know fully, as
    I am fully known.

13 Now these three remain:
    faith, hope, and love.
But the greatest of these is
    love.

## Prophecy: A Superior Gift

**14** Pursue love and desire spiritual gifts, and above all that you may prophesy. [2] For the person who speaks in ⌊another⌋ language is not speaking to men but to God, since no one understands him; however, he speaks mysteries in the Spirit. [3] But the person who prophesies speaks to people for edification, encouragement, and consolation. [4] The person who speaks in ⌊another⌋ language builds himself up, but he who prophesies builds up the church. [5] I wish all of you spoke in other languages, but even more that you prophesied. The person who prophesies is greater than the person who speaks in languages, unless he interprets so that the church may be built up.

[6] But now, brothers, if I come to you speaking in ⌊other⌋ languages, how will I benefit you unless I speak to you with a revelation or knowledge or prophecy or teaching? [7] Even inanimate things producing sounds—whether flute or harp—if they don't make a distinction in the notes, how will what is played on the flute or harp be recognized? [8] In fact, if the trumpet makes an unclear sound, who will prepare for battle? [9] In the same way, unless you use your tongue for intelligible speech, how will what is spoken be known? For you will be speaking into the air. [10] There are doubtless many different kinds of languages in the world, and all have meaning. [11] Therefore, if I do not know the meaning of the

---

[a]**13:3** Other mss read *to boast*

language, I will be a foreigner to the speaker, and the speaker will be a foreigner to me. [12] So also you—since you are zealous in matters of the spirit, seek to excel in building up the church.

[13] Therefore the person who speaks in ⌊another⌋ language should pray that he can interpret. [14] For if I pray in ⌊another⌋ language, my spirit prays, but my understanding is unfruitful. [15] What then? I will pray with the spirit, and I will also pray with my understanding. I will sing with the spirit, and I will also sing with my understanding. [16] Otherwise, if you bless with the spirit, how will the uninformed person say "•Amen" at your giving of thanks, since he does not know what you are saying? [17] For you may very well be giving thanks, but the other person is not being built up. [18] I thank God that I speak in ⌊other⌋ languages more than all of you; [19] yet in the church I would rather speak five words with my understanding, in order to teach others also, than 10,000 words in ⌊another⌋ language.

[20] Brothers, don't be childish in your thinking, but be infants in evil and adult in your thinking. [21] It is written in the law:

By people of other languages
and by the lips of foreigners,
I will speak to this people;
and even then, they will not
listen to Me,[a]

says the Lord. [22] It follows that speaking in other languages is intended as a sign, not to believers but to unbelievers. But prophecy is not for unbelievers but for believers. [23] Therefore if the whole church assembles together, and all are speaking in ⌊other⌋ lan-

guages, and people who are uninformed or unbelievers come in, will they not say that you are out of your minds? [24] But if all are prophesying, and some unbeliever or uninformed person comes in, he is convicted by all and is judged by all. [25] The secrets of his heart will be revealed, and as a result he will fall down on his face and worship God, proclaiming, "God is really among you."

## Order in Church Meetings

[26] How is it then, brothers? Whenever you come together, each one[b] has a psalm, a teaching, a revelation, ⌊another⌋ language, or an interpretation. All things must be done for edification. [27] If any person speaks in ⌊another⌋ language, there should be only two, or at the most three, each in turn, and someone must interpret. [28] But if there is no interpreter, that person should keep silent in the church and speak to himself and to God. [29] Two or three prophets should speak, and the others should evaluate. [30] But if something has been revealed to another person sitting there, the first prophet should be silent. [31] For you can all prophesy one by one, so that everyone may learn and everyone may be encouraged. [32] And the prophets' spirits are under the control of the prophets, [33] since God is not a God of disorder but of peace.

As in all the churches of the saints, [34] the women[c] should be silent in the churches, for they are not permitted to speak, but should be submissive, as the law also says. [35] And if they want to learn something, they should ask their own husbands at home, for it is disgraceful for a woman to speak

[a]14:21 Is 28:11–12  [b]14:26 Other mss add *of you*  [c]14:34 Other mss read *your women*

in the church meeting. [36] Did the word of God originate from you, or did it come to you only?

[37] If anyone thinks he is a prophet or spiritual, he should recognize that what I write to you is the Lord's command. [38] But if anyone ignores this, he will be ignored.[a] [39] Therefore, my brothers, be eager to prophesy, and do not forbid speaking in ⌊other⌋ languages. [40] But everything must be done decently and in order.

## Resurrection Essential to the Gospel

**15** Now brothers, I want to clarify for you the gospel I proclaimed to you; you received it and have taken your stand on it. [2] You are also saved by it, if you hold to the message I proclaimed to you—unless you believed to no purpose. [3] For I passed on to you as most important what I also received:

> that Christ died for our sins
> according to the Scriptures,
> [4] that He was buried,
> that He was raised on the
> third day
> according to the Scriptures,
> [5] and that He appeared to
> •Cephas,
> then to the Twelve.
> [6] Then He appeared to over
> 500 brothers at one
> time,
> most of whom remain to the
> present,
> but some have fallen •asleep.
> [7] Then He appeared to James,
> then to all the apostles.
> [8] Last of all, as to one
> abnormally born,
> He also appeared to me.

[9] For I am the least of the apostles, unworthy to be called an apostle,

> *"If you enter a dry season, don't treat your spiritual life casually. Christians who begin to treat Jesus casually often become casualties."*
> —Tom Sirotnak

because I persecuted the church of God. [10] But by God's grace I am what I am, and His grace toward me was not ineffective. However, I worked more than any of them, yet not I, but God's grace that was with me. [11] Therefore, whether it is I or they, so we preach and so you have believed.

## Resurrection Essential to the Faith

[12] Now if Christ is preached as raised from the dead, how can some of you say, "There is no resurrection of the dead"? [13] But if there is no resurrection of the dead, then Christ has not been raised; [14] and if Christ has not been raised, then our preaching is without foundation, and so is your faith. [15] In addition, we are found to be false witnesses about God, because we have testified about God that He raised up Christ—whom He did not raise up if in fact the dead are not raised. [16] For if the dead are not raised, Christ has not been raised. [17] And if Christ has not been raised, your faith is worthless; you are still in your sins. [18] Therefore those who have fallen asleep in Christ have also perished. [19] If we have placed our hope in Christ for this life only, we should be pitied more than anyone.

[a]14:38 Other mss read *he should be ignored*

## 1 Corinthians 15:21-22

### Man

*The nature of a person without Christ—no matter how bright and bubbly they may look on the out- side—is dark and depressing down where it really counts. The only light that can reach their deepest need is the truth of the gospel. And that light is found in Jesus Christ.*

### Christ's Resurrection Guarantees Ours

20 But now Christ has been raised from the dead, the *firstfruits of those who have fallen asleep. 21 For since death came through a man, the resur- rection of the dead also comes through a man. 22 For just as in Adam all die, so also in Christ all will be made alive. 23 But each in his own order: Christ, the firstfruits; after- ward, at His coming, the people of Christ. 24 Then comes the end, when He hands over the kingdom to God the Father, when He abolishes all rule and all authority and power. 25 For He must reign until He puts all His ene- mies under His feet. 26 The last enemy He abolishes is death. 27 For **He has put everything under His feet.**[a] But when it says "everything" is put under Him, it is obvious that He who puts everything under Him is the exception. 28 And when everything is subject to Him, then the Son Himself will also be subject to Him who sub-

jected everything to Him, so that God may be all in all.

### Resurrection Supported by Christian Experience

29 Otherwise what will they do who are being baptized for the dead? If the dead are not raised at all, then why are people baptized for them?[b] 30 Why are we in danger every hour? 31 I affirm by the pride in you that I have in Christ Jesus our Lord: I die every day! 32 If I fought wild animals in Ephesus with only human hope, what good does that do me? If the dead are not raised, **Let us eat and drink, because tomor- row we die.**[c] 33 Do not be deceived: "Bad company corrupts good morals." 34 Become right-minded and stop sin- ning, because some people are igno- rant about God. I say this to your shame.

### The Nature of the Resurrection Body

35 But someone will say, "How are the dead raised? What kind of body will they have when they come?" 36 Foolish one! What you sow does not come to life unless it dies. 37 And as for what you sow—you are not sowing the future body, but only a seed, per- haps of wheat or another grain. 38 But God gives it a body as He wants, and to each of the seeds its own body. 39 Not all flesh is the same flesh; there is one flesh for humans, another for animals, another for birds, and another for fish. 40 There are heavenly bodies and earthly bodies, but the splendor of the heavenly bodies is different from that of the earthly ones. 41 There is a splen- dor of the sun, another of the moon, and another of the stars; for star differs from star in splendor. 42 So it is with the resurrection of the dead:

---

[a]15:27 Ps 8:6   [b]15:29 Other mss read *for the dead*   [c]15:32 Is 22:13

Sown in corruption, raised in
  incorruption;
43 sown in dishonor, raised in
  glory;
sown in weakness, raised in
  power;
44 sown a natural body, raised a
  spiritual body.

If there is a natural body, there is
also a spiritual body. ⁴⁵ So it is
written: **The first man Adam
became a living being;**ᵃ the last
Adam became a life-giving Spirit.
⁴⁶ However, the spiritual is not first,
but the natural; then the spiritual.

47 The first man was from the
  earth
and made of dust;
the second man isᵇ from
  heaven.
48 Like the man made of dust,
so are those who are made of
  dust;
like the heavenly man,
so are those who are
  heavenly.
49 And just as we have borne
the image of the man made of
  dust,
we will also bear
the image of the heavenly
  man.

## Victorious Resurrection

⁵⁰ Brothers, I tell you this: flesh and
blood cannot inherit the kingdom of
God, and corruption cannot inherit
incorruption. ⁵¹ Listen! I am telling
you a •mystery:

We will not all fall asleep,
but we will all be changed,
52 in a moment, in the twinkling
  of an eye,

at the last trumpet.
For the trumpet will sound,
and the dead will be raised
  incorruptible,
and we will be changed.
53 Because this corruptible
must be clothed with
  incorruptibility,
and this mortal
must be clothed with
  immortality.
54 Now when this corruptible
is clothed with
  incorruptibility,
and this mortal
is clothed with immortality,
then the saying that is
  written will take place:
**Death has been swallowed
up in victory.**ᶜ
55 O Death, where is your
  victory?
**O Death, where is your
sting?**ᵈ
56 Now the sting of death is sin,
and the power of sin is the
  law.
57 But thanks be to God,
who gives us the victory
through our Lord Jesus
  Christ!

═══════════════════════

### 1 Corinthians 15:55-58

*Times will inevitably come when
you're tempted to pull back, when
failure and fatigue try to chain your
faith to the floor. When you feel the
sleepy sighs of spiritual boredom
coming on, stay where you can
hear the alarm. Remember that
faith in God is never a waste of
time.*

ᵃ15:45 Gn 2:7    ᵇ15:47 Other mss add *the Lord*    ᶜ15:54 Is 25:8    ᵈ15:55 Hs 13:14

58 Therefore, my dear brothers, be steadfast, immovable, always abounding in the Lord's work, knowing that your labor in the Lord is not in vain.

## Collection for the Jerusalem Church

**16** Now about the collection for the saints: you should do the same as I instructed the Galatian churches. 2 On the first day of the week, each of you is to set something aside and save to the extent that he prospers, so that no collections will need to be made when I come. 3 And when I arrive, I will send those whom you recommend by letter to carry your gracious gift to Jerusalem. 4 If it is also suitable for me to go, they will travel with me.

## Paul's Travel Plans

5 I will come to you after I pass through Macedonia—for I will be traveling through Macedonia— 6 and perhaps I will remain with you, or even spend the winter, that you may send me on my way wherever I go. 7 I don't want to see you now just in passing, for I hope to spend some time with you, if the Lord allows. 8 But I will stay in Ephesus until Pentecost, 9 because a wide door for effective ministry has opened for me—yet many oppose me. 10 If Timothy comes, see that he has nothing to fear from you, because he is doing the Lord's work, just as I am. 11 Therefore no one should look down on him; but you should send him on his way in peace so he can come to me, for I am expecting him with the brothers.

12 About our brother Apollos: I strongly urged him to come to you with the brothers, but he was not at all willing to come now. However, when he has time, he will come.

## Final Exhortation

13 Be alert, stand firm in the faith, be brave and strong. 14 Your every ⌊action⌋ must be done with love.

15 Brothers, you know the household of Stephanas: they are the *firstfruits of Achaia and have devoted themselves to serving the saints. I urge you 16 also to submit to such people, and to everyone who works and labors with them. 17 I am delighted over the presence of Stephanas, Fortunatus, and Achaicus, because these men have made up for your absence. 18 For they have refreshed my spirit and yours. Therefore recognize such people.

## Conclusion

19 The churches of the Asian province greet you. Aquila and Priscilla greet you heartily in the Lord, along with the church that meets in their home. 20 All the brothers greet you. Greet one another with a holy kiss.

21 This greeting is in my own hand—Paul. 22 If anyone does not love the Lord, a curse be on him. *Maranatha!* 23 The grace of our Lord Jesus be with you. 24 My love be with all of you in Christ Jesus.

# 2 CORINTHIANS

## Greeting

**1** Paul, an apostle of Christ Jesus by God's will, and Timothy our brother:

To God's church at Corinth, with all the saints who are throughout Achaia.

[2] Grace to you and peace from God our Father and the Lord Jesus Christ.

## The God of Comfort

[3] Blessed be the God and Father of our Lord Jesus Christ, the Father of mercies and the God of all comfort. [4] He comforts us in all our affliction, so that we may be able to comfort those who are in any kind of affliction, through the comfort we ourselves receive from God. [5] For as the sufferings of Christ overflow to us, so our comfort overflows through Christ. [6] If we are afflicted, it is for your comfort and salvation; if we are comforted, it is for your comfort, which is experienced in the endurance of the same sufferings that we suffer. [7] And our hope for you is firm, because we know that as you share in the sufferings, so you will share in the comfort.

[8] For we don't want you to be unaware, brothers, of our affliction that took place in the province of Asia: we were completely overwhelmed—beyond our strength—so that we even despaired of life. [9] However, we personally had a death sentence within ourselves so that we would not trust in ourselves, but in God who raises the dead. [10] He has delivered us from such a terrible death, and He will deliver us; we have placed our hope in Him that He will deliver us again. [11] And you can join in helping with prayer for us, so that thanks may be given by many on our[a] behalf for the gift that came to us through ⌊the prayers of⌋ many.

## A Clear Conscience

[12] For our boast is this: the testimony of our conscience that we have conducted ourselves in the world, and especially toward you, with God-given sincerity and purity, not by fleshly wisdom but by God's grace. [13] Now we are writing you nothing other than what you can read and also understand. I hope you will understand completely— [14] as you have partially understood us—that we are your reason for pride, as you are ours, in the day of our[b] Lord Jesus.

## A Visit Postponed

[15] In this confidence, I planned to come to you first, so you could have a double benefit,[c] [16] and to go on to Macedonia with your help, then come to you again from Macedonia and be given a start by you on my journey to Judea. [17] So when I planned this, was I irresponsible? Or what I plan, do I plan in a purely human way so that I say "Yes, yes" and "No, no" ⌊simultaneously⌋? [18] As God is faithful, our message to you is not "Yes and no." [19] For the Son of God, Jesus Christ, who was preached among you by us—by me and Silvanus and Timothy—did not become "Yes and no"; on

[a]1:11 Other mss read *your*   [b]1:14 Other mss omit *our*   [c]1:15 Other mss read *a second joy*

the contrary, "Yes" has come about in Him. [20] For every one of God's promises is "Yes" in Him. Therefore the "Amen" is also through Him for God's glory through us. [21] Now the One who confirms us with you in Christ, and has anointed us, is God; [22] He has also sealed us and given us the Spirit as a down payment in our hearts.

[23] I call on God as a witness against me: it was to spare you that I did not come to Corinth. [24] Not that we have control of your faith, but we are workers with you for your joy, because you

**2** stand by faith. [1] In fact, I made up my mind about this: not to come to you on another painful visit. [2] For if I cause you pain, then who will cheer me other than the one hurt? [3] I wrote this very thing so that when I came I wouldn't have pain from those who ought to give me joy, because I am confident about all of you that my joy is yours. [4] For out of an extremely troubled and anguished heart I wrote to you with many tears—not that you should be hurt, but that you should know the abundant love I have for you.

## A Sinner Forgiven

[5] If anyone has caused pain, he has not caused pain to me, but in some degree—not to exaggerate—to all of you. [6] The punishment by the majority is sufficient for such a person, [7] so now you should forgive and comfort him instead; otherwise, this one may be overwhelmed by excessive grief. [8] Therefore I urge you to confirm your love to him. [9] It was for this purpose I wrote: so I may know your proven character, if you are obedient in everything. [10] Now to whom you forgive anything, I do too. For what I have forgiven, if I have forgiven anything, it is for you in the presence of

Christ, [11] so that we may not be taken advantage of by Satan; for we are not ignorant of his intentions.

## A Trip to Macedonia

[12] When I came to Troas for the gospel of Christ, a door was opened to me by the Lord. [13] I had no rest in my spirit because I did not find my brother Titus, but I said good-bye to them and left for Macedonia.

## A Ministry of Life or Death

[14] But thanks be to God, who always puts us on display in Christ, and spreads through us in every place the scent of knowing Him. [15] For to God we are the fragrance of Christ among those who are being saved and among those who are perishing. [16] To some we are a scent of death leading to death, but to others, a scent of life leading to life. And who is competent for this? [17] For we are not like the many[a] who make a trade in God's message [for profit], but as those with sincerity, we speak in Christ, as from God and before God.

## Living Letters

**3** Are we beginning to commend ourselves again? Or like some, do we need letters of recommendation to you or from you? [2] You yourselves are our letter, written on our hearts, recognized and read by everyone, [3] since it is plain that you are Christ's letter, produced by us, not written with ink but with the Spirit of the living God; not on stone tablets but on tablets that are hearts of flesh.

a **2:17** Other mss read *the rest*

---

---

## Paul's Competence

⁴ We have this kind of confidence toward God through Christ: ⁵ not that we are competent in ourselves to consider anything as coming from ourselves, but our competence is from God. ⁶ He has made us competent to be ministers of a new covenant, not of the letter, but of the Spirit; for the letter kills, but the Spirit produces life.

## New Covenant Ministry

⁷ Now if the ministry of death, chiseled in letters on stones, came with glory, so that the sons of Israel were not able to look directly at Moses' face because of the glory from his face—a fading ⌊glory⌋— ⁸ how will the ministry of the Spirit not be more glorious? ⁹ For if the ministry of condemnation had glory, the ministry of righteousness overflows with even more glory. ¹⁰ In fact, what had been glorious is not glorious in this case because of the glory that surpasses it. ¹¹ For if what was fading away was glorious, what endures will be even more glorious. ¹² Therefore having such a hope, we use great boldness—¹³ not like Moses, who used to put a veil over his face so that the sons of Israel could not look at the end of what was fading away. ¹⁴ But their minds were closed. For to this day, at the reading of the old covenant, the same veil remains; it is not lifted, because it is set aside ⌊only⌋ in Christ. ¹⁵ However, to this day, whenever Moses is read, a veil lies over their hearts, ¹⁶ but whenever a person turns to the Lord, the veil is removed. ¹⁷ Now the Lord is the Spirit; and where the Spirit of the Lord is, there is freedom. ¹⁸ We all, with unveiled faces, are reflecting the glory of the Lord and are being transformed into the same image from glory to glory; this is from the Lord who is the Spirit.

## The Light of the Gospel

4 Therefore, since we have this ministry, as we have received mercy, we do not give up. ² Instead, we have renounced shameful secret things, not walking in deceit or distorting God's message, but in God's sight we commend ourselves to every person's conscience by an open display of the truth. ³ But if, in fact, our gospel is veiled, it is veiled to those who are perishing. ⁴ Regarding them: the god of this age has blinded the minds of the unbelievers so they cannot see the light of the gospel of the glory of Christ, who is the image of God. ⁵ For we are not proclaiming ourselves but Jesus Christ as Lord,

---

and ourselves as your slaves because of Jesus. [6] For God, who said, "Light shall shine out of darkness"—He has shone in our hearts to give the light of the knowledge of God's glory in the face of Jesus Christ.

## Treasure in Clay Jars

[7] Now we have this treasure in clay jars, so that this extraordinary power may be from God and not from us. [8] We are pressured in every way but not crushed; we are perplexed but not in despair; [9] we are persecuted but not abandoned; we are struck down but not destroyed. [10] We always carry the death of Jesus in our body, so that the life of Jesus may also be revealed in our body. [11] For we who live are always given over to death because of Jesus, so that Jesus' life may also be revealed in our mortal flesh. [12] So death works in us, but life in you. [13] And since we have the same spirit of faith in accordance with what is written, **I believed, therefore I spoke,**[a] we also believe, and therefore speak, [14] knowing that the One who raised the Lord Jesus will raise us also with Jesus, and present us with you. [15] For all this is because of you, so that grace, extended through more and more people, may cause thanksgiving to overflow to God's glory.

[16] Therefore we do not give up; even though our outer person is being destroyed, our inner person is being renewed day by day. [17] For our momentary light affliction is producing for us an absolutely incomparable eternal weight of glory. [18] So we do not focus on what is seen, but on what is unseen; for what is seen is temporary, but what is unseen is eternal.

> *"God's primary goal for a person in this life is that he or she comes to know Him in a personal way."*
> —Henry Blackaby

## Our Future after Death

**5** For we know that if our earthly house, a tent, is destroyed, we have a building from God, a house not made with hands, eternal in the heavens. [2] And, in fact, we groan in this one, longing to put on our house from heaven, [3] since, when we are clothed,[b] we will not be found naked. [4] Indeed, we who are in this tent groan, burdened as we are, because we do not want to be unclothed but clothed, so that mortality may be swallowed up by life. [5] And the One who prepared us for this very thing is God, who gave us the Spirit as a down payment.

[6] Therefore, though we are always confident and know that while we are at home in the body we are away from the Lord— [7] for we •walk by faith, not by sight— [8] yet we are confident and satisfied to be out of the body and at home with the Lord. [9] Therefore, whether we are at home or away, we make it our aim to be pleasing to Him. [10] For we must all appear before the judgment seat of Christ, so that each may be repaid for what he has done in the body, whether good or bad.

[11] Knowing, then, the fear of the Lord, we persuade people. We are completely open before God, and I hope we are completely open to your consciences as well. [12] We are not commending ourselves to you

---

[a] **4:13** Ps 116:10 LXX    [b] **5:3** Other mss read *stripped*

again, but giving you an opportunity to be proud of us, so that you may have a reply for those who take pride in the outward appearance rather than in the heart. [13] For if we are out of our mind, it is for God; if we have a sound mind, it is for you. [14] For Christ's love compels us, since we have reached this conclusion: if One died for all, then all died. [15] And He died for all so that those who live should no longer live for themselves, but for the One who died for them and was raised.

## The Ministry of Reconciliation

[16] From now on, then, we do not know anyone in a purely human way. Even if we have known Christ in a purely human way, yet now we no longer know Him like that. [17] Therefore if anyone is in Christ, there is a new creation; old things have passed away, and look, new things[a] have come. [18] Now everything is from God, who reconciled us to Himself through Christ and gave us the ministry of reconciliation: [19] that is, in Christ, God was reconciling the world to Himself,

---

### 2 Corinthians 5:18-21

*This holy God, who could have squished us all like a bug and started over from scratch without a judge in the world to find him guilty, chooses instead to have fellowship with us. Close your eyes and experience the miracle: God loves you.*

---

not counting their trespasses against them, and He has committed the message of reconciliation to us. [20] Therefore, we are ambassadors for Christ; certain that God is appealing through us, we plead on Christ's behalf, "Be reconciled to God." [21] He made the One who did not know sin to be sin for us, so that we might become the righteousness of God in Him.

**6** Working together with Him, we also appeal to you: "Don't receive God's grace in vain." [2] For He says:

> In an acceptable time, I
>   heard you,
> and in the day of salvation, I
>   helped you.[b]

Look, now is the acceptable time; look, now is the day of salvation.

## The Character of Paul's Ministry

[3] We give no opportunity for stumbling to anyone, so that the ministry will not be blamed. [4] But in everything, as God's ministers, we commend ourselves:

> by great endurance, by
>   afflictions,
> by hardship, by pressures,
> [5] by beatings, by
>   imprisonments,
> by riots, by labors,
> by sleepless nights, by times
>   of hunger,
> [6] by purity, by knowledge,
> by patience, by kindness,
> by the Holy Spirit, by sincere
>   love,
> [7] by the message of truth, by the
>   power of God;
> through weapons of
>   righteousness

---

[a]**5:17** Other mss read *look, all new things*    [b]**6:2** Is 49:8

on the right hand and the left,
8 through glory and dishonor,
through slander and good
report;
as deceivers yet true;
9 as unknown yet recognized;
as dying and look—we live;
as being chastened yet not
killed;
10 as grieving yet always
rejoicing;
as poor yet enriching many;
as having nothing yet
possessing everything.

11 We have spoken openly to you, Corinthians; our heart has been opened wide. 12 You are not limited by us, but you are limited by your own affections. 13 Now in like response—I speak as to children—you also should be open to us.

## Separation to God

14 Do not be mismatched with unbelievers. For what partnership is there between righteousness and lawlessness? Or what fellowship does light have with darkness? 15 What agreement does Christ have with Belial? Or what does a believer have in common with an unbeliever? 16 And what agreement does God's sanctuary have with idols? For we[a] are the sanctuary of the living God, as God said:

I will dwell among them and
walk among them,
and I will be their God,[b]
and they will be My people.
17 Therefore, come out from
among them
and be separate, says the
Lord;

do not touch any unclean
thing,
and I will welcome you.[c]
18 I will be a Father to you,
and you will be sons and
daughters to Me,
says the Lord Almighty.[d]

7 Therefore dear friends, since we have such promises, we should wash ourselves clean from every impurity of the flesh and spirit, making our sanctification complete in the fear of God.

---

### 2 Corinthians 7:1

### God's Assurance

*For those who don't see why obedience is all that important after we're saved, seeing as how all our sins are going to be forgiven anyhow, remember that those who are going to be with Christ should long right now to be more like Christ. Anything else just might be unChristian.*

---

## Joy and Repentance

2 Take us into your hearts. We have wronged no one, corrupted no one, defrauded no one. 3 I don't say this to condemn you, for I have already said that you are in our hearts, to die together and to live together. 4 I have great confidence in you; I have great pride in you. I am filled with encouragement; I am overcome with joy in all our afflictions.

---

a **6:16** Other mss read *you*   b**6:16** Lv 26:12; Jr 31:33; 32:38; Ezk 37:26   c**6:17** Is 52:11   d**6:18** 2 Sm 7:14; Is 43:6; 49:22; 60:4; Hs 1:10

[5] In fact, when we came into Macedonia, we had no rest. Instead, we were afflicted in every way: struggles on the outside, fears inside. [6] But God, who comforts the humble, comforted us by the coming of Titus, [7] and not only by his coming, but also by the comfort he received from you. He announced to us your deep longing, your sorrow, your zeal for me, so that I rejoiced even more. [8] For although I grieved you with my letter, I do not regret it—even though I did regret it since I saw that the letter grieved you, though only for a little while. [9] Now I am rejoicing, not because you were grieved, but because your grief led to repentance. For you were grieved as God willed, so that you didn't experience any loss from us. [10] For godly grief produces a repentance not to be regretted and leading to salvation, but worldly grief produces death. [11] For consider how much diligence this very thing—this grieving as God wills—has produced in you: what a desire to clear yourselves, what indignation, what fear, what deep longing, what zeal, what justice! In every way you have commended yourselves to be pure in this matter. [12] So even though I wrote to you, it was not because of the one who did wrong, or because of the one who was wronged, but in order that your diligence for us might be made plain to you in the sight of God. [13] For this reason we have been comforted.

In addition to our comfort, we were made to rejoice even more over the joy Titus had, because his spirit was refreshed by all of you. [14] For if I have made any boast to him about you, I have not been embarrassed; but as I have spoken everything to you in truth, so our boasting to Titus has also turned out to be the truth. [15] And his affection toward you is even greater as he remembers the obedience of all of you, and how you received him with fear and trembling. [16] I rejoice that I have complete confidence in you.

## Appeal to Complete the Collection

**8** We want you to know, brothers, about the grace of God granted to the churches of Macedonia: [2] during a severe testing by affliction, their abundance of joy and their deep poverty overflowed into the wealth of their generosity. [3] I testify that, on their own, according to their ability and beyond their ability, [4] they begged us insistently for the privilege of sharing in the ministry to the saints, [5] and not just as we had hoped. Instead, they gave themselves especially to the Lord, then to us by God's will. [6] So we urged Titus that, just as he had begun, so he should also complete this grace to you. [7] Now as you excel in everything—in faith, in speech, in knowledge, in all diligence, and in your love for us[a]—excel also in this grace.

[8] I am not saying this as a command. Rather, by means of the diligence of others, I am testing the genuineness of your love. [9] For you know the grace of our Lord Jesus Christ: although He was rich, for your sake He became poor, so that by His poverty you might become rich. [10] Now I am giving an opinion on this because it is profitable for you, who a year ago began not only to do something but also to desire it. [11] But now finish the task as well, that just as there was eagerness to desire it, so there may also be a completion from what you have. [12] For if the

---

[a]8:7 Other mss read *in our love for you*

eagerness is there, it is acceptable according to what one has, not according to what he does not have. [13] It is not that there may be relief for others and hardship for you, but it is a question of equality— [14] at the present time your surplus is ⌊available⌋ for their need, so that their abundance may also become ⌊available⌋ for your need, that there may be equality. [15] As it has been written:

**The person who gathered much
did not have too much,
and the person who gathered
little did not have too little.**[a]

## Administration of the Collection

[16] Thanks be to God who put the same diligence for you into the heart of Titus. [17] For he accepted our urging and, being very diligent, went out to you by his own choice. [18] With him we have sent the brother who is praised throughout the churches for his gospel ministry. [19] And not only that, but he was also appointed by the churches to accompany us with this gift that is being administered by us for the glory of the Lord Himself and to show our eagerness ⌊to help⌋. [20] We are taking this precaution so no one can find fault with us concerning this large sum administered by us. [21] For we are making provision for what is honorable, not only before the Lord but also before men. [22] We have also sent with them our brother whom we have often tested, in many circumstances, and found diligent—and now even more diligent because of his great confidence in you. [23] As for Titus, he is my partner and coworker serving you; as for our brothers, they are the messengers of the churches, the glory of Christ.

[24] Therefore, before the churches, show them the proof of your love and of our boasting about you.

## Motivations for Giving

**9** Now concerning the ministry to the saints, it is unnecessary for me to write to you. [2] For I know your eagerness, and I brag about you to the Macedonians: "Achaia has been prepared since last year," and your zeal has stirred up most of them. [3] But I sent the brothers so our boasting about you in the matter would not prove empty, and so you would be prepared just as I said. [4] For if any Macedonians should come with me and find you unprepared, we, not to mention you, would be embarrassed in that situation. [5] Therefore I considered it necessary to urge the brothers to go on ahead to you and arrange in advance the generous gift you promised, so that it will be ready as a gift and not an extortion.

[6] Remember this: the person who sows sparingly will also reap sparingly, and the person who sows generously will also reap generously. [7] Each person should do as he has decided in his heart—not out of regret or out of necessity, for God loves a cheerful giver. [8] And God is able to make every grace overflow to you, so that in every way, always having everything you need, you may excel in every good work. [9] As it is written:

**He has scattered;
He has given to the poor;
His righteousness endures
forever.**[b]

[10] Now the One who provides seed for the sower and bread for food will provide and multiply your seed and

[a] 8:15 Ex 16:18   [b] 9:9 Ps 112:9

increase the harvest of your righteousness, [11] as you are enriched in every way for all generosity, which produces thanksgiving to God through us. [12] For the ministry of this service is not only supplying the needs of the saints, but is also overflowing in many acts of thanksgiving to God. [13] Through the proof of this service, they will glorify God for your obedience to the confession of the gospel of Christ, and for your generosity in sharing with them and with others. [14] And in their prayers for you they will have deep affection for you because of the surpassing grace of God on you. [15] Thanks be to God for His indescribable gift.

## Paul's Apostolic Authority

**10** Now I, Paul, make a personal appeal to you by the gentleness and graciousness of Christ—I who am humble among you in person, but bold toward you when absent. [2] I beg you that when I am present I will not need to be bold with the confidence by which I plan to challenge certain people who think we are walking in a fleshly way. [3] For although we are walking in the flesh, we do not wage war in a fleshly way, [4] since the weapons of our warfare are not fleshly, but are powerful through God for the demolition of strongholds. We demolish arguments [5] and every high-minded thing that is raised up against the knowledge of God, taking every thought captive to the obedience of Christ. [6] And we are ready to punish any disobedience, once your obedience is complete.

[7] Look at what is obvious. If anyone is confident that he belongs to Christ, he should remind himself of this: just as he belongs to Christ, so do we. [8] For if I boast some more about our authority, which the Lord gave for building you up and not for tearing you down, I am not ashamed. [9] I don't want to seem as though I am trying to terrify you with my letters. [10] For it is said, "His letters are weighty and powerful, but his physical presence is weak, and his public speaking is despicable." [11] Such a person should consider this: what we are in the words of our letters when absent, we will be in actions when present.

---

### 2 Corinthians 10:12-18

*Being new to something (like the Christian life) can make you feel outclassed by those who do it so well. But we're not racing each other. We're racing ourselves. There are people in your church who are so neat, who have so much to offer. And you're one of them.*

---

[12] For we don't dare classify or compare ourselves with some who commend themselves. But in measuring themselves by themselves and comparing themselves to themselves, they lack understanding. [13] We, however, will not boast beyond measure, but according to the measure of the area [of ministry] that God has assigned to us, [which] reaches even to you. [14] For we are not overextending ourselves, as if we had not reached you, since we have come to you with the gospel of Christ. [15] We are not bragging beyond measure about other people's labors. But we have the hope that as your faith increases, our area [of ministry] will be

greatly enlarged, [16] so that we may preach the gospel to the regions beyond you, not boasting about what has already been done in someone else's area ⌊of ministry⌋. [17] So **the one who boasts must boast in the Lord.**[a] [18] For it is not the one commending himself who is approved, but the one the Lord commends.

---

*"We don't have to fear being inadequate. Our God is adequate. He will provide everything we need to serve Him."*
—*Chip Ricks*

---

## Paul and the False Apostles

**11** I wish you would put up with a little foolishness from me. Yes, do put up with me. [2] For I am jealous over you with a godly jealousy, because I have promised you in marriage to one husband—to present a pure virgin to Christ. [3] But I fear that, as the serpent deceived Eve by his cunning, your minds may be corrupted from a complete and pure[b] devotion to Christ. [4] For if a person comes and preaches another Jesus, whom we did not preach, or you receive a different spirit, which you had not received, or a different gospel, which you had not accepted, you put up with it splendidly! [5] Now I consider myself in no way inferior to the "super-apostles." [6] Though ⌊untrained⌋ in public speaking, I am certainly not untrained in knowledge. Indeed, we have always made that clear to you in everything. [7] Or did I commit a sin by humbling myself so that you might be exalted, because I preached the gospel of God to you free of charge? [8] I robbed other churches by taking pay ⌊from them⌋ to minister to you. [9] When I was present with you and in need, I did not burden anyone, for the brothers who came from Macedonia supplied my needs. I have kept myself, and will keep myself, from burdening you in any way. [10] As the truth of Christ is in me, this boasting of mine will not be stopped in the regions of Achaia. [11] Why? Because I don't love you? God knows I do!

[12] But I will continue to do what I am doing, in order to cut off the opportunity of those who want an opportunity to be regarded just as we are in what they are boasting about. [13] For such people are false apostles, deceitful workers, disguising themselves as apostles of Christ. [14] And no wonder! For Satan himself is disguised as an angel of light. [15] So it is no great thing if his servants also disguise themselves as servants of righteousness. Their destiny will be according to their works.

## Paul's Sufferings for Christ

[16] I repeat: no one should consider me a fool. But if ⌊you do⌋, at least accept me as a fool, so I too may boast a little. [17] What I say in this matter of boasting, I don't speak as the Lord would, but foolishly. [18] Since many boast from a human perspective, I will also boast. [19] For you gladly put up with fools since you are so smart! [20] In fact, you put up with it if someone enslaves you, if someone devours you, if someone captures you, if someone dominates you, or if someone hits you in the face. [21] I say this to ⌊our⌋ shame: we have been weak.

---

[a]10:17 Jr 9:24   [b]11:3 Other mss omit *and pure*

But in whatever anyone dares ⌊to boast⌋—I am talking foolishly—I also dare:

22 Are they Hebrews? So am I.
Are they Israelites? So am I.
Are they the seed of
Abraham? So am I.
23 Are they servants of Christ?
I'm talking like a madman—
I'm a better one:
with far more labors, many
more imprisonments,
far worse beatings, near
death many times.
24 Five times I received from
the Jews 40 lashes
minus one.
25 Three times I was beaten
with rods.
Once I was stoned.
Three times I was
shipwrecked.
I have spent a night and a day
in the depths of the sea.
26 On frequent journeys, ⌊I faced⌋
dangers from rivers, dangers
from robbers,
dangers from my own
people, dangers from the
Gentiles,
dangers in the city, dangers
in the open country,
dangers on the sea, and
dangers among false
brothers;
27 labor and hardship,
many sleepless nights,
hunger and thirst,
often without food, cold, and
lacking clothing.

28 Not to mention other things, there is the daily pressure on me: my care for all the churches. 29 Who is weak, and I am not weak? Who is made to stumble, and I do not burn with indig-nation? 30 If boasting is necessary, I will boast about my weaknesses. 31 The eternally blessed One, the God and Father of the Lord Jesus, knows I am not lying. 32 In Damascus, the governor under King Aretas guarded the city of the Damascenes in order to arrest me, 33 so I was let down in a basket through a window in the wall and escaped his hands.

## Sufficient Grace

**12** It is necessary to boast; it is not helpful, but I will move on to visions and revelations of the Lord. 2 I know a man in Christ who was caught up into the third heaven 14 years ago. Whether he was in the body or out of the body, I don't know; God knows. 3 I know that this man— whether in the body or out of the body I do not know, God knows— 4 was caught up into paradise. He heard inexpressible words, which a man is not allowed to speak. 5 I will boast about this person, but not about myself, except of my weakness-es. 6 For if I want to boast, I will not be a fool, because I will be telling the truth. But I will spare you, so that no one can credit me with something beyond what he sees in me or hears from me, 7 especially because of the extraordinary revelations. Therefore, so that I would not exalt myself, a thorn in the flesh was given to me, a messenger of Satan to torment me so I would not exalt myself. 8 Concerning this, I pleaded with the Lord three times to take it away from me. 9 But He said to me, "My grace is sufficient for you, for power[a] is perfected in weakness." Therefore, I will most gladly boast all the more about my weaknesses, so that Christ's power may reside in me. 10 So because of

[a]**12:9** Other mss read *My power*

Christ, I am pleased in weaknesses, in insults, in catastrophes, in persecutions, and in pressures. For when I am weak, then I am strong.

## Signs of an Apostle

[11] I have become a fool; you forced it on me. I ought to have been recommended by you, since I am in no way inferior to the "super-apostles," even though I am nothing. [12] The signs of an apostle were performed among you in all endurance—not only signs but also wonders and miracles. [13] So in what way were you treated worse than the other churches, except that I personally did not burden you? Forgive me this wrong!

## Paul's Concern for the Corinthians

[14] Look! I am ready to come to you this third time. I will not burden you, for I am not seeking what is yours, but you. For children are not obligated to save up for their parents, but parents for their children. [15] I will most gladly spend and be spent for you. If I love you more, am I to be loved less? [16] Now granted, I have not burdened you; yet sly as I am, I took you in by deceit! [17] Did I take advantage of you by anyone I sent you? [18] I urged Titus [to come], and I sent the brother with him. Did Titus take advantage of you? Didn't we •walk in the same spirit and in the same footsteps?

[19] You have thought all along that we were defending ourselves to you. [No], in the sight of God we are speaking in Christ, and everything, dear friends, is for building you up. [20] For I fear that perhaps when I come I will not find you to be what I want, and I may not be found by you to be what you want; there may be quarreling, jealousy, outbursts of anger, selfish ambitions, slander, gossip, arrogance, and disorder. [21] I fear that when I come my God will again humiliate me in your presence, and I will grieve for many who sinned before and have not repented of the uncleanness, sexual immorality, and promiscuity they practiced.

## Final Warnings and Exhortations

**13** This is the third time I am coming to you. **On the testimony of two or three witnesses every word will be confirmed.**[a] [2] I gave warning, and I give warning—as when I was present the second time, so now while I am absent—to those who sinned before and to all the rest: if I come again, I will not be lenient, [3] since you seek proof of Christ speaking in me. He is not weak toward you, but powerful among you. [4] In fact, He was crucified in weakness, but He lives by God's power. For we also are weak in Him, yet toward you we will live with Him by God's power.

[5] Test yourselves [to see] if you are in the faith. Examine yourselves. Or do you not recognize for yourselves that Jesus Christ is in you?—unless you fail the test. [6] And I hope you will recognize that we are not failing the test. [7] Now we pray to God that you do nothing wrong, not that we may appear to pass the test, but that you may do what is right, even though we [may appear] to fail. [8] For we are not able to do anything against the truth, but only for the truth. [9] In fact, we rejoice when we are weak and you are strong. We also pray for this: your maturity. [10] This is why I am writing these things while absent, that when I am there I will not use severity, in

[a]**13:1** Dt 17:6; 19:15

keeping with the authority the Lord gave me for building up and not for tearing down.

¹¹ Finally, brothers, rejoice. Be restored, be encouraged, be of the same mind, be at peace, and the God of love and peace will be with you.

¹² Greet one another with a holy kiss. All the saints greet you.

¹³ The grace of the Lord Jesus Christ, and the love of God, and the fellowship of the Holy Spirit be with all of you.

# GALATIANS

## Greeting

**1** Paul, an apostle—not from men or by man, but by Jesus Christ and God the Father who raised Him from the dead— ² and all the brothers who are with me:

To the churches of Galatia.

³ Grace to you and peace from God the Father and our Lordᵃ Jesus Christ, ⁴ who gave Himself for our sins to rescue us from this present evil age, according to the will of our God and Father, ⁵ to whom be the glory forever and ever. •Amen.

## No Other Gospel

⁶ I am amazed that you are so quickly turning away from Him who called you by the grace of Christ, ⌊and are turning⌋ to a different gospel— ⁷ not that there is another ⌊gospel⌋, but there are some who are troubling you and want to change the gospel of Christ. ⁸ But even if we or an angel from heaven should preach to you a gospel other than what we have preached to you, a curse be on him! ⁹ As we have said before, I now say again: if anyone preaches to you a gospel contrary to what you received, a curse be on him!

¹⁰ For am I now trying to win the favor of people, or God? Or am I striving to please people? If I were still trying to please people, I would not be a slave of Christ.

## Paul Defends His Apostleship

¹¹ Now I want you to know, brothers, that the gospel preached by me is not based on a human point of view. ¹² For I did not receive it from a human source and I was not taught it, but it came by a revelation from Jesus Christ. ¹³ For you have heard about my former way of life in Judaism: I persecuted God's church to an extreme degree and tried to destroy it; ¹⁴ and I advanced in Judaism beyond many contemporaries among my people, because I was extremely zealous for the traditions of my ancestors. ¹⁵ But when God, who from my mother's womb set me apart and called me by His grace, was pleased ¹⁶ to reveal His Son in me, so that I could preach Him among the Gentiles, I did not immediately consult with anyone. ¹⁷ I did not go up to Jerusalem to those who had become apostles before me; instead I went to Arabia and came back to Damascus.

¹⁸ Then after three years I did go up to Jerusalem to get to know •Cephas,ᵇ and I stayed with him 15 days. ¹⁹ But I didn't see any of the other apostles except James, the Lord's brother. ²⁰ Now in what I write to you, I'm not lying. God is my witness.

²¹ Afterwards, I went to the regions of Syria and Cilicia. ²² I remained personally unknown to the Judean churches in Christ; ²³ they simply kept hearing: "He who formerly persecuted us now preaches the faith he once tried to destroy." ²⁴ And they glorified God because of me.

## Paul Defends His Gospel at Jerusalem

**2** Then after 14 years I went up again to Jerusalem with Barnabas, taking Titus along also. ² I went up because of a revelation and presented to them the gospel I preach among the Gentiles—but privately to those recognized ⌊as leaders⌋—so that I might not be running, or have run, in vain. [3] But not even Titus who was with me, though he was a Greek, was compelled to be circumcised. [4] ⌊This issue arose⌋ because of false brothers smuggled in, who came in secretly to spy on our freedom that we have in Christ Jesus, in order to enslave us. [5] But we did not yield in submission to these people for even an hour, so that the truth of the gospel would remain for you.

[6] But from those recognized as important (what they really were makes no difference to me; God does not show favoritism)—those recognized as important added nothing to me. [7] On the contrary, they saw that I had been entrusted with the gospel for the uncircumcised, just as Peter was for the circumcised. [8] For He who was at work with Peter in the apostleship to the circumcised was also at work with me among the Gentiles. [9] When James, •Cephas, and John, recognized as pillars, acknowledged the grace that had been given to me, they gave the right hand of fellowship to me and Barnabas, ⌊agreeing⌋ that we should go to the Gentiles and they to the circumcised. [10] ⌊They⌋ asked only that we would remember the poor, which I made every effort to do.

## Freedom from the Law

[11] But when Cephas came to Antioch, I opposed him to his face because he stood condemned. [12] For he used to eat with the Gentiles before certain men came from James. However, when they came, he withdrew and separated himself, because he feared those from the circumcision party. [13] Then the rest of the Jews joined his hypocrisy, so that even Barnabas was carried away by their hypocrisy. [14] But when I saw that they were deviating from the truth of the gospel, I told Cephas[a] in front of everyone, "If you, who are a Jew, live like a Gentile and not like a Jew, how can you compel Gentiles to live like Jews?"

[15] We are Jews by birth and not "Gentile sinners"; [16] yet we know that no one is justified by the works of the law but by faith in Jesus Christ. And we have believed in Christ Jesus, so that we might be justified by faith in Christ and not by the works of the law, because by the works of the law no human being will be justified. [17] But if, while seeking to be justified by Christ, we ourselves are also found to be sinners, is Christ then a promoter of sin? Absolutely not! [18] If I rebuild those things that I tore down, I show myself to be a lawbreaker. [19] For through the law I have died to the law, that I might live to God. I have been crucified with Christ; [20] and I no longer live, but Christ lives in me. The life I now live in the flesh, I live by faith in the Son of God, who loved me and gave Himself for me. [21] I do not set aside the grace of God; for if righteousness comes through the law, then Christ died for nothing.

## Justification through Faith

**3** You foolish Galatians! Who has hypnotized you,[b] before whose eyes Jesus Christ was vividly portrayed[c] as crucified? [2] I only want to learn this from you: Did you receive the Spirit by the works of the law or by hearing with faith? [3] Are you so foolish? After beginning with the Spirit, are you now going to be made complete by the flesh? [4] Did you suffer so much for nothing—if in fact it was for

[a]2:14 Other mss read *Peter*   [b]3:1 Other mss add *not to obey the truth*   [c]3:1 Other mss add *among you*

---

*Galatians 3:1-5*

*You didn't do anything to earn
your salvation. You don't have to
pass a test every five years to keep
it current. You're in. You're staying
in. What's so hard about that? If we
all had to work our way into God's
good graces, heaven would be one
lonely place.*

---

nothing? [5] So then, does God supply
you with the Spirit and work miracles
among you by the works of the law or
by hearing with faith?

[6] Just as Abraham **believed God,
and it was credited to him for righteousness,**[a] [7] so understand that
those who have faith are Abraham's
sons. [8] Now the Scripture foresaw
that God would justify the Gentiles by
faith and foretold the good news to
Abraham, saying, **All the nations will
be blessed in you.**[b] [9] So those who
have faith are blessed with Abraham,
who had faith.

*Law and Promise*

[10] For all who ⌊rely on⌋ the works of
the law are under a curse, because it
is written: **Cursed is everyone who
does not continue doing everything
written in the book of the law.**[c]
[11] Now it is clear that no one is justified before God by the law, because
**the righteous will live by faith.**[d]
[12] But the law is not based on faith;
instead, **the one who does these
things will live by them.**[e] [13] Christ
has redeemed us from the curse of the

law by becoming a curse for us,
because it is written: **Cursed is
everyone who is hung on a tree.**[f]
[14] The purpose was that the blessing
of Abraham would come to the Gentiles in Christ Jesus, so that we could
receive the promise of the Spirit
through faith.

[15] Brothers, I'm using a human illustration. No one sets aside even a
human covenant that has been ratified, or makes additions to it. [16] Now
the promises were spoken to Abraham
and to his seed. He does not say "and
to seeds," as though referring to many,
but **and to your seed,**[g] referring to
one, who is Christ. [17] And I say this:
the law, which came 430 years later,
does not revoke a covenant that was
previously ratified by God,[h] so as to
cancel the promise. [18] For if the inheritance is from the law, it is no longer
from the promise; but God granted it
to Abraham through the promise.

*The Purpose of the Law*

[19] Why the law then? It was added
because of transgressions until the
Seed to whom the promise was made
would come. ⌊The law⌋ was ordered
through angels by means of a mediator.
[20] Now a mediator is not for just one
person, but God is one. [21] Is the law
therefore contrary to God's promises?
Absolutely not! For if a law had been
given that was able to give life, then

---

*"Grace is the unconditional love of
God in Christ freely given to the
sinful, the undeserving, and the
imperfect."*
—*David Seamands*

---

[a]**3:6** Gn 15:6  [b]**3:8** Gn 12:3; 18:18  [c]**3:10** Dt 27:26  [d]**3:11** Hab 2:4  [e]**3:12** Lv 18:5  [f]**3:13** Dt 21:23
[g]**3:16** Gn 12:7; 13:15; 17:8; 24:7  [h]**3:17** Other mss add *in Christ*

righteousness would certainly be by the law. [22] But the Scripture has imprisoned everything under sin's power, so that the promise by faith in Jesus Christ might be given to those who believe. [23] Before this faith came, we were confined under the law, imprisoned until the coming faith was revealed. [24] The law, then, was our guardian until Christ, so that we could be justified by faith. [25] But since that faith has come, we are no longer under a guardian, [26] for you are all sons of God through faith in Christ Jesus.

## Sons and Heirs

[27] For as many of you as have been baptized into Christ have put on Christ. [28] There is no Jew or Greek, slave or free, male or female; for you are all one in Christ Jesus. [29] And if you are Christ's, then you are Abraham's seed, heirs according to the promise.

**4** [1] Now I say that as long as the heir is a child, he differs in no way from a slave, though he is the owner of everything. [2] Instead, he is under guardians and stewards until the time set by his father. [3] In the same way we also, when we were children, were in slavery under the elemental forces of the world. [4] But when the completion of the time came, God sent His Son, born of a woman, born under the law, [5] to redeem those under the law, so that we might receive adoption as sons. [6] And because you are sons, God has sent the Spirit of His Son into our[a] hearts, crying, "•*Abba*, Father!" [7] So you are no longer a slave, but a son; and if a son, then an heir through God.

## Paul's Concern for the Galatians

[8] But in the past, when you didn't know God, you were enslaved to

---

*Galatians 4:3-7*

*God the Father*

*We are not God's children by birth. We can't be. To do that, we would've had to be born perfect, already in full compliance with the law of God. No, for us to be His children, we had to be adopted. And that is what we are—grafted into God's family with the full privileges of a rightful heir.*

---

things that by nature are not gods. [9] But now, since you know God, or rather have become known by God, how can you turn back again to the weak and bankrupt elemental forces? Do you want to be enslaved to them all over again? [10] You observe ⌊special⌋ days, months, seasons, and years. [11] I am fearful for you, that perhaps my labor for you has been wasted.

[12] I beg you, brothers: become like me, for I also became like you. You have not wronged me; [13] you know that previously I preached the gospel to you in physical weakness, [14] and though my physical condition was a trial for you,[b] you did not despise or reject me. On the contrary, you received me as an angel of God, as Christ Jesus ⌊Himself⌋.

[15] What happened to this blessedness of yours? For I testify to you that, if possible, you would have torn out your eyes and given them to me. [16] Have I now become your enemy by telling you the truth? [17] They are enthusiastic about you, but not for

---

[a]4:6 Other mss read *your*   [b]4:14 Other mss read *me*

any good. Instead, they want to isolate you so you will be enthusiastic about them. [18] Now it is always good to be enthusiastic about good—and not just when I am with you. [19] My children, again I am in the pains of childbirth for you until Christ is formed in you. [20] I'd like to be with you right now and change my tone of voice, because I don't know what to do about you.

## Sarah and Hagar: Two Covenants

[21] Tell me, you who want to be under the law, don't you hear the law? [22] For it is written that Abraham had two sons, one by a slave and the other by a free woman. [23] But the one by the slave was born according to the flesh, while the one by the free woman was born as the result of a promise. [24] These things are illustrations, for the women represent the two covenants. One is from Mount Sinai and bears children into slavery—this is Hagar. [25] Now Hagar is Mount Sinai in Arabia and corresponds to the present Jerusalem, for she is in slavery with her children. [26] But the Jerusalem above is free, and she is our mother. [27] For it is written:

**Rejoice, O barren woman
who does not give birth.
Break forth and shout,
you who are not in labor,
for the children of the
    desolate are many,
more numerous than those of
the woman who has a husband.**[a]

[28] Now you, brothers, like Isaac, are children of promise. [29] But just as then the child born according to the flesh

persecuted the one born according to the Spirit, so also now. [30] But what does the Scripture say?

**Throw out the slave and her
son, for the son of the slave
will never inherit with the
son of the free woman.**[b]

[31] Therefore, brothers, we are not children of the slave but of the free woman.

## Freedom of the Christian

**5** Christ has liberated us into freedom. Therefore stand firm and don't submit again to a yoke of slavery. [2] Take note! I, Paul, tell you that if you get circumcised, Christ will not benefit you at all. [3] Again I testify to every man who gets circumcised that he is obligated to keep the entire law. [4] You who are trying to be justified by the law are alienated from Christ; you have fallen from grace! [5] For by the Spirit we eagerly wait for the hope of righteousness from faith. [6] For in Christ Jesus neither circumcision nor uncircumcision accomplishes anything; what matters is faith working through love.

---

*"What would be the result if every church member should begin to do as Jesus would do? It is not easy to go into details of the result."*
*—Charles Sheldon*

---

[7] You were running well. Who prevented you from obeying the truth? [8] This persuasion did not come from Him who called you. [9] A little yeast

[a]4:27 Is 54:1    [b]4:30 Gn 21:10

leavens the whole lump of dough. [10] In the Lord I have confidence in you that you will not accept any other view. But whoever it is who is troubling you will pay the penalty. [11] Now brothers, if I still preach circumcision, why am I still persecuted? In that case the offense of the cross has been abolished. [12] I wish those who are disturbing you might also get themselves castrated!

[13] For you are called to freedom, brothers; only don't use this freedom as an opportunity for the flesh, but serve one another through love. [14] For the entire law is fulfilled in one statement: **You shall love your neighbor as yourself.**[a] [15] But if you bite and devour one another, watch out, or you will be consumed by one another.

---

### Galatians 5:16-18

*As a Christian, you now have the luxury of filtering every decision you make through the timeless wisdom of an all-knowing God. And with the Holy Spirit calling the shots, you're free to make good choices every day—and to have the strength to match.*

---

### The Spirit versus the Flesh

[16] I say then, •walk by the Spirit and you will not carry out the desire of the flesh. [17] For the flesh desires what is against the Spirit, and the Spirit desires what is against the flesh; these are opposed to each other, so that you don't do what you want. [18] But if you

are led by the Spirit, you are not under the law.

[19] Now the works of the flesh are obvious:[b] sexual immorality, moral impurity, promiscuity, [20] idolatry, sorcery, hatreds, strife, jealousy, outbursts of anger, selfish ambitions, dissensions, factions, [21] envy,[c] drunkenness, carousing, and anything similar, about which I tell you in advance—as I told you before—that those who practice such things will not inherit the kingdom of God.

[22] But the fruit of the Spirit is love, joy, peace, patience, kindness, goodness, faith, [23] gentleness, self-control. Against such things there is no law. [24] Now those who belong to Christ Jesus have crucified the flesh with its passions and desires. [25] If we live by the Spirit, we must also follow the Spirit. [26] We must not become conceited, provoking one another, envying one another.

### Carry One Another's Burdens

**6** Brothers, if someone is caught in any wrongdoing, you who are spiritual should restore such a person with a gentle spirit, watching out for yourselves so you won't be tempted also. [2] Carry one another's burdens; in this way you will fulfill the law of Christ. [3] For if anyone considers himself to be something when he is nothing, he is deceiving himself. [4] But each person should examine his own work, and then he will have a reason for boasting in himself alone, and not in respect to someone else. [5] For each person will have to carry his own load.

[6] The one who is taught the message must share his goods with the teacher. [7] Don't be deceived: God is not mocked. For whatever a man sows

[a]5:14 Lv 19:18   [b]5:19 Other mss add *adultery*   [c]5:21 Other mss add *murders*

## Galatians 6:14

### Salvation

*For as long as we live, our greatest struggle will be to let this salvation take hold in our lives—to submit our wills so completely to God that He has full control of our hearts. It is the most freeing experience in the world to hand over the reins to One who really knows how to use them.*

he will also reap, [8] because the one who sows to his flesh will reap corruption from the flesh, but the one who sows to the Spirit will reap eternal life from the Spirit. [9] So we must not get tired of doing good, for we will reap at the proper time if we don't give up. [10] Therefore, as we have opportunity, we must work for the good of all, especially for those who belong to the household of faith.

### Concluding Exhortation

[11] Look at what large letters I have written to you in my own handwriting. [12] Those who want to make a good showing in the flesh are the ones who would compel you to be circumcised—but only to avoid being persecuted for the cross of Christ. [13] For even the circumcised don't keep the law themselves; however, they want you to be circumcised in order to boast about your flesh. [14] But as for me, I will never boast about anything except the cross of our Lord Jesus Christ, through whom the world has been crucified to me, and I to the world. [15] For[a] both circumcision and uncircumcision mean nothing; ⌊what matters⌋ instead is a new creation. [16] May peace be on all those who follow this standard, and mercy also be on the Israel of God!

[17] From now on, let no one cause me trouble, because I carry the marks of Jesus on my body. [18] Brothers, the grace of our Lord Jesus Christ be with your spirit. •Amen.

[a]6:15 Other mss add *in Christ Jesus*

# EPHESIANS

## Greeting

**1** Paul, an apostle of Christ Jesus by God's will:

To the saints and believers in Christ Jesus at Ephesus.[a]

² Grace to you and peace from God our Father and the Lord Jesus Christ.

## God's Rich Blessings

³ Blessed be the God and Father of our Lord Jesus Christ, who has blessed us with every spiritual blessing in the heavens, in Christ; ⁴ for He chose us in Him, before the foundation of the world, to be holy and blameless in His sight. In love ⁵ He predestined us to be adopted through Jesus Christ for Himself, according to His favor and will, ⁶ to the praise of His glorious grace that He favored us with in the Beloved.

⁷ In Him we have redemption through His blood, the forgiveness of our trespasses, according to the riches of His grace ⁸ that He lavished on us with all wisdom and understanding. ⁹ He made known to us the •mystery of His will, according to His good pleasure that He planned in Him ¹⁰ for the administration of the days of fulfillment—to bring everything together in the •Messiah, both things in heaven and things on earth in Him.

¹¹ In Him we were also made His inheritance, predestined according to the purpose of the One who works out everything in agreement with the decision of His will, ¹² so that we who had already put our hope in the Messiah might bring praise to His glory.

¹³ In Him you also, when you heard the word of truth, the gospel of your salvation—in Him when you believed—were sealed with the promised Holy Spirit. ¹⁴ He is the down payment of our inheritance, for the redemption of the possession, to the praise of His glory.

---

### Ephesians 1:15-19

*Since old habits don't go away overnight and may continue to be a nagging source of frustration and (at times) failure for many years, where does the victory start coming in? It comes from not underestimating the struggle of Christian living—or the power that God has put in you.*

---

## Prayer for Spiritual Insight

¹⁵ This is why, since I heard about your faith in the Lord Jesus and your love for all the saints, ¹⁶ I never stop giving thanks for you as I remember you in my prayers. ¹⁷ ⌊I pray⌋ that the God of our Lord Jesus Christ, the glorious Father, would give you a spirit of wisdom and revelation in the knowledge of Him. ¹⁸ ⌊I pray⌋ that the eyes of your heart may be enlightened so you may know what is the hope of His calling, what are the glorious riches of His inheritance among the saints, ¹⁹ and what is the immeasurable greatness of

[a]1:1 Other mss omit *at Ephesus*

*"Just as He delivered us from the overall reign of sin, so He has made ample provision for us to win the daily skirmishes against sin."*
—Jerry Bridges

His power to us who believe, according to the working of His vast strength.

## God's Power in Christ

[20] He demonstrated ⌊this power⌋ in the Messiah by raising Him from the dead and seating Him at His right hand in the heavens— [21] far above every ruler and authority, power and dominion, and every title given, not only in this age but also in the one to come. [22] And **He put everything under His feet**[a] and appointed Him as head over everything for the church, [23] which is His body, the fullness of the One who fills all things in every way.

## From Death to Life

**2** And you were dead in your trespasses and sins [2] in which you previously walked according to this worldly age, according to the ruler of the atmospheric domain, the spirit now working in the disobedient. [3] We too all previously lived among them in our fleshly desires, carrying out the inclinations of our flesh and thoughts, and by nature we were children under wrath, as the others were also. [4] But God, who is abundant in mercy, because of His great love that He had for us, [5] made us alive with the •Messiah even though we were dead in tres-

passes. By grace you are saved! [6] He also raised us up with Him and seated us with Him in the heavens, in Christ Jesus, [7] so that in the coming ages He might display the immeasurable riches of His grace in ⌊His⌋ kindness to us in Christ Jesus. [8] For by grace you are saved through faith, and this is not from yourselves; it is God's gift— [9] not from works, so that no one can boast. [10] For we are His creation—created in Christ Jesus for good works, which God prepared ahead of time so that we should •walk in them.

## Unity in Christ

[11] So then, remember that at one time you were Gentiles in the flesh—called "the uncircumcised" by those called "the circumcised," done by hand in the flesh. [12] At that time you were without the Messiah, excluded from the citizenship of Israel, and foreigners to the covenants of the promise, with no hope and without God in the world. [13] But now in Christ Jesus, you who

---

### Ephesians 2:4-9

### Salvation

*Far too many people believe that when it's all said and done, God will have to notice that they were good people at heart, not nearly as bad as some people they knew. But good, nice, and better has nothing to do with it. Faith and grace are the only ingredients of salvation.*

---

[a]1:22 Ps 8:6

were far away have been brought near by the blood of the Messiah. ¹⁴ For He is our peace, who made both groups one and tore down the dividing wall of hostility. In His flesh, ¹⁵ He did away with the law of the commandments in regulations, so that He might create in Himself one new man from the two, resulting in peace. ¹⁶ ⌊He did this so⌋ that He might reconcile both to God in one body through the cross and put the hostility to death by it. ¹⁷ When ⌊Christ⌋ came, He proclaimed the good news of peace to you who were far away and peace to those who were near. ¹⁸ For through Him we both have access by one Spirit to the Father. ¹⁹ So then you are no longer foreigners and strangers, but fellow citizens with the saints, and members of God's household, ²⁰ built on the foundation of the apostles and prophets, with Christ Jesus Himself as the cornerstone. ²¹ The whole building is being fitted together in Him and is growing into a holy sanctuary in the Lord, ²² in whom you

---

### Ephesians 2:19-22

### The Church

*Church is not an option for the Christian, for it is in community with other believers that we link ourselves into what Christ is doing in the world. We multiply what He has done in us by joining with others who share our faith, who need our gifts, who can bless and refine our lives.*

---

also are being built together for God's dwelling in the Spirit.

## Paul's Ministry to the Gentiles

**3** For this reason, I, Paul, the prisoner of Christ Jesus on behalf of you Gentiles— ² you have heard, haven't you, about the administration of God's grace that He gave to me for you? ³ The •mystery was made known to me by revelation, as I have briefly written above. ⁴ By reading this you are able to understand my insight about the mystery of the •Messiah. ⁵ This was not made known to people in other generations as it is now revealed to His holy apostles and prophets by the Spirit: ⁶ the Gentiles are co-heirs, members of the same body, and partners of the promise in Christ Jesus through the gospel. ⁷ I was made a servant of this ⌊gospel⌋ by the gift of God's grace that was given to me by the working of His power.

⁸ This grace was given to me—the least of all the saints!—to proclaim to the Gentiles the incalculable riches

---

### Ephesians 3:8-12

### God's Grace

*The mystery of the New Testament, which was at least partially hidden in the early part of human history, was that God's grace was for all people, not just the nation of Israel. Imagine people's surprise at this great announcement after so many years of having God in a box.*

of the Messiah, [9] and to shed light for all about the administration of the mystery hidden for ages in God who created all things. [10] This is so that God's multi-faceted wisdom may now be made known through the church to the rulers and authorities in the heavens. [11] This is according to the purpose of the ages, which He made in the Messiah, Jesus our Lord, [12] in whom we have boldness, access, and confidence through faith in Him. [13] So then I ask you not to be discouraged over my afflictions on your behalf, for they are your glory.

## Prayer for Spiritual Power

[14] For this reason I bow my knees before the Father[a] [15] from whom every family in heaven and on earth is named. [16] ⌊I pray⌋ that He may grant you, according to the riches of His glory, to be strengthened with power through His Spirit in the inner man, [17] and that the Messiah may dwell in your hearts through faith. ⌊I pray that⌋ you, being rooted and firmly established in love, [18] may be able to comprehend with all the saints what is the breadth and width, height and depth, [19] and to know the Messiah's love that surpasses knowledge, so you may be filled with all the fullness of God.

[20] Now to Him who is able to do above and beyond all that we ask or think—according to the power that works in you— [21] to Him be glory in the church and in Christ Jesus to all generations, forever and ever. •Amen.

## Unity and Diversity in the Body of Christ

**4** I, therefore, the prisoner in the Lord, urge you to •walk worthy of the calling you have received,

[2] with all humility and gentleness, with patience, accepting one another in love, [3] diligently keeping the unity of the Spirit with the peace that binds ⌊us⌋. [4] There is one body and one Spirit, just as you were called to one hope at your calling; [5] one Lord, one faith, one baptism, [6] one God and Father of all, who is above all and through all and in all.

[7] Now grace was given to each one of us according to the measure of the •Messiah's gift. [8] For it says:

> **When He ascended on high,**
> **He took prisoners into**
> **captivity;**
> **He gave gifts to people.**[b]

[9] But what does "He ascended" mean except that He[c] descended to the lower parts of the earth? [10] The One who descended is the same as the One who ascended far above all the heavens, that He might fill all things. [11] And He personally gave some to be apostles, some prophets, some evangelists, some pastors and teachers, [12] for the training of the saints in the work of ministry, to build up the body of Christ, [13] until we all reach unity in the faith and in the knowledge of God's Son, ⌊growing⌋ into a mature man with a stature measured by Christ's fullness. [14] Then we will no longer be little children, tossed by the waves and blown around by every wind of teaching, by human cunning with cleverness in the techniques of deceit. [15] But speaking the truth in love, let us grow in every way into Him who is the Head—Christ. [16] From Him the whole body, fitted and knit together by every supporting ligament, promotes the growth of the body for building up itself in love by the proper working of each individual part.

---

[a]**3:14** Other mss add *of our Lord Jesus Christ*   [b]**4:8** Ps 68:18   [c]**4:9** Other mss add *first*

## Living the New Life

[17] Therefore, I say this and testify in the Lord: You should no longer walk as the Gentiles walk, in the futility of their thoughts. [18] They are darkened in their understanding, excluded from the life of God, because of the ignorance that is in them and because of the hardness of their hearts. [19] They became callous and gave themselves over to promiscuity for the practice of every kind of impurity with a desire for more and more.

[20] But that is not how you learned about the Messiah, [21] assuming you heard Him and were taught by Him, because the truth is in Jesus: [22] you took off your former way of life, the old man that is corrupted by deceitful desires; [23] you are being renewed in the spirit of your minds; [24] you put on the new man, the one created according to God's |likeness| in righteousness and purity of the truth.

[25] Since you put away lying, **Speak the truth, each one to his neighbor,**[a] because we are members of one another. [26] **Be angry and do not sin.**[b] Don't let the sun go down on your anger, [27] and don't give the Devil an opportunity. [28] The thief must no longer steal. Instead, he must do honest work with his own hands, so that he has something to share with anyone in need. [29] No rotten talk should come from your mouth, but only what is good for the building up of someone

---

*"Being free from sin not only means I can be strong in Him to stop doing wrong. It also means in Him I have the ability to do what's right."*

*—Stuart Briscoe*

---

### Ephesians 4:25-32

*Becoming a Christian doesn't automatically eliminate the bad habits you've formed over the years. But it does give you power to overcome them, one try at a time. Every bad habit opens a window for Satan to climb in again. But God has a way for you to shut him out.*

---

in need, in order to give grace to those who hear. [30] And don't grieve God's Holy Spirit, who sealed you for the day of redemption. [31] All bitterness, anger and wrath, insult and slander must be removed from you, along with all wickedness. [32] And be kind and compassionate to one another, forgiving one another, just as God also forgave you[c] in Christ.

**5** Therefore, be imitators of God, as dearly loved children. [2] And •walk in love, as the •Messiah also loved us and gave Himself for us, a sacrificial and fragrant offering to God. [3] But sexual immorality and any impurity or greed should not even be heard of among you, as is proper for saints. [4] And coarse and foolish talking or crude joking are not suitable, but rather giving thanks. [5] For know and recognize this: no sexually immoral or impure or greedy person, who is an idolater, has an inheritance in the kingdom of the Messiah and of God.

### Light versus Darkness

[6] Let no one deceive you with empty arguments, for because of these things

---

[a]**4:25** Zch 8:16 [b]**4:26** Ps 4:4 [c]**4:32** Other mss read *us*

God's wrath is coming on the disobedient. [7] Therefore, do not become their partners. [8] For you were once darkness, but now ⌊you are⌋ light in the Lord. Walk as children of light— [9] for the fruit of the light[a] ⌊results⌋ in all goodness, righteousness, and truth— [10] discerning what is pleasing to the Lord. [11] Don't participate in the fruitless works of darkness, but instead, expose them. [12] For it is shameful even to mention what is done by them in secret. [13] Everything exposed by the light is made clear, [14] for what makes everything clear is light. Therefore it is said:

> Get up, sleeper,
> and rise up from the dead,
> and the Messiah will shine on you.

## Consistency in the Christian Life

[15] Pay careful attention, then, to how you walk—not as unwise people but as wise— [16] making the most of the time, because the days are evil. [17] So don't be foolish, but understand what the Lord's will is. [18] And don't get drunk with wine, which ⌊leads to⌋ reckless actions, but be filled with the Spirit:

[19]  speaking to one another in
         psalms, hymns, and
         spiritual songs,
      singing and making music to
         the Lord in your heart,
[20]  giving thanks always for everything
         to God the Father in the name
         of our Lord Jesus Christ,
[21]  submitting to one another in
         the fear of Christ.

## Wives and Husbands

[22] Wives, submit[b] to your own husbands as to the Lord, [23] for the husband is head of the wife as also Christ is head of the church. He is the Savior of the body. [24] Now as the church submits to Christ, so wives should ⌊submit⌋ to their husbands in everything. [25] Husbands, love your wives, just as also Christ loved the church and gave Himself for her, [26] to make her holy, cleansing her in the washing of water by the word. [27] He did this to present the church to Himself in splendor, without spot or wrinkle or any such thing, but holy and blameless. [28] In the same way, husbands should love their wives as their own bodies. He who loves his wife loves himself. [29] For no one ever hates his own flesh, but provides and cares for it, just as Christ does for the church, [30] since we are members of His body.[c]

[31]  **For this reason a man will
        leave his father and mother
        and be joined to his wife,
        and the two will become one
        flesh.** [d]

[32] This •mystery is profound, but I am talking about Christ and the church. [33] To sum up, each one of you is to love his wife as himself, and the wife is to respect her husband.

## Children and Parents

**6** Children, obey your parents in the Lord, because this is right. [2] **Honor your father and mother**— which is the first commandment with a promise—[3] **that it may go well with you and that you may have a long life in the land.**[e] [4] And fathers, don't stir up anger in your children, but bring them up in the training and instruction of the Lord.

---

[a]**5:9** Other mss read *fruit of the Spirit;* see Gl 5:22, but compare Eph 5:11-14   [b]**5:22** Other mss omit *submit*
[c]**5:30** Other mss add *and of His flesh and of His bones*   [d]**5:31** Gn 2:24   [e]**6:2–3** Ex 20:12

---

### Ephesians 6:1-4

*The process of discipleship can change the way you think, helping you start paying attention to the important things in life—like the most important people in the world, for example—the ones God has placed right in your living room.*

---

## Slaves and Masters

5 Slaves, obey your human masters with fear and trembling, in the sincerity of your heart, as to Christ. 6 Don't ⌊work only⌋ while being watched, in order to please men, but as slaves of Christ, do God's will from your heart. 7 Render service with a good attitude, as to the Lord and not to men, 8 knowing that whatever good each one does, slave or free, he will receive this back from the Lord. 9 And masters, treat them the same way, without threatening them, because you know that both their and your Master is in heaven, and there is no favoritism with Him.

## Christian Warfare

10 Finally, be strengthened by the Lord and by His vast strength. 11 Put on the full armor of God so that you can stand against the tactics of the Devil. 12 For our battle is not against flesh and blood, but against the rulers, against the authorities, against the world powers of this darkness, against the spiritual forces of evil in the heavens. 13 This is why you must take up the full armor of God, so that

you may be able to resist in the evil day, and having prepared everything, to take your stand. 14 Stand, therefore,

with truth like a belt around
  your waist,
righteousness like armor on
  your chest,
15 and your feet sandaled with
  the readiness of the
  gospel of peace.
16 In every situation take the
  shield of faith,
and with it you will be able to
  extinguish
the flaming arrows of the evil
  one.
17 Take the helmet of salvation,
and the sword of the Spirit,
  which is God's word.

18 With every prayer and request, pray at all times in the Spirit, and stay alert in this, with all perseverance and intercession for all the saints. 19 Pray also for me, that the message may be given to me when I open my mouth to make known with boldness the •mystery of the gospel. 20 For this I am an ambassador in chains. Pray that I might be bold enough in Him to speak as I should.

---

*"Whatever problems your family is facing, healing can and will take place if Jesus is allowed to come into your home and sit at the head of the table."*
—Robert and Debra Bruce

---

## Paul's Farewell

21 Tychicus, our dearly loved brother and faithful servant in the Lord, will tell

you everything so that you also may know how I am and what I'm doing. [22] I am sending him to you for this very reason, to let you know how we are and to encourage your hearts.

[23] Peace to the brothers, and love with faith, from God the Father and the Lord Jesus Christ. [24] Grace be with all who have undying love for our Lord Jesus Christ.[a]

[a]**6:24** Other mss add *Amen.*

# PHILIPPIANS

## Greeting

**1** Paul and Timothy, slaves of Christ Jesus:

To all the saints in Christ Jesus who are in Philippi, including the •overseers and deacons.

[2] Grace to you and peace from God our Father and the Lord Jesus Christ.

## Thanksgiving and Prayer

[3] I give thanks to my God for every remembrance of you, [4] always praying with joy for all of you in my every prayer, [5] because of your partnership in the gospel from the first day until now. [6] I am sure of this, that He who started a good work in you will carry it on to completion until the day of Christ Jesus. [7] It is right for me to think this way about all of you, because I have you in my heart, and you are all partners with me in grace, both in my imprisonment and in the defense and establishment of the gospel. [8] For God is my witness, how I deeply miss all of you with the affection of Christ Jesus. [9] And I pray this: that your love will keep on growing in knowledge and every kind of discernment, [10] so that you can determine what really matters and can be pure and blameless in the day of Christ, [11] filled with the fruit of righteousness that ⌊comes⌋ through Jesus Christ, to the glory and praise of God.

## Advance of the Gospel

[12] Now I want you to know, brothers, that what has happened to me has actually resulted in the advancement of the gospel, [13] so that it has become known throughout the whole imperial guard, and to everyone else, that my imprisonment is for Christ. [14] Most of the brothers in the Lord have gained confidence from my imprisonment and dare even more to speak the message[a] fearlessly. [15] Some, to be sure, preach Christ out of envy and strife, but others out of good will. [16] These do so out of love, knowing that I am appointed for the defense of the gospel; [17] the others proclaim Christ out of rivalry, not sincerely, seeking to cause ⌊me⌋ trouble in my imprisonment. [18] What does it matter? Just that in every way, whether out of false motives or true, Christ is proclaimed. And in this I rejoice. Yes, and I will rejoice [19] because I know this will lead to my deliverance through your prayers and help from the Spirit of Jesus Christ. [20] My eager expectation and hope is that I will not be ashamed about anything, but that now as always, with all boldness, Christ will be highly honored in my body, whether by life or by death.

## Living Is Christ

[21] For me, living is Christ and dying is gain. [22] Now if I live on in the flesh, this means fruitful work for me; and I don't know which one I should choose. [23] I am pressured by both. I have the desire to depart and be with Christ—which is far better— [24] but to remain in the flesh is more necessary for you. [25] Since I am persuaded of this, I know that I will remain and continue with all of you for your advancement and joy in the faith, [26] so

[a]1:14 Other mss add *of God*

that, because of me, your confidence may grow in Christ Jesus when I come to you again.

²⁷ Just one thing: live your life in a manner worthy of the gospel of Christ. Then, whether I come and see you or am absent, I will hear about you that you are standing firm in one spirit, with one mind, working side by side for the faith of the gospel, ²⁸ not being frightened in any way by your opponents. This is evidence of their destruction, but of your deliverance— and this is from God. ²⁹ For it has been given to you on Christ's behalf not only to believe in Him, but also to suffer for Him, ³⁰ having the same struggle that you saw I had and now hear about me.

## Christian Humility

**2** If then there is any encouragement in Christ, if any consolation of love, if any fellowship with the Spirit, if any affection and mercy, ² fulfill my joy by thinking the same way, having the same love, sharing the same feelings, focusing on one goal. ³ Do nothing out of rivalry or conceit, but in humility consider others as more important than yourselves. ⁴ Everyone should look out not

---

### Philippian 2:1-4

*Don't be surprised if you can't see eye-to-eye with everybody at church or everybody who claims to know Christ. But surprise them by loving them anyway. You won't like every person you meet in this family, but with God's help, you can learn to get along.*

---

[only] for his own interests, but also for the interests of others.

## Christ's Humility and Exaltation

⁵ Make your own attitude that of Christ Jesus,

⁶ who, existing in the form of God,
· did not consider equality with God
as something to be used for His own advantage.

⁷ Instead He emptied Himself by assuming the form of a slave,
taking on the likeness of men.
And when He had come as a man in His external form,

⁸ He humbled Himself by becoming obedient to the point of death—
even to death on a cross.

⁹ For this reason God also highly exalted Him
and gave Him the name that is above every name,

¹⁰ so that at the name of Jesus every knee should bow—
of those who are in heaven and on earth and under the earth—

¹¹ and every tongue should confess
that Jesus Christ is Lord,
to the glory of God the Father.

## Lights in the World

¹² So then, my dear friends, just as you have always obeyed, not only in my presence, but now even more in my absence, work out your own salvation with fear and trembling. ¹³ For it is God who is working in you, [enabling you] both to will and to act for His good purpose. ¹⁴ Do everything without grumbling and arguing, ¹⁵ so

> *"As long as our knowledge is imperfect, our preferences vary, and our opinions differ, let's leave a lot of room in areas that don't really matter."*
> —Charles Swindoll

that you may be blameless and pure, children of God who are faultless in a crooked and perverted generation, among whom you shine like stars in the world. [16] Hold firmly the message of life. Then I can boast in the day of Christ that I didn't run in vain or labor for nothing. [17] But even if I am poured out as a drink offering on the sacrifice and service of your faith, I am glad and rejoice with all of you. [18] In the same way you also should rejoice and share your joy with me.

## Timothy and Epaphroditus

[19] Now I hope in the Lord Jesus to send Timothy to you soon so that I also may be encouraged when I hear news about you. [20] For I have no one else like-minded who will genuinely care about your interests; [21] all seek their own interests, not those of Jesus Christ. [22] But you know his proven character, because he has served with me in the gospel ministry like a son with a father. [23] Therefore, I hope to send him as soon as I see how things go with me. [24] And I am convinced in the Lord that I myself will also come quickly.

[25] But I considered it necessary to send you Epaphroditus—my brother, co-worker, and fellow soldier, as well as your messenger and minister to my need— [26] since he has been longing for all of you and was distressed because you heard that he was sick. [27] Indeed, he was so sick that he nearly died. However, God had mercy on him, and not only on him but also on me, so that I would not have one grief on top of another. [28] For this reason, I am very eager to send him so that you may rejoice when you see him again and I may be less anxious. [29] Therefore, welcome him in the Lord with all joy and hold men like him in honor, [30] because he came close to death for the work of Christ, risking his life to make up what was lacking in your ministry to me.

## Knowing Christ

3 Finally, my brothers, rejoice in the Lord. To write to you again about this is no trouble for me and is a protection for you.
[2] Watch out for "dogs," watch out for evil workers, watch out for those who mutilate the flesh. [3] For we are the circumcision, the ones who serve by the Spirit of God, boast in Christ Jesus, and do not put confidence in the flesh— [4] although I once had confidence in the flesh too. If anyone else thinks he has grounds for confidence in the flesh, I have more: [5] circumcised the eighth day; of the nation of Israel, of the tribe of Benjamin, a Hebrew born of Hebrews; as to the law, a *Pharisee; [6] as to zeal, persecuting the church; as to the

> *"We must be content with our daily portion, without anxious thought as to anything that may be whirling around us in God's universe."*
> —Hannah Whitall Smith

righteousness that is in the law, blameless. [7] But everything that was a gain to me, I have considered to be a loss because of Christ. [8] More than that, I also consider everything to be a loss in view of the surpassing value of knowing Christ Jesus my Lord. Because of Him I have suffered the loss of all things and consider them filth, so that I may gain Christ [9] and be found in Him, not having a righteousness of my own from the law, but one that is through faith in Christ—the righteousness from God based on faith. [10] ⌊My goal⌋ is to know Him and the power of His resurrection and the fellowship of His sufferings, being conformed to His death, [11] assuming that I will somehow reach the resurrection from among the dead.

## Reaching Forward to God's Goal

[12] Not that I have already reached ⌊the goal⌋ or am already fully mature, but I make every effort to take hold of it because I also have been taken hold of by Christ Jesus. [13] Brothers, I do not[a] consider myself to have taken hold of it. But one thing I do: forgetting what is behind and reaching forward to what is ahead, [14] I pursue as my goal the prize promised by God's heavenly call in Christ Jesus. [15] Therefore, all who are mature should think this way. And if you think differently about anything, God will reveal this to you also. [16] In any case, we should live up to whatever ⌊truth⌋ we have attained. [17] Join in imitating me, brothers, and observe those who live according to the example you have in us. [18] For I have often told you, and now say again with tears, that many live as enemies of the cross of Christ. [19] Their end is destruction;

their god is their stomach; their glory is in their shame. They are focused on earthly things, [20] but our citizenship is in heaven, from which we also eagerly wait for a Savior, the Lord Jesus Christ. [21] He will transform the body of our humble condition into the likeness of His glorious body, by the power that enables Him to subject everything to Himself.

---

*Philippians 3:12-14*

*The story of the tortoise and the hare isn't found in the Bible, but it's running over with a lesson too many of us learn the hard way: Slow and steady wins the race. People who take life in quick bursts of glory miss the sustained experience of Christian victory.*

---

## Practical Counsel

**4** So then, in this way, my dearly loved brothers, my joy and crown, stand firm in the Lord, dear friends. [2] I urge Euodia and I urge Syntyche to agree in the Lord. [3] Yes, I also ask you, true partner, to help these women who have contended for the gospel at my side, along with Clement and the rest of my co-workers whose names are in the book of life. [4] Rejoice in the Lord always. I will say it again: Rejoice! [5] Let your graciousness be known to everyone. The Lord is near. [6] Don't worry about anything, but in everything, through prayer and petition with thanksgiving, let your requests be made known

---

[a]**3:13** Other mss read *not yet*

to God. [7] And the peace of God, which surpasses every thought, will guard your hearts and your minds in Christ Jesus.

[8] Finally brothers, whatever is true, whatever is honorable, whatever is just, whatever is pure, whatever is lovely, whatever is commendable—if there is any moral excellence and if there is any praise—dwell on these things. [9] Do what you have learned and received and heard and seen in me, and the God of peace will be with you.

## Appreciation of Support

[10] I rejoiced in the Lord greatly that now at last you have renewed your care for me. You were, in fact, concerned about me, but lacked the opportunity [to show it]. [11] I don't say this out of need, for I have learned to be content in whatever circumstances I am. [12] I know both how to have a little, and I know how to have a lot. In any and all circumstances I have learned the secret [of being content]—whether well-fed or hungry, whether in abundance or in need. [13] I am able to do all things through Him[a] who strengthens me. [14] Still, you did well by sharing with me in my hardship.

[15] And you, Philippians, know that in the early days of the gospel, when I left Macedonia, no church shared with me in the matter of giving and receiving except you alone. [16] For even in Thessalonica you sent [gifts] for my need several times. [17] Not that I seek the gift, but I seek the fruit that is increasing to your account. [18] But I have received everything in full, and I have an abundance. I am fully supplied, having received from Epaphroditus what you provided—a fragrant offering, a welcome sacrifice, pleasing to God. [19] And my God will supply all your needs according to His riches in glory in Christ Jesus. [20] Now to our God and Father be glory forever and ever. •Amen.

## Final Greetings

[21] Greet every saint in Christ Jesus. Those brothers who are with me greet you. [22] All the saints greet you, but especially those from Caesar's household. [23] The grace of the Lord Jesus Christ be with your spirit.

[a]4:13 Other mss read *Christ*

# COLOSSIANS

## Greeting

**1** Paul, an apostle of Christ Jesus by God's will, and Timothy our brother:

² To the saints and faithful brothers in Christ in Colossae.

Grace to you and peace from God our Father.ᵃ

## Thanksgiving

³ We always thank God, the Father of our Lord Jesus Christ, when we pray for you, ⁴ for we have heard of your faith in Christ Jesus and of the love you have for all the saints ⁵ because of the hope reserved for you in heaven. You have already heard about ⌊this hope⌋ in the message of truth, ⁶ the gospel that has come to you. It is bearing fruit and growing all over the world, just as it has among you since the day you heard it and recognized God's grace in the truth. ⁷ You learned this from Epaphras, our much loved fellow slave. He is a faithful minister of the •Messiah on yourᵇ behalf, ⁸ and he has told us about your love in the Spirit.

## Prayer for Spiritual Growth

⁹ For this reason also, since the day we heard this, we haven't stopped praying for you. We are asking that you may be filled with the knowledge of His will in all wisdom and spiritual understanding, ¹⁰ so that you may •walk worthy of the Lord, fully pleasing ⌊to Him⌋, bearing fruit in every good work and growing in the knowledge of God. ¹¹ May you be strengthened with all power, according to His glorious might, for all endurance and patience, with joy ¹² giving thanks to the Father, who has enabled youᶜ to share in the saints' inheritance in the light. ¹³ He has rescued us from the domain of darkness and transferred us into the kingdom of the Son He loves, ¹⁴ in whom we have redemption,ᵈ the forgiveness of sins.

---

### Colossians 1:15-20

### God the Son

*In Jesus we see a man, doing human things. In this passage we see the Son, doing things no one ever imagined. We see how complete His authority is, how total His reign, how perfectly qualified He is to bear the penalty for our sins without us ever having to worry that His promise might fail.*

---

## The Centrality of Christ

¹⁵ He is the image of the
    invisible God,
    the firstborn over all
    creation;
¹⁶ because by Him
    everything was created,
    in heaven and on earth,

---

ᵃ1:2 Other mss add *and the Lord Jesus Christ*  ᵇ1:7 Other mss read *our*  ᶜ1:12 Other mss read *us*  ᵈ1:14 Other mss add *through His blood*

the visible and the invisible,
whether thrones or
    dominions
or rulers or authorities—
all things have been created
    through Him and for Him.
[17] He is before all things,
and by Him all things hold
    together.
[18] He is also the head of the
    body, the church;
He is the beginning,
the firstborn from the dead,
so that He might come to
    have first place in
    everything.
[19] Because all the fullness was
    pleased to dwell in Him,
[20] and to reconcile everything to
    Himself through Him
by making peace through the
    blood of His cross[a]—
whether things on earth or
    things in heaven.

[21] And you were once alienated and hostile in mind because of your evil actions. [22] But now He has reconciled you by His physical body through His death, to present you holy, faultless, and blameless before Him—[23] if indeed you remain grounded and steadfast in the faith, and are not shifted away from the hope of the gospel that you heard. [This gospel] has been proclaimed in all creation under heaven, and I, Paul, have become a minister of it.

## Paul's Ministry

[24] Now I rejoice in my sufferings for you, and I am completing in my flesh what is lacking in Christ's afflictions for His body, that is, the church. [25] I have become its minister, according to God's administration that was given to me for you, to make God's message fully known, [26] the *mystery hidden for ages and generations but now revealed to His saints. [27] God wanted to make known to those among the Gentiles the glorious wealth of this mystery, which is Christ in you, the hope of glory. [28] We proclaim Him, warning and teaching everyone with all wisdom, so that we may present everyone mature in Christ. [29] I labor for this, striving with His strength that works powerfully in me.

**2** For I want you to know how great a struggle I have for you, for those in Laodicea, and for all who have not seen me in person. [2] [I want] their hearts to be encouraged and joined together in love, so that they may have all the riches of assured understanding, and have the knowledge of God's *mystery—Christ.[b] [3] In Him all the treasures of wisdom and knowledge are hidden.

---

### Colossians 2:6-10

*It's no big surprise that the Christian way of thinking is totally foreign to the worldly mind. But it has to become second nature to you if you're to have any impact. Everyone operates from a basic belief system. Get to know yours—so you can both practice and defend it.*

---

### Christ versus the Colossian Heresy

[4] I am saying this so that no one will deceive you with persuasive argu-

---

[a]**1:20** Other mss add *through Him*    [b]**2:2** Other mss read *mystery of God, both of the Father and of Christ;* other ms variations exist on this v.

ments. [5] For I may be absent in body, but I am with you in spirit, rejoicing to see your good order and the strength of your faith in Christ.

[6] Therefore as you have received Christ Jesus the Lord, •walk in Him, [7] rooted and built up in Him and established in the faith, just as you were taught, and overflowing with thankfulness.

[8] Be careful that no one takes you captive through philosophy and empty deceit based on human tradition, based on the elemental forces of the world, and not based on Christ. [9] For in Him the entire fullness of God's nature dwells bodily, [10] and you have been filled by Him, who is the head over every ruler and authority. [11] In Him you were also circumcised with a circumcision not done with hands, by putting off the body of flesh, in the circumcision of the •Messiah. [12] Having been buried with Him in baptism, you were also raised with Him through faith in the working of God, who raised Him from the dead. [13] And when you were dead in trespasses and in the uncircumcision of your flesh, He made you alive with Him and forgave us all our trespasses. [14] He erased the certificate of debt, with its obligations, that was against us and opposed to us, and has taken it out of the way by nailing it to the cross. [15] He disarmed the rulers and authorities and disgraced them publicly; He triumphed over them by Him.

[16] Therefore don't let anyone judge you in regard to food and

---

*"Christianity is true, and its truth will be discovered anywhere you look very far."*
—*George Gilder*

---

## Colossians 3:9-11

### Man

*Mankind has only one hope of ever becoming more than he is. That hope is in Jesus Christ, who alone has the power to do away with the "old man"—the habits and restraints of our sinful selves—and to form in us something totally new—a person ruled by our loving Lord and Savior.*

---

drink or in the matter of a festival or a new moon or a sabbath day. [17] These are a shadow of what was to come; the substance is the Messiah. [18] Let no one disqualify you, insisting on ascetic practices and the worship of angels, claiming access to a visionary realm and inflated without cause by his fleshly mind. [19] He doesn't hold on to the Head, from whom the whole body, nourished and held together by its ligaments and tendons, develops with growth from God.

[20] If you died with Christ to the elemental forces of this world, why do you live as if you still belonged to the world? Why do you submit to regulations: [21] "Don't handle, don't taste, don't touch"? [22] All these ⌊regulations⌋ refer to what is destroyed by being used up; they are human commands and doctrines. [23] Although these have a reputation of wisdom by promoting ascetic practices, humility, and severe treatment of the body, they are not of any value against fleshly indulgence.

## The Life of the New Man

**3** So if you have been raised with the •Messiah, seek what is above, where the Messiah is, seated at the right hand of God. [2] Set your minds on what is above, not on what is on the earth. [3] For you have died, and your life is hidden with the Messiah in God. [4] When the Messiah, who is your[a] life, is revealed, then you also will be revealed with Him in glory.

[5] Therefore, put to death whatever in you is worldly: sexual immorality, impurity, lust, evil desire, and greed, which is idolatry. [6] Because of these, God's wrath comes on the disobedient,[h] [7] and you once walked in these things when you were living in them. [8] But now you must also put away all the following: anger, wrath, malice, slander, and filthy language from your mouth. [9] Do not lie to one another, since you have put off the old man with his practices [10] and have put on the new man, who is being renewed in knowledge according to the image of his Creator. [11] Here there is not Greek and Jew, circumcision and uncircumcision, barbarian, Scythian, slave and free; but Christ is all and in all.

## The Christian Life

[12] Therefore, God's chosen ones, holy and loved, put on heartfelt compassion, kindness, humility, gentleness, and patience, [13] accepting one another and forgiving one another if anyone has a complaint against another. Just as the Lord has forgiven you, so also you must ⌊forgive⌋. [14] Above all, ⌊put on⌋ love—the perfect bond of unity. [15] And let the peace of the Messiah, to which you were also called in one body, control your hearts. Be thankful. [16] Let the message about the Messiah dwell richly among you, teaching and admonishing one another in all wisdom, and singing psalms, hymns, and spiritual songs, with gratitude in your hearts to God. [17] And whatever you do, in word or in deed, do everything in the name of the Lord Jesus, giving thanks to God the Father through Him.

## Christ in Your Home

[18] Wives, be submissive to your husbands, as is fitting in the Lord.

[19] Husbands, love your wives and don't become bitter against them.

[20] Children, obey your parents in everything, for this is pleasing in the Lord.

[21] Fathers, do not exasperate your children, so they won't become discouraged.

[22] Slaves, obey your human masters in everything; don't work only while being watched, in order to please men, but ⌊work⌋ wholeheartedly, fearing the Lord.

[23] Whatever you do, do it enthusiastically, as something done for the Lord and not for men, [24] knowing that you will receive the reward of an inheritance from the Lord—you serve the Lord Christ. [25] For the wrongdoer will be paid back for whatever wrong he has done, and there is no favoritism.

**4** [1] Masters, supply your slaves with what is right and fair, since you know that you too have a Master in heaven.

---

a3:4 Other mss read *our*    b3:6 Other mss omit *on the disobedient*

## Speaking to God and Others

2 Devote yourselves to prayer; stay alert in it with thanksgiving. 3 At the same time, pray also for us that God may open a door to us for the message, to speak the *mystery of the *Messiah—for which I am in prison— 4 so that I may reveal it as I am required to speak. 5 *Walk in wisdom toward outsiders, making the most of the time. 6 Your speech should always be gracious, seasoned with salt, so that you may know how you should answer each person.

## Christian Greetings

7 Tychicus, a loved brother, a faithful servant, and a fellow slave in the Lord, will tell you all the news about me. 8 I have sent him to you for this very purpose, so that you may know how we are,[a] and so that he may encourage your hearts. 9 He is with Onesimus, a faithful and loved brother,

---

### Colossians 4:5-6

*Life puts you in contact with a lot of different people. Some are fun to be around. Some are a challenge. But God has put them all into your life for a reason. Friend or foe, relevant or seemingly irrelevant, every person in your life is a ministry opportunity.*

---

---

*"If we will reach out to and hold on to each other, we will find companionship on our journey."*
—*Sheila Walsh*

---

who is one of you. They will tell you about everything here.
10 Aristarchus, my fellow prisoner, greets you, as does Mark, Barnabas' cousin (concerning whom you have received instructions: if he comes to you, welcome him), 11 and so does Jesus who is called Justus. These alone of the circumcision are my co-workers for the kingdom of God, and they have been a comfort to me. 12 Epaphras, who is one of you, a slave of Christ Jesus, greets you. He is always contending for you in his prayers, so that you can stand mature and fully assured[b] in everything God wills. 13 For I testify about him that he works hard[c] for you, for those in Laodicea, and for those in Hierapolis. 14 Luke, the loved physician, and Demas greet you. 15 Give my greetings to the brothers in Laodicea, and to Nympha and the church in her house. 16 And when this letter has been read among you, have it read also in the church of the Laodiceans; and see that you also read the letter from Laodicea. 17 And tell Archippus, "Pay attention to the ministry you have received in the Lord, so that you can accomplish it."
18 This greeting is in my own hand—Paul. Remember my imprisonment. Grace be with you.[d]

---

[a]4:8 Other mss read *that he may know how you are*  [b]4:12 Other mss read *and complete*  [c]4:13 Other mss read *he has a great zeal*  [d]4:18 Other mss add *Amen.*

# 1 THESSALONIANS

## Greeting

**1** Paul, Silvanus, and Timothy:

To the church of the Thessalonians in God the Father and the Lord Jesus Christ.

Grace to you and peace.[a]

## Thanksgiving

[2] We always thank God for all of you, remembering you constantly in our prayers. [3] We recall, in the presence of our God and Father, your work of faith, labor of love, and endurance of hope in our Lord Jesus Christ, [4] knowing your election, brothers loved by God. [5] For our gospel did not come to you in word only, but also in power, in the Holy Spirit, and with much assurance. You know what kind of men we were among you for your benefit, [6] and you became imitators of us and of the Lord when, in spite of severe persecution, you welcomed the message with the joy from the Holy Spirit. [7] As a result, you became an example to all the believers in Macedonia and Achaia. [8] For the Lord's message rang out from you, not only in Macedonia and Achaia, but in every place that your faith in God has gone out, so we don't need to say anything. [9] For they themselves report about us what kind of reception we had from you: how you turned to God from idols to serve the living and true God, [10] and to wait for His Son from heaven, whom He raised from the dead—Jesus, who rescues us from the coming wrath.

## Paul's Conduct

**2** For you yourselves know, brothers, that our visit with you was not without result. [2] On the contrary, after we had previously suffered and been outrageously treated in Philippi, as you know, we were emboldened by our God to speak the gospel of God to you in spite of great opposition. [3] For our exhortation didn't come from error or impurity or an intent to deceive. [4] Instead, just as we have been approved by God to be entrusted with the gospel, so we speak, not to please men, but rather God, who examines our hearts. [5] For we never used flattering speech, as you know, or had greedy motives—God is our witness— [6] and we didn't seek glory from people, either from you or from others. [7] Although we could have been a burden as Christ's apostles, instead we were gentle[b] among you, as a nursing mother nurtures her own children. [8] We cared so much for you that we were pleased to share with you not

[a]1:1 Other mss add *from God our Father and the Lord Jesus Christ*    [b]2:7 Other mss read *infants*

only the gospel of God but also our own lives, because you had become dear to us. [9] For you remember our labor and hardship, brothers. Working night and day so that we would not burden any of you, we preached God's gospel to you. [10] You are witnesses, and so is God, of how devoutly, righteously, and blamelessly we conducted ourselves with you believers. [11] As you know, like a father with his own children, [12] we encouraged, comforted, and implored each one of you to •walk worthy of God, who calls you into His own kingdom and glory.

---

*"Many times our human desire to be acceptable to everyone keeps us from being real in all but the most superficial ways."*
*—Jim Smoke*

---

## Reception and Opposition to the Message

[13] Also, this is why we constantly thank God, because when you received the message about God that you heard from us, you welcomed it not as a human message, but as it truly is, the message of God, which also works effectively in you believers. [14] For you, brothers, became imitators of God's churches in Christ Jesus that are in Judea, since you have also suffered the same things from people of your own country, just as they did from the Jews. [15] They killed both the Lord Jesus and the prophets, and persecuted us; they displease God, and are hostile to everyone, [16] hindering us from speaking to the Gentiles so that they may be saved. As a result, they are always

adding to the number of their sins, and wrath has overtaken them completely.

## Paul's Desire to See Them

[17] But as for us, brothers, after we were forced to leave you for a short time (in person, not in heart), we greatly desired and made every effort to return and see you face to face. [18] So we wanted to come to you— even I, Paul, time and again—but Satan hindered us. [19] For who is our hope, or joy, or crown of boasting in the presence of our Lord Jesus at His coming? Is it not you? [20] For you are our glory and joy!

## Anxiety in Athens

**3** Therefore, when we could no longer stand it, we thought it was better to be left alone in Athens. [2] And we sent Timothy, our brother and God's co-worker[a] in the gospel of Christ, to strengthen and encourage you concerning your faith, [3] so that no one will be shaken by these persecutions. For you yourselves know that we are appointed to this. [4] In fact, when we were with you, we told you previously that we were going to suffer persecution, and as you know, it happened. [5] For this reason, when I could no longer stand it, I also sent to find out about your faith, fearing that the tempter had tempted you and that our labor might be for nothing.

## Encouraged by Timothy

[6] But now Timothy has come to us from you and brought us good news about your faith and love, and that you always have good memories of us, wanting to see us, as we also want to

---

[a]3:2 Other mss read *servant*

see you. [7] Therefore, brothers, in all our distress and persecution, we were encouraged about you through your faith. [8] For now we live, if you stand firm in the Lord. [9] How can we thank God for you in return for all the joy we experience because of you before our God, [10] as we pray earnestly night and day to see you face to face and to complete what is lacking in your faith?

## Prayer for the Church

[11] Now may our God and Father Himself, and our Lord Jesus, direct our way to you. [12] And may the Lord cause you to increase and overflow with love for one another and for everyone, just as we also do for you. [13] May He make your hearts blameless in holiness before our God and Father at the coming of our Lord Jesus with all His saints. *Amen.[a]

## The Call to Sanctification

**4** Finally then, brothers, we ask and encourage you in the Lord Jesus, that as you have received from us how you must *walk and please God—as you are doing—do so even more. [2] For you know what commands we gave you through the Lord Jesus. [3] For this is God's will, your sanctification: that you abstain from sexual immorality, [4] so that each of you knows how to possess his own vessel in sanctification and honor, [5] not with lustful desires, like the Gentiles who don't know God. [6] This means one must not transgress against and defraud his brother in this matter, because the Lord is an avenger of all these offenses, as we also previously told and warned you. [7] For God has not called us to impurity, but to sanctification.

[a]**3:13** Other mss omit *Amen.*

[8] Therefore, the person who rejects this does not reject man, but God, who also gives you His Holy Spirit.

## Loving and Working

[9] About brotherly love: you don't need me to write you because you yourselves are taught by God to love one another. [10] In fact, you are doing this toward all the brothers in the entire region of Macedonia. But we encourage you, brothers, to do so even more, [11] to seek to lead a quiet life, to mind your own business, and to work with your own hands, as we commanded you, [12] so that you may walk properly in the presence of outsiders and not be dependent on anyone.

## The Comfort of Christ's Coming

[13] We do not want you to be uninformed, brothers, concerning those who are *asleep, so that you will not grieve like the rest, who have no hope. [14] Since we believe that Jesus died and rose again, in the same way God will bring with Him those who have fallen asleep through Jesus. [15] For we say this to you by a revelation from the Lord: We who are still

---

### 1 Thessalonians 4:13-18

*Jesus Christ is coming back to earth through a real sky on a real day to take real people to a real paradise. Wouldn't you really like to be here to see that? Just as surely as you believe He lay in a manger, He's going to peel back the sky and call us home.*

---

*"Somewhere, somewhen, somehow, we who are worshiping God here will wake up to see Him as He is, face to face."*
*—John Baillie*

alive at the Lord's coming will certainly have no advantage over those who have fallen asleep. [16] For the Lord Himself will descend from heaven with a shout, with the archangel's voice, and with the trumpet of God, and the dead in Christ will rise first. [17] Then we who are still alive will be caught up together with them in the clouds to meet the Lord in the air; and so we will always be with the Lord. [18] Therefore encourage one another with these words.

## The Day of the Lord

5 About the times and the seasons: brothers, you do not need anything to be written to you. [2] For you yourselves know very well that the Day of the Lord will come just like a thief in the night. [3] When they say, "Peace and security," then sudden destruction comes on them, like labor pains on a pregnant woman, and they will not escape. [4] But you, brothers, are not in the dark, so that this day would overtake you like a thief. [5] For you are all sons of light and sons of the day. We're not of the night or of darkness. [6] So then, we must not sleep, like the rest, but we must stay awake and be sober. [7] For those who sleep, sleep at night, and those who get drunk are drunk at night. [8] But since we are of the day, we must be sober and put the armor of faith and love on our chests, and

put on a helmet of the hope of salvation. [9] For God did not appoint us to wrath, but to obtain salvation through our Lord Jesus Christ, [10] who died for us, so that whether we are awake or *asleep, we will live together with Him. [11] Therefore encourage one another and build each other up as you are already doing.

## Exhortations and Blessings

[12] Now we ask you, brothers, to give recognition to those who labor among you and lead you in the Lord and admonish you, [13] and to esteem them very highly in love because of their work. Be at peace among yourselves. [14] And we exhort you, brothers: warn those who are lazy, comfort the discouraged, help the weak, be patient with everyone. [15] See to it that no one repays evil for evil to anyone, but always pursue what is good for one another and for all.

[16] Rejoice always!
[17] Pray constantly.
[18] Give thanks in everything,

*1 Thessalonians 5:23-24*

*God's Assurance*

*In this passage, we see the three compartments of the human make-up: the spirit, the soul, and the body. And we see the three persons of the Godhead: the Holy Spirit "sanctifying" us, encouraging us to obedience, the Son preparing for His near return, the Father faithfully keeping us ready.*

for this is God's will for you in Christ Jesus.

19 Don't stifle the Spirit.

20 Don't despise prophecies,

21 but test all things.

Hold on to what is good.

22 Stay away from every form of evil.

23 Now may the God of peace Himself sanctify you completely. And may your spirit, soul, and body be kept sound and blameless for the coming of our Lord Jesus Christ. 24 He who calls you is faithful, who also will do it. 25 Brothers, pray for us also. 26 Greet all the brothers with a holy kiss. 27 I charge you by the Lord that this letter be read to all the brothers. 28 May the grace of our Lord Jesus Christ be with you!

# 2 THESSALONIANS

## Greeting

**1** Paul, Silvanus, and Timothy:

To the church of the Thessalonians in God our Father and the Lord Jesus Christ.

² Grace to you and peace from God our Father and the Lord Jesus Christ.

## God's Judgment and Glory

³ We must always thank God for you, brothers, which is fitting, since your faith is flourishing, and the love of every one of you for one another is increasing. ⁴ Therefore we ourselves boast about you among God's churches—about your endurance and faith in all the persecutions and afflictions you endure. ⁵ It is a clear evidence of God's righteous judgment that you will be counted worthy of God's kingdom, for which you also are suffering, ⁶ since it is righteous for God to repay with affliction those who afflict you, ⁷ and ⌊to reward⌋ with rest you who are afflicted, along with us. ⌊This will take place⌋ at the revelation of the Lord Jesus from heaven with His powerful angels, ⁸ taking vengeance with flaming fire on those who don't know God and on those who don't obey the gospel of our Lord Jesus. ⁹ These will pay the penalty of everlasting destruction, away from the Lord's presence and from His glorious strength, ¹⁰ in that day when He comes to be glorified by His saints and to be admired by all those who have believed, because our testimony among you was believed. ¹¹ And in view of this, we always pray for you that our God will consider you worthy of His calling, and will, by His power, fulfill every desire for goodness and the work of faith, ¹² so that the name of our Lord Jesus will be glorified by you, and you by Him, according to the grace of our God and the Lord Jesus Christ.

## The Man of Lawlessness

**2** Now concerning the coming of our Lord Jesus Christ and our being gathered to Him: we ask you, brothers, ² not to be easily upset in mind or troubled, either by a spirit or by a message or by a letter as if from us, alleging that the Day of the Lord[a] has come. ³ Don't let anyone deceive you in any way. For ⌊that day⌋ will not come unless the apostasy comes first and the man of lawlessness[b] is revealed, the son of destruction. ⁴ He opposes and exalts himself above every so-called god or object of worship, so that he sits[c] in God's sanctuary, publicizing that he himself is God.

⁵ Don't you remember that when I was still with you I told you about this? ⁶ And you know what currently restrains ⌊him⌋, so that he will be revealed in his time. ⁷ For the •mystery of lawlessness is already at work; but the one now restraining will do so until he is out of the way, ⁸ and then the lawless one will be revealed. The Lord Jesus will destroy him with the breath of His mouth and will bring him to nothing with the brightness of His coming. ⁹ The coming ⌊of the lawless one⌋ is based on Satan's working,

<hr>

**a2:2** Other mss read *Christ*   **b2:3** Other mss read *man of sin*   **c2:4** Other mss add *as God*

---

*2 Thessalonians 2:13-14*

*God's Grace*

*Glory is a great Bible word. Its definitions make us think of the radiance and brilliant light of Christ's appearance. But no word picture can paint the feeling of His presence in all its dazzling color and expression. God is here, and we get to enjoy Him. That's glory. That's God's desire.*

---

with all kinds of false miracles, signs, and wonders, [10] and with every unrighteous deception among those who are perishing. [They perish] because they did not accept the love of the truth in order to be saved. [11] For this reason God sends them a strong delusion so that they will believe what is false, [12] so that all will be condemned—those who did not believe the truth but enjoyed unrighteousness.

*Stand Firm*

[13] But we must always thank God for you, brothers loved by the Lord, because from the beginning[a] God has chosen you for salvation through sanctification by the Spirit and through belief in the truth. [14] He called you to this through our gospel, so that you might obtain the glory of our Lord Jesus Christ. [15] Therefore, brothers, stand firm and hold to the traditions you were taught, either by our message or by our letter.

[a]**2:13** Other mss read *because as a firstfruit*

[16] May our Lord Jesus Christ Himself and God our Father, who has loved us and given us eternal encouragement and good hope by grace, [17] encourage your hearts and strengthen you in every good work and word.

*Pray for Us*

**3** Finally, pray for us, brothers, that the Lord's message may spread rapidly and be honored, just as it was with you, [2] and that we may be delivered from wicked and evil men, for not all have faith. [3] But the Lord is faithful; He will strengthen and guard you from the evil one. [4] We have confidence in the Lord about you, that you are doing and will do what we command. [5] May the Lord direct your hearts to God's love and Christ's endurance.

*Warning against Irresponsible Behavior*

[6] Now we command you, brothers, in the name of our Lord Jesus Christ, to keep away from every brother who ʼwalks irresponsibly and not according to the tradition received from us. [7] For you yourselves know how you must imitate us: we were not

---

*2 Thessalonians 3:6-10*

*One thing that should look a little different through Christian eyes is the place where you work, the people you work with, and the job that's expected of you. No longer is work or school just the necessary nightmare between you and a fun weekend.*

---

irresponsible among you; [8] we did not eat anyone's bread free of charge; instead, we labored and toiled, working night and day, so that we would not be a burden to any of you. [9] It is not that we don't have the right ⌊to support⌋, but we did it to make ourselves an example to you so that you would imitate us. [10] In fact, when we were with you, this is what we commanded you: "If anyone isn't willing to work, he should not eat." [11] For we hear that there are some among you who walk irresponsibly, not working at all, but interfering with the work ⌊of others⌋. [12] Now we command and exhort such people, by the Lord Jesus Christ, that quietly working, they may eat their own bread. [13] But you, brothers, do not grow weary in doing good.

[14] And if anyone does not obey our instruction in this letter, take note of that person; don't associate with him, so that he may be ashamed. [15] Yet don't treat him as an enemy, but warn him as a brother.

---

*"To follow Jesus means first and foremost to discover in our daily lives God's unique vocation for us."*
—*Henri Nouwen*

---

## Final Greetings

[16] May the Lord of peace Himself give you peace always in every way. The Lord be with all of you. [17] This greeting is in my own hand—Paul. This is a sign in every letter; this is how I write. [18] The grace of our Lord Jesus Christ be with all of you.

# 1 TIMOTHY

## Greeting

**1** Paul, an apostle of Christ Jesus according to the command of God our Savior and of Christ Jesus, our hope:

[2] To Timothy, my true child in the faith.

Grace, mercy, and peace from God the[a] Father and Christ Jesus our Lord.

## False Doctrine and Misuse of the Law

[3] As I urged you when I went to Macedonia, remain in Ephesus so that you may command certain people not to teach other doctrine [4] or to pay attention to myths and endless genealogies. These promote empty speculations rather than God's plan, which operates by faith. [5] Now the goal of our instruction is love from a pure heart, a good conscience, and a sincere faith. [6] Some have deviated from these and turned aside to fruitless discussion. [7] They want to be teachers of the law, although they don't understand what they are saying or what they are insisting on. [8] Now we know that the law is good, provided one uses it legitimately. [9] We know that the law is not meant for a righteous person, but for the lawless and rebellious, for the ungodly and sinful, for the unholy and irreverent, for those who kill their fathers and mothers, for murderers, [10] for the sexually immoral and homosexuals, for kidnappers, liars, perjurers, and for whatever else is contrary to the sound teaching [11] based on the

glorious gospel of the blessed God that was entrusted to me.

## Paul's Testimony

[12] I give thanks to Christ Jesus our Lord, who has strengthened me, because He considered me faithful, appointing me to the ministry— [13] one who was formerly a blasphemer, a persecutor, and a violent man. But I received mercy because I had acted ignorantly in unbelief, [14] and the grace of our Lord overflowed, along with the faith and love that are in Christ Jesus. [15] This saying is trustworthy and deserving of full acceptance: "Christ Jesus came into the world to save sinners"—and I am the worst of them. [16] But I received mercy because of this, so that in me, the worst ⌊of them⌋, Christ Jesus might demonstrate the utmost patience as an example to those who

[a]**1:2** Other mss read *our*

would believe in Him for eternal life. [17] Now to the King eternal, immortal, invisible, the only[a] God, be honor and glory forever and ever. •Amen.

### Engage in Battle

[18] Timothy, my child, I am giving you this instruction in keeping with the prophecies previously made about you, so that by them you may strongly engage in battle, [19] having faith and a good conscience. Some have rejected these and have suffered the shipwreck of their faith. [20] Hymenaeus and Alexander are among them, and I have delivered them to Satan, so that they may be taught not to blaspheme.

### Instructions on Prayer

**2** First of all, then, I urge that petitions, prayers, intercessions, and thanksgivings be made for everyone, [2] for kings and all those who are in authority, so that we may lead a tranquil and quiet life in all godliness and dignity. [3] This is good, and it pleases God our Savior, [4] who wants everyone to be saved and to come to the knowledge of the truth.

[5] For there is one God
and one mediator between
     God and man,
a man, Christ Jesus,
[6] who gave Himself—a ransom
     for all,
a testimony at the proper
     time.

[7] For this I was appointed a herald, an apostle (I am telling the truth;[b] I am not lying), and a teacher of the Gentiles in faith and truth.

---

*1 Timothy 2:5-6*

### God the Son

*A wide chasm yawns to a terrifying depth and an impossible distance across. On your side of the canyon is nothing but death, sin, despair. On the other side is life, freedom, security. Your best jump is a bazillion times too short. But the Father has made a way. The Son has made a bridge.*

---

### Instructions to Men and Women

[8] Therefore I want the men in every place to pray, lifting up holy hands without anger or argument. [9] Also, the women are to dress themselves in modest clothing, with decency and good sense; not with elaborate hairstyles, gold, pearls, or expensive apparel, [10] but with good works, as is proper for women who affirm that they worship God. [11] A woman should learn in silence with full submission. [12] I do not allow a woman to teach or to have authority over a man; instead, she is to be silent. [13] For Adam was created first, then Eve. [14] And Adam was not deceived, but the woman was deceived and transgressed. [15] But she will be saved through childbearing, if they continue in faith, love, and holiness, with good sense.

### Qualifications of Church Leaders

**3** This saying is trustworthy: "If anyone aspires to be an •overseer, he

---

[a]1:17 Other mss add *wise*   [b]2:7 Other mss add *in Christ*

desires a noble work." [2] An overseer, therefore, must be above reproach, the husband of one wife, self-controlled, sensible, respectable, hospitable, an able teacher, [3] not addicted to wine, not a bully but gentle, not quarrelsome, not greedy— [4] one who manages his own household competently, having his children under control with all dignity. [5] (If anyone does not know how to manage his own household, how will he take care of God's church?) [6] He must not be a new convert, or he might become conceited and fall into the condemnation of the Devil. [7] Furthermore, he must have a good reputation among outsiders, so that he does not fall into disgrace and the Devil's trap.

[8] Deacons, likewise, should be worthy of respect, not hypocritical, not drinking a lot of wine, not greedy for money, [9] holding the *mystery of the faith with a clear conscience. [10] And they must also be tested first; if they prove blameless, then they can serve as deacons. [11] Wives, too, must be worthy of respect, not slanderers, self-controlled, faithful in everything. [12] Deacons must be husbands of one wife, managing their children and their own households competently. [13] For those who have served well as deacons acquire a good standing for themselves, and great boldness in the faith that is in Christ Jesus.

## The Mystery of Godliness

[14] I write these things to you, hoping to come to you soon. [15] But if I should be delayed, ⌊I have written⌋ so that you will know how people ought to act in God's household, which is the church of the living God, the pillar and foundation of the truth. [16] And most certainly, the mystery of godliness is great:

a[3:16] Other mss read *God*

He[a] was manifested in the
    flesh,
justified in the Spirit,
seen by angels,
preached among the
    Gentiles,
believed on in the world,
taken up in glory.

## Demonic Influence

4 Now the Spirit explicitly says that in the latter times some will depart from the faith, paying attention to deceitful spirits and the teachings of demons, [2] through the hypocrisy of liars whose consciences are seared. [3] They forbid marriage and demand abstinence from foods that God created to be received with gratitude by those who believe and know the truth. [4] For everything created by God is good, and nothing should be rejected if it is received with thanksgiving, [5] since it is sanctified by the word of God and by prayer.

## A Good Servant of Jesus Christ

[6] If you point these things out to the brothers, you will be a good servant of Christ Jesus, nourished by the words of the faith and of the good teaching that you have followed. [7] But have nothing to do with irreverent and silly myths. Rather, train yourself in godliness, [8] for,

the training of the body has a
    limited benefit,
but godliness is beneficial in
    every way,
since it holds promise for the
    present life
and also for the life to come.

[9] This saying is trustworthy and deserves full acceptance. [10] In fact, we

labor and strive[a] for this, because we have put our hope in the living God, who is the Savior of everyone, especially of those who believe.

## Instructions for Ministry

[11] Command and teach these things. [12] No one should despise your youth; instead, you should be an example to the believers in speech, in conduct, in love,[b] in faith, in purity. [13] Until I come, give your attention to public reading, exhortation, and teaching. [14] Do not neglect the gift that is in you; it was given to you through prophecy, with the laying on of hands by the council of elders. [15] Practice these things; be committed to them, so that your progress may be evident to all. [16] Be conscientious about yourself and your teaching; persevere in these things, for by doing this you will save both yourself and your hearers.

**5** Do not rebuke an older man, but exhort him as a father, younger men as brothers, [2] older women as mothers, and with all propriety, the younger women as sisters.

## The Support of Widows

[3] Support widows who are genuinely widows. [4] But if any widow has children or grandchildren, they should learn to practice their religion toward their own family first and to repay their parents, for this pleases God. [5] The real widow, left all alone, has put her hope in God and continues night and day in her petitions and prayers; [6] however, she who is self-indulgent is dead even while she lives. [7] Command this, so that they won't be blamed. [8] Now if anyone does not provide for his own relatives, and especially for his household, he has denied the faith and is worse than an unbeliever.

[9] No widow should be placed on the official support list unless she is at least 60 years old, has been the wife of one husband, [10] and is well known for good works—that is, if she has brought up children, shown hospitality, washed the saints' feet, helped the afflicted, and devoted herself to every good work. [11] But refuse to enroll younger widows; for when they are drawn away from Christ by desire, they want to marry, [12] and will therefore receive condemnation because they have renounced their original pledge. [13] At the same time, they also learn to be idle, going from house to house; they are not only idle, but are also gossips and busybodies, saying things they shouldn't say. [14] Therefore, I want younger women to marry, have children, manage their households, and give the adversary no opportunity to accuse us. [15] For some have already turned away to follow Satan. [16] If any[c] believing woman has widows, she should help them, and the church should not be burdened, so that it can help those who are genuinely widows.

## Honoring the Elders

[17] The elders who are good leaders should be considered worthy of an ample honorarium, especially those who work hard at preaching and teaching. [18] For the Scripture says:

> **You must not muzzle an ox**
> **that is threshing grain,**[d] and,
> The laborer is worthy of his pay.

[19] Don't accept an accusation against an elder unless it is supported

---

[a]**4:10** Other mss read *and suffer reproach*   [b]**4:12** Other mss add *in spirit*   [c]**5:16** Other mss add *believing man or*   [d]**5:18** Dt 25:4

by two or three witnesses. [20] Publicly rebuke those who sin, so that the rest will also be afraid. [21] I solemnly charge you, before God and Christ Jesus and the elect angels, to observe these things without prejudice, doing nothing out of favoritism. [22] Don't be too quick to lay hands on anyone, and don't share in the sins of others. Keep yourself pure. [23] Don't continue drinking only water, but use a little wine because of your stomach and your frequent illnesses. [24] Some people's sins are evident, going before them to judgment, but ⌊the sins⌋ of others follow them. [25] Likewise, good works are obvious, and those that are not ⌊obvious⌋ cannot remain hidden.

## Honoring Masters

**6** All who are under the yoke as slaves must regard their own masters to be worthy of all respect, so that God's name and His teaching will not be blasphemed. [2] And those who have believing masters should not be disrespectful to them because they are brothers, but should serve them better, since those who benefit from their service are believers and dearly loved.

## False Doctrine and Human Greed

Teach and encourage these things. [3] If anyone teaches other doctrine and does not agree with the sound teaching of our Lord Jesus Christ and with the teaching that promotes godliness, [4] he is conceited, understanding nothing, but having a sick interest in disputes and arguments over words. From these come envy, quarreling, slanders, evil suspicions, [5] and constant disagreement among men whose minds are depraved and deprived of the truth, who imagine that godliness is a way to material gain.[a] [6] But godliness with contentment is a great gain.

---

### 1 Timothy 6:3-10

*You're not going to get everything you want out of life, but God has promised to make sure you get everything you need. And you can learn to be content with that. How much time and energy could you save if you were happy with what you already have?*

---

[7]  For we brought nothing into
        the world,
    and[b] we can take nothing out.
[8]  But if we have food and clothing,
    we will be content with these.

[9] But those who want to be rich fall into temptation, a trap, and many foolish and harmful desires, which plunge people into ruin and destruction. [10] For the love of money is a root of all kinds of evil, and by craving it, some have wandered away from the faith and pierced themselves with many pains.

## Compete for the Faith

[11]  Now you, man of God, run
        from these things;
    but pursue righteousness,
        godliness, faith,
    love, endurance, and
        gentleness.
[12]  Fight the good fight for the faith;
    take hold of eternal life,
    to which you were called

---

**6:5** Other mss add *From such people withdraw yourself.*   [b]**6:7** Other mss add *it is clear that*

*"Contentment is a learned behavior, an acquired skill. It doesn't just happen when you fall into the right set of circumstances."*
—*Mary Hunt*

and have made a good confession before many witnesses.

[13] In the presence of God, who gives life to all, and before Christ Jesus, who gave a good confession before Pontius •Pilate, I charge you [14] to keep the commandment without spot or blame until the appearing of our Lord Jesus Christ, [15] which God will bring about in His own time. ⌊He is⌋

the blessed and only Sovereign,
the King of kings,
and the Lord of lords,
[16] the only One who has
immortality,
dwelling in unapproachable
light,

whom none of mankind has
seen or can see,
to whom be honor and
eternal might.
•Amen.

### Instructions to the Rich

[17] Instruct those who are rich in the present age not to be arrogant or to set their hope on the uncertainty of wealth, but on God,[a] who richly provides us with all things to enjoy. [18] ⌊Instruct them⌋ to do good, to be rich in good works, to be generous, willing to share, [19] storing up for themselves a good foundation for the age to come, so that they may take hold of life that is real.

### Guard the Heritage

[20] Timothy, guard what has been entrusted to you, avoiding irreverent, empty speech and contradictions from the "knowledge" that falsely bears that name. [21] By professing it, some people have deviated from the faith.

Grace be with all of you.

[a]**6:17** Other mss read *on the living God*

# 2 TIMOTHY

## Greeting

**1** Paul, an apostle of Christ Jesus by God's will, for the promise of life in Christ Jesus:

² To Timothy, my dearly loved child.

Grace, mercy, and peace from God the Father and Christ Jesus our Lord.

## Thanksgiving

³ I thank God, whom I serve with a clear conscience as my forefathers did, when I constantly remember you in my prayers night and day. ⁴ Remembering your tears, I long to see you so that I may be filled with joy, ⁵ clearly recalling your sincere faith that first lived in your grandmother Lois, then in your mother Eunice, and that I am convinced is in you also.
⁶ Therefore, I remind you to keep ablaze the gift of God that is in you through the laying on of my hands. ⁷ For God has not given us a spirit of fearfulness, but one of power, love, and sound judgment.

## Not Ashamed of the Gospel

⁸ So don't be ashamed of the testimony about our Lord, or of me His prisoner. Instead, share in suffering for the gospel, relying on the power of God,

⁹ who has saved us
    and called us with a holy calling,
    not according to our works,
    but according to His own
        purpose and grace,

which was given to us in
    Christ Jesus
before time began.
¹⁰ This has now been made
    evident
through the appearing of our
    Savior Christ Jesus,
who has abolished death
and has brought life and
    immortality to light
    through the gospel.

¹¹ For this gospel I was appointed a herald, apostle, and teacher,[a] ¹² and that is why I suffer these things. But I am not ashamed, because I know whom I have believed and am persuaded that He is able to guard what has been entrusted to me until that day.

## Be Loyal to the Faith

¹³ Hold on to the pattern of sound teaching that you have heard from

---

*2 Timothy 1:11-12*

*God's Assurance*

*Suffering is an uncomfortable component of the Christian life. We are not to go out looking for it, or feel like we're competing with others to have more of it, but we're not to avoid it either. Because whatever Christianity costs us on earth will be more than made up for in heaven.*

---

ª**1:11** Other mss add *of the Gentiles*

me, in the faith and love that are in Christ Jesus. [14] Guard, through the Holy Spirit who lives in us, that good thing entrusted to you. [15] This you know: all those in Asia have turned away from me, including Phygelus and Hermogenes. [16] May the Lord grant mercy to the household of One-siphorus, because he often refreshed me and was not ashamed of my chains. [17] On the contrary, when he was in Rome, he diligently searched for me and found me. [18] May the Lord grant that he obtain mercy from the Lord on that day. And you know how much he ministered at Ephesus.

## Be Strong in Grace

2 You, therefore, my child, be strong in the grace that is in Christ Jesus. [2] And what you have heard from me in the presence of many witnesses, commit to faithful men who will be able to teach others also.

[3] Share in suffering as a good soldier of Christ Jesus. [4] To please the recruiter, no one serving as a soldier gets entangled in the concerns of everyday life. [5] Also, if anyone competes as an athlete, he is not crowned unless he competes according to the rules. [6] It is the hardworking farmer who ought to be the first to get a share of the crops. [7] Consider what I say, for the Lord will give you understanding in everything.

[8] Keep in mind Jesus Christ, risen from the dead, descended from David, according to my gospel. [9] For this I suffer, to the point of being bound like a criminal; but God's message is not bound. [10] This is why I endure all things for the elect: so that they also may obtain salvation, which is in Christ Jesus, with eternal glory. [11] This saying is trustworthy:

For if we have died with Him,
we will also live with Him;
[12] if we endure,
we will also reign with Him;
if we deny Him,
He will also deny us;
[13] if we are faithless,
He remains faithful,
for He cannot deny Himself.

---

### 2 Timothy 2:14-16

*The issue is priorities—having a deliberate framework in place to help you make good decisions, avoid lazy distractions, and increase your inclination to obey. When you know who you are, and you know where you're going, you can live for God like you mean it.*

---

## An Approved Worker

[14] Remind them of these things, charging them before God[a] not to fight about words; this is in no way profitable and leads to the ruin of the hearers. [15] Be diligent to present yourself approved to God, a worker who doesn't need to be ashamed, correctly teaching the word of truth. [16] But avoid irreverent, empty speech, for this will produce an even greater measure of godlessness. [17] And their word will spread like gangrene, among whom are Hymenaeus and Philetus. [18] They have deviated from the truth, saying that the resurrection has already taken place, and are overturning the faith of some. [19] Nevertheless, God's solid

---

[a]2:14 Other mss read *before the Lord*

> *"Christianity, if false, is of no importance, and if true, is of infinite importance. The one thing it cannot be is moderately important."*
>
> —C. S. Lewis

foundation stands firm, having this inscription:

**The Lord knows those who are His,**[a] and
Everyone who names the
     name of the Lord
must turn away from
     unrighteousness.

[20] Now in a large house there are not only gold and silver bowls, but also those of wood and earthenware, some for special use, some for ordinary. [21] So if anyone purifies himself from these things, he will be a special instrument, set apart, useful to the Master, prepared for every good work.

[22] Flee from youthful passions, and pursue righteousness, faith, love, and peace, along with those who call on the Lord from a pure heart. [23] But reject foolish and ignorant disputes, knowing that they breed quarrels. [24] The Lord's slave must not quarrel, but must be gentle to everyone, able to teach, and patient, [25] instructing his opponents with gentleness. Perhaps God will grant them repentance to know the truth. [26] Then they may come to their senses and escape the Devil's trap, having been captured by him to do his will.

[a]**2:19** Nm 16:5

## Difficult Times Ahead

**3** But know this: difficult times will come in the last days. [2] For people will be lovers of self, lovers of money, boastful, proud, blasphemers, disobedient to parents, ungrateful, unholy, [3] unloving, irreconcilable, slanderers, without self-control, brutal, without love for what is good, [4] traitors, reckless, conceited, lovers of pleasure rather than lovers of God, [5] holding to the form of religion but denying its power. Avoid these people!

[6] For among them are those who worm their way into households and capture idle women burdened down with sins, led along by a variety of passions, [7] always learning and never able to come to a knowledge of the truth. [8] Just as Jannes and Jambres resisted Moses, so these also resist the truth, men who are corrupt in mind, worthless in regard to the faith. [9] But they will not make further progress, for their lack of understanding will be clear to all, as theirs was also.

---

*2 Timothy 3:14-17*

*The Scriptures*

*Perhaps the biggest word in this passage is the little 3-letter word* All, *because every bit of the Bible has been delivered to us by God. So when we wake in the morning, our first thought shouldn't be "I don't have time to read my Bible" but "Can you believe God wants to speak with me today?"*

## The Sacred Scriptures

[10] But you have followed my teaching, conduct, purpose, faith, patience, love, and endurance, [11] along with the persecutions and sufferings that came to me in Antioch, Iconium, and Lystra. What persecutions I endured! Yet the Lord rescued me from them all. [12] In fact, all those who want to live a godly life in Christ Jesus will be persecuted. [13] Evil people and imposters will become worse, deceiving and being deceived. [14] But as for you, continue in what you have learned and firmly believed, knowing those from whom you learned, [15] and that from childhood you have known the sacred Scriptures, which are able to instruct you for salvation through faith in Christ Jesus. [16] All Scripture is inspired by God and is profitable for teaching, for rebuking, for correcting, for training in righteousness, [17] so that the man of God may be complete, equipped for every good work.

## Fulfill Your Ministry

4 Before God and Christ Jesus, who is going to judge the living and the dead, and by His appearing and His kingdom, I solemnly charge you: [2] proclaim the message; persist in it whether convenient or not; rebuke, correct, and encourage with great patience and teaching. [3] For the time will come when they will not tolerate sound doctrine, but according to their own desires, will accumulate teachers for themselves because they have an itch to hear something new. [4] They will turn away from hearing the truth and will turn aside to myths. [5] But as for you, keep a clear head about everything, endure hard-

ship, do the work of an evangelist, fulfill your ministry.

[6] For I am already being poured out as a drink offering, and the time for my departure is close. [7] I have fought the good fight, I have finished the race, I have kept the faith. [8] In the future, there is reserved for me the crown of righteousness, which the Lord, the righteous Judge, will give me on that day, and not only to me, but to all those who have loved His appearing.

---

### 2 Timothy 4:7-8

### Last Things

*The older we get, the more likely we find ourselves gravitating toward this passage. It's the Apostle Paul's final testimony of the life he'd led and of the blessed hope that awaited him. While we're here, we keep up the good fight, because once we're there, we get to rest forever and ever.*

---

## Final Instructions

[9] Make every effort to come to me soon, [10] for Demas has deserted me, because he loved this present world, and has gone to Thessalonica. Crescens has gone to Galatia, Titus to Dalmatia. [11] Only Luke is with me. Bring Mark with you, for he is useful to me in the ministry. [12] I have sent Tychicus to Ephesus. [13] When you come, bring the cloak I left in Troas with Carpus, as well as the scrolls, especially the parchments. [14] Alexander the coppersmith did great harm to me. The Lord will repay him according to his works.

¹⁵ Watch out for him yourself, because he strongly opposed our words.

¹⁶ At my first defense, no one came to my assistance, but everyone deserted me. May it not be counted against them. ¹⁷ But the Lord stood with me and strengthened me, so that the proclamation might be fully made through me, and all the Gentiles might hear. So I was rescued from the lion's mouth. ¹⁸ The Lord will rescue me from every evil work and will bring me safely into His heavenly kingdom. To Him be the glory forever and ever! •Amen.

## Benediction

¹⁹ Greet Prisca and Aquila, and the household of Onesiphorus. ²⁰ Erastus has remained at Corinth; Trophimus I left sick at Miletus. ²¹ Make every effort to come before winter. Eubulus greets you, as do Pudens, Linus, Claudia, and all the brothers.

²² The Lord be with your spirit. Grace be with you!

# TITUS

## Greeting

**1** Paul, a slave of God, and an apostle of Jesus Christ for the faith of God's elect and the knowledge of the truth that leads to godliness, [2] in the hope of eternal life that God, who cannot lie, promised before time began, [3] and has in His own time revealed His message in the proclamation that I was entrusted with by the command of God our Savior:

[4] To Titus, my true child in our common faith.

Grace and peace from God the Father and Christ Jesus our Savior.

## Titus' Ministry in Crete

[5] The reason I left you in Crete was to set right what was left undone and, as I directed you, to appoint elders in every town: [6] someone who is blameless, the husband of one wife, having faithful children not accused of wildness or rebellion. [7] For an •overseer, as God's manager, must be blameless, not arrogant, not quick tempered, not addicted to wine, not a bully, not greedy for money, [8] but hospitable, loving what is good, sensible, righteous, holy, self-controlled, [9] holding to the faithful message as taught, so that he will be able both to encourage with sound teaching and to refute those who contradict it.

[10] For there are also many rebellious people, idle talkers and deceivers, especially those from Judaism. [11] It is necessary to silence them; they overthrow whole households by teaching for dishonest gain what they should not. [12] One of their very own prophets said,

Cretans are always liars, evil beasts,
  lazy gluttons.

[13] This testimony is true. So, rebuke them sharply, that they may be sound in the faith [14] and may not pay attention to Jewish myths and the commandments of men who reject the truth.
[15] To the pure, everything is pure, but to those who are defiled and unbelieving nothing is pure; in fact, both their mind and conscience are defiled. [16] They profess to know God, but they deny Him by their works. They are detestable, disobedient, and disqualified for any good work.

---

*"God's grace is not a suit meant for Sundays. We should wrap it around our shoulders every day of our lives."*
*—Sheila Walsh*

---

## Sound Teaching

**2** But you must speak what is consistent with sound teaching. [2] Older men are to be self-controlled, worthy of respect, sensible, and sound in faith, love, and endurance. [3] In the same way, older women are to be reverent in behavior, not slanderers, not addicted to much wine. ⌊They are⌋ to teach what is good, [4] so that they may encourage the young women to love their husbands and children, [5] to be sensible, pure, good homemakers, and submissive to their husbands, so that God's message will not be slandered.

[6] Likewise, encourage the young men to be sensible [7] about everything. Set an example of good works yourself, with integrity and dignity[a] in your teaching. [8] Your message is to be sound beyond reproach, so that the opponent will be ashamed, having nothing bad to say about us.

[9] Slaves are to be submissive to their masters in everything, and to be well-pleasing, not talking back [10] or stealing, but demonstrating utter faithfulness, so that they may adorn the teaching of God our Savior in everything. [11] For the grace of God has appeared, with salvation for all people, [12] instructing us to deny godlessness and worldly lusts and to live in a sensible, righteous, and godly way in the present age, [13] while we wait for the blessed hope and the appearing of the glory of our great God and Savior, Jesus Christ. [14] He gave Himself for us to redeem us from all lawlessness and to cleanse for Himself a special people, eager to do good works.

[15] Say these things, and encourage and rebuke with all authority. Let no one disregard you.

## The Importance of Good Works

3 Remind them to be submissive to rulers and authorities, to obey, to be ready for every good work, [2] to slander no one, to avoid fighting, and to be kind, always showing gentleness to all people. [3] For we too were once foolish, disobedient, deceived, captives of various passions and pleasures, living in malice and envy, hateful, detesting one another.

[4]  But when the goodness and love
        for man
      appeared from God our Savior,
[5]  He saved us—
      not by works of righteousness
        that we had done,
      but according to His mercy,
      through the washing of
        regeneration
      and renewal by the Holy Spirit.
[6]  This ⌊Spirit⌋ He poured out on
        us abundantly
      through Jesus Christ our Savior,
[7]  so that having been justified by
        His grace,
      we may become heirs with the
        hope of eternal life.

[8] This saying is trustworthy. I want you to insist on these things, so that those who have believed God might be careful to devote themselves to good works. These are good and profitable for everyone. [9] But avoid foolish debates, genealogies, quarrels, and disputes about the law, for they are

---

### Titus 2:11-14

*It takes some truly amazing grace to turn a hardheaded, rebellious sinner into a child of the living God. But that's not the only amazing thing that grace can do. You are every bit as dependent on the grace of God this minute as you were from the very start.*

---

[a]**2:7** Other mss add *incorruptibility*

unprofitable and worthless. [10] Reject a divisive person after a first and second warning, [11] knowing that such a person is perverted and sins, being self-condemned.

## Final Instructions and Closing

[12] When I send Artemas to you, or Tychicus, make every effort to come to me in Nicopolis, for I have decided to spend the winter there. [13] Diligently help Zenas the lawyer and Apollos on their journey, so that they will lack nothing.

[14] And our people must also learn to devote themselves to good works for cases of urgent need, so that they will not be unfruitful. [15] All those who are with me greet you. Greet those who love us in the faith. Grace be with all of you.

# PHILEMON

## Greeting

**P**aul, a prisoner of Christ Jesus, and Timothy, our brother:

To Philemon, our dear friend and co-worker, [2] to Apphia our sister,[a] to Archippus our fellow soldier, and to the church that meets in your house.

[3] Grace to you and peace from God our Father and the Lord Jesus Christ.

## Philemon's Love and Faith

[4] I always thank my God when I mention you in my prayers, [5] because I hear of your love and faith toward the Lord Jesus and for all the saints. [6] ⌊I pray⌋ that your participation in the faith may become effective through knowing every good thing that is in us[b] for ⌊the glory of⌋ Christ. [7] For I have great joy and encouragement from your love, because the hearts of the saints have been refreshed through you, brother.

## An Appeal for Onesimus

[8] For this reason, although I have great boldness in Christ to command you to do what is right, [9] I appeal, instead, on the basis of love. I, Paul, as an elderly man and now also as a prisoner of Christ Jesus, [10] appeal to you for my child, whom I fathered while in chains—Onesimus. [11] Once he was useless to you, but now he is useful to both you and me. [12] I am sending him—a part of myself—back to you.[c] [13] I wanted to keep him with me, so that in my imprisonment for the gospel he might serve me in your place. [14] But I didn't want to do anything without your consent, so that your good deed might not be out of obligation, but of your own free will. [15] For perhaps this is why he was separated ⌊from you⌋ for a brief time, so that you might get him back permanently, [16] no longer as a slave, but more than a slave—as a dearly loved brother. This is especially so to me, but even more to you, both in the flesh and in the Lord.

---

### Philemon 14

### Christian Influence

*Good deeds done because someone else was watching or because we'd feel guilty otherwise, cost us at least half the fun of letting God use us for important things. Serving God with a sigh and a grunt doesn't earn us any brownie points, and it shows that our hearts are still stuck on ourselves.*

---

[17] So if you consider me a partner, accept him as you would me. [18] And if he has wronged you in any way, or owes you anything, charge that to my account. [19] I, Paul, write this with my own hand: I will repay it—not to mention to you that you owe me even your own self. [20] Yes, brother,

---

a2 Other mss read *our beloved*   b6 Other mss read *in you*   c12 Other mss read *him back. Receive him as a part of myself.*

may I have joy from you in the Lord; refresh my heart in Christ. [21] Since I am confident of your obedience, I am writing to you, knowing that you will do even more than I say. [22] But meanwhile, also prepare a guest room for me, for I hope that through your prayers I will be restored to you.

## Final Greetings

[23] Epaphras, my fellow prisoner in Christ Jesus, greets you, and so do [24] Mark, Aristarchus, Demas, and Luke, my co-workers.

[25] The grace of the Lord[a] Jesus Christ be with your spirit.

[a]25 Other mss read *our Lord*

# HEBREWS

## The Nature of the Son

**1** Long ago God spoke to the fathers by the prophets at different times and in different ways. ² In these last days, He has spoken to us by ⌊His⌋ Son, whom He has appointed heir of all things and through whom He made the universe. ³ He is the radiance of His glory, the exact expression of His nature, and He sustains all things by His powerful word. After making purification for sins,ᵃ He sat down at the right hand of the Majesty on high. ⁴ So He became higher in rank than the angels, just as the name He inherited is superior to theirs.

## The Son Superior to Angels

⁵ For to which of the angels did He ever say, **You are My Son; today I have become Your Father,**ᵇ or again, **I will be His Father, and He will be My Son?**ᶜ ⁶ When He again brings His firstborn into the world, He says, **And all God's angels must worship Him.**ᵈ ⁷ And about the angels He says:

**He makes His angels winds,
and His servants a fiery flame;**ᵉ

⁸ but about the Son:

**Your throne, O God, is
forever and ever,
and the scepter of Your kingdom
is a scepter of justice.**
⁹ **You have loved righteousness
and hated lawlessness;
this is why God, Your God,
has anointed You,**

**rather than Your companions,
with the oil of joy.**ᶠ

¹⁰ And:

**In the beginning, Lord, You
established the earth,
and the heavens are the
works of Your hands;**
¹¹ **they will perish, but You remain.
They will all wear out like
clothing;**
¹² **You will roll them up like a
cloak,**ᵍ
**and they will be changed like
a robe.
But You are the same,
and Your years will never end.**ʰ

¹³ Now to which of the angels has He ever said:

**Sit at My right hand
until I make Your enemies
Your footstool?**ⁱ

¹⁴ Are they not all ministering spirits sent out to serve those who are going to inherit salvation?

## Warning against Neglect

**2** We must therefore pay even more attention to what we have heard, so that we will not drift away. ² For if the message spoken through angels was legally binding, and every transgression and disobedience received a just punishment, ³ how will we escape if we neglect such a great salvation? It was first spoken by the Lord and was confirmed to us by those who heard

ᵃ1:3 Other mss read *for our sins by Himself*  ᵇ1:5 Ps 2:7  ᶜ1:5 2 Sm 7:14; 1 Ch 17:13  ᵈ1:6 Dt 32:43 LXX; Ps 97:7  ᵉ1:7 Ps 104:4  ᶠ1:8–9 Ps 45:6–7  ᵍ1:12 Other mss omit *like a cloak*  ʰ1:10–12 Ps 102:25–27  ⁱ1:13 Ps 110:1

Him. [4] At the same time, God also testified by signs and wonders, various miracles, and distributions ⌊of gifts⌋ from the Holy Spirit according to His will.

---

## Hebrews 2:1-3

### Salvation

*God wasn't under obligation to extend salvation to us, but because of His great love, He chose to give us a way out of death and punishment. There is no other reason for this turn of events. And those who turn away from His salvation are rejecting the best thing they've ever been given.*

---

## Jesus and Humanity

[5] For He has not subjected to angels the world to come that we are talking about. [6] But one has somewhere testified:

**What is man, that You
 remember him,
or the •son of man, that You
 care for him?
[7] You made him lower than
 the angels for a short time;
You crowned him with glory
 and honor [a]
[8] and subjected everything
 under his feet.[b]**

For in **subjecting everything** to him, He left nothing not subject to him. As it is, we do not yet see **everything**

**subjected** to him. [9] But we do see Jesus—**made lower than the angels for a short time** so that by God's grace He might taste death for everyone—crowned with glory and honor because of the suffering of death.

[10] For it was fitting, in bringing many sons to glory, that He, for whom and through whom all things exist, should make the source of their salvation perfect through sufferings. [11] For the One who sanctifies and those who are sanctified all have one Father. That is why He is not ashamed to call them brothers, [12] saying:

**I will proclaim Your name to
 My brothers;
I will sing hymns to You in the
 congregation.[c]**

[13] Again, **I will trust in Him.[d]** And again, **Here I am with the children God gave Me.[e]**
[14] Now since the children have flesh and blood in common, He also shared in these, so that through His death He might destroy the one holding the power of death—that is, the Devil— [15] and free those who were held in slavery all their lives by the fear of death. [16] For it is clear that He does not reach out to help angels, but to help Abraham's offspring. [17] Therefore He had to be like His brothers in every way, so that He could become a merciful and faithful high priest in service to God, to make propitiation for the sins of the people. [18] For since He Himself was tested and has suffered, He is able to help those who are tested.

## Our Apostle and High Priest

**3** Therefore, holy brothers and companions in a heavenly calling, con-

---

[a]**2:7** Other mss add *and set him over the works of your hands* [b]**2:6–8** Ps 8:5–7 LXX [c]**2:12** Ps 22:22
[d]**2:13** Is 8:17 LXX; 12:2 LXX; 2 Sm 22:3 LXX [e]**2:13** Is 8:18 LXX

sider Jesus, the apostle and high priest of our confession; [2] He was faithful to the One who appointed Him, just as Moses was in all God's household. [3] For Jesus is considered worthy of more glory than Moses, just as the builder has more honor than the house. [4] Now every house is built by someone, but the One who built everything is God. [5] Moses was faithful as a servant in all God's household, as a testimony to what would be said ⌊in the future⌋. [6] But Christ was faithful as a Son over His household, whose household we are if we hold on to the courage and the confidence of our hope.[a]

---

*"I believe if a man gets close to a true spiritual champion, he will become one. We become like the people we associate with."*
—*Ronnie Floyd*

---

## Warning against Unbelief

[7] Therefore, as the Holy Spirit says:

Today, if you hear His voice,
[8]  do not harden your hearts as in the rebellion,
 on the day of testing in the desert,
[9] where your fathers tested Me, tried ⌊Me⌋,
 and saw My works
[10] for 40 years.
 Therefore I was provoked with this generation
 and said, "They always go astray in their hearts,
 and they have not known My ways."
[11] So I swore in My anger,

*Hebrews 3:12-14*

*More than just on Sunday morning, you need a face-to-face connection with a few close Christian friends who can help keep you living what you say you believe. God can help you be the person you want to be, but seek out somebody who'll help you see to it.*

---

### "They will not enter My rest."[b]

[12] Watch out, brothers, so that there won't be in any of you an evil, unbelieving heart that departs from the living God. [13] But encourage each other daily, while it is still called **today**, so that none of you is hardened by sin's deception. [14] For we have become companions of the •Messiah if we hold firmly until the end the reality that we had at the start. [15] As it is said:

Today, if you hear His voice,
do not harden your hearts as in the rebellion.[c]

[16] For who heard and rebelled? Wasn't it really all who came out of Egypt under Moses? [17] And with whom was He "provoked for 40 years"? Was it not with those who sinned, whose bodies fell in the desert? [18] And to whom did He "swear that they would not enter His rest," if not those who disobeyed? [19] So we see that they were unable to enter because of unbelief.

---

[a]**3:6** Other mss add *firm to the end*   [b]**3:7–11** Ps 95:7–11   [c]**3:15** Ps 95:7–8

## The Promised Rest

**4** Therefore, while the promise remains of entering His rest, let us fear so that none of you should miss it. ² For we also have received the good news just as they did; but the message they heard did not benefit them, since they were not united with those who heard it in faith[a] ³ (for we who have believed enter the rest), in keeping with what He has said:

> So I swore in My anger,
> they will not enter My rest.[b]

And yet His works have been finished since the foundation of the world, ⁴ for somewhere He has spoken about the seventh day in this way:

> And on the seventh day
> God rested from all His works.[c]

⁵ Again, in that passage ⌊He says⌋, **"They will never enter My rest."**[d] ⁶ Since it remains for some to enter it, and those who formerly received the good news did not enter because of disobedience, ⁷ again, He specifies a certain day—**"today"**—speaking through David after such a long time, as previously stated:

> **Today if you hear His voice,**
> **do not harden your hearts.**[e]

⁸ For if Joshua had given them rest, He would not have spoken later about another day. ⁹ A Sabbath rest remains, therefore, for God's people. ¹⁰ For the person who has entered His rest has rested from his own works, just as God did from His. ¹¹ Let us then make every effort to enter that rest, so that no one will fall into the same pattern of disobedience.

¹² For the word of God is living and effective and sharper than any two-edged sword, penetrating as far as to divide soul, spirit, joints, and marrow; it is a judge of the ideas and thoughts of the heart. ¹³ No creature is hidden from Him, but all things are naked and exposed to the eyes of Him to whom we must give an account.

---

### Hebrews 4:14-16

### God the Son

*We are saved through faith in Christ, but we don't become like Him in a day, a year, or even a lifetime. That's why the Son continues to stand in as our substitute before the Father, until the day that sin has had its last chance at us. That's why we are told to keep coming boldly, receiving His mercy.*

---

### Our Great High Priest

¹⁴ Therefore since we have a great high priest who has passed through the heavens—Jesus the Son of God—let us hold fast to the confession. ¹⁵ For we do not have a high priest who is unable to sympathize with our weaknesses, but One who has been tested in every way as we are, yet without sin. ¹⁶ Therefore let us approach the throne of grace with boldness, so that we may receive mercy and find grace to help us at the proper time.

---

[a]**4:2** Other mss read *since it was not united by faith in those who heard*  [b]**4:3** Ps 95:11  [c]**4:4** Gn 2:2
[d]**4:5** Ps 95:11  [e]**4:7** Ps 95:7–8

## The Messiah, a High Priest

**5** For every high priest taken from men is appointed in service to God for the people, to offer both gifts and sacrifices for sins. [2] He is able to deal gently with those who are ignorant and are going astray, since he himself is also subject to weakness. [3] Because of this, he must make a sin offering for himself as well as for the people. [4] No one takes this honor on himself; instead, a person is called by God, just as Aaron was. [5] In the same way, the •Messiah did not exalt Himself to become a high priest, but the One who said to Him, **You are My Son; today I have become Your Father,**[a] [6] also said in another passage, **You are a priest forever in the order of Melchizedek.**[b]

[7] During His earthly life, He offered prayers and appeals, with loud cries and tears, to the One who was able to save Him from death, and He was heard because of His reverence. [8] Though a Son, He learned obedience through what He suffered. [9] After He was perfected, He became the source of eternal salvation to all who obey Him, [10] and He was declared by God a high priest "in the order of Melchizedek."

## The Problem of Immaturity

[11] We have a great deal to say about this, and it's difficult to explain, since you have become slow to understand. [12] For though by this time you ought to be teachers, you need someone to teach you again the basic principles of God's revelation. You need milk, not solid food. [13] Now everyone who lives on milk is inexperienced with the message about righteousness, because he is an infant. [14] But solid food is for

---

### Hebrews 5:7-10

### Salvation

*Jesus did everything that was asked of Him. He avoided all manner of sin. He lived in perfect fellowship with the Father. He suffered the highest indignity in human history. And He became all we could ever want in a Savior. (Oh, and about Melchizedek, you can read about him in chapter 7.)*

---

the mature—for those whose senses have been trained to distinguish between good and evil.

## Warning against Regression

**6** Therefore, leaving the elementary message about the •Messiah, let us go on to maturity, not laying again the foundation of repentance from dead works, faith in God, [2] teaching about ritual washings, laying on of hands, the resurrection of the dead, and eternal judgment. [3] And we will do this if God permits.

[4] For it is impossible to renew to repentance those who were once enlightened, who tasted the heavenly gift, became companions with the Holy Spirit, [5] tasted God's good word and the powers of the coming age, [6] and who have fallen away, because, to their own harm, they are recrucifying the Son of God and holding Him up to contempt. [7] For ground that has drunk the rain that has often fallen on it, and that produces vegetation

[a]**5:5** Ps 2:7   [b]**5:6** Ps 110:4; Gn 14:18–20

useful to those it is cultivated for, receives a blessing from God. [8] But if it produces thorns and thistles, it is worthless and about to be cursed, and will be burned at the end.

[9] Even though we are speaking this way, dear friends, in your case we are confident of the better things connected with salvation. [10] For God is not unjust; He will not forget your work and the love[a] you showed for His name when you served the saints—and you continue to serve them. [11] Now we want each of you to demonstrate the same diligence for the final realization of your hope, [12] so that you won't become lazy, but imitators of those who inherit the promises through faith and perseverance.

## Inheriting the Promise

[13] For when God made a promise to Abraham, since He had no one greater to swear by, He swore by Himself:

[14] **I will most certainly bless you, and I will greatly multiply you.**[b]

[15] And so, after waiting patiently, Abraham obtained the promise. [16] For men swear by something greater than themselves, and for them a confirming oath ends every dispute. [17] Because God wanted to show His unchangeable purpose even more clearly to the heirs of the promise, He guaranteed it with an oath, [18] so that through two unchangeable things, in which it is impossible for God to lie, we who have fled for refuge might have strong encouragement to seize the hope set before us. [19] We have this ⌊hope⌋—like a sure and firm anchor of the soul—that enters the in-

ner sanctuary behind the curtain. [20] Jesus has entered there on our behalf as a forerunner, because He has become a "high priest forever in the order of Melchizedek."

## The Greatness of Melchizedek

**7** For this Melchizedek—

King of Salem, priest of the Most High God,
who met Abraham and blessed him as he returned
from defeating the kings,
[2] and Abraham gave him a tenth of everything;
first, his name means "king of righteousness,"
then also, "king of Salem,"
meaning "king of peace";
[3] without father, mother, or genealogy,
having neither beginning of days nor end of life,
but resembling the Son of God—
remains a priest forever.

---

*"God delights in hearing prayer and answering it. He gave His Son that Christ might always pray for us and with us."*
*—Andrew Murray*

---

[4] Now consider how great this man was, to whom even Abraham the patriarch gave a tenth of the plunder! [5] The sons of Levi who receive the priestly office have a commandment according to the law to collect a tenth from the people—that is, from their brothers—though they

have ⌊also⌋ descended from Abraham. ⁶ But one without this lineage collected tithes from Abraham and blessed the one who had the promises. ⁷ Without a doubt, the inferior is blessed by the superior. ⁸ In the one case, men who will die receive tithes; but in the other case, ⌊Scripture⌋ testifies that he lives. ⁹ And in a sense Levi himself, who receives tithes, has paid tithes through Abraham, ¹⁰ for he was still within his forefather when Melchizedek met him.

## A Superior Priesthood

¹¹ If, then, perfection came through the Levitical priesthood (for under it the people received the law), what further need was there for another priest to arise in the order of Melchizedek, and not to be described as being in the order of Aaron? ¹² For when there is a change of the priesthood, there must be a change of law as well. ¹³ For the One about whom these things are said belonged to a different tribe, from which no one has served at the altar. ¹⁴ Now it is evident that our Lord came from Judah, and about that tribe Moses said nothing concerning priests.

¹⁵ And this becomes clearer if another priest like Melchizedek arises, ¹⁶ who doesn't become a ⌊priest⌋ based on a legal command concerning physical descent but based on the power of an indestructible life. ¹⁷ For it has been testified:

**You are a priest forever
in the order of Melchizedek.**ᵃ

¹⁸ So the previous commandment is annulled because it was weak and unprofitable ¹⁹ (for the law perfected nothing), but a better hope is introduced, through which we draw near to God.

²⁰ None of this ⌊happened⌋ without an oath. For others became priests without an oath, ²¹ but He with an oath made by the One who said to Him:

**The Lord has sworn, and He
will not change His mind,
You are a priest forever.**ᵇ

²² So Jesus has also become the guarantee of a better covenant.

²³ Now many have become ⌊Levitical priests⌋, since they are prevented by death from remaining in office. ²⁴ But because He remains forever, He holds His priesthood permanently. ²⁵ Therefore He is always able to save those who come to God through Him, since He always lives to intercede for them.

---

### Hebrews 7:23-28

*When Jesus rose from the grave and ascended back home into the heavens, He took His seat at the right hand of God's throne. And He took on Himself a new job— High Priest. So even in your quiet time, you're not really alone. Jesus is there to pray even harder than you do.*

---

²⁶ For this is the kind of high priest we need: holy, innocent, undefiled, separated from sinners, and exalted above the heavens. ²⁷ He doesn't need

ᵃ**7:17** Ps 110:4     ᵇ**7:21** Ps 110:4

to offer sacrifices every day, as high priests do—first for their own sins, then for those of the people. He did this once for all when He offered Himself. <sup>28</sup> For the law appoints as high priests men who are weak, but the promise of the oath, which came after the law, ⌊appoints⌋ a Son, who has been perfected forever.

## A Heavenly Priesthood

**8** Now the main point of what is being said is this: we have this kind of high priest, who sat down at the right hand of the throne of the Majesty in the heavens, <sup>2</sup> a minister of the sanctuary and the true *tabernacle, which the Lord set up, and not man. <sup>3</sup> For every high priest is appointed to offer gifts and sacrifices; therefore it was necessary for this ⌊priest⌋ also to have something to offer. <sup>4</sup> Now if He were on earth, He wouldn't be a priest, since there are those[a] offering the gifts prescribed by the law. <sup>5</sup> These serve as a copy and shadow of the heavenly things, as Moses was warned when he was about to complete the tabernacle. For He said, **Be careful that you make everything according to the pattern that was shown to you on the mountain.**[b] <sup>6</sup> But Jesus has now obtained a superior ministry, and to that degree He is the mediator of a better covenant, which has been legally enacted on better promises.

## A Superior Covenant

<sup>7</sup> For if that first ⌊covenant⌋ had been faultless, no opportunity would have been sought for a second one. <sup>8</sup> But finding fault with His people, He says:[c]

"Look, the days are
    coming," says the Lord,
"when I will make a new
    covenant
with the house of Israel
and with the house of
    Judah—
<sup>9</sup> not like the covenant
that I made with their fathers
on the day I took them by
    their hand
to lead them out of the land
    of Egypt.
Because they did not
    continue in My covenant,
I disregarded them," says
    the Lord.
<sup>10</sup> "But this is the covenant that
I will make with
    the house of Israel
after those days," says the
    Lord:
"I will put My laws into their
    minds,
and I will write them on their
    hearts,
and I will be their God,
and they will be My people.
<sup>11</sup> And each person will not
    teach his fellow citizen,[d]
and each his brother, saying,
    'Know the Lord,'
because they will all know
    Me,
from the least to the greatest
    of them.
<sup>12</sup> For I will be merciful to their
    wrongdoing,
and I will never again
    remember their sins."[e][f]

<sup>13</sup> By saying, "a new ⌊covenant⌋," He has declared that the first is old. And what is old and aging is about to disappear.

---

[a]**8:4** Other mss read *priests*   [b]**8:5** Ex 25:40   [c]**8:8** Other mss read *finding fault, He says to them*   [d]**8:11** Other mss read *neighbor*   [e]**8:12** Other mss add *and their lawless deeds*   [f]**8:8–12** Jr 31:31–34

## Old Covenant Ministry

**9** Now the first ⌊covenant⌋ also had regulations for ministry and an earthly sanctuary. [2] For a *tabernacle was set up; and in the first room, which is called "the holy place," were the lampstand, the table, and the presentation loaves. [3] Behind the second curtain, the tabernacle was called "the holy of holies." [4] It contained the gold altar of incense and the ark of the covenant, covered with gold on all sides, in which there was a gold jar containing the manna, Aaron's rod that budded, and the tablets of the covenant. [5] The cherubim of glory were above it overshadowing the mercy seat. It is not possible to speak about these things in detail right now.

[6] These things having been set up this way, the priests enter the first room repeatedly, performing their ministry. [7] But the high priest alone enters the second room, and that only once a year, and never without blood, which he offers for himself and for the sins of the people committed in ignorance. [8] The Holy Spirit was making it clear that the way into the holy of holies had not yet been disclosed while the first tabernacle was still standing. [9] This is a symbol for the present time, during which gifts and sacrifices are offered that cannot perfect the worshiper's conscience. [10] They are physical regulations and only deal with food, drink, and various washings imposed until the time of restoration.

## New Covenant Ministry

[11] Now the *Messiah has appeared, high priest of the good things that have come.[a] In the greater and more perfect tabernacle not made with hands (that is, not of this creation), [12] He entered the holy of holies once for all, not by the blood of goats and calves, but by His own blood, having obtained eternal redemption. [13] For if the blood of goats and bulls and the ashes of a heifer sprinkling those who are defiled, sanctify for the purification of the flesh, [14] how much more will the blood of the Messiah, who through the eternal Spirit offered Himself without blemish to God, cleanse our[b] consciences from dead works to serve the living God?

[15] Therefore He is the mediator of a new covenant, so that those who are called might receive the promise of the eternal inheritance, because a death has taken place for redemption from the transgressions ⌊committed⌋ under the first covenant. [16] Where a will exists, the death of the testator must be established. [17] For a will is valid only when people die, since it is never in force while the testator is living. [18] That is why even the first covenant was inaugurated with blood. [19] For when every commandment had been proclaimed by Moses to all the people according to the law, he took the blood of calves and goats, along with water, scarlet wool, and hyssop, and sprinkled the scroll itself and all the people, [20] saying, **This is the blood of the covenant that God has commanded for you.**[c] [21] In the same way, he sprinkled the tabernacle and all the vessels of worship with blood. [22] According to the law almost everything is purified with blood, and without the shedding of blood there is no forgiveness.

[23] Therefore it was necessary for the copies of the things in the heavens to be purified with these ⌊sacrifices⌋, but

---

[a]9:11 Other mss read *that are to come*    [b]9:14 Other mss read *your*    [c]9:20 Ex 24:8

## Hebrews 9:24-28

### God the Son

*In the Old Testament, the high priest entered a room called the Holy of Holies once a year to offer sacrifices for the sins of the people. The Son has entered an even holier place—the visible presence of almighty God—to make one sacrifice that need never be repeated.*

the heavenly things themselves ⌊to be purified⌋ with better sacrifices than these. [24] For the Messiah did not enter a sanctuary made with hands (only a model of the true one) but into heaven itself, that He might now appear in the presence of God for us. [25] He did not do this to offer Himself many times, as the high priest enters the sanctuary yearly with the blood of another. [26] Otherwise, He would have had to suffer many times since the foundation of the world. But now He has appeared one time, at the end of the ages, for the removal of sin by the sacrifice of Himself. [27] And just as it is appointed for people to die once—and after this, judgment— [28] so also the Messiah, having been offered once to bear the sins of many, will appear a second time, not to bear sin, but to bring salvation to those who are waiting for Him.

### The Perfect Sacrifice

**10** Since the law has ⌊only⌋ a shadow of the good things to come, and not the actual form of those realities, it can never perfect the worshipers by the same sacrifices they continually offer year after year. [2] Otherwise, wouldn't they have stopped being offered, since the worshipers, once purified, would no longer have any consciousness of sins? [3] But in the sacrifices there is a reminder of sins every year. [4] For it is impossible for the blood of bulls and goats to take away sins.

[5] Therefore, as He was coming into the world, He said:

> **You did not want sacrifice**
> **and offering,**
> **but You prepared a body for**
> **Me.**
> [6] **You did not delight**
> **in whole burnt offerings and**
> **sin offerings.**
> [7] **Then I said, "See, I have**
> **come—**
> **it is written about Me**
> **in the volume of the scroll—**
> **to do Your will, O God!"** [a]

*"What a surge of hope and adrenaline to know that because I have chosen to follow Christ, I am a victor in the only game that really matters."*

—*Lucinda Secrest McDowell*

[8] After He says above, **You did not desire or delight in sacrifices and offerings, whole burnt offerings and sin offerings,** (which are offered according to the law), [9] He then says, **See, I have come to do Your will.** [b] He takes away the first to establish the

---

[a]10:5–7 Ps 40:6–8    [b]10:9 Other mss add *O God*

second. [10] By this will, we have been sanctified through the offering of the body of Jesus Christ once and for all.

[11] Now every priest stands day after day ministering and offering time after time the same sacrifices, which can never take away sins. [12] But this man, after offering one sacrifice for sins forever, sat down at the right hand of God. [13] He is now waiting until His enemies are made His footstool. [14] For by one offering He has perfected forever those who are sanctified. [15] The Holy Spirit also testifies to us about this. For after He had said:

[16] This is the covenant that I
    will make with them
  after those days, says the
    Lord:
  I will put My laws on their
    hearts,
  and I will write them on their
    minds,

[17] ⌊He adds⌋:

  I will never again remember
  their sins and their lawless acts.[a]

[18] Now where there is forgiveness of these, there is no longer an offering for sin.

## Exhortations to Godliness

[19] Therefore, brothers, since we have boldness to enter the sanctuary through the blood of Jesus, [20] by the new and living way that He has inaugurated for us, through the curtain (that is, His flesh); [21] and since we have a great high priest over the house of God, [22] let us draw near with a true heart in full assurance of faith, our hearts sprinkled ⌊clean⌋ from an evil conscience and our bodies washed in pure water. [23] Let us hold on to the confession of our hope without wavering, for He who promised is faithful. [24] And let us be concerned about one another in order to promote love and good works, [25] not staying away from our meetings, as some habitually do, but encouraging each other, and all the more as you see the day drawing near.

## Warning against Willful Sin

[26] For if we deliberately sin after receiving the knowledge of the truth, there no longer remains a sacrifice for sins, [27] but a terrifying expectation of judgment, and the fury of a fire about to consume the adversaries. [28] If anyone disregards Moses' law, he dies without mercy, based on the testimony of two or three witnesses. [29] How much worse punishment, do you think one will deserve who has trampled on the Son of God, regarded as profane the blood of the covenant by which he was sanctified, and insulted the Spirit of grace? [30] For we know the One who has said, **Vengeance belongs to Me, I will repay,**[bc] and again, **The Lord will judge His people.**[d] [31] It is a terrifying thing to fall into the hands of the living God!

[32] Remember the earlier days when, after you had been enlightened, you endured a hard struggle with sufferings. [33] Sometimes you were publicly exposed to taunts and afflictions, and at other times you were companions of those who were treated that way. [34] For you sympathized with the prisoners[e] and accepted with joy the confiscation of your possessions, knowing that you yourselves have a better and enduring possession.[f] [35] So don't throw away your confidence, which

[a]10:16–17 Jr 31:33–34  [b]10:30 Other mss add *says the Lord*  [c]10:30 Dt 32:35  [d]10:30 Dt 32:36
[e]10:34 Other mss read *sympathized with my imprisonment*  [f]10:34 Other mss add *in heaven*

has a great reward. [36] For you need endurance, so that after you have done God's will, you may receive what was promised.

---

### Hebrews 10:32-36

*Most people do well if they can wait a week to see the fruit of their decisions. But the Christian life doesn't promise to pay off in a hurry—or in the way you think. You've got forever to see the truth win out, to get your questions answered. Are you willing to wait?*

---

[37] For in yet **a very little while, the Coming One will come and not delay.**
[38] **But My righteous one[a] will live by faith; and if he draws back, My soul has no pleasure in him.[b]**

[39] But we are not those who draw back and are destroyed, but those who have faith and obtain life.

## Heroes of Faith

11 Now faith is the reality of what is hoped for, the proof of what is not seen. [2] For by it our ancestors were approved.

[3] By faith we understand that the universe was created by the word of God, so that what is seen has been made from things that are not visible.

[4] By faith Abel offered to God a better sacrifice than Cain ⌊did⌋. By this he was approved as a righteous man, because God approved his gifts, and even though he is dead, he still speaks through this.

[5] By faith, Enoch was taken away so that he did not experience death, and **he was not to be found because God took him away.[c]** For prior to his transformation he was approved, having pleased God. [6] Now without faith it is impossible to please God, for the one who draws near to Him must believe that He exists and rewards those who seek Him.

[7] By faith Noah, after being warned about what was not yet seen, in reverence built an ark to deliver his family. By this he condemned the world and became an heir of the righteousness that comes by faith.

[8] By faith Abraham, when he was called, obeyed and went out to a place he was going to receive as an inheritance; he went out, not knowing where he was going. [9] By faith he stayed as a foreigner in the land of promise, living in tents with Isaac and Jacob, co-heirs of the same promise. [10] For he was looking forward to the

---

### Hebrews 11:6

### God the Father

*The beginning point of faith is the belief that God exists—not just any god, not a somewhere god, not an "Everything is God" god. We're talking about the one true and living God, the only One with the power to do what He wants and the love to give us what we need . . . Him.*

---

[a]10:38 Other mss read *the righteous one*   [b]10:37–38 Is 26:20 LXX; Hab 2:3–4   [c]11:5 Gn 5:21–24

city that has foundations, whose architect and builder is God.

¹¹ By faith even Sarah herself, when she was barren, received power to conceive offspring, even though she was past the age, since she considered that the One who had promised was faithful. ¹² And therefore from one man—in fact, from one as good as dead—came offspring as numerous as the stars of heaven and as innumerable as the grains of sand by the seashore.

¹³ These all died in faith without having received the promises, but they saw them from a distance, greeted them, and confessed that they were foreigners and temporary residents on the earth. ¹⁴ Now those who say such things make it clear that they are seeking a homeland. ¹⁵ If they had been remembering that land they came from, they would have had opportunity to return. ¹⁶ But they now aspire to a better land—a heavenly one. Therefore God is not ashamed to be called their God, for He has prepared a city for them.

¹⁷ By faith Abraham, when he was tested, offered up Isaac; he who had received the promises was offering up his •one and only son, ¹⁸ about whom it had been said, **In Isaac your seed will be called.**ᵃ ¹⁹ He considered God to be able even to raise someone from the dead, from which he also got him back as an illustration.

²⁰ By faith Isaac blessed Jacob and Esau concerning things to come. ²¹ By faith Jacob, when he was dying, blessed each of the sons of Joseph, and, **he worshiped, leaning on the top of his staff.**ᵇ ²² By faith Joseph, as he was nearing the end of his life, mentioned the exodus of the sons of Israel and gave instructions concerning his bones.

²³ By faith Moses, after he was born, was hidden by his parents for three months, because they saw that the child was beautiful, and they didn't fear the king's edict. ²⁴ By faith Moses, when he had grown up, refused to be called the son of Pharaoh's daughter ²⁵ and chose to suffer with the people of God rather than to enjoy the short-lived pleasure of sin. ²⁶ For he considered reproach for the sake of the •Messiah to be greater wealth than the treasures of Egypt, since his attention was on the reward.

²⁷ By faith he left Egypt behind, not being afraid of the king's anger, for he persevered, as one who sees Him who is invisible. ²⁸ By faith he instituted the •Passover and the sprinkling of the blood, so that the destroyer of the firstborn might not touch them. ²⁹ By faith they crossed the Red Sea as though they were on dry land. When the Egyptians attempted to do this, they were drowned.

³⁰ By faith the walls of Jericho fell down after being encircled for seven days. ³¹ By faith Rahab the prostitute received the spies in peace and didn't perish with those who disobeyed.

³² And what more can I say? Time is too short for me to tell about Gideon, Barak, Samson, Jephthah, of David and Samuel and the prophets, ³³ who by faith conquered kingdoms, administered justice, obtained promises, shut the mouths of lions, ³⁴ quenched the raging of fire, escaped the edge of the sword, gained strength after being weak, became mighty in battle, and put foreign armies to flight. ³⁵ Women received their dead raised to life again. Some men were tortured, not accepting release, so that they might gain a

ᵃ**11:18** Gn 21:12    ᵇ**11:21** Gn 47:31

better resurrection, [36] and others experienced mockings and scourgings, as well as bonds and imprisonment. [37] They were stoned,[a] they were sawed in two, they died by the sword, they wandered about in sheepskins, in goatskins, destitute, afflicted, and mistreated. [38] The world was not worthy of them. They wandered in deserts, mountains, caves, and holes in the ground.

[39] All these were approved through their faith, but they did not receive what was promised, [40] since God had provided something better for us, so that they would not be made perfect without us.

## The Call to Endurance

**12** Therefore since we also have such a large cloud of witnesses surrounding us, let us lay aside every weight and the sin that so easily ensnares us, and run with endurance the race that lies before us, [2] keeping our eyes on Jesus, the source and perfecter of our faith, who for the joy that lay before Him endured a cross and despised the shame, and has sat down at the right hand of God's throne.

## Fatherly Discipline

[3] For consider Him who endured such hostility from sinners against Himself, so that you won't grow weary and lose heart. [4] In struggling against sin, you have not yet resisted to the point of shedding your blood. [5] And you have forgotten the exhortation that addresses you as sons:

**My son, do not take the
Lord's discipline lightly,**

---

*Hebrews 12:5-11*

*God the Father*

*Good fathers are not the ones who give their children everything they ask for. They're the ones who love their kids too much to let them always have their own foolish way—the ones who are willing to apply pressure now to avoid implosion later. That's the kind of Father we have.*

---

**or faint when you are
reproved by Him;
[6] for the Lord disciplines
the one He loves,
and punishes every son
whom He receives. [b]**

[7] Endure it as discipline: God is dealing with you as sons. For what son is there whom a father does not discipline? [8] But if you are without discipline—which all receive—then you are illegitimate children and not sons. [9] Furthermore, we had natural fathers discipline us, and we respected them. Shouldn't we submit even more to the Father of spirits and live? [10] For they disciplined us for a short time based on what seemed good to them, but He does it for our benefit, so that we can share His holiness. [11] No discipline seems enjoyable at the time, but painful. Later on, however, it yields the fruit of peace and righteousness to those who have been trained by it. [12] Therefore strengthen your tired hands and weakened knees, [13] and

---

[a]**11:37** Other mss add *they were tempted*   [b]**12:6** Pr 3:11–12

make straight paths for your feet, so that what is lame may not be dislocated, but healed instead.

## Warning against Rejecting God's Grace

[14] Pursue peace with everyone, and holiness—without it no one will see the Lord. [15] See to it that no one falls short of the grace of God and that no root of bitterness springs up, causing trouble and by it, defiling many. [16] And see that there isn't any immoral or irreverent person like Esau, who sold his birthright in exchange for one meal. [17] For you know that later, when he wanted to inherit the blessing, he was rejected because he didn't find any opportunity for repentance, though he sought it with tears.

[18] For you have not come to what could be touched, to a blazing fire, to darkness, gloom, and storm, [19] to the blast of a trumpet, and the sound of words. (Those who heard it begged that not another word be spoken to them, [20] for they could not bear what was commanded: **And if even an animal touches the mountain, it must be stoned!**[a] [21] And the appearance was so terrifying that Moses said, **I am terrified and trembling.**)[b] [22] Instead, you have come to Mount Zion, to the city of the living God (the heavenly Jerusalem), to myriads of angels in festive gathering, [23] to the assembly of the firstborn whose names have been written in heaven, to God who is the judge of all, to the spirits of righteous people made perfect, [24] to Jesus (mediator of a new covenant), and to the sprinkled blood, which says better things than the ⌊blood⌋ of Abel.

[25] See that you do not reject the One who speaks; for if they did not escape when they rejected Him who warned them on earth, even less will we if we turn away from Him who warns us from heaven. [26] His voice shook the earth at that time, but now He has promised, **Yet once more I will shake not only the earth but also heaven.**[c] [27] Now this expression, "Yet once more," indicates the removal of what can be shaken—that is, created things—so that what is not shaken might remain. [28] Therefore, since we are receiving a kingdom that cannot be shaken, let us hold on to grace. By it, we may serve God acceptably, with reverence and awe; [29] for our God is a consuming fire.

## Final Exhortations

**13** Let brotherly love continue. [2] Don't neglect to show hospitality, for by doing this some have welcomed angels as guests without knowing it. [3] Remember the prisoners, as though you were in prison with them, and the mistreated, as though you yourselves were suffering bodily. [4] Marriage must be respected by all, and the marriage

---

### Hebrews 13:1-3

*The table is set for you to be a chosen tool in the hand of God, to be the lens that people look through to feel His love, experience His grace, and find His life. The happiest you will ever be is when you're giving of yourself to others. Try it and see.*

---

[a]12:20 Ex 19:12   [b]12:21 Dt 9:19   [c]12:26 Hg 2:6

bed kept undefiled, because God will judge immoral people and adulterers. ⁵ Your life should be free from the love of money. Be satisfied with what you have, for He Himself has said, **I will never leave you or forsake you.**[a] ⁶ Therefore, we may boldly say:

**The Lord is my helper;
I will not be afraid.
What can man do to me?**[b]

⁷ Remember your leaders who have spoken God's word to you. As you carefully observe the outcome of their lives, imitate their faith. ⁸ Jesus Christ is the same yesterday, today, and forever. ⁹ Don't be led astray by various kinds of strange teachings; for it is good for the heart to be established by grace and not by foods, since those involved in them have not benefited. ¹⁰ We have an altar from which those who serve the •tabernacle do not have a right to eat. ¹¹ For the bodies of those animals whose blood is brought into the holy of holies by the high priest as a sin offering are burned outside the camp. ¹² Therefore Jesus also suffered outside the gate, so that He might sanctify the people by His own blood. ¹³ Let us then go to Him outside the camp, bearing His disgrace. ¹⁴ For here we do not have an enduring city; instead, we seek the one to come. ¹⁵ Therefore, through Him let us continually offer up to God a sacrifice of praise, that is, the fruit of our lips that confess His name. ¹⁶ Don't neglect to do good and to share, for God is pleased with such sacrifices. ¹⁷ Obey your leaders and submit to them, for they keep watch over your souls as those who will give an account, so that they can do this with joy and not with grief, for that would be unprofitable for you. ¹⁸ Pray for us; for we are convinced that we have a clear conscience, wanting to conduct ourselves honorably in everything. ¹⁹ And I especially urge you to pray that I may be restored to you very soon.

*"Jesus is the leader. I am the follower. My goal today is to follow His schedule, accomplish His agenda, and love whoever He sends my way."*
*—John Kramp*

### Benediction and Farewell

²⁰ Now may the God of peace, who brought up from the dead our Lord Jesus—the great Shepherd of the sheep—with the blood of the everlasting covenant, ²¹ equip you with all that is good to do His will, working in us what is pleasing in His sight, through Jesus Christ, to whom be glory forever and ever.[c] •Amen.
²² Brothers, I urge you to receive this word of exhortation, for I have written to you in few words. ²³ Be aware that our brother Timothy has been released. If he comes soon enough, he will be with me when I see you. ²⁴ Greet all your leaders and all the saints. Those who are from Italy greet you. ²⁵ Grace be with all of you.

[a]**13:5** Dt 31:6   [b]**13:6** Ps 118:6   [c]**13:21** Other mss omit *and ever*

# JAMES

## Greeting

**1** James, a slave of God and of the Lord Jesus Christ:

To the 12 tribes in the Dispersion.

Greetings.

## Trials and Maturity

[2] Consider it a great joy, my brothers, whenever you experience various trials, [3] knowing that the testing of your faith produces endurance. [4] But endurance must do its complete work, so that you may be mature and complete, lacking nothing.

[5] Now if any of you lacks wisdom, he should ask God, who gives to all generously and without criticizing, and it will be given to him. [6] But let him ask in faith without doubting. For the doubter is like the surging sea, driven and tossed by the wind. [7] That person should not expect to receive anything from the Lord. [8] An indecisive man is unstable in all his ways.

[9] The brother of humble circumstances should boast in his exaltation; [10] but the one who is rich ⌊should boast⌋ in his humiliation, because he will pass away like a flower of the field. [11] For the sun rises with its scorching heat and dries up the grass; its flower falls off, and its beautiful appearance is destroyed. In the same way, the rich man will wither away while pursuing his activities.

[12] Blessed is a man who endures trial, because when he passes the test he will receive the crown of life that He[a] has promised to those who love Him.

[13] No one undergoing a trial should say, "I am being tempted by God." For God is not tempted by evil, and He Himself doesn't tempt anyone. [14] But each person is tempted when he is drawn away and enticed by his own evil desires. [15] Then after desire has conceived, it gives birth to sin, and when sin is fully grown, it gives birth to death.

[16] Don't be deceived, my dearly loved brothers. [17] Every generous act and every perfect gift is from above, coming down from the Father of lights; with Him there is no variation or shadow cast by turning. [18] By His own choice, He gave us a new birth by the message of truth so that we would be the •firstfruits of His creatures.

---

### James 1:19-25

*Christ has saved you from sin, but the temptation to keep dabbling in it will keep you busy the rest of your life. The way to start battling it is to fill your mind so full with the Word of God that the devil's lies can't find any room to work.*

---

## Hearing and Doing the Word

[19] My dearly loved brothers, understand this: everyone must be quick to hear, slow to speak, and slow to anger, [20] for man's anger does not accomplish

God's righteousness. [21] Therefore, ridding yourselves of all moral filth and evil excess, humbly receive the implanted word, which is able to save you.

---

*"The light Jesus brings helps us to see ourselves more clearly and not to be fooled by what is hidden inside."*

—*James Houston*

---

[22] But be doers of the word and not hearers only, deceiving yourselves. [23] Because if anyone is a hearer of the word and not a doer, he is like a man looking at his own face in a mirror; [24] for he looks at himself, goes away, and right away forgets what kind of man he was. [25] But the one who looks intently into the perfect law of freedom and perseveres in it, and is not a forgetful hearer but a doer who acts—this person will be blessed in what he does.

[26] If anyone[a] thinks he is religious, without controlling his tongue but deceiving his heart, his religion is useless. [27] Pure and undefiled religion before our God and Father is this: to look after orphans and widows in their distress and to keep oneself unstained by the world.

## The Sin of Favoritism

**2** My brothers, hold your faith in our glorious Lord Jesus Christ without showing favoritism. [2] For suppose a man comes into your meeting wearing a gold ring, dressed in fine clothes, and a poor man dressed in dirty clothes also comes in. [3] If you look with favor on the man wearing the fine clothes so that you say, "Sit here in a good place," and yet you say to the poor man, "Stand over there," or, "Sit here on the floor by my footstool," [4] haven't you discriminated among yourselves and become judges with evil thoughts?

[5] Listen, my dear brothers: Didn't God choose the poor in this world to be rich in faith and heirs of the kingdom that He has promised to those who love Him? [6] Yet you dishonored that poor man. Don't the rich oppress you and drag you into the courts? [7] Don't they blaspheme the noble name that you bear?

[8] If you really carry out the royal law prescribed in Scripture, **You shall love your neighbor as yourself,**[b] you are doing well. [9] But if you show favoritism, you commit sin and are convicted by the law as transgressors. [10] For whoever keeps the entire law, yet fails in one point, is guilty of ⌊breaking it⌋ all. [11] For He who said, **Do not commit adultery,**[c] also said, **Do not murder.**[d] So if you do not commit adultery, but you do murder, you are a lawbreaker.

[12] Speak and act as those who will be judged by the law of freedom. [13] For judgment is without mercy to the one who hasn't shown mercy. Mercy triumphs over judgment.

## Faith and Works

[14] What good is it, my brothers, if someone says he has faith, but does not have works? Can his faith save him? [15] If a brother or sister is without clothes and lacks daily food, [16] and one of you says to them, "Go in peace, keep warm, and eat well," but you don't give them what the body needs, what good is it? [17] In the same way faith, if it doesn't have works, is dead by itself.

---

[a]**1:26** Other mss add *among you*   [b]**2:8** Lv 19:18   [c]**2:11** Ex 20:14; Dt 5:18   [d]**2:11** Ex 20:13; Dt 5:17

*James 2:15-17*

## Christian Influence

*"I'll be praying for you" has a powerful place in the vocabulary of the believer, but it doesn't exempt us from getting our hands dirty, from doing without, from going out of our way to meet the immediate needs of those who are hot, hungry, tired, and discouraged.*

---

[18] But someone will say, "You have faith, and I have works." Show me your faith without works, and I will show you faith from my works.[a] [19] You believe that God is one; you do well. The demons also believe—and they shudder.

[20] Foolish man! Are you willing to learn that faith without works is useless? [21] Wasn't Abraham our father justified by works when he offered Isaac his son on the altar? [22] You see that faith was active together with his works, and by works, faith was perfected. [23] So the Scripture was fulfilled that says, **Abraham believed God, and it was credited to him for righteousness,**[b] and he was called God's friend. [24] You see that a man is justified by works and not by faith alone. [25] And in the same way, wasn't Rahab the prostitute also justified by works when she received the messengers and sent them out by a different route? [26] For just as the body without the spirit is dead, so also faith without works is dead.

## Controlling the Tongue

**3** Not many should become teachers, my brothers, knowing that we will receive a stricter judgment; [2] for we all stumble in many ways. If anyone does not stumble in what he says, he is a mature man who is also able to control his whole body.

[3] Now when we put bits into the mouths of horses to make them obey us, we also guide the whole animal. [4] And consider ships: though very large and driven by fierce winds, they are guided by a very small rudder wherever the will of the pilot directs. [5] So too, though the tongue is a small part ⌊of the body⌋, it boasts great things. Consider how large a forest a small fire ignites. [6] And the tongue is a fire. The tongue, a world of unrighteousness, is placed among the parts of our ⌊bodies⌋; it pollutes the whole body, sets the course of life on fire, and is set on fire by •hell.

[7] For every creature—animal or bird, reptile or fish—is tamed and has been tamed by man, [8] but no man can tame the tongue. It is a restless evil, full of deadly poison. [9] With it we bless our Lord and Father, and with it we curse men who are made in God's likeness. [10] Out of the same mouth come blessing and cursing. My brothers, these things should not be this way. [11] Does a spring pour out sweet and bitter water from the same opening? [12] Can a fig tree produce olives, my brothers, or a grapevine ⌊produce⌋ figs? Neither can a salt-water spring yield fresh water.

## The Wisdom from Above

[13] Who is wise and understanding among you? He should show his works by good conduct with wisdom's

---

a[2:18] Other mss read *Show me your faith from your works, and from my works I will show you my faith*
b[2:23] Gn 15:6

*"You can't testify to your righteousness and His at the same time. You can only give witness to His righteousness in you."*
—*Jim Gilbert*

gentleness. [14] But if you have bitter envy and selfish ambition in your heart, don't brag and lie in defiance of the truth. [15] Such wisdom does not come down from above, but is earthly, sensual, demonic. [16] For where envy and selfish ambition exist, there is disorder and every kind of evil. [17] But the wisdom from above is first pure, then peace-loving, gentle, compliant, full of mercy and good fruits, without favoritism and hypocrisy. [18] And the fruit of righteousness is sown in peace by those who make peace.

## Proud or Humble

4 What is the source of the wars and the fights among you? Don't they come from the cravings that are at war within you? [2] You desire and do not have. You murder and covet and cannot obtain. You fight and war. You do not have because you do not ask. [3] You ask and don't receive because you ask wrongly, so that you may spend it on your desires for pleasure. [4] Adulteresses![a] Do you not know that friendship with the world is hostility toward God? So whoever wants to be the world's friend becomes God's enemy. [5] Or do you think it's without reason the Scripture says that the Spirit He has caused to live in us yearns jealously?

[6] But He gives greater grace. Therefore He says:

**God resists the proud,
but gives grace to the humble.[b]**

[7] Therefore, submit to God. But resist the Devil, and he will flee from you. [8] Draw near to God, and He will draw near to you. Cleanse your hands, sinners, and purify your hearts, double-minded people! [9] Be miserable and mourn and weep. Your laughter must change to mourning and your joy to sorrow. [10] Humble yourselves before the Lord, and He will exalt you.

[11] Don't criticize one another, brothers. He who criticizes a brother or judges his brother criticizes the law and judges the law. But if you judge the law, you are not a doer of the law but a judge. [12] There is one lawgiver and judge[c] who is able to save and to destroy. But who are you to judge your neighbor?

## Our Will and His Will

[13] Come now, you who say, "Today or tomorrow we will travel to such

James 4:7-10

*No amount of personal improvement or bootstraps reform measures can help you defeat temptation. You'll reach the end of your willpower quicker than you think. We like to think we can will our way past the tight spots of life. We think too highly of ourselves.*

---

[a]4:4 Other mss read *Adulterers and adulteresses*   [b]4:6 Pr 3:34   [c]4:12 Other mss omit *and judge*

and such a city and spend a year there and do business and make a profit." [14] You don't even know what tomorrow will bring—what your life will be! For you are a bit of smoke that appears for a little while, then vanishes.

[15] Instead, you should say, "If the Lord wills, we will live and do this or that." [16] But as it is, you boast in your arrogance. All such boasting is evil. [17] So, for the person who knows to do good and doesn't do it, it is a sin.

### Warning to the Rich

5 Come now, you rich people! Weep and wail over the miseries that are coming on you. [2] Your wealth is ruined: your clothes are moth-eaten; [3] your silver and gold are corroded, and their corrosion will be a witness against you and will eat your flesh like fire. You stored up treasure in the last days! [4] Look! The pay that you withheld from the workers who reaped your fields cries out, and the outcry of the harvesters has reached the ears of the Lord of Hosts. [5] You have lived luxuriously on the land and have indulged yourselves. You have fattened your hearts for the day of slaughter. [6] You have condemned— you have murdered—the righteous man; he does not resist you.

### Waiting for the Lord

[7] Therefore, brothers, be patient until the Lord's coming. See how the farmer waits for the precious fruit of the earth and is patient with it until it receives the early and the late rains. [8] You also must be patient. Strengthen your hearts, because the Lord's coming is near.

---

*James 5:7-8*

*Last Things*

*Things we've had to wait for mean all that much more when they finally get here. It'll be like that with Christ's coming. If He happens to come before we die—but after we've been through hard times, hurt feelings, and scrapes with danger—we'll know that all the waiting was worth it.*

---

[9] Brothers, do not complain about one another, so that you will not be judged. Look, the judge stands at the door!

[10] Brothers, take the prophets who spoke in the Lord's name as an example of suffering and patience. [11] See, we count as blessed those who have endured. You have heard of Job's endurance and have seen the outcome from the Lord: the Lord is very compassionate and merciful.

### Truthful Speech

[12] Now above all, my brothers, do not swear, either by heaven or by earth or with any other oath. Your "yes" must be "yes," and your "no" must be "no," so that you won't fall under judgment.[a]

### Effective Prayer

[13] Is anyone among you suffering? He should pray. Is anyone cheerful?

[a]5:12 Other mss read *fall into hypocrisy*

He should sing praises. [14] Is anyone among you sick? He should call for the elders of the church, and they should pray over him after anointing him with olive oil in the name of the Lord. [15] The prayer of faith will save the sick person, and the Lord will raise him up; and if he has committed sins, he will be forgiven. [16] Therefore, confess your sins to one another and pray for one another, so that you may be healed. The intense prayer of the righteous is very powerful. [17] Elijah was a man with a nature like ours; yet he prayed earnestly that it would not rain, and for three years and six months it did not rain on the land. [18] Then he prayed again, and the sky gave rain and the land produced its fruit.

[19] My brothers, if any among you strays from the truth, and someone turns him back, [20] he should know that whoever turns a sinner from the error of his way will save his *life from death and cover a multitude of sins.

# 1 PETER

## Greeting

1 Peter, an apostle of Jesus Christ:

To the temporary residents of the Dispersion in the provinces of Pontus, Galatia, Cappadocia, Asia, and Bithynia, chosen ² according to the foreknowledge of God the Father and set apart by the Spirit for obedience and ⌊for the⌋ sprinkling with the blood of Jesus Christ.

May grace and peace be multiplied to you.

## A Living Hope

³ Blessed be the God and Father of our Lord Jesus Christ. According to His great mercy, He has given us a new birth into a living hope through the resurrection of Jesus Christ from the dead, ⁴ and into an inheritance that is imperishable, uncorrupted, and unfading, kept in heaven for you, ⁵ who are being protected by God's power through faith for a salvation that is ready to be revealed in the last time. ⁶ You rejoice in this, though now for a short time you have had to be distressed by various trials ⁷ so that the genuineness of your faith—more valuable than gold, which perishes though refined by fire—may result in praise, glory, and honor at the revelation of Jesus Christ. ⁸ You love Him, though you have not seen Him. And though not seeing Him now, you believe in Him and rejoice with inexpressible and glorious joy, ⁹ because you are receiving the goal of your[a] faith, the salvation of your souls.

¹⁰ Concerning this salvation, the prophets who prophesied about the grace that would come to you, searched and carefully investigated. ¹¹ They inquired into what time or what circumstances the Spirit of Christ within them was indicating when He testified in advance to the messianic sufferings and the glories that would follow. ¹² It was revealed to them that they were not serving themselves but you concerning things that have now been announced to you through those who preached the gospel to you by the Holy Spirit sent from heaven. Angels desire to look into these things.

## A Call to Holy Living

¹³ Therefore, get your minds ready for action, being self-disciplined, and set your hope completely on the grace to be brought to you at the revelation of Jesus Christ. ¹⁴ As obedient children, do not be conformed to the desires of your former ignorance ¹⁵ but, as the One who called you is holy, you also are to be holy in all your conduct; ¹⁶ for it is written, **Be holy, because I am holy.**[b]

¹⁷ And if you address as Father the One who judges impartially based on each one's work, you are to conduct yourselves in reverence during this time of temporary residence. ¹⁸ For you know that you were redeemed from your empty way of life inherited from the fathers, not with perishable things, like silver or gold, ¹⁹ but with the precious blood of Christ, like that of a lamb without defect or blemish. ²⁰ He was destined before the foundation of the

a1:9 Other mss read *our*, or omit the possessive pronoun   b1:16 Lv 11:44–45; 19:2; 20:7

*1 Peter 1:17*

*God the Father*

*God is perfectly holy and eternal.
And what difference does that
make? It means that we should try
to be as much like Him as we can
(as near perfection as humanly
possible) and that we should let
our minds think bigger than this
world, for there is more to life than
what we see.*

world, but was revealed at the end of
the times for you [21] who through Him
are believers in God, who raised Him
from the dead and gave Him glory, so
that your faith and hope are in God.
[22] By obedience to the truth,[a]
having purified yourselves for sincere love of the brothers, love one
another earnestly from a pure[b]
heart, [23] since you have been born
again—not of perishable seed but
of imperishable—through the living and enduring word of God.
[24] For

**All flesh is like grass,
and all its glory like a flower
of the grass.
The grass withers,
and the flower drops off,
[25] but the word of the Lord
endures forever.[c]**

And this is the word that was preached
as the gospel to you.

*The Living Stone and a Holy People*

**2** So rid yourselves of all wickedness,
all deceit, hypocrisy, envy, and all
slander. [2] Like newborn infants, desire
the unadulterated spiritual milk, so that
you may grow by it in ⌊your⌋ salvation,[d]
[3] since **you have tasted that the Lord
is good.**[e] [4] Coming to Him, a living
stone—rejected by men but chosen
and valuable to God— [5] you yourselves, as living stones, are being built
into a spiritual house for a holy priesthood to offer spiritual sacrifices acceptable to God through Jesus Christ. [6] For
it stands in Scripture:

**Look! I lay a stone in Zion,
a chosen and valuable
cornerstone,
and the one who believes in
Him
will never be put to shame!**[f]

[7] So the honor is for you who believe;
but for the unbelieving,

**The stone that the builders
rejected—
this One has become the
cornerstone,**[g]

and

[8] **A stone that causes men to
stumble,
and a rock that trips them up.**[h]

They stumble by disobeying the message; they were destined for this.

[9] But you are **a chosen race,**[i] **a
royal priesthood,**[j]
**a holy nation,**[k] **a people for
His possession,**[l]

[a]**1:22** Other mss add *through the Spirit*   [b]**1:22** Other mss omit *pure*   [c]**1:24–25** Is 40:6–8   [d]**2:2** Other mss omit
*in your salvation*   [e]**2:3** Ps 34:8   [f]**2:6** Is 28:16 LXX   [g]**2:7** Ps 118:22   [h]**2:8** Is 8:14   [i]**2:9** Is 43:20 LXX; Dt 7:6;
10:15   [j]**2:9** Ex 19:6; 23:22 LXX; Is 61:6   [k]**2:9** Ex 19:6; 23:22 LXX   [l]**2:9** Ex 19:5; 23:22 LXX; Dt 4:20; 7:6;
Is 43:21 LXX

*1 Peter 2:9-10*

*You are part of a family who can trace its bloodline back 2,000 years to a hillside in Jerusalem—and to a place in the plan of God, dating back before time began. Every color, every nation, every age and generation. We're not the world. We're the family of God.*

**so that you may proclaim the praises**[a]
of the One who called you
      out of darkness
into His marvelous light.
[10] Once you were not a
      people,
but now you are God's
      people;
you had not received mercy,
but now you have received
      mercy.

## A Call to Good Works

[11] Dear friends, I urge you as aliens and temporary residents to abstain from fleshly desires that war against you. [12] Conduct yourselves honorably among the Gentiles, so that in a case where they speak against you as those who do evil, they may, by observing your good works, glorify God in a day of visitation. [13] Submit to every human institution because of the Lord, whether to the Emperor as the supreme authority, [14] or to governors as those sent out by him to punish those who do evil and to praise those who do good.

[15] For it is God's will that you, by doing good, silence the ignorance of foolish people. [16] As God's slaves, ⌊live⌋ as free people, but don't use your freedom as a way to conceal evil. [17] Honor everyone. Love the brotherhood. Fear God. Honor the Emperor.

## Submission of Slaves to Masters

[18] Household slaves, submit yourselves to your masters with all respect, not only to the good and gentle but also to the cruel. [19] For it ⌊brings⌋ favor[b] if, because of conscience toward God,[c] someone endures grief from suffering unjustly. [20] For what credit is there if you endure when you sin and are beaten? But when you do good and suffer, if you endure, it brings favor with God.

[21] For you were called to this,
      because Christ also suffered
         for you,
      leaving you an example,
      so that you should follow in
         His steps.
[22] He **did not commit sin,
      and no deceit was found in
         His mouth;**[d]
[23] when reviled, He did not
         revile in return;
      when suffering, He did not
         threaten,
      but committed Himself to the
         One who judges justly.
[24] He Himself bore our sins

*"Christians are people whose activities are not so much determined by their past as they are by their future."*
*—Timothy R. Phillips*

[a]**2:9** Is 42:12; 43:21   [b]**2:19** Other mss add *with God*   [c]**2:19** Other mss read *because of a good conscience*
[d]**2:22** Is 53:9

in His body on the tree,
so that, having died to sins,
we might live for
   righteousness;
by **His wounding you have
   been healed.** [a]

25 For you **were like sheep
   going astray,**[b]
but you have now returned
to the shepherd and guardian
   of your souls.

## Wives and Husbands

**3** Wives, in the same way, submit yourselves to your own husbands so that, even if some disobey the [Christian] message, they may be won over without a message by the way their wives live, [2] when they observe your pure, reverent lives. [3] Your beauty should not be the outer beauty of elaborate hairstyles and the wearing of gold ornaments or of fine clothes; [4] rather, it should be an inner beauty with the imperishability of a gentle and quiet spirit, which is very valuable in God's eyes. [5] For in the past, the holy women who hoped in God also beautified themselves in this way, submitting to their own husbands, [6] just as Sarah obeyed Abraham, calling him lord. You have become her children when you do good and aren't frightened by anything alarming.

[7] Husbands, in the same way, live with your wives with understanding of their weaker nature yet showing them honor as co-heirs of the grace of life, so that your prayers will not be hindered.

## Do No Evil

[8] Now finally, all of you should be like-minded and sympathetic, should love believers, and be compassionate and humble,[c] [9] not paying back evil for evil or insult for insult but, on the contrary, giving a blessing, since you were called for this, so that you can inherit a blessing.

10 For **the one who wants to
   love life
and to see good days
must keep his tongue from evil
and his lips from speaking
   deceit,**
11 **and he must turn away from
   evil and do good.
He must seek peace and
   pursue it,**
12 **because the eyes of the Lord
   are on the righteous
and His ears are open to
   their request.
But the face of the Lord is
   against those who do evil.**[d]

## Undeserved Suffering

[13] And who will harm you if you are passionate for what is good? [14] But even if you should suffer for righteousness, you are blessed. **Do not fear what they fear or be disturbed,**[e] [15] but set apart the Messiah[f] as Lord in your hearts, and always be ready to give a defense to anyone who asks you a reason for the hope that is in you. [16] However, do this with gentleness and respect, keeping your conscience clear, so that when you are accused,[g] those who denounce your Christian life will be put to shame. [17] For it is better to suffer for doing good, if that should be God's will, than for doing evil.

18 For Christ also suffered for
   sins once for all,[h]

---

[a]**2:24** Is 53:5  [b]**2:25** Is 53:6  [c]**3:8** Other mss read *courteous*  [d]**3:10–12** Ps 34:12–16  [e]**3:14** Is 8:12
[f]**3:15** Other mss read *set God*  [g]**3:16** Other mss read *when they speak against you as evildoers*  [h]**3:18** Other
mss read *died for sins on our behalf,* other mss read *died for our sins;* other mss read *died for sins on your behalf*

the righteous for the
    unrighteous,
that He might bring you[a] to
    God,
after being put to death in the
    fleshly realm
but made alive in the spiritual
    realm.

19 In that state He also went and made a proclamation to the spirits in prison 20 who in the past were disobedient, when God patiently waited in the days of Noah while an ark was being prepared; in it, a few—that is, eight people—were saved through water. 21 Baptism, which corresponds to this, now saves you (not the removal of the filth of the flesh, but the pledge of a good conscience toward God) through the resurrection of Jesus Christ. 22 Now that He has gone into heaven, He is at God's right hand, with angels, authorities, and powers subjected to Him.

## Following Christ

**4** Therefore, since Christ suffered[b] in the flesh, arm yourselves also with the same resolve—because the One who suffered in the flesh has finished with sin— 2 in order to live the remaining time in the flesh, no longer for human desires, but for God's will. 3 For there has already been enough time spent in doing the will of the pagans: carrying on in unrestrained behavior, evil desires, drunkenness, orgies, carousing, and lawless idolatry. 4 In regard to this, they are surprised that you don't plunge with them into the same flood of dissipation—and they slander you. 5 They will give an account to the One who stands ready to judge the

living and the dead. 6 For this reason the gospel was also preached to ⌊those who are now⌋ dead, so that, although they might be judged by men in the fleshly realm, they might live by God in the spiritual realm.

---

### 1 Peter 4:7-11

### Christian Influence

*Our goal in loving other people is that they will see in us the love of Christ. Not all of us do this in the same way. God has equipped each of us individually with gifts and abilities, interests and inclinations, that He will use to make our service to Him exactly what the people around us need.*

---

## End-time Ethics

7 Now the end of all things is near; therefore, be clear-headed and disciplined for prayer. 8 Above all, keep your love for one another at full strength, since **love covers a multitude of sins.**[c] 9 Be hospitable to one another without complaining. 10 Based on the gift they have received, everyone should use it to serve others, as good managers of the varied grace of God. 11 If anyone speaks, ⌊his speech should be⌋ like the oracles of God; if anyone serves, ⌊his service should be⌋ from the strength God provides, so that in everything God may be glorified through Jesus Christ. To Him belong the glory and the power forever and ever. •Amen!

---

a3:18 Other mss read *us*   b4:1 Other mss read *suffered for us*   c4:8 Pr 10:12

## Christian Suffering

[12] Dear friends, when the fiery ordeal arises among you to test you, don't be surprised by it, as if something unusual were happening to you. [13] Instead, as you share in the sufferings of the *Messiah rejoice, so that you may also rejoice with great joy at the revelation of His glory. [14] If you are ridiculed for the name of Christ, you are blessed, because the Spirit of glory and of God rests on you.[a] [15] None of you, however, should suffer as a murderer, a thief, an evildoer, or as a meddler. [16] But if ⌊anyone suffers⌋ as a Christian, he should not be ashamed, but should glorify God with that name. [17] For the time has come for judgment to begin with God's household; and if it begins with us, what will the outcome be for those who disobey the gospel of God?

[18] And **if the righteous is saved
   with difficulty,
   what will become of the
   ungodly and the sinner?**[b]

[19] So those who suffer according to God's will should, in doing good, entrust themselves to a faithful Creator.

## About the Elders

**5** Therefore, as a fellow elder and witness to the sufferings of the *Messiah, and also a participant in the glory about to be revealed, I exhort the elders among you: [2] shepherd God's flock among you, not overseeing[c] out of compulsion but freely, according to God's ⌊will⌋;[d] not for the money but eagerly; [3] not lording it over those entrusted to you, but being examples to the flock. [4] And when the chief Shepherd appears, you will receive the unfading crown of glory.

[5] Likewise, you younger men, be subject to the elders. And all of you clothe yourselves with humility toward one another, because

**God resists the proud,
   but gives grace to the
   humble.**[e]

[6] Humble yourselves therefore under the mighty hand of God, so that He may exalt you in due time, [7] casting all your care upon Him, because He cares about you.

## Conclusion

[8] Be sober! Be on the alert! Your adversary the Devil is prowling around like a roaring lion, looking for anyone he can devour. [9] Resist him, firm in the faith, knowing that the same sufferings are being experienced by your brothers in the world.

---

### 1 Peter 5:8-9

*One of the few people who knows your weak spots as well as you do is the devil. But you can learn how to use this inside knowledge to beat him at his own game. You can paint temptation into a corner by sealing off its favorite points of entry into your life.*

---

[10] Now the God of all grace, who called you to His eternal glory in

---

[a]**4:14** Other mss add *He is blasphemed because of them, but He is glorified because of you.*   [b]**4:18** Pr 11:31 LXX   [c]**5:2** Other mss omit *overseeing*   [d]**5:2** Other mss omit *according to God's will*   [e]**5:5** Pr 3:34 LXX

Christ Jesus, will personally restore, establish, strengthen, and support you after you have suffered a little. [11] To Him be the dominion[a] forever.[b] •Amen!

[12] Through Silvanus, whom I consider a faithful brother, I have written briefly, encouraging you and testifying that this is the true grace of God. Take your stand in it! [13] She who is in Babylon, also chosen, sends you greetings, as does Mark, my son. [14] Greet one another with a kiss of love. Peace to all of you who are in Christ.[c]

> "Everything can be taken from a man but one thing: the last of human freedoms—to choose one's attitude in any given set of circumstances."
> —Viktor Frankl

[a]5:11 Other mss read *dominion and glory*; other mss read *glory and dominion*   [b]5:11 Other mss read *forever and ever*   [c]5:14 Other mss read *Christ Jesus. Amen.*

# 2 PETER

## Greeting

**1** Simeon Peter, a slave and an apostle of Jesus Christ:

To those who have obtained a faith of equal privilege with ours through the righteousness of our God and Savior Jesus Christ.

2 May grace and peace be multiplied to you through the knowledge of God and of Jesus our Lord.

## Growth in the Faith

3 For His divine power has given us everything required for life and godliness, through the knowledge of Him who called us by His own glory and goodness. 4 By these He has given us very great and precious promises, so that through them you may share in the divine nature, escaping the corruption that is in the world because of evil desires. 5 For this very reason, make every effort to supplement your faith with goodness, goodness with knowledge, 6 knowledge with self-control, self-control with endurance, endurance with godliness, 7 godliness with brotherly affection, and brotherly affection with love. 8 For if these qualities are yours and are increasing, they will keep you from being useless or unfruitful in the knowledge of our Lord Jesus Christ. 9 The person who lacks these things is blind and shortsighted, and has forgotten the cleansing from his past sins. 10 Therefore, brothers, make every effort to confirm your calling and election, because if you do these things you will never stumble. 11 For in this way, entry into the eternal kingdom of our Lord and Savior Jesus Christ will be richly supplied to you.

12 Therefore I will always remind you about these things, even though you know them and are established in the truth you have. 13 I consider it right, as long as I am in this tent, to wake you up with a reminder, 14 knowing that I will soon lay aside my tent, as our Lord Jesus Christ has also shown me. 15 And I will also make every effort that after my departure you may be able to recall these things at any time.

---

*"Knowing what is right and wrong, we have a way to have order and freedom simultaneously."*
—*Francis Schaeffer*

---

## The Trustworthy Prophetic Word

16 For we did not follow cleverly contrived myths when we made known to you the power and coming of our Lord Jesus Christ; instead, we were eyewitnesses of His majesty. 17 For when He received honor and glory from God the Father, a voice came to Him from the Majestic Glory:

This is My beloved Son.[a]
I take delight in Him!

a 1:17 Other mss read *My Son, My Beloved*

---

*2 Peter 1:16-21*

*Before you can really do what God says, you have to square it away in your mind that His Word is true, His commands are justified, and His authority is real. The truth is not the truth just because God says so. The truth is the truth because the truth is the truth.*

---

[18] And we heard this voice when it came from heaven while we were with Him on the holy mountain. [19] So we have the prophetic word strongly confirmed. You will do well to pay attention to it, as to a lamp shining in a dismal place, until the day dawns and the morning star arises in your hearts. [20] First of all, you should know this: no prophecy of Scripture comes from one's own interpretation, [21] because no prophecy ever came by the will of man; instead, moved by the Holy Spirit, men spoke from God.

## The Judgment of False Teachers

**2** But there were also false prophets among the people, just as there will be false teachers among you. They will secretly bring in destructive heresies, even denying the Master who bought them, and will bring swift destruction on themselves. [2] Many will follow their unrestrained ways, and because of them the way of truth will be blasphemed. [3] In their greed they will exploit you with deceptive words. Their condem-

nation, ⌊pronounced⌋ long ago, is not idle, and their destruction does not sleep.

[4] For if God didn't spare the angels who sinned, but threw them down into Tartarus and delivered them to be kept in chains^a of darkness until judgment; [5] and if He didn't spare the ancient world, but protected Noah, a preacher of righteousness, and seven others, when He brought a flood on the world of the ungodly; [6] and if He reduced the cities of Sodom and Gomorrah to ashes and condemned them to ruin,^b making them an example to those who were going to be ungodly;^c [7] and if He rescued righteous Lot, distressed by the unrestrained behavior of the immoral [8] (for as he lived among them, that righteous man tormented himself day by day with the lawless deeds he saw and heard), [9] then the Lord knows how to rescue the godly from trials and to keep the unrighteous under punishment until the day of judgment, [10] especially those who follow the polluting desires of the flesh and despise authority.

Bold, arrogant people! They do not tremble when they blaspheme the glorious ones; [11] however, angels, who are greater in might and power, do not bring a slanderous charge against them before the Lord.^d [12] But these people, like irrational animals—creatures of instinct born to be caught and destroyed—speak blasphemies about things they don't understand, and in their destruction they too will be destroyed, [13] suffering harm as the payment for unrighteousness. They consider it a pleasure to carouse in the daytime. They are blots and blemishes, delighting in their deceptions^e as they feast with

---

^a **2:4** Other mss read *in pits*   ^b **2:6** Other mss omit *to ruin*   ^c **2:6** Other mss read *an example of what is going to happen to the ungodly*   ^d **2:11** Other mss read *them from the Lord*   ^e **2:13** Other mss read *delighting in the love feasts*

you, [14] having eyes full of adultery and always looking for sin, seducing unstable people, and with hearts trained in greed. Accursed children! [15] By abandoning the straight path, they have gone astray and have followed the path of Balaam, the son of Bosor,[a] who loved the wages of unrighteousness, [16] but received a rebuke for his transgression: a speechless donkey spoke with a human voice and restrained the prophet's madness.

[17] These people are springs without water, mists driven by a whirlwind. The gloom of darkness has been reserved for them. [18] For uttering bombastic, empty words, they seduce, by fleshly desires and debauchery, people who have barely escaped from those who live in error. [19] They promise them freedom, but they themselves are slaves of corruption, since people are enslaved to whatever defeats them. [20] For if, having escaped the world's impurity through the knowledge of our Lord and Savior Jesus Christ, they are again entangled in these things and defeated, the last state is worse for them than the first. [21] For it would have been better for them not to have known the way of righteousness than, after knowing it, to turn back from the holy commandment delivered to them. [22] It has happened to them according to the true proverb: **A dog returns to its own vomit,**[b] and, "a sow, after washing itself, wallows in the mud."

## The Day of the Lord

**3** Dear friends, this is now the second letter I've written you; in both, I awaken your pure understanding with a reminder, [2] so that you can remember the words previously spoken by the holy prophets, and the commandment of our Lord and Savior ⌊given⌋ through your apostles. [3] First, be aware of this: scoffers will come in the last days to scoff, following their own lusts, [4] saying, "Where is the promise of His coming? For ever since the fathers fell •asleep, all things continue as they have been since the beginning of creation." [5] They willfully ignore this: long ago the heavens and the earth existed out of water and through water by the word of God. [6] Through these the world of that time perished when it was flooded by water. [7] But by the same word the present heavens and earth are held in store for fire, being kept until the day of judgment and destruction of ungodly men.

[8] Dear friends, don't let this one thing escape you: with the Lord one day is like 1,000 years, and 1,000 years like one day. [9] The Lord does not delay His promise, as some understand delay, but is patient with you, not wanting any to perish, but all to come to repentance.

---

*"There is no sweeter manner of living in the world than continuous communion with God. Only those who have experienced it can understand."*
—*Brother Lawrence*

---

[10] But the Day of the Lord will come like a thief;[c] on that ⌊day⌋ the heavens will pass away with a loud noise, the elements will burn and be dissolved, and the earth and the works on it will be disclosed.[d] [11] Since all these things

---

[a]2:15 Other mss read *Beor*    [b]2:22 Pr 26:11    [c]3:10 Other mss add *in the night*    [d]3:10 Other mss read *will be burned up*

*2 Peter 3:8-9*

## Last Things

*God has not forgotten about us.
But His concept of time and His
purpose for coming varies from
anything our human minds can
grasp. He will not come just in
time for you to avoid going to the
dentist, but He will come just in
time to help some people you
know avoid going to hell.*

are to be destroyed in this way, ⌊it is
clear⌋ what sort of people you should
be in holy conduct and godliness [12] as
you wait for and earnestly desire the
coming of the day of God, because of
which the heavens will be on fire and
be dissolved, and the elements will
melt with the heat. [13] But based on
His promise, we wait for new heavens
and a new earth, where righteousness
will dwell.

## Conclusion

[14] Therefore, dear friends, while
you wait for these things, make
every effort to be found in peace
without spot or blemish before Him.
[15] Also, regard the patience of our
Lord as ⌊an opportunity for⌋ salvation, just as our dear brother Paul,
according to the wisdom given to
him, has written to you. [16] He
speaks about these things in all his
letters, in which there are some
matters that are hard to understand.
The untaught and unstable twist
them to their own destruction, as
they also do with the rest of the
Scriptures.
[17] Therefore, dear friends, since you
have been forewarned, be on your
guard, so that you are not led away by
the error of the immoral and fall from
your own stability. [18] But grow in the
grace and knowledge of our Lord and
Savior Jesus Christ. To Him be the
glory both now and to the day of eternity. •Amen.[a]

*2 Peter 3:17-18*

*Since up to now you've always
counted on your gut instincts and
willpower, don't expect trusting
God to come naturally. Be prepared to hit a learning curve. Like
starting a new job or moving to a
new city, learning to think like a
Christian takes some time. You
grow into it.*

[a]**3:18** Other mss omit *Amen.*

# 1 John

## Prologue

**1** What was from the beginning,
what we have heard,
what we have seen with our
eyes,
what we have observed,
and have touched with our
hands,
concerning the Word of life—
² that life was revealed,
and we have seen it
and we testify and declare to
you
the eternal life that was with
the Father
and was revealed to us—
³ what we have seen and heard
we also declare to you,
so that you may have
fellowship along with us;
and indeed our fellowship is
with the Father
and with His Son Jesus Christ.
⁴ We are writing these things[a]
so that our[b] joy may be
complete.

## Fellowship with God

⁵ Now this is the message we have heard from Him and declare to you: God is light, and there is absolutely no darkness in Him. ⁶ If we say, "We have fellowship with Him," and •walk in darkness, we are lying and are not practicing the truth. ⁷ But if we walk in the light as He Himself is in the light, we have fellowship with one another, and the blood of Jesus His Son cleanses us from all sin. ⁸ If we say, "We have no sin," we are deceiving ourselves, and the truth is not in us. ⁹ If we confess our sins, He is faithful and righteous to forgive us our sins and to cleanse us from all unrighteousness. ¹⁰ If we say, "We have not sinned," we make Him a liar, and His word is not in us.

**2** My little children, I am writing you these things so that you may not sin. But if anyone does sin, we have an •advocate with the Father— Jesus Christ the righteous One. ² He Himself is the propitiation for our sins, and not only for ours, but also for those of the whole world.

---

*"God's intention is that we be free from this world's mindset. When we think like God thinks, we are free from the bonds of Satan."*
—*T. W. Hunt*

---

## God's Commands

³ This is how we are sure that we have come to know Him: by keeping His commands. ⁴ The one who says, "I have come to know Him," without keeping His commands, is a liar, and the truth is not in him. ⁵ But whoever keeps His word, truly in him the love of God is perfected. This is how we know we are in Him: ⁶ the one who says he remains in Him should •walk just as He walked.

⁷ Dear friends, I am not writing you a new command, but an old command that you have had from the beginning.

---

[a]**1:4** Other mss add *to you*   [b]**1:4** Other mss read *your*

The old command is the message you have heard. ⁸ Yet I am writing you a new command, which is true in Him and in you, because the darkness is passing away and the true light is already shining. ⁹ The one who says he is in the light but hates his brother is in the darkness until now. ¹⁰ The one who loves his brother remains in the light, and there is no cause for stumbling in him. ¹¹ But the one who hates his brother is in the darkness, walks in the darkness, and doesn't know where he's going, because the darkness has blinded his eyes.

## Reasons for Writing

¹² I am writing to you, little
children,
because your sins have been
forgiven on account of
His name.
¹³ I am writing to you, fathers,
because you have come to
know the One who is
from the beginning.
I am writing to you, young
men,
because you have had victory
over the evil one.
¹⁴ I have written to you,
children,
because you have come to
know the Father.
I have written to you,
fathers,
because you have come to
know the One who is
from the beginning.
I have written to you, young
men,
because you are strong,
God's word remains in you,
and you have had victory
over the evil one.

## A Warning about the World

¹⁵ Do not love the world or the things that belong to the world. If anyone loves the world, love for the Father is not in him. Because everything that belongs to the world— ¹⁶ the lust of the flesh, the lust of the eyes, and the pride in one's lifestyle— is not from the Father, but is from the world. ¹⁷ And the world with its lust is passing away, but the one who does God's will remains forever.

## The Last Hour

¹⁸ Children, it is the last hour. And as you have heard, "Antichrist is coming," even now many antichrists have come. We know from this that it is the last hour. ¹⁹ They went out from us, but they did not belong to us; for if they had belonged to us, they would have remained with us. However, they went out so that it might be made clear that none of them belongs to us. ²⁰ But you have an anointing from the Holy One, and you all have

knowledge.ᵃ ²¹ I have not written to you because you don't know the truth, but because you do know it, and because no lie comes from the truth. ²² Who is the liar, if not the one who denies that Jesus is the •Messiah? He is the antichrist, the one who denies the Father and the Son. ²³ No one who denies the Son can have the Father; he who confesses the Son has the Father as well.

## Remaining with God

²⁴ What you have heard from the beginning must remain in you. If what you have heard from the beginning remains in you, then you will remain in the Son and in the Father. ²⁵ And this is the promise that He Himself made to us: eternal life. ²⁶ I have written these things to you about those who are trying to deceive you.

²⁷ The anointing you received from Him remains in you, and you don't need anyone to teach you. Instead, His anointing teaches you about all things, and is true and is not a lie; just as it has taught you, remain in Him.

## God's Children

²⁸ So now, little children, remain in Him, so that when He appears we may have boldness and not be ashamed before Him at His coming. ²⁹ If you know that He is righteous, you know this as well: everyone who does what is right has been born of Him.

**3** ¹ Look at how great a love the Father has given us, that we should be called God's children. And we are! The reason the world does not know us is that it didn't know Him. ² Dear friends, we are God's children now, and what we will be has not yet been revealed. We know that when He appears, we will be like Him, because we will see Him as He is. ³ And everyone who has this hope in Him purifies himself just as He is pure.

⁴ Everyone who commits sin also breaks the law; sin is the breaking of law. ⁵ You know that He was revealed so that He might take away sins,ᵇ and there is no sin in Him. ⁶ Everyone who remains in Him does not sin; everyone who sins has not seen Him or known Him.

⁷ Little children, let no one deceive you! The one who does what is right is righteous, just as He is righteous. ⁸ The one who commits sin is of the Devil, for the Devil has sinned from the beginning. The Son of God was revealed for this purpose: to destroy the Devil's works. ⁹ Everyone who has been born of God does not sin, because His seed remains in him; he is not able to sin, because he has been born of God. ¹⁰ This is how God's children—and the Devil's children—are made evident.

### 1 John 3:2-3

### Last Things

*"We will be like Him." We don't really know what all that means. We will never be God, for example, but when we "see Him as He is" at His coming, we will look at ourselves and be amazed at what can happen when an ordinary old us is filled with the extraordinary character of Christ.*

---

ᵃ2:20 Other mss read *and you know all things* ᵇ3:5 Other mss read *our sins*

## Love's Imperative

Whoever does not do what is right is not of God, especially the one who does not love his brother. [11] For this is the message you have heard from the beginning: we should love one another, [12] unlike Cain, who was of the evil one and murdered his brother. And why did he murder him? Because his works were evil, and his brother's were righteous. [13] Do not be surprised, brothers, if the world hates you. [14] We know that we have passed from death to life because we love our brothers. The one who does not love remains in death. [15] Everyone who hates his brother is a murderer, and you know that no murderer has eternal life residing in him.

## Love in Action

[16] This is how we have come to know love: He laid down His life for us. We should also lay down our lives for our brothers. [17] If anyone has this world's goods and sees his brother in need but shuts off his compassion from him— how can God's love reside in him? [18] Little children, we must not love in word or speech, but in deed and truth; [19] that is how we will know we are of the truth, and will convince our hearts in His presence, [20] because if our hearts condemn us, God is greater than our hearts and knows all things. [21] Dear friends, if our hearts do not condemn ⌊us⌋ we have confidence before God, [22] and can receive whatever we ask from Him because we keep His commands and do what is pleasing in His sight. [23] Now this is His command: that we believe in the name of His Son Jesus Christ, and love one another as He commanded us. [24] The one who keeps His commands remains in Him, and He in him. And the way we know that He remains in us is from the Spirit He has given us.

## The Spirit of Truth and the Spirit of Error

4 Dear friends, do not believe every spirit, but test the spirits to determine if they are from God, because many false prophets have gone out into the world. [2] This is how you know the Spirit of God: Every spirit who confesses that Jesus Christ has come in the flesh is from God. [3] But every spirit who does not confess Jesus[a] is not from God. This is the spirit of the antichrist; you have heard that he is coming, and he is already in the world now. [4] You are from God, little children, and you have conquered them, because the One who is in you is greater than the one who is in the world. [5] They are from the world. Therefore what they say is from the world, and the world listens to them. [6] We are from God. Anyone who knows God listens to us; anyone who is not from God does not listen to us. From this we know the Spirit of truth and the spirit of deception.

---

*"Can you learn to love those unlovely people whom God seems to love just as much as He loves you?"*
—Calvin Miller

---

[a]**4:3** Other mss read *confess that Jesus has come in the flesh*

## Knowing God through Love

[7] Dear friends, let us love one another, because love is from God, and everyone who loves has been born of God and knows God. [8] The one who does not love does not know God, because God is love. [9] God's love was revealed among us in this way: God sent His *One and Only Son into the world so that we might live through Him. [10] Love consists in this: not that we loved God, but that He loved us and sent His Son to be the propitiation for our sins. [11] Dear friends, if God loved us in this way, we also must love one another. [12] No one has ever seen God. If we love one another, God remains in us and His love is perfected in us.

---

### 1 John 4:7-12

*Put all the qualities of the Christian life into one nice package. Pile them up as high as you like. But make sure they're wrapped in only one ribbon—the ribbon of love. Life can get you into some difficult situations. But love can get you through anything.*

---

[13] This is how we know that we remain in Him and He in us: He has given to us from His Spirit. [14] And we have seen and we testify that the Father has sent the Son as Savior of the world. [15] Whoever confesses that Jesus is the Son of God—God remains in him and he in God. [16] And we have come to know and to believe the love that God has for us. God is love, and the one who remains in love remains in God, and God remains in him.

[17] In this, love is perfected with us so that we may have confidence in the day of judgment; for we are as He is in this world. [18] There is no fear in love; instead, perfect love drives out fear, because fear involves punishment. So the one who fears has not reached perfection in love. [19] We love[a] because He first loved us.

## Keeping God's Commands

[20] If anyone says, "I love God," yet hates his brother, he is a liar. For the person who does not love his brother whom he has seen cannot love[b] God whom he has not seen. [21] And we have this command from Him: the one who loves God must also love his brother.

**5** Everyone who believes that Jesus is the *Messiah has been born of God, and everyone who loves the parent also loves his child. [2] This is how we know that we love God's children when we love God and obey[c] His commands. [3] For this is what love for God is: to keep His commands. Now His commands are not a burden, [4] because whatever has been born of God conquers the world. This is the victory that has conquered the world: our faith. [5] And who is the one who conquers the world but the one who believes that Jesus is the Son of God?

## The Sureness of God's Testimony

[6] Jesus Christ—He is the One who came by water and blood; not by water only, but by water and by blood.

---

[a]**4:19** Other mss add *Him*   [b]**4:20** Other mss read *seen, how is he able to love . . . seen?* (as a question)   [c]**5:2** Other mss read *keep*

And the Spirit is the One who testifies, because the Spirit is the truth. [7] For there are three that testify:[a] [8] the Spirit, the water, and the blood—and these three are in agreement. [9] If we accept the testimony of men, God's testimony is greater, because it is God's testimony that He has given about His Son. [10] (The one who believes in the Son of God has the testimony in himself. The one who does not believe God has made Him a liar, because he has not believed in the testimony that God has given about His Son.) [11] And this is the testimony: God has given us eternal life, and this life is in His Son.

[12] The one who has the Son has life. The one who doesn't have the Son of God does not have life. [13] I have written these things to you who believe in the name of the Son of God, so that you may know that you have eternal life.

### Effective Prayer

[14] Now this is the confidence we have before Him: whenever we ask anything according to His will, He hears us. [15] And if we know that He hears whatever we ask, we know that we have what we have asked Him for.

[16] If anyone sees his brother committing a sin that does not bring death, he should ask, and God will give life to him—to those who commit sin that doesn't bring death. There is sin that brings death. I am not saying he should pray about

---

*1 John 5:12-13*

*God's Assurance*

*Can John make this any clearer? Those who are saved but aren't sure they are going to heaven need only to read these couple of verses, for God has given us His Word and His Son so that we may know— yes, know—that our faith is in a Father big enough to keep His promises.*

---

that. [17] All unrighteousness is sin, and there is sin that does not bring death.

### Conclusion

[18] We know that everyone who has been born of God does not sin, but the One who is born of God keeps him,[b] and the evil one does not touch him. [19] We know that we are of God, and the whole world is under the sway of the evil one. [20] And we know that the Son of God has come and has given us understanding so that we may know the true One.[c] We are in the true One—that is, in His Son Jesus Christ. He is the true God and eternal life. [21] Little children, guard yourselves from idols.

---

[a]**5:7-8** Other mss (the Lat Vg and a few late Gk mss) read *testify in heaven, the Father, the word, and the Holy Spirit, and these three are One. [8] And there are three who bear witness on earth: the Spirit*   [b]**5:18** Other mss read *himself*   [c]**5:20** Other mss read *the true God*

# 2 JOHN

## Greeting

The Elder:

To the elect lady and her children, whom I love in truth—and not only I, but also all who have come to know the truth— ² because of the truth that remains in us and will be with us forever.

³ Grace, mercy, and peace will be with us from God the Father and from Jesus Christ, the Son of the Father, in truth and love.

## Truth and Deception

⁴ I was very glad to find some of your children walking in truth, in keeping with a command we have received from the Father. ⁵ So now I urge you, lady—not as if I were writing you a new command, but one we have had from the beginning—that we love one another. ⁶ And this is love: that we •walk according to His commands. This is the command as you have heard it from the beginning: you must walk in love.

⁷ Many deceivers have gone out into the world; they do not confess the coming of Jesus Christ in the flesh. This is the deceiver and the antichrist. ⁸ Watch yourselves so that you don't lose what we[a] have worked for, but you may receive a full reward. ⁹ Anyone who does not remain in the teaching about Christ, but goes beyond it, does not have God. The one who remains in that teaching, this one has both the Father and the Son. ¹⁰ If anyone comes to you and does not bring this teaching, do not receive him into your home, and don't say, "Welcome," to him; ¹¹ for the one who says, "Welcome," to him shares in his evil works.

## Farewell

¹² Though I have many things to write to you, I don't want to do so with paper and ink. Instead, I hope to be with you and talk face to face so that our joy may be complete.

¹³ The children of your elect sister send you greetings.

---

a8 Other mss read *you*

# 3 JOHN

## Greeting

T he Elder:
   To my dear friend Gaius, whom I love in truth.

² Dear friend, I pray that you may prosper in every way and be in good health, just as your soul prospers. ³ For I was very glad when some brothers came and testified to your ⌊faithfulness⌋ to the truth—how you are walking in the truth. ⁴ I have no greater joy than this: to hear that my children are walking in the truth.

## Gaius Commended

⁵ Dear friend, you are showing your faith by whatever you do for the brothers, and this ⌊you are doing⌋ for strangers; ⁶ they have testified to your love before the church. You will do well to send them on their journey in a manner worthy of God, ⁷ since they set out for the sake of the name, accepting nothing from pagans. ⁸ Therefore, we ought to support such men, so that we can be co-workers with the truth.

## Diotrephes and Demetrius

⁹ I wrote something to the church, but Diotrephes, who loves to have first place among them, does not receive us. ¹⁰ This is why, if I come, I will remind him of the works he is doing, slandering us with malicious words. And he is not satisfied with that! He not only refuses to welcome the brothers himself, but he even stops those who want to do so and expels them from the church.

¹¹ Dear friend, do not imitate what is evil, but what is good. The one who does good is of God; the one who does evil has not seen God. ¹² Demetrius has a ⌊good⌋ testimony from everyone, and from the truth itself. And we also testify for him, and you know that our testimony is true.

## Farewell

¹³ I have many things to write you, but I don't want to write to you with pen and ink. ¹⁴ I hope to see you soon, and we will talk face to face.

Peace be with you. The friends send you greetings. Greet the friends by name.

# JUDE

## Greeting

Jude, a slave of Jesus Christ, and a brother of James:

To those who are the called, loved[a] by God the Father and kept by Jesus Christ.

[2] May mercy, peace, and love be multiplied to you.

## Jude's Purpose in Writing

[3] Dear friends, although I was eager to write you about our common salvation, I found it necessary to write and exhort you to contend for the faith that was delivered to the saints once for all. [4] For certain men, who were designated for this judgment long ago, have come in by stealth; they are ungodly, turning the grace of our God into promiscuity and denying our only Master and Lord, Jesus Christ.

## Apostates: Past and Present

[5] Now I want to remind you, though you know all these things: the Lord, having first of all[b] saved a people out of Egypt, later destroyed those who did not believe; [6] and He has kept, with eternal chains in darkness for the judgment of the great day, angels who did not keep their own position but deserted their proper dwelling. [7] In the same way, Sodom and Gomorrah and the cities around them committed sexual immorality and practiced perversions, just as they did, and serve as an example by undergoing the punishment of eternal fire.

[8] Nevertheless, these dreamers likewise defile their flesh, despise authority, and blaspheme glorious beings. [9] Yet Michael the archangel, when he was disputing with the Devil in a debate about Moses' body, did not dare bring an abusive condemnation against him, but said, "The Lord rebuke you!" [10] But these people blaspheme anything they don't understand, and what they know by instinct, like unreasoning animals—they destroy themselves with these things. [11] Woe to them! For they have traveled in the way of Cain, have abandoned themselves to the error of Balaam for profit, and have perished in Korah's rebellion.

## The Apostates' Doom

[12] These are the ones who are like dangerous reefs at your love feasts. They feast with you, nurturing only themselves without fear. They are waterless clouds carried along by winds; trees in late autumn—fruitless, twice dead, pulled out by the roots;

---

*"Through true guilt, the Holy Spirit seeks to draw us closer to God. Through false, incriminating guilt, Satan seeks to separate us from God."*

*—Jim Henry*

---

[a]1 Other mss read *sanctified*   [b]5 Other mss place *first of all* after *remind you*

13 wild waves of the sea, foaming up their shameful deeds; wandering stars for whom is reserved the blackness of darkness forever!

14 And Enoch, in the seventh ⌊generation⌋ from Adam, prophesied about them:

Look! The Lord comes with
   thousands of His holy ones
15 to execute judgment on all,
   and to convict them
of all their ungodly deeds
   that they have done in an
   ungodly way,
and of all the harsh things
   ungodly sinners
have said against Him.

16 These people are discontented grumblers, walking according to their desires; their mouths utter arrogant words, flattering people for their own advantage.

17 But you, dear friends, remember the words foretold by the apostles of our Lord Jesus Christ; 18 they told you, "In the end time there will be scoffers walking according to their own ungodly desires." 19 These people create divisions and are merely natural, not having the Spirit.

## Exhortation and Benediction

20 But you, dear friends, building yourselves up in your most holy faith and praying in the Holy Spirit, 21 keep yourselves in the love of God, expecting the mercy of our Lord Jesus Christ for eternal life. 22 Have mercy on some who doubt; 23 save others by snatching ⌊them⌋ from the fire; on others have mercy in fear, hating even the garment defiled by the flesh.

24 Now to Him who is able to protect you from stumbling and to make you stand in the presence of His glory, blameless and with great joy, 25 to the only God our Savior, through Jesus Christ our Lord,[a] be glory, majesty, power, and authority before all time,[b] now, and forever. •Amen.

> ### Jude 24
>
> *Even though you know God's for-given you, you can still carry around guilt for the things you've done. At times you may wonder if you'll ever be able to get past your past. But God has chosen to make you blameless in His sight. Embrace it as a gift, and wear it for His glory.*

[a]25 Other mss omit *through Jesus Christ our Lord*   [b]25 Other mss omit *before all time*

# REVELATION

## Prologue

**1** The revelation of Jesus Christ that God gave Him to show His slaves what must quickly take place. He sent it and signified it through His angel to His slave John, ² who testified to God's word and to the testimony about Jesus Christ, in all he saw. ³ Blessed is the one who reads and blessed are those who hear the words of this prophecy and keep what is written in it, because the time is near!

⁴ John:

To the seven churches in the province of Asia.

Grace and peace to you from[a] the One who is, who was, and who is coming; from the seven spirits before His throne; ⁵ and from Jesus Christ, the faithful witness, the firstborn from the dead and the ruler of the kings of the earth.

To Him who loves us and has set us free[b] from our sins by His blood, ⁶ and made us a kingdom,[c] priests to His God and Father—to Him be the glory and dominion forever and ever. •Amen.

⁷ Look! He is coming with
   the clouds,
and every eye will see Him,
   including those who
   pierced Him.
And all the families of the
   earth[d]
will mourn over Him.[e]

This is certain! Amen!

⁸ "I am the •Alpha and the Omega," says the Lord God, "the One who is, who was, and who is coming, the Almighty."

## John's Vision of the Risen Lord

⁹ I, John, your brother and partner in the tribulation, kingdom, and perseverance in Jesus, was on the island called Patmos because of God's word and the testimony about Jesus. ¹⁰ I was in the Spirit on the Lord's day, and I heard behind me a loud voice like a trumpet ¹¹ saying, "Write on a scroll what you see and send it to the seven churches: Ephesus, Smyrna, Pergamum, Thyatira, Sardis, Philadelphia, and Laodicea."

¹² I turned to see the voice that was speaking to me. When I turned I saw seven gold lampstands, ¹³ and among the lampstands was One like the •Son of Man, dressed in a long robe, and with a gold sash wrapped around His chest. ¹⁴ His head and hair were white like wool—white as snow, His eyes like a fiery flame, ¹⁵ His feet like fine bronze fired in a furnace, and His voice like the sound of cascading waters. ¹⁶ In His right hand He had seven stars; from His mouth came a sharp two-edged sword; and His face was shining like the sun at midday. ¹⁷ When I saw Him, I fell at His feet like a dead man. He laid His right hand on me, and said, "Don't be afraid! I am the First and the Last, ¹⁸ and the Living One. I was dead, but look—I am alive forever and ever, and I hold the keys of death and •Hades. ¹⁹ Therefore write what

---

ª1:4 Other mss add *God*   ᵇ1:5 Other mss read *has washed us*   ᶜ1:6 Other mss read *kings and*   ᵈ1:7 Gn 12:3; 28:14; Zch 14:17   ᵉ1:7 Dn 7:13; Zch 12:10

---

*Revelation 1:20*

*The Church*

*This awesome picture of Christ, with His eyes like fire and His face like a noonday sun, reveals Him in all of His power and might. Among His most astounding features are these: His guardian presence in the midst of His church and His protection of her in the palm of His hand.*

---

you have seen, what is, and what will take place after this. <sup>20</sup> The secret of the seven stars you saw in My right hand, and of the seven gold lampstands, is this: the seven stars are the angels of the seven churches, and the seven lampstands[a] are the seven churches.

## THE LETTERS TO THE SEVEN CHURCHES

### The Letter to Ephesus

**2** "To the angel of the church in Ephesus write:
"The One who holds the seven stars in His right hand and who walks among the seven gold lampstands says: <sup>2</sup> I know your works, your labor, and your endurance, and that you cannot tolerate evil. You have tested those who call themselves apostles and are not, and you have found them to be liars. <sup>3</sup> You also possess endurance and have tol-

erated ⌊many things⌋ because of My name, and have not grown weary. <sup>4</sup> But I have this against you: you have abandoned the love ⌊you had⌋ at first. <sup>5</sup> Remember then how far you have fallen; repent, and do the works you did at first. Otherwise, I will come to you[b] and remove your lampstand from its place—unless you repent. <sup>6</sup> Yet you do have this: you hate the practices of the Nicolaitans, which I also hate.

<sup>7</sup> "Anyone who has an ear should listen to what the Spirit says to the churches. I will give the victor the right to eat from the tree of life, which is in[c] the paradise of God.

### The Letter to Smyrna

<sup>8</sup> "To the angel of the church in Smyrna write:
"The First and the Last, the One who was dead and came to life, says: <sup>9</sup> I know your[d] tribulation and poverty, yet you are rich. ⌊I know⌋ the slander of those who say they are Jews and are not, but are a •synagogue of Satan. <sup>10</sup> Don't be afraid of what you are about to suffer. Look, the Devil is about to throw some of you into prison to test you, and you will have tribulation for 10 days. Be faithful until death, and I will give you the crown of life.

<sup>11</sup> "Anyone who has an ear should listen to what the Spirit says to the churches. The victor will never be harmed by the second death.

### The Letter to Pergamum

<sup>12</sup> "To the angel of the church in Pergamum write:
"The One who has the sharp, two-edged sword says: <sup>13</sup> I know[e] where

---

[a]**1:20** Other mss add *that you saw*   [b]**2:5** Other mss add *quickly*   [c]**2:7** Other mss read *in the midst of*
[d]**2:9** Other mss add *works and*   [e]**2:13** Other mss add *your works and*

you live—where Satan's throne is! And you are holding on to My name and did not deny your faith in Me, even in the days of Antipas, My faithful witness, who was killed among you, where Satan lives. [14] But I have a few things against you. You have some there who hold to the teaching of Balaam, who taught Balak to place a stumbling block in front of the sons of Israel: to eat meat sacrificed to idols and to commit sexual immorality. [15] In the same way, you also have those who hold to the teaching of the Nicolaitans.[a] [16] Therefore repent! Otherwise, I will come to you quickly and fight against them with the sword of My mouth.

[17] "Anyone who has an ear should listen to what the Spirit says to the churches. I will give the victor some of the hidden manna.[b] I will also give him a white stone, and on the stone a new name is inscribed that no one knows except the one who receives it.

### The Letter to Thyatira

[18] "To the angel of the church in Thyatira write:

"The Son of God, the One whose eyes are like a fiery flame, and whose feet are like fine bronze says: [19] I know your works—your love, faithfulness, service, and endurance. Your last works are greater than the first. [20] But I have this against you: you tolerate the woman Jezebel, who calls herself a prophetess, and teaches and deceives My slaves to commit sexual immorality and to eat meat sacrificed to idols. [21] I gave her time to repent, but she does not want to repent of her sexual immorality. [22] Look! I will throw her into a sickbed, and those who commit adultery with her into great tribulation, unless they repent of her[c] practices. [23] I will kill her children with the plague. Then all the churches will know that I am the One who examines minds and hearts, and I will give to each of you according to your works. [24] I say to the rest of you in Thyatira, who do not hold this teaching, who haven't known the deep things of Satan—as they say—I do not put any other burden on you. [25] But hold on to what you have until I come. [26] The victor and the one who keeps My works to the end: I will give him authority over the nations—

[27] **and He will shepherd them
with an iron scepter;
He will shatter them like
pottery**—[d]

just as I have received this from My Father. [28] I will also give him the morning star.

[29] "Anyone who has an ear should listen to what the Spirit says to the churches.

### The Letter to Sardis

**3** "To the angel of the church in Sardis write:

"The One who has the seven spirits of God and the seven stars says: I know your works; you have a reputation for being alive, but you are dead. [2] Be alert and strengthen[e] what remains, which is about to die, for I have not found your works complete before My God. [3] Remember therefore what you have received and heard; keep it, and repent. But if you are not alert, I will come[f] like a thief, and you have no idea at what hour I will come against you. [4] But you have

---

[a]**2:15** Other mss add *which I hate*    [b]**2:17** Other mss add *to eat*    [c]**2:22** Other mss read *their*    [d]**2:27** Ps 2:9
[e]**3:2** Other mss read *guard*    [f]**3:3** Other mss add *upon you*

## Revelation 3:5

### God's Assurance

*God has a book, containing the names of all the saved of all the ages. And God has an eraser, which He uses to rub out the long, filthy record of sin that was stockpiled in our standing account. But when God writes our name in His book, He writes it in blood. And it can't be erased.*

---

a few people in Sardis who have not defiled their clothes, and they will •walk with Me in white, because they are worthy. [5] In the same way, the victor will be dressed in white clothes, and I will never erase his name from the book of life, but will acknowledge his name before My Father and before His angels.

[6] "Anyone who has an ear should listen to what the Spirit says to the churches.

### The Letter to Philadelphia

[7] "To the angel of the church in Philadelphia write:

"The Holy One, the True One, the One who has the key of David, who opens and no one will close, and closes and no one opens says: [8] I know your works. Look, I have placed before you an open door that no one is able to close; because you have limited strength, have kept My word, and have not denied My name. [9] Take note! I will make those from the •synagogue of Satan, who claim to be Jews and are not, but are lying— note this—I will make them come

and bow down at your feet, and they will know that I have loved you. [10] Because you have kept My command to endure, I will also keep you from the hour of testing that is going to come over the whole world to test those who live on the earth. [11] I am coming quickly. Hold on to what you have, so that no one takes your crown. [12] The victor: I will make him a pillar in the sanctuary of My God, and he will never go out again. I will write on him the name of My God, and the name of the city of My God— the new Jerusalem, which comes down out of heaven from My God— and My new name.

[13] "Anyone who has an ear should listen to what the Spirit says to the churches.

### The Letter to Laodicea

[14] "To the angel of the church in Laodicea write:

"The •Amen, the faithful and true Witness, the Originator of God's creation says: [15] I know your works, that you are neither cold nor hot. I wish that you were cold or hot. [16] So, because you are lukewarm, and neither hot nor cold, I am going to vomit you out of My mouth. [17] Because you say, 'I'm rich; I have become wealthy, and need nothing,' and you don't know that you are wretched, pitiful, poor, blind, and naked, [18] I advise you to buy from Me gold refined in the fire so that you may be rich, and white clothes so that you may be dressed and your shameful nakedness not be exposed, and ointment to spread on your eyes so that you may see. [19] As many as I love, I rebuke and discipline. So be committed and repent. [20] Listen! I stand at the door and knock. If anyone hears My voice and opens the door, I will come in to him and have dinner with

---

## Revelation 4:9-11

### God the Father

*Many people today still don't believe in God. If you want to realize how tragic that is, stand with the gathered saints around His throne, see Him for who He really is, and imagine what your friends stand to lose by not knowing the thrill and joy of looking into your Father's face.*

---

him, and he with Me. [21] The victor: I will give him the right to sit with Me on My throne, just as I also won the victory and sat down with My Father on His throne.

[22] "Anyone who has an ear should listen to what the Spirit says to the churches."

### The Throne Room of Heaven

**4** After this I looked, and there in heaven was an open door. The first voice that I had heard speaking to me like a trumpet said, "Come up here, and I will show you what must take place after this."

[2] Immediately I was in the Spirit, and there in heaven a throne was set. One was seated on the throne, [3] and the One seated[a] looked like jasper and carnelian stone. A rainbow that looked like an emerald surrounded the throne. [4] Around that throne were 24 thrones, and on the thrones sat 24 elders dressed in white clothes, with gold crowns on their heads. [5] From the throne came flashes of lightning, rumblings, and thunder. Burning before the throne were seven fiery torches, which are the seven spirits of God. [6] Also before the throne was something like a sea of glass, similar to crystal. In the middle and around the throne were four living creatures covered with eyes in front and in back. [7] The first living creature was like a lion; the second living creature was like a calf; the third living creature had a face like a man; and the fourth living creature was like a flying eagle. [8] Each of the four living creatures had six wings; they were covered with eyes around and inside. Day and night they never stop, saying:

> Holy, holy, holy,[b]
> Lord God, the Almighty,
> who was, who is, and who is
>     coming.

[9] Whenever the living creatures give glory, honor, and thanks to the One seated on the throne, the One who lives forever and ever, [10] the 24 elders fall down before the One seated on the throne, worship the One who lives forever and ever, cast their crowns before the throne, and say:

> [11]  Our Lord and God,[c]
> You are worthy to receive
> glory and honor and power,
> because You have created all
>     things,
> and because of Your will
> they exist and were created.

### The Lamb Takes the Scroll

**5** Then I saw in the right hand of the One seated on the throne a scroll with writing on the inside

---

[a]4:3 Other mss omit *and the One seated*   [b]4:8 Other mss read *holy* nine times   [c]4:11 Other mss add *the Holy One;* other mss read *O Lord*

and on the back, sealed with seven seals. ² I also saw a mighty angel proclaiming in a loud voice, "Who is worthy to open the scroll and break its seals?" ³ But no one in heaven or on earth or under the earth was able to open the scroll or even to look in it. ⁴ And I cried and cried because no one was found worthy to open[a] the scroll or even to look in it.

⁵ Then one of the elders said to me, "Stop crying. Look! The Lion from the tribe of Judah, the Root of David, has been victorious so that He may open the scroll and[b] its seven seals." ⁶ Then I saw one like a slaughtered lamb standing between the throne and the four living creatures and among the elders. He had seven horns and seven eyes, which are the seven spirits of God sent into all the earth. ⁷ He came and took ⌊the scroll⌋ out of the right hand of the One seated on the throne.

---

### Revelation 5:8-10

#### God the Son

*The reason that faith in Christ is the only way to be saved is because no one else is worthy to obtain salvation for us. He was God and became a man, lived a perfect life, was killed in innocence, but took upon Himself the sins of people from every time, nation, and race. He is it. And we are His.*

---

### The Lamb Is Worthy

⁸ When He took the scroll, the four living creatures and the 24 elders fell down before the Lamb. Each one had a harp and gold bowls filled with incense, which are the prayers of the saints. ⁹ And they sang a new song:

You are worthy to take the
   scroll
and to open its seals;
because You were
   slaughtered,
and You redeemed ⌊people⌋[c]
   for God by Your blood
from every tribe and
   language and people
   and nation.
¹⁰ You made them a kingdom[d]
   and priests to our God,
and they will reign on the
   earth.

¹¹ Then I looked, and heard the voice of many angels around the throne, and also of the living creatures, and of the elders. Their number was countless thousands, plus thousands of thousands. ¹² They said with a loud voice:

The Lamb who was
   slaughtered is worthy
to receive power and
   riches
and wisdom and strength
and honor and glory and
   blessing!

¹³ I heard every creature in heaven, on earth, under the earth, on the sea, and everything in them say:

Blessing and honor and glory
   and dominion

[a]5:4 Other mss add *and read*  [b]5:5 Other mss add *loose*  [c]5:9 Other mss read *us*  [d]5:10 Other mss read *them kings*

to the One seated on the
   throne,
and to the Lamb, forever and
   ever!

[14] The four living creatures said,
"•Amen," and the elders fell down
and worshiped.

## The First Seal on the Scroll

**6** Then I saw the Lamb open one
of the seven[a] seals, and I heard
one of the four living creatures say
with a voice like thunder, "Come!"[b]
[2] I looked, and there was a white
horse. The horseman on it had a
bow; a crown was given to him, and
he went out as a victor to conquer.

## The Second Seal

[3] When He opened the second
seal, I heard the second living creature say, "Come!"[c] [4] Then another
horse went out, a fiery red one, and
its horseman was empowered to
take peace from the earth, so that
people would slaughter one
another. And a large sword was
given to him.

## The Third Seal

[5] When He opened the third seal,
I heard the third living creature say,
"Come!"[c] And I looked, and there
was a black horse. The horseman on
it had a balance scale in his hand.
[6] Then I heard something like a
voice among the four living creatures say, "A quart of wheat for a
denarius, and three quarts of barley
for a •denarius—but do not harm the
olive oil and the wine."

## The Fourth Seal

[7] When He opened the fourth seal, I
heard the voice of the fourth living
creature say, "Come!"[c] [8] And I
looked, and there was a pale green
horse. The horseman on it was named
Death, and •Hades was following after
him. Authority was given to them[d]
over a fourth of the earth, to kill by the
sword, by famine, by plague, and by
the wild animals of the earth.

## The Fifth Seal

[9] When He opened the fifth seal, I
saw under the altar the souls of those
slaughtered because of God's word
and the testimony they had.[e] [10] They
cried out with a loud voice: "O Lord,
holy and true, how long until You
judge and avenge our blood from
those who live on the earth?" [11] So a
white robe was given to each of them,
and they were told to rest a little while
longer until ⌊the number of⌋ their fellow slaves and their brothers, who
were going to be killed just as they had
been, would be completed.

## The Sixth Seal

[12] Then I saw Him open the sixth
seal. A violent earthquake occurred;
the sun turned black like sackcloth
made of goat hair; the entire moon
became like blood; [13] the stars of
heaven fell to the earth as a fig tree
drops its unripe figs when shaken by
a high wind; [14] the sky separated
like a scroll being rolled up; and
every mountain and island was
moved from its place.
[15] Then the kings of the earth, the
nobles, the military commanders, the
rich, the powerful, and every slave and
free person hid in the caves and among

[a]6:1 Other mss omit *seven*    [b]6:1 Other mss add *and see*
read *him*    [e]6:9 Other mss add *about the Lamb*    [c]6:3,5,7 Other mss add *and see*    [d]6:8 Other mss

the rocks of the mountains. [16] And they said to the mountains and to the rocks, "Fall on us and hide us from the face of the One seated on the throne and from the wrath of the Lamb, [17] because the great day of their[a] wrath has come! And who is able to stand?"

## The Sealed of Israel

**7** After this I saw four angels standing at the four corners of the earth, restraining the four winds of the earth so that no wind could blow on the earth or on the sea or on any tree. [2] Then I saw another angel rise up from the east, who had the seal of the living God. He cried out in a loud voice to the four angels who were empowered to harm the earth and the sea: [3] "Don't harm the earth or the sea or the trees until we seal the slaves of our God on their foreheads." [4] And I heard the number of those who were sealed:

144,000 sealed from every
    tribe of the sons of Israel:
[5] 12,000 sealed from the tribe
    of Judah,
12,000[b] from the tribe of
    Reuben,
12,000 from the tribe of Gad,
[6] 12,000 from the tribe of
    Asher,
12,000 from the tribe of
    Naphtali,
12,000 from the tribe of
    Manasseh,
[7] 12,000 from the tribe of
    Simeon,
12,000 from the tribe of Levi,
12,000 from the tribe of
    Issachar,
[8] 12,000 from the tribe of
    Zebulun,
12,000 from the tribe of Joseph,

12,000 sealed from the tribe
    of Benjamin.

## A Multitude from the Great Tribulation

[9] After this I looked, and there was a vast multitude from every nation, tribe, people, and language, which no one could number, standing before the throne and before the Lamb. They were robed in white with palm branches in their hands. [10] And they cried out in a loud voice:

Salvation belongs to our God,
    who is seated on the throne,
    and to the Lamb!

[11] All the angels stood around the throne, the elders, and the four living creatures, and they fell on their faces before the throne and worshiped God, [12] saying:

•Amen! Blessing and glory and
    wisdom
and thanksgiving and honor
and power and strength,
be to our God forever and
    ever. Amen.

[13] Then one of the elders asked me, "Who are these people robed in white, and where did they come from?" [14] I said to him, "Sir, you know." Then he told me:

These are the ones coming
    out of the great tribulation.
They washed their robes and
    made them white
in the blood of the Lamb.
[15] For this reason they are
    before the throne of God,
and they serve Him day and
    night in His sanctuary.

[a]6:17 Other mss read *His*  [b]7:5-8 Other mss add *sealed* after each number

*Revelation 7:16-17*

*Last Things*

*A day is coming—as sure as the
sunrise—when we will be transported into the Lord's presence
and surrounded by His glory. It will
be an everlasting experience of
freedom from sin and temptation,
from sadness and fear, from doubt
and despair. It will be wonderful!
And it will be forever!*

The One seated on the
    throne will shelter them:
16 no longer will they hunger; no
    longer will they thirst;
no longer will the sun strike
    them, or any heat.
17 Because the Lamb who is at
    the center of the throne
    will shepherd them;
He will guide them to springs
    of living waters,
and God will wipe away every
    tear from their eyes.

## The Seventh Seal

**8** When He opened the seventh seal, there was silence in heaven for about half an hour. 2 Then I saw the seven angels who stand in the presence of God; seven trumpets were given to them. 3 Another angel, with a gold incense burner, came and stood at the altar. He was given a large amount of incense to offer with the prayers of all the saints on the gold altar in front of the throne. 4 The smoke of the incense, with the prayers of the saints, went up in the presence of God from the angel's hand. 5 The angel took the incense burner, filled it with fire from the altar, and hurled it to the earth; there were thunders, rumblings, lightnings, and an earthquake. 6 And the seven angels who had the seven trumpets prepared to blow them.

### The First Trumpet

7 The first ⌊angel⌋ blew his trumpet, and hail and fire, mixed with blood, were hurled to the earth. So a third of the earth was burned up, a third of the trees were burned up, and all the green grass was burned up.

### The Second Trumpet

8 The second angel blew his trumpet, and something like a great mountain ablaze with fire was hurled into the sea. So a third of the sea became blood, 9 a third of the living creatures in the sea died, and a third of the ships were destroyed.

### The Third Trumpet

10 The third angel blew his trumpet, and a great star, blazing like a torch, fell from heaven. It fell on a third of the rivers and springs of water. 11 The name of the star is Wormwood, and a third of the waters became wormwood. So, many of the people died from the waters, because they had been made bitter.

### The Fourth Trumpet

12 The fourth angel blew his trumpet, and a third of the sun was struck,

a third of the moon, and a third of the stars, so that a third of them were darkened. A third of the day was without light, and the night as well.

[13] I looked, and I heard an eagle,[a] flying in mid-heaven, saying in a loud voice, "Woe! Woe! Woe to those who live on the earth, because of the remaining trumpet blasts that the three angels are about to sound!"

## The Fifth Trumpet

**9** The fifth angel blew his trumpet, and I saw a star that had fallen from heaven to earth. The key to the shaft of the •abyss was given to him. [2] He opened the shaft of the abyss, and smoke came up out of the shaft like smoke from a great[b] furnace so that the sun and the air were darkened by the smoke from the shaft. [3] Then out of the smoke locusts came to the earth, and power was given to them like the power that scorpions have on the earth. [4] They were told not to harm the grass of the earth, or any green plant, or any tree, but only people who do not have God's seal on their foreheads. [5] They were not permitted to kill them, but were to torment ⌊them⌋ for five months; their torment is like the torment caused by a scorpion when it strikes a man. [6] In those days people will seek death and will not find it; they will long to die, but death will flee from them.

[7] The appearance of the locusts was like horses equipped for battle. On their heads were something like gold crowns; their faces were like men's faces; [8] they had hair like women's hair; their teeth were like lions' teeth; [9] they had chests like iron breastplates; the sound of their wings was like the sound of chariots with many horses rushing into battle; [10] and they had tails with stingers, like scorpions, so that with their tails they had the power to harm people for five months. [11] They had as their king the angel of the abyss; his name in Hebrew is Abaddon, and in Greek he has the name Apollyon. [12] The first woe has passed. There are still two more woes to come after this.

## The Sixth Trumpet

[13] The sixth angel blew his trumpet. From the four[c] horns of the gold altar that is before God, I heard a voice [14] say to the sixth angel who had the trumpet, "Release the four angels bound at the great river Euphrates." [15] So the four angels who were prepared for the hour, day, month, and year were released to kill a third of the human race. [16] The number of mounted troops was 200 million;[d] I heard their number. [17] This is how I saw the horses in my vision: The horsemen had breastplates that were fiery red, hyacinth blue, and sulfur yellow. The heads of the horses were like lions' heads, and from their mouths came fire, smoke, and sulfur. [18] A third of the human race was killed by these three plagues—by the fire, the smoke, and the sulfur that came from their mouths. [19] For the power of the horses is in their mouths and in their tails, because their tails, like snakes, have heads, and they inflict injury with them.

[20] The rest of the people, who were not killed by these plagues, did not repent of the works of their

[a]8:13 Other mss read *angel*  [b]9:2 Other mss omit *great*  [c]9:13 Other mss omit *four*  [d]9:16 Other mss read *100 million*

hands to stop worshiping demons and idols of gold, silver, bronze, stone, and wood, which are not able to see, hear, or walk. [21] And they did not repent of their murders, their sorceries, their sexual immorality, or their thefts.

### The Mighty Angel and the Small Scroll

**10** Then I saw another mighty angel coming down from heaven, surrounded by a cloud, with a rainbow over his head. His face was like the sun, his legs were like fiery pillars, [2] and he had a little scroll opened in his hand. He put his right foot on the sea, his left on the land, [3] and he cried out with a loud voice like a roaring lion. When he cried out, the seven thunders spoke with their voices. [4] And when the seven thunders spoke, I was about to write. Then I heard a voice from heaven, saying, "Seal up what the seven thunders said, and do not write it down!"

[5] Then the angel that I had seen standing on the sea and on the land raised his right hand to heaven. [6] He swore an oath by the One who lives forever and ever, who created heaven and what is in it, the earth and what is in it, and the sea and what is in it: "There will no longer be an interval of time, [7] but in the days of the sound of the seventh angel, when he will blow his trumpet, then God's hidden plan will be completed, as He announced to His servants the prophets."

[8] Now the voice that I heard from heaven spoke to me again and said, "Go, take the scroll that lies open in the hand of the angel who is standing on the sea and on the land."

[9] So I went to the angel and asked him to give me the little scroll. He said to me, "Take and eat it; it will be bitter in your stomach, but it will be as sweet as honey in your mouth."

[10] Then I took the little scroll from the angel's hand and ate it. It was as sweet as honey in my mouth, but when I ate it, my stomach became bitter. [11] And I was told, "You must prophesy again about many peoples, nations, languages, and kings."

### The Two Witnesses

**11** Then I was given a measuring reed like a rod,[a] with these words: "Go and measure God's sanctuary and the altar, and ⌊count⌋ those who worship there. [2] But exclude the courtyard outside the sanctuary. Don't measure it, because it is given to the nations, and they will trample the holy city for 42 months. [3] I will empower my two witnesses, and they will prophesy for 1,260 days, dressed in sackcloth." [4] These are the two olive trees and the two lampstands that stand before the Lord[b] of the earth. [5] If anyone wants to harm them, fire comes from their mouths and consumes their enemies; if anyone wants to harm them, he must be killed in this way. [6] These men have the power to close the sky so that it does not rain during the days of their prophecy. They also have power over the waters to turn them into blood, and to strike the earth with any plague whenever they want.

### The Witnesses Martyred

[7] When they finish their testimony, the beast that comes up out of the •abyss will make war with them, conquer them, and kill them. [8] Their dead bodies will lie in the public square of the great city, which is

---

[a]11:1 Other mss add *and the angel stood up*  [b]11:4 Other mss read *God*

called, prophetically, Sodom and Egypt, where also their Lord was crucified. ⁹ And representatives from the peoples, tribes, languages, and nations will view their bodies for three and a half days and not permit their bodies to be put into a tomb. ¹⁰ Those who live on the earth will gloat over them and celebrate and send gifts to one another, because these two prophets tormented those who live on the earth.

## The Witnesses Resurrected

¹¹ But after the three and a half days, the breath of life from God entered them, and they stood on their feet. So great fear fell on those who saw them. ¹² Then they heard[a] a loud voice from heaven saying to them, "Come up here." They went up to heaven in a cloud, while their enemies watched them. ¹³ At that moment a violent earthquake took place, a tenth of the city fell, and 7,000 people were killed in the earthquake. The survivors were terrified and gave glory to the God of heaven. ¹⁴ The second woe has passed. Take note: the third woe is coming quickly!

## The Seventh Trumpet

¹⁵ The seventh angel blew his trumpet, and there were loud voices in heaven saying:

> The kingdom of the world
>     has become the ⌊kingdom⌋
> of our Lord and of His
>     •Messiah,
> and He will reign forever and
>     ever!

¹⁶ The 24 elders, who were seated before God on their thrones, fell on their faces and worshiped God, ¹⁷ saying:

---

*Revelation 11:15*

*The Kingdom*

*The Egyptians, the Greeks, the Romans, the Turks—yes, even the Americans—all these proud kingdoms and nations have fallen or will fall. For only one kingdom is ultimately destined to lead us into the brightness of eternal peace and freedom. Only one King deserves our true·loyalty.*

---

> We thank You, Lord God, the
>     Almighty, who is and who
>     was,[b]
> because You have taken Your
>     great power and have
>     begun to reign.
> ¹⁸ The nations were angry, but
>     Your wrath has come.
> The time has come for the
>     dead to be judged,
> and to give the reward to
>     Your servants the
>     prophets,
> to the saints, and to those
>     who fear Your name,
>     both small and great,
> and the time has come to
>     destroy those who destroy
>     the earth.

¹⁹ God's sanctuary in heaven was opened, and the ark of His covenant[c] appeared in His sanctuary. There were lightnings, rumblings, thunders, an earthquake,[d] and severe hail.

---

[a]11:12 Other mss read *Then I heard*   [b]11:17 Other mss add *and who is to come*   [c]11:19 Other mss read *ark of the covenant of the Lord*   [d]11:19 Other mss omit *an earthquake*

## The Woman, the Child, and the Dragon

**12** A great sign appeared in heaven: a woman clothed with the sun, with the moon under her feet, and a crown of 12 stars on her head. [2] She was pregnant and cried out in labor and agony to give birth. [3] Then another sign appeared in heaven: There was a great fiery red dragon having seven heads and 10 horns, and on his heads were seven diadems. [4] His tail swept away a third of the stars in heaven and hurled them to the earth. And the dragon stood in front of the woman who was about to give birth, so that when she did give birth he might devour her child. [5] But she gave birth to a Son— a male who is going to shepherd all nations with an iron scepter—and her child was caught up to God and to His throne. [6] The woman fled into the wilderness, where she had a place prepared by God, to be fed there for 1,260 days.

## The Dragon Thrown Out of Heaven

[7] Then war broke out in heaven: Michael and his angels fought against the dragon. The dragon and his angels also fought, [8] but he could not prevail, and there was no place for them in heaven any longer. [9] So the great dragon was thrown out—the ancient serpent, who is called the Devil and Satan, the one who deceives the whole world. He was thrown to earth, and his angels with him. [10] Then I heard a loud voice in heaven say:

The salvation and the power
and the kingdom of our God
and the authority of His
      •Messiah have now come,
because the accuser of our
      brothers has been thrown out:
the one who accuses them
      before our God day and night.
[11] They conquered him by the
      blood of the Lamb
and by the word of their
      testimony,
for they did not love their
      lives in the face of death.
[12] Therefore rejoice,
      O heavens, and you who
      dwell in them!
Woe to the earth and the sea,
for the Devil has come down
      to you with great fury,
because he knows he has a
      short time.

## The Woman Persecuted

[13] When the dragon saw that he had been thrown to earth, he persecuted the woman who gave birth to the male. [14] The woman was given two wings of a great eagle, so that she could fly from the serpent's presence to her place in the wilderness, where she was fed for a time, times, and half a time. [15] From his mouth the serpent spewed water like a river after the woman, to sweep her away in a torrent. [16] But the earth helped the woman: the earth opened its mouth and swallowed up the river that the dragon had spewed from his mouth. [17] So the dragon was furious with the woman and left to wage war against the rest of her offspring—those who keep the commandments of God and have the testimony about Jesus. [18] He[a] stood on the sand of the sea.

[a]**12:18** Other mss read *I*. "He" is apparently a reference to the dragon.

*The Beast from the Sea*

**13** And I saw a beast coming up out of the sea. He had 10 horns and seven heads. On his horns were 10 diadems, and on his heads were blasphemous names.[a] [2] The beast I saw was like a leopard, his feet were like a bear's, and his mouth was like a lion's mouth. The dragon gave him his power, his throne, and great authority. [3] One of his heads appeared to be fatally wounded, but his fatal wound was healed. The whole earth was amazed and followed the beast. [4] They worshiped the dragon because he gave authority to the beast. And they worshiped the beast, saying, "Who is like the beast? Who is able to wage war against him?"

[5] A mouth was given to him to speak boasts and blasphemies. He was also given authority to act[b] for 42 months. [6] He began to speak blasphemies against God: to blaspheme His name and His dwelling—those who dwell in heaven. [7] And he was permitted to wage war against the saints and to conquer them. He was also given authority over every tribe, people, language, and nation. [8] All those who live on the earth will worship him, everyone whose name was not written from the foundation of the world in the book of life of the Lamb who was slaughtered.

[9] If anyone has an ear, he should listen:

[10] If anyone is destined for captivity,
    into captivity he goes.
If anyone is to be killed[c] with
    a sword,
with a sword he will be killed.

Here is the endurance and the faith of the saints.

*The Beast from the Earth*

[11] Then I saw another beast coming up out of the earth; he had two horns like a lamb, but he sounded like a dragon. [12] He exercises all the authority of the first beast on his behalf and compels the earth and those who live on it to worship the first beast, whose fatal wound was healed. [13] He also performs great signs, even causing fire to come down from heaven to earth before people. [14] He deceives those who live on the earth because of the signs that he is permitted to perform on behalf of the beast, telling those who live on the earth to make an image of the beast who had the sword wound yet lived. [15] He was permitted to give a spirit to the image of the beast, so that the image of the beast could both speak and cause whoever would not worship the image of the beast to be killed. [16] And he requires everyone—small and great, rich and poor, free and slave—to be given a mark on his right hand or on his forehead, [17] so that no one can buy or sell unless he has the mark: the beast's name or the number of his name. [18] Here is wisdom: The one who has understanding must calculate the number of the beast, because it is the number of a man. His number is 666.[d]

*The Lamb and the 144,000*

**14** Then I looked, and there on Mount Zion stood the Lamb, and with Him were 144,000 who had His name and His Father's name written on their foreheads. [2] I heard a sound

[a]13:1 Other mss read *heads was a blasphemous name*   [b]13:5 Other mss read *wage war*   [c]13:10 Other mss read *anyone kills*   [d]13:18 One Gk ms plus other ancient evidence read *616*

from heaven like the sound of cascading waters and like the rumbling of loud thunder. The sound I heard was also like harpists playing on their harps. [3] They sang[a] a new song before the throne and before the four living creatures and the elders, but no one could learn the song except the 144,000 who had been redeemed from the earth. [4] These are the ones not defiled with women, for they have kept their virginity. These are the ones who follow the Lamb wherever He goes. They were redeemed[b] from the human race as the •firstfruits for God and the Lamb. [5] No lie was found in their mouths; they are blameless.

## The Proclamation of Three Angels

[6] Then I saw another angel flying in mid-heaven, having the eternal gospel to announce to the inhabitants of the earth—to every nation, tribe, language, and people. [7] He spoke with a loud voice: "Fear God and give Him glory, because the hour of His judgment has come. Worship the Maker of heaven and earth, the sea and springs of water."

[8] A second angel followed, saying: "It has fallen, Babylon the Great has fallen,[c] who made all nations drink the wine of her sexual immorality, which brings wrath."

[9] And a third angel followed them and spoke with a loud voice: "If anyone worships the beast and his image

---

*"A person of faith may experience loss but not emptiness, disappointment but not despair, adversity but not defeat."*

*—Dorothy Kelley Patterson*

---

and receives a mark on his forehead or on his hand, [10] he will also drink the wine of God's wrath, which is mixed full strength in the cup of His anger. He will be tormented with fire and sulfur in the sight of the holy angels and in the sight of the Lamb, [11] and the smoke of their torment will go up forever and ever. There is no rest day or night for those who worship the beast and his image, or anyone who receives the mark of his name. [12] Here is the endurance of the saints, who keep the commandments of God and the faith in Jesus."

---

## Revelation 14:9-13

*Faith is not wishful thinking, nor is it a stubborn demand that God work something out for us just the way we want him to. Faith is hanging your every hope on both the wisdom and the goodness of God and knowing that He's got everything under control.*

---

[13] Then I heard a voice from heaven saying, "Write: Blessed are the dead who die in the Lord from now on."

"Yes," says the Spirit, "let them rest from their labors, for their works follow them!"

## Reaping the Earth's Harvest

[14] Then I looked, and there was a white cloud, and One like the •Son of Man was seated on the cloud, with a gold crown on His head and a sharp sickle in His hand. [15] Another angel came out of the sanctuary, crying out in a loud voice to the One

---

[a]**14:3** Other mss add *as it were*   [b]**14:4** Other mss add *by Jesus*   [c]**14:8** Other mss omit the second *has fallen*

who was seated on the cloud, "Use your sickle and reap, for the time to reap has come, since the harvest of the earth is ripe." [16] So the One seated on the cloud swung His sickle over the earth, and the earth was harvested.

[17] Then another angel who also had a sharp sickle came out of the sanctuary in heaven. [18] Yet another angel, who had authority over fire, came from the altar, and he called with a loud voice to the one who had the sharp sickle, "Use your sharp sickle and gather the clusters of grapes from earth's vineyard, because its grapes have ripened." [19] So the angel swung his sickle toward earth and gathered the grapes from earth's vineyard, and he threw them into the great winepress of God's wrath. [20] Then the press was trampled outside the city, and blood flowed out of the press up to the horses' bridles for about 180 miles.

## Preparation for the Bowl Judgments

**15** Then I saw another great and awesome sign in heaven: seven angels with the seven last plagues, for with them, God's wrath will be completed. [2] I also saw something like a sea of glass mixed with fire, and those who had won the victory from the beast, his image,[a] and the number of his name, were standing on the sea of glass with harps from God. [3] They sang the song of God's servant Moses, and the song of the Lamb:

Great and awesome are Your
    works, Lord God, the Almighty;
righteous and true are Your
    ways, King of the Nations.
[4]   Who will not fear, Lord, and

glorify Your name?
Because You alone are holy,
because all the nations will
    come and worship before You,
because Your righteous acts
    have been revealed.

[5] After this I looked, and the heavenly sanctuary—the •tabernacle of testimony—was opened. [6] Out of the sanctuary came the seven angels with the seven plagues, dressed in clean, bright linen, with gold sashes wrapped around their chests. [7] One of the four living creatures gave the seven angels seven gold bowls filled with the wrath of God who lives forever and ever. [8] Then the sanctuary was filled with smoke from God's glory and from His power, and no one could enter the sanctuary until the seven plagues of the seven angels were completed.

## The First Bowl

**16** Then I heard a loud voice from the sanctuary saying to the seven angels, "Go and pour out the seven[b] bowls of God's wrath on the earth." [2] The first went and poured out his bowl on the earth, and severely painful sores broke out on the people who had the mark of the beast and who worshiped his image.

## The Second Bowl

[3] The second[c] poured out his bowl into the sea. It turned to blood like a dead man's, and all life in the sea died.

## The Third Bowl

[4] The third[c] poured out his bowl into the rivers and the springs of

[a]15:2 Other mss add *his mark*   [b]16:1 Other mss omit *seven*   [c]16:3-4 Other mss read *The angel*

water, and they became blood. [5] I heard the angel of the waters say:

> You are righteous, who is and
> who was, the Holy One,
> for You have decided these
> things.
> [6] Because they poured out the
> blood of the saints and
> the prophets,
> You also gave them blood to
> drink; they deserve it!

[7] Then I heard someone from the altar say:

> Yes, Lord God, the Almighty,
> true and righteous are Your
> judgments.

## The Fourth Bowl

[8] The fourth[a] poured out his bowl on the sun. He was given the power to burn people with fire, [9] and people were burned by the intense heat. So they blasphemed the name of God who had the power over these plagues, and they did not repent and give Him glory.

## The Fifth Bowl

[10] The fifth[a] poured out his bowl on the throne of the beast, and his kingdom was plunged into darkness. People gnawed their tongues from pain [11] and blasphemed the God of heaven because of their pains and their sores, yet they did not repent of their actions.

## The Sixth Bowl

[12] The sixth[a] poured out his bowl on the great river Euphrates, and its water was dried up to prepare the way for the kings from the east. [13] Then I saw three unclean spirits like frogs [coming] from the dragon's mouth, from the beast's mouth, and from the mouth of the false prophet. [14] For they are spirits of demons performing signs, who travel to the kings of the whole world to assemble them for the battle of the great day of God, the Almighty. [15] "Look, I am coming like a thief. Blessed is the one who is alert and remains clothed so that he may not go naked, and they see his shame." [16] So they assembled them at the place called in Hebrew Armagedon.[b]

## The Seventh Bowl

[17] Then the seventh[c] poured out his bowl into the air, and a loud voice came out of the sanctuary,[d] from the throne, saying, "It is done!" [18] There were lightnings, rumblings, and thunders. And a severe earthquake occurred like no other since man has been on the earth—so great was the quake. [19] The great city split into three parts, and the cities of the nations fell. Babylon the Great was remembered in God's presence; He gave her the cup filled with the wine of His fierce anger. [20] Every island fled, and the mountains disappeared. [21] Enormous hailstones, each weighing about 100 pounds, fell from heaven on the people, and they blasphemed God for the plague of hail because that plague was extremely severe.

## The Woman and the Scarlet Beast

**17** Then one of the seven angels who had the seven bowls came

---

[a]16:8,10,12 Other mss read *The angel*  [b]16:16 Other mss read *Armageddon*; other mss read *Harmegedon*; other mss read *Mageddon*; other mss read *Magedon*  [c]16:17 Other mss add *angel*  [d]16:17 Other mss add *of heaven*

and spoke with me: "Come, I will show you the judgment of the notorious prostitute who sits on many waters. [2] The kings of the earth committed sexual immorality with her, and those who live on the earth became drunk on the wine of her sexual immorality." [3] So he carried me away in the Spirit to a desert. I saw a woman sitting on a scarlet beast that was covered with blasphemous names, having seven heads and 10 horns. [4] The woman was dressed in purple and scarlet, adorned with gold, precious stones, and pearls. She had a gold cup in her hand filled with everything vile and with the impurities of her[a] prostitution. [5] On her forehead a cryptic name was written:

> BABYLON THE GREAT
> THE MOTHER OF PROSTITUTES
> AND OF THE VILE THINGS OF THE EARTH

[6] Then I saw that the woman was drunk on the blood of the saints and on the blood of the witnesses to Jesus. When I saw her, I was utterly astounded.

## The Meaning of the Woman and of the Beast

[7] Then the angel said to me, "Why are you astounded? I will tell you the secret meaning of the woman and of the beast, with the seven heads and the 10 horns, that carries her. [8] The beast that you saw was, and is not, and is about to come up from the •abyss and go to destruction. Those who live on the earth whose names were not written in the book of life from the foundation of the world will be astounded when they see the beast

that was, and is not, and will be present ⌊again⌋.

[9] "Here is the mind with wisdom: the seven heads are seven mountains on which the woman is seated. [10] They are also seven kings: five have fallen, one is, the other has not yet come, and when he comes, he must remain for a little while. [11] The beast that was and is not, is himself the eighth, yet is of the seven and goes to destruction. [12] The 10 horns you saw are 10 kings who have not yet received a kingdom, but they will receive authority as kings with the beast for one hour. [13] These have one purpose, and they give their power and authority to the beast. [14] These will make war against the Lamb, but the Lamb will conquer them because he is Lord of lords and King of kings. Those with him are called and elect and faithful."

[15] He also said to me, "The waters you saw, where the prostitute was seated, are peoples, multitudes, nations, and languages. [16] The 10 horns you saw, and the beast, will hate the prostitute. They will make her desolate and naked, devour her flesh, and burn her up with fire. [17] For God has put it into their hearts to carry out His plan by having one purpose, and to give their kingdom to the beast until God's words are accomplished. [18] And the woman you saw is the great city that has an empire over the kings of the earth."

## The Fall of Babylon the Great

**18** After this I saw another angel with great authority coming down from heaven, and the earth was illuminated by his splendor. [2] He cried in a mighty voice:

---

[a]17:4 Other mss read *of earth's*

It has fallen,[a] Babylon the
  Great has fallen!
She has become a dwelling
  for demons,
a haunt for every unclean spirit,
a haunt for every unclean
  bird,
and a haunt for every
  unclean and despicable
  beast.[b]
3 For all the nations have
  drunk[c]
the wine of her sexual
  immorality, which brings
  wrath.
The kings of the earth have
  committed sexual
  immorality with her,
and the merchants of the
  earth have grown wealthy
  from her excessive
  luxury.

4 Then I heard another voice from
heaven:

Come out of her, My people,
  so that you will not share in
  her sins,
or receive any of her plagues.
5 For her sins are piled up to
  heaven,
and God has remembered
  her crimes.
6 Pay her back the way she also
  paid,
and double it according to
  her works.
In the cup in which she
  mixed,
mix a double portion for her.
7 As much as she glorified
  herself and lived
  luxuriously,
give her that much torment
  and grief.

Because she says in her
  heart, 'I sit as queen;
I am not a widow, and I will
  never see grief,'
8 therefore her plagues will
  come in one day—
death, and grief, and famine.
She will be burned up with
  fire,
because the Lord God who
  judges her is mighty.

## The World Mourns Babylon's Fall

9 The kings of the earth who have
committed sexual immorality and
lived luxuriously with her will weep
and mourn over her when they see
the smoke of her burning. 10 They
stand far off in fear of her torment,
saying:

Woe, woe, the great city,
Babylon, the mighty city!
For in a single hour
your judgment has come.

11 The merchants of the earth will
also weep and mourn over her,
because no one buys their merchandise any longer— 12 merchandise of
gold, silver, precious stones, and
pearls; fine fabrics of linen, purple,
silk, and scarlet; all kinds of fragrant
wood products; objects of ivory;
objects of expensive wood, brass,
iron, and marble; 13 cinnamon,
spice,[d] incense, myrrh, and frankincense; wine, olive oil, fine wheat
flour, and grain; cattle and sheep;
horses and carriages; and human
bodies and souls.

14 The fruit you craved has left
  you.

---

[a]18:2 Other mss omit *It has fallen*   [b]18:2 Other mss omit the words *and a haunt for every unclean beast*. The
words *and despicable* then refer to the *bird* of the previous line.   [c]18:3 Other mss read *have collapsed*; other
mss read *have fallen*   [d]18:13 Other mss omit *spice*

All your splendid and
   glamorous things are
   gone;
they will never find them
   again.

15 The merchants of these things, who became rich from her, will stand far off in fear of her torment, weeping and mourning, 16 saying:

Woe, woe, the great city,
clothed in fine linen, purple,
   and scarlet,
adorned with gold, precious
   stones, and pearls;
17 because in a single hour such
   fabulous wealth was
   destroyed!

And every shipmaster, seafarer, the sailors, and all who do business by sea, stood far off 18 as they watched the smoke from her burning and kept crying out: "Who is like the great city?" 19 They threw dust on their heads and kept crying out, weeping, and mourning:

Woe, woe, the great city,
where all those who have
   ships on the sea
became rich from her wealth;
because in a single hour she
   was destroyed.
20 Rejoice over her, heaven:
   saints, apostles and
   prophets;
because God has executed
   your judgment on her!

## The Finality of Babylon's Fall

21 Then a mighty angel picked up a stone like a large millstone and threw it into the sea, saying:

In this way, Babylon the great
   city will be thrown

down violently
and never be found again.
22 The sound of harpists,
   musicians, flutists,
   and trumpeters
will never be heard in you again;
no craftsman of any trade
will ever be found in you again;
the sound of a mill
will never be heard in you
   again;
23 the light of a lamp will never
   shine in you again;
and the voice of a groom and
   bride
will never be heard in you
   again.
⌊All this will happen⌋
because your merchants
   were the nobility
   of the earth,
because all the nations were
   deceived by your
   sorcery,
24 and the blood of prophets
   and saints,
and all those slaughtered on
   earth, was found in you.

## Heaven Exults over Babylon

19 After this I heard something like the loud voice of a vast multitude in heaven, saying:

Hallelujah!
Salvation, glory, and power
   belong to our God,
2 because His judgments are
   true and righteous,
because He has judged the
   notorious prostitute
who corrupted the earth
   with her sexual
   immorality;
and He has avenged the
   blood of His servants that
   was on her hands.

³ A second time they said:

> Hallelujah!
> Her smoke ascends forever
>     and ever!

⁴ Then the 24 elders and the four living creatures fell down and worshiped God, who is seated on the throne, saying:

> •Amen! Hallelujah!

⁵ A voice came from the throne, saying:

> Praise our God,
> all you His servants, you who
>     fear Him,
> both small and great!

## Marriage of the Lamb Announced

⁶ Then I heard something like the voice of a vast multitude, like the sound of cascading waters, and like the rumbling of loud thunder, saying:

> Hallelujah—because our Lord
>     God, the Almighty,
> has begun to reign!
> ⁷ Let us be glad, rejoice, and
>     give Him glory,
> because the marriage of the
>     Lamb has come,
> and His wife has prepared
>     herself.
> ⁸ She was permitted to wear
>     fine linen, bright
>     and pure.

For the fine linen represents the righteous acts of the saints. ⁹ Then he said to me, "Write: Blessed are those invited to the marriage feast of the Lamb!" He also said to me, "These words of God are true." ¹⁰ Then I fell at his feet to worship him, but he said to me, "Don't do that! I am a fellow slave with you and your brothers who have the testimony about Jesus. Worship God, because the testimony about Jesus is the spirit of prophecy."

## The Rider on a White Horse

¹¹ Then I saw heaven opened, and there was a white horse! Its rider is called Faithful and True, and in righteousness He judges and makes war. ¹² His eyes were like a fiery flame, and on His head were many crowns. He had a name written that no one knows except Himself. ¹³ He wore a robe stained with blood, and His name is called the Word of God. ¹⁴ The armies that were in heaven followed Him on white horses, wearing pure white linen. ¹⁵ From His mouth came a sharp[a] sword, so that with it He might strike the nations. He will shepherd them with an iron scepter. He will also trample the winepress of the fierce anger of God, the Almighty. ¹⁶ And on His robe and on His thigh He has a name written:

> ### KING OF KINGS
> ### AND LORD OF LORDS

## The Beast and His Armies Defeated

¹⁷ Then I saw an angel standing in the sun, and he cried out in a loud voice, saying to all the birds flying in mid-heaven, "Come, gather together for the great supper of God, ¹⁸ so that you may eat the flesh of kings, the flesh of commanders, the flesh of mighty men, the flesh of horses and of their riders, and the

---

[a]19:15 Other mss add *double-edged*

flesh of everyone, both free and slave, small and great."

¹⁹ Then I saw the beast, the kings of the earth, and their armies gathered together to wage war against the rider on the horse and against His army. ²⁰ But the beast was taken prisoner, and along with him the false prophet, who had performed signs on his authority, by which he deceived those who accepted the mark of the beast and those who worshiped his image. Both of them were thrown alive into the lake of fire that burns with sulfur. ²¹ The rest were killed with the sword that came from the mouth of the rider on the horse, and all the birds were filled with their flesh.

## Satan Bound

**20** Then I saw an angel coming down from heaven with the key to the •abyss and a great chain in his hand. ² He seized the dragon, that ancient serpent who is the Devil and Satan,ᵃ and bound him for 1,000 years. ³ He threw him into the abyss, closed it, and put a seal on it so that he would no longer deceive the nations until the 1,000 years were completed. After that, he must be released for a short time.

## The Saints Reign with the Messiah

⁴ Then I saw thrones, and people seated on them who were given authority to judge. [I] also [saw] the souls of those who had been beheaded because of their testimony about Jesus and because of God's word, who had not worshiped the beast or his image, and who had not accepted the mark on their foreheads or their hands. They came to life and reigned with the

•Messiah for 1,000 years. ⁵ The rest of the dead did not come to life until 1,000 years were completed. This is the first resurrection. ⁶ Blessed and holy is the one who shares in the first resurrection! The second death has no power over these, but they will be priests of God and the Messiah, and they will reign with Him for 1,000 years.

## Satanic Rebellion Crushed

⁷ When the 1,000 years are completed, Satan will be released from his prison ⁸ and will go out to deceive the nations at the four corners of the earth, Gog and Magog, to gather them for battle. Their number is like the sand of the sea. ⁹ They came up over the surface of the earth and surrounded the encampment of the saints, the beloved city. Then fire came down from heavenᵇ and consumed them. ¹⁰ The Devil who deceived them was thrown into the lake of fire and sulfur where the beast and the false prophet are, and they will be tormented day and night forever and ever.

## The Great White Throne Judgment

¹¹ Then I saw a great white throne and One seated on it. Earth and heaven fled from His presence, and no place was found for them. ¹² I also saw the dead, the great and the small, standing before the throne, and books were opened. Another book was opened, which is the book of life, and the dead were judged according to their works by what was written in the books. ¹³ Then the sea gave up its dead, and Death and •Hades gave up their

ᵃ**20:2** Other mss add *who deceives the whole world*  ᵇ**20:9** Other mss add *from God*

dead; all were judged according to their works. ¹⁴ Death and Hades were thrown into the lake of fire. This is the second death, the lake of fire.ᵃ ¹⁵ And anyone not found written in the book of life was thrown into the lake of fire.

### The New Creation

**21** Then I saw a new heaven and a new earth, for the first heaven and the first earth had passed away, and the sea existed no longer. ² I also saw the Holy City, new Jerusalem, coming down out of heaven from God, prepared like a bride adorned for her husband.

³ Then I heard a loud voice from the throne:ᵇ

Look! God's dwelling is with
    men,
and He will live with them.
They will be His people,
and God Himself will be with
    them and be their God.ᶜ
⁴ He will wipe away every tear
    from their eyes.
Death will exist no longer;
grief, crying, and pain will
    exist no longer,
because the previous things
    have passed away.

⁵ Then the One seated on the throne said, "Look! I am making everything new." He also said, "Write, because these wordsᵈ are faithful and true." ⁶ And He said to me, "It is done! I am the •Alpha and the Omega, the Beginning and the End. I will give to the thirsty from the spring of living water as a gift. ⁷ The victor will inherit these things, and I will be his God, and he

---

### Revelation 21:2-3

#### The Church

*Few things are more beautiful than a man's first glimpse of his bride in flowing white, walking to him amid strewn flowers and stately music, softly hidden behind her wedding veil. About the only thing more beautiful is the sight of the church to the eyes of its Savior. That's how He sees us.*

---

will be My son. ⁸ But the cowards, unbelievers,ᵉ vile, murderers, sexually immoral, sorcerers, idolaters, and all liars—their share will be in the lake that burns with fire and sulfur, which is the second death."

### The New Jerusalem

⁹ Then one of the seven angels, who had held the seven bowls filled with the seven last plagues, came and spoke with me: "Come, I will show you the bride, the wife of the Lamb." ¹⁰ He then carried me away in the Spirit to a great and high mountain and showed me the holy city, Jerusalem, coming down out of heaven from God, ¹¹ arrayed with God's glory. Her radiance was like a very precious stone, like a jasper stone, bright as crystal. ¹² ⌊The city⌋ had a massive high wall, with 12 gates. Twelve angels were at the gates; ⌊on the gates⌋, names were inscribed, the names of the 12 tribes of the sons of

---

ᵃ20:14 Other mss omit *the lake of fire*  ᵇ21:3 Other mss read *from heaven*  ᶜ21:3 Other mss omit *and be their God*  ᵈ21:5 Other mss add *of God*  ᵉ21:8 Other mss add *the sinful*

Israel. [13] There were three gates on the east, three gates on the north, three gates on the south, and three gates on the west. [14] The city wall had 12 foundations, and on them were the 12 names of the Lamb's 12 apostles.

[15] The one who spoke with me had a gold measuring rod to measure the city, its gates, and its wall. [16] The city is laid out in a square; its length and width are the same. He measured the city with the rod at 12,000 *stadia*. Its length, width, and height are equal. [17] Then he measured its wall, 144 cubits according to human measurement, which the angel used. [18] The building material of its wall was jasper, and the city was pure gold like clear glass.

[19] The foundations of the city wall were adorned with every kind of precious stone:

the first foundation jasper,
the second sapphire,
the third chalcedony,
the fourth emerald,
[20] the fifth sardonyx,
the sixth carnelian,
the seventh chrysolite,
the eighth beryl,
the ninth topaz,
the tenth chrysoprase,
the eleventh jacinth,
the twelfth amethyst.

[21] The 12 gates are 12 pearls; each individual gate was made of a single pearl. The broad street of the city was pure gold, like transparent glass.

[22] I did not see a sanctuary in it, because the Lord God the Almighty and the Lamb are its sanctuary. [23] The city does not need the sun or the moon to shine on it, because God's glory illuminates it, and its lamp is the Lamb. [24] The nations[a] will •walk in its light, and the kings of the earth will bring their glory into it.[b] [25] Each day its gates will never close because it will never be night there. [26] They will bring the glory and honor of the nations into it.[c] [27] Nothing profane will ever enter it: no one who does what is vile or false, but only those written in the Lamb's book of life.

## The Source of Life

**22** Then he showed me the river[d] of living water, sparkling like crystal, flowing from the throne of God and of the Lamb [2] down the middle of the broad street ⌊of the city⌋. On both sides of the river was the tree of life bearing 12 kinds of fruit, producing its fruit every month. The leaves of the tree are for healing the nations, [3] and there will no longer be any curse. The throne of God and of the Lamb will be in the city, and His servants will serve Him. [4] They will see His face, and His name will be on their foreheads. [5] Night will no longer exist, and people will not need lamplight or sunlight, because the Lord God will give them light. And they will reign forever and ever.

## The Time Is Near

[6] Then he said to me, "These words are faithful and true. And the Lord, the God of the spirits of the prophets,[e] has sent His angel to show His servants what must quickly take place."

---

[a]21:24 Other mss add *of those who are saved*   [b]21:24 Other mss read *will bring to Him the nations' glory and honor*   [c]21:26 Other mss add *in order that they might go in*   [d]22:1 Other mss read *pure river*   [e]22:6 Other mss read *God of the holy prophets*

## Revelation 22:1-5

*Heaven is more real than the room you're sitting in. With that in your future, you can stand anything. So even when life scratches you hard enough to break the skin, you have a glorious hope—hope that no defeat is ever final. God's people last forever.*

⁷ "Look, I am coming quickly! Blessed is the one who keeps the prophetic words of this book."

⁸ I, John, am the one who heard and saw these things. When I heard and saw them, I fell down to worship at the feet of the angel who had shown them to me. ⁹ But he said to me, "Don't do that! I am a fellow slave with you, your brothers the prophets, and those who keep the words of this book. Worship God." ¹⁰ He also said to me, "Don't seal the prophetic words of this book, because the time is near. ¹¹ Let the unrighteous go on in unrighteousness; let the filthy go on being made filthy; let the righteous go on in righteousness; and let the holy go on being made holy."

¹² "Look! I am coming quickly, and My reward is with Me to repay each person according to what he has done. ¹³ I am the •Alpha and the Omega, the First and the Last, the Beginning and the End.

¹⁴ "Blessed are those who wash their robes,ᵃ so that they may have the right to the tree of life and may enter the city by the gates. ¹⁵ Outside are the dogs, the sorcerers, the sexually immoral, the murderers, the idolaters, and everyone who loves and practices lying.

¹⁶ "I, Jesus, have sent My angel to attest these things to you for the churches. I am the Root and the Offspring of David, the Bright Morning Star."

¹⁷ Both the Spirit and the bride say, "Come!" Anyone who hears should say, "Come!" And the one who is thirsty should come. Whoever desires should take the living water as a gift.

¹⁸ I testify to everyone who hears the prophetic words of this book: If anyone adds to them, God will add to him the plagues that are written in this book. ¹⁹ And if anyone takes away from the words of this prophetic book, God will take away his share of the tree of life and the holy city, written in this book.

²⁰ He who testifies about these things says, "Yes, I am coming quickly."

•Amen! Come, Lord Jesus!

²¹ The grace of the Lord Jesusᵇ be with all the saints.ᶜ Amen.ᵈ

---

*"To pretend to describe heaven by the most artful composition of words would be but to darken and cloud it."*

*—Jonathan Edwards*

---

ᵃ**22:14** Other mss read *who keep His commandments*   ᵇ**22:21** Other mss add *Christ*   ᶜ**22:21** Other mss omit *the saints*   ᵈ**22:21** Other mss omit *Amen.*

# PSALMS

## BOOK I
## (PSALMS 1–41)

### The Two Ways

**1** How happy is the man
  who does not
    follow the advice
    of the wicked,
  or take the path of sinners,
  or join a group of mockers!
2 Instead, his delight is
    in the LORD's instruction,
  and he meditates on it day
    and night.
3 He is like a tree planted
    beside streams of water
  that bears its fruit in season
  and whose leaf does
    not wither.
  Whatever he does prospers.

4 The wicked are not like this;
  instead, they are like husks
    that the wind blows away.
5 Therefore the wicked
    will not survive the
    judgment,
  and sinners will not be
    in the community
    of the righteous.

6 For the LORD watches over
    the way of the righteous,
  but the way of the wicked
    leads to ruin.

### Coronation of the Son

**2** Why do the nations rebel
  and the peoples plot in vain?
2 The kings of the earth take
    their stand

and the rulers conspire
    together
against the LORD and
    His Anointed One:
3 "Let us tear off their chains
and free ourselves
    from their restraints."

4 The One enthroned in heaven
    laughs;
the Lord ridicules them.
5 Then He speaks to them
    in His anger
and terrifies them
    in His wrath:
6 "I have consecrated My King
on Zion, My holy mountain."

7 I will declare
    the LORD's decree:
He said to Me, "You are
    My Son;
today I have become
    Your Father.

---

*Psalm 2:7-9*

*God the Son*

*God the Son has existed from
eternity. Yet somewhere in the
mysteries of God, the Father chose
to send His Son to earth, to suffer
for the sins of mankind, to redeem
the believing, and ultimately to
reign over all things in heaven and
earth. The Bible is the story of this
plan unfolding.*

---

8 Ask of Me, and I will make
    the nations
    Your inheritance
  and the ends of the earth
    Your possession.
9 You will break[a] them
    with a rod of iron;
  You will shatter them
    like pottery."

10 So now, kings, be wise;
    receive instruction, you judges
    of the earth.
11 Serve the LORD
    with reverential awe,
  and rejoice with trembling.
12 Pay homage to the Son,
    or He will be angry,
  and you will perish
    in your rebellion,
  for His anger may ignite
    at any moment.
  All those who take refuge
    in Him are happy.

## Confidence in Troubled Times

*A psalm of David when he fled
from his son Absalom.*

**3** LORD, how my foes increase!
  There are many who attack
    me.
2 Many say about me,
  "There is no help for him
    in God."          •*Selah*

3 But You, LORD, are a shield
    around me,
  my glory, and the One
    who lifts up my head.
4 I cry aloud to the LORD,
  and He answers me
    from His holy mountain.
                            *Selah*

5 I lie down and sleep;

I wake again because the LORD
    sustains me.
6 I am not afraid
    of the thousands of people
  who have taken their stand
    against me on every side.

7 Rise up, LORD!
  Save me, my God!
  You strike all my enemies
    on the cheek;
  You break the teeth
    of the wicked.
8 Salvation belongs to the LORD;
  may Your blessing be
    on Your people.       *Selah*

## A Night Prayer

*For the choir director:
with stringed instruments.
A Davidic psalm.*

**4** Answer me when I call,
  O God who vindicates me.
  You freed me from affliction;
  be gracious to me and hear
    my prayer.

2 How long, exalted men,
    will my honor be insulted?

  [How long] will you love
    what is worthless
    and pursue a lie?    •*Selah*
3 Know that the LORD has
    set apart the faithful
    for Himself;
  the LORD will hear when I call
    to Him.
4 Be angry and do not sin;
  on your bed, reflect
    in your heart and be still.
                            *Selah*

5 Offer sacrifices
    in righteousness
  and trust in the LORD.

---

[a] 2:9 LXX, Syr, Tg read *shepherd*

6 Many are saying,
   "Who can show us
      anything good?"
   Look on us with favor, LORD.

7 You have put more joy
      in my heart
   than they have when
      their grain and new wine
      abound.

8 I will both lie down and sleep
      in peace,
   for You alone, LORD, make me
      live in safety.

---

## Psalm 5:1-3

*The moments spent with no one
else but God build the best foundation to a Christian's day. It's one of
those basic, everyday disciplines of
Christian living that you'll likely
find challenging to maintain, but
get good at it. It's the best way for
you to get to know God.*

---

### The Refuge of the Righteous

*For the choir director:
with the flutes. A Davidic psalm.*

**5** Listen to my words, LORD;
   consider my sighing.
2   Pay attention to the sound
      of my cry,
   my King and my God,
   for I pray to You.

3 At daybreak, LORD, You hear
      my voice;
   at daybreak I plead my case
      to You and watch
      expectantly.

4 For You are not a God
      who delights
      in wickedness;
   evil cannot lodge with You.
5 The boastful cannot stand
      in Your presence;
   You hate all evildoers.
6 You destroy those who tell lies;
   the LORD abhors a man
      of bloodshed
      and treachery.

7 But I enter Your house
      by the abundance
      of Your faithful love;
   I bow down toward
      Your holy temple
      in reverential awe of You.
8 LORD, lead me
      in Your righteousness,
   because of my adversaries;
   make Your way straight
      before me.

9 For there is nothing reliable
      in what they say;
   destruction is within them;
   their throat is an open grave;
   they flatter
      with their tongues.
10 Punish them, God;
   let them fall by
      their own schemes.
   Drive them out because of
      their many crimes,
   for they rebel against You.

---

*"If you meet the Lord before you
meet anyone else, you'll be
pointed in the right direction for
whatever comes."*
—*Elisabeth Elliot*

---

11   But let all who take refuge
        in You rejoice;

let them shout for joy forever.
May You shelter them,
and may those who love
    Your name boast about You.
12 For You, LORD, bless
    the righteous one;
You surround him with favor
    like a shield.

## A Prayer for Mercy

*For the choir director:*
*with stringed instruments,*
*according to* •Sheminith.
*A Davidic psalm.*

**6** LORD, do not rebuke me
    in Your anger;
do not discipline me
    in Your wrath.
2 Be gracious to me, LORD,
    for I am weak;
heal me, LORD, for my bones
    are shaking;
3 my whole being is shaken
    with terror.
And You, LORD—how long?

4 Turn, LORD! Rescue me;
save me because of
    Your faithful love.
5 For there is no remembrance
    of You in death;
who can thank You in •Sheol?

6 I am weary from my groaning;
with my tears I dampen
    my pillow
and drench my bed
    every night.
7 My eyes are swollen
    from grief;
they[a] grow old because of all
    my enemies.

8 Depart from me, all evildoers,

for the LORD has heard
    the sound of my weeping.
9 The LORD has heard my plea
    for help;
the LORD accepts my prayer.
10 All my enemies will be
    ashamed and shake
    with terror;
they will turn back
    and suddenly be disgraced.

## Prayer for Justice

*A Shiggaion of David, which he sang*
*to the LORD concerning the words*
*of Cush,*[b] *a Benjaminite.*

**7** LORD my God, I seek refuge
    in You;
save me from all my pursuers
    and rescue me,
2 or they will tear me
    like a lion,
ripping me apart, with no one
    to rescue me.

3 LORD my God, if I have done
    this,
if there is injustice
    on my hands,
4 if I have done harm to one
    at peace with me
or have
    plundered my adversary
    without cause,
5 may an enemy pursue
    and overtake me;
may he trample me
    to the ground
and leave my honor
    in the dust.     •*Selah*

6 Rise up, LORD, in Your anger;
lift Yourself up against the fury
    of my adversaries;
awake for me;[c]

[a] **6:7** LXX, Aq, Sym, Jer read *I*   [b] LXX, Aq, Sym, Theod, Jer read *of the Cushite*   [c] **7:6** LXX reads *awake, Lord my God*

You have ordained
a judgment.
7 Let the assembly of peoples
gather around You;
take Your seat[a] on high over it.
8 The LORD judges the peoples;
vindicate me, LORD,
according to my righteousness
and my integrity.

9 Let the evil of the wicked
come to an end,
but establish the righteous.
The One who examines
the thoughts and emotions
is a righteous God.
10 My shield is with God,
who saves the upright
in heart.
11 God is a righteous judge,
and a God who executes
justice every day.

12 If anyone does not repent,
God will sharpen
His sword;
He has strung His bow
and made it ready.
13 He has prepared
His deadly weapons;
He tips His arrows with fire.

14 See, he is pregnant with evil,
conceives trouble,
and gives birth to deceit.
15 He dug a pit and hollowed it
out,
but fell into the hole
he had made.
16 His trouble comes back
on his own head,
and his violence falls
on the top of his head.

17 I will thank the LORD
for His righteousness;

---

### Psalm 8:3-5

#### Man

*Many people think they're worth less than nothing. They feel unloved, unappreciated, and incapable of doing anything right. But what could give a person more significance than being made by the one and only God, created in His incredible image, loved by the Maker of everything?*

---

I will sing about the name
of the LORD,
the •Most High.

### God's Glory, Man's Dignity
*For the choir director:
on the •Gittith. A Davidic psalm.*

**8** O LORD, our Lord,
how magnificent is Your name
throughout the earth!

You have covered the heavens
with Your majesty.
2 Because of Your adversaries,
You have established
a stronghold[b]
from the mouths of children
and nursing infants,
to silence the enemy
and the avenger.

3 When I observe Your heavens,
the work of Your fingers,
the moon and the stars,
which You set in place,

---

[a]7:7 MT reads *and return*  [b]8:2 LXX reads *established praise*

4  what is man
   that You remember him,
the son of man that You look
   after him?
5  You made him little less
   than God[a]
and crowned him with glory
   and honor.
6  You made him lord
   over the works
   of Your hands;
You put everything
   under his feet:
7  all the sheep and oxen,
as well as animals
   in the wild,
8  birds of the sky,
and fish of the sea
passing through the currents
   of the seas.

9  O LORD, our Lord,
   how magnificent is Your name
      throughout the earth!

### Celebration of God's Justice

*For the choir director:*
*according to* Muth-labben.
*A Davidic psalm.*

**9**  I will thank the LORD with all
         my heart;
I will declare all
   Your wonderful works.
2  I will rejoice and boast
   about You;
I will sing about Your name,
   *Most High.

3  When my enemies retreat,
they stumble and perish
   before You.
4  For You have upheld
   my just cause;
You are seated on Your throne
   as a righteous judge.

5  You have rebuked the nations;
   You have destroyed
   the wicked;
You have erased their name
   forever and ever.
6  The enemy has come
   to eternal ruin;
You have uprooted the cities,
and the very memory of them
   has perished.

7  But the LORD sits enthroned
   forever;
He has established His throne
   for judgment.
8  He judges the world
   with righteousness;
He executes judgment
   on the peoples
   with fairness.
9  The LORD is a refuge
   for the oppressed,
a refuge in times of trouble.
10 Those who know Your name
   trust in You
because You have not
   abandoned those who seek
   You, LORD.

11 Sing to the LORD, who dwells
   in Zion;
proclaim His deeds
   among the peoples.
12 For the One who seeks
   an accounting
   for bloodshed remembers
   them;
He does not forget the cry
   of the afflicted.

13 Be gracious to me, LORD;
consider my affliction
   at the hands of those
   who hate me.
Lift me up from the gates
   of death,

[a] 8:5 LXX reads *angels*

14 so that I may declare all
        Your praises.
    I will rejoice in Your salvation
    within the gates
        of Daughter Zion.

15 The nations have fallen
        into the pit they made;
    their foot is caught in the net
        they have concealed.
16 The LORD has revealed
        Himself;
    He has executed justice,
    striking down the wicked[a]
        by the work of their hands.
                *Higgaion. *Selah*

17 The wicked will return
        to *Sheol—
    all the nations that forget God.
18 For the oppressed will not
        always be forgotten;
    the hope of the afflicted[b]
        will not perish forever.

19 Rise up, LORD! Do not let man
        prevail;
    let the nations be judged
        in Your presence.
20 Put terror in them, LORD;
    let the nations know they are
        only men.                    *Selah*

**10** LORD,[c] why do You stand
        so far away?
    Why do You hide in times
        of trouble?
2    In arrogance the wicked
        relentlessly pursue
        the afflicted;
    let them be caught
        in the schemes
        they have devised.

3    For the wicked one boasts
        about his own cravings;

the one who is greedy
    curses and despises
    the LORD.
4 In all his scheming,
    the wicked arrogantly
        thinks:
    "There is no accountability,
    ⌊since⌋ God does not
        exist."
5 His ways are always secure;
    Your lofty judgments are
        beyond his sight;
    he scoffs at all his adversaries.
6 He says to himself, "I will
        never be moved—
    from generation to generation
        without calamity."
7 Cursing, deceit, and violence
        fill his mouth;
    trouble and malice are under
        his tongue.
8 He waits in ambush
        near the villages;
    he kills the innocent
        in secret places;
    his eyes are on the lookout
        for the helpless.
9 He lurks in secret like a lion
        in a thicket.
    He lurks in order to seize
        the afflicted.
    He seizes the afflicted
        and drags him in his net.
10 He crouches and bends down;
    the helpless fall because of
        his strength.
11 He says to himself,
    "God has forgotten;
    He hides His face and will
        never see."
12 Rise up, LORD God! Lift up
        Your hand.
    Do not forget the afflicted.
13 Why has the wicked despised
        God?

---

[a]9:16 LXX, Aq, Syr, Tg read *justice, the wicked is trapped*   [b]9:18 Alt Hb tradition reads *humble*   [c]10:1 A few Hb
mss and LXX connect Pss 9–10. Together these 2 psalms form a partial *acrostic.

He says to himself, "You will
   not demand an account."
14 But You Yourself have seen
   trouble and grief,
observing it in order to take
   the matter into Your hands.
The helpless entrusts himself
   to You;
You are a helper
   of the fatherless.
15 Break the arm of the wicked
   and evil person;
call his wickedness
   into account until nothing
   remains of it.

16 The LORD is King forever
   and ever;
the nations will perish
   from His land.
17 LORD, You have heard
   the desire of the humble;[a]
You will strengthen
   their hearts.
You will listen carefully,
18 doing justice for the fatherless
   and the oppressed,
so that men of the earth may
   terrify ⌊them⌋ no more.

## Refuge in the LORD

*For the choir director. Davidic.*

**11** I have taken refuge
   in the LORD.
How can you say to me,
   "Escape to the mountain
   like a bird![b]
2 For look, the wicked string
   the bow;
they put the arrow
   on the bowstring
to shoot from the shadows
   at the upright in heart.

3 When the foundations
   are destroyed,
what can the righteous do?"

4 The LORD is in
   His holy temple;
the LORD's throne is in heaven.
His eyes watch; He
   examines •everyone.
5 The LORD examines
   the righteous
   and the wicked.
He hates the lover of violence.
6 He will rain burning coals
   and sulfur[c] on the wicked;
a scorching wind will be
   their portion.
7 For the LORD is righteous;
   He loves righteous deeds.
The upright will see His face.

## Oppression by the Wicked

*For the choir director:
according to •Sheminith.
A Davidic psalm.*

**12** Help, LORD, for no
   faithful one remains;
the loyal have disappeared
   from the •human race.
2 They lie to one another;
   they speak with flattering lips
   and deceptive hearts.
3 May the LORD cut off all
   flattering lips
and the tongue that speaks
   boastfully.
4 They say, "Through
   our tongues
   we have power;
our lips are our own—
   who can be our master?"

5 "Because of the oppression
   of the afflicted

---

[a]10:17 Other Hb mss, LXX, Syr read *afflicted*  [b]11:1 LXX, Syr, Jer, Tg; Hb reads *to your mountain, bird*
[c]11:6 Sym; Hb reads *rain snares, fire*; the difference between the 2 Hb words is 1 letter

and the groaning
of the poor,
I will now rise up,"
says the LORD.
"I will put in a safe place
the one who longs for it."

6   The words of the LORD
are pure words,
like silver refined
in an earthen furnace,
purified seven times.

7   You, LORD, will guard us;ª
You will protect us[b]
from this generation forever.
8   The wicked
wander everywhere,
and what is worthless
is exalted
by the human race.

## A Plea for Deliverance

*For the choir director.*
*A Davidic psalm.*

**13** LORD, how long will You
continually forget me?
How long will You hide
Your face from me?
2   How long will I store up
anxious
concerns within me,
agony in my mind every day?
How long will my enemy
dominate me?

3   Consider me and answer,
LORD, my God.
Restore brightness to my eyes;
otherwise, I will sleep
in death,
4   my enemy will say,
"I have triumphed
over him,"

and my foes will rejoice
because I am defeated.

5   But I have trusted in
Your faithful love;
my heart will rejoice in
Your deliverance.
6   I will sing to the LORD
because He has treated me
generously.

## A Portrait of Sinners

*For the choir director. Davidic.*

**14** The fool says in his heart,
"God does not exist."
They are corrupt; their actions
are revolting.
There is no one who does
good.
2   The LORD looks down
from heaven
on the •human race
to see if there is one who is wise,
one who seeks God.
3   All have turned away;
they have all become
corrupt.
There is no one who does
good,
not even one.[c]

4   Will evildoers never
understand?
They consume my people
as they consume bread;
they do not call on the LORD.

5   Then they will be filled
with terror,
for God is with those
who are righteous.
6   You ⌊sinners⌋ frustrate
the plans of the afflicted,
but the LORD is his refuge.

---

ª 12:7 Some Hb mss, LXX, Jer; other Hb mss read *them*   [b] 12:7 Some Hb mss, LXX; other Hb mss read *him*
[c] 14:3 Two Hb mss, some LXX mss add the material found in Rm 3:13–18

7 Oh, that Israel's deliverance
      would come from Zion!
   When the LORD restores
      His captive people,
   Jacob will rejoice;
      Israel will be glad.

## A Description of the Godly

*A Davidic psalm.*

**15** LORD, who can dwell
      in Your tent?
   Who can live on
      Your holy mountain?

2 The one who lives honestly,
      practices righteousness,
   and acknowledges the truth
      in his heart—
3 who does not slander
      with his tongue,
   who does not harm his friend
   or discredit his neighbor,
4 who despises the one rejected
      by the LORD,
   but honors those who •fear
      the LORD,
   who keeps his word whatever
      the cost,
5 who does not lend his money
      at interest
   or take a bribe
      against the innocent—
   the one who does these things
      will never be moved.

## Confidence in the LORD

*A Davidic •Miktam.*

**16** Protect me, God, for I take
      refuge in You.
2   I[a] said to the LORD, "You are
      my Lord;
   I have no good besides You."

3 As for the holy people who are
      in the land,
   they are the noble ones
      in whom is all my delight.
4 The sorrows of those who take
      another ⌊god⌋
      for themselves multiply;
   I will not pour out
      their drink offerings
      of blood,
   and I will not speak
      their names with my lips.

5 LORD, You are
      my portion and my cup
      ⌊of blessing⌋;
   You hold my future.
6 The boundary lines have fallen
      for me in pleasant places;
   indeed, I have a beautiful
      inheritance.

7 I will praise the LORD
      who counsels me—
   even at night my conscience
      instructs me.
8 I keep the LORD
      in mind always.
   Because He is
      at my right hand, I will not
      be defeated.

9 Therefore my heart is glad,
      and my spirit[b] rejoices;
   my body also rests securely.
10 For You will not abandon me
      to •Sheol;
   You will not allow
      Your Faithful One to see
      the •Pit.[c]
11 You reveal the path of life
      to me;
   in Your presence is
      abundant joy;

---

[a]16:2 Some Hb mss, LXX, Syr, Jer; other Hb mss read *You*   [b]16:9 LXX reads *tongue*   [c]16:10 LXX reads *see decay*

in Your right hand are
   eternal pleasures.

## A Prayer for Protection
*A Davidic prayer.*

**17** LORD, hear a just cause;
   pay attention to my cry;
listen to my prayer—
   from lips free of deceit.
2 Let my vindication come
     from You,
   ⌊for⌋ You see what is right.
3 You have tested my heart;
You have visited by night;
You have tried me and found
     nothing ⌊evil⌋;[a]
I have determined that
   my mouth will not sin.
4 Concerning what people do:
   by the word of Your lips
I have avoided the ways
   of the violent.
5 My steps are on Your paths;
   my feet have not slipped.

6 I call on You, God, because
   You will answer me;
listen closely to me; hear
   what I say.
7 Display the wonders
   of Your faithful love, Savior
   of all who seek refuge
from those who rebel against
   Your right hand.
8 Guard me as the apple
   of Your eye;
hide me in the shadow
   of Your wings
9 from the wicked who treat me
   violently,
my deadly enemies
   who surround me.

10 They have become hardened;
   their mouths speak arrogantly.

11 They advance against me; now
   they surround me.
They are determined to throw
   ⌊me⌋ to the ground.
12 They are like a lion eager
   to tear,
like a young lion lurking
   in ambush.

13 Rise up, LORD!
Confront him; bring him
   down.
With Your sword, save me
   from the wicked.
14 With Your hand, LORD,
   ⌊save me⌋ from men,
from men of the world,
   whose portion is
   in this life:
You fill their bellies with what
   You have in store,
their sons are satisfied,
and they leave their surplus
   to their children.

15 But I will see Your face
   in righteousness;
when I awake, I will be
   satisfied
   with Your presence.

## Praise for Deliverance
*For the choir director. Of the servant
of the LORD, David, who spoke the
words of this song to the LORD on
the day the LORD rescued him from
the hand of all his enemies and from
the hand of Saul. He said:*

**18** I love You, LORD,
   my strength.
2 The LORD is my rock,
   my fortress,
   and my deliverer,
my God, my mountain where
   I seek refuge,

[a] 17:3 LXX, Aq, Sym, Syr, Jer read *found no unrighteousness*

my shield and the *horn
    of my salvation, my
    stronghold.
3 I called to the LORD, who is
    worthy of praise,
and I was saved
    from my enemies.

4 The ropes of death
    were wrapped around me;
the torrents of destruction
    terrified me.
5 The ropes of *Sheol entangled me;
the snares of death stared me
    in the face.
6 I called to the LORD
    in my distress,
and I cried to my God for help.
From His temple He heard
    my voice,
and my cry to Him reached
    His ears.

7 Then the earth shook
    and trembled;
the foundations
    of the mountains quaked;
they shook because He burned
    with anger.
8 Smoke rose from His nostrils,
and consuming fire ⌊came⌋
    from His mouth;
coals were set ablaze by it.
9 He parted the heavens
    and came down,
a dark cloud beneath His feet.
10 He rode on a cherub and flew,
soaring on the wings
    of the wind.
11 He made darkness
    His hiding place,
dark storm clouds His canopy
    around Him.
12 From the radiance
    of His presence,
His clouds swept onward
    with hail and blazing coals.

13 The LORD thundered
    from[a] heaven;
the *Most High projected
    His voice.[b]
14 He shot His arrows
    and scattered them;
He hurled lightning bolts
    and routed them.
15 The depths of the sea became
    visible,
the foundations of the world
    were exposed,
at Your rebuke, LORD,
at the blast of the breath
    of Your nostrils.

16 He reached down
    from on high and took hold
    of me;
He pulled me out of
    deep water.
17 He rescued me
    from my powerful enemy
and from those who hated me,
    for they were too strong
    for me.
18 They confronted me in the day
    of my distress,
but the LORD was my support.
19 He brought me out to a wide-
    open place;
He rescued me because
    He delighted in me.

20 The LORD rewarded me
    according to
    my righteousness;
He repaid me according
    to the cleanness
    of my hands.
21 For I have kept the ways
    of the LORD
and have not turned
    from my God
    to wickedness.
22 Indeed, I have kept all
    His ordinances in mind

[a] 18:13 Some Hb mss, LXX, Tg, Jer; other Hb mss read *in*   [b] 18:13 Other Hb mss read *voice, with hail and fiery coals*

and have not disregarded
His statutes.

23 I was blameless toward Him
and kept myself from sinning.

24 So the LORD repaid me
according to
my righteousness,
according to the cleanness
of my hands in His sight.

25 With the faithful You prove
Yourself faithful;
with the blameless man
You prove Yourself
blameless;

26 with the pure You prove
Yourself pure,
but with the crooked
You prove Yourself shrewd.

27 For You rescue
an afflicted people,
but You humble those
with haughty eyes.

28 LORD, You light my lamp;
my God illuminates
my darkness.

29 With You I can attack
a barrier,
and with my God I can leap
a wall.

30 God—His way is perfect;
the word of the LORD is pure.
He is a shield to all who take
refuge in Him.

31 For who is God besides
the LORD?
And who is a rock?
Only our God.

32 God—He clothes me
with strength
and makes my way perfect.

33 He makes my feet like the feet
of a deer
and sets me securely
on the heights.

34 He trains my hands for war;

my arms can bend a bow
of bronze.

35 You have given me the shield
of Your salvation;
Your right hand upholds me,
and Your humility exalts me.

36 You widen ⌊a place⌋ beneath
me for my steps,
and my ankles do not
give way.

37 I pursue my enemies
and overtake them;
I do not turn back until
they are wiped out.

38 I crush them, and they cannot
get up;
they fall beneath my feet.

39 You have clothed me
with strength for battle;
You subdue my adversaries
beneath me.

40 You have made my enemies
retreat before me;
I annihilate those who hate
me.

41 They cry for help, but there is
no one to save ⌊them⌋—
to the LORD, but He does not
answer them.

42 I pulverize them like dust
before the wind;
I trample them[a] like mud
in the streets.

43 You have freed me
from the feuds
among the people;
You have appointed me
the head of nations;
a people I had not known
serve me.

44 As soon as they
hear, they obey me;
foreigners submit to me
grudgingly.

45 Foreigners lose heart

a18:42 Some Hb mss, LXX, Syr, Tg; other Hb mss read *I poured them out*

and come trembling
   from their fortifications.

46 The LORD lives—may my rock
   be praised!
The God of my salvation
   is exalted.
47 God—He gives me vengeance
and subdues peoples
   under me.
48 He frees me from my enemies.
You exalt me above
   my adversaries;
You rescue me
   from the violent man.
49 Therefore I will praise You,
   LORD, among the nations;
I will sing about Your name.
50 He gives great victories
   to His king;
He shows loyalty
   to His anointed,
to David and his descendants
   forever.

### The Witness of Creation and Scripture

*For the choir director.*
*A Davidic psalm.*

**19** The heavens declare
   the glory of God,
and the sky proclaims
   the work of His hands.
2 Day after day they pour out
   speech;
night after night they
   communicate knowledge.
3 There is no speech; there are
   no words;
their voice is not heard.
4 Their message[a] has gone out
   to all the earth,
and their words to the ends
   of the inhabited world.

---

### Psalm 19:7-11

*Hope you're ready to carve out a
spot in your day that's earmarked
for just you and God to enjoy
together. But what are you supposed to fill up a quiet time with?
The surest way to God's heart is
through His Word. When you start
there, you'll never go wrong.*

---

In the heavens He has pitched
   a tent for the sun.
5 It is like a groom coming from
   the bridal chamber;
it rejoices like an athlete
   running a course.
6 It rises from one end
   of the heavens
and circles to their other end;
nothing is hidden
   from its heat.

7 The instruction of the LORD
   is perfect, reviving the soul;
the testimony of the LORD
   is trustworthy, making
   the inexperienced wise.
8 The precepts of the LORD are
   right, making the heart glad;
the commandment
   of the LORD is radiant,
   making the eyes light up.
9 The •fear of the LORD is pure,
   enduring forever;
the ordinances of the LORD
   are reliable and altogether
   righteous.
10 They are more desirable
   than gold—

---

[a] 19:4 LXX, Sym, Syr, Vg; Hb reads *line*

than an abundance
of pure gold;
and sweeter than honey—
than honey dripping
from the comb.
11 In addition, Your servant
is warned by them;
there is great reward
in keeping them.

12 Who perceives
his unintentional sins?
Cleanse me
from my hidden faults.
13 Moreover, keep Your servant
from willful sins;
do not let them rule over me.
Then I will be innocent,
and cleansed
from blatant rebellion.
14 May the words of my mouth
and the meditation
of my heart
be acceptable to You,
O LORD, my rock
and my Redeemer.

## Deliverance in Battle

*For the choir director.*
*A Davidic psalm.*

**20** May the LORD answer you
in a day of trouble;
may the name of Jacob's God
protect you.

---

*"The Bible gives us heart and hope*
*to make earth like heaven, and to*
*make our hearts and homes a*
*habitation for Christ."*
*—A. T. Robertson*

---

2 May He send you help
from the sanctuary
and sustain you from Zion.
3 May He remember all
your offerings
and accept
your *burnt offering. *Selah

4 May He give you what
your heart desires
and fulfill your whole purpose.
5 Let us shout for joy
at your victory
and lift the banner
in the name of our God.
May the LORD fulfill all
your requests.

6 Now I know that the LORD
gives victory
to His anointed;
He will answer him
from His holy heaven
with miraculous victories
from[a] His right hand.
7 Some take pride in a chariot,
and others in horses,
but we take pride in the name
of the LORD our God.
8 They collapse and fall,
but we rise and stand firm.
9 LORD, give victory to the king!
May He answer us on the day
that we call.

## The King's Victory

*For the choir director.*
*A Davidic psalm.*

**21** LORD, the king finds joy
in Your strength.
How greatly he rejoices
in Your victory!
2 You have given him
his heart's desire

---

[a] 20:6 Other Hb mss, Aq, Sym, Jer, Syr read *with the victorious might of*

and have not denied
   the request of his lips.
                    •*Selah*

3 For You meet him
   with rich blessings;
You place a crown of pure gold
   on his head.
4 He asked You for life, and You
   gave it to him—
length of days forever
   and ever.
5 His glory is great
   through Your victory;
You confer majesty
   and splendor on him.
6 You give him blessings forever;
You cheer him with joy
   in Your presence.
7 For the king relies
   on the LORD;
through the faithful love
   of the •Most High he is
   not shaken.

8 Your hand will capture all
   your enemies;
your right hand will seize
   those who hate you.
9 You will make them ⌊burn⌋
   like a fiery furnace
   when you appear;
the LORD will engulf them
   in His wrath,
and fire will devour them.
10 You will wipe
   their descendants
   from the earth
and their offspring
   from the •human race.
11 Though they intend
   to harm you
and devise a wicked plan,
   they will not prevail.
12 Instead, you will put them
   to flight
when you aim
   your bow at their faces.

13 Be exalted, LORD,
   in Your strength;
we will sing and praise
   Your might.

## From Suffering to Praise

*For the choir director: according to*
*"The Deer of the Dawn."*
*A Davidic psalm.*

**22** My God, my God, why have
   You forsaken me?
⌊Why are You⌋ so far
   from my deliverance
and from my words
   of groaning?
2 My God, I cry by day, but You
   do not answer,
by night, yet I have no rest.
3 But You are holy,
   enthroned on the praises
   of Israel.
4 Our fathers trusted in You;
   they trusted, and You rescued
   them.
5 They cried to You and were
   set free;
they trusted in You and were
   not disgraced.

6 But I am a worm and not
   a man,
scorned by men and despised
   by people.
7 Everyone who sees me
   mocks me;
they sneer and shake
   their heads:
8 "He relies on the LORD; let
   Him rescue him;
let the LORD deliver him,
   since He takes pleasure
   in him."

9 You took me from the womb,

making me secure
while at my mother's
breast.
10 I was given over to You
at birth;
You have been my God
from my mother's womb.

11 Do not be far from me,
because distress is near
and there is no one to help.

12 Many bulls surround me;
strong ones of Bashan encircle
me.
13 They open their mouths
against me—
lions, mauling and roaring.
14 I am poured out like water,
and all my bones
are disjointed;
my heart is like wax,
melting within me.
15 My strength is dried up
like baked clay;
my tongue sticks to the roof
of my mouth.
You put me into the dust
of death.
16 For dogs have surrounded me;
a gang of evildoers
has closed in on me;
they pierced[a] my hands
and my feet.
17 I can count all my bones;
people look and stare at me.
18 They divided my garments
among themselves,
and they cast lots
for my clothing.

19 But You, LORD, don't be
far away;
my strength, come quickly
to help me.
20 Deliver my life
from the sword,

my very life from the power
of the dog.
21 Save me from the mouth
of the lion!
You have rescued me
from the horns
of the wild oxen.

22 I will proclaim Your name
to my brothers;
I will praise You
in the congregation.
23 You who *fear the LORD,
praise Him!
All you descendants of Jacob,
honor Him!
All you descendants of Israel,
revere Him!
24 For He has not despised
or detested the torment
of the afflicted.
He did not hide His face
from him,
but listened when he cried
to Him for help.

25 I will give praise in the great
congregation because of
You;
I will fulfill my vows
before those who fear You.
26 The humble will eat
and be satisfied;
those who seek the LORD
will praise Him.
May your hearts live forever!

27 All the ends of the earth
will remember and turn
to the LORD.
All the families of the nations
will bow down before You,
28 for kingship belongs
to the LORD;
He rules over the nations.
29 All who prosper on earth
will eat and bow down;

[a]22:16 Some Hb mss, LXX, Syr; other Hb mss read *me; like a lion*

all those who go down
   to the dust
will kneel before Him—
even the one who cannot
   preserve his life.
30 Descendants will serve Him;
the next generation
   will be told about the Lord.
31 They will come and tell
   a people yet to be born
about His righteousness—
what He has done.

## The Good Shepherd
*A Davidic psalm.*

**23** The LORD is my shepherd;
there is nothing I lack.
2 He lets me lie down
   in green pastures;
He leads me beside
   quiet waters.
3 He renews my life;
He leads me along
   the right paths for His
   name's sake.
4 Even when I walk
   through the darkest valley,
I fear no danger,
for You are with me;
Your rod and Your staff—
   they comfort me.

5 You prepare a table before me
in the presence of my enemies;
You anoint my head with oil;
my cup overflows.
6 Only goodness
   and faithful love will pursue
   me all the days of my life,
and I will dwell in the house
   of the LORD as long as
   I live.

## The King of Glory
*A Davidic psalm.*

**24** The earth and everything
   in it,
the world and its inhabitants,
   belong to the LORD;
2 for He laid its foundation
   on the seas
and established it
   on the rivers.
3 Who may ascend the mountain
   of the LORD?
Who may stand
   in His holy place?
4 The one who has clean hands
   and a pure heart,
who has not set his mind on
   what is false,
and who has not sworn
   deceitfully.
5 He will receive blessing
   from the LORD,
and righteousness
   from the God
   of his salvation.
6 Such is the generation of those
   who seek Him,
who seek the face of the God
   of Jacob.[a]   •*Selah*

7 Lift up your heads, O gates!
Rise up, O ancient doors!
Then the King of glory
   will come in.
8 Who is this King of glory?
The LORD, strong and mighty,
the LORD, mighty in battle.
9 Lift up your heads, O gates!
Rise up, O ancient doors!
Then the King of glory
   will come in.

[a]**24:6** Some Hb mss, LXX, Syr; other Hb mss read *seek Your face, Jacob*

¹⁰ Who is He, this King of glory?
The LORD of •Hosts,
He is the King of glory.  *Selah*


*Dependence on the LORD*

*Davidic.*

**25** LORD, I turn my hope
to You.
² My God, I trust in You.
Do not let me be disgraced;
do not let my enemies gloat
over me.
³ Not one person who waits
for You will be disgraced;
those who act treacherously
without cause will be
disgraced.

⁴ Make Your ways known to me,
LORD;
teach me Your paths.
⁵ Guide me in Your truth
and teach me,
for You are the God
of my salvation;
I wait for You all day long.
⁶ Remember, LORD,
Your compassion
and Your faithful love,
for they ⌊have existed⌋
from antiquity.
⁷ Do not remember the sins
of my youth or my acts
of rebellion;
in keeping with
Your faithful love,
remember me
because of Your goodness,
LORD.

⁸ The LORD is good and upright;
therefore He shows sinners
the way.
⁹ He leads the humble in what
is right

and teaches them His way.
¹⁰ All the LORD's ways ⌊show⌋
faithful love and truth
to those who keep
His covenant and decrees.
¹¹ Out of regard for Your name,
LORD,
forgive my sin, for it is great.

¹² Who is the person who •fears
the LORD?
He will show him the way
he should choose.
¹³ He will live a good life,
and his descendants
will inherit the land.
¹⁴ The secret counsel of the LORD
is for those who fear Him,
and He reveals His covenant
to them.
¹⁵ My eyes are always
on the LORD,
for He will pull my feet
out of the net.

¹⁶ Turn to me and be gracious
to me,
for I am alone and afflicted.
¹⁷ The distresses of my heart
increase;
bring me out of my
sufferings.
¹⁸ Consider my affliction
and trouble,
and take away all my sins.
¹⁹ Consider my enemies;
they are numerous,
and they hate me violently.
²⁰ Guard me and deliver me;
do not let me be put to shame,
for I take refuge in You.
²¹ May integrity and uprightness
keep me,
for I wait for You.

²² Redeem Israel, O God, from all
its distresses.

*Prayer for Vindication*

*Davidic.*

**26** Vindicate me, LORD,
because I have lived
with integrity
and have trusted in the LORD
without wavering.
2  Test me, LORD, and try me;
examine my heart and mind.
3  For Your faithful love is
before my eyes,
and I live by Your truth.

4  I do not sit with the worthless
or associate with hypocrites.
5  I hate a crowd of evildoers,
and I do not sit
with the wicked.
6  I wash my hands in
innocence
and go around Your altar,
LORD,
7  raising my voice
in thanksgiving
and telling about
Your wonderful works.

8  LORD, I love the house where
You dwell,
the place where Your glory
resides.
9  Do not destroy me
along with sinners,
or my life along with men
of bloodshed
10  in whose hands are
evil schemes,
and whose right hands
are filled with bribes.

11  But I live with integrity;
redeem me and be gracious
to me.
12  My foot stands
on level ground;

I will praise the LORD
in the assemblies.

*My Stronghold*

*Davidic.*

**27** The LORD is my light
and my salvation—
whom should I fear?
The LORD is the stronghold
of my life—
of whom should I be afraid?
2  When evildoers came
against me to devour
my flesh,
my foes and my enemies
stumbled and fell.
3  Though an army deploy
against me,
my heart is not afraid;
though war break out
against me,
still I am confident.

4  I have asked one thing
from the LORD; it is what
I desire:
to dwell in the house
of the LORD all the days
of my life,
gazing on the beauty
of the LORD
and seeking [Him]
in His temple.
5  For He will conceal me
in His shelter in the day
of adversity;
He will hide me
under the cover of His tent;
He will set me high on a rock.
6  Then my head will be high
above my enemies
around me;
I will offer sacrifices
in His tent with shouts
of joy.

I will sing and make music
    to the LORD.

7   LORD, hear my voice
    when I call;
be gracious to me and answer
    me.
8   In Your behalf my heart says,
    "Seek My face."
LORD, I will seek Your face.
9   Do not hide Your face
    from me;
do not turn Your servant away
    in anger.
You have been my help;
do not leave me or abandon
    me,
O God of my salvation.
10  Even if my father and mother
    abandon me,
the LORD cares for me.

11  Because of my adversaries,
show me Your way, LORD,
and lead me on a level path.
12  Do not give me over
    to the will of my foes,
for false witnesses rise up
    against me, breathing
    violence.

13  I am certain that I will see
    the LORD's goodness
in the land of the living.
14  Wait for the LORD;
be courageous and let
    your heart be strong.
Wait for the LORD.

## My Strength
*Davidic.*

**28** LORD, I call to You;
my rock, do not be deaf to me.
If You remain silent to me,
I will be like those going down
    to the •Pit.

2   Listen to the sound
    of my pleading when I cry
    to You for help,
when I lift up my hands
    toward Your holy sanctuary.

3   Do not drag me away
    with the wicked,
with the evildoers,
who speak in friendly ways
    with their neighbors,
while malice is
    in their hearts.
4   Repay them according to what
    they have done—
according to the evil
    of their deeds.
Repay them according to
    the work of their hands;
give them back
    what they deserve.
5   Because they do not consider
    what the LORD has done
or the work of His hands,
He will tear them down
    and not rebuild them.

6   May the LORD be praised,
for He has heard the sound
    of my pleading.
7   The LORD is my strength
    and my shield;
my heart trusts in Him,
    and I am helped.
Therefore my heart rejoices,
and I praise Him
    with my song.

8   The LORD is the strength
    of His people;[a]
He is a stronghold
    of salvation
    for His anointed.
9   Save Your people, bless
    Your possession,
shepherd them, and carry
    them forever.

---

[a] **28:8** Some Hb mss, LXX, Syr; other Hb mss read *strength for them*

## The Voice of the LORD

*A Davidic psalm.*

**29** Give the LORD—
  you heavenly beings—
give the LORD glory
  and strength.
2  Give the LORD the glory due
    His name;
worship the LORD
  in holy splendor.

3  The voice of the LORD is above
    the waters.
The God of glory thunders—
  the LORD, above vast waters,
4  the voice of the LORD
    in power,
the voice of the LORD
  in splendor.
5  The voice of the LORD breaks
    the cedars;
the LORD shatters the cedars
  of Lebanon.
6  He makes Lebanon skip
    like a calf,
and Sirion, like a young wild
  ox.
7  The voice of the LORD flashes
    flames of fire.
8  The voice of the LORD shakes
    the wilderness;
the LORD shakes
  the wilderness of Kadesh.
9  The voice of the LORD makes
    the deer give birth
and strips the woodlands
  bare.

In His temple all cry, "Glory!"

10  The LORD sat enthroned
    at the flood;
the LORD sits enthroned, King
  forever.

11  The LORD gives His people
    strength;
the LORD blesses His people
  with peace.

## Joy in the Morning

*A psalm; a dedication song
for the house. Davidic.*

**30** I will exalt You, LORD,
  because You have lifted
    me up
and have not allowed
  my enemies to triumph
    over me.
2  O LORD my God,
I cried to You for help,
  and You healed me.
3  O LORD, You brought me up
    from *Sheol;
You spared me from among
  those going down[a]
    to the *Pit.

4  Sing to the LORD, you
    His faithful ones,
and praise His holy name.
5  For His anger lasts
    only a moment,
but His favor, a lifetime.

---

### Psalm 30:1-5

*Anybody can smile big. But the only people who can be really happy—deep down where it counts, in any situation—are those who've made Jesus Christ the joy of their lives. There's something only Christ can give that's a whole lot better than happiness. Enjoy!*

---

a**30:3** Some Hb mss, LXX, Theod, Orig, Syr; other Hb mss, Aq, Sym, Tg, Jer read *from going down*

> "Wherever you are, be all there.
> Live to the hilt every situation
> you believe to be the will
> of God."
> —Jim Elliot

Weeping may spend
the night,
but there is joy
in the morning.

6 When I was secure,
I said,
"I will never be shaken."
7 LORD, when You showed
Your favor,
You made me stand
like a strong mountain;
when You hid Your face,
I was terrified.
8 LORD, I called to You;
I sought favor
from my Lord:
9 "What gain is there
in my death,
in my descending
to the Pit?
Will the dust praise You?
Will it proclaim Your truth?
10 LORD, listen and be gracious
to me;
LORD, be my helper."

11 You turned my lament
into dancing;
You removed my •sackcloth
and clothed me
with gladness,
12 so that I can sing to You
and not be silent.
LORD my God, I will praise You
forever.

## A Plea for Protection

For the choir director.
A Davidic psalm.

**31** LORD, I seek refuge in You;
let me never be disgraced.
Save me
by Your righteousness.
2 Listen closely to me;
rescue me quickly.
Be a rock of refuge for me,
a mountain fortress to save me.
3 For You are my rock
and my fortress;
You lead and guide me
because of Your name.
4 You will free me
from the net that is secretly
set for me,
for You are my refuge.
5 Into Your hand I entrust
my spirit;
You redeem me, LORD,
God of truth.

6 I[a] hate those who are devoted
to worthless idols,
but I trust in the LORD.
7 I will rejoice and be glad
in Your faithful love
because You have seen
my affliction.
You have known the troubles
of my life
8 and have not handed me over
to the enemy.
You have set my feet
in a spacious place.

9 Be gracious to me, LORD,
because I am in distress;
my eyes are worn out
from angry sorrow—
my whole being as well.

[a]31:6 One Hb ms, LXX, Syr, Vg, Jer read You

¹⁰ Indeed, my life is consumed
    with grief,
and my years with groaning;
my strength has failed
    because of my sinfulness,ᵃ
and my bones waste away.
¹¹ I am ridiculed by all
    my adversaries
and even by my neighbors.
I am an object of dread
    to my acquaintances;
those who see me in the street
    run from me.
¹² I am forgotten:
    gone from memory
like a dead person—
    like broken pottery.
¹³ I have heard the gossip
    of many;
terror is on every side.
When they conspired
    against me,
they plotted to take my life.

¹⁴ But I trust in You, LORD;
I say, "You are my God."
¹⁵ The course of my life is
    in Your power;
deliver me from the power
    of my enemies and from
    my persecutors.
¹⁶ Show Your favor
    to Your servant;
save me by Your faithful love.
¹⁷ LORD, do not let me
    be disgraced when I call
    on You.
Let the wicked be disgraced;
let them be silentᵇ in *Sheol.
¹⁸ Let lying lips be quieted;
they speak arrogantly
    against the righteous
    with pride and contempt.

¹⁹ How great is Your goodness
that You have stored up
    for those who *fear You,

and accomplished in the sight
    of *everyone
for those who take refuge
    in You.
²⁰ You hide them
    in the protection
    of Your presence;
You conceal them in a shelter
from the schemes of men,
from quarrelsome tongues.
²¹ May the LORD be praised,
for He has wonderfully shown
    His faithful love to me
in a city under siege.
²² In my alarm I had said,
"I am cut off from Your sight."
But You heard the sound
    of my pleading
when I cried to You for help.

²³ Love the LORD, all
    His faithful ones.
The LORD protects the loyal,
but fully repays the arrogant.
²⁴ Be strong and courageous,
all you who hope in the LORD.

### The Joy of Forgiveness

*Davidic. A *Maskil.

**32** How happy is the one whose
    transgression is forgiven,
whose sin is covered!
² How happy is the man
    whom the LORD
    does not charge with sin,
and in whose spirit is
    no deceit!

³ When I kept silent, my bones
    became brittle
from my groaning all day long.
⁴ For day and night Your hand
    was heavy on me;
my strength was drained
    as in the summer's heat.
                    *Selah

---

ᵃ31:10 LXX, Syr, Sym read *affliction*   ᵇ31:17 LXX reads *brought down*

5 Then I acknowledged my sin
    to You
and did not conceal
    my iniquity.
I said, "I will confess
    my transgressions
    to the LORD,"
and You took away the guilt
    of my sin.                *Selah*

6 Therefore let everyone
    who is faithful pray to You
at a time that You may be
    found.
When great floodwaters come,
they will not reach him.
7 You are my hiding place;
You protect me from trouble.
You surround me
    with joyful shouts
    of deliverance.          *Selah*

8 I will instruct you and show
    you the way to go;
with My eye on you,
    I will give counsel.
9 Do not be like a horse or mule,
    without understanding,
that must be controlled
    with bit and bridle,
or else it will not come
    near you.

10 Many pains come
    to the wicked,
but the one who trusts
    in the LORD
will have faithful love
    surrounding him.
11 Be glad in the LORD
    and rejoice,
    you righteous ones;
shout for joy, all you upright
    in heart.

*Praise to the Creator*

**33** Rejoice in the LORD, O you
        righteous ones;
    praise from the upright
        is beautiful.
2 Praise the LORD with the lyre;
    make music to Him with a ten-
        stringed harp.
3 Sing a new song to Him;
    play skillfully on the strings,
        with a joyful shout.

4 For the word of the LORD
        is right,
    and all His work
        is trustworthy.
5 He loves righteousness
        and justice;
    the earth is full of the LORD's
        unfailing love.

6 The heavens were made
        by the word of the LORD,
    and all the stars, by the breath
        of His mouth.
7 He gathers the waters
        of the sea into a heap;[a]
    He puts the depths
        into storehouses.
8 Let the whole earth tremble
        before the LORD;
    let all the inhabitants
        of the world stand in awe
        of Him.
9 For He spoke, and it came
        into being;
    He commanded, and it came
        into existence.

10 The LORD frustrates
        the counsel of the nations;
    He thwarts the plans
        of the peoples.
11 The counsel of the LORD
        stands forever,

[a] **33:7** LXX, Tg, Syr, Vg, Jer read *sea as in a bottle*

the plans of His heart
   from generation
   to generation.
12 Happy is the nation
   whose God is the LORD—
the people He has chosen
   to be His own possession!

13 The LORD looks down
   from heaven;
He observes everyone.
14 He gazes on all the inhabitants
   of the earth
from His dwelling place.
15 He alone crafts their hearts;
He considers all their works.
16 A king is not saved by
   a large army;
a warrior will not be delivered
   by great strength.
17 The horse is a false hope
   for safety;
it provides no escape by
   its great power.

18 Now the eye of the LORD is
   on those who *fear Him—
those who depend on
   His faithful love
19 to deliver their souls
   from death
and to keep them alive
   in famine.

20 We wait for the LORD;
He is our help and shield.
21 For our hearts rejoice in Him,
because we trust in
   His holy name.
22 May Your faithful love rest
   on us, LORD,
for we hope in You.

### The LORD Delivers the Righteous

*Concerning David, when he pretended to be insane in the presence of Abimelech, who drove him out, and he departed.*

**34** I will praise the LORD
   at all times;
His praise will always be
   on my lips.
2 I will boast in the LORD;
the humble will hear
   and be glad.
3 Proclaim with me
   the LORD's greatness;
let us exalt His name together.

4 I sought the LORD,
   and He answered me
and delivered me from all
   my fears.
5 Those who look to Him are[a]
   radiant with joy;
their faces will never
   be ashamed.
6 This poor man cried,
   and the LORD heard ⌊him⌋
and saved him from all
   his troubles.
7 The angel of the LORD
   encamps
around those who *fear Him,
   and rescues them.

8 Taste and see that the LORD
   is good.
How happy is the man
   who takes refuge in Him!
9 Fear the LORD, you His saints,
for those who fear Him lack
   nothing.
10 Young lions[b] lack food
   and go hungry,
but those who seek the LORD
   will not lack any
   good thing.

11 Come, children, listen to me;
I will teach you the fear
   of the LORD.

[a] **34:5** Some Hb mss, LXX, Aq, Syr, Jer read *Look to Him and be*    [b] **34:10** LXX, Syr, Vg read *The rich*

12 Who is the man who delights
  in life,
 loving a long life to enjoy
  what is good?
13 Keep your tongue
  from evil
 and your lips
  from deceitful speech.
14 Turn away from evil
  and do good;
 seek peace and
  pursue it.

15 The eyes of the LORD are
  on the righteous,
 and His ears are open
  to their cry for help.
16 The face of the LORD is set
  against those who do evil,
 to erase all memory
  of them from the earth.
17 The righteous cry out,
  and the LORD hears,
 and delivers them from all
  their troubles.
18 The LORD is near
  the brokenhearted;
 He saves those crushed
  in spirit.

19 Many adversities come
  to the one who is
  righteous,
 but the LORD delivers him
  from them all.
20 He protects all his bones;
 not one of them is broken.
21 Evil brings death to the sinner,
 and those who hate
  the righteous
  will be punished.
22 The LORD redeems the life
  of His servants,
 and all who take refuge
  in Him will not
  be punished.

*Prayer for Victory*

*Davidic.*

**35** Oppose my opponents, LORD;
 fight those who fight me.
2 Take Your shields—
  large and small—
 and come to my aid.
3 Draw the spear and javelin
  against my pursuers,
 and assure me: "I am
  your deliverance."

4 Let those who seek to kill me
 be disgraced and humiliated;
 let those who plan to harm me
 be turned back and ashamed.
5 Let them be like husks
  in the wind,
 with the angel of the LORD
  driving them away.
6 Let their way be dark
  and slippery,
 with the angel of the LORD
  pursuing them.
7 They hid their net for me
  without cause;
 they dug a pit for me
  without cause.
8 Let ruin come on him
  unexpectedly,
 and let the net that he hid
  ensnare him;
 let him fall into it—to his ruin.

9 Then I will rejoice
  in the LORD;
 I will delight
  in His deliverance.
10 My very bones will say,
 "LORD, who is like You,
 rescuing the poor from one
  too strong for him,
 the poor or the needy
  from one who robs him?"

11 Malicious witnesses come
      forward;
   they question me about things
      I do not know.
12 They repay me evil
      for good,
   making me desolate.
13 Yet when they were sick,
   my clothing was •sackcloth;
   I humbled myself
      with fasting,
   and my prayer was genuine.
14 I went about ⌊grieving⌋ as if
      for my friend or brother;
   I was bowed down with grief,
      like one mourning
      a mother.
15 But when I stumbled,
      they gathered in glee;
   they gathered against me.
   Assailants I did not know
   tore at me and did not stop.
16 With godless mockery
   they gnashed their teeth
      at me.

17 Lord, how long will You
      look on?
   Rescue my life
      from their ravages,
   my very life
      from the young lions.
18 I will praise You
      in the great congregation;
   I will exalt You
      among many people.
19 Do not let
      my deceitful enemies
      rejoice over me;
   do not let those who hate me
      without cause look at me
      maliciously.
20 For they do not speak
      in friendly ways,

but contrive
      deceitful schemes
against those who live
      peacefully in the land.
21 They open their mouths wide
      against me and say,
   "Aha, aha! We saw it!"

22 You saw it, LORD; do not
      be silent.
   Lord, do not be far from me.
23 Wake up and rise
      to my defense,
   to my cause, my God and my
      Lord!
24 Vindicate me, LORD, my God,
   in keeping with
      Your righteousness,
   and do not let them rejoice
      over me.
25 Do not let them say
      in their hearts,
   "Aha! Just what we wanted."
   Do not let them say,
   "We have swallowed
      him up!"
26 Let those who rejoice
      at my misfortune
   be disgraced and humiliated;
   let those who exalt themselves
      over me
   be clothed with shame
      and reproach.

27 Let those who want
      my vindication
   shout for joy and be glad;
   let them continually say,
   "The LORD be exalted,
   who wants His servant's
      well-being."
28 And my tongue will proclaim
      Your righteousness,
   Your praise all day long.

## Human Wickedness and God's Love

*For the choir director. ⌊A psalm⌋ of David, the LORD's servant.*

**36** An oracle within my[a] heart
concerning the
transgression of the wicked:
There is no dread of God
before his eyes,
2  for in his own eyes he flatters
himself ⌊too much⌋
to discover and hate his sin.
3  The words of his mouth
are malicious
and deceptive;
he has stopped acting wisely
and doing good.
4  Even on his bed he makes
malicious plans.
He sets himself on a path
that is not good
and does not reject evil.

5  LORD, Your faithful love
⌊reaches⌋ to heaven,
Your faithfulness
to the skies.
6  Your righteousness is
like the highest
mountain;
Your judgments,
like the deepest sea.
LORD, You preserve man
and beast.
7  God, Your faithful love
is so valuable
that •people take refuge
in the shadow
of Your wings.
8  They are filled
from the abundance
of Your house;
You let them drink from Your
refreshing stream,
9  for with You is life's fountain.
In Your light we will see light.

10  Spread Your faithful love
over those who know You,
and Your righteousness
over the upright in heart.
11  Do not let the foot
of the arrogant come near me
or the hand of the wicked
drive me away.
12  There the evildoers fall;
they have been thrown down
and cannot rise.

## Instruction in Wisdom

*Davidic.*

**37** Do not be agitated
by evildoers;
do not envy those
who do wrong.
2  For they wither quickly
like grass
and wilt like tender
green plants.

3  Trust in the LORD and do good;
dwell in the land
and live securely.
4  Take delight in the LORD,
and He will give you
your heart's desires.

---

### Psalm 37:1-4

*While you're building your spiritual muscles on the free weights of joy, here's another good exercise to help you take off those unsightly inches of flesh in your life. It's not easy to do, but it's actually very simple: Put God first, and the rest will take care of itself.*

---

[a] **36:1** Some Hb mss; other Hb mss, LXX, Syr, Jer, Vg read *his*

5 Commit your way to the LORD;
  trust in Him, and He will act,
6 making your righteousness
      shine like the dawn,
  your justice like the noonday.

---

*"Holy simplicity is a life that has
become simple in its integrity,
devotion, and inner freedom, a life
that simply belongs to God alone."*
—*James Houston*

---

7 Be silent before the LORD
      and wait expectantly
      for Him;
  do not be agitated by one
      who prospers in his way,
  by the man who carries out
      evil plans.

8 Refrain from anger and give up
      [your] rage;
  do not be agitated—it can only
      bring harm.
9 For evildoers will be
      destroyed,
  but those who hope
      in the LORD will inherit
      the land.

10 A little while, and the wicked
      will be no more;
   though you look for him,
      he will not be there.
11 But the humble will inherit
      the land
   and will enjoy abundant
      prosperity.

12 The wicked schemes
      against the righteous
   and gnashes his teeth at him.
13 The Lord laughs at him
   because He sees that his day
      is coming.

14 The wicked have drawn
      the sword and strung
      the bow
   to bring down the afflicted
      and needy
   and to slaughter those
      whose way is upright.

15 Their swords will enter
      their own hearts,
   and their bows will be
      broken.

16 Better the little
      that the righteous man has
   than the abundance
      of many wicked people.
17 For the arms of the wicked
      will be broken,
   but the LORD supports
      the righteous.

18 The LORD watches over
      the blameless all their days,
   and their inheritance will last
      forever.
19 They will not be disgraced
      in times of adversity;
   they will be satisfied in days
      of hunger.

20 But the wicked will perish;
   the LORD's enemies,
      like the glory
      of the pastures,
      will fade away—
   they will fade away
      like smoke.

21 The wicked borrows
      and does not repay,
   but the righteous is gracious
      and giving.
22 Those who are blessed by Him
      will inherit the land,
   but those cursed by Him
      will be destroyed.

23  A man's steps are established
        by the LORD,
    and He takes pleasure
        in his way.
24  Though he falls, he will not be
        overwhelmed,
    because the LORD holds
        his hand.

25  I have been young and now
        I am old,
    yet I have not seen
        the righteous abandoned
    or his children begging bread.
26  He is always generous,
        always lending,
    and his children are a blessing.

27  Depart from evil and do good,
    and dwell there forever.
28  For the LORD loves justice
    and will not abandon
        His faithful ones.
    They are kept safe forever,
    but the children of the wicked
        will be destroyed.
29  The righteous will inherit
        the land
    and dwell in it permanently.

30  The mouth of the righteous
        utters wisdom;
    his tongue speaks what is just.
31  The instruction of his God is
        in his heart;
    his steps do not falter.

32  The wicked lies in wait
        for the righteous
    and seeks to kill him;
33  the LORD will not leave him
        in his hand
    or allow him to be condemned
        when he is judged.

34  Wait for the LORD and keep
        His way,
    and He will exalt you
        to inherit the land.
    You will watch
        when the wicked
        are destroyed.

35  I have seen a wicked,
        violent man
    well-rooted like a flourishing
        native tree.[a]
36  Then I passed by and[b] noticed
        he was gone;
    I searched for him,
        but he could not be
        found.

37  Watch the blameless
        and observe the upright,
    for the man of peace will have
        a future.
38  But transgressors will all be
        eliminated;
    the future of the wicked
        will be destroyed.

39  The salvation of the righteous
        is from the LORD,
    their refuge in a time
        of distress.
40  The LORD helps and delivers
        them;
    He will deliver them
        from the wicked
        and will save them
    because they take refuge
        in Him.

## Prayer of a Suffering Sinner
*A Davidic psalm for remembrance.*

**38** O LORD, do not punish me
        in Your anger

---

[a] **37:35** LXX reads *man, lifting himself up like the cedars of Lebanon*   [b] **37:36** DSS, LXX, Syr, Vg, Jer; MT reads *Then he passed away, and I*

or discipline me
 in Your wrath.
2 For Your arrows have sunk
 into me,
and Your hand has pressed
 down on me.

3 There is no soundness
 in my body because of
 Your indignation;
there is no health in my bones
 because of my sin.
4 For my sins have flooded
 over my head;
they are a burden too heavy
 for me to bear.
5 My wounds are foul
 and festering
because of my foolishness.
6 I am bent over and brought
 low;
all day long I go around
 in mourning.
7 For my loins are full of
 burning pain,
and there is no health
 in my body.
8 I am faint and severely
 crushed;
I groan because of the anguish
 of my heart.

9 Lord, my every desire
 is known to You;
my sighing is not hidden
 from You.
10 My heart races, my strength
 leaves me,
and even the light of my eyes
 has faded.
11 My loved ones and friends
 stand back
 from my affliction,
and my relatives stand
 at a distance.
12 Those who seek my life
 set traps,

and those who want to harm
 me threaten to destroy me;
they plot treachery all day
 long.

13 I am like a deaf person;
 I do not hear.
I am like a speechless person
 who does not open
 his mouth.
14 I am like a man
 who does not hear
and has no arguments
 in his mouth.
15 I hope in You, LORD;
 You will answer, Lord my God.
16 For I said, "Don't let them
 rejoice over me—
those who are arrogant
 toward me
 when I stumble."
17 For I am about to fall,
 and my pain is constantly
 with me.
18 So I confess my guilt;
 I am anxious because of
 my sin.
19 But my enemies are vigorous
 and powerful;
many hate me for no reason.
20 Those who repay evil for good
 attack me for pursuing good.

21 LORD, do not abandon me;
 my God, do not be far
 from me.
22 Hurry to help me,
 O Lord, my Savior.

## The Fleeting Nature of Life

*For the choir director,*
*for Jeduthun. A Davidic psalm.*

**39** I said, "I will guard my ways
 so that I may not sin
 with my tongue;

I will guard my mouth
  with a muzzle
as long as the wicked are
  in my presence."
2 I was speechless and quiet;
I kept silent, even from
  ⌊speaking⌋ good,
and my pain intensified.
3 My heart grew hot within me;
as I mused, a fire burned.
I spoke with my tongue:

4 "LORD, reveal to me the end
  of my life
and the number of my days.
Let me know how transitory
  I am.
5 You, indeed, have made
  my days short in length,
and my life span as nothing
  in Your sight.
Yes, every mortal man is
  only a vapor. •Selah
6 Certainly, man walks about
  like a mere shadow.
Indeed, they frantically rush
  around in vain,
gathering possessions
  without knowing
who will get them.

7 "Now, Lord, what do I wait for?
My hope is in You.
8 Deliver me from all
  my transgressions;
do not make me the taunt
  of fools.
9 I am speechless; I do not open
  my mouth
because of what You have
  done.
10 Remove Your torment
  from me;
I fade away because of
  the force of Your hand.
11 You discipline a man
  with punishment for sin,

consuming like a moth
  what is precious to him;
every man is a mere vapor.
     *Selah*

12 "Hear my prayer, LORD,
and listen to my cry for help;
do not be silent at my tears.
For I am a foreigner residing
  with You,
a sojourner like all my fathers.
13 Turn Your angry gaze from me
  so that I may be cheered up
before I die and am gone."

### Thanksgiving and a Cry for Help

*For the choir director.
A Davidic psalm.*

**40** I waited patiently
  for the LORD,
and He turned to me
  and heard my cry for help.
2 He brought me up
  from a desolate pit,
out of the muddy clay,
and set my feet on a rock,
making my steps secure.
3 He put a new song
  in my mouth,
a hymn of praise to our God.
Many will see and fear,
and put their trust
  in the LORD.

4 How happy is the man
who has put his trust
  in the LORD
and has not turned
  to the proud
or to those who run after lies!
5 LORD my God, You have done
  many things—
Your wonderful works
  and Your plans for us;
none can compare with You.

If I were to report and speak
⌊of them⌋,
they are more than can
be told.

6 You do not delight in sacrifice
and offering;
You open my ears to listen.
You do not ask for
a whole •burnt offering
or a •sin offering.
7 Then I said, "See,
I have come;
it is written about me
in the volume of the scroll.
8 I delight to do Your will,
my God;
Your instruction resides
within me."

9 I proclaim righteousness
in the great assembly;
see, I do not keep my mouth
closed—as You know,
LORD.
10 I did not hide
Your righteousness
in my heart;
I spoke about Your faithfulness
and salvation;
I did not conceal
Your constant love
and truth
from the great assembly.

11 LORD, do not withhold
Your compassion from me;
Your constant love and truth
will always guard me.
12 For troubles without number
have surrounded me;
my sins have overtaken me;
I am unable to see.
They are more than the hairs
of my head,
and my courage leaves me.
13 LORD, be pleased to deliver me;
hurry to help me, LORD.

14 Let those who seek to take
my life
be disgraced and confounded.
Let those who wish me harm
be driven back and humiliated.
15 Let those who say to me,
"Aha, aha!"
be horrified because of
their shame.

16 Let all who seek You rejoice
and be glad in You;
let those who love
Your salvation continually
say,
"Great is the LORD!"
17 Though I am afflicted
and needy,
the Lord thinks of me.
You are my help
and my deliverer;
my God, do not delay.

## Victory in spite of Betrayal

*For the choir director.*
*A Davidic psalm.*

**41** Happy is one who cares
for the poor;
the LORD will save him
in a day of adversity.
2 The LORD will keep him
and preserve him;
he will be blessed in the land.
You will not give him over
to the desire
of his enemies.
3 The LORD will sustain him
on his sickbed;
You will heal him on the bed
where he lies.

4 I said, "LORD, be gracious
to me;
heal me, for I have sinned
against You."

5  My enemies speak maliciously
        about me:
   "When will he die
        and be forgotten?"
6  When one ⌊of them⌋ comes
        to visit, he speaks
        deceitfully;
   he stores up evil in his heart;
   he goes out and talks.
7  All who hate me whisper
        together about me;
   they plan to harm me.
8  "Lethal poison has been
        poured into him,
   and he won't rise again
        from where he lies!"
9  Even my friend in whom
        I trusted,
   one who ate my bread,
   has lifted up his heel
        against me.

10  But You, LORD, be gracious
        to me
        and raise me up;
    then I will repay them.
11  By this I know that You delight
        in me:
    my enemy does not shout
        in triumph over me.
12  You supported me because of
        my integrity
    and set me in Your presence
        forever.

13  May the LORD, the God
        of Israel, be praised
    from everlasting to everlasting.
    Amen and amen.

# BOOK II

## (PSALMS 42–72)

### Longing for God

*For the choir director. A •Maskil
of the sons of Korah.*

**42** As a deer longs for streams
        of water,

so I long for You, God.
2  I thirst for God, the living God.
   When can I come and appear
        before God?
3  My tears have been my food
        day and night,
   while all day long people say
        to me,
   "Where is your God?"
4  I remember this as I pour out
        my heart:
   how I walked with many,
   leading the festive procession
        to the house of God,
   with joyful
        and thankful shouts.

5  Why am I so depressed?
   Why this turmoil within me?
   Hope in God, for I will still
        praise Him,
   my Savior and my God.
6  I[a] am deeply depressed;
   therefore I remember You
        from the land of Jordan
   and the peaks of Hermon,
   from Mount Mizar.
7  Deep calls to deep
        in the roar
        of Your waterfalls;
   all Your breakers
        and Your billows
        have swept over me.
8  The LORD will send
        His faithful love by day;
   His song will be with me
        in the night—
   a prayer to the God of my life.

9  I will say to God, my rock,
   "Why have You forgotten me?
   Why must I go about in sorrow
   because of the enemy's
        oppression?"
10  My adversaries taunt me,
    as if crushing my bones,
    while all day long they say
        to me,

[a] 42:5–6 Some Hb mss, LXX, Syr; other Hb mss read *Him, the salvation of His presence.* [b] *My God, I*

"Where is your God?"
11 Why am I so depressed?
Why this turmoil within me?
Hope in God, for I will still
    praise Him,
my Savior and my God.

**43** <sup>a</sup> Vindicate me, God,
    and defend my cause
against an ungodly nation;
rescue me from the deceitful
    and unjust man.
2   For You are the God
    of my refuge.
Why have You rejected me?
Why must I go about
    in sorrow
because of the enemy's
    oppression?

3   Send Your light and Your truth;
    let them lead me.
Let them bring me
    to Your holy mountain,
to Your dwelling place.
4   Then I will come to the altar
    of God,
to God, my greatest joy.
I will praise You with the lyre,
O God, my God.

5   Why am I so depressed?
Why this turmoil within me?
Hope in God, for I will still
    praise Him,
my Savior and my God.

## Israel's Complaint

*For the choir director. A •Maskil
of the sons of Korah.*

**44** God, we have heard
    with our ears—
our forefathers have told us—

---

*Psalm 44:4-8*

*Worship looks as good in your
weekday outfits as it does in your
Sunday clothes. Praising God
through the day will dress up the
way you think, act, and feel. Wish
you had the words to thank God
for all He's done for you? You'll
find them when you worship.*

---

the work You accomplished
    in their days,
in days long ago:
2   to plant them, You drove out
    the nations with Your hand;
to settle them, You crushed
    the peoples.
3   For they did not take the land
    by their sword—
their arm did not bring them
    victory—
but by Your right hand,
    Your arm, and the light
    of Your face,
for You were pleased
    with them.

4   You are my King, My God,
who ordains<sup>b</sup> victories
    for Jacob.
5   Through You we drive back
    our foes;
through Your name
    we trample our enemies.
6   For I do not trust in my bow,
and my sword does not bring
    me victory.
7   But You give us victory
    over our foes
and let those who hate us
    be disgraced.

---

<sup>a</sup>**Ps 43** Many Hb mss connect **Pss 42–43**    <sup>b</sup>**44:4** LXX, Syr, Aq; MT reads *King, God; ordain*

8 We boast in God all day
    long;
  we will praise Your name
    forever.                      *Selah*

9 But You have rejected
    and humiliated us;
  You do not march out
    with our armies.
10 You make us retreat
    from the foe,
  and those who hate us
    have taken plunder
    for themselves.
11 You hand us over to be eaten
    like sheep
  and scatter us
    among the nations.
12 You sell Your people
    for nothing;
  You make no profit
    from selling them.
13 You make us an object
    of reproach
    to our neighbors,
  a source of mockery
    and ridicule to those
    around us.
14 You make us a joke
    among the nations,
  a laughingstock among
    the peoples.
15 My disgrace is before
    me all day long,

---

*"When we are empowered by
worship, our day-to-day lives at
home, at work, and at leisure take
on a new dimension. They rise to
the new life."*
—Robert Webber

---

  and shame has covered
    my face,
16 because of the voice
    of the scorner and reviler,
  because of the enemy
    and avenger.
17 All this has happened to us,
    but we have not forgotten
    You
  or betrayed Your covenant.
18 Our hearts have not turned
    back;
  our steps have not strayed
    from Your path.
19 But You have crushed us
    in a haunt of jackals
  and have covered us
    with deepest darkness.
20 If we had forgotten the name
    of our God
  and spread out our hands
    to a foreign god,
21 wouldn't God have found
    this out,
  since He knows the secrets
    of the heart?
22 Because of You we are slain all
    day long;
  we are counted as sheep
    to be slaughtered.

23 Wake up, LORD! Why are You
    sleeping?
  Get up! Don't reject us
    forever!
24 Why do You hide Yourself
  and forget our affliction
    and oppression?
25 For we have sunk down
    to the dust;
  our bodies cling to the ground.
26 Rise up! Help us!
  Redeem us because of
    Your faithful love.

## A Royal Wedding Song

*For the choir director: according to "The Lilies." A •Maskil of the sons of Korah. A love song.*

**45** My heart is moved
by a noble theme
as I recite my verses
to the king;
my tongue is the pen
of a skillful writer.

2 You are the most handsome
of •men;
grace flows from your lips.
Therefore God has blessed you
forever.

3 Mighty warrior, strap
your sword at your side.
In your majesty
and splendor—

4 in your splendor ride
triumphantly
in the cause of truth, humility,
and justice.
May your right hand show
your awe-inspiring deeds.

5 Your arrows pierce the hearts
of the king's enemies;
the peoples fall under you.

6 Your throne, God, is forever
and ever;
the scepter of Your kingdom is
a scepter of justice.

7 You love righteousness
and hate wickedness;
therefore God, your God,
has anointed you,
more than your companions,
with the oil of joy.

8 Myrrh, aloes, and cassia
⌊perfume⌋ all
your garments;

from ivory palaces harps bring
you joy.

9 Kings' daughters are among
your honored women;
the queen, adorned with gold
from Ophir, stands
at your right hand.

10 Listen, daughter, pay attention
and consider:
forget your people
and your father's house,

11 and the king will desire
your beauty.
Bow down to him, for he is
your lord.

12 The daughter of Tyre,
the wealthy people,
will seek your favor with gifts.

13 In ⌊her chamber⌋,
the royal daughter is all
glorious,
her clothing embroidered
with gold.

14 In colorful garments she is led
to the king;
after her, the virgins,
her companions,
are brought to you.

15 They are led in with gladness
and rejoicing;
they enter the king's palace.

16 Your sons will succeed
your ancestors;
you will make them
princes
throughout the land.

17 I will cause your name
to be remembered for all
generations;
therefore the peoples
will praise you forever
and ever.

## God Our Refuge

*For the choir director. A song*
*of the sons of Korah. According to*
Alamoth.

**46** God is our refuge
         and strength,
a helper who is always found
    in times of trouble.
2    Therefore we will not be
        afraid, though the earth
        trembles
and the mountains topple
    into the depths of the seas,
3    though its waters roar
        and foam
and the mountains quake
    with its turmoil.        *Selah

4    ⌊There is⌋ a river—its streams
        delight the city of God,
the holy dwelling place
    of the *Most High.
5    God is within her; she will
        not be toppled.
God will help her
    when the morning dawns.
6    Nations rage, kingdoms topple;
the earth melts when He lifts
    His voice.
7    The LORD of *Hosts is with us;
the God of Jacob is
    our stronghold.        *Selah*

8    Come, see the works
        of the LORD,
who brings devastation
    on the earth.
9    He makes wars cease
        throughout the earth.
He shatters bows and cuts
    spears to pieces;
He burns up the chariots.[a]
10   "Stop ⌊your fighting⌋—
        and know that I am God,

exalted among the nations,
    exalted on the earth."
11   The LORD of Hosts is with us;
the God of Jacob is
    our stronghold.        *Selah*

## God Our King

*For the choir director. A psalm*
*of the sons of Korah.*

**47** Clap your hands, all you
         peoples;
shout to God
    with a jubilant cry.
2    For the LORD *Most High
        is awe-inspiring,
a great King over all the earth.
3    He subdues peoples under us
and nations under our feet.
4    He chooses for us
        our inheritance—
the pride
    of Jacob, whom He loves.
                              *Selah*

5    God ascends amid shouts
        of joy,
the LORD, amid the sound
    of trumpets.
6    Sing praise to God, sing praise;
sing praise to our King,
    sing praise!
7    Sing a song of instruction,
for God is King of all the earth.

8    God reigns over the nations;
God is seated
    on His holy throne.
9    The nobles of the peoples
        have assembled
⌊with⌋ the people of the God
    of Abraham.
For the leaders of the earth
    belong to God;
He is greatly exalted.

---

[a] **46:9** Other Hb mss, LXX, Tg read *shields*

## Zion Exalted

*A song. A psalm of the sons
of Korah.*

**48** The LORD is great and is
    highly praised
in the city of our God.
His holy mountain, ² rising
    splendidly,
is the joy of the whole earth.
Mount Zion on the slopes
    of the north
is the city of the great King.
³ God is known as a stronghold
in its citadels.

⁴ Look! The kings assembled;
they advanced together.
⁵ They looked, and froze
    with fear;
they fled in terror.
⁶ Trembling seized them there,
agony like that of a woman
    in labor,
⁷ as You wrecked the ships
    of Tarshish
with the east wind.

⁸ Just as we heard,
    so we have seen
in the city of the LORD
    of •Hosts,
in the city of our God;
God will establish it forever.
               •*Selah*

⁹ God, within Your temple,
we contemplate
    Your faithful love.
¹⁰ Your name, God,
    like Your praise,
reaches to the ends
    of the earth;
Your right hand is filled
    with justice.

¹¹ Mount Zion is glad.
The towns of Judah rejoice
because of Your judgments.

¹² Go around Zion, encircle it;
count its towers,
¹³ note its ramparts; tour
    its citadels
so that you can tell
    a future generation:
¹⁴ "This God, our God forever
    and ever—
He will lead us eternally."[a]

## Misplaced Trust in Wealth

*For the choir director. A psalm
of the sons of Korah.*

**49** Hear this, all you peoples;
    listen, all who inhabit
        the world,
² both low and high,
rich and poor together.
³ My mouth speaks wisdom;
my heart's meditation ⌊brings⌋
    understanding.
⁴ I turn my ear to a proverb;
I explain my riddle with a lyre.

⁵ Why should I fear in times
    of trouble?
The iniquity of my foes
    surrounds me.
⁶ They trust in their wealth
and boast of their abundant
    riches.
⁷ Yet these cannot redeem
    a person
or pay his ransom to God—
⁸ since the price of redeeming
    him is too costly,
one should forever stop
    trying—
⁹ so that he may live forever
and not see the •Pit.

---

a **48:14** Some Hb mss, LXX; other Hb mss read *over death*

10 For one can see that wise men
     die;
   the foolish and the senseless
     also pass away.
   Then they leave their wealth
     to others.
11 Their graves are
     their eternal homes,[a]
   their homes from generation
     to generation,
   though they have named
     estates after themselves.
12 But despite ⌊his⌋ assets,
     man will not last;
   he is like the animals
     that perish.

13 This is the way of those
     who are arrogant,
   and of their followers,
     who approve
     of their words.        •*Selah*
14 Like sheep they are headed
     for •Sheol;
   Death will shepherd them.
   The upright will rule over
     them in the morning,
   and their form will waste away
     in Sheol, far
     from their lofty abode.
15 But God will redeem my life
     from the power of Sheol,
   for He will take me.        *Selah*

16 Do not be afraid when a man
     gets rich,
   when the wealth of his house
     increases.
17 For when he dies, he will take
     nothing at all;
   his wealth will not follow him
     down.
18 Though he praises himself
     during his lifetime—
   and people praise you
     when you do well
     for yourself—

19 he will go to the generation
     of his fathers;
   they will never see the light.
20 A man with valuable
     possessions but without
     understanding
   is like the animals that perish.

## God as Judge

*A psalm of Asaph.*

**50** God, the LORD God speaks;
   He summons the earth
     from east to west.
2 From Zion, the perfection
     of beauty,
   God appears in radiance.
3 Our God is coming;
   He will not be silent!
   Devouring fire precedes Him,
   and a storm rages around Him.
4 On high, He summons heaven
     and earth
   in order to judge His people.
5 "Gather My faithful ones
     to Me,
   those who made a covenant
     with Me by sacrifice."
6 The heavens proclaim
     His righteousness,
   for God is the judge.        •*Selah*

7 "Listen, My people,
     and I will speak;
   I will testify against you, Israel.
   I am God, your God.
8 I do not rebuke you
     for your sacrifices
   or for your •burnt offerings,
     which are continually
     before Me.
9 I will not accept a bull
     from your household
   or male goats from your pens,
10 for every animal of the forest is
     Mine,

[a]49:11 LXX, Syr, Tg; MT reads *Their inner thought is that their houses are eternal*

the cattle on a thousand hills.
11 I know every bird
of the mountains,
and the creatures of the field
are Mine.
12 If I were hungry, I would not
tell you,
for the world and everything
in it is Mine.
13 Do I eat the flesh of bulls
or drink the blood of goats?
14 Sacrifice a thank
offering to God,
and pay your vows
to the *Most High.
15 Call on Me in a day of trouble;
I will rescue you,
and you will honor Me."

16 But God says to the wicked:
"What right do you have
to recite My statutes
and to take My covenant
on your lips?
17 You hate instruction
and turn your back
on My words.
18 When you see a thief,
you make friends with him,
and you associate
with adulterers.
19 You unleash your mouth
for evil
and harness your tongue
for deceit.
20 You sit, maligning
your brother,
slandering your mother's son.
21 You have done these things,
and I kept silent;
you thought I was just
like you.
But I will rebuke you
and lay out the case
before you.

22 "Understand this,
you who forget God,

or I will tear you apart,
and there will be
no rescuer.
23 Whoever sacrifices
a thank offering honors Me,
and whoever orders
his conduct,
I will show him the salvation
of God."

## A Prayer for Restoration

*For the choir director.*
*A Davidic psalm, when Nathan the*
*prophet came to him after he had*
*gone to Bathsheba.*

**51** Be gracious to me, God,
according to
Your faithful love;
according to Your abundant
compassion, blot out
my rebellion.
2 Wash away my guilt,
and cleanse me from my sin.
3 For I am conscious
of my rebellion,
and my sin is always
before me.
4 Against You—You alone—
I have sinned
and done this evil
in Your sight.
So You are right
when You pass
sentence;
You are blameless
when You judge.
5 Indeed, I was guilty
⌊when I⌋ was born;
I was sinful when my mother
conceived me.

6 Surely You desire integrity
in the inner self,
and You teach me wisdom
deep within.

## Psalm 51:4-5

### Man

*This is a hard pill to swallow. It seems so unfair. The Bible says we start out sinful nine months before we're born. But isn't that what we see? Do children have to be taught to fight and argue, to whine and rebel, and want their own way? Obedience is work. But selfishness is natural.*

7   Purify me with hyssop,
        and I will be clean;
    wash me, and I will be whiter
        than snow.
8   Let me hear joy and gladness;
    let the bones You have crushed
        rejoice.
9   Turn Your face away
        from my sins
    and blot out all my guilt.

10  God, create a clean heart
        for me
    and renew a steadfast spirit
        within me.
11  Do not banish me
        from Your presence
    or take Your Holy Spirit
        from me.
12  Restore the joy
        of Your salvation to me,
    and give me a willing spirit.
13  Then I will teach
        the rebellious Your ways,
    and sinners will return to You.

14  Save me from the guilt
        of bloodshed, God, the God
    of my salvation,
    and my tongue will sing
        of Your righteousness.
15  Lord, open my lips,
    and my mouth will declare
        Your praise.
16  You do not want a sacrifice,
        or I would give it;
    You are not pleased
        with a burnt offering.
17  The sacrifice pleasing to God
        is a broken spirit.
    God, You will not despise
        a broken
        and humbled heart.

18  In Your good pleasure, cause
        Zion to prosper;
    build the walls of Jerusalem.
19  Then You will delight
        in righteous sacrifices,
        whole *burnt offerings;
    then bulls will be offered
        on Your altar.

### God Judges the Proud

*For the choir director.
A Davidic *Maskil. When Doeg the Edomite went and reported to Saul, telling him, "David went to Ahimelech's house."*

**52** Why brag about evil,
        you hero!
    God's faithful love
        is constant.
2   Like a sharpened razor,
    your tongue devises
        destruction,
    working treachery.
3   You love evil instead
        of good,
    lying instead of speaking
        truthfully.          *Selah
4   You love any words
        that destroy,
    you treacherous tongue!

5 This is why God will bring you
  down forever.
He will take you, ripping you
  out of your tent;
He will uproot you
  from the land of the living.
                    *Selah*
6 The righteous will look on
  with awe
and will ridicule him:
7 "Here's the man
  who would not make God
  his refuge,
but trusted in the abundance
  of his riches,
taking refuge in his destructive
  behavior."

8 But I am like a flourishing
  olive tree in the house
  of God;
I trust in God's faithful love
  forever and ever.
9 I will praise You forever
  for what You have done.
In the presence
  of Your faithful people,
I will place my hope
  in Your name, for it is good.

### A Portrait of Sinners

*For the choir director:
on* Mahalath. *A Davidic* •Maskil.

**53** The fool says in his heart,
  "God does not exist."
They are corrupt, and they do
  vile deeds.
There is no one
  who does good.
2 God looks down from heaven
  on the •human race
to see if there is anyone
  who is wise
and who seeks God.
3 Everyone has turned aside;
they have all become corrupt.

There is no one
  who does good,
not even one.

4 Will those who practice sin
  never understand?
They consume My people
  as they consume bread;
they do not call on God.
5 Then they will be filled
  with terror—
terror like no other—
because God will scatter
  the bones of those
  who besiege you.
You will put them to shame,
  for God has rejected them.

6 Oh, that Israel's deliverance
  would come from Zion!
When God restores
  His captive people,
Jacob will rejoice;
  Israel will be glad.

### Prayer for Deliverance

*For the choir director:
with stringed instruments.
A Davidic* •Maskil. *When the
Ziphites went and said to Saul, "Is
David not hiding among us?"*

**54** God, save me by Your name,
  and vindicate me
  by Your might!
2 God, hear my prayer;
listen to the words
  of my mouth.
3 For strangers rise up
  against me,
and violent men seek my life.
They have no regard
  for God.          •*Selah*

4 God is my helper;
the Lord is the sustainer
  of my life.

5   He will repay my adversaries
        for ⌊their⌋ evil.
    Because of Your faithfulness,
        annihilate them.

6   I will sacrifice
        a freewill offering to You.
    I will praise Your name, LORD,
        because it is good.
7   For He has delivered me
        from every trouble,
    and my eye has looked down
        on my enemies.

## Betrayal by a Friend

*For the choir director:*
*with stringed instruments.*
*A Davidic* •Maskil.

**55** God, listen to my prayer
        and do not ignore my plea
            for help.
2   Pay attention to me
        and answer me.
    I am restless and in turmoil
        with my complaint,
3   because of the enemy's voice,
        because of the pressure
            of the wicked.
    For they bring down disaster
        on me
    and harass me in anger.

4   My heart shudders within me;
    terrors of death sweep
        over me.
5   Fear and trembling come
        upon me;
    horror has overwhelmed me.
6   I said, "If only I had wings
        like a dove!
    I would fly away and find rest.
7   How far away I would flee;
    I would stay in the wilderness.
                            •Selah
8   I would hurry to my shelter

    from the raging wind
        and the storm."

9   Lord, confuse and confound
        their speech,
    for I see violence and strife
        in the city;
10  day and night they make
        the rounds on its walls.
    Crime and trouble are
        within it;
11  destruction is inside it;
    oppression and deceit never
        leave its marketplace.

12  Now, it is not an enemy
        who insults me—
    otherwise I could bear it;
    it is not a foe who rises up
        against me—
    otherwise I could hide
        from him.
13  But it is you, a man who is
        my peer,
    my companion
        and good friend!
14  We used to have
        close fellowship;
    we walked with the crowd
        into the house of God.

15  Let death take them
        by surprise;
    let them go down to •Sheol
        alive,
    because evil is in their homes
        and within them.
16  But I call to God,
    and the LORD will save me.
17  I complain and groan morning,
        noon, and night,
    and He hears my voice.
18  Though many are against me,
    He will redeem me
        from my battle unharmed.
19  God, the One enthroned
        from long ago,

will hear, and will humiliate
    them                       *Selah*
because they do not change
and do not •fear God.

20 He acts violently against those
        at peace with him;
    he violates his covenant.
21 His buttery words are smooth,[a]
    but war is in his heart.
    His words are softer than oil,
    but they are drawn swords.

22 Cast your burden on the LORD,
    and He will support you;
    He will never allow
        the righteous to be shaken.

23 You, God, will bring them
        down to the pit
        of destruction;
    men of bloodshed
        and treachery
        will not live out half
        their days.
    But I will trust in You.

## A Call for God's Protection

*For the choir director: according to
"A Silent Dove Far Away."
A Davidic* •Miktam. *When the
Philistines seized him in Gath.*

**56** Be gracious to me, God, for
        man tramples me;
    he fights and oppresses me
        all day long.
2 My adversaries trample me
        all day,
    for many arrogantly fight
        against me.

3 When I am afraid,
    I will trust in You.
4 In God, whose word I praise,

in God I trust; I will not fear.
What can man do to me?

5 They twist my words all day
        long;
    all their thoughts
        are against me for evil.
6 They stir up strife, they lurk;
    they watch my steps
    while they wait to take
        my life.
7 Will they escape in spite of
        such sin?
    God, bring down the nations
        in wrath.

8 You Yourself have recorded
        my wanderings.
    Put my tears in Your bottle.
    Are they not in Your records?
9 Then my enemies will retreat
        on the day when I call.
    This I know: God is for me.

10 In God, whose word I praise,
    in the LORD, whose word
        I praise,
11 in God I trust; I will not fear.
    What can man do to me?

12 I am obligated by vows to You,
        God;
    I will make
        my thank offerings to You.
13 For You delivered me
        from death,
    even my feet from stumbling,
    to walk before God in the light
        of life.

## Praise for God's Protection

*For the choir director:
"Do Not Destroy."
A Davidic* •Miktam. *When he fled
before Saul into the cave.*

**57** Be gracious to me, God,
        be gracious to me,
    for I take refuge in You.

---

[a] **55:21** Other Hb mss, Sym, Syr, Tg, Jer read *His speech is smoother than butter*

I will seek refuge
   in the shadow
   of Your wings
until danger passes.
2 I call to God *Most High,
to God who fulfills
   [His purpose] for me.
3 He reaches down from heaven
   and saves me,
challenging the one
   who tramples me.   *Selah
God sends His faithful love
   and truth.
4 I am in the midst of lions;
I lie down with those
   who devour *men.
Their teeth are spears
   and arrows;
their tongues
   are sharp swords.
5 God, be exalted
   above the heavens;
let Your glory be above
   the whole earth.
6 They prepared a net
   for my steps;
I was downcast.
They dug a pit ahead of me,
but they fell into it!   *Selah*

7 My heart is confident, God,
   my heart is confident.
I will sing, I sing praises.
8 Wake up, my soul!
Wake up, harp and lyre!
I will wake up the dawn.
9 I will praise You, Lord,
   among the peoples;
I will sing praises to You
   among the nations.
10 For Your faithful love is
   as high as the heavens;
Your faithfulness reaches
   to the clouds.
11 God, be exalted
   above the heavens;
let Your glory be
   over the whole earth.

## A Cry against Injustice

*For the choir director:*
*"Do Not Destroy." A Davidic* *Miktam.

**58** Do you really
   speak righteously,
   you mighty ones?
Do you judge *people fairly?
2 No, you practice injustice
   in your hearts;
with your hands
   you weigh out violence
   in the land.

3 The wicked go astray
   from the womb;
liars err from birth.
4 They have venom
   like the venom of a snake,
like the deaf cobra
   that stops up its ears,
5 that does not listen
   to the sound
   of the charmers
who skillfully weave spells.

6 God, knock the teeth out
   of their mouths;
LORD, tear out
   the young lions' fangs.
7 They will vanish like water
   that flows by;
they will aim
   their useless arrows.
8 Like a slug that moves along
   in slime,
like a woman's miscarried
   [child], they will not see
   the sun.

9 Before your pots can feel
   the heat of the thorns—
whether green or burning—
   He will sweep them away.
10 The righteous will rejoice
   when he sees
   the retribution;

he will wash his feet
    in the blood of the wicked.
11 Then people will say, "Yes,
    there is a reward
    for the righteous!
    There is a God who judges
    on earth!"

## God Our Stronghold

*For the choir director:*
*"Do Not Destroy." A Davidic •Miktam.*
*When Saul sent men to watch the*
*house to kill him.*

**59** Deliver me
    from my enemies, my God;
    protect me from those
    who rise up against me.
2 Deliver me from those
    who practice sin,
    and save me from men
    of bloodshed.
3 LORD, look! They set
    an ambush for me.
    Powerful men attack me,
    but not because of any sin
    or rebellion of mine.
4 For no fault of mine, they run
    and take up a position.
    Awake to help me,
    and take notice.
5 You, LORD God of •Hosts,
    God of Israel,
    rise up to punish all
    the nations;
    do not show grace
    to any wicked traitors.
                •*Selah*

6 They return at evening,
    snarling like dogs
    and prowling around the city.
7 Look, they spew
    from their mouths—
    sharp words from their lips.

"For who," ⌊they say,⌋
    "will hear?"
8 But You laugh at them, LORD;
    You ridicule all the nations.
9 I will keep watch for You,
    my[a] strength,
    because God is my stronghold.
10 My faithful God[b] will come
    to meet me;
    God will let me look down on
    my adversaries.

11 Do not kill them; otherwise,
    my people will forget.
    By Your power, make them
    homeless wanderers
    and bring them down,
    O Lord, our shield.
12 The sin of their mouths is
    the word of their lips,
    so let them be caught
    in their pride.
    They utter curses and lies.
13 Consume ⌊them⌋ in rage;
    consume ⌊them⌋ until they are
    gone.
    Then they will know
    to the ends of the earth
    that God rules over Jacob.
                *Selah*

14 And they return at evening,
    snarling like dogs
    and prowling around the city.
15 They scavenge for food;
    they growl if they are not
    satisfied.

16 But I will sing of Your strength
    and will joyfully proclaim
    Your faithful love
    in the morning.
    For You have been
    a stronghold for me,
    a refuge in my day of trouble.

---

[a] 59:9 Some Hb mss, LXX, Vg, Tg; other Hb mss read *his*    [b] 59:10 Alt Hb traditions read *God in His faithful love*, or *My God, His faithful love*

17 To You, my strength, I sing
praises,
because God is
my stronghold—
my faithful God.

## Prayer in Difficult Times

*For the choir director: according to
"The Lily of Testimony."
A Davidic •Miktam for teaching.
When he fought with Aram-naharaim
and Aram-zobah, and Joab returned
and struck Edom in the Valley
of Salt, ⌊killing⌋ 12,000.*

**60** God, You have rejected us;
You have broken out
against us;
You have been angry.
Restore us!
2 You have shaken the land
and split it open.
Heal its fissures,
for it shudders.
3 You have made Your people
suffer hardship;
You have given us a wine
to drink that made us
stagger.
4 You have given a signal flag
to those who •fear You,
so that they can flee
before the archers.   •Selah
5 Save with
Your right hand, and
answer me,
so that those You love may be
rescued.

6 God has spoken
in His sanctuary:
"I will triumph! I will
divide up Shechem.
I will apportion the Valley
of Succoth.
7 Gilead is Mine,
Manasseh is Mine,

and Ephraim is My helmet;
Judah is My scepter.
8 Moab is My washbasin;
on Edom I throw My sandal.
Over Philistia I shout
in triumph."

9 Who will bring me
to the fortified city?
Who will lead me to Edom?
10 Is it not You, God, who have
rejected us?
God, You do not march out
with our armies.
11 Give us aid against the foe,
for human help is worthless.
12 With God we will perform
valiantly;
He will trample our foes.

## Security in God

*For the choir director:
on stringed instruments. Davidic.*

**61** God, hear my cry;
pay attention to my prayer.
2 I call to You from the ends
of the earth when my heart
is without strength.
Lead me to a rock that is high
above me,
3 for You have been a refuge
for me,
a strong tower in the face
of the enemy.
4 I will live in Your tent forever,
take refuge under the shelter
of Your wings.   •Selah

5 God, You have heard my vows;
You have given a heritage
to those who fear
Your name.
6 Add days to the king's life;
may his years span
many generations.

7 May he sit enthroned
    before God forever;
appoint faithful love and truth
    to guard him.
8 Then I will continually sing
    of Your name,
fulfilling my vows day by day.

### Trust in God Alone

*For the choir director:*
*according to Jeduthun.*
*A Davidic psalm.*

**62** I am at rest in God alone;
my salvation comes from Him.
2 He alone is my rock
    and my salvation,
my stronghold; I will not be
    greatly shaken.

3 How long will you threaten
    a man?
Will all of you attack[a]
as if he were a leaning wall
or a tottering stone fence?
4 They only plan to bring him
    down
    from his high position.
They take pleasure in lying;
they bless with their mouths,
but they curse
    inwardly.     •*Selah*

5 Rest in God alone, my soul,
for my hope comes from Him.
6 He alone is my rock
    and my salvation,
my stronghold; I will not
    be shaken.
7 My salvation and glory depend
    on God;
my strong rock, my refuge,
    is in God.
8 Trust in Him at all times,
    you people;

pour out your hearts
    before Him.
God is our refuge.     *Selah*

9 •Men are only a vapor;
exalted men, an illusion.
On a balance scale, they go up;
together they ⌊weigh⌋ less than
    a vapor.
10 Place no trust in oppression,
or false hope in robbery.
If wealth increases,
pay no attention to it.

11 God has spoken once;
I have heard this twice:
strength belongs to God,
12 and faithful love belongs
    to You, LORD.
For You repay each
    according to his works.

### Praise God Who Satisfies

*A Davidic psalm. When he was*
*in the wilderness of Judah.*

**63** O God, You are my God;
    I eagerly seek You.
My soul thirsts for You;
   my body faints for You
in a land that is dry, desolate,
    and without water.
2 So I gaze on You
    in the sanctuary
to see Your strength
    and Your glory.

3 My lips will glorify You
because Your faithful love
    is better than life.
4 So I will praise You as long as
    I live;
at Your name, I will lift up
    my hands.
5 You satisfy me as with
    rich food;
my mouth will praise You
    with joyful lips.

[a]**62:3** Other Hb mss read *you be struck down*

⁶ When, on my bed, I think
    of You,
I meditate on You during
    the night watches
⁷ because You are my help;
I will rejoice in the shadow
    of Your wings.
⁸ I follow close to You;
Your right hand holds on
    to me.

⁹ But those who seek to destroy
    my life
will go into the depths
    of the earth.
¹⁰ They will be given over
    to the power of the sword;
they will become
    the jackals' prey.
¹¹ But the king will rejoice
    in God;
all who swear
    by Him will boast,
for the mouths of liars
    will be shut.

## Protection from Evildoers

*For the choir director.*
*A Davidic psalm.*

**64** God, hear my voice
    when I complain.
Protect my life from the terror
    of the enemy.
² Hide me from the scheming
    of the wicked,
from the mob of evildoers,
³ who sharpen their tongues
    like swords
and aim bitter words
    like arrows,
⁴ shooting from concealed
    places at the innocent.
They shoot at him suddenly
    and are not afraid.

⁵ They encourage each other
    in an evil plan;
they talk about hiding
    traps and say,
"Who will see them?"
⁶ They devise crimes ⌊and say,⌋
"We have perfected
    a secret plan."
The inner man and the heart
    are mysterious.

⁷ But God will shoot them
    with arrows;
suddenly, they will be
    wounded.
⁸ They will be made to stumble;
their own tongues work
    against them.
All who see them will shake
    their heads.
⁹ Then everyone will fear
and will tell about God's work,
for they will understand
    what He has done.

¹⁰ The righteous rejoice
    in the LORD and take refuge
    in Him;
all the upright in heart offer
    praise.

## God's Care for the Earth

*For the choir director.*
*A Davidic psalm. A song.*

**65** Praise is rightfully Yours,ᵃ
    God, in Zion;
vows to You will be fulfilled.
² All humanity will come to You,
the One who hears prayer.
³ Iniquities overwhelm me;
only You can atone
    for our rebellions.

ᵃ65:1 LXX, Syr read *is due to You*

4 How happy is the one
    You choose
and bring near to live
    in Your courts!
We will be satisfied
    with the goodness
    of Your house,
the holiness of Your temple.

5 You answer us
    in righteousness, with
    awe-inspiring works,
God of our salvation,
the hope of all the ends
    of the earth
    and of the distant seas;
6 You establish the mountains
    by Your power,
robed with strength;
7 You silence the roar
    of the seas, the roar
    of their waves,
and the tumult of the nations.
8 Those who live far away
    are awed by Your signs;
You make east and west shout
    for joy.

9 You visit the earth and water it
    abundantly, enriching it
    greatly.
God's stream is filled
    with water,
for You prepare
    the earth in this way,
    providing ⌊people⌋
    with grain.
10 You soften it with showers
    and bless its growth,
soaking its furrows
    and leveling its ridges.
11 You crown the year
    with Your goodness;
Your ways overflow
    with plenty.
12 The wilderness pastures
    overflow,
and the hills are robed
    with joy.

13 The pastures are clothed
    with flocks,
and the valleys covered
    with grain.
They shout in triumph;
    indeed, they sing.

## Praise for God's Mighty Acts

*For the choir director. A song.*
*A psalm.*

**66** Shout joyfully to God,
    all the earth!
2 Sing the glory of His name;
    make His praise glorious.
3 Say to God, "How awe-
    inspiring are Your works!
Your enemies will cringe
    before You
because of Your great
    strength.
4 All the earth will worship
    You and sing praise to You.
They will sing praise
    to Your name."          *Selah

5 Come and see the works of God;
His acts toward *mankind are
    awe-inspiring.
6 He turned the sea
    into dry land,
and they crossed the river
    on foot.
There we rejoiced in Him.
7 He rules forever by His might;
He keeps His eye
    on the nations.
The rebellious should not exalt
    themselves.          *Selah*
8 Praise our God, you peoples;
let the sound of His praise
    be heard.
9 He keeps us alive
and does not allow our feet
    to slip.
10 For You, God, tested us;
You refined us as silver
    is refined.
11 You lured us into a trap;

You placed burdens
  on our backs.
12 You let men ride
  over our heads;
we went through fire
  and water,
but You brought us out
  to abundance.

13 I will enter Your house
  with *burnt offerings;
I will pay You my vows
14 that my lips promised
and my mouth spoke
  during my distress.
15 I will offer You fattened sheep
  as burnt offerings,
with the fragrant smoke
  of rams;
I will sacrifice oxen with goats.
                              *Selah*

16 Come and listen, all who *fear
  God,
and I will tell what
  He has done for me.
17 I cried out to Him
  with my mouth,
and praise was on my tongue.
18 If I had been aware of malice
  in my heart,
the Lord would not have
  listened.
19 However, God has listened;
He has paid attention
  to the sound of my prayer.
20 May God be praised!
He has not turned away
  my prayer
or turned His faithful love
  from me.

## All Will Praise God

*For the choir director:*
*with stringed instruments. A psalm.*
*A song.*

**67** May God be gracious to us
      and bless us;
look on us with favor     *Selah*

2 so that Your way
  may be known on earth,
Your salvation among all
  nations.

3 Let the peoples praise You,
  God;
let all the peoples praise You.
4 Let the nations rejoice
  and shout for joy,
for You judge the peoples
  with fairness
and lead the nations on earth.
                              *Selah*
5 Let the peoples praise You,
  O God,
let all the peoples praise You.

6 The earth has produced
  its harvest;
God, our God, blesses us.
7 God will bless us,
and all the ends of the earth
  will *fear Him.

## God's Majestic Power

*For the choir director.*
*A Davidic psalm. A song.*

**68** God arises. His enemies
      scatter,
and those who hate
  Him flee
  from His presence.
2 As smoke is blown away,
so You blow ⌊them⌋ away.
As wax melts before the fire,
so the wicked are destroyed
  before God.
3 But the righteous are glad;
they rejoice before God
  and celebrate with joy.

4 Sing to God! Sing praises
  to His name.
Exalt Him who rides
  on the clouds—

His name is •Yahweh—
and rejoice before Him.

5 A father of the fatherless
and a champion of widows
is God in His holy dwelling.

6 God provides homes for those
who are deserted.
He leads out the prisoners
to prosperity,
but the rebellious live
in a scorched land.

7 God, when You went out
before Your people,
when You marched
through the desert,   •Selah

8 the earth trembled,
and the skies poured down
⌊rain⌋
before God, the God of Sinai,
before God, the God of Israel.

9 You, God, showered
abundant rain;
You revived Your inheritance
when it languished.

10 Your people settled in it;
by Your goodness You provided
for the poor, God.

---

*"We place ourselves in great peril if
we seek to render God as a play-
thing of our piety, an ornamental
decoration on the religious life."*
—David Wells

---

11 The Lord gave the command;
a great company of women
brought the good news:

12 "The kings of the armies
flee—they flee!"
She who stays at home divides
the spoil.

13 While you lie among
the sheepfolds,

the wings of a dove
are covered with silver,
and its feathers
with glistening gold.

14 When the Almighty scattered
kings in the land,
it snowed on Zalmon.

15 Mount Bashan is God's
towering mountain;
Mount Bashan is a mountain
of many peaks.

16 Why gaze with envy, you
mountain peaks,
at the mountain God desired
for His dwelling?
The LORD will live ⌊there⌋
forever!

17 God's chariots are tens
of thousands, thousands
and thousands;
the Lord is among them
in the sanctuary as He was
at Sinai.[a]

18 You ascended to the heights,
taking away captives;
You received gifts from
people,
even from the rebellious,
so that the LORD God
might live ⌊there⌋.

19 May the Lord be praised!
Day after day He bears
our burdens;
God is our salvation.      *Selah*

20 Our God is a God
of salvation,
and escape from death belongs
to the Lord GOD.

21 Surely God crushes the heads
of His enemies,
the hairy head of one
who goes on
in his guilty acts.

22 The Lord said, "I will bring
⌊them⌋ back from Bashan;

[a]**68:17** Some emend text to *Lord came from Sinai into the holy place*

I will bring ⌊them⌋ back
    from the depths of the sea
23 so that your foot may wade[a]
    in blood
and your dogs' tongues
    may have their share
    from the enemies."
24 People have seen
    Your procession, God,
the procession of my God,
    my King, in the sanctuary.
25 Singers[b] lead the way,
    with musicians following;
among them are young women
    playing tambourines.
26 Praise God in the assemblies;
⌊praise⌋ the LORD
    from the fountain of Israel.
27 There is Benjamin,
    the youngest, leading them,
the rulers of Judah
    in their assembly,
the rulers of Zebulun,
    the rulers of Naphtali.

28 Your God has decreed
    your strength.
Show Your strength, God,
You who have acted
    on our behalf.
29 Because of Your temple
    at Jerusalem,
kings will bring tribute to You.
30 Rebuke the beast in the reeds,
the herd of bulls
    with the calves
    of the peoples.
Trample underfoot those
    with bars of silver.
Scatter the peoples
    who take pleasure in war.
31 Ambassadors
    will come from Egypt;
Cush will stretch out
    its hands to God.

32 Sing to God, you kingdoms
    of the earth;

---

### Psalm 68:32-35

*We may think our favorite singing group is awesome. We may think water skiing is awesome. We may think three-cheese nachos are awesome. No—God is awesome. Yes, He's our Father. He's our Friend. But this God of ours is holy. And we do well to remember it.*

---

    sing praise to the Lord,  *Selah*
33 to Him who rides
    in the ancient,
    highest heavens.
Look, He thunders
    with His powerful voice!
34 Ascribe power to God.
His majesty is over Israel,
His power among the clouds.
35 God, You are awe-inspiring
    in Your sanctuaries.
The God of Israel gives power
    and strength to His people.
May God be praised!

### A Plea for Rescue
*For the choir director: according to "The Lilies." Davidic.*

**69** Save me, God,
for the water has risen
    to my neck.
2 I have sunk in deep mud
    with no footing;
I have come into deep waters,
and a flood sweeps over me.
3 I am weary from my crying;
    my throat is parched.
My eyes fail, looking
    for my God.
4 Those who hate me
    without cause

---

[a]68:23 LXX, Syr read *dip*   [b]68:25 Some Hb mss, LXX, Syr read *Officials*

are more numerous
    than the hairs of my head;
my deceitful enemies,
    who would destroy me,
    are powerful.
Though I did not steal,
    I must repay.

5 God, You know
    my foolishness,
and my guilty acts are
    not hidden from You.
6 Do not let those who hope
    in You be disgraced
    because of me,
Lord GOD of •Hosts;
do not let those who seek You
    be humiliated
    because of me,
God of Israel.
7 For I have endured insults
    because of You,
and shame has covered
    my face.
8 I have become a stranger
    to my brothers
and a foreigner
    to my mother's sons
9 because zeal for Your house
    has consumed me,
and the insults of those
    who insult You have fallen
    on me.
10 I mourned and fasted,
    but it brought me insults.
11 I wore sackcloth
    as my clothing,
and I was a joke to them.
12 Those who sit at the city gate
    talk about me,
and drunkards make up songs
    about me.

13 But as for me, LORD,
    my prayer to You is
    for a time of favor.
In Your abundant, faithful love,
    God,

answer me with
    Your sure salvation.
14 Rescue me
    from the miry mud;
    don't let me sink.
Let me be rescued from those
    who hate me,
and from the deep waters.
15 Don't let the floodwaters
    sweep over me
or the deep swallow me up;
don't let the pit close
    its mouth over me.
16 Answer me, LORD,
    for Your faithful love is
    good;
in keeping with
    Your great compassion, turn
    to me.
17 Don't hide Your face
    from Your servant,
for I am in distress.
Answer me quickly!
18 Draw near to me and redeem
    me;
ransom me because of
    my enemies.

19 You know the insults
    I endure—my shame
    and disgrace.
You are aware of all
    my adversaries.
20 Insults have broken my heart,
    and I am in despair.
I waited for sympathy,
    but there was none;
for comforters, but found
    no one.
21 Instead, they gave me
    gall for my food,
and for my thirst they gave me
    vinegar to drink.

22 Let their table set before them
    be a snare,
and let it be a trap
    for ⌊their⌋ allies.

23 Let their eyes grow too dim
      to see,
   and let their loins continually
      shake.
24 Pour out Your rage on them,
   and let Your burning anger
      overtake them.
25 Make their fortification
      desolate;
   may no one live in their tents.
26 For they persecute the one
      You struck
   and talk about the pain
      of those You wounded.
27 Add guilt to their guilt;
   do not let them share
      in Your righteousness.
28 Let them be erased
      from the book of life
   and not be recorded
      with the righteous.

29 But as for me—poor
      and in pain—
   let Your salvation protect me,
      God.
30 I will praise God's name
      with song
   and exalt Him
      with thanksgiving.
31 That will please the LORD
      more than an ox,
   more than a bull with horns
      and hooves.
32 The humble will see it
      and rejoice.
   You who seek God, take heart!
33 For the LORD listens
      to the needy
   and does not despise His own
      who are prisoners.

34 Let heaven and earth praise
      Him,
   the seas and everything
      that moves in them,
35 for God will save Zion

   and build up the cities
      of Judah.
   They will live there
      and possess it.
36 The descendants
      of His servants will inherit
      it,
   and those who love His name
      will live in it.

## A Call for Deliverance

*For the choir director. Davidic.*
*To bring remembrance.*

**70** God, deliver me.
      Hurry to help me, LORD!

2  Let those who seek my life
      be disgraced and confounded;
   let those who wish me harm
      be driven back and humiliated.
3  Let those who say, "Aha, aha!"
   retreat because of
      their shame.

4  Let all who seek You rejoice
      and be glad in You;
   let those who love
      Your salvation
   continually say,
      "God is great!"
5  But I am afflicted and needy;
   hurry to me, God.
   You are my help
      and my deliverer;
   LORD, do not delay.

## God's Help in Old Age

**71** LORD, I seek refuge in You;
      never let me be disgraced.
2  In Your justice, rescue
      and deliver me;
   listen closely to me and save
      me.
3  Be a rock of refuge[a] for me,

---

[a] 71:3 Some Hb mss, LXX, Sym, Tg; other Hb mss read *habitation*

where I can always go.
Give the command to save me,
for You are my rock
and fortress.
4 Deliver me, My God,
from the hand
of the wicked,
from the grasp of the unjust
and oppressive.
5 For You are my hope,
Lord GOD,
my confidence from my youth.
6 I have leaned on You
from birth;
You took me from
my mother's womb.
My praise is always about You.
7 I have become
an ominous sign to many,
but You are my strong refuge.
8 My mouth is full of praise
and honor to You all day long.

9 Don't discard me
in my old age:
as my strength fails,
do not abandon me.
10 For my enemies talk about me,
and those who spy on me plot
together,
11 saying, "God has abandoned
him;
chase him and catch him,
for there is no one to rescue
⌊him⌋."
12 God, do not be far from me;
my God, hurry to help me.
13 May my adversaries
be disgraced
and confounded;
may those who seek my harm
be covered with disgrace
and humiliation.
14 But I will hope continually
and will praise You more
and more.

15 My mouth will tell
about Your righteousness
and Your salvation all day long,
though I cannot sum them up.
16 I come because of
the mighty acts[a]
of the Lord GOD;
I will proclaim
Your righteousness,
Yours alone.

17 God, You have taught me
from my youth,
and I still proclaim
Your wonderful works.
18 Even when I am old and gray,
God, do not abandon me.
Then I will proclaim
Your power to ⌊another⌋
generation,
Your strength to all who are
to come.
19 Your righteousness reaches
heaven, God,
You who have done
great things;
God, who is like You?
20 You caused me[b] to experience
many troubles
and misfortunes,
but You will revive me[c] again.
You will bring me[d] up again,
even from the depths
of the earth.
21 You will increase my honor
and comfort me once again.
22 Therefore, with a lute
I will praise You
for Your faithfulness, my God;
I will sing to You with a harp,
Holy One of Israel.
23 My lips will shout for joy
when I sing praise to You,
because You have
redeemed me.

[a]71:16 Some Hb mss, LXX, Jer read *come with the might*    [b]71:20 Alt Hb tradition, Aq read *us*    [c]71:20 Alt Hb
tradition, Tg, Jer read *us*    [d]71:20 Other Hb mss, Tg, Jer read *us*

24 Therefore, my tongue
will proclaim
Your righteousness all day
long,
for those who seek my harm
will be disgraced
and confounded.

## A Prayer for the King

*Solomonic.*

**72** God, give Your justice
to the king
and Your righteousness
to the king's son.
2 He will judge Your people
with righteousness
and Your afflicted ones
with justice.
3 May the mountains
bring prosperity
to the people,
and the hills, righteousness.
4 May he vindicate the afflicted
among the people,
help the poor,
and crush the oppressor.

5 May he continue[a]
while the sun endures,
and as long as the moon,
throughout all generations.
6 May he be like rain that falls
on the cut grass,
like spring showers that water
the earth.
7 May the righteous[b] flourish
in his days,
and prosperity abound
till the moon is no more.

8 And may he rule from sea
to sea
and from the Euphrates
to the ends of the earth.

9 May desert tribes kneel
before him
and his enemies lick the dust.
10 May the kings of Tarshish
and the coastlands bring
tribute,
the kings of Sheba and Seba
offer gifts.
11 And let all kings bow down
to him,
all nations serve him.

12 For he will rescue the poor
who cry out
and the afflicted who have
no helper.
13 He will have pity on the poor
and helpless
and save the lives of the poor.
14 He will redeem them
from oppression
and violence,
for their lives
are precious in his sight.

15 May he live long!
May gold from Sheba be given
to him.
May prayer be offered for him
continually,
and may he be blessed all day
long.
16 May there be plenty of grain
in the land;
may it wave on the tops
of the mountains.
May its crops be like Lebanon.
May people flourish
in the cities like the grass
of the field.
17 May his name endure forever;
as long as the sun shines, may
his fame increase.
May all nations be blessed
by him and call him
blessed.

---

[a] **72:5** LXX; MT reads *May they fear you*   [b] **72:7** Some Hb mss, LXX, Syr, Jer read *May righteousness*

18 May the LORD God, the God
     of Israel, be praised,
   who alone does wonders.
19 May His glorious name
     be praised forever;
   . the whole earth is filled
     with His glory.
   Amen and amen.
20 The prayers of David
     son of Jesse are concluded.

# BOOK III

## (PSALMS 73–89)

### God's Ways Vindicated

*A psalm of Asaph.*

**73** God is indeed good to Israel,
   to the pure in heart.
2   But as for me, my feet
      almost slipped;
    my steps nearly went astray.
3   For I envied the arrogant;
    I saw the prosperity
      of the wicked.

4   They have an easy time
      until they die,
    and their bodies are well-fed.
5   They are not in trouble
      like others;
    they are not afflicted
      like most people.
6   Therefore, pride is
      their necklace,
    and violence covers them
      like a garment.
7   Their eyes bulge out
      from fatness;
    the imaginations
      of their hearts run wild.
8   They mock, and they speak
      maliciously;
    they arrogantly threaten
      oppression.

9   They set their mouths
      against heaven,
    and their tongues strut
      across the earth.
10  Therefore His people turn
      to them
    and drink in their overflowing
      waters.
11  They say, "How can God
      know?
    Does the •Most High know
      everything?"
12  Look at them—the wicked!
    They are always at ease,
      and they increase
      their wealth.

13  Did I purify my heart
    and wash my hands
      in innocence for nothing?
14  For I am afflicted all day long,
    and punished every morning.
15  If I had decided to say
      these things ⌊aloud⌋,
    I would have betrayed
      Your people.
16  When I tried to understand all
      this,
    it seemed hopeless
17  until I entered
      God's sanctuary.
    Then I understood
      their destiny.
18  Indeed You put them
      in slippery places;
    You make them fall into ruin.
19  How suddenly they become
      a desolation!
    They come to an end,
      swept away by terrors.
20  Like one waking
      from a dream,
    Lord, when arising, You will
      despise their image.

21  When I became embittered
    and my innermost
      being was wounded,

22 I was a fool
   and didn't understand;
   I was an unthinking animal
   toward You.
23 Yet I am always with You;
   You hold my right hand.
24 You guide me
   with Your counsel,
   and afterward You will take me
   up in glory.
25 Whom do I have in heaven
   but You?
   And I desire nothing on earth
   but You.
26 My flesh and my heart
   may fail,
   but God is
   the strength of my heart,
   my portion forever.
27 Those far from You will
   certainly perish;
   You destroy all who are
   unfaithful to You.
28 But as for me, God's presence
   is my good.
   I have made the Lord GOD
   my refuge,
   so I can tell about all You do.

## Prayer for Israel
*A* °Maskil *of Asaph.*

**74** Why have You rejected ⌊us⌋
    forever, God?
    Why does Your anger burn
    against the sheep
    of Your pasture?
2  Remember Your congregation,
   which You purchased
   long ago
   and redeemed as the tribe
   for Your own possession.
   ⌊Remember⌋ Mount Zion
   where You dwell.
3  Make Your
   way to the everlasting ruins,
   to all that the enemy
   has destroyed
   in the sanctuary.

4  Your adversaries roared
   in the meeting place
   where You met with us.
   They set up their emblems
   as signs.
5  It was like men in a thicket
   of trees,
   wielding axes,
6  then smashing all the carvings
   with hatchets and picks.
7  They set Your sanctuary
   on fire;
   they utterly desecrated
   the dwelling place
   of Your name.
8  They said in their hearts,
   "Let us oppress them
   relentlessly."
   They burned down every place
   throughout the land where
   God met with us.
9  We don't see any signs for us.
   There is no longer a prophet.
   And none of us knows
   how long this will last.
10 God, how long will the foe
   mock?
   Will the enemy insult
   Your name forever?
11 Why do You hold back
   Your hand?
   Stretch out Your right hand
   and destroy ⌊them⌋!

12 God my king is
   from ancient times,
   performing saving acts
   on the earth.
13 You divided the sea
   with Your strength;
   You smashed the heads
   of the sea monsters
   in the waters;
14 You crushed the heads
   of Leviathan;
   You fed him to the creatures
   of the desert.
15 You opened up springs
   and streams;

You dried up ever-flowing
    rivers.
16 The day is Yours, also
    the night;
    You established the moon
    and the sun.
17 You set all the boundaries
    of the earth;
    You made summer
    and winter.


18 Remember this: the enemy
    has mocked the LORD,
    and a foolish people
    has insulted Your name.
19 Do not give the life
    of Your dove to beasts;[a]
    do not forget the lives
    of Your poor people forever.
20 Consider the covenant,
    for the dark places of the land
    are full of violence.
21 Do not let the oppressed
    turn away in shame;
    let the poor and needy praise
    Your name.
22 Arise, God, defend
    Your cause!
    Remember the insults that
    fools bring against You all
    day long.
23 Do not forget the clamor
    of Your adversaries,
    the tumult of Your opponents
    that goes up constantly.

### God Judges the Wicked

*For the choir director:*
*"Do Not Destroy." A psalm*
*of Asaph. A song.*

**75** We give thanks to You, God;
    we give thanks to You,
    for Your name is near.
    People tell about
    Your wonderful works.

2 "When I choose a time,
    I will judge fairly.
3 When the earth and all
    its inhabitants shake,
    I am the One who steadies
    its pillars.      *•Selah*
4 I say to the boastful,
    'Do not boast,'
    and to the wicked, 'Do not
    lift up your •horn.
5 Do not lift up your horn
    against heaven
    or speak arrogantly.' "

6 Exaltation does not come
    from the east, the west,
    or the desert,
7 for God is the judge:
    He brings down one and exalts
    another.
8 For there is a cup
    in the LORD's hand,
    full of wine blended
    with spices, and He pours
    from it.
    All the wicked of the earth
    will drink,
    draining it to the dregs.

9 As for me, I will tell about Him
    forever;
    I will sing praise to the God
    of Jacob.

10 "I will cut off all the horns
    of the wicked,
    but the horns of the righteous
    will be lifted up."

### God, the Powerful Judge

*For the choir director:*
*with stringed instruments. A psalm*
*of Asaph. A song.*

**76** God is known in Judah;
    His name is great in Israel.

---

a **74:19** One Hb ms, LXX, Syr read *Do not hand over to beasts a soul that praises You*

2   His tent is in Salem,
    His dwelling place in Zion.
3   There He shatters the bow's
        flaming arrows,
    the shield, the sword,
        and the weapons of war.
                                    •Selah

4   You are resplendent
        and majestic
    ⌊coming down⌋
        from the mountains of prey.
5   The brave-hearted
        have been plundered;
    they have slipped
        into their ⌊final⌋ sleep.
    None of the warriors was able
        to lift a hand.
6   At Your rebuke, God of Jacob,
    both chariot and horse lay still.

7   And You—You are to be
        •feared.
    When You are angry,
        who can stand before You?
8   From heaven You pronounced
        judgment.
    The earth feared and grew
        quiet
9   when God rose up to judge
    and to save all the lowly
        of the earth.            Selah
10  Even human wrath will praise
        You;
    You will clothe Yourself with
        their remaining wrath.

11  Make and keep your vows
        to the LORD your God;
    let all who are around Him
        bring tribute to the awe-
        inspiring One.
12  He humbles the spirit
        of leaders;
    He is feared by the kings
        of the earth.

## Confidence in a Time of Crisis

*For the choir director: according to
Jeduthun. Of Asaph. A psalm.*

**77**  I cry aloud to God,
        aloud to God, and He will hear
        me.
2   In my day of trouble I sought
        the Lord.
    My hands were lifted up all
        night long;
    I refused to be comforted.
3   I think of God; I groan;
    I meditate; my spirit becomes
        weak.              •Selah

4   You have kept me from closing
        my eyes;
    I am troubled and cannot
        speak.
5   I consider days of old,
    years long past.
6   At night I remember
        my music;
    I meditate in my heart,
        and my spirit ponders.

7   "Will the Lord reject forever
    and never again show favor?
8   Has His faithful love ceased
        forever?
    Is ⌊His⌋ promise at an end
        for all time?
9   Has God forgotten to be
        gracious?
    Has He in anger withheld
        His compassion?"        Selah

10  So I say, "It is my sorrow
    that the right hand
        of the •Most High
        has changed."
11  I will remember
        the LORD's works;
    yes, I will remember
        Your ancient wonders.

12 I will reflect on all
    You have done
and meditate on Your actions.

13 God, Your way is holy.
    What god is great like God?
14 You are the God who works
    wonders;
You revealed Your strength
    among the peoples.
15 With power You redeemed
    Your people,
the descendants of Jacob
    and Joseph.    *Selah*

16 The waters saw You, God.
The waters saw You;
    they trembled.
Even the depths shook.
17 The clouds poured down
    water.
The storm clouds thundered;
Your arrows flashed back
    and forth.
18 The sound of Your thunder
    was in the whirlwind;
lightning lit up the world.
The earth shook and quaked.
19 Your way went
    through the sea,
and Your path through
    the great waters,
but Your footprints
    were unseen.
20 You led Your people
    like a flock
by the hand of Moses
    and Aaron.

## Lessons from Israel's Past
A •Maskil *of Asaph.*

**78** My people, hear
    my instruction;
listen to what I say.

### Psalm 78:1-8

*Not every person in need of your Christian witness is at work or around the corner. The ones you'll have the best chance of reaching are the ones right in your own home. Let's never be so busy taking our message to the world that we forget the little ones right at our feet.*

2 I will declare wise sayings;
I will speak mysteries
    from the past—
3 things we have heard
    and known
and that our fathers have
    passed down to us.
4 We must not hide them
    from their children,
but must tell
    a future generation
    the praises of the LORD,
His might,
    and the wonderful works
    He has performed.
5 He established a testimony
    in Jacob
and set up a law in Israel,
which He commanded
    our fathers
to teach to their children
6 so that a future generation—
    children yet to be born—
    might know.
They were to rise and tell
    their children
7 so that they might put
    their confidence in God
and not forget God's works,
but keep His commandments.

455

8 Then they would not be
   like their fathers,
a stubborn and rebellious
   generation,
a generation whose heart
   was not loyal
and whose spirit was not
   faithful to God.

9 The Ephraimite archers
   turned back
on the day of battle.
10 They did not keep
   God's covenant
and refused to live by His law.
11 They forgot what
   He had done,
the wonderful works
   He had shown them.
12 He worked wonders
   in the sight of their fathers,
in the land of Egypt, the region
   of Zoan.
13 He split the sea and brought
   them across;
the water stood up
   like a wall.
14 He led them with a cloud
   by day
and with a fiery light
   throughout the night.
15 He split rocks
   in the wilderness
and gave them drink
   as abundant as the deep.
16 He brought streams out of
   the stone

"If we abandon our vision for our
children, we are left to wander
aimlessly with no direction other
than our own self-interest."
—Susan Card

and made water flow down
   like rivers.

17 But they continued to sin
   against Him,
rebelling in the desert against
   the *Most High.
18 They deliberately tested God,
demanding the food
   they craved.
19 They spoke against God,
saying, "Is God able to provide
   food in the wilderness?
20 Look! He struck the rock
   and water gushed out;
torrents overflowed.
But can He also provide bread
or furnish meat
   for His people?"
21 Therefore, the LORD heard
   and became furious;
then fire broke out
   against Jacob,
and anger flared up
   against Israel
22 because they did not believe
   God
or rely on His salvation.
23 He gave a command
   to the clouds above
and opened the doors
   of heaven.
24 He rained manna for them
   to eat;
He gave them grain
   from heaven.
25 People ate the bread
   of angels.
He sent them
   an abundant supply
   of food.
26 He made the east wind blow
   in the skies
and drove the south wind
   by His might.
27 He rained meat on them
   like dust,

and winged birds like the sand
    of the seas.
28  He made ⌊them⌋ fall
    in His camp,
    all around His tent.ᵃ
29  They ate and were completely
        satisfied,
    for He gave them
        what they craved.
30  Before they had satisfied
        their desire,
    while the food was still
        in their mouths,
31  God's anger flared up
        against them,
    and He killed some of
        their best men.
    He struck down Israel's choice
        young men.

32  Despite all this, they kept
        sinning
    and did not believe
        His wonderful works.
33  He made their days end
        in futility,
    their years in sudden disaster.
34  When He killed
        ⌊some of⌋ them, ⌊the rest⌋
        began to seek Him;
    they repented and searched
        for God.
35  They remembered that God
        was their rock,
    the Most High
    God, their Redeemer.
36  But they deceived Him
        with their mouths,
    they lied to Him
        with their tongues,
37  their hearts were insincere
        toward Him,
    and they were unfaithful
        to His covenant.
38  Yet He was compassionate;
    He atoned for ⌊their⌋ guilt

and did not destroy ⌊them⌋.
He often turned His anger
    aside
and did not unleash all
    His wrath.
39  He remembered that
        they were ⌊only⌋ flesh,
    a wind that passes
        and does not return.

40  How often they rebelled
        against Him
    in the wilderness
    and grieved Him in the desert.
41  They constantly tested God
    and provoked the Holy One
        of Israel.
42  They did not remember
        His power ⌊shown⌋
    on the day He redeemed them
        from the foe,
43  when He performed
        His miraculous signs
        in Egypt
    and His marvels in the region
        of Zoan.
44  He turned their rivers
        into blood,
    and they could not drink
        from their streams.
45  He sent among them swarms
        of flies, which fed on them,
    and frogs, which devastated
        them.
46  He gave their crops
        to the caterpillar
    and the fruit of their labor
        to the locust.
47  He killed their vines with hail
    and their sycamore-fig trees
        with a flood.
48  He handed over their livestock
        to hail
    and their cattle
        to lightning bolts.

ᵃ **78:28** LXX, Syr read *in their camp . . . their tents*

49 He sent His burning anger
      against them:
  fury, indignation,
      and calamity—
  a band of deadly messengers.
50 He cleared a path
      for His anger.
  He did not spare them
      from death,
  but delivered their lives
      to the plague.
51 He struck all the firstborn
      in Egypt,
  the first progeny of the tents
      of Ham.
52 He led His people out
      like sheep
  and guided them like a flock
      in the wilderness.
53 He led them safely,
      and they were not afraid;
  but the sea covered
      their enemies.
54 He brought them
      to His holy land,
  to the mountain His right hand
      acquired.
55 He drove out nations
      before them.
  He apportioned
      their inheritance by lot
  and settled the tribes of Israel
      in their tents.

56 But they rebelliously tested
      the Most High God,
  for they did not keep
      His decrees.
57 They treacherously
      turned away
      like their fathers;
  they became warped
      like a faulty bow.
58 They enraged Him
      with their high places
  and provoked His jealousy
      with their carved images.

59 God heard and
      became furious;
  He completely rejected Israel.
60 He abandoned the tabernacle
      at Shiloh,
  the tent where He resided
      among men.
61 He gave up
      His strength to captivity
  and His splendor to the hand
      of a foe.
62 He surrendered His people
      to the sword
  because He was enraged
      with His heritage.
63 Fire consumed His chosen
      young men,
  and His young women had no
      wedding songs.
64 His priests fell by the sword,
  but the widows could not
      lament.

65 Then the Lord awoke as if
      from sleep,
  like a warrior from the effects
      of wine.
66 He beat back His foes;
  He gave them lasting shame.
67 He rejected the tent of Joseph
  and did not choose the tribe
      of Ephraim.
68 He chose instead the tribe
      of Judah,
  Mount Zion, which He loved.
69 He built His sanctuary
      like the heights,
  like the earth that
      He established forever.
70 He chose David His servant
  and took him
      from the sheepfolds;
71 He brought him from tending
      ewes
  to be shepherd
      over His people Jacob—
  over Israel, His inheritance.

72 He shepherded
   them with a pure heart
and guided them
   with his skillful hands.

## Faith amid Confusion
*A psalm of Asaph.*

**79** God, the nations
   have invaded
   Your inheritance,
desecrated Your holy temple,
and turned Jerusalem
   into ruins.
2 They gave the corpses
   of Your servants
to the birds of the sky
   for food,
the flesh of Your godly ones
   to the beasts of the earth.
3 They poured out their blood
   like water all
   around Jerusalem,
and there was no one to bury
   ⌊them⌋.
4 We have become an object
   of reproach
   to our neighbors,
a source of mockery
   and ridicule to those
   around us.

5 How long, LORD? Will You
   be angry forever?
Will Your jealousy
   keep burning like fire?
6 Pour out Your wrath
   on the nations that don't
   acknowledge You,
on the kingdoms that don't
   call on Your name,
7 for they have devoured Jacob
and devastated his homeland.
8 Do not hold past
   sins against us;
let Your compassion come
   to us quickly,
for we have become weak.

9 God of our salvation,
   help us—
for the glory of Your name.
Deliver us
   and atone for our sins,
for Your name's sake.
10 Why should the nations ask,
   "Where is their God?"
Before our eyes, let vengeance
   for the shed blood
   of Your servants
be known among
   the nations.
11 Let the groans of the prisoners
   reach You;
according to Your great power,
preserve those condemned
   to die.

12 Pay back sevenfold
   to our neighbors
the reproach they have hurled
   at You, Lord.
13 Then we, Your people,
   the sheep of Your pasture,
will thank You forever;
we will declare Your praise
   to generation
   after generation.

## A Prayer for Restoration
*For the choir director: according to
"The Lilies." A testimony
of Asaph. A psalm.*

**80** Listen, Shepherd of Israel,
   who guides Joseph
   like a flock;
You who sit enthroned
   on the cherubim, rise up
2 at the head of Ephraim,
   Benjamin, and Manasseh.
Rally Your power and come
   to save us.
3 Restore us, God;

look ⌊on us⌋
   with favor, and we will
   be saved.

4 LORD God of *Hosts,
   how long will You be angry
      with Your people's prayers?
5 You fed them the bread
    of tears
and gave them
   a full measure of tears
   to drink.
6 You set us at strife
   with our neighbors;
our enemies make fun of us.
7 Restore us, God of Hosts;
look ⌊on us⌋ with favor, and we
   will be saved.

8 You uprooted a vine
   from Egypt;
You drove out
   the nations and planted it.
9 You cleared ⌊a place⌋ for it;
it took root and filled the land.
10 The mountains were covered
   by its shade,
and the mighty
   cedars with its branches.
11 It sent out sprouts
   toward the Sea
and shoots toward the River.

12 Why have You broken down
   its walls
so that all who pass by pick
   its fruit?
13 The boar from the forest
   gnaws at it,
and creatures of the field feed
   on it.
14 Return, God of Hosts.
Look down from heaven
   and see;
take care of this vine,
15 the root Your right hand
   has planted,

the shoot that
   You made strong
   for Yourself.
16 It was cut down
   and burned up;
they perish at the rebuke
   of Your countenance.
17 Let Your hand be with the man
   at Your right hand,
with the son of man
   You have made strong
   for Yourself.
18 Then we will not turn away
   from You;
revive us, and we will call
   on Your name.
19 Restore us, LORD God
   of Hosts;
look ⌊on us⌋ with favor,
   and we will be saved.

### A Call to Obedience

*For the choir director:*
*on the *Gittith. Of Asaph.*

**81** Sing for joy to God
   our strength;
shout in triumph to the God
   of Jacob.
2 Lift up a song—play
   the tambourine,
the melodious lyre,
   and the harp.
3 Blow the horn during
   the new moon
and during the full moon,
   on the day of our feast.
4 For this is a statute for Israel,
a judgment of the God
   of Jacob.
5 He set it up as an ordinance
   for Joseph
when He went throughout [a]
   the land of Egypt.

I heard an unfamiliar language:

6 "I relieved his shoulder
    from the burden;
his hands were freed from
    ⌊carrying⌋ the basket.
7 You called out in distress,
    and I rescued you;
I answered you
    from the thundercloud.
I tested you at the waters
    of Meribah.    •Selah
8 Listen, My people, and I will
    admonish you.
O Israel, if you would only
    listen to Me!
9 There must not be
    a strange god among you;
you must not bow down
    to a foreign god.
10 I am •Yahweh your God,
who brought you up
    from the land of Egypt.
Open your mouth wide,
    and I will fill it.

11 "But My people did not listen
    to Me;
Israel did not obey Me.
12 So I gave them over
    to their stubborn hearts
to follow their own plans.
13 If only My people would listen
    to Me
and Israel would follow
    My ways,
14 I would quickly subdue
    their enemies
and turn My hand
    against their foes."
15 Those who hate the LORD
    would pretend submission
    to Him;
their doom would last forever.
16 But He would feed
    Israel with the best wheat.
"I would satisfy you
    with honey
    from the rock."

## A Plea for Righteous Judgment

*A psalm of Asaph.*

**82** God has taken His place
    in the divine assembly;
He judges among the gods:
2 "How long will you judge
    unjustly
and show partiality
    to the wicked?    •Selah
3 Provide justice for the needy
    and the fatherless;
uphold the rights
    of the oppressed
    and the destitute.
4 Rescue the poor and needy;
save them from the hand
    of the wicked."

5 They do not know
    or understand;
they wander in darkness.
All the foundations
    of the earth are shaken.

6 I said, "You are gods;
you are all sons
    of the •Most High.
7 However, you will die
    like men
and fall like any other ruler."

8 Rise up, God, judge the earth,
for all the nations belong
    to You.

## Prayer against Enemies

*A song. A psalm of Asaph.*

**83** God, do not keep silent.
Do not be deaf, God; do not
    be idle.
2 See how Your enemies make
    an uproar;
those who hate You have acted
    arrogantly.

3   They devise clever schemes
      against Your people;
    they conspire against
      Your treasured ones.
4   They say, "Come, let us wipe
      them out as a nation
    so that Israel's name will
      no longer be remembered."
5   For they have conspired
      with one mind;
    they form an
      alliance against You—
6   the tents of Edom
      and the Ishmaelites,
    Moab and the Hagrites,
7   Gebal, Ammon, and Amalek,
    Philistia with the inhabitants
      of Tyre.
8   Even Assyria has joined them;
    they lend support to the sons
      of Lot.                    *Selah

9   Deal with them as ⌊You did⌋
      with Midian,
    as ⌊You did⌋ with Sisera
      and Jabin
      at the Kishon River.
10  They were destroyed at
      En-dor;
    they became manure
      for the ground.
11  Make their nobles like Oreb
      and Zeeb,
    and all their tribal leaders
      like Zebah and Zalmunna,
12  who said, "Let us seize
      God's pastures
      for ourselves."

13  Make them like tumbleweed,
      my God,
    like straw before the wind.
14  As fire burns a forest,
    as a flame blazes
      through mountains,
15  so pursue them
      with Your tempest

    and terrify them
      with Your storm.
16  Cover their faces with shame
    so that they will seek
      Your name, LORD.
17  Let them be put to shame
      and terrified forever;
    let them perish in disgrace.
18  May they know that You
      alone—
    whose name is *Yahweh—
    are the *Most High over all
      the earth.

## Longing for God's House

*For the choir director:
on the *Gittith. A psalm of the sons
of Korah.*

**84** How lovely is
      Your dwelling place,
    LORD of *Hosts.
2   My soul longs, even
      languishes,
    for the courts of the LORD;
    my heart and flesh cry out
      for the living God.

3   Even a sparrow finds a home,
    and a swallow, a nest
      for herself
    where she places her young—
    near Your altars, LORD
      of Hosts,
    my King and my God.
4   How happy are those
      who reside in Your house,
    who praise You continually.
                              *Selah

5   Happy are the people
      whose strength is in You,
    whose hearts are set
      on pilgrimage.
6   As they pass
      through the Valley of Baca,

they make it a source
of springwater;
even the autumn rain
will cover it
with blessings.
7 They go from strength
to strength;
each appears before God
in Zion.

8 LORD God of Hosts, hear
my prayer;
listen, God of Jacob.      *Selah*
9 Consider our shield, God;
look on the face
of Your anointed one.

10 Better a day in Your courts
than a thousand
[anywhere else].
I would rather be at the door
of the house of my God
than to live in the tents
of the wicked.
11 For the LORD God is a sun
and shield.
The LORD gives
grace and glory;
He does not withhold the good
from those who live
with integrity.
12 LORD of Hosts,
happy is the person who trusts
in You!

## Restoration of Favor

*For the choir director. A psalm
of the sons of Korah.*

**85** LORD, You showed favor
to Your land;
You restored Jacob's prosperity.
2 You took away
Your people's guilt;
You covered all their sin.
                                    •*Selah*
3 You withdrew all Your fury;

You turned from Your
burning anger.

4 Return to us, God
of our salvation,
and abandon Your displeasure
with us.
5 Will You be angry with us
forever?
Will You prolong Your anger
for all generations?
6 Will You not revive us again
so that Your people
may rejoice in You?
7 Show us Your faithful love,
LORD,
and give us Your salvation.

8 I will listen to what God
will say;
surely the LORD will declare
peace to His people,
His godly ones,
and not let them go back
to foolish ways.
9 His salvation is very near those
who fear Him,
so that glory may dwell
in our land.

10 Faithful love
and truth will join
together;
righteousness and peace
will embrace.
11 Truth will spring up
from the earth,
and righteousness will look
down from heaven.
12 Also, the LORD will provide
what is good,
and our land will yield
its crops.
13 Righteousness will go
before Him
to prepare the way
for His steps.

## Lament and Petition

*A Davidic prayer.*

**86** Listen, LORD, and answer me,
for I am poor and needy.
² Protect my life, for I am faithful.
You are my God; save
Your servant who trusts in You.
³ Be gracious to me, Lord,
for I call to You all day long.
⁴ Bring joy
to Your servant's life,
since I set my hope on You, Lord.

⁵ For You, Lord, are kind
and ready to forgive,
abundant in faithful love to all
who call on You.
⁶ LORD, hear my prayer;
listen to my plea for mercy.
⁷ I call on You in the day
of my distress,
for You will answer me.

⁸ Lord, there is no one like You
among the gods,
and there are no works
like Yours.
⁹ All the nations You have made
will come and bow down
before You, Lord,
and will honor Your name.
¹⁰ For You are great and perform wonders;
You alone are God.

¹¹ Teach me Your way, LORD,
and I will live by Your truth.
Give me an undivided mind
to fear Your name.
¹² I will praise You with all
my heart, Lord my God,

and will honor Your name forever.
¹³ For Your faithful love for me is great,
and You deliver my life
from the depths of •Sheol.

¹⁴ God, arrogant people
have attacked me;
a gang of ruthless men seeks my life.
They have no regard for You.
¹⁵ But You, Lord, are
a compassionate
and gracious God,
slow to anger and abundant
in faithful love and truth.
¹⁶ Turn to me and be gracious to me.
Give Your strength
to Your servant;
save the son
of Your female servant.
¹⁷ Show me a sign
of Your goodness;
my enemies will see
and be put to shame
because You, LORD, have helped
and comforted me.

## Zion, the City of God

*A psalm of the sons
of Korah. A song.*

**87** His foundation is
on the holy mountains.
² The LORD loves the gates of Zion
more than all the dwellings of Jacob.
³ Glorious things are said
about you,
city of God. •Selah

⁴ "I will mention those
who know Me:

Rahab, Babylon, Philistia, Tyre,
and Cush—
each one was born there."
5 And it will be said of Zion,
"This one and that one
were born in her."
The •Most High Himself
will establish her.
6 When He registers
the peoples, the LORD
will record,
"This one was born there."
*Selah*
7 Singers and dancers alike
⌊will say⌋,
"All my springs are in you."

### A Cry of Desperation

*A song. A psalm of the sons
of Korah. For the choir director:
according to* Mahalath
Leannoth. *A* •Maskil *of Heman
the Ezrahite.*

**88** O LORD, God of my salvation,
I cry out before You day
and night.
2 May my prayer reach
Your presence;
listen to my cry.

3 For I have had enough
troubles,
and my life is near •Sheol.
4 I am counted among those
going down to the •Pit.
I am like a man
without strength,
5 abandoned among the dead.
I am like the slain lying
in the grave,
whom You no longer
remember,
and who are cut off
from Your care.

6 You have put me
in the lowest part
of the Pit,
in the darkest places,
in the depths.
7 Your wrath weighs heavily
on me;
You have overwhelmed me
with all Your waves.
•*Selah*
8 You have distanced my friends
from me;
You have made me repulsive
to them.
I am shut in and cannot
go out.
9 My eyes are worn out
from crying.
LORD, I cry out to You all day
long;
I spread out my hands to You.

10 Do You work wonders
for the dead?
Do departed spirits rise up
to praise You? *Selah*
11 Will Your faithful love
be declared in the grave,
Your faithfulness
in •Abaddon?
12 Will Your wonders be known
in the darkness,
or Your righteousness
in the land of oblivion?

13 But I call to You for help, LORD;
in the morning my prayer
meets You.
14 LORD, why do You reject me?
Why do You hide Your face
from me?
15 From my youth, I have been
afflicted and near death.
I suffer Your horrors;
I am desperate.
16 Your wrath sweeps over me;
Your terrors destroy me.
17 They surround me like water
all day long;

they close in on me
    from every side.
18 You have distanced loved one
    and neighbor from me;
    darkness is my ⌊only⌋ friend.


## Perplexity about God's Promises

A •Maskil *of Ethan the Ezrahite.*

**89** I will sing about the LORD's
    faithful love forever;
    with my mouth I will proclaim
    Your faithfulness
    to all generations.
2 For I will declare,
    "Faithful love is built up
    forever;
    You establish Your faithfulness
    in the heavens."

3 ⌊The LORD said,⌋ "I have made
    a covenant
    with My chosen one;
    I have sworn an oath to David
    My servant:
4 'I will establish your offspring
    forever
    and build up your throne
    for all generations.' "
                              •*Selah*

5 LORD, the heavens praise
    Your wonders—
    Your faithfulness also—
    in the assembly
    of the holy ones.
6 For who in the skies
    can compare
    with the LORD?
    Who among the heavenly
    beings is like the LORD?
7 God is greatly feared
    in the council
    of the holy ones,
    more awe-inspiring than all
    who surround Him.
8 O LORD God of •Hosts,

who is strong like You, LORD?
    Your faithfulness surrounds
    You.
9 You rule the raging sea;
    when its waves surge,
    You still them.
10 You crushed Rahab like one
    who is slain;
    You scattered Your enemies
    with Your powerful arm.
11 The heavens are Yours;
    the earth also is Yours.
    The world and everything
    in it—You founded them.
12 North and south—
    You created them.
    Tabor and Hermon shout
    for joy at Your name.
13 You have a mighty arm;
    Your hand is powerful;
    Your right hand is lifted
    high.
14 Righteousness and justice are
    the foundation
    of Your throne;
    faithful love and truth go
    before You.
15 Happy are the people
    who know the joyful shout;
    LORD, they walk in the light
    of Your presence.
16 They rejoice in Your name all
    day long,
    and they are exalted
    by Your righteousness.
17 For You are
    their magnificent strength;
    by Your favor our •horn
    is exalted.
18 Surely our shield belongs to
    the LORD,
    our king to the Holy One
    of Israel.

19 You once spoke in a vision
    to Your loyal ones and said:
    "I have granted help
    to a warrior;

I have exalted one
  chosen from the people.
20 I have found David
    My servant;
  I have anointed him with
    My sacred oil.
21 My hand will always be
    · with him,
  and My arm will strengthen
    him.
22 The enemy will not afflict him;
  no wicked man will oppress
    him.
23 I will crush his foes before him
  and strike those who hate him.
24 My faithfulness and love
    will be with him,
  and through My name
    his horn will be exalted.
25 I will extend his power
    to the sea
  and his right hand
    to the rivers.
26 He will call to Me, 'You are
    my Father,
  my God, the rock
    of my salvation.'
27 I will also make him
    My firstborn,

---

### Psalm 89:26-29

### God the Father

*King David was a picture of the
King to come, the One who would
reign "as long as heaven lasts."
That's why when you read this passage, you should not only see
David but the One who would be
born in the city of David—the Savior, Christ the Lord: The eternal
gift of the Father.*

---

greatest of the kings
    of the earth.
28 I will always preserve
    My faithful love for him,
  and My covenant with him
    will endure.
29 I will establish his line forever,
  his throne as long as heaven
    lasts.
30 If his sons forsake
    My instruction
  and do not live
    by My ordinances,
31 if they dishonor My statutes
  and do not keep
    My commandments,
32 then I will call their rebellion
    to account with the rod,
  their sin with blows.
33 But I will not withdraw
    My faithful love from him
  or betray My faithfulness.
34 I will not violate My covenant
  or change what My lips
    have said.
35 Once and for all I have sworn
    an oath by My holiness;
  I will not lie to David.
36 His offspring will continue
    forever,
  his throne like the sun
    before Me,
37 like the moon, established
    forever,
  a faithful witness in the sky."
                              *Selah*

38 But You have spurned
    and rejected him;
  You have become enraged
    with Your anointed.
39 You have repudiated
    the covenant
    with Your servant;
  You have completely
    dishonored his crown.
40 You have broken down all
    his walls;

You have reduced
his fortified cities to ruins.

41 All who pass by plunder him;
he has become a joke
to his neighbors.

42 You have lifted high
the right hand of his foes;
You have made all his enemies
rejoice.

43 You have also turned back
his sharp sword
and have not let him stand
in battle.

44 You have made his splendor
cease
and have overturned
his throne.

45 You have shortened the days
of his youth;
You have covered him
with shame.                    *Selah*

46 How long, LORD?
Will You hide Yourself
forever?
Will Your anger keep burning
like fire?

47 Remember how short my
life is.
Have You created •everyone
for nothing?

48 What man can live and never
see death?
Who can save himself
from the power of •Sheol?
                                        *Selah*

49 Lord, where are
the former acts
of Your faithful love
that You swore to David
in Your faithfulness?

50 Remember, Lord, the ridicule
against Your servants—
in my heart I carry ⌊abuse⌋
from all the peoples—

51 how Your enemies
have ridiculed, LORD,
how they have ridiculed
every step of Your anointed.

52 May the LORD be praised
forever.
Amen and amen.

# BOOK IV
## (PSALMS 90–106)

*Eternal God and Mortal Man*

*A prayer of Moses the man of God.*

**90** Lord, You have been
our refuge[a]
in every generation.
2   Before the mountains
were born,
before You gave birth
to the earth and the world,[b]
from eternity to eternity, You
are God.

3   You return mankind
to the dust,
saying, "Return, descendants
of Adam."
4   For in Your sight
a thousand years
are like yesterday that
passes by,
like a few hours of the night.
5   You end their life; they sleep.
They are like grass that grows
in the morning—
6   in the morning it sprouts
and grows;
by evening it withers
and dries up.

7   For we are consumed
by Your anger;

[a]90:1 A few Hb mss, LXX; MT reads *dwelling place*   [b]90:2 LXX, Aq, Sym, Jer, Tg read *before the earth and the world were brought forth*

we are terrified by Your wrath.

8 You have set our unjust ways
   before You,
our secret sins in the light
   of Your presence.

9 For all our days ebb away
   under Your wrath;
we end our years like a sigh.

10 Our lives last 70 years
   or, if we are strong,
   80 years.
Even the best of them are[a] toil
   and sorrow;
indeed, they pass quickly
   and we fly away.

11 Who understands the power
   of Your anger?
Your wrath matches the fear
   that is due You.

12 Teach us to number our days
   carefully
so that we may develop
   wisdom in our hearts.

13 LORD—how long?
Turn and have compassion
   on Your servants.

14 Satisfy us in the morning
   with Your faithful love
so that we may shout with joy
   and be glad all our days.

15 Make us rejoice for as many
   days as You have
   humbled us,
for as many years as
   we have seen adversity.

16 Let Your work be seen
   by Your servants,
and Your splendor
   by their children.

17 Let the favor of the Lord
   our God be upon us;
establish for us the work
   of our hands—
establish the work
   of our hands!

## The Protection of the Most High

91 The one who lives
   under the protection
   of the •Most High
dwells in the shadow
   of the Almighty.

2 I will say[b] to the LORD,
   "My refuge
   and my fortress,
my God, in whom I trust."

3 He Himself will deliver you
   from the hunter's net,
from the destructive
   plague.

4 He will cover you
   with His feathers;
you will take refuge
   under His wings.
His faithfulness will be
   a protective shield.

5 You will not fear the terror
   of the night,
the arrow that flies by day,

6 the plague that stalks
   in darkness,
or the pestilence that ravages
   at noon.

7 Though a thousand fall
   at your side
and ten thousand
   at your right hand,
the pestilence will not reach
   you.

8 You will only see it
   with your eyes
and witness the punishment
   of the wicked.

9 Because you have made
   the LORD—my refuge,
the Most High—
   your dwelling place,

10 no harm will come to you;

---

[a] 90:10 LXX, Tg, Syr, Vg read *Even their breadth is*; Hb uncertain   [b] 91:1–2 LXX, Syr, Jer read *Almighty, saying*, or *Almighty, he will say*

no plague will come near
    your tent.
11 For He will give His angels
    orders concerning you,
to protect you in all your ways.
12 They will support you
    with their hands
so that you will not strike
    your foot against a stone.
13 You will tread on the lion
    and the cobra;
you will trample
    the young lion
    and the serpent.

14 Because he is lovingly devoted
    to Me, I will deliver him;
I will exalt him because
    he knows My name.
15 When he calls out to Me, I will
    answer him;
I will be with him in trouble.
I will rescue him and give him
    honor.
16 I will satisfy him
    with a long life
and show him My salvation.

## God's Love and Faithfulness

*A psalm. A song for the Sabbath day.*

**92** It is good to praise the LORD,
to sing praise to Your name,
    •Most High,
2 to declare Your faithful love
    in the morning
and Your faithfulness at night,
3 with a ten-stringed harp
and the music of a lyre.

4 For You have made me rejoice,
    LORD, by what
    You have done;
I will shout for joy because of
    the works of Your hands.
5 How magnificent are
    Your works, LORD,

how profound Your thoughts!
6 A stupid person does not
    know,
a fool does not understand
    this:
7 though the wicked sprout
    like grass
and all evildoers flourish,
they will be eternally
    destroyed.
8 But You, LORD, are exalted
    forever.
9 For indeed, LORD,
    Your enemies—
indeed, Your enemies
    will perish;
all evildoers will be scattered.
10 You have lifted up
    my •horn like that
    of a wild ox;
I have been anointed with oil.
11 My eyes look down on
    my enemies;
my ears hear evildoers
    when they attack me.

12 The righteous thrive
    like a palm tree
and grow like a cedar tree
    in Lebanon.
13 Planted in the house
    of the LORD,
they thrive in the courtyards
    of our God.
14 They will still bear fruit
    in old age,
healthy and green,
15 to declare: "The LORD is just;
He is my rock, and there is no
    unrighteousness in Him."

## God's Eternal Reign

**93** The LORD reigns! He is robed
    in majesty;
The LORD is robed, enveloped
    in strength.

The world is firmly
    established; it cannot
    be shaken.
2 Your throne has been
    established
    from the beginning;
You are from eternity.
3 The floods have lifted up,
    LORD,
    the floods have lifted up
        their voice;
    the floods lift up
        their pounding waves.
4 Greater than the roar
    of many waters—
    the mighty breakers
    of the sea—
    the LORD on high is majestic.

5 LORD, Your testimonies are
    completely reliable;
    holiness is the beauty
    of Your house
    for all the days to come.

### The Just Judge

**94** LORD, God of vengeance—
    God of vengeance, appear.
2 Rise up, Judge of the earth;
    repay the proud what
        they deserve.
3 LORD, how long will
        the wicked—
    how long will
        the wicked gloat?

4 They pour out arrogant words;
    all the evildoers boast.
5 LORD, they crush Your people;
    they afflict Your heritage.
6 They kill the widow
        and the foreigner
    and murder the fatherless.
7 They say, "The LORD
        doesn't see it.
    The God of Jacob doesn't pay
        attention."

8 Pay attention, you
        stupid people!
    Fools, when will you be
        wise?
9 Can the One who shaped
        the ear not hear,
    the One who formed the eye
        not see?
10 The One who instructs
        nations,
    the One who teaches man
        knowledge—
    does He not discipline?
11 The LORD knows
        man's thoughts;
    they are meaningless.

12 LORD, happy is the man
        You discipline
    and teach from Your law
13 to give him relief
        from troubled times
    until a pit is dug
        for the wicked.
14 The LORD will not forsake
        His people
    or abandon His heritage,
15 for justice will again be
        righteous,
    and all the upright in heart
        will follow it.

---

### Psalm 94:12-15

*If you want to receive the blessings
of God's continual presence, you'll
also have to accept His right to
offer correction and rebuke. It's for
your own good. Honest. God will
clip the wings on your freedom at
times in order to help you learn
what true freedom is.*

> *"Until we accept the fact that our Father is willing to discipline us, we'll never be able to comprehend what He's doing in our lives."*
> —James Lucas

16 Who stands up for me against
     the wicked?
   Who takes a stand for me
     against evildoers?
17 If the LORD had not been
     my help,
   I would soon rest
     in the silence
     ⌊of death⌋.
18 If I say, "My foot is slipping,"
   Your faithful love will support
     me, LORD.
19 When I am filled with cares,
   Your comfort brings me joy.

20 Can a corrupt throne—
   one that creates trouble
     by law—
   become Your ally?
21 They band together against
     the life of the righteous
   and condemn the innocent
     to death.
22 But the LORD is my refuge;
   my God is the rock
     of my protection.
23 He will pay them back
     for their sins
   and destroy them
     for their evil.
   The LORD our God will destroy
     them.

## Worship and Warning

**95** Come, let us shout joyfully
      to the LORD,

shout triumphantly to the rock
     of our salvation!
2 Let us enter His presence
     with thanksgiving;
   let us shout triumphantly
     to Him in song.

3 For the LORD is a great God,
   a great King above all gods.
4 The depths of the earth are
     in His hand,
   and the mountain peaks are
     His.
5 The sea is His; He made it.
   His hands formed
     the dry land.

6 Come, let us worship and bow
     down;
   let us kneel before the LORD
     our Maker.
7 For He is our God,
   and we are the people
     of His pasture, the sheep
     under His care.

   Today, if you hear His voice:
8 "Do not harden your hearts
     as at Meribah,
   as on that day at Massah
     in the wilderness
9 where your fathers
     tested Me;
   they tried Me, though
     they had seen what I did.
10 For 40 years I was disgusted
     with that generation;
   I said, 'They are a people
     whose hearts go astray;
   they do not know My ways.'
11 So I swore in My anger,
   'They will not enter
     My rest.' "

## King of the Earth

**96** Sing a new song to the LORD;
      sing to the LORD, all the earth.

2 Sing to the LORD, praise
      His name;
    proclaim His
      salvation from day to day.
3 Declare His glory among
      the nations,
    His wonderful works among all
      peoples.

4 For the LORD is great and is
      highly praised;
    He is feared above all gods.
5 For all the gods of the peoples
      are idols,
    but the LORD made
      the heavens.
6 Splendor and majesty are
      before Him;
    strength and beauty are
      in His sanctuary.

7 Ascribe to the LORD, families
      of the peoples,
    ascribe to the LORD glory
      and strength.
8 Ascribe to the LORD the glory
      of His name;
    bring an offering and enter
      His courts.
9 Worship the LORD
      in His holy majesty;
    tremble before Him, all
      the earth.

10 Say among the nations:
      "The LORD reigns.
    The world is firmly
      established; it cannot
      be shaken.
    He judges the peoples fairly."
11 Let the heavens be glad
      and the earth rejoice;
    let the sea and all that fills it
      resound.
12 Let the fields and everything
      in them exult.

Then all the trees of the forest
      will shout for joy
13 before the LORD,
      for He is coming—
    for He is coming to judge
      the earth.
    He will judge the world
      with righteousness
    and the peoples
      with His faithfulness.

## The Majestic King

**97** The LORD reigns! Let
      the earth rejoice;
    let the many islands be glad.

2 Clouds and thick darkness
      surround Him;
    righteousness and justice are
      the foundation
      of His throne.
3 Fire goes before Him
    and burns up His foes
      on every side.
4 His lightning lights up
      the world;
    the earth sees and trembles.
5 The mountains melt like wax
      at the presence
      of the LORD—
    at the presence of the Lord
      of all the earth.

6 The heavens proclaim
      His righteousness;
    all the peoples see His glory.

7 All who serve carved images,
    those who boast in idols,
      will be put to shame.
    All the gods[a] will
      worship Him.

8 Zion hears and is glad,
    and the towns of Judah rejoice

---

[a] **97:7** LXX, Syr read *All His angels;* Heb 1:6

because of
Your judgments, LORD.
9 For You, LORD, are
the •Most High over all
the earth;
You are exalted above all
the gods.

10 You who love the LORD,
hate evil!
He protects the lives
of His godly ones;
He rescues them
from the hand
of the wicked.
11 Light dawns^a for the righteous,
gladness for the upright
in heart.
12 Be glad in the LORD,
you righteous ones,
and praise His holy name.

## Praise the King

*A psalm.*

**98** Sing a new song
to the LORD,
for He has performed wonders;
His right hand and holy arm
have won Him victory.
2 The LORD has made His victory
known;
He has revealed
His righteousness
in the sight of the nations.
3 He has remembered His love
and faithfulness
to the house of Israel;
all the ends of the earth
have seen
our God's victory.

4 Shout to the LORD, all
the earth;
be jubilant, shout for joy,
and sing.

5 Sing to the LORD with the lyre,
with the lyre and melodious
song.
6 With trumpets and the blast
of the ram's horn
shout triumphantly
in the presence
of the LORD, our King.

7 Let the sea and all that fills it,
the world and those who live
in it, resound.
8 Let the rivers clap their hands;
let the mountains shout
together for joy
9 before the LORD,
for He is coming to judge
the earth.
He will judge the world
righteously
and the peoples fairly.

## The King Is Holy

**99** The LORD reigns! Let
the peoples tremble.
He is enthroned
above the cherubim.
Let the earth quake.
2 The LORD is great in Zion;
He is exalted above all
the peoples.
3 Let them praise Your great
and awe-inspiring name.
He is holy.

4 The mighty King loves justice.
You have established fairness;
You have administered justice
and righteousness in Jacob.
5 Exalt the LORD our God;
bow in worship
at His footstool.
He is holy.

6 Moses and Aaron were
among His priests;

^a 97:11 One Hb ms, LXX, other versions read *rises to shine*

Samuel also was among
    those calling on His name.
They called to the LORD,
    and He answered them.
7 He spoke to them in a pillar
    of cloud;
they kept His decrees
    and the statutes He gave
    them.
8 O LORD our God,
    You answered them.
You were a God who forgave
    them,
but punished their misdeeds.

9 Exalt the LORD our God;
bow in worship
    at His holy mountain,
for the LORD our God is holy.

## Be Thankful
*A psalm of thanksgiving.*

**100** Shout triumphantly
    to the LORD, all the earth.
2 Serve the LORD with gladness;
come before Him
    with joyful songs.
3 Acknowledge that the LORD
    is God.
He made us,
    and we are His[a]—
His people, the sheep
    of His pasture.
4 Enter His gates
    with thanksgiving
and His courts with praise.
Give thanks to Him and praise
    His name.
5 For the LORD is good,
    and His love is eternal;
His faithfulness endures
    through all generations.

---

### Psalm 101:1-4

*You're probably not going to like this. And granted, it's an easy target to pick on. But the things that entertain you shouldn't be the things Christ died for. What goes for family viewing these days can become one of a Christian's prime-time problems.*

---

## A Vow of Integrity

*A Davidic psalm.*

**101** I will Sing of faithful love
    and justice;
I will sing praise to You, LORD.
2 I will pay attention to the way
    of integrity.
When will You come to me?
I will live with integrity
    of heart in my house.
3 I will not set anything godless
    before my eyes.
I hate the doing
    of transgression;
it will not cling to me.
4 A devious heart will be far
    from me;
I will not be involved
    with evil.

---

*"We cannot afford the luxury of entertaining ourselves with sin if we want to maintain our moral purity."*
—*Bill and Kathy Peel*

---

a **100:3** Alt Hb tradition, other Hb mss, LXX, Syr, Vg read *and not we ourselves*

475

5 I will destroy anyone
who secretly slanders
his neighbor;
I cannot tolerate anyone
with haughty eyes
or an arrogant heart.
6 My eyes ⌊favor⌋ the faithful
of the land
so that they may sit down
with me.
The one who follows the way
of integrity may serve me.
7 No one who acts deceitfully
will live in my palace;
no one who tells
lies will remain in
my presence.
8 Every morning I will destroy
all the wicked of the land,
eliminating all evildoers
from the LORD's city.

### Affliction in Light of Eternity

*A prayer of an afflicted person
who is weak and pours out
his lament before the LORD.*

**102** LORD, hear my prayer;
let my cry for help come
before You.
2 Do not hide Your face from me
in my day of trouble.
Listen closely to me;
answer me quickly
when I call.

3 For my days vanish
like smoke,
and my bones burn
like a furnace.
4 My heart is afflicted, withered
like grass;
I even forget to eat my food.
5 Because of the sound
of my groaning,
my flesh sticks to
my bones.

6 I am like a desert owl,
like an owl among the ruins.
7 I stay awake;
I am like a solitary bird
on a roof.
8 My enemies taunt me all day
long;
they ridicule and curse me.
9 I eat ashes like bread
and mingle my drinks
with tears
10 because of Your indignation
and wrath;
for You have picked me up
and thrown me aside.
11 My days are like
a lengthening shadow,
and I wither away like grass.

12 But You, LORD, are enthroned
forever;
Your fame ⌊endures⌋ to all
generations.
13 You will arise and have
compassion on Zion,
for it is time to show favor
to her—
the appointed time has come.
14 For Your servants take delight
in its stones
and favor its dust.

15 Then the nations will fear
the name of the LORD,
and all the kings of the earth
Your glory,
16 for the LORD will rebuild Zion;
He will appear in His glory.
17 He will pay attention
to the prayer
of the destitute
and will not despise
their prayer.

18 This will be written for a later
generation,
and a newly created people
will praise the LORD:

19 He looked down from
      His holy heights—
   the LORD gazed out
      from heaven to earth—
20 to hear a prisoner's groaning,
      to set free those condemned
      to die,
21 so that they might declare
      the name of the LORD
      in Zion
   and His praise in Jerusalem,
22 when peoples and kingdoms
      are assembled
   to serve the LORD.

23 He has broken my[a] strength
      in midcourse;
   He has shortened my days.
24 I say: "My God, do not take
      me in the middle of my life!
   Your years continue through
      all generations.
25 Long ago You established
      the earth,
   and the heavens are the work
      of Your hands.
26 They will perish, but You
      will endure;
   all of them will wear out
      like clothing.
   You will change them
      like a garment, and they
      will pass away.
27 But You are the same,
   and Your years will never end.
28 Your servants' children
      will dwell ⌊securely⌋,
   and their offspring will be
      established before You."

## The Forgiving God
*Davidic.*

**103** My soul, praise the LORD,
      and all that is within me,
      praise His holy name.

---

*Psalm 103:11-14*

*Before you start a new job, you
need to know who the boss is—
not just who He is, but what He's
like, what He's looking for, and
how you can expect to be treated.
God goes by many names that
describe His nature and character.
But you can just call Him . . .
Father.*

---

2 My soul, praise the LORD,
   and do not forget all
      His benefits.

3 He forgives all your sin;
   He heals all your diseases.
4 He redeems your life
      from the •Pit;
   He crowns you
      with faithful love
      and compassion.
5 He satisfies
      you with goodness;
   your youth is renewed
      like the eagle.

6 The LORD executes acts
      of righteousness
   and justice for all
      the oppressed.
7 He revealed His ways
      to Moses,
   His deeds to the people
      of Israel.
8 The LORD is compassionate
      and gracious,
   slow to anger and full
      of faithful love.
9 He will not always accuse ⌊us⌋
   or be angry forever.

---

a 102:23 Other Hb mss, LXX read *His*

10 He has not dealt with us as
our sins deserve
or repaid us according to
our offenses.

11 For as high as the heavens
are above the earth,
so great is His faithful love
toward those who fear Him.
12 As far as the east is
from the west,
so far has He removed
our transgressions from us.
13 As a father has compassion
on his children,
so the LORD has compassion
on those who fear Him.
14 For He knows what we are
made of,
remembering
that we are dust.

15 As for man, his days are
like grass—
he blooms like a flower
of the field;
16 when the wind passes over it,
it vanishes,
and its place is no longer
known.
17 But from eternity to eternity
the LORD's faithful love is
toward those who fear Him,
and His righteousness toward
the grandchildren
18 of those who keep
His covenant,

"God will go out of His way to
make His children feel His love for
them and know their privilege and
security as members of His family."
—J. I. Packer

who remember to observe
His instructions.
19 The LORD has established
His throne in heaven,
and His kingdom rules over all.

20 Praise the LORD, ⌊all⌋
His angels of great strength,
who do His word,
obedient to His command.
21 Praise the LORD, all
His armies,
His servants who do His will.
22 Praise the LORD, all His works
in all the places
where He rules.
My soul, praise the LORD!

### God the Creator

**104** My soul, praise the LORD!
LORD my God, You are
very great;
You are clothed with majesty
and splendor.
2 He wraps Himself in light as if
it were a robe,
spreading out the sky
like a canopy,
3 laying the beams of His palace
on the waters ⌊above⌋,
making the clouds His chariot,
walking on the wings
of the wind,
4 and making the winds
His messengers,
flames of fire His servants.

5 He established the earth
on its foundations;
it will never be shaken.
6 You covered it with the deep
as if it were a garment;
the waters stood
above the mountains.
7 At Your rebuke the waters
fled;

at the sound of Your thunder
   they hurried away—
8 mountains rose and valleys
   sank—
to the place You established
   for them.
9 You set a boundary
   they cannot cross;
they will never cover the earth
   again.

10 He causes the springs to gush
   into the valleys;
they flow
   between the mountains.
11 They supply water
   for every wild beast;
the wild donkeys quench
   their thirst.
12 The birds of the sky live beside
   ⌊the springs⌋;
they sing among the foliage.
13 He waters the mountains
   from His palace;
the earth is satisfied
   by the fruit of Your labor.

14 He causes grass to grow
   for the livestock
and ⌊provides⌋ crops for man
   to cultivate,
producing food from the earth,
15 wine that makes man's heart
   glad—
making his face shine
   with oil—
and bread that sustains
   man's heart.

16 The trees of the LORD
   flourish,
the cedars of Lebanon
   that He planted.
17 There the birds make
   their nests;
the stork makes its home
   in the pine trees.

18 The high mountains are
   for the wild goats;
the cliffs are a refuge
   for hyraxes.

19 He made the moon to mark
   the seasons;
the sun knows when to set.
20 You bring darkness,
   and it becomes night,
when all the forest animals
   stir.
21 The young lions roar
   for their prey
and seek their food from God.
22 The sun rises; they go back
and lie down in their dens.
23 Man goes out to his work
and to his labor until
   evening.

24 How countless are Your works,
   LORD!
In wisdom You have made
   them all;
the earth is full of
   Your creatures.
25 Here is the sea, vast
   and wide,
teeming with creatures
   beyond number—
living things both large
   and small.
26 There the ships move about,
and Leviathan, which
   You formed to play there.

27 All of them wait for You
to give them their food
   at the right time.
28 When You give it to them,
   they gather it;
when You open Your hand,
   they are satisfied
   with good things.
29 When You hide Your face,
   they are terrified;

when You take away
   their breath, they die
   and return to the dust.
30 When You send
   Your breath, they are created,
   and You renew the face
   of the earth.

31 May the glory of the LORD
   endure forever;
   may the LORD rejoice
   in His works.
32 He looks at the earth,
   and it trembles;
   He touches the mountains,
   and they pour out smoke.
33 I will sing to the LORD all
   my life;
   I will sing praise to my God
   while I live.
34 May my meditation
   be pleasing to Him;
   I will rejoice in the LORD.
35 May sinners vanish
   from the earth
   and the wicked be no more.
   My soul, praise the LORD!
   *Hallelujah!

### God's Faithfulness to His People

**105** Give thanks to the LORD,
   call on His name;
   proclaim His deeds among
   the peoples.
2 Sing to Him, sing praise
   to Him;
   tell about all
   His wonderful works!
3 Honor His holy name;
   let the hearts of those
   who seek the LORD rejoice.
4 Search for the LORD and for
   His strength;
   seek His face always.
5 Remember
   the wonderful works
   He has done,

His wonders,
   and the judgments
   He has pronounced,
6 O offspring of Abraham
   His servant,
   O descendants of Jacob—
   His chosen ones.

7 He is the LORD our God;
   His judgments ⌊govern⌋
   the whole earth.
8 He forever remembers
   His covenant,
   the promise He ordained
   for a thousand
   generations—
9 ⌊the covenant⌋ He made
   with Abraham,
   swore to Isaac,
10 and confirmed to Jacob
   as a decree
   and to Israel
   as an everlasting covenant:
11 "To you I will give the land
   of Canaan
   as your inherited portion."

12 When they were few
   in number,
   very few indeed,
   and temporary residents
   in Canaan,
13 wandering from nation
   to nation,
   from one kingdom to another,
14 He allowed no one to oppress
   them;
   He rebuked kings
   on their behalf:
15 "Do not touch
   My anointed ones,
   or harm My prophets."

16 He called down famine against
   the land
   and destroyed
   the entire food supply.

17 He had sent a man ahead
of them—
Joseph, who was sold
as a slave.
18 They hurt his feet
with shackles;
his neck was put in
an iron collar.
19 Until the time his prediction
came true,
the word of the LORD tested
him.
20 The king sent ⌊for him⌋
and released him;
the ruler of peoples set him
free.
21 He made him master
of his household,
ruler over all his possessions—
22 binding[a] his officials at will
and instructing his elders.

23 Then Israel went to Egypt;
Jacob lived as a foreigner
in the land of Ham.
24 The LORD made His people
very fruitful;
He made them more
numerous than their foes,
25 whose hearts He turned
to hate His people
and to deal deceptively
with His servants.
26 He sent Moses His servant,
and Aaron,
whom He had chosen.
27 They performed
His miraculous signs
among them,
and wonders in the land
of Ham.
28 He sent darkness,
and it became dark—
for did they not defy
His commands?

29 He turned their waters
into blood
and caused their fish to die.
30 Their land was overrun
with frogs,
even in their kings' chambers.
31 He spoke, and insects came—
gnats throughout
their country.
32 He gave them hail for rain,
and lightning throughout
their land.
33 He struck their vines
and fig trees
and shattered the trees
of their territory.
34 He spoke and locusts came—
young locusts without number.
35 They devoured all
the vegetation in their land
and consumed the produce
of their soil.
36 He struck all the firstborn
in their land,
all their first progeny.

37 Then He brought Israel out
with silver and gold,
and no one among His tribes
stumbled.
38 Egypt was glad when they left,
for dread of Israel had fallen
on them.
39 He spread a cloud
as a covering
and ⌊gave⌋ a fire to light up
the night.
40 They asked, and He brought
quail
and satisfied them with bread
from heaven.
41 He opened a rock, and water
gushed out;
it flowed like a stream
in the desert.

a 105:22 LXX, Syr, Vg read *teaching*

42 For He remembered
His holy promise
to Abraham His servant.
43 He brought His people out
with rejoicing,
His chosen ones with shouts
of joy.
44 He gave them the lands
of the nations,
and they inherited what
other peoples had
worked for.

45 ⌊All this happened⌋ so that
they might keep
His statutes
and obey His laws.
•Hallelujah!

## Israel's Unfaithfulness to God

**106** •Hallelujah!
Give thanks to the LORD,
for He is good;
His faithful love endures
forever.
2 Who can declare the LORD's
mighty acts
or proclaim all the praise due
Him?
3 How happy are those
who uphold justice,
who practice righteousness
at all times.

4 Remember me, LORD,
when You show favor
to Your people.
Come to me
with Your salvation
5 so that I may enjoy
the prosperity
of Your chosen ones,
rejoice in the joy
of Your nation,
and boast about Your heritage.

6 Both we and our fathers
have sinned;
we have gone astray
and have acted wickedly.
7 Our fathers in Egypt did not
grasp ⌊the significance of⌋
Your wonderful works
or remember Your many acts
of faithful love;
instead, they rebelled
by the sea—the •Red Sea.
8 Yet He saved them
for His name's sake,
to make His power known.
9 He rebuked the Red Sea,
and it dried up;
He led them through
the depths as through
a desert.
10 He saved them from the hand
of the adversary;
He redeemed them
from the hand
of the enemy.
11 Water covered their foes;
not one of them remained.
12 Then they believed
His promises
and sang His praise.

13 They soon forgot His works
and would not wait
for His counsel.
14 They were seized with craving
in the desert
and tested God
in the wilderness.
15 He gave them what
they asked for,
but sent a wasting disease
among them.

16 In the camp they were envious
of Moses
and of Aaron,
the LORD's holy one.
17 The earth opened up
and swallowed Dathan;

it covered the assembly
of Abiram.

18 Fire blazed throughout
their assembly;
flames consumed the wicked.

19 At Horeb they made a calf
and worshiped
the cast metal image.

20 They exchanged their glory
for the image
of a grass-eating ox.

21 They forgot God their Savior,
who did great things in Egypt,

22 wonderful works in the land
of Ham,
awe-inspiring deeds
at the Red Sea.

23 So He said He would have
destroyed them—
if Moses His chosen one
had not
stood before Him
in the breach
to turn His wrath away
from destroying ⌊them⌋.

24 They despised
the pleasant land
and did not believe
His promise.

25 They grumbled in their tents
and did not listen
to the LORD's voice.

26 So He raised His hand
against them ⌊with an oath⌋
that He would make them fall
in the desert

27 and would disperse
their descendants
among the nations,
scattering them
throughout the lands.

28 They aligned themselves
with Baal of Peor

and ate sacrifices offered
to lifeless gods.

29 They provoked the LORD
with their deeds,
and a plague broke out
against them.

30 But Phinehas stood up
and intervened,
and the plague was stopped.

31 It was credited to him
as righteousness
throughout all generations
to come.

32 They angered ⌊the LORD⌋
at the waters of Meribah,
and Moses suffered because of
them;

33 for they embittered his spirit,[a]
and he spoke rashly
with his lips.

34 They did not destroy
the peoples
as the LORD had commanded
them,

35 but mingled with the nations
and adopted their ways.

36 They served their idols,
which became a snare
to them.

37 They sacrificed their sons
and daughters to demons.

38 They shed innocent blood—
the blood of their sons
and daughters
whom they sacrificed
to the idols of Canaan;
so the land became polluted
with blood.

39 They defiled themselves
by their actions
and prostituted themselves
by their deeds.

[a] 106:33 Some Hb mss, LXX, Syr, Vg; other Hb mss read *they rebelled against His Spirit*

40 Therefore the LORD's anger
        burned against His people,
    and He abhorred
        His own inheritance.
41 He handed them over
        to the nations;
    those who hated them ruled
        them.
42 Their enemies oppressed them,
    and they were subdued
        under their power.
43 He rescued them many times,
    but they continued to rebel
        deliberately
    and were beaten down
        by their sin.

44 When He heard their cry,
    He took note of their distress,
45 remembered His covenant
        with them,
    and relented according to
        the abundance
        of His faithful love.
46 He caused them to be pitied
    before all their captors.

47 Save us, LORD our God,
    and gather us
        from the nations,
    so that we may give thanks
        to Your holy name
    and make Your praise
        our pride.

48 May the LORD, the God
        of Israel, be praised
    from everlasting to everlasting.
    Let all the people say,
        "Amen!"
    Hallelujah!

# BOOK V

## (PSALMS 107–150)

*Thanksgiving for God's Deliverance*

**107** Give thanks to the LORD,
        for He is good;

His faithful love endures
        forever.
2 Let the redeemed of the LORD
        proclaim
    that He has redeemed them
        from the hand of the foe
3 and has gathered them
        from the lands—
    from the east and the west,
    from the north and the south.

4 Some wandered
        in the desolate wilderness,
    finding no way to a city where
        they could live.
5 They were hungry and thirsty;
    their spirits
        failed within them.
6 Then they cried out
        to the LORD
        in their trouble;
    He rescued them
        from their distress.
7 He led them by the right path
    to go to a city where
        they could live.
8 Let them give thanks
        to the LORD
        for His faithful love
    and His wonderful works
        for the *human race.
9 For He has satisfied the thirsty
    and filled the hungry
        with good things.

10 Others sat in darkness
        and gloom—
    prisoners in cruel chains—
11 because they rebelled against
        God's commands
    and despised the counsel
        of the *Most High.
12 He broke their spirits
        with hard labor;
    they stumbled, and there was
        no one to help.

13 Then they cried out
     to the LORD
     in their trouble;
   He saved them
     from their distress.
14 He brought them
     out of darkness and gloom
   and broke their chains apart.
15 Let them give thanks
     to the LORD
     for His faithful love
   and His wonderful works
     for the human race.
16 For He has broken down
     the bronze gates
   and cut through the iron bars.

17 Fools suffered affliction
   because of
     their rebellious ways
     and their sins.
18 They loathed all food
   and came near the gates
     of death.
19 Then they cried out
     to the LORD
     in their trouble;
   He saved them
     from their distress.
20 He sent His word and healed
     them;
   He rescued them
     from the •Pit.
21 Let them give thanks
     to the LORD
     for His faithful love
   and His wonderful works
     for the human race.
22 Let them offer sacrifices
     of thanksgiving
   and announce His works
     with shouts of joy.

23 Others went to sea in ships,
   conducting trade
     on the vast waters.
24 They saw the LORD's works,

His wonderful works
     in the deep.
25 He spoke and raised a tempest
   that stirred up the waves
     of the sea.
26 Rising up to the sky,
     sinking down to the
     depths,
   their courage melting away
     in anguish,
27 they reeled and staggered
     like drunken men,
   and all their skill was useless.
28 Then they cried out
     to the LORD
     in their trouble,
   and He brought them
     out of their distress.
29 He stilled the storm
     to a murmur,
   and the waves
     of the sea were hushed.
30 They rejoiced
     when the waves grew quiet.
   Then He guided them
     to the harbor
     they longed for.
31 Let them give thanks
     to the LORD
     for His faithful love
   and His wonderful works
     for the human race.
32 Let them exalt Him
     in the assembly
     of the people
   and praise Him in the council
     of the elders.

33 He turns rivers into desert,
   springs of water
     into thirsty ground,
34 and fruitful land
     into salty wasteland,
   because of the wickedness
     of its inhabitants.
35 He turns a desert into a pool
     of water,
   dry land into springs of water.

36 He causes the hungry to settle
    there,
and they establish a city where
    they can live.
37 They sow fields and plant
    vineyards
that yield a fruitful harvest.
38 He blesses them,
    and they multiply greatly;
He does not let their livestock
    decrease.

39 When they are diminished
    and are humbled
by cruel oppression
    and sorrow,
40 He pours contempt on nobles
and makes them wander
    in trackless wastelands.
41 But He lifts the needy out of
    their suffering
and makes their families
    ⌊multiply⌋ like flocks.
42 The upright see it and rejoice,
and all injustice shuts
    its mouth.

43 Let whoever is wise
    pay attention to
    these things
and consider the LORD's acts
    of faithful love.

*A Plea for Victory*

*A song. A Davidic psalm.*

**108** My heart is confident, God;
I will sing; I will sing praises
    with the whole
    of my being.
2 Wake up, harp and lyre!
I will wake up the dawn.
3 I will praise You, LORD,
    among the peoples;
I will sing praises to You
    among the nations.

4 For Your faithful love is higher
    than the heavens;
Your faithfulness reaches
    the clouds.
5 Be exalted above the heavens,
    God;
let Your glory be over
    the whole earth.
6 Save with Your right hand
    and answer me
so that those You love may be
    rescued.

7 God has spoken
    in His sanctuary:
"I will triumph!
I will divide up Shechem.
I will apportion the Valley
    of Succoth.
8 Gilead is Mine, Manasseh is
    Mine,
and Ephraim is My helmet;
Judah is My scepter.
9 Moab is My washbasin;
on Edom I throw My sandal.
Over Philistia I shout
    in triumph."

10 Who will bring me
    to the fortified city?
Who will lead me to Edom?
11 Have You not rejected us, God?
God, You do not march out
    with our armies.
12 Give us aid against the foe,
for human help is worthless.
13 With God we will perform
    valiantly;
He will trample our foes.

*Prayer against an Enemy*

*For the choir director.*
*A Davidic psalm.*

**109** O God of my praise,
do not be silent.

2 For wicked
   and deceitful mouths open
   against me;
 they speak against me
   with lying tongues.
3 They surround me
   with hateful words
 and attack me without cause.
4 In return for my love
   they accuse me,
 but I continue to pray.
5 They repay me evil for good,
 and hatred for my love.

6 Set a wicked person
   over him;
 let an accuser stand
   at his right hand.
7 When he is judged, let him
   be found guilty,
 and let his prayer be counted
   as sin.
8 Let his days be few;
 let another take over
   his position.
9 Let his children be fatherless
 and his wife a widow.
10 Let his children wander
   as beggars,
 searching [for food] far
   from their demolished
   homes.
11 Let a creditor seize all he has;
 let strangers plunder
   what he has worked for.
12 Let no one show him
   kindness,
 and let no one be gracious
   to his fatherless children.
13 Let the line of his descendants
   be cut off;
 let their name be blotted out
   in the next generation.
14 Let his forefathers' guilt
   be remembered
   before the LORD,
 and do not let his mother's sin
   be blotted out.

15 Let their sins always remain
   before the LORD,
 and let Him cut off [all]
   memory of them
   from the earth.

16 For he did not think to show
   kindness,
 but pursued
   the wretched poor
   and the brokenhearted
 in order to put them to death.
17 He loved cursing—let it fall
   on him;
 he took no delight
   in blessing—let it be far
   from him.
18 He wore cursing like
   his coat—
 let it enter his body like water
 and go into his bones like oil.
19 Let it be like a robe he wraps
   around himself,
 like a belt he always wears.
20 Let this be the LORD's payment
   to my accusers,
 to those who speak evil
   against me.

21 But You, GOD my Lord,
 deal [kindly] with me
   for Your name's sake;
 deliver me because of
   the goodness
   of Your faithful love.
22 For I am poor and needy;
 my heart is wounded
   within me.
23 I fade away like a lengthening
   shadow;
 I am shaken off like a locust.
24 My knees are weak
   from fasting,
 and my body is emaciated.
25 I have become an object
   of ridicule to my accusers;
 when they see me, they shake
   their heads [in scorn].

26 Help me, LORD my God;
   save me according to
      Your faithful love
27 so they may know that this is
      Your hand
   and that You, LORD,
      have done it.
28 Though they curse,
      You will bless.
   When they rise up, they will
      be put to shame,
   but Your servant will rejoice.
29 My accusers will be clothed
      with disgrace;
   they will wear their shame
      like a cloak.
30 I will fervently thank the LORD
      with my mouth;
   I will praise Him
      in the presence of many.
31 For He stands at the right hand
      of the needy,
   to save him from those who
      would condemn him.

## The Priestly King

*A Davidic psalm.*

**110** The LORD declared
      to my Lord:
   "Sit at My right hand
   until I make Your enemies
      Your footstool."
2  The LORD will extend
      Your mighty scepter
      from Zion.
   Rule[a] over
      Your surrounding enemies.
3  Your people will volunteer
   on Your day of battle.
   In holy splendor,
      from the womb
      of the dawn,
   the dew of Your youth belongs
      to You.

4  The LORD has sworn an oath
      and will not take it back:
   "Forever, You are a priest
   like Melchizedek."

5  The Lord is at Your right hand;
   He will crush kings on the day
      of His anger.
6  He will judge the nations,
      heaping up corpses;
   He will crush leaders
      over the entire world.
7  He will drink from the brook
      by the road;
   therefore, He will lift up
      His head.

## Praise for the LORD's Works

**111** *Hallelujah!
   I will praise the LORD
      with all my heart
   in the assembly of the upright
      and in the congregation.

2  The LORD's works are great,
   studied by all who delight
      in them.
3  All that He does is splendid
      and majestic;
   His righteousness endures
      forever.
4  He has caused
      His wonderful works
      to be remembered.
   The LORD is gracious
      and compassionate.
5  He has provided food for those
      who fear Him;
   He remembers His covenant
      forever.
6  He has shown His people
      the power of His works
   by giving them the inheritance
      of the nations.

---

[a] 110:2 One Hb ms, LXX, Tg read *You will rule*

7 The works of His hands
    are truth and justice;
all His instructions
    are trustworthy.
8 They are established forever
    and ever,
enacted in truth
    and uprightness.
9 He has sent redemption
    to His people.
He has ordained His covenant
    forever.
His name is holy and awe-
    inspiring.

10 The *fear of the LORD is
    the beginning of wisdom;
all who follow His instructions
    have good insight.
His praise endures forever.

### The Traits of the Righteous

**112** *Hallelujah!
Happy is the man
    who *fears the LORD,
taking great delight
    in His commandments.

2 His descendants will be
    powerful in the land;
the generation of the upright
    will be blessed.
3 Wealth and riches are
    in his house,
and his righteousness endures
    forever.
4 Light shines in the darkness
    for the upright.
He is gracious, compassionate,
    and righteous.
5 Good will come to a man
    who lends generously
and conducts his business
    fairly.
6 He will never be shaken.
The righteous will be
    remembered forever.

7 He will not fear bad news;
his heart is confident, trusting
    in the LORD.
8 His heart is assured;
    he will not fear.
In the end he will look
    in triumph on his foes.
9 He distributes freely
    to the poor;
his righteousness endures
    forever.
His *horn will be exalted
    in honor.

10 The wicked man will see ⌊it⌋
    and be angry;
he will gnash his teeth
    in despair.
The desire of the wicked will
    come to nothing.

### Praise to the Merciful God

**113** *Hallelujah!
Give praise, servants
    of the LORD;
praise the name of the LORD.
2 Let the name of the LORD
    be praised
both now and forever.
3 From the rising of the sun
    to its setting,
let the name of the LORD
    be praised.

4 The LORD is exalted above all
    the nations,
His glory above the heavens.
5 Who is like the LORD
    our God—
the One enthroned on high,
6 who stoops down to look
on the heavens and the earth?
7 He raises the poor
    from the dust
and lifts the needy
    from the garbage heap

8 in order to seat them
    with nobles—
with the nobles of His people.
9 He gives the childless woman
    a household,
⌊making her⌋ the joyful mother
    of children.
Hallelujah!

### God's Deliverance of Israel

**114** When Israel came out
    of Egypt—
the house of Jacob
    from a people
who spoke
    a foreign language—
2 Judah became His sanctuary,
Israel, His dominion.

3 The sea looked and fled;
the Jordan turned back.
4 The mountains skipped
    like rams,
the hills, like lambs.
5 Why was it, sea, that you fled?
Jordan, that you turned back?
6 Mountains, that you skipped
    like rams?
Hills, like lambs?

7 Tremble, earth,
    at the presence of the Lord,
at the presence of the God
    of Jacob,
8 who turned the rock
    into a pool of water,
the flint into a spring of water.

### Glory to God Alone

**115** Not to us, LORD, not to us,
    but to Your name give glory
because of Your faithful love,
    because of Your truth.
2 Why should the nations say,
    "Where is their God?"

3 Our God is in heaven
and does whatever He pleases.

4 Their idols are silver and gold,
made by human hands.
5 They have mouths,
    but cannot speak,
eyes, but cannot see.
6 They have ears,
    but cannot hear,
noses, but cannot smell.
7 They have hands,
    but cannot feel,
feet, but cannot walk.
They cannot make a sound
    with their throats.
8 Those who make them are just
    like them,
as are all who trust in them.

9 Israel,[a] trust in the LORD!
He is their help and shield.
10 House of Aaron, trust
    in the LORD!
He is their help and shield.
11 You who •fear the LORD,
    trust in the LORD!
He is their help and shield.
12 The LORD remembers us
    and will bless ⌊us⌋.
He will bless the house
    of Israel;
He will bless the house
    of Aaron;
13 He will bless those who fear
    the LORD—
small and great alike.

14 May the LORD add to
    ⌊your numbers⌋,
both yours
    and your children's.
15 May you be blessed
    by the LORD,
the Maker of heaven
    and earth.
16 The heavens are the LORD's,

---

a 115:9 Other Hb mss, LXX, Syr read *House of Israel*

but the earth He has given
   to the *human race.
17 It is not the dead who praise
   the LORD,
nor any of those descending
   into the silence ⌊of death⌋.
18 But we will praise the LORD,
both now and forever.
*Hallelujah!

## Thanks to God for Deliverance

**116** I love the LORD
   because He has heard
my appeal for mercy.
2 Because He has turned His ear
   to me,
I will call ⌊out to Him⌋
   as long as I live.

3 The ropes of death
   were wrapped around me,
and the torments of *Sheol
   overcame me;
I encountered trouble
   and sorrow.
4 Then I called on the name
   of the LORD:
"LORD, save me!"

5 The LORD is gracious
   and righteous;
our God is compassionate.
6 The LORD guards
   the inexperienced;
I was helpless, and He saved me.
7 Return to your rest, my soul,
for the LORD has been good
   to you.
8 For You, ⌊LORD,⌋ rescued me
   from death,
my eyes from tears,
my feet from stumbling.
9 I will walk before the LORD
in the land of the living.
10 I believed, even when I said,

"I am severely afflicted."
11 In my alarm I said,
"Everyone is a liar."

12 How can I repay the LORD
all the good He has done
   for me?
13 I will take the cup of salvation
and worship the LORD.
14 I will fulfill my vows
   to the LORD
in the presence of all
   His people.

15 In the sight of the LORD
the death of His faithful ones
   is costly.
16 LORD, I am indeed
   Your servant;
I am Your servant, the son
   of Your female servant.
You have loosened my bonds.

17 I will offer You a sacrifice
   of thanksgiving
and will worship the LORD.
18 I will fulfill my vows
   to the LORD,
in the very presence of all
   His people,
19 in the courts
   of the LORD's house—
within you, Jerusalem.
*Hallelujah!

## Universal Call to Praise

**117** Praise the LORD, all nations!
   Glorify Him, all peoples!
2 For great is His faithful love
   to us;
the LORD's faithfulness
   endures forever.
*Hallelujah!

491

PSALM 118:23

## Thanksgiving for Victory

**118** Give thanks to the LORD,
for He is good;
His faithful love endures
forever.
² Let Israel say,
"His faithful love endures
forever."
³ Let the house of Aaron say,
"His faithful love endures
forever."
⁴ Let those who fear the LORD
say,
"His faithful love endures
forever."

⁵ I called to the LORD in distress;
the LORD answered me
⌊and put me⌋ in a spacious
place.
⁶ The LORD is for me;
I will not be afraid.
What can man do to me?
⁷ With the LORD for me as
my helper,
I will look in triumph on those
who hate me.

⁸ It is better to take refuge
in the LORD
than to trust in man.
⁹ It is better to take refuge
in the LORD
than to trust in nobles.

¹⁰ All the nations surrounded me;
in the name of the LORD
I destroyed them.
¹¹ They surrounded me, yes,
they surrounded me;
in the name of the LORD
I destroyed them.
¹² They surrounded me
like bees;

they were extinguished
like a fire among thorns;
in the name of the LORD
I destroyed them.
¹³ You pushed meᵃ hard to make
me fall,
but the LORD helped me.
¹⁴ The LORD is my strength
and my song;
He has become my salvation.

¹⁵ There are shouts of joy
and victory
in the tents of the righteous:
"The LORD's right hand strikes
with power!
¹⁶ The LORD's right hand
is raised!
The LORD's right hand strikes
with power!"
¹⁷ I will not die, but I will live
and proclaim what the LORD
has done.
¹⁸ The LORD disciplined me
severely
but did not give me over
to death.

¹⁹ Open the gates
of righteousness for me;
I will enter through them
and give thanks
to the LORD.
²⁰ This is the gate of the LORD;
the righteous will enter
through it.
²¹ I will give thanks to You because
You have answered me
and have become
my salvation.
²² The stone that the builders
rejected
has become the cornerstone.
²³ This came from the LORD;
it is wonderful in our eyes.

ᵃ118:13 LXX, Syr, Jer read *I was pushed*

24 This is the day the LORD
     has made;
   let us rejoice and be glad in it.

25 LORD, save us!
   LORD, please grant us success!
26 Blessed is he who comes
     in the name of the LORD.
   From the house of the LORD
     we bless you.
27 The LORD is God and has given
     us light.
   Bind the festival sacrifice
     with cords to the horns
     of the altar.
28 You are my God,
     and I will give You thanks.
   ⌊You are⌋ my God;
     I will exalt You.
29 Give thanks to the LORD,
     for He is good;
   His faithful love endures
     forever.

## Delight in God's Word

### א Alef

**119** How happy are those whose
     way is blameless,
   who live according to the law
     of the LORD!
2 Happy are those who keep
     His decrees
   and seek Him with all
     their heart.
3 They do nothing wrong;
   they follow His ways.
4 You have commanded that
     Your precepts
   be diligently kept.
5 If only my ways
     were committed
   to keeping Your statutes!
6 Then I would not be ashamed
   when I think about all
     Your commands.

---

### Psalm 119:9-16

*You're likely to forget a lot of what
you read in the Bible if all you do is
just read it. To really let it sink in
deep, you've got to lock it away for
safekeeping, memorizing the
verses that are speaking to you. It'll
take some work, but it'll pay off
with a life that's lived by the Book.*

---

7 I will praise You
     with a sincere heart
   when I learn
     Your righteous judgments.
8 I will keep Your statutes;
   never abandon me.

### ב Bet

9 How can a young man keep
     his way pure?
   By keeping Your word.
10 I have sought You with all
     my heart;
    don't let me wander
      from Your commands.
11 I have treasured Your word
      in my heart
    so that I may not sin
      against You.
12 LORD, may You be praised;
    teach me Your statutes.
13 With my lips I proclaim
    all the judgments
      from Your mouth.
14 I rejoice in the way
      ⌊revealed by⌋ Your decrees
    as much as in all riches.
15 I will meditate on
      Your precepts
    and think about Your ways.

16 I will delight in Your statutes;
I will not forget Your word.

### ג Gimel

17 Deal generously
with Your servant so that
I might live;
then I will keep Your word.
18 Open my eyes so that
I may see
wonderful things in Your law.
19 I am a stranger on earth;
do not hide Your commands
from me.
20 I am continually overcome
by longing for Your judgments.
21 You rebuke the proud,
the accursed,
who wander
from Your commands.
22 Take insult and contempt away
from me,
for I have kept Your decrees.
23 Though princes sit together
speaking against me,
Your servant will think
about Your statutes;
24 Your decrees are my delight
and my counselors.

### ד Dalet

25 My life is down in the dust;
give me life through
Your word.
26 I told You about my life,
and You listened to me;
teach me Your statutes.
27 Help me understand
the meaning
of Your precepts
so that I can meditate on
Your wonders.
28 I am weary from grief;
strengthen me through
Your word.
29 Keep me from the way
of deceit,

and graciously give me
Your instruction.
30 I have chosen the way
of truth;
I have set Your ordinances
⌊before me⌋.
31 I cling to Your decrees;
LORD, do not put me to shame.
32 I pursue the way of
Your commands,
for You broaden
my understanding.

### ה He

33 Teach me, LORD, the meaning
of Your statutes,
and I will always keep them.
34 Help me understand
Your instruction, and I will
obey it
and follow it with all my
heart.
35 Help me stay on the path
of Your commands,
for I take pleasure in it.
36 Turn my heart to Your decrees
and not to material gain.
37 Turn my eyes from looking at
what is worthless;
give me life in Your ways.[a]
38 Confirm what You said
to Your servant,
for it produces reverence
for You.
39 Turn away the disgrace
I dread;
indeed, Your judgments
are good.
40 How I long for Your precepts!
Give me life through
Your righteousness.

### ו Vav

41 Let Your faithful love come
to me, LORD,
Your salvation,
as You promised.

[a] 119:37 Other Hb mss, Tg read word

42 Then I can answer the one
      who taunts me,
   for I trust in Your word.
43 Never take the word of truth
      from my mouth,
   for I hope in Your judgments.
44 I will always keep Your law,
   forever and ever.
45 I will walk freely
      in an open place
   because I seek Your precepts.
46 I will speak of Your decrees
      before kings
   and not be ashamed.
47 I delight in Your commands,
   which I love.
48 I will lift up my
      hands to Your commands,
      which I love,
   and will meditate
      on Your statutes.

### ז Zayin

49 Remember ⌊Your⌋ word
      to Your servant,
   through which You have given
      me hope.
50 This is my comfort
      in my affliction:
   Your promise has given me
      life.
51 The arrogant constantly
      ridicule me,
   but I do not turn away
      from Your instruction.
52 LORD, I remember
      Your judgments
      from long ago
   and find comfort.
53 Rage seizes me because of
      the wicked
   who reject Your instruction.
54 Your statutes are
      ⌊the theme of⌋ my song
   during my earthly life.
55 I remember Your name
      in the night, LORD,

and I keep Your law.
56 This is my ⌊practice⌋:
   I obey Your precepts.

---

*"One of the primary reasons for
studying the Bible is to provide
Him with the Word to bring to our
remembrance—when we need it."*
**—Evelyn Christenson**

---

### ח Khet

57 The LORD is my portion;
   I have promised to keep
      Your words.
58 I have sought Your favor
      with all my heart;
   be gracious to me according to
      Your promise.
59 I thought about my ways
   and turned my steps back
      to Your decrees.
60 I hurried, not hesitating
   to keep Your commands.
61 Though the ropes
      of the wicked
      were wrapped around me,
   I did not forget Your law.
62 I rise at midnight to thank You
   for Your righteous judgments.
63 I am a friend to all
      who °fear You,
   to those who keep
      Your precepts.
64 LORD, the earth is filled with
      Your faithful love;
   teach me Your statutes.

### ט Tet

65 LORD, You have treated
      Your servant well,
   just as You promised.
66 Teach me good judgment
      and discernment,

for I rely on Your commands.
67 Before I was afflicted
    I went astray,
but now I keep Your word.
68 You are good, and You do
    what is good;
teach me Your statutes.
69 The arrogant have smeared me
    with lies,
but I obey Your precepts
    with all my heart.
70 Their hearts are hard
    and insensitive,
but I delight in
    Your instruction.
71 It was good for me
    to be afflicted
so that I could learn
    Your statutes.
72 Instruction from Your lips
    is better for me
than thousands of gold
    and silver pieces.

### ’ *Yod*

73 Your hands made me
    and formed me;
give me understanding
    so that I can learn
    Your commands.
74 Those who fear You will see
    me and rejoice,
for I hope in Your word.
75 I know, LORD, that Your
    judgments are just
and that You have afflicted me
    fairly.
76 May Your faithful love
    comfort me,
as You promised Your servant.
77 May Your compassion come
    to me so that I may live,
for Your instruction is
    my delight.
78 Let the arrogant be put to
    shame for slandering me
    with lies;

I will meditate on
    Your precepts.
79 Let those who fear You,
those who know Your decrees,
    turn to me.
80 May my heart be blameless
    regarding Your statutes
so that I will not be put
    to shame.

### כ *Kaf*

81 I long for Your salvation;
I hope in Your word.
82 My eyes grow weary ⌊looking⌋
    for what You have
    promised;
I ask, "When will You
    comfort me?"
83 Though I have become
    like a wineskin ⌊dried⌋
    by smoke,
I do not forget Your statutes.
84 How many days ⌊must⌋
    Your servant ⌊wait⌋?
When will You execute
    judgment
    on my persecutors?
85 The arrogant have dug pits
    for me;
they violate Your instruction.
86 All Your commands are true;
people persecute me
    with lies—help me!
87 They almost ended my life
    on earth,
but I did not abandon
    Your precepts.
88 Give me life in accordance
    with Your faithful love,
and I will obey the decree
    You have spoken.

### ל *Lamed*

89 LORD, Your word is forever;
it is firmly fixed in heaven.
90 Your faithfulness is for all
    generations;

You established the earth,
and it stands firm.

91 They stand today
in accordance with
Your judgments,
for all things are Your servants.

92 If Your instruction had not
been my delight,
I would have died
in my affliction.

93 I will never forget
Your precepts,
for You have given me life
through them.

94 I am Yours; save me,
for I have sought
Your precepts.

95 The wicked hope to destroy me,
but I contemplate
Your decrees.

96 I have seen a limit to all
perfection,
but Your command is
without limit.

### מ Mem

97 How I love Your teaching!
It is my meditation all
day long.

98 Your command makes me
wiser than my enemies,
for it is always with me.

99 I have more insight than all
my teachers
because Your decrees are
my meditation.

100 I understand more than
the elders
because I obey Your precepts.

101 I have kept my feet from every
evil path
to follow Your word.

102 I have not turned from
Your judgments,
for You Yourself have
instructed me.

103 How sweet Your word is
to my taste—
⌊sweeter⌋ than honey
to my mouth.

104 I gain understanding from
Your precepts;
therefore I hate
every false way.

### נ Nun

105 Your word is a lamp
for my feet
and a light on my path.

106 I have solemnly sworn
to keep Your righteous
judgments.

107 I am severely afflicted;
LORD, give me life
through Your word.

108 LORD, please accept
my willing offerings
of praise,
and teach me Your judgments.

109 My life is constantly
in danger,
yet I do not forget
Your instruction.

110 The wicked have set a trap
for me,
but I have not wandered
from Your precepts.

111 I have Your decrees
as a heritage forever;
indeed, they are the joy
of my heart.

112 I am resolved to obey
Your statutes
to the very end.

### ס Samek

113 I hate the double-minded,
but I love Your instruction.

114 You are my shelter
and my shield;
I hope in Your word.

115 Depart from me, you evil ones,

so that I may obey
   my God's commands.
116 Sustain me as You promised,
   and I will live;
   do not let me be ashamed of
   my hope.
117 Sustain me so that I can
   be safe
   and be concerned with
   Your statutes continually.
118 You reject all who stray from
   Your statutes,
   for their deceit is a lie.
119 You remove all the wicked
   on earth as if they were[a]
   dross;
   therefore, I love Your decrees.
120 I shudder in awe of You;
   I fear Your judgments.

### ע Ayin

121 I have done what is just
   and right;
   do not leave me to
   my oppressors.
122 Guarantee Your servant's
   well-being;
   do not let the arrogant
   oppress me.
123 My eyes grow weary
   ⌊looking for⌋ Your salvation
   and for Your righteous
   promise.
124 Deal with Your servant
   based on Your faithful love;
   teach me Your statutes.
125 I am Your servant; give me
   understanding
   so that I may know
   Your decrees.
126 It is time for the LORD to act,
   ⌊for⌋ they have broken
   Your law.
127 Since I love
   Your commandments

more than gold,
   even the purest gold,
128 I carefully follow all
   Your precepts
   and hate every false way.

### פ Pe

129 Your decrees are wonderful;
   therefore I obey them.
130 The revelation of Your words
   brings light
   and gives understanding
   to the inexperienced.
131 I pant with open mouth
   because I long
   for Your commands.
132 Turn to me and be gracious
   to me,
   as is ⌊Your⌋ practice toward
   those who love Your name.
133 Make my steps steady
   through Your promise;
   don't let sin dominate me.
134 Redeem me
   from human oppression,
   and I will keep Your precepts.
135 Show favor to Your servant,
   and teach me Your statutes.
136 My eyes pour out streams
   of tears
   because people do not follow
   Your instruction.

### צ Tsade

137 You are righteous, LORD,
   and Your judgments are just.
138 The decrees You issue
   are righteous
   and altogether trustworthy.
139 My anger overwhelms me
   because my foes forget
   Your words.
140 Your word is completely pure,
   and Your servant loves it.

---

[a] 119:119 Other Hb mss, DSS, LXX, Aq, Sym, Jer read *All the wicked of the earth You count as*

141 I am insignificant
and despised,
but I do not forget
Your precepts.
142 Your righteousness is
an everlasting
righteousness,
and Your instruction is true.
143 Trouble and distress
have overtaken me,
but Your commands are
my delight.
144 Your decrees are righteous
forever.
Give me understanding,
and I will live.

ק *Qof*

145 I call with all my heart;
answer me, LORD.
I will obey Your statutes.
146 I call to You; save me,
and I will keep Your decrees.
147 I rise before dawn and cry out
for help;
I hope in Your word.
148 I am awake through
each watch of the night
to meditate on Your promise.
149 In keeping with
Your faithful love,
hear my voice.
LORD, give me life,
in keeping with
Your justice.
150 Those who pursue evil plans[a]
come near;
they are far from
Your instruction.
151 You are near, LORD,
and all Your commands
are true.
152 Long ago I learned from
Your decrees

that You have established them
forever.

ר *Resh*

153 Consider my affliction
and rescue me,
for I have not forgotten
Your instruction.
154 Defend my cause, and
redeem me;
give me life, as You promised.
155 Salvation is far
from the wicked
because they do not seek
Your statutes.
156 Your compassions are many,
LORD;
give me life, according to
Your judgments.
157 My persecutors and foes
are many.
I have not turned
from Your decrees.
158 I have seen the disloyal
and feel disgust
because they do not keep
Your word.
159 Consider how I love
Your precepts;
LORD, give me life,
according to
Your faithful love.
160 The entirety of Your word
is truth,
and all Your righteous
judgments endure forever.

ש *Sin/* ש *Shin*

161 Princes have persecuted me
without cause,
but my heart fears ⌊only⌋
Your word.
162 I rejoice over Your promise

---

[a] 119:150 Some Hb mss, LXX, Sym, Jer read *who maliciously persecute me*

like one who finds
   vast treasure.
163 I hate and abhor falsehood,
⌊but⌋ I love Your instruction.
164 I praise You seven times a day
for Your righteous judgments.
165 Abundant peace belongs to
   those who love
   Your instruction;
nothing makes them stumble.
166 LORD, I hope for Your salvation
and carry out Your commands.
167 I obey Your decrees
and love them greatly.
168 I obey Your precepts
   and decrees,
for all my ways are before You.

ת *Tav*

169 Let my cry reach You, LORD;
give me understanding
   according to Your word.
170 Let my plea reach You;
rescue me according to
   Your promise.
171 My lips pour out praise,
for You teach me Your statutes.
172 My tongue sings
   about Your promise,
for all Your commandments
   are righteous.
173 May Your hand be ready
   to help me,
for I have chosen
   Your precepts.
174 I long for Your salvation, LORD,
and Your instruction is
   my delight.
175 Let me live, and I will praise
   You;
may Your judgments help me.
176 I wander like a lost sheep;
seek Your servant,
for I do not forget
   Your commands.

### A Cry for Truth and Peace

A •*song of ascents.*

**120** In my distress I called
   to the LORD,
and He answered me:
2 "LORD, deliver me
   from lying lips
and a deceitful tongue."

3 What will He give you,
and what will He do to you,
you deceitful tongue?
4 A warrior's sharp arrows,
with burning charcoal!

5 What misery that I have stayed
   in Meshech,
that I have lived among
   the tents of Kedar!
6 I have lived too long
with those who hate peace.
7 I am for peace;
   but when I speak,
they are for war.

### The LORD Our Protector

A •*song of ascents.*

**121** I raise my eyes toward
   the mountains.
Where will my help
   come from?
2 My help comes from the LORD,
the Maker of heaven
   and earth.

3 He will not allow your foot
   to slip;
your Protector will not
   slumber.
4 Indeed, the Protector of Israel
does not slumber or sleep.

5 The LORD protects you;

the LORD is a shelter right by
    your side.
6 The sun will not strike you
    by day,
or the moon by night.

7 The LORD will protect you
    from all harm;
He will protect your life.
8 The LORD will protect
    your coming and going
both now and forever.

## A Prayer for Jerusalem

A Davidic °song of ascents.

**122** I rejoiced with those
    who said to me,
"Let us go to the house
    of the LORD."
2 Our feet are standing
within your gates,
    Jerusalem—

3 Jerusalem, built as a city
    ⌊should be⌋,
solidly joined together,
4 where the tribes, the tribes
    of the LORD, go up
to give thanks to the name
    of the LORD.
(This is an ordinance
    for Israel.)
5 There, thrones for judgment
    are placed,
thrones of the house of David.

6 Pray for the peace
    of Jerusalem:
"May those who love you
    prosper;
7 may there be peace
    within your walls,
prosperity
    within your fortresses."
8 For the sake of my brothers
    and friends,

I will say, "Peace be
    with you."
9 For the sake of the house
    of the LORD our God,
I will seek your good.

## Looking for God's Favor

A °song of ascents.

**123** I lift my eyes to You,
    the One enthroned
    in heaven.
2 Like a servant's eyes
    on His master's hand,
like a servant girl's eyes
    on her mistress's hand,
so our eyes are on the LORD
    our God
until He shows us favor.

3 Show us favor, LORD, show us
    favor,
for we've had more than
    enough contempt.
4 We've had more than enough
scorn from the arrogant
⌊and⌋ contempt
    from the proud.

## The LORD Is on Our Side

A Davidic °song of ascents.

**124** If the LORD had not been
    on our side—
let Israel say—
2 If the LORD had not been
    on our side
when men attacked us,
3 then they would have
    swallowed us alive
in their burning anger
    against us.
4 Then the waters would have
    engulfed us;
the torrent would have swept
    over us;

5 the raging waters would have
  swept over us.

6 Praise the LORD,
  who has not let us be
    ripped apart by their teeth.
7 We have escaped like a bird
  from the hunter's net;
  the net is torn,
    and we have escaped.
8 Our help is in the name
  of the LORD,
  the Maker of heaven
  and earth.

## Israel's Stability

A •song of ascents.

**125** Those who trust
  in the LORD are
  like Mount Zion.
  It cannot be shaken; it remains
    forever.
2 Jerusalem—the mountains
  surround her.
  And the LORD surrounds
  His people,
  both now and forever.

3 The scepter of the wicked
  will not remain
  over the land allotted
  to the righteous,
  so that the righteous
  will not apply their hands
  to injustice.
4 Do good, LORD, to the good,
  to those whose hearts
  are upright.
5 But as for those who turn aside
  to crooked ways,
  the LORD will banish them
  with the evildoers.

Peace be with Israel.

## Zion's Restoration

A •song of ascents.

**126** When the LORD restored
  the fortunes of Zion,
  we were like those
  who dream.
2 Our mouths were filled
  with laughter then,
  and our tongues with shouts
  of joy.
  Then they said
  among the nations,
  "The LORD has done
  great things for them."
3 The LORD had done
  great things for us;
  we were joyful.

4 Restore our fortunes, LORD,
  like watercourses
  in the Negev.
5 Those who sow in tears
  will reap with shouts of joy.
6 Though one goes along
  weeping,
  carrying the bag of seed,
  he will surely come back
  with shouts of joy,
  carrying his sheaves.

## The Blessing of the LORD

A Solomonic •song of ascents.

**127** Unless the LORD builds
  a house,
  its builders labor over it
  in vain;
  unless the LORD watches over
  a city,
  the watchman stays alert
  in vain.
2 In vain you get up early
  and stay up late,
  eating food earned
  by hard work;

certainly He gives sleep
   to the one He loves.

3  Sons are indeed a heritage
     from the LORD,
  children, a reward.
4  Like arrows in the hand
     of a warrior
  are the sons born in
     one's youth.
5  Happy is the man
     who has filled his quiver
     with them.
  Such men will never be put
     to shame
  when they speak
     with ⌊their⌋ enemies
     at the city gate.

## Blessings for Those Who Fear God

A •song of ascents.

**128**  How happy is everyone
     who •fears the LORD,
  who walks in His ways!
2  You will surely eat what
     your hands
     have worked for.
  You will be happy,
     and it will go well for you.
3  Your wife will be
     like a fruitful vine
     within your house,
  your sons,
     like young olive trees
     around your table.
4  In this very way the man
     who fears the LORD
  will be blessed.

5  May the LORD bless you
     from Zion,
  so that you will see
     the prosperity of Jerusalem
  all the days of your life,
6  and will see your children's
     children!

Peace be with Israel.

## Protection of the Oppressed

A •song of ascents.

**129**  Since my youth they have
     often attacked me—
  let Israel say—
2  Since my youth they have
     often attacked me,
  but they have not prevailed
     against me.
3  Plowmen plowed
     over my back;
  they made their furrows long.
4  The LORD is righteous;
  He has cut the ropes
     of the wicked.

5  Let all who hate Zion
     be driven back in disgrace.
6  Let them be like grass
     on the rooftops,
  which withers before
     it grows up
7  and can't even fill the hands
     of the reaper
  or the arms of the one
     who binds sheaves.
8  Then none who pass by
     will say,
  "May the LORD's blessing be
     on you."

  We bless you in the name
     of the LORD.

## Awaiting Redemption

A •song of ascents.

**130**  Out of the depths I call
     to You, LORD!
2  Lord, listen to my voice;
  let Your ears be attentive
     to my cry for help.

3  LORD, if You considered sins,
  Lord, who could stand?

⁴ But with You there is
forgiveness,
so that You may be revered.

⁵ I wait for the LORD; I wait,
and put my hope in His word.
⁶ I ⌊wait⌋ for the Lord
more than watchmen
for the morning—
more than watchmen
for the morning.

⁷ Israel, hope in the LORD.
For there is faithful love
with the LORD,
and with Him is redemption
in abundance.
⁸ And He will redeem Israel
from all its sins.

## A Childlike Spirit

A Davidic •song of ascents.

**131** LORD, my heart is not
proud; my eyes are not
haughty.
I do not get involved
with things too great
or too difficult for me.
² Instead, I have calmed
and quieted myself
like a little weaned child
with its mother;
I am like a little child.

³ Israel, hope in the LORD,
both now and forever.

## David and Zion Chosen

A •song of ascents.

**132** LORD, remember David
and all the hardships
he endured,

² and how he swore an oath
to the LORD,
making a vow
to the Mighty One of Jacob:
³ "I will not enter my house
or get into my bed,
⁴ I will not allow my eyes
to sleep
or my eyelids to slumber
⁵ until I find a place
for the LORD,
a dwelling for the Mighty One
of Jacob."

⁶ We heard of ⌊the ark⌋
in Ephrathah;
we found it in the fields
of Jaar.
⁷ Let us go
to His dwelling place;
let us worship at His footstool.
⁸ Arise, LORD, come to
Your resting place,
You and the ark ⌊that shows⌋
Your strength.
⁹ May Your priests be clothed
with righteousness,
and may Your godly people
shout for joy.
¹⁰ Because of Your servant David,
do not reject
Your anointed one.

¹¹ The LORD swore an oath
to David,
a promise He will not
abandon:
"I will set one of your
descendants on your
throne.
¹² If your sons keep My covenant
and My decrees
that I will teach them,
their sons will also sit
on your throne, forever."

¹³ For the LORD has chosen Zion;

He has desired it
   for His home:
14  "This is My resting place
       forever;
   I will make My home here
       because I have desired it.
15  I will abundantly bless its food;
   I will satisfy its needy
       with bread.
16  I will clothe its priests
       with salvation,
   and its godly people will shout
       for joy.
17  There I will make
       a *horn grow for David;
   I have prepared a lamp for
       My anointed one.
18  I will clothe his enemies
       with shame,
   but the crown he
       wears will be glorious."

## Living in Harmony

*A Davidic *song of ascents.*

**133** How good and pleasant it is
       when brothers can live
       together!
2  It is like fine oil on the head,
   running down on the beard,
   running down Aaron's beard,
   onto his robes.
3  It is like the dew of Hermon
   falling on the mountains
       of Zion.
   For there the LORD
       has appointed
       the blessing—
   life forevermore.

## Call to Evening Worship

*A *song of ascents.*

**134** Now praise the LORD, all
       you servants of the LORD

who stand in the LORD's house
   at night!
2  Lift up your hands
   in the holy place,
   and praise the LORD!

3  May the LORD, Maker
       of heaven and earth,
   bless you from Zion.

## The LORD Is Great

**135** *Hallelujah!
   Praise the name
       of the LORD.
   Give praise, you servants
       of the LORD
2  who stand in the house
       of the LORD,
   in the courts of the house
       of our God.
3  Praise the LORD, for the LORD
       is good;
   sing praise to His name, for
       it is delightful.
4  For the LORD has chosen Jacob
       for Himself,
   Israel as His treasured
       possession.

5  For I know that the LORD
       is great;
   our Lord is greater
       than all gods.
6  The LORD does whatever
       He pleases
   in heaven and on earth,
   in the seas and all the depths.
7  He causes the clouds to rise
       from the ends of the earth.
   He makes lightning
       for the rain
   and brings the wind from
       His storehouses.

8  He struck down the firstborn
       of Egypt,
   both people and animals.

9 He sent signs and wonders
    against you, Egypt,
against Pharaoh and all
    his officials.
10 He struck down many nations
and slaughtered mighty kings:
11 Sihon king of the Amorites,
Og king of Bashan,
and all the kings of Canaan.
12 He gave their land
    as an inheritance,
an inheritance to His people
    Israel.

13 LORD, Your name ⌊endures⌋
    forever,
Your reputation, LORD,
    through all generations.
14 For the LORD will judge
    His people
and have compassion
    on His servants.

15 The idols of the nations are
    of silver and gold,
the work of human hands.
16 They have mouths,
    but cannot speak,
eyes, but cannot see.
17 They have ears,
    but cannot hear;
indeed, there is no breath
    in their mouths.
18 Those who make them are just
    like them,
as are all who trust in them.

19 House of Israel,
    praise the LORD!
House of Aaron,
    praise the LORD!
20 House of Levi,
    praise the LORD!
You who revere the LORD,
    praise the LORD!

21 May the LORD be praised
    from Zion;
He dwells in Jerusalem.
Hallelujah!

### God's Love Is Eternal

**136** Give thanks to the LORD,
    for He is good.
        *His love is eternal.*

2 Give thanks to the God
    of gods.
        *His love is eternal.*

3 Give thanks to the Lord
    of lords.
        *His love is eternal.*

4 He alone does great wonders.
        *His love is eternal.*

5 He made the heavens
    skillfully.
        *His love is eternal.*

6 He spread the land
    on the waters.
        *His love is eternal.*

7 He made the great lights:
        *His love is eternal.*

8 the sun to rule by day,
        *His love is eternal.*

9 the moon and stars to rule
    by night.
        *His love is eternal.*

10 He struck the firstborn
    of the Egyptians
        *His love is eternal.*

11 and brought Israel out
    from among them
        *His love is eternal.*

12 with a strong hand
     and outstretched arm.
          *His love is eternal.*

13 He divided the •Red Sea
          *His love is eternal.*

14 and led Israel through,
          *His love is eternal.*

15 but hurled Pharaoh
     and his army
     into the Red Sea.
          *His love is eternal.*

16 He led His people
     in the wilderness.
          *His love is eternal.*

17 He struck down great kings
          *His love is eternal.*

18 and slaughtered
     famous kings—
          *His love is eternal.*

19 Sihon king of the Amorites
          *His love is eternal.*

20 and Og king of Bashan—
          *His love is eternal.*

21 and gave their land as
     an inheritance,
          *His love is eternal.*

22 an inheritance to Israel
     His servant.
          *His love is eternal.*

23 He remembered us
     in our humiliation
          *His love is eternal.*

24 and rescued us from our foes.
          *His love is eternal.*

25 He gives food
     to every creature.
          *His love is eternal.*

26 Give thanks to the God
     of heaven!
          *His love is eternal.*

## Lament of the Exiles

**137** By the rivers of Babylon—
     there we sat down
     and wept
     when we remembered Zion.
2 There we hung up our lyres
     on the poplar trees,
3 for our captors there asked us
          for songs,
     and our tormentors,
          for rejoicing:
     "Sing us one of the songs
          of Zion."

4 How can we sing
     the LORD's song
     on foreign soil?
5 If I forget you, Jerusalem,
     may my right hand forget
     ⌊its skill⌋.
6 May my tongue stick
     to the roof of my mouth
     if I do not remember you,
     if I do not exalt Jerusalem as
          my greatest joy!

7 Remember, LORD, ⌊what⌋
     the Edomites said
     that day at Jerusalem:
     "Destroy it! Destroy it
     down to its foundations!"
8 Daughter Babylon, doomed
     to destruction,
     happy is the one who pays you
          back
     what you have done to us.

<sup>9</sup> Happy is he who takes
   your little ones
and dashes them against
   the rocks.

## A Thankful Heart
*Davidic.*

**138** I will give You thanks with
   all my heart;
I will sing Your praise before
   the heavenly beings.
<sup>2</sup> I will bow down toward
   Your holy temple
and give thanks to Your name
for Your constant love
   and faithfulness.
You have exalted Your name
   and Your promise above
   everything else.
<sup>3</sup> On the day I called,
   You answered me;
You increased strength
   within me.

<sup>4</sup> All the kings on earth will give
   You thanks, LORD,
when they hear
   what You have promised.
<sup>5</sup> They will sing of
   the LORD's ways,
for the LORD's glory is great.
<sup>6</sup> Though the LORD is exalted,
He takes note of the humble;
but He knows the haughty
   from afar.

<sup>7</sup> If I walk in the thick of danger,
You will preserve my life
   from the anger
   of my enemies.
You will extend Your hand;
Your right hand will save me.
<sup>8</sup> The LORD will fulfill
   [His purpose] for me.
LORD, Your love is eternal;

do not abandon the work
   of Your hands.

## The All-Knowing, Ever-Present God
*For the choir director.*
*A Davidic psalm.*

**139** LORD, You have searched
   me and known me.
<sup>2</sup> You know when I sit down
   and when I stand up;
You understand my thoughts
   from far away.
<sup>3</sup> You observe my travels
   and my rest;
You are aware of all my ways.
<sup>4</sup> Before a word is on
   my tongue,
You know all about it, LORD.
<sup>5</sup> You have encircled me;
You have placed Your hand
   on me.
<sup>6</sup> [This] extraordinary
   knowledge is beyond me.
It is lofty; I am unable
   to [reach] it.

---

*Psalm 139:7-10*

### God the Holy Spirit

*There is nowhere we can go that
the Spirit of God doesn't go there
with us. We are never separated
from Him, never forgotten. One of
our great tasks as Christians is to
live in such a way that His constant
presence is something we desire
rather than something we wish we
could hide from.*

---

7  Where can I go to escape
   Your Spirit?
   Where can I flee from
   Your presence?
8  If I go up to heaven,
   You are there;
   if I make my bed
   in *Sheol, You are there.
9  If I live at the eastern horizon
   ⌊or⌋ settle at the western limits,
10 even there Your hand will lead
   me;
   Your right hand will hold on
   to me.
11 If I say, "Surely the darkness
   will hide me,
   and the light around me will
   become night"—
12 even the darkness is not too
   dark for You.
   The night shines like the day;
   darkness and light are alike
   to You.

13 For it was You who created
   my inward parts;
   You knit me together
   in my mother's womb.
14 I will praise You
   because I am[a] unique
   in remarkable ways.
   Your works are wonderful,
   and I know ⌊this⌋ very well.
15 My bones were not hidden
   from You
   when I was made in secret,
   when I was formed
   in the depths of the earth.
16 Your eyes saw me when
   I was formless;
   all ⌊my⌋ days were written
   in Your book and planned
   before a single one of them
   began.

17 God, how difficult
   Your thoughts are for me

   ⌊to comprehend⌋;
   how vast their sum is!
18 If I counted them, they would
   outnumber the grains
   of sand;
   when I wake up,[b] I am still
   with You.

19 God, if only You would kill
   the wicked
   (stay away from me, you
   bloodthirsty men)
20 who invoke You deceitfully.
   Your enemies swear ⌊by You⌋
   falsely.
21 LORD, don't I hate those
   who hate You,
   and detest those who rebel
   against You?
22 I hate them with
   extreme hatred;
   I consider them my enemies.

23 Search me, God, and know
   my heart;
   test me and know
   my concerns.
24 See if there is any
   offensive way in me;
   lead me in the everlasting way.

## Prayer for Rescue

*For the choir director.*
*A Davidic psalm.*

**140** Rescue me, LORD,
        from evil men.
   Keep me safe
   from violent men
2  who plan evil in their hearts.
   They stir up wars all day long.
3  They make their tongues
   as sharp as a snake's bite;
   viper's venom is under
   their lips.            *Selah

---

a 139:14 DSS, some LXX mss, Syr, Jer read *because You are*   b 139:18 Other Hb mss read *I come to an end*

4  Protect me, LORD,
       from the clutches
       of the wicked.
   Keep me safe
       from violent men
   who plan to make me
       stumble.
5  The proud hide a trap
       with ropes for me;
   they spread a net along
       the path
   and set snares for me.     *Selah*

6  I say to the LORD, "You
       are my God."
   Listen, LORD, to my cry
       for help.
7  Lord GOD, my strong Savior,
   You shield my head on the day
       of battle.
8  LORD, do not grant the desires
       of the wicked;
   do not let them achieve
       their goals.
   ⌊Otherwise,⌋ they will become
       proud.                  *Selah*

9  As for the heads of those who
       surround me,
   let the trouble their lips cause
       overwhelm ⌊them⌋.
10 Let hot coals fall on them.
   Let them be thrown
       into the fire,
   into the abyss, never again
       to rise.
11 Do not let a slanderer stay
       in the land.
   Let evil relentlessly hunt down
       a violent man.

12 I[a] know that the LORD upholds
       the just cause of the poor,
   justice for the needy.
13 Surely the righteous will praise
       Your name;

the upright will live in
    Your presence.

## Protection from Sin and Sinners
*A Davidic psalm.*

**141** LORD, I call on You; hurry
       to ⌊help⌋ me.
   Listen to my voice when I call
       on You.
2  May my prayer be set
       before You as incense,
   the raising of my hands as
       the evening offering.

3  LORD, set up a guard for
       my mouth;
   keep watch at the door
       of my lips.
4  Do not let my heart turn to any
       evil thing
   or wickedly perform
       reckless acts
   with men who commit sin.
   Do not let me feast
       on their delicacies.
5  Let the righteous one strike
       me—it is ⌊an act of⌋
       faithful love;
   let him rebuke me—it is oil for
       my head;
   let me not refuse it.
   Even now my prayer is against
       the evil acts of the wicked.
6  When their rulers will be
       thrown off the sides
       of a cliff,
   the people will listen to
       my words, for they are
       pleasing.

7  As when one plows and
       breaks up the soil,
   ⌊turning up rocks⌋,

---

a 140:12 Alt IIb tradition reads *You*

so our[a] bones have been
   scattered at the mouth
   of •Sheol.

8 But my eyes ⌊look⌋ to You,
   Lord GOD.
I seek refuge in You; do not let
   me die.
9 Protect me from the trap
   they have set for me,
and from the snares
   of evildoers.
10 Let the wicked fall into
   their own nets,
while I pass ⌊safely⌋ by.

## A Cry of Distress

*A Davidic •Maskil. When he was
in the cave. A prayer.*

**142** I cry aloud to the LORD;
   I plead aloud to the LORD
   for mercy.
2 I pour out my complaint
   before Him;
I reveal my trouble to Him.
3 Although my spirit is weak
   within me,
You know my way.

Along this path I travel
they have hidden a trap
   for me.
4 Look to the right and see:[b]
no one stands up for me;
there is no refuge for me;
no one cares about me.

5 I cry to You, LORD;
I say, "You are my shelter,
my portion in the land
   of the living."
6 Listen to my cry,
for I am very weak.
Rescue me from those who
   pursue me,

*Psalm 143:5-6*

*Prayer helps you put your thoughts
into words, but journaling helps
you remember what they were—
and what God did in your life along
the way. You'll be so glad you kept
a record of your journey, because it
will give you a lasting track record
of God's power and faithfulness.*

for they are too strong for me.
7 Free me from prison
so that I can praise Your name.
The righteous will gather
   around me
because You deal generously
   with me.

## A Cry for Help

*A Davidic psalm.*

**143** LORD, hear my prayer.
   In Your faithfulness listen
   to my plea,
and in Your righteousness
   answer me.
2 Do not bring Your servant
   into judgment,
for no one alive is righteous
   in Your sight.

3 For the enemy has pursued
   me,
crushing me to the ground,
making me live in darkness
like those long dead.
4 My spirit is weak within me;
my heart is overcome
   with dismay.

5 I remember the days of old;

[a] **141:7** DSS reads *my*; some LXX mss, Syr read *their*  [b] **142:4** DSS, LXX, Syr, Vg, Tg read *I look to the right and I see*

I meditate on all You have
   done;
I reflect on the work
   of Your hands.
6 I spread out my hands to You;
I am like parched land
   before You.            •Selah

---

*"Informed by the past, we can
speak to God with specific hopes
for the future, and with certain
assurances about the present."*
                    *—Welton Gaddy*

---

7 Answer me quickly, LORD;
my spirit fails.
Don't hide Your face from me,
or I will be like those going
   down to the •Pit.
8 Let me experience
   Your faithful love
   in the morning,
for I trust in You.
Reveal to me the way I
   should go,
because I long for You.
9 Rescue me from my enemies,
   LORD;
I come to You for protection.
10 Teach me to do Your will, for
   You are my God.
May Your gracious Spirit lead
   me on level ground.

11 For Your name's sake, LORD,
   let me live.
In Your righteousness
   deliver me from trouble,
12 and in Your faithful love
   destroy my enemies.
Wipe out all those who
   attack me,
for I am Your servant.

---

*A King's Prayer*

*Davidic.*

**144** May the LORD my rock
         be praised,
who trains my hands
   for battle
and my fingers for warfare.
2 He is my faithful love
   and my fortress,
my stronghold
   and my deliverer.
He is my shield, and I take
   refuge in Him;
He subdues my people[a]
   under me.

3 LORD, what is man, that
   You care for him,
the son of man, that You think
   of him?
4 Man is like a breath;
his days are like
   a passing shadow.

5 LORD, part Your heavens and
   come down.
Touch the mountains,
   and they will smoke.
6 Flash ⌊Your⌋ lightning
   and scatter the foe;
shoot Your arrows and rout
   them.
7 Reach down from on high;
rescue me from deep water,
   and set me free
from the grasp of foreigners
8 whose mouths speak lies,
whose right hands
   are deceptive.

9 God, I will sing a new song
   to You;
I will play on a ten-stringed
   harp for You—

---

a 144:2 Other Hb mss, DSS, Aq, Syr, Tg, Jer read *subdues peoples*; Ps 18:47; 2 Sm 22:48

10 the One who gives victory
        to kings,
    who frees His servant David
        from the deadly sword.
11 Set me free and rescue me
        from the grasp of foreigners
    whose mouths speak lies,
    whose right hands
        are deceptive.

12 Then our sons will be like
        plants nurtured
        in their youth,
    our daughters, like
        corner pillars that
        are carved
        in the palace style.
13 Our storehouses will be full,
        supplying all kinds of
        produce;
    our flocks will increase
        by thousands
    and tens of thousands in
        our open fields.
14 Our cattle will be well fed.
    There will be no breach
        ⌊in the walls⌋, no going
        ⌊into captivity⌋,
    and no cry of lament in
        our public squares.
15 Happy are the people with
        such ⌊blessings⌋.
    Happy are the people
        whose God is the LORD.

## Praising God's Greatness

*A Davidic hymn.*

**145** I exalt You,
            my God the King,
    and praise Your name forever
        and ever.
2 I will praise You every day;
    I will honor Your name forever
        and ever.

3 The LORD is great
        and is highly praised;
    His greatness is unsearchable.
4 One generation will declare
        Your works to the next
    and will proclaim
        Your mighty acts.
5 I[a] will speak of
        Your glorious splendor
    and[b] Your wonderful works.
6 They will proclaim the power
        of Your awesome works,
    and I will declare
        Your greatness.[c]
7 They will give a testimony of
        Your great goodness
    and will joyfully sing
        of Your righteousness.

8 The LORD is gracious
        and compassionate,
    slow to anger and great
        in faithful love.
9 The LORD is good to everyone;
    His compassion ⌊rests⌋ on all
        He has made.
10 All You have made will praise
        You, LORD;
    the godly will bless You.
11 They will speak of the glory of
        Your kingdom
    and will declare Your might,
12 informing ⌊all⌋ people
        of Your mighty acts
    and of the glorious splendor
        of Your kingdom.
13 Your kingdom is
        an everlasting kingdom;
    Your rule is for all
        generations.[d]

14 The LORD helps all who fall;
    He raises up all who are
        oppressed.

---

[a] 145:5 LXX, Syr read *They*   [b] 145:5 LXX, Syr read *and they will tell of*   [c] 145:6 Alt Hb tradition, Jer read *great deeds*   [d] 145:13 One Hb ms, LXX, Syr add *The LORD is faithful in His words and gracious in all His actions.*

15 All eyes look to You,
   and You give them their food
      in due time.
16 You open Your hand
   and satisfy the desire of every
      living thing.

17 The LORD is righteous in all
      His ways
   and gracious in all His acts.
18 The LORD is near all who
      call out to Him,
   all who call out to Him
      with integrity.
19 He fulfills the desires of those
      who *fear Him;
   He hears their cry for help
      and saves them.
20 The LORD guards all those
      who love Him,
   but He destroys all the wicked.
21 My mouth will declare
      the LORD's praise;
   let every living thing praise
      His holy name forever
      and ever.

## The God of Compassion

**146** *Hallelujah!
      My soul, praise the LORD.
2  I will praise the LORD all
      my life;
   I will sing to the LORD
      as long as I live.

3  Do not trust in nobles,
   in man, who cannot save.
4  When his breath leaves him,
      he returns to the ground;
   on that day his plans die.

5  Happy is the one whose help is
      the God of Jacob,
   whose hope is in the LORD
      his God,
6  the Maker of heaven
      and earth,

the sea and everything
   in them.
He remains faithful forever,
7  executing justice
      for the exploited
   and giving food to the hungry.
   The LORD frees prisoners.
8  The LORD opens ⌊the eyes of⌋
      the blind.
   The LORD raises up those
      who are oppressed.
   The LORD loves the righteous.
9  The LORD protects foreigners
   and helps the fatherless
      and the widow,
   but He frustrates the ways
      of the wicked.

10 The LORD reigns forever;
   your God, O Zion, ⌊reigns⌋ for
      all generations.
   Hallelujah!

## God Restores Jerusalem

**147** *Hallelujah!
      How good it is to sing
      to our God,
   for praise is pleasant
      and lovely.

2  The LORD rebuilds Jerusalem;
   He gathers Israel's exiled
      people.
3  He heals the brokenhearted
   and binds up their wounds.
4  He counts the number
      of the stars;
   He gives names to all of them.
5  Our Lord is great, vast
      in power;
   His understanding is infinite.
6  The LORD helps the afflicted
   but brings the wicked
      to the ground.

7  Sing to the LORD
      with thanksgiving;

play the lyre to our God,
8 who covers the sky
   with clouds,
prepares rain for the earth,
and causes grass to grow
   on the hills.
9 He provides the animals
   with their food,
and the young ravens,
   what they cry for.

10 He is not impressed
   by the strength of a horse;
He does not value
   the power of a man.
11 The LORD values those
   who fear Him,
those who hope in
   His faithful love.

12 Exalt the LORD, Jerusalem;
   praise your God, Zion!
13 For He strengthens the bars
   of your gates
and blesses your children
   within you.
14 He endows your territory
   with prosperity;
He satisfies you with
   the finest wheat.

15 He sends His command
   throughout the earth;
His word runs swiftly.
16 He spreads snow like wool;
He scatters frost like ashes;
17 He throws His hailstones
   like crumbs.
Who can withstand His cold?
18 He sends His word and melts
   them;
He unleashes His winds,
   and the waters flow.

19 He declares His word to Jacob,
His statutes and judgments
   to Israel.
20 He has not done this
   for any nation;
they do not know[a]
   ⌊His⌋ judgments.
Hallelujah!

## Creation's Praise of the LORD

**148** 'Hallelujah!
Praise the LORD
   from the heavens;
praise Him in the heights.
2 Praise Him, all His angels;
praise Him, all His hosts.
3 Praise Him, sun and moon;
praise Him, all
   you shining stars.
4 Praise Him, highest heavens,
and you waters above
   the heavens.
5 Let them praise the name
   of the LORD,
for He commanded,
   and they were created.
6 He set them in position forever
   and ever;
He gave an order that will
   never pass away.

7 Praise the LORD
   from the earth,
all sea monsters
   and ocean depths,
8 lightning and hail, snow
   and cloud,
powerful wind that executes
   His command,
9 mountains and all hills,
fruit trees and all cedars,
10 wild animals and all cattle,
creatures that crawl
   and flying birds,

---

[a] **147:20** DSS, LXX, Syr, Tg read *He has not made known to them*

11  kings of the earth
        and all peoples,
    princes and all judges
        of the earth,
12  young men as well as
        young women,
    old and young together.
13  Let them praise the name
        of the LORD,
    for His name alone is exalted.
    His majesty covers heaven
        and earth.
14  He has raised up a •horn
        for His people,
    praise from all His godly ones,
    from the Israelites, the people
        close to Him.
    Hallelujah!

## Praise for God's Triumph

**149** •Hallelujah!
    Sing to the LORD
        a new song,
    His praise in the assembly
        of the godly.
2   Let Israel celebrate its
        Maker;
    let the children of Zion
        rejoice in their King.
3   Let them praise His name
        with dancing
    and make music to Him
        with tambourine and lyre.
4   For the LORD takes pleasure
        in His people;
    He adorns the humble
        with salvation.
5   Let the godly celebrate
        in triumphal glory;
    let them shout for joy
        on their beds.

6   Let the exaltation of God be
        in their mouths
    and a two-edged sword
        in their hands,
7   inflicting vengeance
        on the nations
    and punishment
        on the peoples,
8   binding their kings
        with chains
    and their dignitaries
        with iron shackles,
9   carrying out the judgment
        decreed against them.
    This honor is for all
        His godly people.
    Hallelujah!

## Praise the LORD

**150** •Hallelujah!
    Praise God in His sanctuary.
    Praise Him
        in His mighty heavens.
2   Praise Him
        for His powerful acts;
    praise Him
        for His abundant greatness.
3   Praise Him with trumpet blast;
    praise Him with harp
        and lyre.
4   Praise Him with tambourine
        and dance;
    praise Him with flute
        and strings.
5   Praise Him
        with resounding cymbals;
    praise Him
        with clashing cymbals.
6   Let everything that breathes
        praise the LORD.
    •Hallelujah!

# PROVERBS

## The Purpose of Proverbs

**1** The proverbs of Solomon
   son of David, king of Israel:
2 For gaining wisdom and being
      instructed;
   for understanding
      insightful sayings;
3 for receiving wise instruction
   ⌊in⌋ righteousness, justice,
      and integrity;
4 for teaching shrewdness
      to the inexperienced,
   knowledge and discretion
      to a young man—
5 a wise man will listen
      and increase his learning,
   and a discerning man will
      obtain guidance—
6 for understanding a proverb
      or a parable,
   the words of the wise,
      and their riddles.

7 The °fear of the LORD is
      the beginning
      of knowledge;
   fools despise wisdom
      and instruction.

## Avoid the Path of the Violent

8 Listen, my son, to your father's
      instruction,
   and don't reject your mother's
      teaching,
9 for they will be a garland
      of grace on your head
   and a ⌊gold⌋ chain around
      your neck.
10 My son, if sinners entice you,
      don't be persuaded.
11 If they say—"Come with us!
   Let's set an ambush and kill
      someone.

Let's attack
   some innocent person
   just for fun!
12 Let's swallow them alive,
      like °Sheol,
   still healthy as they go down
      to the °Pit.
13 We'll find all kinds
      of valuable property
   and fill our houses
      with plunder.
14 Throw in your lot with us,
   and we'll all share
      our money"—
15 my son, don't travel that road
      with them
   or set foot on their path,
16 because their feet run
      toward trouble
   and they hurry to commit
      murder.
17 It is foolish to spread a net
   where any bird can see it,
18 but they set an ambush to kill
      themselves;
   they attack their own lives.
19 Such are the paths of all
      who pursue gain
      dishonestly;
   it takes the lives of those
      who profit from it.

## Wisdom's Plea

20 Wisdom calls out in the street;
   she raises her voice
      in the public squares.
21 She cries out above
      the commotion;
   she speaks at the entrance
      of the city °gates:
22 "How long, foolish ones,
      will you love ignorance?

⌊How long⌋ will ⌊you⌋ mockers
  enjoy mocking
and ⌊you⌋ fools hate
  knowledge?
23  If you turn to my
      discipline,
    then I will pour out my spirit
      on you
    and teach you my words.
24  Since I called out
      and you refused,
    extended my hand and no one
      paid attention,
25  since you neglected all
      my counsel
    and did not accept
      my correction,
26  I, in turn, will laugh at
      your calamity.
    I will mock when terror
      strikes you,
27  when terror strikes you
      like a storm
    and your calamity comes
      like a whirlwind,
    when trouble and stress
      overcome you.
28  Then they will call me,
      but I won't answer;
    they will search for me,
      but won't find me.
29  Because they hated
      knowledge,
    didn't choose to fear
      the LORD,
30  were not interested
      in my counsel,
    and rejected all
      my correction,
31  they will eat the fruit
      of their way
    and be glutted with
      their own schemes.
32  For the waywardness
      of the inexperienced
      will kill them,
    and the complacency of fools
      will destroy them.

33  But whoever listens to me
      will live securely
    and be free from the fear
      of danger."

## Wisdom's Worth

2 My son, if you accept my words
    and store up my commands
      within you,
2   listening closely to wisdom
      and directing your heart
        to understanding;
3   furthermore, if you call out
        to insight
      and lift your voice
        to understanding,
4   if you seek it like silver
      and search for it like
        hidden treasure,
5   then you will understand
        the *fear of the LORD
      and discover the knowledge
        of God.
6   For the LORD gives wisdom;
      from His mouth come
        knowledge
      and understanding.
7   He stores up
        success for the upright;
    He is a shield for those
        who live with integrity
8   so that He may guard the paths
        of justice
      and protect the way
        of His loyal followers.
9   Then you will understand
        righteousness, justice,
      and integrity—
        every good path.
10  For wisdom will enter
        your heart,
      and knowledge will delight
        your soul.
11  Discretion will watch
        over you,
      and understanding will guard
        you,

12 rescuing you from the way
  of evil—
from the one who says
  perverse things,
13 ⌊from⌋ those who abandon
  the right paths
to walk in ways of darkness,
14 ⌊from⌋ those who enjoy
  doing evil
and celebrate perversity,
15 whose paths are crooked,
and whose ways are devious.
16 It will rescue you from
  a forbidden woman,
from a stranger
  with her flattering talk,
17 who abandons the companion
  of her youth
and forgets the covenant
  of her God;
18 for her house sinks down
  to death
and her ways to the land
  of the departed spirits.
19 None return who go to her;
none reach the paths of life.
20 So follow the way
  of good people,
and keep to the paths
  of the righteous.
21 For the upright will inhabit
  the land,
and those of integrity
  will remain in it;
22 but the wicked will be cut off
  from the land,
and the treacherous uprooted
  from it.

## Trust the LORD

**3** My son, don't forget
  my teaching,
but let your heart keep
  my commands;
2 for they will bring you
many days, a full life,
  and well-being.

3 Never let loyalty and
  faithfulness leave you.
Tie them around your neck;
write them on the tablet
  of your heart.
4 Then you will find favor
  and high regard
in the sight of God and man.

---

*"Learn to be unknown. To think of
oneself as nothing, and to think
well and highly of others is the best
and most perfect wisdom."*
—*Thomas á Kempis*

---

5 Trust in the LORD with all
  your heart,
and do not rely on your own
  understanding;
6 think about Him in all
  your ways,
and He will guide you
  on the right paths.
7 Don't consider yourself
  to be wise;
•fear the LORD and turn away
  from evil.
8 This will be healing
  for your body
and strengthening
  for your bones.
9 Honor the LORD
  with your possessions
and with the first produce
  of your entire harvest;
10 then your barns will be
  completely filled,
and your vats will overflow
  with new wine.
11 Do not despise
  the LORD's instruction,
  my son,
and do not loathe
  His discipline;

12 for the LORD disciplines
    the one He loves,
just as a father, the son
    he delights in.

## Wisdom Brings Happiness

13 Happy is a man who finds
    wisdom
and who acquires
    understanding,
14 for she is more profitable
    than silver,
and her revenue is better
    than gold.
15 She is more precious
    than jewels;
nothing you desire compares
    with her.
16 Long life is in her right hand;
in her left, riches and honor.
17 Her ways are pleasant,
and all her paths, peaceful.
18 She is a tree of life to those
    who embrace her,
and those who hold on to her
    are happy.

19 The LORD founded the earth
    by wisdom
and established the heavens
    by understanding.
20 By His knowledge
    the watery depths
    broke open,
and the clouds dripped
    with dew.

21 Maintain ⌊your⌋ competence
    and discretion.
My son, don't lose sight
    of them.
22 They will be life for you
and adornment for your neck.
23 Then you will go safely
    on your way;
your foot will not stumble.

24 When you lie down,
    you will not be afraid;
you will lie down,
    and your sleep will be
    pleasant.
25 Don't fear sudden danger
or the ruin of the wicked
    when it comes,
26 for the LORD will be
    your confidence
and will keep your foot
    from a snare.

## Treat Others Fairly

27 When it is in your power,
don't withhold good
    from the one to whom
    it is due.
28 Don't say to your neighbor,
    "Go away! Come back later.
I'll give it tomorrow"—
    when it is there with you.
29 Don't plan any harm against
    your neighbor,
for he trusts you and lives
    near you.
30 Don't accuse anyone
    without cause,
when he has done you
    no harm.

---

### Proverbs 3:27-35

*Humble people don't tend to attract a lot of attention—not because they feel inferior, but because they know the value of serving people where only God can see it. Want to feel good about yourself when you lie down at night? Think about others through the day.*

31 Don't envy a violent man
   or choose any of his ways;
32 for the devious are detestable
      to the LORD,
   but He is a friend
      to the upright.
33 The LORD's curse is
      on the household
      of the wicked,
   but He blesses the home
      of the righteous;
34 He mocks those who mock,
   but gives grace to the humble.
35 The wise will inherit honor,
   but He holds up fools
      to dishonor.

## A Father's Example

**4** Listen, ⌊my⌋ sons, to a father's
         discipline,
   and pay attention so that
      you may gain understanding,
2 for I am giving you good
      instruction.
   Don't abandon my teaching.
3 When I was a son
      with my father,
   tender and precious
      to my mother,
4 he taught me and said:
   "Your heart must hold on to
      my words.
   Keep my commands and live.
5 Get wisdom,
      get understanding;
   don't forget or turn away
      from the words
      of my mouth.
6 Don't abandon wisdom,
      and she will watch over
      you;
   love her, and she will guard
      you.
7 Wisdom is supreme—
      so get wisdom.
   And whatever else you get, get
      understanding.

8 Cherish her, and she will
      exalt you;
   if you embrace her, she will
      honor you.
9 She will place a garland
      of grace on your head;
   she will give you a crown
      of beauty."

## Two Ways of Life

10 Listen, my son.
      Accept my words,
   and you will live many years.
11 I am teaching you the way
      of wisdom;
   I am guiding you
      on straight paths.
12 When you walk, your steps
      will not be hindered;
   when you run, you will not
      stumble.
13 Hold on to instruction;
      don't let go.
   Guard it, for it is your life.
14 Don't set foot on the path
      of the wicked;
   don't proceed in the way
      of evil ones.
15 Avoid it; don't travel on it.
   Turn away from it,
      and pass it by.
16 For they can't sleep unless
      they have done evil;
   they are robbed of sleep unless
      they make someone
      stumble.
17 They eat the bread
      of wickedness
   and drink the wine
      of violence.
18 The path of the righteous is
      like the light of dawn,
   shining brighter and brighter
      until midday.
19 But the way of the wicked is
      like the darkest gloom;

they don't know what makes
  them stumble.

*The Straight Path*

20  My son, pay attention to
      my words;
    listen closely to my sayings.
21  Don't lose sight of them;
    keep them within your heart.
22  For they are life to those
      who find them,
    and health to
      one's whole body.
23  Guard your heart
      above all else,
    for it is the source of life.
24  Don't let your mouth speak
      dishonestly,
    and don't let your lips talk
      deviously.
25  Let your eyes look forward;
    fix your gaze straight ahead.
26  Carefully consider
      the path for your feet,
    and all your ways will be
      established.
27  Don't turn to the right
      or to the left;
    keep your feet away from evil.

*Avoid Seduction*

**5** My son, pay attention
      to my wisdom;
    listen closely
      to my understanding
2   so that ⌊you⌋ may maintain
      discretion
    and your lips safeguard
      knowledge.
3   Though the lips
      of the forbidden woman
      drip honey
    and her words are smoother
      than oil,
4   in the end she's as bitter
      as •wormwood

and as sharp as a double-
  edged sword.
5   Her feet go down to death;
    her steps head straight
      for •Sheol.
6   She doesn't consider the path
      of life;
    she doesn't know that
      her ways are unstable.

7   So now, ⌊my⌋ sons, listen
      to me,
    and don't turn away
      from the words
      of my mouth.
8   Keep your way far from her.
    Don't go near the door
      of her house.
9   Otherwise, you will give up
      your vitality to others
    and your years
      to someone cruel;
10  strangers will drain
      your resources,
    and your earnings will end up
      in a foreigner's house.
11  At the end of your life,
      you will lament
    when your physical body
      has been consumed,
12  and you will say, "How I hated
      discipline,
    and how my heart despised
      correction.
13  I didn't obey my teachers
    or listen closely to my mentors.
14  I was on the verge of
      complete ruin
    before the entire community."

*Enjoy Marriage*

15  Drink water from
      your own cistern,
    water flowing from
      your own well.
16  Should your springs flow
      in the streets,

streams of water
in the public squares?

17 They should be for you alone
and not for you ⌊to share⌋
with strangers.

18 Let your fountain be blessed,
and take pleasure in the wife
of your youth.

19 A loving doe,
a graceful fawn—
let her breasts always
satisfy you;
be lost in her love forever.

20 Why, my son, would you
be infatuated with
a forbidden woman
or embrace the breast
of a stranger?

21 For a man's ways are
before the LORD's eyes,
and He considers all his paths.

22 A wicked man's iniquities
entrap him;
he is entangled in the ropes
of his own sin.

23 He will die because there is no
instruction,
and be lost because of
his great stupidity.

## Financial Entanglements

**6** My son, if you have put up
security for your neighbor
or entered into an agreement
with a stranger,

2 you have been trapped
by the words of your lips—
ensnared by the words
of your mouth.

3 Do this, then, my son,
and free yourself,
for you have put yourself
in your neighbor's power:
Go, humble yourself,
and plead
with your neighbor.

4 Don't give sleep to your eyes
or slumber to your eyelids.

5 Escape like a gazelle
from a hunter,
like a bird from a fowler's trap.

## Laziness

6 Go to the ant, you slacker!
Observe its ways and become
wise.

7 Without leader, administrator,
or ruler,

8 it prepares its provisions
in summer;
it gathers its food
during harvest.

9 How long will you stay in bed,
you slacker?
When will you get up
from your sleep?

10 A little sleep, a little slumber,
a little folding of the arms
to rest,

11 and your poverty will come
like a robber,
your need, like a bandit.

## The Malicious Man

12 A worthless person,
a wicked man,
who goes around speaking
dishonestly,

13 who winks his eyes, signals
with his feet,
and gestures with his fingers,

14 who plots evil with perversity
in his heart—
he stirs up trouble
constantly.

15 Therefore calamity will strike
him suddenly;
he will be shattered
instantly—
beyond recovery.

## What the LORD Hates

<sup>16</sup> Six things the LORD hates;
in fact, seven are detestable
to Him:
<sup>17</sup> arrogant eyes, a lying tongue,
hands that shed
innocent blood,
<sup>18</sup> a heart that plots
wicked schemes,
feet eager to run to evil,
<sup>19</sup> a lying witness who gives false
testimony,
and one who stirs up trouble
among brothers.

## Warning against Adultery

<sup>20</sup> My son, keep
your father's command,
and don't reject
your mother's teaching.
<sup>21</sup> Always bind them
to your heart;
tie them around your neck.
<sup>22</sup> When you walk here
and there, they will
guide you;
when you lie down, they will
watch over you;
when you wake up, they will
talk to you.
<sup>23</sup> For a commandment is a lamp,
teaching is a light,
and corrective instructions are
the way to life.
<sup>24</sup> They will protect you from
an evil woman,<sup>a</sup>
from the flattering tongue
of a stranger.
<sup>25</sup> Don't lust in your heart for
her beauty
or let her captivate you with
her eyelashes.
<sup>26</sup> For a prostitute's fee is only
a loaf of bread,

but an adulteress goes after
[your] very life.
<sup>27</sup> Can a man embrace fire
and his clothes not be burned?
<sup>28</sup> Can a man walk on coals
without scorching his feet?
<sup>29</sup> So it is with the one
who sleeps with another
man's wife;
no one who touches her will
go unpunished.
<sup>30</sup> People don't despise the thief
if he steals
to satisfy himself when he is
hungry.
<sup>31</sup> Still, if caught, he must pay
seven times as much;
he must give up all the wealth
in his house.
<sup>32</sup> The one who commits
adultery lacks sense;
whoever does so destroys
himself.
<sup>33</sup> He will get a
beating and dishonor,
and his disgrace will never
be removed.
<sup>34</sup> For jealousy enrages
a husband,
and he will show no mercy
when he takes revenge.
<sup>35</sup> He will not be appeased
by anything
or be persuaded by lavish gifts.

**7** My son, obey my words,
and treasure my commands.
<sup>2</sup> Keep my commands and live;
protect my teachings as
you would the pupil
of your eye.
<sup>3</sup> Tie them to your fingers;
write them on the tablet
of your heart.
<sup>4</sup> Say to wisdom, "You are
my sister,"

<sup>a</sup> 6:24 LXX reads *from a married woman*

and call understanding
⌊your⌋ relative.
5 She will keep you
from a forbidden woman,
a stranger with
her flattering talk.

## A Story of Seduction

6 At the window of my house
I looked through my lattice.
7 I saw among
the inexperienced,
I noticed among the youths,
a young man lacking sense.
8 Crossing the street
near her corner,
he strolled down the road
to her house
9 at twilight, in the evening,
in the dark of the night.
10 A woman came to meet him,
dressed like a prostitute,
having a hidden agenda.
11 She is loud and defiant;
her feet do not stay at home.
12 Now in the street, now
in the squares,
she lurks at every corner.
13 She grabs him and kisses him;
she brazenly says to him,
14 "I've made
fellowship offerings;
today I've fulfilled my vows.
15 So I came out to meet you,
to search for you,
and I've found you.
16 I've spread coverings
on my bed—
richly colored linen
from Egypt.
17 I've perfumed my bed
with myrrh, aloes,
and cinnamon.
18 Come, let's drink deeply
of lovemaking
until morning.

Let's feast on
each other's love!
19 My husband isn't home;
he went on a long journey.
20 He took a bag of money
with him
and will come home
at the time
of the full moon."
21 She seduces him with
her persistent pleading;
she lures
with her flattering talk.
22 He follows her impulsively
like an ox going
to the slaughter,
like a deer bounding
toward a trap[a]
23 until an arrow pierces
its liver,
like a bird darting
into a snare—
he doesn't know it will cost
him his life.

24 Now, ⌊my⌋ sons, listen to me,
and pay attention to the words
of my mouth.
25 Don't let your heart turn aside
to her ways;
don't stray onto her paths.
26 For she has brought many
down to death;
her victims are countless.
27 Her house is the road
to *Sheol,
descending to the chambers
of death.

## Wisdom's Appeal

8 Doesn't Wisdom call out?
Doesn't Understanding make
her voice heard?
2 At the heights overlooking
the road,

---

[a] 7:22 Hb emended; lit *like shackles for the discipline of a fool*

## Proverbs 8:4-11

*Sometimes your choices are not between right and wrong but between good, better, and best. Then the only way to make the best decision is to determine what God would want you to do in that particular situation or with that certain amount of time.*

at the crossroads, she takes
  her stand.
3 Beside the gates at the entry
    to the city,
  at the main entrance,
    she cries out:
4 "People, I call out to you;
  my cry is to mankind.
5 Learn to be shrewd, you
    who are inexperienced;
  develop common sense, you
    who are foolish.
6 Listen, for I speak
    of noble things,
  and what my lips say is right.
7 For my mouth tells the truth,
  and wickedness is detestable
    to my lips.
8 All the words of my mouth
    are righteous;
  none of them are deceptive
    or perverse.
9 All of them are clear
    to the perceptive,
  and right to those
    who discover knowledge.
10 Accept my instruction
    instead of silver,
  and knowledge rather than
    pure gold.
11 For wisdom is better than
    precious stones,

and nothing desirable
  can compare with it.
12 I, Wisdom, share a home
    with shrewdness
  and have knowledge
    and discretion.
13 To *fear the LORD is to
    hate evil.
  I hate arrogant pride,
    evil conduct,
    and perverse speech.
14 I possess good advice
    and competence;
  I have understanding
    and strength.
15 It is by me that kings reign
  and rulers enact just law;
16 by me, princes lead,
  as do nobles ⌊and⌋ all
    righteous judges.
17 I love those who love me,
  and those who search for me
    find me.
18 With me are riches and honor,
  lasting wealth
    and righteousness.
19 My fruit is better than
    solid gold,
  and my harvest than
    pure silver.
20 I walk in the way
    of righteousness,
  along the paths of justice,
21 giving wealth
    as an inheritance to those
    who love me,
  and filling their treasuries.

22 The LORD made me
    at the beginning
    of His creation,
  before His works of long ago.
23 I was formed
    before ancient times,
  from the beginning,
    before the earth began.

> *"We are free to say no to good opportunities in order to say yes to the best, to do a few things without feeling we have to do everything."*
> —*Peg Rankin*

24 I was brought forth when
    there were no
    watery depths
and no springs filled
    with water.
25 I was brought forth
before the mountains and hills
    were established,
26 before He made the land,
    the fields,
or the first soil on earth.
27 I was there
    when He established
    the heavens,
when He laid out the horizon
    on the surface of the
    ocean,
28 when He placed the skies
    above,
when the fountains
    of the ocean gushed forth,
29 when He set a limit for the sea
so that the waters would not
    violate His command,
when He laid out
    the foundations
    of the earth.
30 I was a skilled
    craftsman beside Him.
I was His[a] delight every day,
    always rejoicing before Him.
31 I was rejoicing in
    His inhabited world,
    delighting in the human race.

32 And now, ⌊my⌋ sons,
    listen to me;
those who keep my ways
    are happy.
33 Listen to instruction
    and be wise;
don't ignore it.
34 Anyone who listens to me
    is happy,
watching at my doors
    every day,
waiting by the posts
    of my doorway.
35 For the one who finds me
    finds life
and obtains favor
    from the LORD,
36 but the one who sins against
    me harms himself;
all who hate me love death."

## Wisdom versus Foolishness

9 Wisdom has built her house;
  she has carved out
    her seven pillars.
2 She has prepared her meat;
    she has mixed her wine;
she has also set her table.
3 She has sent out her
    servants;
she calls out from
    the highest points
    of the city:
4 "Whoever is inexperienced,
    enter here!"
To the one who lacks sense,
    she says,
5 "Come, eat my bread,
and drink the wine
    I have mixed.
6 Leave inexperience behind,
    and you will live;
pursue the way
    of understanding.

[a] 8:30 LXX; Hb omits *His*

7 The one who corrects
    a mocker will bring
    dishonor on himself;
the one who rebukes
    a wicked man will get hurt.
8 Don't rebuke a mocker,
    or he will hate you;
rebuke a wise man,
    and he will love you.
9 Instruct a wise man,
    and he will be wiser still;
teach a righteous man,
    and he will learn more.

10 The •fear of the LORD is
    the beginning of wisdom,
and the knowledge
    of the Holy One is
    understanding.
11 For by Wisdom your days
    will be many,
and years will be added
    to your life.
12 If you are wise, you are wise
    for your own benefit;
if you mock, you alone
    will bear
    ⌊the consequences⌋."
13 The woman Folly is rowdy;
she is gullible and knows
    nothing.
14 She sits by the doorway
    of her house,
on a seat at the highest point
    of the city,
15 calling to those who pass by,
who go straight ahead
    on their paths:
16 "Whoever is inexperienced,
    enter here!"
To the one who lacks sense,
    she says,
17 "Stolen water is sweet,
and bread ⌊eaten⌋ secretly
    is tasty!"
18 But he doesn't know that
    the departed spirits
    are there,

that her guests are
    in the depths of •Sheol.

## A Collection of Solomon's Proverbs

**10** Solomon's proverbs:

A wise son brings joy
    to his father,
but a foolish son, heartache
    to his mother.

2 Ill-gotten gains do not profit
    anyone,
but righteousness rescues
    from death.

3 The LORD will not let
    the righteous go hungry,
but He denies the wicked
    what they crave.

4 Idle hands make one poor,
but diligent hands bring
    riches.

5 The son who gathers
    during summer is prudent;
the son who sleeps
    during harvest
    is disgraceful.

6 Blessings are on the head
    of the righteous,
but the mouth of the wicked
    conceals violence.

7 The remembrance
    of the righteous is
    a blessing,
but the name of the wicked
    will rot.

8 A wise heart accepts
    commands,
but foolish lips will be
    destroyed.

9 The one who lives
     with integrity lives
     securely,
   but whoever perverts his ways
     will be found out.

10 A sly wink of the eye causes
     grief,
   and foolish lips will be
     destroyed.

11 The mouth of the righteous is
     a fountain of life,
   but the mouth of the wicked
     conceals violence.

12 Hatred stirs up conflicts,
   but love covers all offenses.

13 Wisdom is found on the lips
     of the discerning,
   but a rod is for the back
     of the one who lacks sense.

14 The wise store up knowledge,
   but the mouth of the fool
     hastens destruction.

15 A rich man's wealth is
     his fortified city;
   the poverty of the poor is
     their destruction.

16 The labor of the righteous
     leads to life;
   the activity of the wicked leads
     to sin.

17 The one who follows
     instruction is on the path
     to life,
   but the one who rejects
     correction goes astray.

18 The one who conceals hatred
     has lying lips,
   and whoever spreads slander
     is a fool.

19 When there are many words,
     sin is unavoidable,
   but the one who controls
     his lips is wise.

20 The tongue of the righteous is
     pure silver;
   the heart of the wicked is
     of little value.

21 The lips of the righteous feed
     many,
   but fools die for lack of sense.

22 The LORD's blessing enriches,
   and toil adds nothing to it.

23 As shameful conduct is
     pleasure for a fool,
   so wisdom is for a man
     of understanding.

24 What the wicked dreads
     will come upon him,
   but what the righteous desires
     will be given to him.

25 When the whirlwind passes,
     the wicked are no more,
   but the righteous are secure
     forever.

26 Like vinegar to the teeth
     and smoke to the eyes,
   so the slacker is to the one
     who sends him
     ⌊on an errand⌋.

27 The •fear of the LORD prolongs
     life,
   but the years of the wicked
     are cut short.

28 The hope of the righteous
     is joy,
   but the expectation
     of the wicked comes
     to nothing.

"A good steward recognizes the value of what he possesses, and wisely manages it to the glory of the one who owns it."
—Jack Taylor

29  The way of the LORD
      is a stronghold
      for the honorable,
    but destruction awaits
      the malicious.

30  The righteous will never
      be shaken,
    but the wicked will not remain
      on the earth.

31  The mouth of the righteous
      produces wisdom,
    but a perverse tongue will be
      cut out.

32  The lips of the righteous know
      what is appropriate,
    but the mouth of the wicked,
      ⌊only⌋ what is perverse.

**11** Dishonest scales are detestable
      to the LORD,
    but an accurate weight is
      His delight.

2   When pride comes, disgrace
      follows,
    but with humility comes
      wisdom.

3   The integrity of the upright
      guides them,
    but the perversity
      of the treacherous destroys
      them.

4   Wealth is not profitable
      on a day of wrath,
    but righteousness rescues
      from death.

5   The righteousness
      of the blameless clears
      his path,
    but the wicked person will fall
      because of his wickedness.

6   The righteousness
      of the upright rescues
      them,
    but the treacherous
      are trapped by
      their own desires.

7   When the wicked dies,
      his expectation comes
      to nothing,
    and hope placed in wealth[a]
      vanishes.

8   The righteous is rescued
      from trouble;
    in his place, the wicked
      goes in.

9   With his mouth the ungodly
      destroys his neighbor,
    but through knowledge
      the righteous are rescued.

10  When the righteous thrive,
      a city rejoices,
    and when the wicked die,
      there is joyful shouting.

11  A city is exalted
      by the blessing
      of the upright,
    but it is overthrown
      by the mouth
      of the wicked.

12  Whoever shows contempt for

[a] 11:7 LXX reads *hope of the ungodly*

his neighbor lacks sense,
but a man with understanding
keeps silent.

<sup>13</sup> A gossip goes around revealing
a secret,
but the trustworthy keeps
a confidence.

<sup>14</sup> Without guidance, people fall,
but with many counselors
there is deliverance.

<sup>15</sup> If someone puts up security
for a stranger,
he will suffer for it,
but the one who hates
such agreements
is protected.

<sup>16</sup> A gracious woman gains
honor,
but violent men gain ⌊only⌋
riches.

<sup>17</sup> A kind man benefits himself,
but a cruel man brings disaster
on himself.

<sup>18</sup> The wicked man earns
an empty wage,
but the one who sows
righteousness,
a true reward.

<sup>19</sup> Genuine righteousness ⌊leads⌋
to life,
but pursuing evil ⌊leads⌋
to death.

<sup>20</sup> Those with twisted minds
are detestable
to the LORD,
but those with blameless
conduct are His delight.

<sup>21</sup> Be assured that the wicked

---

*Proverbs 11:24-25*

*Your house is His. Your car is His.
Your money is His. Your family is
His. Every single thing you have is
His. You're just taking care of it for
Him. Aren't you? God is awfully
generous to let us borrow all these
things. Are you willing to start
giving them back?*

---

will not go unpunished,
but the offspring
of the righteous
will escape.

<sup>22</sup> A beautiful woman
who rejects good sense
is like a gold ring
in a pig's snout.

<sup>23</sup> The desire of the righteous
⌊turns out⌋ well,
but the hope of the wicked
⌊leads to⌋ wrath.

<sup>24</sup> One person gives freely,
yet gains more;
another withholds
what is right, only
to become poor.

<sup>25</sup> A generous person will be
enriched,
and the one who gives
a drink of water
will receive water.

<sup>26</sup> People will curse anyone
who hoards grain,
but a blessing will come
to the one who sells it.

27 The one who searches for
        what is good finds favor,
    but if someone looks for
        trouble, it will come to him.

28 Anyone trusting in his riches
        will fall,
    but the righteous will flourish
        like foliage.

29 The one who brings ruin
        on his household
        will inherit the wind,
    and a fool will be a slave
        to someone whose heart
        is wise.

30 The fruit of the righteous is
        a tree of life,
    but violence[a] takes lives.

31 If the righteous will be repaid
        on earth,
    how much more the wicked
        and sinful.

**12** Whoever loves instruction
        loves knowledge,
    but one who hates correction
        is stupid.

2 The good obtain favor
        from the LORD,
    but He condemns a man
        who schemes.

3 Man cannot be made secure
        by wickedness,
    but the root of the righteous is
        immovable.

4 A capable wife is
        her husband's crown,
    but a wife who causes shame
        is like rottenness
        in his bones.

5 The thoughts of the righteous
        ⌊are⌋ just,
    but guidance from the wicked
        ⌊leads to⌋ deceit.

6 The words of the wicked are
        a deadly ambush,
    but the speech of the upright
        rescues them.

7 The wicked are overthrown
        and perish,
    but the house of the righteous
        will stand.

8 A man is praised
        for his insight,
    but a twisted mind is despised.

9 Better to be dishonored,
        yet have a servant,
    than to act important but have
        no food.

10 A righteous man cares about
        his animal's health,
    but ⌊even⌋ the merciful acts
        of the wicked are cruel.

11 The one who works his land
        will have plenty of food,
    but whoever chases fantasies
        lacks sense.

12 The wicked desire what
        evil men have,
    but the root of the righteous
        produces ⌊fruit⌋.

13 An evil man is trapped by
        ⌊his⌋ rebellious speech,
    but the righteous escapes
        from trouble.

14 A man will be satisfied with
        good by the words

---

a 11:30 LXX, Syr; Hb reads *but a wise one*

of his mouth,
and the work of a man's hands
will reward him.

15 A fool's way is right
in his own eyes,
but whoever listens to counsel
is wise.

16 A fool's displeasure is known
at once,
but whoever ignores an insult
is sensible.

17 Whoever speaks the truth
declares what is right,
but a false witness, deceit.

18 There is one who speaks
rashly, like a piercing
sword;
but the tongue of the wise
⌊brings⌋ healing.

19 Truthful lips endure forever,
but a lying tongue,
only a moment.

20 Deceit is in the hearts of those
who plot evil,
but those who promote peace
have joy.

21 No disaster ⌊overcomes⌋
the righteous,
but the wicked are full
of misery.

22 Lying lips are detestable
to the LORD,
but faithful people
are His delight.

23 A shrewd person conceals
knowledge,
but a foolish heart publicizes
stupidity.

24 The diligent hand will rule,
but laziness will lead to
forced labor.

25 Anxiety in a man's heart
weighs it down,
but a good word cheers it up.

26 A righteous man is careful
in dealing
with his neighbor,
but the ways of wicked men
lead them astray.

27 A lazy man doesn't roast
his game,
but to a diligent man,
his wealth is precious.

28 There is life in the path
of righteousness,
but another path leads
to death.

**13** A wise son ⌊hears his⌋
father's instruction,
but a mocker doesn't listen
to rebuke.

_Proverbs 12:25_

_Christian Influence_

_The bottom line is that people are
hurting, suffering from loneliness,
guilt, pointlessness, shame. Reel-
ing from betrayal and injustice,
dealing with aches and pains. Your
smile, or thank you, or thoughtful
note, or genuine "How-are-
you?"—they make a difference.
They draw people to Christ._

2 From the words of his mouth,
    a man will enjoy
    good things,
but treacherous people have
    an appetite for violence.

3 The one who guards his mouth
    protects his life;
the one who opens his lips
    invites his own ruin.

4 The slacker craves,
    yet has nothing,
but the diligent is fully
    satisfied.

5 The righteous hate lying,
but the wicked act disgustingly
    and disgracefully.

6 Righteousness guards people
    of integrity,
but wickedness undermines
    the sinner.

7 One man pretends to be rich
    but has nothing;
another pretends to be poor
    but has great wealth.

8 Riches are a ransom
    for a man's life,
but a poor man hears
    no threat.

9 The light of the righteous
    shines brightly,
but the lamp of the wicked
    is extinguished.

10 Arrogance leads to nothing
    but strife,
but wisdom is gained by those
    who take advice.

11 Wealth obtained by fraud
    will dwindle,
but whoever earns it through
    labor will multiply it.

12 Delayed hope makes the heart
    sick,
but fulfilled desire is a tree
    of life.

13 The one who has contempt
    for instruction will pay
    the penalty,
but the one who respects
    a command will be
    rewarded.

14 A wise man's instruction is
    a fountain of life,
turning people away
    from the snares of death.

15 Good sense wins favor,
but the way of the treacherous
    never changes.

16 Every sensible person acts
    knowledgeably,
but a fool displays his stupidity.

17 A wicked messenger falls
    into trouble,
but a trustworthy courier
    ⌊brings⌋ healing.

18 Poverty and disgrace ⌊come to⌋
    those who ignore
    instruction,
but the one who accepts
    rebuke will be honored.

19 Desire fulfilled is sweet
    to the taste,
but fools hate to turn
    from evil.

20 The one who walks
    with the wise will become
    wise,

but a companion of fools will
suffer harm.

21   Disaster pursues sinners,
but good rewards
the righteous.

22   A good man leaves
an inheritance
to his grandchildren,
but the sinner's wealth
is stored up
for the righteous.

23   The field of the poor yields
abundant food,
but without justice, it is
swept away.

24   The one who will not use
the rod hates his son,
but the one who loves him
disciplines him diligently.

25   A righteous man eats until
he is satisfied,
but the stomach of the wicked
is empty.

14 Every wise woman builds
her house,
but a foolish one tears it down
with her own hands.

2   Whoever lives with integrity
•fears the LORD,
but the one who is devious
in his ways despises Him.

3   The proud speech of a fool
⌊brings⌋ a rod ⌊of discipline⌋,
but the lips of the wise protect
them.

4   Where there are no oxen,
the feed-trough is empty,

but an abundant harvest
⌊comes⌋
through the strength
of an ox.

5   An honest witness does not
deceive,
but a dishonest witness utters
lies.

6   A mocker seeks wisdom
and doesn't find it,
but knowledge ⌊comes⌋ easily
to the perceptive.

7   Stay away from a foolish man;
you will gain no knowledge
from his speech.

8   The sensible man's wisdom is
to consider his way,
but the stupidity of fools
deceives ⌊them⌋.

9   Fools mock at making
restitution,
but there is goodwill
among the upright.

10   The heart knows
its own bitterness,
and no outsider shares
in its joy.

11   The house of the wicked
will be destroyed,
but the tent of the upright
will stand.

12   There is a way that seems
right to a man,
but its end is the way
to death.

13   Even in laughter a heart
may be sad,
and joy may end in grief.

14 The disloyal will get what
     their conduct deserves,
and a good man, what
     his ⌊deeds deserve.⌋

15 The inexperienced believe
     anything,
but the sensible
     watch their steps.

16 A wise man is cautious
     and turns from evil,
but a fool is easily angered
     and is careless.

17 A quick-tempered man acts
     foolishly,
and a man who schemes
     is hated.

18 The gullible inherit
     foolishness,
but the sensible are crowned
     with knowledge.

19 The evil bow before those
     who are good,
the wicked, at the gates
     of the righteous.

20 A poor man is hated even
     by his neighbor,
but there are many who love
     the rich.

21 The one who despises
     his neighbor sins,
but whoever shows kindness
     to the poor will be happy.

22 Don't those who plan evil
     go astray?
But those who plan good find
     loyalty and faithfulness.

23 There is profit in all
     hard work,
but endless talk leads only
     to poverty.

24 The crown of the wise is
     their wealth,
but the foolishness of fools
     produces foolishness.

25 A truthful witness rescues
     lives,
but one who utters lies
     is deceitful.

26 In the fear of the LORD one has
     strong confidence
and his children have
     a refuge.

27 The fear of the LORD is
     a fountain of life,
turning people from the snares
     of death.

28 A large population is
     a king's splendor,
but a shortage of people is
     a ruler's devastation.

29 A patient person ⌊shows⌋ great
     understanding,
but a quick-tempered one
     promotes foolishness.

30 A tranquil heart is life
     to the body,
but jealousy is rottenness
     to the bones.

31 The one who oppresses
     the poor insults
     their Maker,
but one who is kind
     to the needy honors Him.

32 The wicked are thrown down
     by their own sin,
but the righteous have a refuge
     when they die.

33 Wisdom resides in the heart
        of the discerning;
    she is known[a] even
        among fools.

34 Righteousness exalts a nation,
    but sin is a disgrace
        to any people.

35 A king favors a wise servant,
    but his anger falls on
        a disgraceful one.

---

### Proverbs 15:1-2

*One of the biggest enemies in your
fight for Christian victory is a foe
so small you could easily overlook
it but it's so close to your heart that
it's hard to control. Your words will
tell you a lot about who you really
are. What are your words saying
about you?*

---

**15** A gentle answer turns away
        anger,
    but a harsh word stirs up
        wrath.

2 The tongue of the wise makes
        knowledge attractive,
    but the mouth of fools
        blurts out foolishness.

3 The eyes of the LORD are
        everywhere,
    observing the wicked
        and the good.

4 The tongue that heals is a tree
        of life,

but a devious tongue breaks
        the spirit.

5 A fool despises his father's
        instruction,
    but a person who heeds
        correction is sensible.

6 The house of the righteous has
        great wealth,
    but trouble accompanies
        the income of the wicked.

7 The lips of the wise broadcast
        knowledge,
    but not so the heart of fools.

8 The sacrifice of the wicked
        is detestable to the LORD,
    but the prayer of the upright is
        His delight.

9 The LORD detests the way
        of the wicked,
    but He loves the one who
        pursues righteousness.

10 Discipline is harsh for the one
        who leaves the path;
    the one who hates correction
        will die.

11 •Sheol and •Abaddon lie open
        before the LORD—
    how much more,
        human hearts.

12 A mocker doesn't love one
        who corrects him;
    he will not consult the wise.

13 A joyful heart makes a face
        cheerful,
    but a sad heart ⌊produces⌋
        a broken spirit.

[a] 14:33 LXX reads *unknown*

14   A discerning mind seeks
         knowledge,
     but the mouth of fools feeds
         on foolishness.

15   All the days of the oppressed
         are miserable,
     but a cheerful heart has
         a continual feast.

16   Better a little with the *fear
         of the LORD
     than great treasure
         with turmoil.

----

*"Let your words be few, lest you
say with your tongue what you will
afterward repent with your heart."*
—*George MacDonald*

----

17   Better a meal of vegetables
         where there is love
     than a fattened calf
         with hatred.

18   A hot-tempered man stirs up
         conflict,
     but a man slow to anger calms
         strife.

19   A slacker's way is like
         a thorny hedge,
     but the path of the upright is
         a highway.

20   A wise son brings joy
         to his father,
     but a foolish one despises
         his mother.

21   Foolishness brings joy to one
         without sense,
     but a man with understanding
         walks a straight path.

22   Plans fail when there is
         no counsel,
     but with many advisers
         they succeed.

23   A man takes joy in giving
         an answer;
     and a timely word—how good
         that is!

24   For the discerning the path
         of life leads upward,
     so that he may avoid
         going down to Sheol.

25   The LORD destroys the house
         of the proud,
     but He protects
         the widow's territory.

26   The LORD detests the plans
         of an evil man,
     but pleasant words are pure.

27   The one who profits
         dishonestly troubles
         his household,
     but the one who hates bribes
         will live.

28   The mind of the righteous
         person thinks
         before answering,
     but the mouth of the wicked
         blurts out evil things.

29   The LORD is far
         from the wicked,
     but He hears the prayer
         of the righteous.

30   Bright eyes cheer the heart;
     good news
         strengthens the bones.

31   An ear that listens to life-
         giving rebukes

will be at home
    among the wise.

32  Anyone who ignores
        instruction despises himself,
    but whoever listens
        to correction acquires
        good sense.

33  The fear of the LORD is
        wisdom's instruction,
    and humility comes
        before honor.

**16** The reflections of the heart
        belong to man,
    but the answer of the tongue
        is from the LORD.

2   All a man's ways seem right
        in his own eyes,
    but the LORD weighs
        the motives.

3   Commit your activities
        to the LORD
    and your plans will be
        achieved.

4   The LORD has prepared
        everything for His purpose—
    even the wicked for the day
        of disaster.

5   Everyone with a proud heart is
        detestable to the LORD;
    be assured, he will not go
        unpunished.

6   Wickedness is atoned for
        by loyalty and faithfulness,
    and one turns from evil
        by the •fear of the LORD.

7   When a man's ways please
        the LORD,
    He makes even his enemies
        to be at peace with him.

8   Better a little
        with righteousness
    than great income
        with injustice.

9   A man's heart plans his way,
    but the LORD determines
        his steps.

10  God's verdict is on the lips
        of a king;
    his mouth should not err
        in judgment.

11  Honest balances and scales are
        the LORD's;
    all the weights in the bag are
        His concern.

12  Wicked behavior is detestable
        to kings,
    since a throne is established
        through righteousness.

13  Righteous lips are a king's
        delight,
    and he loves one
        who speaks honestly.

14  A king's fury is a messenger
        of death,
    but a wise man appeases it.

15  When a king's face lights up,
        there is life;
    his favor is like a cloud
        with spring rain.

16  Acquire wisdom—
        how much better it is
        than gold!
    And acquire understanding—
        it is preferable to silver.

17  The highway of the upright
        avoids evil;
    the one who guards his way
        protects his life.

18  Pride comes before
        destruction,
    and an arrogant spirit before
        a fall.

19  Better to be lowly of spirit
        with the humble[a]
    than to divide plunder
        with the proud.

20  The one who understands
        a matter finds success,
    and the one who trusts
        in the LORD will be happy.

21  Anyone with a wise heart
        is called discerning,
    and pleasant speech increases
        learning.

22  Insight is a fountain
        of life for its possessor,
    but folly is the instruction
        of fools.

23  A wise heart instructs
        its mouth
    and increases learning
        with its speech.

24  Pleasant words are
        a honeycomb:
    sweet to the soul and healing
        to the bones.

25  There is a way that seems
        right to a man,
    but in the end it is the way
        of death.

26  A worker's appetite works
        for him
    because his
        hunger urges him on.

27  A worthless man digs up evil,

and his speech is like
    a scorching fire.

28  A contrary man spreads
        conflict,
    and a gossip separates friends.

29  A violent man lures
        his neighbor,
    leading him in a way that is
        not good.

30  The one who narrows his eyes
        is planning deceptions;
    the one who compresses
        his lips brings about evil.

31  Gray hair is a glorious crown;
    it is found in the way
        of righteousness.

32  Patience is better than power,
    and controlling one's
        temper, than capturing
        a city.

33  The lot is cast into the lap,
    but its every decision is
        from the LORD.

**17** Better a dry crust with peace
    than a house full of feasting
        with strife.

2   A wise servant will rule over
        a disgraceful son
    and share an inheritance
        among brothers.

3   A crucible is for silver
        and a smelter for gold,
    but the LORD is a tester
        of hearts.

4   A wicked person listens to
        malicious talk;

[a] 16:19 Alt Hb tradition reads *afflicted*

a liar pays attention to
    a destructive tongue.

5  The one who mocks the poor
    insults his Maker,
and one who rejoices over
    disaster will not go
    unpunished.

6  Grandchildren are the crown
    of the elderly,
and the pride of sons is
    their fathers.

7  Excessive speech is not
    appropriate on a fool's lips;
how much worse are lies
    for a ruler.

8  A bribe seems like
    a magic stone to its owner;
wherever he turns,
    he succeeds.

9  Whoever conceals an offense
    promotes love,
but whoever gossips about it
    separates friends.

10  A rebuke cuts into
    a perceptive person
more than a hundred lashes
    into a fool.

11  An evil man seeks only rebellion;
a cruel messenger will be sent
    against him.

12  Better for a man to meet a bear
    robbed of her cubs
than a fool in his foolishness.

13  If anyone returns evil for good,
evil will never depart
    from his house.

14  To start a conflict is to release
    a flood;
stop the dispute before
    it breaks out.

15  Acquitting the guilty
    and condemning the just—

both are detestable
    to the LORD.

16  Why does a fool have money
    in his hand
with no intention of buying
    wisdom?

17  A friend loves at all times,
and a brother is born for
    a difficult time.

18  One without sense enters
    an agreement
and puts up security
    for his friend.

19  One who loves to offend loves
    strife;
one who builds
    a high threshold invites
    injury.

20  One with a twisted mind
    will not succeed,
and one with deceitful speech
    will fall into ruin.

21  A man fathers a fool
    to his own sorrow;
the father of a fool has no joy.

22  A joyful heart is
    good medicine,
but a broken spirit dries up
    the bones.

23  A wicked man secretly takes
    a bribe
to subvert the course
    of justice.

24  Wisdom is the focus
    of the perceptive,
but a fool's eyes roam
    to the ends of the earth.

25  A foolish son is grief
    to his father
and bitterness to the one
    who bore him.

26 It is certainly not good to fine
       an innocent person,
   or to beat a noble
       for his honesty.

27 The intelligent person
       restrains his words,
   and one who keeps
       a cool head is a man
       of understanding.

28 Even a fool is considered wise
       when he keeps silent,
   discerning, when he seals
       his lips.

**18** One who isolates himself
       pursues ⌊selfish⌋ desires;
   he rebels against all
       sound judgment.

2 A fool does not delight
       in understanding,
   but only wants to show off
       his opinions.

3 When a wicked man comes,
       shame does also,
   and along with dishonor,
       disgrace.

4 The words of a man's mouth
       are deep waters,
   a flowing river, a fountain
       of wisdom.

5 It is not good to show partiality
       to the guilty
   by perverting the justice due
       the innocent.

6 A fool's lips lead to strife,
   and his mouth provokes
       a beating.

7 A fool's mouth is
       his devastation,

and his lips are a trap
       for his life.

8 A gossip's words are like
       choice food
   that goes down to
       one's innermost being.

9 The one who is truly lazy
       in his work
   is brother to a vandal.

10 The name of the LORD is
       a strong tower;
   the righteous run to it
       and are protected.

11 A rich man's wealth is
       his fortified city;
   in his imagination it is like
       a high wall.

12 Before his downfall
       a man's heart is proud,
   but before honor comes
       humility.

13 The one who gives an answer
       before he listens—
   this is foolishness and disgrace
       for him.

14 A man's spirit can endure
       sickness,
   but who can survive
       a broken spirit?

15 The mind of the discerning
       acquires knowledge,
   and the ear of the wise seeks it.

16 A gift opens doors for a man
   and brings him before
       the great.

17 The first to state his case
       seems right

until another comes and cross-
examines him.

18 ⌊Casting⌋ the lot ends quarrels
and separates
     powerful opponents.

19 An offended brother is
     ⌊harder to reach⌋ than
     a fortified city,
and quarrels are like the bars
     of a fortress.

20 From the fruit of his mouth
     a man's stomach
     is satisfied;
he is filled with the product
     of his lips.

21 Life and death are
     in the power of the tongue,
and those who love it will eat
     its fruit.

22 A man who finds a wife finds
     a good thing
and obtains favor
     from the LORD.

23 The poor man pleads,
but the rich one answers
     roughly.

24 A man with many friends
     may be harmed,[a]
but there is a friend who stays
     closer than a brother.

**19** Better a poor man who walks
     in integrity
than someone who has
     deceitful lips and is a fool.

2 Even zeal is not good
     without knowledge,

and the one who acts
     hastily sins.

3 A man's own foolishness leads
     him astray,
yet his heart rages against
     the LORD.

4 Wealth attracts many friends,
but a poor man is separated
     from his friend.

5 A false witness will not go
     unpunished,
and one who utters lies
     will not escape.

6 Many seek the favor of a ruler,
and everyone is a friend of one
     who gives gifts.

7 All the brothers of a poor man
     hate him;
how much more do his friends
     keep their distance
     from him!
He may pursue ⌊them with⌋
     words, ⌊but⌋ they are not
     ⌊there⌋.

8 The one who acquires
     good sense loves himself;
one who safeguards
     understanding finds success.

9 A false witness will not go
     unpunished,
and one who utters lies
     perishes.

10 Luxury is not appropriate
     for a fool—
how much less for a slave
     to rule over princes!

11 A person's insight gives him
     patience,

a 18:24 Some LXX mss, Syr, Tg, Vg read *friends must be friendly*

and his virtue is to overlook
    an offense.

12  A king's rage is like
    a lion's roar,
but his favor is like dew
    on the grass.

13  A foolish son is
    his father's ruin,
and a wife's nagging is
    an endless dripping.

14  A house and wealth
    are inherited from fathers,
but a sensible wife is
    from the LORD.

15  Laziness induces deep sleep,
and a lazy person will go
    hungry.

16  The one who keeps commands
    preserves himself;
one who disregards his ways
    will die.

17  Kindness to the poor is a loan
    to the LORD,
and He will give a reward
    to the lender.

18  Discipline your son while
    there is hope;
don't be intent on killing
    him.

19  A person with great anger
    bears the penalty;
if you rescue him, you'll have
    to do it again.

20  Listen to counsel and receive
    instruction
so that you may be wise
    in later life.

21  Many plans are
    in a man's heart,
but the LORD's decree
    will prevail.

22  A man's desire should be
    loyalty to the covenant;
better to be a poor man than
    a perjurer.

23  The •fear of the LORD leads
    to life;
one will sleep
    at night without danger.

24  The slacker buries his hand
    in the bowl;
he doesn't even bring it back
    to his mouth.

25  Strike a mocker,
    and the inexperienced
    learn a lesson;
rebuke the discerning,
    and he gains knowledge.

26  The one who assaults
    his father and evicts
    his mother
is a disgraceful
    and shameful son.

27  If you stop listening
    to instruction, my son,
you will stray from the words
    of knowledge.

28  A worthless witness mocks
    justice,
and a wicked mouth swallows
    iniquity.

29  Judgments are prepared
    for mockers,
and beatings for the backs
    of fools.

**20** Wine is a mocker, beer is
        a brawler,
and whoever staggers
        because of them
        is not wise.

2  A king's terrible wrath is like
        the roaring of a lion;
anyone who provokes him
        endangers himself.

3  It is honorable for a man
        to resolve a dispute,
but any fool can get himself
        into a quarrel.

4  The slacker does not plow
        during planting season;
at harvest time
        he looks, and there is
        nothing.

5  Counsel in a man's heart is
        deep water;
but a man of understanding
        draws it up.

6  Many a man proclaims
        his own loyalty,
but who can find
        a trustworthy man?

7  The one who lives
        with integrity is righteous;
his children who come
        after him will be happy.

8  A king sitting on a throne
        to judge
sifts out all evil with his eyes.

9  Who can say, "I have kept
        my heart pure;
I am cleansed from my sin"?

10  Differing weights
        and varying measures—

both are detestable
        to the LORD.

11  Even a young man is known
        by his actions—
by whether his behavior
        is pure and upright.

12  The hearing ear
        and the seeing eye—
the LORD made them both.

13  Don't love sleep, or you will
        become poor;
open your eyes,
        and you'll have enough
        to eat.

14  "It's worthless, it's worthless!"
        the buyer says,
but after he is on his way,
        he gloats.

15  There is gold and a multitude
        of jewels,
but knowledgeable lips are
        a rare treasure.

16  Take his garment, for he has
        put up security
        for a stranger;
get collateral if it is
        for foreigners.

17  Food gained by fraud is sweet
        to a man,
but afterward his mouth is full
        of gravel.

18  Finalize plans through counsel,
and wage war with sound
        guidance.

19  The one who reveals secrets is
        a constant gossip;
avoid someone
        with a big mouth.

545

PROVERBS 21:5

<sup>20</sup> Whoever curses his father
  or mother—
his lamp will go out
  in deep darkness.

<sup>21</sup> An inheritance gained
  prematurely
will not be blessed ultimately.

<sup>22</sup> Don't say, "I will avenge
  this evil!"
Wait on the LORD, and He will
  rescue you.

<sup>23</sup> Differing
  weights are detestable
  to the LORD,
and dishonest scales
  are unfair.

<sup>24</sup> A man's steps are determined
  by the LORD,
so how can anyone understand
  his own way?

<sup>25</sup> It is a trap for anyone
  to dedicate something
  rashly
and later to reconsider
  his vows.

<sup>26</sup> A wise king separates out
  the wicked
and drives
  the threshing wheel
  over them.

<sup>27</sup> A person's breath is the lamp
  of the LORD,
searching the innermost parts.

<sup>28</sup> Loyalty and faithfulness deliver
  a king;
through loyalty he maintains
  his throne.

<sup>29</sup> The glory of young men is
  their strength,
and the splendor of old men is
  gray hair.

<sup>30</sup> Lashes and wounds
  purge away evil,
and beatings cleanse
  the innermost parts.

**21** A king's heart is
  a water channel
  in the LORD's hand:
He directs it wherever
  He chooses.

<sup>2</sup> All the ways of a man
  seem right to him,
but the LORD evaluates
  the motives.

<sup>3</sup> Doing what is righteous
  and just
is more acceptable to the LORD
  than sacrifice.

<sup>4</sup> The lamp[a] that guides
  the wicked—
haughty eyes
  and an arrogant heart—
  is sin.

<sup>5</sup> The plans of the diligent
  certainly lead to profit,

*"Giving from a grateful heart and expecting nothing in return is a sweet offering to the One who owns everything you have anyway."*
—*Mary Hunt*

[a] **21:4** Other mss read *tillage*

but anyone who is reckless
   only becomes poor.

6   Making a fortune
     through a lying tongue
  is a vanishing mist, a pursuit
     of death.[a]

7   The violence of the wicked
     sweeps them away
  because they refuse
     to act justly.

8   A guilty man's conduct
     is crooked,
  but the behavior
     of the innocent is upright.

9   Better to live on the corner
     of a roof
  than to share a house
     with a nagging wife.

10  A wicked person desires evil;
  he has no consideration
     for his neighbor.

11  When a mocker is punished,
     the inexperienced
     become wiser;
  when one teaches a wise man,
     he acquires knowledge.

12  The Righteous One considers
     the house of the wicked;
  He brings the wicked to ruin.

13  The one who shuts his ears
     to the cry of the poor
  will himself also call out
     and not be answered.

14  A secret gift soothes anger,
  and a covert bribe,
     fierce rage.

15  Justice executed is a joy
     to the righteous
  but a terror to those
     who practice iniquity.

16  The man who strays
     from the way of wisdom
  will come to rest
     in the assembly
     of the departed spirits.

17  The one who loves pleasure
     will become a poor man;
  whoever loves wine and oil
     will not get rich.

18  The wicked are a ransom
     for the righteous,
  and the treacherous,
     for the upright.

19  Better to live in a wilderness
  than with a nagging and hot-
     tempered wife.

20  Precious treasure and oil are
     in the dwelling
     of the wise,
  but a foolish man consumes
     them.

21  The one who pursues
     righteousness
     and faithful love
  will find life, righteousness,
     and honor.

22  The wise conquer a city
     of warriors
  and bring down
     its mighty fortress.

23  The one who guards his mouth
     and tongue
  keeps himself out of trouble.

---

[a] 21:6 Other Hb mss, LXX, Vg read *a snare of death*

## Proverbs 21:25-26

*One of the most powerful lifestyles
you can adopt is the freedom of letting God's blessings flow through
you into the lives of others. When
you hold on too tightly to what's
yours, you miss the whole point of
why God gave it to you.*

24   The proud and arrogant
       person, named
       "Mocker,"
     acts with excessive pride.

25   A slacker's craving will kill
       him
     because his hands refuse
       to work.
26   He is filled
       with craving all day long,
     but the righteous give
       and don't hold back.

27   The sacrifice
       of a wicked person
       is detestable—
     how much more so when
       he brings it
       with ulterior motives!

28   A lying witness will perish,
     but the one who listens
       will speak successfully.

29   A wicked man puts on
       a bold face,
     but the upright man considers
       his way.

30   No wisdom, no understanding,
       and no counsel
     ⌊will prevail⌋ against the LORD.

31   A horse is prepared for the day
       of battle,
     but victory comes
       from the LORD.

**22** A good name is to be chosen
       over great wealth;
     favor is better than silver
       and gold.

2    The rich and the poor have
       this in common:
     the LORD made them both.

3    A sensible person sees danger
       and takes cover,
     but the inexperienced
       keep going
       and are punished.

4    The result of humility is *fear
       of the LORD,
     along with wealth, honor,
       and life.

5    There are thorns and snares
       on the path
       of the crooked;
     the one who guards himself
       stays far from them.

6    Teach a youth about the way
       he should go;
     even when he is old
       he will not depart from it.

7    The rich rule over the poor,
     and the borrower is a slave
       to the lender.
8    The one who sows injustice
       will reap disaster,
     and the rod of his fury will be
       destroyed.

9    A generous person will be
       blessed,
     for he shares his food
       with the poor.

10 Drive out a mocker,
    and conflict goes too;
then lawsuits and dishonor
    will cease.

11 The one who loves
    a pure heart
and gracious lips—the king is
    his friend.

12 The LORD's eyes keep watch
    over knowledge,
but He overthrows the words
    of the treacherous.

13 The slacker says,
    "There's a lion outside!
I'll be killed in the streets!"

14 The mouth
    of the forbidden woman is
    a deep pit;
a man cursed by the LORD
    will fall into it.

15 Foolishness is tangled up
    in the heart of a youth;
the rod of discipline
    will drive it away
    from him.

16 Oppressing the poor to enrich
    oneself,
and giving to the rich—both
    lead only to poverty.

## Words of the Wise

17 Listen closely, pay attention
    to the words of the wise,
and apply your mind
    to my knowledge.
18 For it is pleasing
    if you keep them
    within you

and if they are constantly
    on your lips.
19 I have instructed you today—
    even you—
so that your confidence may be
    in the LORD.
20 Haven't I written for you
    previously[a]
about counsel and knowledge,
21 in order to teach you true
    and reliable words,
so that you may give
    a dependable report
    to those who sent you?

22 Don't rob a poor man because
    he is poor,
and don't crush the oppressed
    at the •gate,
23 for the LORD will take up
    their case
and will plunder those
    who plunder them.

24 Don't make friends
    with an angry man,
and don't be a companion
    of a hot-tempered man,
25 or you will learn his ways
and entangle yourself
    in a snare.

26 Don't be one of those
    who enter agreements,
who put up security for loans.
27 If you have no money to pay,
even your bed will be taken
    from under you.

28 Don't move an ancient
    property line
that your fathers set up.

29 Do you see a man skilled
    in his work?

---

[a]22:20 Alt Hb tradition reads *excellent things;* LXX, Syr, Tg, Vg read *three times;* some emend to read *30 sayings.*

He will stand in the presence
    of kings.
He will not stand
    in the presence
    of unknown men.

**23** When you sit down to dine
    with a ruler,
consider carefully what is
    before you,
2 and stick a knife in your throat
    if you have a big appetite;
3 don't desire his choice food,
    for that food is deceptive.

4 Don't wear yourself out
    to get rich;
stop giving your attention to it.
5 As soon as your eyes fly to it,
    it disappears,
for it makes wings for itself
    and flies like an eagle
    to the sky.

6 Don't eat
    a stingy person's bread,
and don't desire
    his choice food,
7 for as he thinks
    within himself, so he is.
"Eat and drink,"
    he says to you,
but his heart is not with you.
8 You will vomit the little
    you've eaten
and waste
    your pleasant words.

9 Don't speak to a fool,
for he will despise the insight
    of your words.

10 Don't move an ancient
    property line,
and don't encroach
    on the fields
    of the fatherless,
11 for their Redeemer is strong,

and He will take up their case
    against you.

12 Apply yourself to instruction
and listen to words
    of knowledge.

13 Don't withhold correction
    from a youth;
if you beat him with a rod,
    he will not die.
14 Strike him with a rod,
and you will rescue his life
    from *Sheol.

15 My son, if your heart is wise,
my heart will indeed rejoice.
16 My innermost being will cheer
when your lips say
    what is right.

17 Don't be jealous of sinners;
instead, always *fear the LORD.
18 For then you will have
    a future,          •
and your hope will never
    fade.

19 Listen, my son, and be wise;
keep your mind
    on the right course.
20 Don't associate with those
    who drink too much wine,
or with those who gorge
    themselves on meat.
21 For the drunkard
    and the glutton
    will become poor,
and grogginess will clothe
    ⌊them⌋ in rags.

22 Listen to your father who gave
    you life,
and don't despise your mother
    when she is old.
23 Buy—and do not sell—truth,
wisdom, instruction,
    and understanding.

24 The father of a righteous son
        will rejoice greatly,
     and one who fathers
        a wise son will delight
        in him.
25 Let your father and mother
        have joy,
     and let her who gave birth
        to you rejoice.

26 My son, give me your heart,
     and let your eyes observe
        my ways.
27 For a prostitute is a deep pit,
     and a forbidden woman is
        a narrow well;
28 indeed, she sets an ambush
        like a robber
     and increases those
        among men who are
        unfaithful.

29 Who has woe?
        Who has sorrow?
     Who has conflicts?
        Who has complaints?
     Who has wounds
        for no reason?
     Who has red eyes?
30 Those who linger over wine,
     those who go looking
        for mixed wine.
31 Don't gaze at wine
        when it is red,
     when it gleams in the cup
     and goes down smoothly.
32 In the end it bites like a snake
     and stings like a viper.
33 Your eyes will see
        strange things,
     and you will say absurd things.
34 You'll be like someone
        sleeping out at sea
     or lying down on the top
        of a ship's mast.
35 "They struck me, but I feel
        no pain!

They beat me, but I didn't
        know it!
     When will I wake up?
     I'll look for another ⌊drink⌋."

**24** Don't envy evil men
        or desire to be with them,
2    for their hearts plan violence,
     and their words stir up trouble.

3    A house is built by wisdom,
     and it is established
        by understanding;
4    by knowledge the rooms
        are filled
     with every precious
        and beautiful treasure.

5    A wise warrior is better than
        a strong one,
     and a man of knowledge than
        one of strength;
6    for you should wage war
        with sound guidance—
     victory comes with
        many counselors.

7    Wisdom is inaccessible
        to a fool;
     he does not open his mouth
        at the •gate.
8    The one who plots evil
     will be called a schemer.
9    A foolish scheme is sin,
     and a mocker is detestable
        to people.

10   If you do nothing in
        a difficult time,
     your strength is limited.
11   Rescue those being taken off
        to death,
     and save those stumbling
        toward slaughter.
12   If you say,
        "But we didn't know
        about this,"

won't He who weighs hearts
    consider it?
Won't He who protects
    your life know?
Won't He repay a person
    according to his work?

13 Eat honey, my son,
    for it is good,
and the honeycomb is sweet
    to your palate;
14 realize that wisdom is
    the same for you.
If you find it, you will have
    a future,
and your hope will never
    fade.

15 Don't set an ambush,
    wicked man, at the camp
    of the righteous man;
don't destroy his dwelling.
16 Though a righteous man falls
    seven times, he will
    get up,
but the wicked will stumble
    into ruin.

17 Don't gloat when your enemy
    falls,
and don't let your heart rejoice
    when he stumbles,
18 or the LORD will see,
    be displeased,
and turn His wrath away
    from him.

19 Don't worry because of
    evildoers,
and don't envy the wicked.
20 For the evil have no future;
    the lamp of the wicked will be
    put out.

21 My son, •fear the LORD,
    as well as the king,
and don't associate
    with rebels,

22 for their destruction will come
    suddenly;
who knows what disaster
    these two can bring?

23 These ⌊sayings⌋ also belong
    to the wise:

It is not good
    to show partiality
    in judgment.
24 Whoever says to the guilty,
    "You are innocent"—
people will curse him,
    and tribes will denounce
    him;
25 but it will go well with those
    who convict the guilty,
and a generous blessing
    will come upon them.

26 He who gives
    an honest answer
gives a kiss on the lips.

27 Complete your outdoor work,
    and prepare your field;
afterwards, build your house.

28 Don't testify against
    your neighbor
    without cause.
Don't deceive with your lips.
29 Don't say, "I'll do to him
    what he did to me;
I'll repay the man for what
    he has done."

30 I went by the field of a slacker
and by the vineyard of a man
    lacking sense.
31 Thistles had come up
    everywhere,
weeds covered the ground,
and the stone wall was ruined.
32 I saw, and took it to heart;
I looked, and received
    instruction:

33 a little sleep, a little slumber,
   a little folding of the arms
       to rest,
34 and your poverty will come
       like a robber,
   your need, like a bandit.

## Hezekiah's Collection

**25** These too are proverbs
       of Solomon,
   which the men of Hezekiah,
       king of Judah, copied.

2  It is the glory of God
       to conceal a matter
   and the glory of kings
       to investigate a matter.
3  As the heaven is high
       and the earth is deep,
   so the hearts of kings cannot
       be investigated.

4  Remove impurities from
       silver,
   and a vessel will be produced
       for a silversmith.
5  Remove the wicked
       from the king's presence,
   and his throne
       will be established
       in righteousness.

6  Don't brag about yourself
       before the king,
   and don't stand in the place
       of the great;
7  for it is better for him to say
       to you, "Come up here!"
   than to demote you
       in plain view of a noble.

8  Don't take a matter to court
       hastily.
   Otherwise, what will you do
       afterwards
   if your opponent humiliates
       you?

9  Make your case
       with your opponent
   without revealing
       another's secret;
10 otherwise, the one who hears
       will disgrace you,
   and you'll never live it down.

11 A word spoken
       at the right time
   is like golden apples
       on a silver tray.
12 A wise correction
       to a receptive ear
   is like a gold ring
       or an ornament of gold.

13 To those who send him,
       a trustworthy messenger
   is like the coolness of snow
       on a harvest day;
   he refreshes the life
       of his masters.

14 The man who boasts about a gift
       that does not exist
   is like clouds and wind
       without rain.
15 A ruler can be persuaded
       through patience,
   and a gentle tongue can break
       a bone.
16 If you find honey, eat only
       what you need;
   otherwise, you'll get sick
       from it and vomit.
17 Seldom set foot
       in your neighbor's house;
   otherwise, he'll get sick of you
       and hate you.

18 A man giving false testimony
       against his neighbor
   is like a club, a sword,
       or a sharp arrow.

19 Trusting an unreliable person
    in a time of trouble
is like a rotten tooth
    or a faltering foot.

20 Singing songs
    to a troubled heart
is like taking off clothing
    on a cold day,
or like ⌊pouring⌋ vinegar
    on soda.

21 If your enemy is hungry,
    give him food to eat,
and if he is thirsty, give him
    water to drink;
22 for you will heap coals
    on his head,
and the LORD will reward you.

23 The north wind produces rain,
and a backbiting tongue,
    angry looks.
24 Better to live on the corner
    of a roof
than in a house shared
    with a nagging wife.
25 Good news from a distant land
is like cold water
    to a parched throat.
26 A righteous person who yields
    to the wicked
is like a muddied spring
    or a polluted well.
27 It is not good to eat too much
    honey,
or to seek glory after glory.
28 A man who does not control
    his temper
is like a city whose wall
    is broken down.

**26** Like snow in summer and rain
    at harvest,
honor is inappropriate
    for a fool.
2 Like a flitting sparrow
    or a fluttering swallow,

an undeserved curse goes
    nowhere.
3 A whip for the horse, a bridle
    for the donkey,
and a rod for the backs
    of fools.
4 Don't answer a fool
    according to
    his foolishness,
or you'll be like him
    yourself.
5 Answer a fool according to
    his foolishness,
or he'll become wise
    in his own eyes.
6 The one who sends a message
    by a fool's hand
cuts off his own feet
    and drinks violence.
7 A proverb in the mouth
    of a fool
is like lame legs that hang
    limp.
8 Giving honor to a fool
is like binding a stone
    in a sling.
9 A proverb in the mouth
    of a fool
is like a stick with thorns,
    brandished by the hand
    of a drunkard.
10 The one who hires a fool,
    or who hires those
    passing by,
is like an archer who wounds
    everyone.
11 As a dog returns to its vomit,
so a fool repeats
    his foolishness.
12 Do you see a man who is wise
    in his own eyes?
There is more hope for a fool
    than for him.
13 The slacker says,
    "There's a lion
    in the road—
a lion in the public square!"
14 A door turns on its hinge,

and a slacker, on his bed.

15 The slacker buries his hand
    in the bowl;
he is too weary to bring it
    to his mouth.

16 In his own eyes, a slacker
    is wiser
than seven men
    who can answer sensibly.

17 A passer-by who meddles
    in a quarrel that's not his
is like one who grabs a dog
    by the ears.

18 Like a madman who throws
    flaming darts
    and deadly arrows,

19 so is the man who deceives
    his neighbor
and says, "I was only joking!"

20 Without wood, fire goes out;
without a gossip,
    conflict dies down.

21 As charcoal for embers
    and wood for fire,
so is a quarrelsome man
    for kindling strife.

22 A gossip's words are
    like choice food
that goes down to
    one's innermost being.

23 Smooth[a] lips with an evil heart
are like glaze
    on an earthen vessel.

24 A hateful person disguises
    himself with his speech
and harbors deceit within.

25 When he speaks graciously,
    don't believe him,
for there are
    seven abominations
    in his heart.

26 Though his hatred is concealed
    by deception,

his evil will be revealed
    in the assembly.

27 The one who digs a pit will fall
    into it,
and whoever rolls a stone—
    it will come back on him.

28 A lying tongue hates those
    it crushes,
and a flattering mouth causes
    ruin.

**27** Don't boast about tomorrow,
for you don't know what a day
    might bring.

2 Let another praise you,
    and not your own mouth—
a stranger, and not
    your own lips.

3 A stone is heavy and sand,
    a burden,
but aggravation from a fool
    outweighs them both.

4 Fury is cruel, and anger is
    a flood,
but who can withstand
    jealousy?

5 Better an open reprimand
than concealed love.

6 The wounds of a friend
    are trustworthy,
but the kisses of an enemy
    are excessive.[b]

7 A person who is full tramples
    on a honeycomb,
but to a hungry person,
    any bitter thing is sweet.

8 A man wandering
    from his home

[a]26:23 LXX; Hb reads *Burning*   [b]27:6 Others emend the text to read *deceitful.*

is like a bird wandering
    from its nest.

9   Oil and incense bring joy
    to the heart,
and the sweetness of a friend
    is better than self-counsel.[a]

10  Don't abandon your friend
    or your father's friend,
and don't go
    to your brother's house
    in your time of calamity;
better a neighbor nearby
    than a brother far away.

11  Be wise, my son, and bring
    my heart joy,
so that I can answer anyone
    who taunts me.

12  The sensible see danger
    and take cover;
the foolish keep going
    and are punished.

13  Take his garment, for he has
    put up security
    for a stranger;
get collateral if it is
    for foreigners.

14  If one blesses his neighbor
    with a loud voice early
    in the morning,
it will be counted as a curse
    to him.

15  An endless dripping
    on a rainy day
and a nagging wife are alike.
16  The one who controls her
    controls the wind
and grasps oil
    with his right hand.

17  Iron sharpens iron,
and one man sharpens
    another.

18  Whoever tends a fig tree
    will eat its fruit,
and whoever looks after
    his master will be honored.

19  As the water reflects the face,
so the heart reflects
    the person.

20  *Sheol and *Abaddon are never
    satisfied,
and people's eyes are never
    satisfied.

21  Silver is ⌊tested⌋ in a crucible,
    gold in a smelter,
and a man, by the praise
    he receives.

22  Though you grind a fool
    in a mortar with a pestle
    along with grain,
you will not separate
    his foolishness from him.

23  Know well the condition
    of your flock,
and pay attention
    to your herds,
24  for wealth is not forever;
not even a crown lasts
    for all time.
25  When hay is removed
    and new growth appears
and the grain from the hills
    is gathered in,
26  lambs will provide
    your clothing,
and goats, the price of a field;
27  there will be enough
    goat's milk for your food—

---

[a]27:9 LXX reads *heart, but the soul is torn up by affliction*

food for your household
and nourishment
for your servants.

**28** The wicked flee when no one
is pursuing ⌊them⌋,
but the righteous are as bold
as a lion.

2   When a land is in rebellion,
it has many rulers,
but with a discerning
and knowledgeable person,
it endures.

3   A destitute leader[a]
who oppresses the poor
is like a driving rain that leaves
no food.

4   Those who reject the law
praise the wicked,
but those who keep the law
battle against them.

5   Evil men do not understand
justice,
but those who seek the LORD
understand everything.

6   Better a poor man who lives
with integrity
than a rich man who distorts
right and wrong.

7   A discerning son keeps
the law,
but a companion of gluttons
humiliates his father.

8   Whoever increases his wealth
through excessive interest
collects it for one who is kind
to the poor.

9   Anyone who turns his ear

away from hearing
the law—
even his prayer is detestable.

10   The one who leads the upright
into an evil way
will fall into his own pit,
but the blameless will inherit
what is good.

11   A rich man is wise in
his own eyes,
but a poor man
who has discernment sees
through him.

12   When the righteous triumph,
there is great rejoicing,
but when the wicked come
to power, people hide
themselves.

13   The one who conceals his sins
will not prosper,
but whoever confesses
and renounces them
will find mercy.

14   Happy is the one who is
always reverent,
but one who hardens his heart
falls into trouble.

---

### Proverbs 28:13-14

*An important step in growing as a
Christian is learning how to keep
your life an open book before God,
to let nothing come between you.
Nobody expects you to be perfect,
but by owning up to your sins, you
get a whole lot closer to it.*

---

[a] **28:3** LXX reads *A wicked man*

15  A wicked ruler over
        a helpless people
    is like a roaring lion
        or a charging bear.

16  A leader who lacks
        understanding is very
        oppressive,
    but one who hates unjust gain
        prolongs his life.

17  A man burdened by blood-guilt
    will be a fugitive until death.
    Let no one help him.

18  The one who lives
        with integrity will be
        helped,
    but one who distorts right
        and wrong will suddenly fall.

19  The one who works his land
        will have plenty of food,
    but whoever chases fantasies
        will have his fill of poverty.

20  A faithful man will have
        many blessings,
    but one in a hurry to get rich
        will not go unpunished.

21  It is not good to show
        partiality—
    yet a man may sin for a piece
        of bread.

22  A greedy man is in a hurry
        for wealth;
    he doesn't know that poverty
        will come to him.

23  One who rebukes a person
        will later find more favor
    than one who
        flatters with his tongue.

24  The one who robs his father
        or mother and says,

> "Christianity is strange. It orders
> man to acknowledge that he is evil,
> even abominable. Yet it also bids
> him to be like God."
> —Blaise Pascal

    "That's no sin,"
    is a companion to a man
        who destroys.

25  A greedy person provokes
        conflict,
    but whoever trusts
        in the LORD will prosper.

26  The one who trusts
        in himself is a fool,
    but one who walks in wisdom
        will be safe.

27  The one who gives to the poor
        will not be in need,
    but one who turns his eyes
        away will receive
        many curses.

28  When the wicked come
        to power, people hide,
    but when they are destroyed,
        the righteous flourish.

29  One who becomes stiff-necked
        after many reprimands
    will be broken suddenly—
        and without a remedy.

2   When the righteous flourish,
        the people rejoice,
    but when the wicked rule,
        people groan.

3   A man who loves wisdom
        brings joy to his father,

but one who consorts
   with prostitutes destroys
   his wealth.

4  By justice a king brings
     stability to a land,
  but a man ⌊who demands⌋
     "contributions"
     demolishes it.

5  A man who
     flatters his neighbor
  spreads a net for his feet.

6  An evil man is caught
     by sin,
  but the righteous one sings
     and rejoices.

7  The righteous person knows
     the rights of the poor,
  but the wicked one does not
     understand these concerns.

8  Mockers inflame a city,
  but the wise turn away anger.

9  If a wise man goes to court
     with a fool,
  there will be ranting
     and raving
     but no resolution.

10  Bloodthirsty men hate
     an honest person,
  but the upright care
     about him.

11  A fool gives full vent
     to his anger,
  but a wise man holds it
     in check.

12  If a ruler listens to lies,
  all his servants will be wicked.

13  The poor and the oppressor
     have this in common:

the LORD gives light
   to the eyes of both.

14  A king who judges the poor
     with fairness—
  his throne will be established
     forever.

15  A rod of correction imparts
     wisdom,
  but a youth left to himself is
     a disgrace to his mother.

16  When the wicked increase,
     rebellion increases,
  but the righteous will see
     their downfall.

17  Discipline your son,
     and he will give you
     comfort;
  he will also give you delight.

18  Without revelation people run
     wild,
  but one who keeps the law
     will be happy.

19  A servant cannot be
     disciplined by words;
  though he understands,
     he doesn't respond.

20  Do you see a man who speaks
     too soon?
  There is more hope for a fool
     than for him.

21  A slave pampered
     from his youth
  will become arrogant later on.

22  An angry man stirs up conflict,
  and a hot-tempered
     man increases rebellion.

23  A person's pride will humble
     him,

but a humble spirit will gain
   honor.

24 To be a thief's partner is
      to hate oneself;
   he hears the curse but will not
      testify.

25 The fear of man is a snare,
   but the one who trusts
      in the LORD is protected.

26 Many seek a ruler's favor,
   but a man receives justice
      from the LORD.

27 An unjust man is detestable
      to the righteous,
   and one whose way is upright
      is detestable to the wicked.

## The Words of Agur

**30** The words of Agur
      son of Jakeh. The oracle.
   The man's oration to Ithiel,
      to Ithiel and Ucal:[a]

2 I am the least intelligent
      of men,
   and I lack man's ability
      to understand.
3 I have not gained wisdom,
   and I have no knowledge
      of the Holy One.
4 Who has gone up to heaven
      and come down?
   Who has gathered the wind
      in His hands?
   Who has bound up the waters
      in a cloak?
   Who has established
      all the ends of the earth?
   What is His name, and what is
      the name of His Son—

---

### Proverbs 30:5-6

### The Scriptures

*We may wish God had said a little
more about certain things. Like
where the dinosaurs came in. Or
whether or not our pets will be in
heaven. Or where Noah's Ark is.
But we know this: the Bible tells us
everything we need to know. What
God hasn't said has been withheld
for a reason.*

---

   if you know?
5 Every word of God is pure;
   He is a shield to those
      who take refuge in Him.
6 Don't add to His words,
   or He will rebuke you,
      and you will be proved
      a liar.

7 Two things I ask of You;
   don't deny them to me
      before I die:
8 Keep falsehood
      and deceitful words far
      from me.
   Give me neither poverty
      nor wealth;
   feed me with the food I need.
9 Otherwise, I might have
      too much
   and deny You, saying,
      "Who is the LORD?"
   or I might have nothing
      and steal,
   profaning the name
      of my God.

---

[a] **30:1** Hb uncertain. Sometimes emended to *oration: I am weary, God, I am weary, God, and I am exhausted*, or *oration: I am not God, I am not God, that I should prevail*. LXX reads *My son, fear my words and when you have received them repent. The man says these things to the believers in God, and I pause.*

10 Don't slander a servant
    to his master,
or he will curse you,
    and you will become guilty.

11 There is a generation
    that curses its father
and does not bless its mother.
12 There is a generation
    that is pure in its own eyes,
yet is not washed from its filth.
13 There is a generation—
    how haughty its eyes
and pretentious its looks.
14 There is a generation
    whose teeth are swords,
whose fangs are knives,
devouring the oppressed
    from the land
and the needy from among
    mankind.

15 The leech has two daughters:
    Give, Give.
Three things are never
    satisfied;
four never say, "Enough!":
16 *Sheol; a barren womb;
earth, which is never satisfied
    with water;
and fire, which never says,
    "Enough!"

17 As for the eye that ridicules
    a father
and despises obedience
    to a mother,
may ravens of the valley pluck
    it out
and young vultures eat it.

18 Three things are beyond me;
four I can't understand:
19 the way of an eagle in the sky,
the way of a snake on a rock,
the way of a ship at sea,

and the way of a man
    with a young woman.
20 This is the way
    of an adulteress:
she eats and wipes her mouth
and says, "I've done
    nothing wrong."

21 The earth trembles
    under three things;
it cannot bear up under four:
22 a servant when he becomes
    king,
a fool when he is stuffed
    with food,
23 an unloved woman
    when she marries,
and a serving girl
    when she ousts her lady.

24 Four things on earth are small,
yet they are extremely wise:
25 the ants are not
    a strong people,
yet they store up their food
    in the summer;
26 hyraxes are not
    a mighty people,
yet they make their homes
    in the cliffs;
27 locusts have no king,
yet all of them march in ranks;
28 a lizard can be caught
    in your hands,
yet it lives in kings' palaces.

29 Three things are stately
    in their stride,
even four are stately
    in their walk:
30 a lion, which is mightiest
    among beasts
and doesn't retreat
    before anything,
31 a strutting rooster, a goat,

and a king at the head
of his army.ª

32 If you have been foolish
by exalting yourself,
or if you've been scheming,
put your hand
over your mouth.
33 For the churning of milk
produces butter,
and twisting a nose draws
blood,
and stirring up anger produces
strife.

## The Words of Lemuel

**31** The words of King Lemuel,
an oracle that his mother
taught him:

2 What ⌊should I say⌋, my son?
What, O son of my womb?
What, O son of my vows?
3 Don't spend your energy
on women
or your efforts on those
who destroy kings.
4 It is not for kings, Lemuel,
it is not for kings to drink wine
or for rulers ⌊to desire⌋ beer.
5 Otherwise, they will drink,
forget what is decreed,
and pervert justice for all
the oppressed.
6 Give beer to one who is dying,
and wine to one whose life
is bitter.
7 Let him drink so that
he can forget his poverty
and remember his trouble
no more.
8 Speak up for those who have
no voice,
for the justice of all who are
dispossessed.

9 Speak up, judge righteously,
and defend
the cause of the oppressed
and needy.

## In Praise of a Capable Wife

10 Who can find a capable wife?
She is far more precious
than jewels.
11 The heart of her husband
trusts in her,
and he will not lack anything
good.
12 She rewards him with good,
not evil,
all the days of her life.
13 She selects wool and flax
and works with willing hands.
14 She is like the merchant ships,
bringing her food
from far away.
15 She rises while it is still night
and provides food
for her household
and portions for her servants.
16 She evaluates a field
and buys it;
she plants a vineyard
with her earnings.
17 She draws on her strength
and reveals that her arms
are strong.
18 She sees that her profits
are good,
and her lamp never goes out
at night.
19 She extends her hands
to the spinning staff,
and her hands hold
the spindle.
20 Her hands reach out
to the poor,
and she extends her hands
to the needy.

ª**30:31** LXX reads *king haranguing his people*

21 She is not afraid
    for her household
    when it snows,
 for all in her household
    are doubly clothed.ᵃ

22 She makes her own bed
    coverings;
 her clothing is fine linen
    and purple.

23 Her husband is known
    at the city •gates,
 where he sits among
    the elders of the land.

24 She makes and sells
    linen garments;
 she delivers belts
    to the merchants.

25 Strength and honor are
    her clothing,
 and she can laugh at the time
    to come.

26 She opens her mouth
    with wisdom,
 and loving instruction is
    on her tongue.

27 She watches over the activities
    of her household
 and is never idle.

28 Her sons rise up and call her
    blessed.
 Her husband also praises her:

29 "Many women are capable,
 but you surpass them all!"

30 Charm is deceptive and beauty
    is fleeting,
 but a woman who •fears
    the Lᴏʀᴅ will be praised.

31 Give her the reward
    of her labor,
 and let her works praise her
    at the city gates.

ᵃ**31:21** LXX, Vg; Hb reads *are dressed in scarlet*

# THE TOP 10 TRUTHS OF THE BIBLE

Fortunately for all of us, God doesn't force us to know a bunch of things before He'll let us become a part of His family. There's no initiation test, no entrance exam, no password but the name of Jesus Christ needed in order to gain admission into His household.

Once we're in, however, we find that the Bible is just full of important information. Since it is God's Word to us, it tells us everything we need to know about who He is and what He expects—the way things are and the way things ought to be.

But even then, this exploding mine of spiritual riches doesn't weigh on our shoulders like material we need to know for a test, like a dreaded list of rules and regulations to memorize. That's because the truths of the Bible are not just words on a page, disconnected from our weekends and Wednesdays. They are living realities that help us make sense of what we're going through, living instructions that rebound with blessing, living hopes that place our lives in the middle of a timeless, eternal Kingdom—and make every day an adventure with the God of the universe.

So here is a list of 10 important things you need to know from the Bible—not to keep your certification current, but to keep from wasting your life on silliness and sideshows when you can be enjoying the main event . . . all the time!

Right after you read the brief summaries of these Bible truths (or doctrines), you'll find a few Scriptures you can look up to help you see where these ideas come from. This is by no means a complete list of verses. We've had to skip over some really good ones, just so you'd be able to read this Bible without getting bogged down by study note boxes. But if you'll work through these selected verses—along with the others that are linked with the devotionals from the front pages of this Bible—you'll be off to a good start at understanding who God is, who you are as a result of what He has done, and what you can be doing today—yes, today—to honor Him with your life.

## *Truth 1: The Scriptures*

The Bible is the record of God's revelation of Himself to the human race, written by men who were divinely inspired. Exactly how God imparted His Word to them, we don't really know. He says in the Scriptures that every book was written under the guiding hand of the Holy Spirit. And apparently, that's all we really need to know.

The Bible was composed over a period of around 1,500 years by many different people—many who had no knowledge of what others had written—yet it is miraculously united around one central theme (God's redemptive purpose), one central figure (Jesus Christ), and one central goal (God being supreme in a redeemed universe). God is the author of Scripture, salvation is its purpose, and truth lines its pages—without any mixture of error.

It reveals the principles by which God judges us, and it will remain the supreme standard of human conduct and religious opinion to the end of the world.

| | |
|---|---|
| *Acts 17:11* | The Scripture is our guide to all things godly. |
| *Proverbs 30:5-6* | It contains everything God wants to say to us. |
| *Matthew 5:17-18* | God's Word is the same today as it's always been. |
| *Luke 24:44-48* | The Bible teaches us what God has done to save us. |
| *Luke 21:33* | His Word will never change, grow old, or get outdated. |
| *Matthew 22:29* | The only truth available in all the world is found in here. |
| *2 Timothy 3:14-17* | Our job is to stay in it and to keep obeying it. |

## Truth 2: God the Father

There is one and only one living and true God. He is an intelligent, spiritual, and personal Being—the Creator, the Redeemer, the Sustainer, and the Ruler of the universe. He is infinite in holiness, perfect in every way, and we owe Him our highest love, reverence, and obedience.

This eternal God reveals Himself to us as Father, Son, and Holy Spirit, each with distinct personal qualities but without any division of nature, essence, or being.

God as Father reigns with care over the universe and all His creatures, even ruling over the course of human history according to the purposes of His grace. He is all-powerful, all-loving, and all-wise, fatherly in His attitude toward all people, yet a Father in truth to those who become His children through faith in Jesus Christ.

| | |
|---|---|
| *Hebrews 11:6* | Truth 101: God exists, and He wants us close to Him. |
| *1 Corinthians 8:6* | There is one God, and He created everything. |
| *1 Timothy 1:17* | He has always been, always is, and will always be. |
| *Psalm 89:26-29* | The Father's love is steady as a rock. |
| *John 17:3-5* | The Son and the Father have always been together. |
| *Matthew 11:27* | When we see the Son, we have seen the Father. |
| *Galatians 4:3-7* | The Father has adopted us into His family. |
| *Hebrews 12:9* | The Father knows exactly what His children need. |
| *Revelation 4:9-11* | One day the whole world will know that He is God. |

## Truth 3: God the Son

The Son of God has existed forever. He was active in the creation of the universe. He became a man as Jesus Christ, being conceived of the Holy Spirit and born of the virgin Mary, taking upon Himself the limitations, vulnerabilities, and weaknesses of human nature.

Yet He never sinned. And in this way, He fulfilled the requirements of the divine law. The Father, then, accepted His death as an atoning sacrifice for the sinfulness of mankind—for all those who believe in Christ through faith.

He was raised from the dead with a glorified body and ascended into heaven, where He is now exalted at the right hand of God and stands in for us as our high priest before the heavenly throne. He will return one day in power and glory to judge the world and to welcome the redeemed to Himself.

| | |
|---|---|
| *Psalm 2:7-9* | The Son was prophesied long ago. |
| *Colossians 1:15-20* | He has been granted full authority by the Father. |
| *Luke 1:31-35* | The Son came to earth, born of a virgin. |
| *Matthew 3:16-17* | His mission met with the Father's approval. |
| *Matthew 16:13-18* | His followers recognized Jesus as the Son. |
| *Matthew 27:54* | Even some not so near recognized who He was. |
| *John 14:6* | The Son is the only way to the Father. |
| *1 Timothy 2:5-6* | He is the bridge that leads us to life. |
| *Hebrews 9:24-28* | Today He lives at the right hand of the Father. |
| *Hebrews 4:14-16* | We can go to Him with all of our problems. |
| *Revelation 5:8-10* | Christ alone is able to pay the price for our sins. |

## Truth 4: God the Holy Spirit

 The Holy Spirit is the Spirit of God, eternal in His nature, bearing all the attributes of God. He inspired the men in years past who wrote the Scriptures and continues to illuminate the Bible today so that we can understand the truth of what we read.

 He convicts people of sin, pointing out our need for a Savior. He convicts us of righteousness, allowing us to see what kind of life is pleasing to God. And He convicts mankind of judgment, making clear to us that life on earth is but a temporary experience.

 He comforts believers in our sorrows and persecutions and gives us spiritual gifts to help us serve God through His church. He empowers us in our worship and evangelism, and His presence in our lives gives us the assurance that God will keep His promises, that we will continue to become more like Christ, and will ultimately see the full reward of our salvation.

| | |
|---|---|
| Psalm 139:7-10 | The Holy Spirit is present everywhere. |
| Acts 2:38 | He comes to live in us as we repent and receive Christ's salvation. |
| Luke 11:13 | The Spirit is a gift to us from the Father. |
| Luke 4:18-21 | He gives us the power we need to serve God. |
| Luke 12:11-12 | He puts the right words in our mouths. |
| John 16:12-15 | He reveals to us what the Bible is really saying. |
| Romans 8:8-11 | His presence in us transforms us into life. |
| Romans 8:26-27 | He helps us pray according to God's will. |

## Truth 5: Man

Mankind was created by the special act of God—created in His own image—and is the crowning work of God's creation. God's creation of male and female is a part of the goodness of God's creation.

In the beginning man was innocent of sin and enjoyed a God-given freedom of choice. He used this free choice, however, to sin against His Creator. This act not only invited God's punishment of death on the first humans as individuals (Adam and Eve) but introduced sin into the human race, a condition that every person since then has inherited by birth. And as soon as any person is able, he confirms his inheritance by committing sin himself.

Only the grace of God can bring us into holy fellowship with Him and enable us to fulfill the purpose He intended for us. God affirmed the value He places on us by giving His Son to die for us. Therefore, every man and woman possesses dignity and is worthy of respect and Christian love.

| | |
|---|---|
| Psalm 8:3-5 | Being created by God gives us ultimate significance. |
| Romans 1:18-21 | We have an inborn knowledge of God and of our own sin. |
| 1 Corinthians 1:20-25 | We are not as smart as we sometimes think we are. |
| Psalm 51:4-5 | We start out sinners before we even have a chance to sin. |
| 1 Corinthians 15:21-22 | The curse comes through Adam, the cure through Christ. |
| Colossians 3:9-11 | Only through Christ are we able to become new people. |

## Truth 6: Salvation

Salvation is offered freely to all who accept Jesus Christ as Lord and Savior. This new birth (sometimes called regeneration) is a work of God's grace that literally makes us different people than we were before—new creatures in Christ Jesus.

As the Holy Spirit convinces us that we are sinful, and as we respond by turning away from our sins and turning to God, He performs a change of heart in us, and we accept Jesus Christ by faith and commit our whole selves to Him. In this transaction we are justified, our record wiped clean by God's grace—with Christ's righteousness being put in its place—giving us a pure relationship of peace and favor with God.

For the rest of our lives, then, we who have been redeemed are in the process of sanctification, being set apart for God's purposes, progressing toward moral and spiritual perfection through the presence and power of the Holy Spirit who dwells in us. We'll never quite get there on earth, but we look forward to the ultimate reward of our salvation—glorification—eternal life in heaven with God.

| | |
|---|---|
| John 1:12-13 | It was God's desire to extend salvation to us. |
| Ephesians 2:4-9 | Salvation can't be earned through being good. |
| Romans 4:1-5 | Faith has always been the means of salvation. |
| John 3:16-18 | Our salvation was the reason Christ came. |
| Hebrews 5:7-10 | He alone can give us the hope of eternal life. |
| John 3:4-6 | Being saved is like being born again. |
| John 5:24 | God literally rescues us from the jaws of death. |
| Romans 10:8-10 | The leap can be hard, but the terms are easy. |
| Romans 13:11 | We look forward to salvation's ultimate reward. |
| Hebrews 2:1-3 | What an incredible second chance God has given. |
| Galatians 6:14 | Being a Christian is all that really matters. |

Election can be defined as the gracious purpose of God—the incredible love and wisdom that He exercises in drawing sinners to Himself. This is not inconsistent with the fact that He has given us the responsibility of free choice, but is rather a display of His immeasurable grace. None of us deserves or can claim the right to be saved. God alone in His goodness has extended salvation to us. He draws, and we come.

People who truly come to Him by faith—those whom God has accepted in Christ and has sanctified by His Spirit—will never run the risk of losing their salvation. Believers may fall into sin through neglect and temptation. As a result, we lose much of what God intended for us: we grieve the Holy Spirit, trouble ourselves with a guilty conscience, bring reproach on the name of Christ, and suffer the consequences of our foolish actions. Yet we are assured of being kept by the power of God, for our salvation rests on His grace, not on our works.

| | |
|---|---|
| Matthew 25:34 | We were known by God before we were even born. |
| Romans 11:33-36 | We don't fully know how He does what He does. |
| Ephesians 3:8-12 | His grace is a mystery but not a mistake. |
| 2 Thessalonians 2:13-14 | It is His desire to share Christ's glory with us. |
| Luke 19:9-10 | Christ's mission was to seek and save the lost. |
| John 10:27-30 | The redeemed are protected in the palm of His hand. |
| 1 Thessalonians 5:23-24 | We are kept safe and sound by a faithful God. |
| 2 Timothy 1:11-12 | He can be trusted to keep all His promises. |
| 1 John 5:12-13 | We can know beyond a doubt that we are saved. |
| Revelation 3:5 | Our name is forever written in His book of life. |
| 2 Corinthians 7:1 | Our response to His grace is grateful obedience. |

## Truth 8: The Church and the Kingdom

The church is a body of Christian believers who are associated by covenant (or promise), having faith and fellowship in the gospel, being committed to the Bible's teaching, exercising the gifts and privileges invested in them by the Holy Spirit, observing the practices of baptism and Communion (also called the Lord's Supper), and seeking to extend the good news to the ends of the earth. The church is represented both as individual congregations operating under the lordship of Jesus Christ, as well as the global body of Christ which includes all the redeemed of all the ages.

The kingdom of God includes both His general rule over the universe and His specific kingship over those who willfully acknowledge Him as King, those who have entered into the kingdom through a childlike commitment to Jesus Christ. We should pray and work that God's kingdom may come—and that His will may be done—on earth, always realizing, however, that the final victory of His kingdom awaits the return of Jesus Christ and the end of this age.

| | |
|---|---|
| Acts 2:43-47 | The church shares a common faith and fellowship. |
| Acts 5:12-14 | The church is a growing group of believers. |
| Acts 6:3-6 | The church has different jobs for people to do. |
| Ephesians 2:19-22 | It is not a club but the living body of Christ. |
| Revelation 21:2-3 | The church is His bride, and He is the bridegroom. |
| Matthew 4:17 | Jesus began His ministry preaching about the kingdom. |
| Matthew 13:11 | Not everyone understood what He was talking about. |
| Matthew 6:31-33 | We are to live for things that matter in His kingdom. |
| Luke 23:42-43 | The kingdom has both a present and a future aspect. |
| John 18:36 | It is involved in this world, but it's not from this world. |
| Revelation 11:15 | Christ's kingdom will stand when all others have fallen. |

## Truth 9: Evangelism and Influence

It is the duty of every follower of Christ and of every church of the Lord Jesus Christ to endeavor to make disciples of all nations. That's because along with our new birth comes the birth of our love for others and our desire that they experience the same forgiveness God has granted us. The Bible clearly teaches that proclaiming the gospel of Jesus Christ to others is both a duty and a privilege of every child of God.

We are likewise under obligation to live in such a way that not only is the will of God supreme in our own lives but also in human society. We should be ready to work with all men of good will in any good cause, but we must always remember that mankind's greatest and most permanent need is for the saving grace of Jesus Christ. We are free—even commanded—to act in the spirit of love toward others, as long as we do so without compromising our loyalty to Christ or to His truth.

| | |
|---|---|
| *Mark 6:7* | Jesus sent His followers to tell others about Him. |
| *Matthew 9:37-38* | He saw them as workers going to gather a harvest. |
| *Matthew 28:19-20* | Our commission is to take His gospel to the world. |
| *Romans 15:1-2* | God wants us to be concerned for the welfare of all. |
| *Proverbs 12:25* | People are hurting, and our words can cheer them up. |
| *James 2:15-17* | It's not enough to just talk about helping others. |
| *Philemon 14* | We give because we want to, not because we have to. |
| *1 Peter 4:7-11* | Our calling is to love others, to help them see Jesus. |

## *Truth 10: Last Things*

God, in His own time and in His own way, will one day bring the world to its appropriate end. According to His promise, Jesus Christ will return personally and visibly in glory to the earth. At that time the dead will be raised, those who are redeemed and are still alive will meet the Lord in the air, and Christ will judge all men according to His perfect standard of righteousness.

The unrighteous will be consigned to hell, the place of everlasting punishment, while the righteous (in our resurrected and glorified bodies) will receive the final and lasting reward of our salvation—the sudden and complete end of all death, sorrow, sin, and evil—and we will live forever in heaven with our precious Lord and with the redeemed of all the ages.

| | |
|---|---|
| *2 Peter 3:8-9* | The Lord will come at the perfect time in history. |
| *1 Corinthians 4:3-5* | His judgment will reveal everything about everyone. |
| *James 5:7-8* | We can look forward to this certainty with patience. |
| *2 Timothy 4:7-8* | We are to keep up the fight while we're waiting. |
| *1 John 3:2-3* | We want to be like Him when we finally see Him. |
| *Revelation 7:16-17* | Living with our Lord forever is going to be wonderful. |

# HCSB BULLET NOTES™

Among the unique features of the *Holman Christian Standard Bible*® are the HCSB *Bullet Notes*™. These notes explain words or terms that are marked with a bullet in the biblical text (for example: •fear of the LORD). Please note that the particular word or term is marked with a bullet on its first occurrence within a chapter of the biblical text. Words like "everyone", "men", or "people" are marked with bullets only when the use of the word fits the definitions given below.

## New Testament HCSB Bullet Notes™

| | |
|---|---|
| *Abba* | Aram word for "father" |
| abyss | Or *the bottomless pit*, or *the depths* (of the sea); the prison for Satan and the demons |
| advocate | (see "Counselor/advocate") |
| Alpha and Omega | First and last letters of the Gk alphabet; used to refer to God the Father in Rv 1:8 and 21:6, and to Jesus, God the Son in Rv 22:13 |
| Amen | Transliteration of a Hb word signifying that something is certain, valid, truthful, or faithful; often used at the end of biblical songs, hymns, and prayers |
| asleep | Term used in reference to believers who have died |
| Beelzebul | Term of slander, variously interpreted "lord of flies," "lord of dung," or "ruler of demons"; 2 Kg 1:2; Mk 3:22 |
| centurion | A Roman officer who commanded about 100 soldiers |
| Cephas | Aram word for *rock* parallel to Gk *petros* from which the Eng name Peter is derived; Jn 1:42; 1 Co 1:12 |
| chief priest(s) | In Judaism a group of temple officers that included the high priest, captain of the temple, temple overseers, and treasurers |

| company/ regiment | Or *cohort*, a Roman military unit that numbered as many as 600 men |
|---|---|
| convert/ proselyte | A person from another race/religion who went through a prescribed ritual to become a Jew |
| Counselor/ advocate | Gk *parakletos;* one called alongside to help, counsel, or protect; used of the Holy Spirit in Jn and in 1 Jn |
| cubit | An OT measurement of distance; about 18 inches. |
| Decapolis | Originally a federation of 10 Gentile towns east of the Jordan River |
| denarius | Small silver Roman coin equal to a day's wages for a common laborer |
| engaged | Jewish engagement was a binding agreement that could only be broken by divorce |
| firstfruits | The first products of agriculture given to God as an offering; also used to mean the first of more to come |
| Hades | The Gk word for the place of the dead, corresponding to the Hb word *Sheol* |
| headquarters/ palace | Lat *Praetorium* used by Gk writers for the residence of the Roman governor; may also refer to military headquarters, the imperial court, or the emperor's guard |
| hell/hellfire | Gk *gehenna*; Aram for Valley of Hinnom on the south side of Jerusalem; formerly a place of human sacrifice, and in NT times, a place for the burning of garbage; place of final judgment for those rejecting Christ |
| Herod | Name of the Idumean family ruling Palestine from 37 B.C. to A.D. 95; the main rulers from this family mentioned in the NT are: |

| | |
|---|---|
| Herod I | (37 B.C.–4 B.C.) also known as Herod the Great; built the great temple in Jerusalem and massacred the male babies in Bethlehem |
| Herod Antipas | (4 B.C.–A.D. 39) son of Herod the Great; ruled one-fourth of his father's kingdom (Galilee and Perea); killed John the Baptist and mocked Jesus |
| Agrippa I | (A.D. 37–44) grandson of Herod the Great; beheaded James the apostle and imprisoned Peter |
| Agrippa II | (A.D. 52–c. 95) great-grandson of Herod the Great; tried Paul |
| •Herodians | Political supporters of Herod the Great and his family |
| *Hosanna* | A term of praise derived from the Hb word for save |
| I assure you | In Mt, Mk, and Lk, a translation of lit *Amen, I say to you*, and in Jn, a translation of lit *Amen, amen, I say to you*; a phrase used only by Jesus to testify to the certainty and importance of His words. |
| life/soul | The same Gk word (*psyche*) can be translated *life* or *soul*. |
| Mary Magdalene | Or *Mary of Magdala*; Magdala was most likely a town on the western shore of the Sea of Galilee and north of Tiberias. |
| Messiah | Or *the Christ*; Gk *Christos*, meaning "the anointed one" |
| mina(s) | Gk coin worth 100 drachma or about 100 days' wages. |
| Mount of Olives | A mountain east of Jerusalem across the Kidron valley |

| | |
|---|---|
| mystery | Transliteration of Gk *mysterion*, a secret hidden in the past but now revealed |
| Nazarene | A person from Nazareth; growing up in Nazareth was an aspect of the Messiah's humble beginnings; see Jn 1:46. |
| One and Only | Or *only begotten*, or *one of a kind,* or *incomparable*; the Gk word could refer to someone's only child; see Lk 7:12; 8:42; 9:38. It could also refer to someone's special child; see Heb 11:17. |
| overseer(s) | Or *elder(s)*, or *bishop(s)* |
| palace | (see "headquarters/palace") |
| Passover | The Jewish ritual meal celebrating Israel's deliverance from slavery in Egypt |
| Pharisee(s) | In Judaism a religious sect that followed the whole written and oral law |
| Pilate | Pontius Pilate was governor of the province of Judea A.D. 26–36. |
| proconsul | Chief Roman government official in a senatorial province who presided over Roman court hearings. |
| proselyte | (see "convert/proselyte") |
| Rabbi | *Rabbi* = *my great one* in Hb, used of a recognized teacher of the Scriptures |
| regiment | (see "company/regiment") |
| sacred bread | Lit *bread of presentation*; 12 loaves, representing the 12 tribes of Israel, put on the table in the holy place in the tabernacle, and later in the temple. The priests ate the previous week's loaves; see Ex 25:30; 29:32; Lv 24:5-9. |

| | |
|---|---|
| Sadducee(s) | In Judaism a religious sect that followed primarily the first five books of the OT (Torah or Pentateuch) |
| Samaritan(s) | People of mixed, Gentile/Jewish ancestry who lived between Galilee and Judea and were hated by the Jews |
| Sanhedrin | The seventy-member supreme council of Judaism, patterned after Moses' 70 elders |
| scribe(s) | A professional group in Judaism that copied the law of Moses and interpreted it, especially in legal cases |
| soul | (see "life/soul") |
| Son of Man | Most frequent title Jesus used for Himself; see Dn 7:13. |
| synagogue | A place where the Jewish people met for prayer, worship and teaching of the Scriptures |
| tabernacle | Or *tent*, or *shelter*, terms used for temporary housing |
| tassel | Fringes that devout Jews wore on their clothing to remind them to keep the law; see Nm 15:37-41. |
| temple complex | In the Jerusalem temple, the sanctuary (the holy place and the holy of holies), at least four courtyards (for priests, Jews, women, and Gentiles), numerous gates, and several covered walkways. |
| Unleavened Bread | A seven-day festival celebrated in conjunction with the Passover; see Ex 12:1-20 |
| walk | Term often used in a figurative way to mean "way of life" or "behavior" |

| | |
|---|---|
| wise men | Gk *magoi;* "magi," based on Persian word; eastern sages who observed the heavens for signs and omens |

## Old Testament HCSB Bullet Notes™ for Psalms and Proverbs

| | |
|---|---|
| Abaddon | Either the grave or realm of the dead |
| acrostic | A device in Hb poetry in which each verse begins with a successive letter of the Hb alphabet |
| burnt offering(s) | Or *holocaust*, an offering completely burned to ashes; used in connection with worship, seeking God's favor, expiating sin, or averting judgment. |
| everyone | Lit *sons of man*, or *sons of Adam* |
| fear(s) God/the LORD | (see "fear of the LORD") |
| fear of the LORD | No single Eng word conveys every aspect of the word *fear* in this phrase. The meaning includes worshipful submission, reverential awe, and obedient respect to the covenant-keeping God of Israel. |
| gate(s) | The center for community discussions, political meetings, and trying of court cases |
| *Gittith* | Perhaps a musical term, an instrument or tune from Gath, or a song for the grape harvest |
| Hallelujah! | Lit *Praise Yah!* (a shortened form of *Yahweh*), or *Praise the LORD!* |
| *Higgaion* | Perhaps a musical notation |
| high place(s) | An ancient place of worship most often associated with pagan religions, usually built on an elevated location |

| | |
|---|---|
| horn | Symbol of power based on the strength of animal horns |
| Hosts | The military forces consisting of God's angels; sometimes the sun, moon, and stars are included. |
| human race | Lit *sons of man*, or *sons of Adam* |
| mankind | Lit *sons of man*, or *sons of Adam* |
| *Maskil* | From a Hb word meaning to be prudent or to have insight; possibly a contemplative, instructive, or wisdom psalm |
| men | Lit *sons of man*, or *sons of Adam* |
| *Miktam* | Perhaps a musical term |
| Most High | Hb *Elyon;* often used with other names of God, such as Hb *El* (God) or Hb *Yahweh* (LORD); used to refer to God as the supreme being |
| people | Lit *sons of man*, or *sons of Adam* |
| Pit | Either the grave or the realm of the dead |
| Red Sea | Lit *Sea of Reeds* |
| sackcloth | Garment made of poor quality material and worn as a sign of grief and mourning |
| *Selah* | A Hb word whose meaning is uncertain; various interpretations include: (1) a musical notation, (2) a pause for silence, (3) a signal for worshipers to fall prostrate on the ground, (4) a term for the worshipers to call out, (5) a word meaning "forever." |
| *Sheminith* | Hb musical term meaning *instruments* or *on the instrument of eight strings* |
| Sheol | Either the grave or the realm of the dead |

| | |
|---|---|
| sin offering | In the OT the *sin* (or *purification*) *offering* is the most important sacrifice for cleansing from impurities. It provided purification from sin and certain forms of ceremonial uncleanness. |
| song of ascents | Probably the songs pilgrims sang as they traveled the roads going up to worship in Jerusalem; Pss 120–134 |
| testimony | A reference to either the Mosaic law in general or to a specific section of the law, the Ten Commandments, that was written on stone tablets and placed in the ark of the covenant (also called the ark of the testimony) |
| wormwood | A small shrub used as a medicinal herb, noted for its bitter taste |
| Yahweh | Or *The LORD*; the personal name of God in Hb |

# CONCISE TOPICAL CONCORDANCE

## A

*Action*
On Jesus' words. Mt 7:24-27.
Command to take action.
Mt 28:18-20.
Will not save you. Ti 3:5.
Show your faith by. Jms 2:14.

*Adultery*
Jesus defines. Mt 5:27-30.

*Angels*
Are ministering spirits. Ps 68:17;
Lk 16:22; Ac 12:7-11; 27:23;
Heb 1:7,14.
Not to be worshiped. Col 2:18;
Rv 19:10; 22:8-9.
Know and delight in the gospel.
1 Tm 3:16; 1 Pt 1:12.
Rejoice over every repentant sinner.
Lk 15:7,10.
Will attend Christ at His second
coming. Mt 16:27; 25:31;
Mk 8:38; 2 Th 1:7.

*Anger*
Be slow to. Pr 15:18; 16:32; 19:11;
Ti 1:7; Jms 1:19.
Characteristic of fools. Pr 12:16;
14:29; 27:3.
Children should not be stirred up
to. Eph 6:4; Col 3:21.
Pray without. 1 Tm 2:8.
A work of sinful nature. Gl 5:20.

*Anxiety*
The cure for. Mt 6:25-34; Php 2:28;
1 Pt 5:7.
Prevented. Ps 121:4; 1 Pt 5:7.

*Appearance*
Can be deceiving. Mt 23:27-28.
Do not judge by. Jms 2:2-4.
Inner versus outward. 1 Pt 3:1-6.

*Assurance*
Abundant in understanding the gos-
pel. Col 2:2; 1 Th 1:5.
Comfort in affliction. 2 Co 4:8-10,
16-18.
Eternal life. 1 Jn 5:13.
Peace with God by Christ. Rm 5:1.

*Authority*
Jesus demonstrates. Mk 1:22,27-28;
Lk 4:32,36-37.

## B

*Baptism*
Jesus was baptized. Mt 3:13-16.
Believers were baptized at Pente-
cost. Ac 2:41.
The Ethiopian eunuch. Ac 8:36.
Paul was baptized. Ac 9:18.
A sign of repentance and sins for-
given. Mk 1:4.
Shows identification with Jesus
Christ. Rm 6:3-8.
A command for all believers.
Mt 28:18-20.

*Believers*
Attentive to Christ's voice.
Jn 10:3-4.
Belong to Christ. Ps 31:23; 34:9;
Rm 1:7.
Want to do good works. Ti 2:14;
3:8.
Fear God. Ac 10:2.
Follow Christ. Jn 10:4,27.
Humble. Ps 34:2; 1 Pt 5:5.
Poor in spirit. Mt 5:3.

*Bible*
Inspired by God. 2 Tm 3:14-17.
Inspired by the Holy Spirit. Ac 1:16;
2 Pt 1:21.
Points to Christ. Jn 5:39; Ac 18:28.
Learn about salvation from.
2 Tm 3:15.
An unerring guide. 2 Pt 1:19.
Sharp as a sword. Eph 6:17;
Heb 4:12.
Hearing is not enough. Jms 1:22.
Received message, not from men,
but from God. 1 Th 2:13.
Those who search, are truly noble.
Ac 17:11.
Warning against those who add to or
take from. Rv 22:18-19.

*Body*
Is the temple of Holy Spirit.
1 Co 6:19.
Will be resurrected. 1 Co 15:12-58.

# C

## Celibacy
Jesus' teaching concerning.
Mt 19:10-12.
Paul's teaching concerning.
1 Co 7:1-9,25-26,32-39.
Wrongly insisted on. 1 Tm 4:1-3.

## Children
Christ taught. Mk 10:13-16.
Should honor the aged. 1 Pt 5:5.
Should obey parents. Pr 6:20;
Eph 6:1.
Should take care of parents.
1 Tm 5:4.
Should be treated with respect.
Eph 6:4.

## Christ
Pre-existence. Jn 1:1-18.
Genealogy traced through Joseph.
Mt 1:1-17.
Genealogy traced through Mary.
Lk 3:23-38.
Birth of. Mt 1:18-25; Lk 2:1-20.
Circumcision and naming of.
Lk 2:21.
Childhood. Lk 2:41-52.
Baptism. Mt 3:13-17.
Tempted by Satan. Mt 4:1-11;
Mk 1:12-13; Lk 4:1-13.
Calls His first disciples. Jn 1:35-51.
Mission. Lk 4:16-21.
Manner of relating to people.
Mt 12:18-21.
Sinless. Jn 8:46; 2 Co 5:21;
Heb 4:14-16.
Forgives sins. Col 3:13; Mk 2:7,
10-11.
One with the Father. Jn 10:30,38;
12:45; 14:7-10; 17:10.
Fully God. Col 2:9; Heb 1:3.
Eternally the same. Heb 1:12; 13:8.
Fully human. Jn 1:14; Heb 2:14.
The only mediator between God
and man. 1 Tm 2:5.

## Church
Christ will build. Mt 16:18.
Commission of. Mt 28:18-20.
Is the bride of Christ. Rv 19:7-8.
Christ is the head. Col 1:18.
Is like a body. 1 Co 12:12-13.

## Confession of Sin
Followed by forgiveness. Ps 32:5;
1 Jn 1:9.
Illustrated. Lk 15:21; 18:13.

## Civil rights
Exercised by Paul. Ac 16:35-40;
22:24-29.
To fair wages. Jms 5:4.

## Confrontation
Jesus with money changers in the
temple. Jn 2:13-25.
Jesus with Samaritan woman.
Jn 4:5-44.
Jesus with the people of His home-
town. Lk 4:16-31.

## Contentment
With wages and possessions.
Lk 3:14; Heb 13:5.
With food and clothing. 1 Tm 6:8.
With godliness is great gain.
Ps 37:16; 1 Tm 6:6.

## Correction
For our good. Heb 12:5-11.
From the Scriptures. 2 Tm 3:16-17.
Of children. Pr 13:24; 19:15.

## Creation
By Christ. Jn 1:3,10; Col 1:16.
By the command of God. Ps 33:9;
Heb 11:3.
For God's pleasure. Pr 16:4;
Rv 4:11.

## Criticism
Jesus' warning. Lk 6:39-42.

## Cursing
Do not curse people. Jms 5:12.
Speech should be an example.
1 Tm 4:12.

# D

## Death
A consequence of sin. Rm 5:12-14;
6:23.
Christ delivers from the fear of.
Heb 2:15.
Conquered by Christ. Rm 6:9;
Rv 1:18.
Described as sleep. Jn 11:11-14;
Ac 7:59-60; 13:36; 1 Co 15:6.
Everyone will experience. 1 Tm
6:7; Heb 9:27.
For believers, a passage to God.
2 Co 5:1-8; Php 1:21-24.
For believers, a place of rest.
Lk 16:22,25; Rv 14:13.
Precious in God's sight. Ps 116:15.

## Debt
Borrower is slave of lender. Pr 22:7.

Rely on God for daily bread.
Mt 6:11.
Owe no one anything. Rm 13:8.
Creditors often cruel. Mt 18:28-30.

Demon
Jesus casts out. Mk 1:21-26;
Lk 4:31-35.

Devil
Assumes the form of an angel of
light. 2 Co 11:14.
Believers should resist. Jms 4:7;
1 Pt 5:9.
Cast down to hell. 2 Pt 2:4; Jd 6;
Rv 20:10.
Subtle. 2 Co 11:3,13.

Discipleship
Command to. Mt 28:18-20.
Cost of. Mt 16:24-28.
Tests of. Mt 10:32-39; Lk 14:26-
27,33; Jn 21:15-19.

Disease
Relationship to sin. Ps 107:17;
Mt 9:1-8; Mk 2:1-12; Lk 5:17-26;
Jn 9:1-5; Ac 5:1-11; Ac 12:20-25;
Rm 1:26-27; 1 Co 11:27-34;
2 Co 12:1-10.

Divorce
Jesus' teaching concerning.
Mt 19:1-10; Mk 10:2-12.

Doubt
Jesus' response to. Mt 11:1-19;
Mk 9:14-29; Jn 20:24-29.

Drugs
Honor God with body. 1 Co 6:20.
Mind should stay alert. 1 Pt 1:13;
1 Th 5:6.

Drunkenness
Avoid those given to. Pr 23:20;
1 Co 5:11.
Forbidden. Eph 5:18.
Excluded from heaven. 1 Co 6:10;
Gl 5:21.

E

Earth
Believers will inherit. Ps 25:13;
Mt 5:5.
Is the Lord's. 1 Co 10:26.
Not to be flooded again. 2 Pt 3:6-7.
To be renewed. 2 Pt 3:13.
Eagerly longs for redemption. Rm
8:19-22.

Endurance
God gives. Rm 15:5.

Enemies
Should be loved. Mt 5:44.
Should be prayed for. Ac 7:60.
Christ forgave. Lk 23:34.

Escapism
Mind should stay ready for action.
1 Pt 1:13; 1 Th 5:6.

Evangelism
Commanded by Christ. Mt 28:8-20.

Evolution
Contrary to the consistent teaching
of Scripture.
Jn 1:1-3; Col 1:16-17; Heb 11:3.

Eternal life
May have assurance of. 1 Jn 5:13.
To know God and Christ is. Jn 17:3.
To those who believe in Christ.
Jn 3:15-16; 6:40,47.

F

Faith
Demonstrated by a pagan soldier.
Lk 7:1-10.
All things should be done in.
Rm 14:22.
Have full assurance of. 2 Tm 1:12;
Heb 10:22.
The gift of God. Rm 12:3; Eph 2:8;
6:23; Philippians1:29.
Christ the source and perfecter of.
Heb 12:2.
Evidence of things not seen.
Heb 11:1.
Examine whether you are in.
2 Co 13:5.
A gift of the Holy Spirit. 1 Co 12:9.
Right with God by. Rm 4:16.
Necessary in prayer. Mt 21:22;
Jms 1:6.
Produces confidence. 1 Pt 2:6.
Scripture designed to produce.
Jn 20:31; 2 Tm 3:14-16.
The wicked often profess.
Ac 8:9-24.

Family
Believers' families blessed.
Ps 128:3-6.
Honoring God in. Eph 5:22–6:9.
Jesus' family. Mk 3:31-35.
Paul's family. Ac 23:16.
Timothy's family. 2 Tm 1:5.
Overseer's family. 1 Tm 3:1-7.
Deacon's family. 1 Tm 3:8-13.

*Fasting*
Not to be made a subject of display.
Mt 6:16.
Promises connected with. Mt 6:18.

*Father*
God in heaven. Mt 6:9; 23:9.
Duties of Christian.  Eph 6:4.
To be honored. Eph 6:2; Col 3:17.

*Fear*
Advantages of. Pr 15:16; 19:23.
Of God, perfects holiness. 2 Co 7:1.
Love drives out. 1 Jn 4:18.

*Flattery*
God despises. Ps 12:3.
Characteristic of enemies. Ps 5:9.
Of self. Ps 36:2.
Beware of. Rm 16:18; Jd 16.

*Flood*
Came suddenly and unexpectedly.
Mt 24:38-39.
Face of the whole earth changed by.
2 Pt 3:5-6.
Noah warned of. Heb 11:7.
Wicked warned of. 1 Pt 3:19-20;
2 Pt 2:5.

*Forgiveness*
Consequences of. Mt 6:14-15.
Of God. Ps 103:1-4.

*Freedom*
Of God. Ac 4:24-28.
Result of truth. Jn 8:32.
From condemnation. Rm 8:1,33-39.
From sin's power. Rm 8:2-4; Rv 1:5.

*Friends*
Constancy of. Pr 17:17.
Jesus called His disciples. Jn 15:13-
15.
Mary, Martha, Lazarus, and Jesus.
Lk 10:38-42.
Paul, Priscilla, and Aquila.
Rm 16:3-4.

# G

*Genders, Relationship between*
Virtuous woman. Pr 31:10-31.
God created two genders. Mk 10:6.
Interdependence of man and
woman. 1 Co 11:7-11.
Male and females equals regarding
salvation. Gl 3:28.
The man is the head of the woman.
1 Co 11:3.

*Generosity*
Blessings connected with. Ps 41:1;
Pr 22:9; Ac 20:35.
Encouraged by Jesus. Lk 6:38
Toward enemies. Pr 25:21.

*Glory*
Present afflictions are not worthy
compared to. Rm 8:18.
Do all to His. 1 Co 10:31.
Afflictions produce. 2 Co 4:17.

*God*
Is good. Ps 25:8; 119:68.
Unchanging. Ps 102:26-27;
Jms 1:17.
Our father. Mt 6:9.
All powerful. Lk 1:37; Rv 1:8.
Is spirit. Jn 4:23.
All knowing. Rm 11:33.
Is knowable. Eph 1:17.
Living. 1 Tm 4:10.
Judge. Jms 4:12.
Is Love. 1 Jn 4:16.
Kind. Rm 2:4.
Is holy. 1 Pt 1:15-16.

*Golden Rule*
Summarizes the Law and Prophets.
Mt 7:12.
Stated by Christ. Lk 6:31.

*Gospel*
Described. 1 Co 15:1-4.
Brings peace. Lk 2:10-14.
Veiled to the lost. 2 Co 4:3.
There is only one. Gl 1:8.
Must be believed. Mk 1:15;
Heb 4:2.
The power of God for salvation.
Rm 1:16; 1 Co 1:18; 1 Th 1:5.
Produces hope. 1 Co 1:23.

*Government*
Instituted by God.  Rm 13:1.
Boundaries of. Ac 4:19; 5:29.
Honor good leaders. 2 Pt 2:17.
Purpose of. 1 Pt 2:13-14.
Believers should pray for authori-
ties. 1 Tm 2:1-2.

*Grace*
Came by Christ. Jn 1:17; Rm 5:15.
Believers should grow in. 2 Pt 3:18.
God's work completed in believers
by. 2 Th 1:11-12.
Justifies sinners. Rm 5:1-21.
Not to be abused. Rm 3:8; 6:1,15;
Jd 4.
Salvation by. Ac 15:11; Eph 2:1-10;
Ti 2:11.

## Grow Up
Christ did. Lk 2:52.
Avoid youthful passions. 2 Tm 2:22.
No one should despise your youth.
1 Tm 4:12.
Grow in grace and knowledge of
Jesus. 2 Pt 3:18.
With solid food. 1 Co 3:1-2;
Heb 5:12-14.
Through the use of Scripture.
2 Tm 3:16-17.

## Guidance
Of believers. Ps 32:8; Jn 10:3.
God guides Joseph. Mt 1:18-25;
2:13-15,19-23.
Spirit leads. Rm 8:14.

## Guilt
The whole world has. Rm 3:9-20.
Blood of Christ alone takes away.
Heb 9:14; 10:2-10, 22.

# H

## Hate
Embitters life. Pr 15:17.
Believers should expect. Mt 10:22;
Jn 15:18-19.
Return good for. Mt 5:44.

## Healing
Comes from God. Ps 103:3.
Proof that Jesus is the Messiah.
Mt 11:5.
Son of a royal official. Jn 4:46-54.

## Hearing
Faith comes by. Rm 10:4,17.
Contrasted with doing. Rm 2:13;
Jms 1:19-25.

## Heart
God enlightens. 2 Co 4:6; Eph 1:18.
Blessings of a pure. Ps 24:4-5;
Mt 5:8.
Believe with. Ac 8:37; Rm 10:10.
Love God with all. Mt 22:37.
Love one another with a pure.
1 Pt 1:22.
Set the Messiah apart in. 1 Pt 3:15.

## Heaven
Believers rewarded in. Mt 5:12;
1 Pt 1:4.
Jesus entered. Ac 3:21; Heb 6:20.
God's dwelling place. Mt 6:9.
Believers names are written in.
Lk 10:20; Heb 12:23.
Wicked are excluded from. Gl 5:21;
Eph 5:5; Rv 22:15.

## Hell
The beast, false prophet, and the
Devil thrown into. Rv 19:20;
20:10.
Body suffers in. Mt 5:29; 10:28.
Described as everlasting fire.
Mt 25:41,46.
Destruction, away from God's
presence. 2 Th 1:9.
Strive to keep others from. Jd 23.

## Heresy
Forbidden. Ti 3:10-11; 2 Jn 10-11.
Teachers of. Ac 15:24; 2 Co 11:4;
Gl 1:7; 2:4; 2 Pt 2:1-22; Jd 3-16.

## History
Bible is account of actual. Lk 1:1-4;
Ac 1:1-4.
Preached by the apostles. Ac 4:2;
17:18-21; 24:15.
Jesus' resurrection, a true event in.
1 Co 15:5-8.
Jesus' life took place in. Lk 24:35-
43; Jn 20:20,27; 1 Jn 1:1-2.

## Holy Spirit
Believers receive. 1 Jn 2:20.
Guides into all truth. Jn 16:13;
1 Jn 2:27.
Baptism of, through Christ. Ti 3:6.
Abides with believers. Jn 14:16.
Communicates joy. Rm 14:17;
Gl 5:22; 1 Th 1:6.
Given by the Father. Jn 14:15-18.
Gives the new birth. Jn 3:5-6.
Called God. Ac 5:3-4.
Convinces of sin. Jn 16:8-11.
Lives in believers. Jn 14:17;
1 Co 3:16; 6:19.
Blasphemy against is unpardonable.
Mt 12:31-32; 1 Jn 5:16.
Can be grieved. Eph 4:30.
Believers sealed by. 2 Co 1:22;
Eph 1:13; 4:30.

## Hope
In God. Ps 39:7; 1 Pt 1:21.
Be ready to give a reason for your.
1 Pt 3:15.
Believers rejoice in. Rm 5:2; 12:12.
Believers wait for the blessed.
Ti 2:13.
Leads to patience. Rm 8:25;
1 Th 1:3.
Abraham believed with. Rm 4:18.

## Human nature
Assumed by Christ without sin.
Jn 1:14; Php 2:7.

Created after the image of God.
Jms 3:9.
Distorted by sin. Rm 3:23.
Affected by Adam's sin. Rm 5:12.

*Husbands*
To love wife. Eph 5:25-30;
Col 3:19.
To respect wife. 1 Pt 3:7.
Should have only one wife. Mt 19:3-
9; Mk 10:6-8; 1 Co 7:2-4.

# I

*Idols*
Believers should be free from.
1 Co 10:14.
Change glory of God into. Rm 1:23;
Ac 17:29.

*Immortality*
Jesus' promise of. Jn 6:39-58.

# J

*Jealousy*
Destructive consequences of.
Mt 2:16-18.

*Jerusalem*
Christ wept over. Mt 23:37;
Lk 19:41.
Was to be destroyed. Lk 19:42-44.

*Jesus (see Christ)*

*Joy*
Commanded to believers. Ps 32:11;
Php 3:1.
Over sinners who repent.
Lk 15:1-32.
In answer to prayer. Jn 16:24.
In fellowship. 2 Tm 1:4; 1 Jn 1:3-4;
2 Jn 12.
The coming of Christ will bring.
1 Pt 4:14.
A fruit of the Spirit. Gl 5:22.

*Judgment*
By God for words spoken. Mt 12:36.
Of Christians. Rm 14:10; 2 Co 5:10.
After death. Heb 9:27.
Not by outward appearances.
Jn 7:24.
Will be in righteousness. Ps 98:9;
Ac 17:31.

*Justice*
Receive joy in doing. Pr 21:15.
Requires two or more witnesses.
Jn 8:17; 2 Co 13:1.

# K

*Kindness*
An attribute of God. Eph 2:7;
Ti 3:4-7.
A quality of believers. Col 3:12;
2 Pt 1:7; 1 Co 13:4.

*Knowledge*
Fear of the Lord is the beginning of.
Pr 1:7.
Of God universal among human
beings. Rm 1:20.
Command to grow in. 2 Pt 3:18.
Jesus' disciples have. Lk 8:10.
Every disciple's goal. Php 3:10.
Of God's will. Col 1:9.
Of salvation. Lk 1:77; 1 Jn 5:13.
Needed to guide zeal. Rm 10:2-3.

# L

*Law*
Jesus fulfills. Mt 5:17-20.
Jesus' interpretation of. Mt 12:9-14;
Mk 2:23-28.
Man's sinful nature and the law.
Rm 7:7-25.

*Lawsuits*
Among believers. 1 Co 6:1-8.

*Life*
God is the author of. Ac 17:28.
God created with intricate design.
Ps 139:13-15.

*Lips*
Requires control. Ps 19:14;
Mt 5:37; Col 4:6.
Reveal the heart. Mt 12:34.
Source of good or evil. Pr 18:21;
Jms 3:9-10.

*Love*
Covers sin. Pr 10:12.
For God. Mt 22:36-40.
Described. 1 Co 13:4-7.
Fulfills the law. Rm 13:8.
God is. 1 Jn 4:7-8,16.
Marks the child of God. Jn 13:35;
1 Jn 4:7.

*Lust*
Flee youthful. 2 Tm 2:22.
Must be controlled by God.
Rm 13:14; Gl 5:17.
Same as committing adultery.
Mt 5:27-28.
Results in aberrant sexual behavior.
Rm 1:26-27.

## Lying
Destestable to the Lord. Pr 12:22.
A characteristic of unbelief.
1 Th 2:9; 1 Tm 4:2; 1 Jn 2:4.
The Devil is the father of. Jn 8:44.
Forbidden. Col 3:9.

# M

## Mankind
Made in God's image. Jms 3:9.
All have sinned. Rm 3:23.
More valuable than animals.
Mt 12:11-12.
Object of God's love. Jn 3:16.

## Marriage
Jesus blesses. Jn 2:1-11.
Honorable for all. Heb 13:4.
Should be permanent. Mt 19:6.
Not to be forbidden. 1 Tm 4:3.

## Materialism
More to life than. Lk 12:15.
Root of all evil. 1 Tm 6:10.
Makes entry into God's kingdom
difficult. Mk 10:23-25.
Can't provide what humans need
most. 1 Pt 1:18-19.

## Metaphysics
Reality more than physical or
material. Ac 17:16-34.

## Mind
Love God with. Mt 22:36-40.
Renewed, key to spirituality.
Rm 12:2; Eph 4:23.
To be prepared before taking action.
1 Pt 1:13.
God puts law in believer's.
Heb 8:10.
Have a sound. 2 Tm 1:7.
Use while praying or singing.
1 Co 14:15-16.

## Ministry
All believers have. Eph 4:12.
Civic leaders have. Rm 13:1-7.
Church pastors have. 1 Pt 5:2.
Parents have. Eph 6:4.

## Miracles
Purpose is to encourage belief in
Christ. Jn 20:30-31.
Insufficient to produce conversion.
Lk 16:31.
Jesus proved to be the Messiah by.
Mt 11:4-6; Lk 7:20-22; Jn 5:36.
Performed by false prophets. Mt
24:24; Rv 19:20.

## Missionaries
All believers are called to be. Mt
28:18-20.

## Money
Must choose between God or
money. Mt 6:24.
Use your money to benefit others.
Lk 16:9.
Test of repentance. Lk 3:10-14.
Longing for it is dangerous.
1 Tm 6:9.
Love of is root of all evil. 1 Tm 6:10.

## Mother
To be honored and cared for. Jn
19:27; Eph 6:2.
Gift of God. Ps 113:9.

## Murder
Jesus defines. Mt 5:21-22.
God hates. Pr 6:16-17.

# N

## Neighbor
Care for. Pr 3:28-29; Mt 25:34-46.
Love as you love yourself. Lk 10:25-
37; Rm 13:8-10; Gl 5:13-15;
Jms 2:8.

## New Creation
Christ brings about. Rm 6:4;
2 Co 5:14-17; Gl 6:14-15.
Will transform the entire universe.
Rm 8:18-21; 2 Pt 3:7-13;
Rv 21:1-8.

# O

## Occult
Belongs to sinful nature. Gl 5:20.
Girl involved with. Ac 16:16.
Sons of Sceva. Ac 19:14-15.
Books of, destroyed. Ac 19:19.

## Orphans
Defend. Ps 82:3.
Their treatment expresses true reli-
gion. Jms 1:27.

# P

## Pain
No existence in heaven. Rv 21:4.
Presence in hell. Lk 16:24;
Rv 16:10.

## Pantheists
Spoken to by Paul. Ac 17:16-34.

## Parties
Wedding, Jesus attended. Jn 2:1-12.

Avoid wild. Rm 13:13-14;
2 Pt 2:13-17.

*Pastoral leadership*
Qualifications for. 1 Tm 3:1-7;
Ti 1:5-9.
To be examples to the flock.
1 Pt 5:1-4.
Personal qualities of. 2 Co 6:3-10.

*Patience*
Waiting for God. Ps 37:7; 40:1.
Believers receive from God.
Col 1:11.
Exercise, toward all. 1 Th 5:14.
Running the race with. Heb 12:1.

*Peace*
Seek it. Ps 34:14.
Believers have in Christ. Rm 5:1;
Jn 14:27; Col 1:19-20.
Takes the place of worry. Php 4:6-7.
Wicked do not know. Rm 3:17.

*Persecution*
Christ's followers will have.
Mt 16:21-26; 2 Tm 3:12.

*Plans*
Importance of. Lk 14:28,31.
Subject to change by God.
Jms 4:13-17.

*Popularity*
Moses rejected. Heb 11:24-26.
Not John's goal. Jn 3:30.

*Poor*
Jesus preached to. Lk 4:18.
Do not despise. Pr 14:21;
Jms 2:2-17.

*Praise*
Offered continually. Ps 35:28; 71:6.
Christ is worthy of. Rv 5:1-14.
Offered in psalms and hymns.
Eph 5:19; Col 3:16.

*Prayer*
Jesus' way. Mt 6:5-13.
Acceptable through Christ.
Jn 14:13-14.
Husband and wife relationship
important for. 1 Pt 3:7.
To be offered with boldness.
Heb 4:16.
At all times. 1 Th 5:17.
Regarding everything. Php 4:6.
For others. 1 Tm 2:1; Jms 5:13-18.

*Preaching*
Purpose of. 2 Tm 4:1-4.

*Pride*
Do not give way to. Ps 131:1.
Warnings against. 1 Co 8:1-2;
10:12.
Comes from the heart. Mk 7:21-23.
God sees and judges. Lk 1:51.

*Prisoners*
To be visited. Mt 25:35-46.

*Prophecy*
Blessing for those who hear and
keep what is heard. Rv 1:3; 22:7.
Does not come by human will.
2 Pt 1:20-21.
Do not despise. 1 Th 5:20.

*Protection*
God provides. Ps 5:11; 46:1-3;
2 Pt 1:5; Jd 24.
From evil. 2 Th 3:3.

*Purity*
Persuasiveness of. 1 Pt 3:1-2.
Impurity is punished. 1 Co 3:16-17;
Eph 5:5-6; Heb 13:4.
Commanded. Pr 31:3; Rm 13:13;
Col 3:5.

# Q

*Quiet Spirit*
Valuable in God's sight. 1 Pt 3:4.

# R

*Racism*
Rejected since all are from one man.
Ac 17:26.
No racial distinction in Christ.
Gl 3:28-29; Eph 2:19; Rv 5:9-10.

*Reason*
Give as an answer for hope.
1 Pt 3:15.
Must be completed by God's revelation. 1 Co 1:18.

*Redemption*
In abundance. Ps 130:7.
Is by the blood of Christ. Heb 9:12;
1 Pt 1:18-19; Rv 5:9.
Of the body. Rm 8:23.

*Repentance*
Given by God. Ac 11:18; 2
Tm 2:25.
Godly grief produces. 2 Co 7:10.
Jesus commands. Mk 1:15.
Results are changed attitudes and
behavior. Lk 3:7-14.

**Rest**
Christ's call to. Mt 11:28-30.
Eternal. Rv 14:13.

**Resurrection**
Of Jesus, the historical event.
Mt 28:5-10.
Preached by the Apostles. Ac 4:2.
Of the body. 1 Co 15:42-45.
First principle of the gospel.
1 Co 15:1-19.

**Revenge**
Jesus' substitute for. Mt 5:38-42.

**Righteousness**
Receive, from God. Ps 24:5.
God's, shown through the gospel.
Rm 3:25-26.
Believers desire. Mt 5:6.
Believers do not trust their own.
Php 3:4-11.
Does not save. Ti 3:5.

# S

**Salvation**
God of. Ps 18:46; 24:5; 25:5; 27:9;
51:14; 65:5; 68:20; 79:9; 85:4;
88:1.
In Jesus alone. Ac 4:11-12.
Gospel is power of God to. Rm 1:16.

**Satan (see Devil)**

**Second Coming of Christ**
Jesus predicted. Mt 25:31; Jn 14:3.
Be ready for. Mt 24:44; Lk 12:40.
In same way as He ascended into
heaven. Ac 1:9-11.
Sudden. Mk 13:32-37.
As a thief. 1 Th 5:1-11;
2 Pt 3:10-13.
Will complete salvation of believers.
Heb 9:28.
Time of, unknown. Mt 24:36.
Wicked will be unprepared.
2 Th 1:3-12.

**Seeking God**
Leads to joy. Ps 70:4; 105:3.
Commanded, with promises.
Mt 6:33.
Will be rewarded. Heb 11:6.

**Senses**
God uses to reveal Himself.
1 Jn 1:1-3.
Are used to receive the gospel. Rm
10:14-18.
Exercised to discern good from evil.
Heb 5:14.

**Sex**
Good in marriage. Heb 13:4.
Not to be withheld in marriage.
1 Co 7:3-5.
Lust is sin. Mt 5:28.
With same gender is perverse.
Rm 1:26-27.

**Sin**
God's word protection against.
Ps 119:11.
All have committed. Rm 3:23.
Begins in the mind. Mt 5:27-28;
Jms 1:14-15.
Confession of followed by forgive-
ness. Ps 32:5; 1 Jn 1:9.
Christ blood cleanses from. 1 Jn 1:7.

**Sinners**
Sought by Jesus. Mt 9:9-13.

**Singing**
Commanded. Ps 100:2; Eph 5:19;
Col 3:16; Jms 5:13.
Fom God. Ps 40:3.

**Soldier**
Man of great faith. Lk 7:1-10.

**Speech**
Acceptable to God Ps 19:14.
Evil or deceitful. Ps 34:13.
Guarding one's. Ps 39:1; 141:3.
Benefits of wise. Pr 10:11-13.
Jesus' prescription for. Mt 5:33-37.

**Spirit**
God is, and must be worshiped in.
Jn 4:24.
Be filled with. Eph 5:18.
Test the spirits. 1 Jn 4:1.

**Stealing**
From the poor, specially forbidden.
Pr 22:22.
Do honest work instead. Eph 4:28.

**Suffering**
Christ, for us. Mk 8:31; Lk 24:26;
1 Pt 2:21.
Essential to sharing in His glory. Rm
8:17.

**Syncretism**
Incompatible with the gospel. Gl
1:6-9.

# T

**Tears**
Observed by God. Ps 56:8.
Jesus had them. Jn 11:35.
None in heaven. Rv 21:4.

*Thankfulness*
Commanded. Ps 50:14; Php 4:6.
In all things. 1 Th 5:18; Eph 5:20.

*Time*
Jesus beyond the bounds of. Jn 8:58.
Use wisely. Eph 5:16.

*Tribulation*
Able to overcome. 2 Co 4:7-15.

*Trinity*
Evident at Jesus' baptism.
Mt 3:16-17.
To be baptized in the name of.
Mt 28:18-20.
The apostolic benediction.
2 Co 13:13.

*Truth*
Endures forever. Pr 12:19.
Sets us free. Jn 8:31-32.
Jesus is. Jn 14:6.
God's Word is. Jn 17:17.
Worship God in. Jn 4:23.

# U

*Unbelief*
Is sin. Jn 16:8-11.
Believers should not partner with
unbelievers. 2 Co 6:14-18.
Questions truthfulness of God.
1 Jn 5:10.

*Understanding*
God's is infinite. Ps 147:5.
Pray and sing with. 1 Co 14:15-17.

# V

*Victory*
Is in Christ. 1 Co 15:57.

*Virtues*
List of. Col 3:12-17.

# W

*Way*
Jesus is. Jn 14:6.
To destruction is broad. Mt 7:13.

*Wise Men*
Seek Jesus. Mt 2:1-12.

*Witness*
Samaritan woman to the people of
Sychar. Jn 4:27-42.

*Wives*
Are a blessing to husbands. Pr 12:4;
31:10,12.
Submissive to their husbands.
Eph 5:22-33.
Win unbelieving husband by their
life. 1 Pt 3:1-2.

*Women*
Financial sponsors of Christ and dis-
ciples. Lk 8:1-3.
First to witness resurrection.
Lk 24:1-12; Jn 20:1-18.

*Work*
Believers should. 2 Th 3:7-15.

*Worship*
With fear and reverence. Ps 5:7;
96:9.
Authentic. Jn 4:19-26.

# YZ

*Youth*
Cleansing of. Ps 119:9.
Should be an example. 1 Tm 4:12.

*Zeal*
Christ an example. Jn 2:13-25.
Should be guided by knowledge.
Rm 10:2-3.